SELECTED POEMS

26/12
£1

SELECTED POEMS

PERCY BYSSHE SHELLEY

———

Edited with an Introduction
and Notes by
EDMUND BLUNDEN

COLLINS
LONDON AND GLASGOW

GENERAL EDITOR: G. F. MAINE

First published in this form 1954
Latest reprint, 1990

ISBN 0 00 424631 4

Printed and bound in Great Britain by
William Clowes Limited,
Beccles and London

CONTENTS

PERCY BYSSHE SHELLEY

HIS LIFE AND WRITINGS

SHELLEY'S LIFE AND WRITINGS

I. Origins and Boyhood

ALTHOUGH the county of Sussex has not produced many of the best English poets it claims one: Percy Bysshe Shelley, whose name continues to bring to the mind a feeling of the beautiful, the impassioned and the generous. It has been often remarked that the arising of such a poet from the family which included him is one of the mysteries of human history. That family however was seen to possess ability and character and to take its part in the country's affairs apart from the poet's achievement.

'The Shelleys,' Leigh Hunt observes, 'are of old standing, and have branched out into three several baronetcies, one of which has become the representative of the kindred of Sir Philip Sidney.' Of the two other branches, the older established itself at Lewes, the Sussex county town, and that baronetcy was attained in 1611 when King James I first created the order. The younger, to which the poet belongs, grew rather in Western Sussex, where its memorials may still be found in churches and place-names, and it waited for its baronetcy until 1806.

The individual whose services to the Whig party were recognized in this honour was Bysshe Shelley, born in 1731, an adventurous and determined man. His childhood was spent in America, but he made his fortune in England, and devoted himself to increasing the Shelley estates. We hear of him as an eccentric and combative being. Sir Bysshe Shelley, as he became, saw the world, kept his pack of hounds, had a library, and was the father of three families, the last of them without the formality of marriage. He had married first a Horsham heiress, Mary Catherine Michell, who died in 1760 aged twenty-five; and nine years later Elizabeth Perry, heiress to the estate of Sir Philip Sidney, so that Sir Bysshe Shelley is part of the history of Penshurst Place. His eldest son by Elizabeth took the name Shelley Sidney and was made a baronet in 1818; his grandson Philip became Lord de L'Isle and Dudley in 1835. This connection was one that the poet Shelley held in respect.

By his first wife Sir Bysshe had a son Timothy, born in 1753, whom he sent to University College, Oxford. Timothy took his degree there, made the tour of Europe, and returned to his native place to marry, farm, and serve conscientiously as a member of parliament on the side of the Whigs. Timothy possessed properties of his own, to which additions were made by his marrying Elizabeth Pilfold, of another well-known Horsham family. Elizabeth had been brought up among people who knew all about horse-racing, but she had a taste in poetry, and her sister who became Mrs. Thomas Grove was something of a painter. In 1791 Timothy and Elizabeth Shelley occupied one of the family's houses, Field Place near Horsham, and their eldest child Percy Bysshe was born there on 4 August 1792. He was the heir to his grandfather's estates, and for this boy the old man was now building, in view of his expected eminence in society, on land overlooking the English Channel, the very curious and spacious residence called Castle Goring. It stands as a relic of Sir Bysshe's fantasy and that of his architect Mr. Rebecca—but also as a symbol of the vanity of human wishes.

Other babies arrived in the Field Place household, and all but one grew up; the rest were Elizabeth, Mary, Hellen, Margaret and lastly John, born in 1806. The girls were beautiful and mildly artistic; John was a country character. Percy himself is called 'Happy P.' in a letter from his mother of 1795 or so,—and she says, 'Bysshe eats a partridge every other day, you never saw a Fellow enjoy anything more than he does boiled partridge and bread sauce.' The boy was certainly the pride of his parents and a favourite all round. His education was begun without delay. Timothy Shelley, M.A. himself gave him lessons and sent him for others to the Rev. Evan Edwards, curate of Warnham. Mrs. Shelley read some English poems to her son, and was delighted with him when, after becoming acquainted with Thomas Gray's *Ode on a Favourite Cat* he at once had it by heart.

Field Place, as wayfarers may still easily see,—for it has not greatly changed,—was a charming little kingdom for the Shelley children. Within there was much to explore; the gardens were finely various, and beyond was good meadowland with big trees. The Place has its own pond, but Shelley's father kept a boat or two on the great millpond at Warnham which of course was much visited. Parks and woods and streams were ever near.

At home the conversation of Timothy and his friends ran much upon the politics of the day (with the French Revolution in progress) and theories of social development. Percy's idea of responsibility and of being useful to the public was aroused. Riding his pony beside his father's steward from farm to farm he did what he could for the poor and needy. It must be remembered that Field Place was not merely a country residence: it was a farmer's house. Timothy Shelley's ordinary appearance in grey coat, breeches and gaiters betokened his agricultural concerns; and in this he resembled his friend and patron the Duke of Norfolk, lord of Horsham and owner of Arundel Castle not far away.

The picture of the poet Shelley's childhood is serenely happy until he is placed at school, at the age of ten. The school was one of many such preparatory schools round London,—Sion House Academy at Isleworth. The teaching was good enough, the supervision insufficient, and boys like Shelley with girlish faces and no enthusiasm for games were bullied. But here Shelley found some companions in his liking for tales of the supernatural, then supplied in profusion at the circulating library. At Sion House Academy too he had his introduction to the 'matchless Vale of Thames' which charmed him present or absent for the rest of his life; he spent one delightful day at Richmond with his cousin Tom Medwin.

Some of his uncles had been at Eton, and to Eton Shelley went in 1804. He spent six years at this great school, where much freedom existed side by side with much severity; many stories have been handed down concerning Shelley's erratic doings and his sufferings. He seems to have led a mutiny against the 'fagging' system, although we get a glimpse of him quite contentedly doing what was required by it. He was provoked into fights with other boys. He experimented on an ancient tree with a burning-glass and gunpowder. By mischance, demonstrating his electrical machine, he gave his tutor a shock. He was 'mad Shelley' to many, and undoubtedly when he was being goaded he flamed up extraordinarily.

Nevertheless, Shelley at Eton worked regularly at his classics and other studies, and among competitors of high quality won his prizes and came near the top of the list in July 1810. He provided himself with a knowledge of the mythology, history and literature of the ancients which was of use to his later purposes in authorship. Already he ventured to publish things in prose and verse, some of which were printed at Horsham; his grandfather, who was watching his course amiably and hopefully, paid the printer's bill. But one of Shelley's early works succeeded in bringing him a profit, which was liquidated in a supper given by him to several schoolfellows. The book was a wild romance, such as other Etonians were scribbling in those days, entitled *Zastrozzi* (1809), and Shelley went on to write another of the kind called *St. Irvyne; or, The Rosicrucian*, which came out after his farewell to Eton.

The Eton years gave him a number of pleasant friendships, although they made some enemies for him where his escapades and even his idealism were resented; and he had time for frequent excursions along the Thames or away into the villages. It was now that his appreciation of the poetry of Thomas Gray, his predecessor at Eton, began to mature. Among living poets he rejoiced in Southey for his 'wild and wondrous song' and in Walter Scott for his Northern romances. In the holidays Shelley entertained his sisters with his own tales of wonder involving Field Place and Warnham Ponds, played his part among relatives and guests, took his gun for a little snipe-shooting, rode meditatively through the bridle-paths, and at last supposed himself in love. The girl was his cousin Harriet Grove, with whom he passed sweet hours in her Wiltshire home, at Field Place, and in London. For a time it appeared likely, young as both were, that they would duly marry, but Shelley's departures from orthodoxy in matters of sport, religious speculation and social convention are thought to have disquieted Harriet's father, and during Shelley's last months at school Mr Grove requested that the affair should be given up. Probably that would have been the course of events even without family dissuasions, for Harriet Grove had hardly imagination enough to sympathize deeply with Shelley as his power unfolded, and her attachment to him was (as her diary shows) less than that of a unique love.

For a short time, round the year 1805, there was at Eton a boy named Edward Ellerker Williams, a son of Captain John Williams of the Indian Army. No record exists of the meeting of Shelley and Williams at Eton, but the strange and tragic sequel to their early association in being contemporaries there will be read further on in this memoir.

II. DISASTER AT OXFORD

Thirty-six years after his father, Shelley signed his name in the same book of Admissions at University College, Oxford, and Timothy travelled there with him in October 1810 to see him safely and comfortably started on what promised to be a valuable course of four years or so. He was eighteen years old,—the age was quite usual for freshmen. Timothy was in an excellent mood, and among other thoughtful attentions introduced him to an old friend's son who had gone into business as a bookseller and publisher; the firm,

Slatter & Munday, had already had the honour of publishing the 1803 edition of W. S. Landor's classic poem *Gebir*. Timothy told Mr. Slatter that his son would be his customer, and requested him, as the youth was 'already an author,' to 'indulge him in his printing freaks.'

University College was a small community, with a dozen or so new Admissions in a year. The Master, the Rev. Dr. Griffith, had been in office two years; he was a mild man with a talent as an amateur artist, and had a room in the College for his beloved experiments in the craft of burning pictures in wood with a poker. The Dean, the Rev. George Rowley, one of Shelley's two tutors, was not an artist; he was more dominant and irritable. He succeeded as Master in 1821. There were one or two younger tutors and lecturers, such as Matthew Rolleston, who was expounding Logic; and the student had also the chance of hearing the University professors and readers on their subjects. Examinations of course took place, but the severer and more complicated system which has now been long in operation was not yet developed. Altogether an undergraduate could make good academic progress without being driven by his College; he was regarded as having character enough to employ his time at Oxford advantageously. It should be added however that a certain change of spirit was beginning about the time of Shelley's arrival. It was to affect him greatly. The feeling was growing that tutors should direct their pupils and maintain order in morality more conscientiously than before. In the end this became a great religious movement.

Shelley soon struck up a friendship with a learned, sceptical, and reserved youth named Thomas Jefferson Hogg, another newcomer, whose home was in the north country. The two went about together with an air of superiority, and in their rooms they had long and critical conversations on the universe, and local phenomena. Hogg was very willing to assist Shelley in his literary plans, which were numerous and mostly what his father had called 'freaks.' The printers were kept busy, and the secrecy in which Shelley pretended to be working was of the kind which pleases university gossips; so that by the early months of 1811 he had quite a reputation as a new Oxford poet of an incalculable kind. Among his printed pieces one was a poem on *The Existing State of Things* which has escaped all the hunters, and must have been a protest against our institutions; that it was not merely advertised is proved by its being catalogued by reviewers among books newly published. Nobody at Oxford seems to have mistaken Hogg for a wild poet though he was noticed as an eccentric person.

In the winter of 1810 Shelley's father became aware of his son's increasing purpose of campaigning against orthodox religion. Timothy Shelley was not a vigorous believer himself, but he thought that the ordinary assumption of the existence of a deity and attendance at a place of worship were things no man of sense would rush to attack in public. His son was rather of the temper of Sir Bysshe, and at this stage imagined that he was sent into the world with a mission only to be fulfilled by speaking out. At Oxford P.B.Shelley was instructed in Logic, and he as well as Hogg delighted in the clear statement of a reasoning. The two students therefore prepared a short argument, to present the case that nobody could prove the existence of God and that belief was illogical. This, they or at least Shelley hoped, would be a challenge to all the divines and professors and elicit a logical answer—if there was one. Shelley took the manuscript to his printers neither at Oxford, nor at Horsham, but (the detail illustrates what an extraordinary boy he was) at Worthing.

The Necessity of Atheism, anonymously, was advertised in February 1811, and in March Shelley went out of college early one morning and filled Slatter & Munday's window and book-tables with copies. But that was not all. He sent copies to all the Heads of Houses at Oxford and Cambridge, to the Bishops, and to other celebrities whose theology he meant to disturb; and letters signed with false names went with them. Old Miss Hannah More, the tireless missionary, opened her packet to read the request that should she find the argument sound she would not hinder the circulation through mere intolerance.

Hardly had Shelley made his early call at his booksellers when a clergyman from New College dropped in to browse on novelties. He looked at the tract with the detestable title, and sent for Slatter and Munday, who had not so far seen even the title; he recommended them to ensure that the whole edition was destroyed, and stood by while they burned the copies dumped on them. But when they had Shelley in the shop again, and tried to plant discretion if not divinity in his mind, they were met with an absolute refusal; and he continued his distribution of the pamphlet by all remaining methods. The picture is laughable, or else it is tragic.

It seems that the University, after trying officially to ignore the Atheist, was provoked into desiring the Atheist's own College to use its discipline. He was therefore called to appear before the Master and Fellows on the morning of 25 March 1811. These meetings, it can be supposed, are not held without previous discussion of the troublesome agenda; and probably the Dean had not succeeded in persuading the Master that the young Atheist should be treated as a criminal. When Shelley, then, stood before the seated Fellows, the Master began carefully. He showed the wicked pamphlet and asked, 'Are you the author of this?' But Shelley would not say—he could not, perhaps—yes or no. The Master was cornered. After some useless exchanges he told Shelley that he would have to be expelled; and the youth retired. Hogg, surely, was quite ready for the emergency, and he went up to the Common Room to face the Fellows with his claim that, if Shelley was guilty, he shared the guilt. Thus the Fellows included him in their sentence. But we must remember that when the paper displaying it was shown on the College hall door, the reason given was their 'contumacy' in refusing to answer the Master, and that the Master had caused the Dean to sign it as well as himself and so accept part of the displeasing responsibility.

To those who have inner knowledge of College life, it seems that the history of Shelley's Oxford disaster, although Hogg gave a copious account of it and many other contributions are extant, lacks some important circumstances. The first activities of any brilliant boy on being transferred from school to university may well be fantastic, and University College had seen such fireworks before Shelley came. However, the word Atheism was as damning as it could be; it conveyed, where the ground was ready, all the demons of revolutionary France! 'No more of that,' said Oxford in 1811. Yet Shelley's dismissal still perplexes us.

It perplexed him. Under the bravado of his expressions at the time, the word 'logic' can be seen as his steady point. 'I have come into the home of the reasoners. They teach me the right form of reasoning. I will take the most important proposition I can, and do my utmost; and they, as men to whom thought is free, will meet me fairly.' Whoever reads *The Necessity of Atheism* is likely to be surprised not by its audacity but by its restraint; 'the language,' Shelley's American biographer Newman White has well judged, 'was temperate and the conclusions were no more than agnostic.' But in the end Shelley was formally expelled not for his exercise of an ancient Oxford diversion; contumacy came in and, they say, other provocations to a small and sleepy society.

Shelley's Oxford life was all over and done in six months. Hogg had been his principal companion through that period, but the rarity of allusions to him in contemporary comments on Shelley the undergraduate seems to mean that Shelley was not invariably seen with Hogg; the poet's school friendships were continuing in their own way until the expulsion. So far Shelley had written nothing of much merit in prose or verse although he had tried to startle and disconcert the world with his extravagances in metre and in prose. He was chiefly distinguished at the age of eighteen by his eagerness to dispute accepted opinion and in general his love of reasoning; his quickness and daring in argument were certainly increased by the brief experience he had of university lectures and discussions. In Godwin's book *Political Justice*, which had become a back number for most people, he discovered the sort of analysis and the sort of manifesto which he dreamed of. As for practical benevolence, which as a small boy he had taken to be the duty of persons in his position, he set about it at Oxford as willingly as ever, but with greater dangers; thus, he undertook responsibility for several hundred pounds paid to a ridiculous but artful man who demanded subsidy as the author of a mass of manuscript about the Northern Courts.

It is not surprising that the sentence passed by University College on Shelley found him short of money, and Hogg was unable to produce any; but they were required to leave Oxford at once. Shelley borrowed £20 from one of the Slatter family and on 26 March he and his fellow-exile were on the coach for London.

III. HARRIET

The reason for Shelley's going to London at this point was mainly that at Field Place he could expect no applause for his valour on behalf of logic and no leave to go on with the argument against all hypotheses of a deity. His father was not prepared to have the younger children enlightened on the necessity of atheism; he and Sir Bysshe required Shelley to submit himself unconditionally to plans for his next discipline. One was that he should travel in Greece, another that he should be controlled by a private tutor, and a third that he should become M.P. for Horsham. The last proposal was urged by the Duke of Norfolk with whom Timothy and his son dined. Nothing would satisfy Shelley, unless (so he said) he could be convinced of error in his precious demonstration, contained in the notorious pamphlet.

So he drifted on in London. At last his father was induced to allow him £200 a year for subsistence. Hogg saw fit to moderate his own 'contumacy' and went off to York and a lawyer's office. Shelley found something more romantic to occupy him. It happened that two of his sisters were at Mrs. Fenning's school at Clapham, and he already knew one of their friends there, a brilliant girl named Harriet Westbrook. Shelley reflected that she might become a convert to his atheism, and found occasion to instruct her; she would not agree, but after the Easter holidays found herself most unpopular at school on the rumour that she had done so.

Harriet Westbrook, three years younger than Shelley, was one of the two surviving daughters of John Westbrook of Chapel Street, Grosvenor Square. He was a wealthy man, perhaps the proprietor of the Cocoa Tree, a club-house long in high favour. Mrs. Westbrook was an invalid, and Harriet was chiefly in charge of her elder sister Elizabeth, who was nine years to a day older than Shelley. Both girls were ready to receive a little novelty and variety; the ordinary conversation of their domestic circle was limited and sectarian. Eliza (so she was usually called) found Shelley interesting in a way different from the school-girl's, and the hint of an adventure arose.

But if Eliza dreamed that her talks with Shelley at 23 Chapel Street would grow into the love affair she seems not to have yet experienced, she and all concerned were soon to be surprised. Harriet's miseries at school, as she explained them to Shelley in person or by letter, disturbed him; he was the cause of them. He confronted Mr West-brook with the advice that he should take his daughter from the school, but the veteran appeared beyond reason. Harriet at last told Shelley that she would run away with him. He made the arrangements; on 25 August 1811 she joined him at a coffee-house in Mount Street and off they went in the Edinburgh coach. On the way Shelley found out the method of getting married in Scotland, and on 28 August, describing himself as a Sussex farmer, he made Harriet his wife.

This lyrical episode duly added to the bewilderment of Timothy Shelley, but apparently did not altogether displease old Sir Bysshe. Another interested party was Hogg, who joined the couple at Edinburgh, and presently, at York, while Shelley was absent in pursuit of funds from Sussex, made violent love to Harriet. She seems to have called upon Eliza to deal with Hogg, and Shelley on his return decided that it was not safe for them to remain in that mistaken friend's neighbourhood. With the two women he removed to Keswick, where he met the poet Robert Southey and resented his confident counsels. Even there, moreover, the Duke of Norfolk was trying to relieve his difficulties; Shelley, Harriet and Eliza spent the first week of December 1811 as his guests at Greystoke Castle. The result was that Shelley's quarrel with his father became less furious, and John Westbrook allowed Harriet £200 a year.

Shelley was writing away, in any time that his problems spared, but action was what he called for, and he now felt himself destined to assist Catholic Emancipation in Ireland. Southey's dissuasion only increased his resolve. At the beginning of February 1812 his trio arrived in Dublin, and *An Address to the Irish People* was soon printed and distributed. Harriet treated the campaign as a great joke—and, for she was all for her husband, as a noble design. He made one public speech which did not quite end in his being mobbed; he produced more pamphlets for Ireland's and humanity's good; but before long admitted that he was unsuccessful. Besides, there were new applicants with bundles of manuscript, desiring ready cash.

In April 1812 the Shelleys returned from Ireland, and lived at one place and another in Wales and Devon; at Barnstaple Shelley was watched by government agents. He was distributing his own *Declaration of Rights* and a seditious *Letter to Lord Ellenborough* aerially by balloons and nautically in dark green bottles. The third 'programme' of 1812 took Shelley, Harriet and Eliza up to Tremadoc in North Wales, where a man of many projects, W. A. Madocks M.P., was reclaiming a large swamp, building an embankment and constructing a new town. Shelley subscribed £100 to this scheme and gave his time and attention to the office work and what is now called publicity. At the end of February 1813 an attempt to murder or maim him during a night of storm ended his services to Madocks, and Harriet probably persuaded him that a holiday at Killarney was necessary to his health. This period had been additionally vexatious because one more of Shelley's ardent plans had failed. He had invited a Sussex schoolmistress, Elizabeth Hitchener, who appeared to share his or William Godwin's political philosophy, to join his household; discord of course quickly arose, and even Shelley was unable to end the situation gracefully.

Most of the poems which Shelley was composing in 1812 and 1813 appear to have remained unprinted, though Harriet, to whom the wisest and best of them were addressed, kept them together with fond care. But there was one long composition which did not remain with the others, and which was intended by the young reformer to be a literary instrument for the progress of free and active opinion. It may even have begun without being distinctly designed while Shelley was at Eton and continued, still in a sketchy way, at Oxford, but at Tremadoc he shaped the work as he had come to see it comprehensively; and its title was *Queen Mab: a Philosophical Poem.* When he submitted it to Thomas Hookham, a London bookseller who also published numerous not over-popular productions, Shelley was prepared to find that *Queen Mab* would be judged too dangerous material to be published in the regular manner. Hookham pardonably declined to take the risk of prosecution.

Accordingly Shelley accepted the labour of printing and circulating his poem himself, and one small mystery is that he gave Mr. Westbrook's address, 23 Chapel Street, on the title-page; perhaps his father-in-law indulged him in that without bothering his head over the nature of the book. Shelley sent copies to the leading writers, including Lord Byron, who treated it as 'a poem of great power and imagination;' but Shelley meant *Queen Mab* for something nearer a guide to modernism. Within the framework of a tale of wonder, he presented a series of discussions on the past, present and future; his scientific notions, his charges against the forms which Christianity had taken, his enthusiasm for the vegetarian diet, his criticism of the institution of marriage where it appears to him to become bondage, his protest against political machines where they destroy human nature, and other striking subjects were marshalled in the strange light of the supernatural opening. In the fashion of the period Shelley reinforced the poetical display with a strong body of prose notes, part original and part quotations.

The contents of the poem itself, to be sure, were also part original and part transmitted; for the ideas which Shelley rejoiced in as the keys to a magnificent and benevolent state of life, not immediately attainable but certain to come in the centuries ahead, were some of them of great antiquity. Most had been appearing, even in authors whose names were held in honour everywhere, during the eighteenth century. What Shelley, not yet twenty-one years of age, had specially to offer was youthful intensity—and that in an astonishing degree. The phenomenon was familiar, but not its absolute force and fiery courage; but then Shelley at the time was so moved by his observations and reflections that he believed himself to be sent into the world as a means of profound change and illumination.

Queen Mab was one of those books which are read by a few and rumoured about by many; the obvious reputation for such a privately circulated revolutionary appeal was that it was sheer wickedness, blasphemy and obscenity. Towards the end of his life Shelley announced that he had not seen a copy for years, and was willing to suppose it crude and abrupt; but he never abandoned the idealism which made him write it. It was used in the bare mention to provoke loathing for his name and to bring suffering on him; but that was not the end. When Shelley was beyond human conflicts, *Queen Mab* was boldly reprinted again and again—illegally—so that anybody could afford to buy it, and it became a classic among the early socialists of England and America. Another historical side of it belongs to the long prose note on vegetarianism which Shelley presently published in separate form as *A Vindication of Natural Diet;* this essay continues to reappear and may be counted as one of the 'sacred books' of the vegetarians.

IV. MARY GODWIN

After his second visit to Ireland Shelley took Harriet from place to place with rapidity, but they passed some time in London, and their daughter Eliza Ianthe was born there in June. They next occupied High Elms House, Bracknell, in Shelley's favourite English landscape. In London Shelley had seen something of William Godwin, who paid him marked attention, but the problem was how to endure Godwin's second wife; and Harriet gave up the attempt. Shelley was indiscreet enough to tell Godwin as much, and it may be that more of subsequent happenings originated in that admission than we have been told. Another man of letters becomes noteworthy in Shelley's life during 1813, the novelist Thomas Love Peacock, who as yet was concerned principally with his hopes as a poet. It is said that Shelley, always trying to be a Liberal in personal actions, allowed Peacock £100 a year, but when that assistance began to be given is unknown. Peacock, though he had his faults, was one of the soundest and most observant friends whom Shelley ever found.

Peacock was amused rather than impressed by a set of clever and unconventional people with whom Shelley was delighted to spend his time at Bracknell. One was a gallant vegetarian and paradox-lover named J. F. Newton; another was his beautiful sister-in-law Mrs. de Boinville, who had with her an even more beautiful daughter Cornelia Turner; and these and other sympathetic spirits made up an artistic and intellectual society in which Shelley was swiftly at home.

That August Shelley greeted Harriet's birthday as his custom was with a poem apparently inspired by happy love, but at Bracknell he showed signs of discontent while Eliza Westbrook remained with his family. However, things went on as usual; and the party, with Peacock too, went north in Harriet's new carriage a little later. Finding no house in the Lakes for them they came back to Windsor, and the deep winter of 1813 closed round them. It is striking, in the light of what happened later, that Shelley and Harriet were re-married on 24 March 1814 with Harriet's father as a witness at St. George's, Hanover Square. Eliza Westbrook is seen leaving the Shelley household in mid-April, and Shelley goes to the home of

Mrs. Boinville by himself. He leaves his friends abruptly and in desolate mood, if a poem of the moment is an actual record of crisis, and something seems to have intervened between him and Harriet, whom he rejoins in London. Nobody has discovered precisely what had endangered their marriage.

But one more of the wild flyings-off which characterize the early life of Shelley quickly ensued. He was detained in London several days without his wife and child to suit the convenience of William Godwin, for whom he had undertaken to raise no less than £3000. In this time he became possessed with the thought of going off with Mary, the daughter of Godwin and Mary Wollstonecraft—a girl who apparently wanted nothing more longingly. Shelley at least called Harriet to him from her holiday at Bath to tell her this and to propose that she, Mary and he might live together, Mary 'as his wife.' Harriet was not sound enough in the new school of Virtue to reach the needed impersonality. Nothing, however, not even Shelley's own recurrent doubt nor Peacock's mediations, could check developments. At the end of July 1814 Shelley and Mary raced over the Channel—but, in case they could have simplified their affairs, it was fated that Jane Clairmont the daughter of Mrs. Godwin by her first husband should go with them. She was never again really to leave them alone together; Eliza Westbrook was comparatively a mild penalty.

Had Shelley returned from the Continental trip with the two girls to his amazed but constant Harriet, he could not have escaped the tongue of rumour. He had already, at twenty-two, provided 'the world' with enough to work on,—the expulsion from Oxford for a campaign of atheism, the elopement with a school-girl from a respectable home, the circulation of subversive and outrageous writings,—and now, taking two of Godwin's daughters into France, he had obviously purchased two mistresses from that despised and money-grubbing philosopher.

Mrs. Godwin pursued the travellers as far as Calais, but failed to detach her daughter Jane from the party, an account of whose adventures was published anonymously in a small volume typical of the Regency era entitled a *History of a Six Weeks' Tour through a Part of France, Switzerland, Germany, and Holland*. One of the wonders of this trip was the manner in which Shelley managed to collect ready money, but it was the lack of this commodity which prevented an intended visit to Italy and turned the travellers homeward. Among the memorable moments, there was a sunny day in a boat carrying merchandise down the upper Rhine, and

Shelley helped the time along by reading aloud Mary Wollstonecraft's *Letters from Norway*. Evening came on with exceptional beauty. 'Suddenly the river grew narrow, and the boat dashed with inconceivable rapidity round the base of a rocky hill covered with pines; a ruined tower, with its desolated windows, stood on the summit of another hill that jutted into the river; beyond, the sunset was illuminating the distant mountains and clouds, casting the reflection of its rich and purple hues on the agitated river. The brilliance and contrasts of the colours on the circling whirlpools of the stream, was an appearance entirely new and most beautiful; the shades grew darker as the sun descended below the horizon, and after we had landed, as we walked to our inn round a beautiful bay, the full moon arose with divine splendour, casting its silver light on the before purpled waves.'

From scenes like that Shelley brought the girls back to London and serio-comic perplexities. William Godwin, supported by his wife, kept him out of the house and demanded money. Harriet, who endured Shelley's violent letters and requests for occasional assistance very well, did not easily give way to the claims of Mary and the plan of a formal separation. On 30 November 1814 her second child, Charles Bysshe Shelley, was born a month before the expected time. Mary's first baby, a girl, a seven months' child, was born about 22 February 1815, and died after a week or so.

At the beginning of 1815 Shelley's grandfather Sir Bysshe died at Horsham, and in the usual way the family assembled soon afterwards to hear the will read. Shelley arrived at Field Place for the occasion but was compelled by his father to remain outside the front door, where he heard (correctly) from his uncle John Shelley Sidney that it was a most extraordinary will. But Sir Timothy and his lawyer judged that something could be done to straighten things out, and Shelley agreed to sell a minor estate (now his property) to his father for a lump sum and £1000 a year. In June 1815 he was able to allow Harriet £200 a year and to make something like a new home with Mary. A furnished house in the Thames Valley—at Bishopsgate on the edge of Windsor Park—was taken, and since for the time Jane Clairmont was in Devonshire the couple were allowed some peace.

After a voyage up the Thames shared with Mary, Charles Clairmont and T. L. Peacock, Shelley passed many autumnal hours under the great trees of Windsor, and composed a long poem expressive of an altering conception of his own destiny. In *Queen Mab* he was prompted by the conviction that he could and must reform the world;

but *Alastor, or the Spirit of Solitude*, is an attempt to depict the mystery of things and to portray the spiritual travels of an idealist who fails to overcome isolation. Shelley had been reading more contemplative and mystical literature than formerly, and his tone in *Alastor* is accordingly deepened and subtilized. The poem is faulty enough, and the story in it is like many of his stories in verse—incredible as well as disjointed; but *Alastor* is not to be read for the story. Its studies of nature and of a romantic temper are the thing here, and the beauty of these is peculiar to this one poem—a sad loveliness.

Alastor was published at the beginning of 1816. As a specimen of the reviewing of that time and the disdainful style to which Shelley had to accustom himself when he received press notices of his books, we may read in *The British Critic*: 'If this gentleman is not blessed with the inspiration, he may at least console himself with the madness of a poetic mind. In the course of our critical labours, we have been often condemned to pose over much profound and prosing stupidity; we are therefore not a little delighted with the nonsense which mounts, which rises, which spurns the earth, and all its dull realities; we love to fly with our author to a silent nook.

> One silent nook
> Was there. Even on the edge of that vast mountain
> Upheld by knotty roots and fallen rocks
> It overlooked in its serenity
> The dark earth and the bending vault of stars.

Tolerably high, this aforesaid nook, to overlook the stars: but

> Hither the poet came. His eyes beheld
> Their own wan light through the reflected lines
> Of his thin hair, distinct in the dark depths
> Of that still fountain.

Vastly intelligible. Perhaps, if his poet had worn a wig, the case might have been clearer ... But this aforesaid hair is endowed with strange qualities.

> his scattered hair
> Sered by the autumn of strange suffering,
> Sung dirges in the wind.

This can only be interpreted by supposing, that the poet's hair was entwined in a fiddle-stick, and being seared with "the autumn of strange sufferings," *alias* rosin, "scraped discords in the wind", for so the last line should evidently be read' ...

V. A Year of Vicissitude

The year 1816 was to bring several new and important factors into Shelley's life, and one of these was the work of the audacious Jane Clairmont. In any case Lord Byron, the author of *Childe Harold* and hitherto the hero of London society, must have played some part in Shelley's history; but it was through Jane, who now began to call herself Claire, that he soon became singularly connected with his daily life.

Early in 1816 the girl forced herself upon Byron and in consequence found herself pregnant. Byron, when rumours about his relations with his half-sister turned society against him, flung away from England on 25 April. Jane, or Claire, now resumed her place with Shelley and Mary. It happened that they were preparing to find relief from the antipathy which often pained them in England by revisiting the Continent. This project was agreeable to Claire, and when they set out in the first week of May 1816 (with their son William, born on 24 January) she accompanied them. All stayed at a hotel in Geneva, and late in the month Byron arrived with his 'staff.'

Claire's affair with him was hopeless; but Byron and Shelley got on well together, and their conversations on poetry and philosophy left both of them stimulated. They enjoyed one famous excursion by boat round the Lake of Geneva, and its associations historic and literary. During this voyage a sudden storm threatened to capsize their boat, and Shelley who could not swim made sure of not involving Byron in an attempt to save him. A noteworthy visitor to Geneva and Byron interested Shelley particularly as one whose tales of terror had magnetized him in boyhood: this was 'Monk' Lewis, and even now, when this affable man served up some gruesome stories, Shelley took the trouble to copy them down at some length. Legal bothers in England dragged Shelley northwards soon after, and on 29 August 1816 his household began the return journey. He had the honour of carrying with him the manuscript of Byron's *Childe Harold*, Canto III—an awkward honour, for he was to negotiate about it with a cold enemy, the publisher John Murray. This Canto shows that Byron had learned something of the interpretation of the universe as a poetical purpose from his new and admiring friend.

Soon after Shelley's resumption of a nomadic and persecuted existence in England, a tragedy occurred which plunged him into misery; and yet it was nothing for which he could reproach himself.

William Godwin's family included a young woman known as Fanny Godwin, the daughter of Mary Wollstonecraft and Captain Imlay. She was incurably 'in disgrace with fortune.' She also had a feeling for Shelley very much like love, to which he had responded with his generous kindness. There was no room for her in his home, and disappointments persuaded her that there was no room for her anywhere this side the grave. On 10 October she committed suicide in a hotel at Swansea, where Shelley, alarmed by a letter from her, arrived too late to dissuade her. He was not quickly able to escape from the reflection that, on his last meeting with her, her manner had given signs of the despair within, if only he had read them aright.

Scarcely had Fanny's death become a thing of yesterday when another catastrophe rushed upon Shelley. He had been assuming that Harriet, with the two children, was secure enough in her father's home in Chapel Street. So, perhaps, she had usually been, but in the autumn of 1816 some situation of which we do not know the details came to a height there. Her father and her sister Eliza seem to have opposed her in a personal decision she was making, and she left the house, to be brought back to it dead ten days later. She had been found drowned in the Serpentine. The news reached Shelley who was in lodgings at Bath; he hastened to London (December 16) in order at least to take charge of his children, but not surprisingly found that Eliza Westbrook, blaming him for her sister's ruin, was minded to prevent him.

It must be said here that the episodes leading to Harriet's death are still obscure, and the present writer's opinion is that a letter supposed to have been written by her before committing suicide is a hateful forgery. Whether she had found and been deserted by a lover is an undecided question. That she had undergone moods of deep dejection, in which she sometimes resorted to her friend Mrs. Boinville, is observable; and that her disaster cut Shelley to the heart, though he did not often talk of it, is a fact witnessed by his undramatic companion Peacock.

The next change was due to the difficult position of Mary, whom Shelley married at a city church—St. Mildred's, Bread Street—on 30 December 1816. Meanwhile a legal battle over the custody of his and Harriet's children was beginning. The Westbrooks, in whose care Ianthe and Charles had so long been, duly made their application to the Lord Chancellor, and that authority at length decided that Shelley, on account of his 'immoral and vicious' principles of conduct, should not be given his children. They were to be placed at a school approved by the Court. (In the end, this plan meant that Eliza Westbrook became the guardian of the girl, and the boy was sent to Sir Timothy Shelley). The indignation of Shelley in face of the decision is best seen in his poetical attack on Lord Eldon for making it.

Yet one more complication befell Shelley at this period. On 13 January 1817 Claire Clairmont gave birth to Byron's daughter Allegra. Her only hope was that Shelley would give her and the baby a home, and he proceeded to do so, but the misinterpretation inevitable in the circumstances must have been a heavier price for him to pay for his kindness than the obvious expense.

If we look for a brighter side to Shelley's concerns in the winter of 1816, one can readily be recognized. For the first time he enjoyed the society of poets and poetical men, gathering freely and talking with gusto. Early in December he had been elated to find himself announced by Leigh Hunt in the *Examiner* as one of three young poets, the other two being John Keats and less decidedly John Hamilton Reynolds, who promised to reanimate poetry in England. Shelley made his way to Hunt's cottage in the Vale of Health, Hampstead, and was quickly accepted as being not only a man of genius but as one of the family. The cottage was itself an entertainment, so many remarkable people arrived to converse with Hunt and with one another, so unusual were the family of Hunt and his wife, so varied even if not mighty their accomplishments. And Hampstead Heath in those days, as Constable's pictures and many others attest, was a surprising pastoral in sight of St. Paul's Cathedral. Shelley delighted especially in its ponds, on which he and the Hunt children sailed their paper boats while all else was forgotten.

In Leigh Hunt Shelley found a friend of much sensibility, a man of taste, a musician, above all a believer in the essential joy of human life. One of Hunt's particular pleasures was to bring his new poets Keats and Shelley together. He found that Shelley took to Keats better than Keats to Shelley, and possibly this was caused in part by Shelley's advising his young rival to postpone the publication of the volume of verse on which at that date Keats's heart was set. However, within the cottage there was plenty of good temper and discourse, and even competition in verse-writing. Leigh Hunt himself was the poet of whom the public had heard and read something, and he rejoiced in these little ceremonies and the sense of having a Parnassus of his own.

Shelley through Hunt met the critic and painter William Hazlitt, who was not sure whether to idolize him or to ridicule him; Hazlitt discerned an extraordinary beauty, physical and spiritual, in this poet, but was impatient with the impossibilities which he saw in such a figure's combat with the shrewd and powerful world. An unlucky acquaintance was that with the artist B. R. Haydon, who was affronted by Shelley's refusal of Christianity and of roast beef. But the malice of Haydon was compensated by the sympathy of another of Hunt's circle, a stockbroker in daily life, named Horace Smith. Not sharing Shelley's religious views himself, this eminent man, who had helped to amuse the age with the parodies called *Rejected Addresses*, and who wrote graceful mythological poems, could listen with amazement to the eloquence with which the young reformer presented them. Horace Smith became to Shelley a friend scarcely less valued than Hunt, and as ready to serve him. It has to be noticed, however, that the friend who stood at Shelley's side all through the exhausting Chancery law-case, and was prepared to make a temporary home under his roof for Shelley's children, was Leigh Hunt.

VI. 'THE HERMIT'

Now that he had married Mary, and no doubt in response to her wishes, Shelley proposed to give up his wandering style of existence and take a house. The locality was never in much doubt—the Thames valley; and in March 1817 he occupied Albion House, Great Marlow, on a lease of twenty-one years. The title of his pamphlet *A Proposal for putting Reform to the Vote, throughout the Kingdom: By the Hermit of Marlow*, illustrates at once his political passion and the dream of tranquil retirement which he was enjoying. His friend Peacock knew Marlow well and was one of his most frequent visitors there, where indeed Shelley's retirement proved to be a constant exercise of hospitality and coming and going of reformists and their relations. It was his delight also to organize a scheme of distributing money, medicine and supplies among the poor inhabitants of Marlow and even beyond.

Within the house there was excellent furniture, a beautiful piano (for Claire) and a numerous collection of books; outside, Shelley commanded a good garden and some meadowland, but he also had his boat on the river and made good use of it for many excursions suited to his readings in English history and his love of natural scenery. He had his favourite seat in Bisham Woods above the Thames. These blessings were clouded a little by the peevishness of Mary, who might be forgiven if she found Claire's presence sometimes on her nerves, besides the restlessness of 'open house' and even the matter of accounts rendered. But she found time for authorship, as of course her husband did; and his long, involved, defiant poem *Laon and Cythna*, afterwards called *The Revolt of Islam*, was the fruit of his months at Marlow. It is claimed to have been composed in competition with John Keats, who was giving his imagination full play through 1817 in his narrative poem *Endymion;* and, to keep up the 'triangular tournament' begun at Hampstead at the beginning of the year, Leigh Hunt was writing his less lengthy vision of *The Nymphs* at the same period.

Both Shelley and Keats met with a publisher in the Hampstead set. This was Charles Ollier, who with his brother James was starting out in the trade, and had more of the literary gift himself than most of the trade then showed. Keats soon left Ollier when his first small volume, *Poems*, made no headway; but Shelley was somewhat differently placed, and though he often meditated on the chances of finding a more effective publisher he never did. Ollier was as near being a Reformist as anybody in the business, but even Ollier took alarm when a few copies of *Laon and Cythna* had been sold. There were passages in the text which threatened to call down a prosecution for blasphemy or for sedition on both poet and publisher; and so after a correspondence Ollier was called to a conference at Albion House. The text was more or less made safe against the dangers of the law; and the title was altered to *The Revolt of Islam*.

However neatly Shelley made his concessions to Ollier and orthodoxy for the re-issue of the poem, one thing was impossible of alteration: the whole thing had no chance of becoming popular, and accordingly one of the writer's chief intentions was unfulfilled. The reader, no matter if he was friendly disposed towards Shelley's opinions or otherwise, could not be expected to sort out the narrative proper, overlaid as it was with an enormous introductory vision. Even the use of the symbol of the Serpent at the beginning, not as representing Evil but as the emblem of Good (and at the same time a supernatural lover of Cythna), is obstructive. Leigh Hunt, with the candour which he knew that his friend would prefer to sleek praise, at once assessed the poem's faults as well as its beauties: especially, 'too great a sameness and gratuitousness of image and metaphor, too (often) drawn from the elements, particularly the sea. The book is full of humanity; and yet it certainly does not go the best way to work for appealing to it through the medium of its common knowledges.'

No work was ever more remote from normal life in passage after passage, and yet it contains intervals of realism and simplicity which suggest that Shelley might have written a romance of peace and war to be read by many. For that matter, the conception of the heroine Cythna comes very near what we might hope to get from a master of the novel. Cythna is not entirely of this world, but a great deal of the story and characterization bring her before us as a woman of a modern type, feminine without denial but capable of daring action in the course of advancing a thought-out civilization. Shelley presumably had Mary Wollstonecraft in mind as he drew this Cythna.

Returning to the happenings of life in 1817 at Albion House, we find Mary's occupations varied by the arrival of a baby, Clara Everina, on 2 September, and Shelley in trouble with ophthalmia as well as the pecuniary embarrassments of his father-in-law, and (when was it not so?) the menaces of his own creditors. It was not simple, either, to maintain a calm mind at Marlow where the 'better class' regarded him as a villain and as nearly a madman, although he found friends among the shopkeepers, and even one or two who admired his genius. Both Mary and he became interested in the old hope of leaving their troubles behind by going to the Continent—and in Italy surely Shelley would find health. In December he advertised Albion House as to be let, furnished or unfurnished, with immediate possession; and his migration from England began to be more than a daydream. It was in February 1818 that Shelley left Marlow, where his brief residence has never been forgotten.

VII. ITALIAN DAYS

The opening months of 1818 seem to have been, in large measure, Mary Shelley's months; for they were spent partly in London and in a holiday spirit. Shelley yielded to the inclinations of his wife and the enthusiasms of his friends and went about with Mary and some of the circle to exhibitions, to plays and to operas. The intimacy with the Leigh Hunts, who had moved to Paddington, went on as light-heartedly and easily as ever; and the last evening that Shelley was to pass in his native land found the editor of the *Examiner* and his wife Marianne with him at 119 Great Russell Street. While Shelley was packing up his possessions the boy Thornton Hunt was allowed to examine an item which we do not commonly think of as part of Shelley's equipment but which had been noticed with suspicion by his contemporaries at University College, Oxford. It was his pair of pistols, and he knew how to use them.

Then the poet and Mary, William, Clara, Claire and Allegra, a young girl and a houseboy from Marlow, were on their way south. The journey through France was uneventful, and their thoughts ran ahead of their horses; but as yet they had not made a choice of their resting-place except all Italy. A reconnaissance of Lake Como almost settled the question, but on Mayday 1818 they moved off for Pisa, and once more their life looked like being a rapid succession of lodgings. They stayed at Leghorn and then at the Baths of Lucca. The problem of Byron, Claire and Allegra continued to be entwined with their direct affairs, and in August it necessitated a journey first by Shelley and next by Mary to Venice where Byron was living. That dutiful undertaking had one result which darkened the pleasant brightness brought into their world by the skies, landscapes and classical relics of Italy; for on the way the child Clara became ill, and at Venice she died.

Byron welcomed Shelley and talked with him as cordially as he could desire, but the wild and consuming excesses of his life at Venice could not be missed, and Shelley was torn between wonder at the intellectual and poetical powers of his friend and depression over the probable outcome of his degradations. The first of these feelings was expressed in a poem of intense beauty as well as lucidity, the *Lines Written Among the Euganean Hills*, in which Shelley includes a lament over the decay of Venice in the matter of political freedom and virtue and suggests that only the fact that the poet Byron lived there will redeem the city's name in days to come.

It is typical of Shelley that he did not regard the long picture-lyric just mentioned as among his considerable poems—it was just *Lines*; but while he was in Byron's neighbourhood he began to shape a work which may be said to be in the sequence of *Queen Mab* and *The Revolt of Islam* and to continue but to purge or refine the philosophy within those imperfect poems. The influence of Italy upon his style and his judgment of a poetical design was already working, and working deeply. The new work, of which more will be seen in a moment, was called *Prometheus Unbound*. Even as he experimented with the first movement of this symphony Shelley was active along a different track of poetry, but then the fascination of Byron's personality was strong upon him, and what he wrote in prophetic and heraldic fashion concerning that poet in the *Lines* was not what he was urged to perpetuate in the strange epistolary poem *Julian and Maddalo*. Whatever may be thought of the spasmodic evocation of the Madman in that piece, the character-study of Count Maddalo, a kind of Byron, is as clever as it is clear.

From Este, where the poet had perhaps tried to forget the bitterness of losing his daughter so suddenly in a special attention to poetry, the Shelleys set forth for Naples, a long journey with Rome as one of the cities on the way. Shelley's letter to Peacock describing the first stage of this travel is worth quoting at some length as expressing the 'Sussex farmer' as well as picturesque observer in him:—

'Ferrara, Nov.8th, 1818.

'My dear Peacock,—We left Este yesterday on our journey towards Naples. The roads were particularly bad; we have, therefore, accomplished only two days' journey of eighteen and twenty-four miles each, and you may imagine that our horses must be tolerably good ones, to drag our carriage, with five people and heavy luggage, through deep and clayey roads. The roads are, however, good during the rest of the way.

'The country is flat, but intersected by lines of wood, trellised with vines, whose broad leaves are now stamped with the redness of their decay. Every here and there one sees people employed in agricultural labours, and the plough, the harrow, or the cart, drawn by long teams of milk-white or dove-coloured oxen of immense size and exquisite beauty. This, indeed, might be the country of Pasiphaes. In one farm-yard I was shown sixty-three of these lovely oxen, tied to their stalls, in excellent condition. A farmyard in this part of Italy is somewhat different from one in England. First, the house, which is large and high, with strange-looking unpainted window-shutters, generally closed, and dreary beyond conception. The farm-yard and out-buildings, however, are usually in the neatest order. The threshing-floor is not under cover, but like that described in the Georgics, usually flattened by a broken column, and neither the mole, nor the toad, nor the ant, can find on its area a crevice for their dwelling. Around it, at this season, are piled the stacks of the leaves and stalks of Indian corn, which has lately been threshed and dried upon its surface. At a little distance are vast heaps of many-coloured zucche or pumpkins, some of enormous size, piled as winter food for the hogs. There are turkeys, too, and fowls wandering about, and two or three dogs, who bark with a sharp hylactism. The people who are occupied with the care of these things seem neither ill-clothed nor ill-fed, and the blunt incivility of their manners has an English air with it, very discouraging to those who are accustomed to the impudent and polished lying of the inhabitants of the cities.'

On this occasion Shelley paused for a week in Rome, a week of supreme delight in all its art and antiquity; thence, going ahead alone, he soon found a lodging in Naples for all the family, looking across the royal gardens upon 'the blue waters of the bay, forever changing, yet forever the same.' These waters were soon to undulate through one of his best known minor poems, headed *Stanzas, Written in Dejection, near Naples*. What, apart from his poor health and the burden of accumulated griefs, was the cause of that dejection? It is possibly connected with the circumstances in which at this time he became the guardian of an infant whose name is unknown, a girl; she died in the summer of 1820 and that loss again threw him into dejection, deeper than before.

VIII. Rome and Elsewhere

No suffering could seriously check Shelley's explorations of Italy, where he was beginning to find merits even among the inhabitants; and Naples was an excellent centre. He recorded what he saw, at Pompeii for instance, and Paestum, in long letters to Peacock, unchallenged for beauty of delineation. What he saw moved him according to his nature to speculate on something which he had never seen—the Greece of his studies and longings. 'If such is Pompeii, what was Athens? What scene was exhibited from the Acropolis, the Parthenon, and the temples of Hercules, and Theseus, and the Winds? The islands and the Ægean sea, the mountains of Argolis, and the peaks of Pindus and Olympus, and the darkness of the Boeotian forests interspersed?' But for wars, he reflected, Athens might have escaped ruin; 'to what an eminence might not humanity have arrived!' The Grecian genius was more than ever in his mind now as he went forward with his new and, some will say, his greatest poem.

It was from Rome on 6 April 1819 that Shelley announced to Peacock what he supposed at the moment to be the completion of that work: 'My *Prometheus Unbound* is just finished, and in a month or two I shall send it. It is a drama, with characters and mechanism of a kind yet unattempted; and I think the execution is better than any of my former attempts.' Shelley had in fact written three acts of this play for the theatre of the imagination only, and might well believe that the scheme was wholly attained since the action appeared to be completed. He put the manuscript by, and very soon another theme caught his attention—it was the history of the extinction of a noble family in Rome in the year 1599. This, communicated to him by a friend, appeared to offer the fabric for a tragic drama, and after failing to convince Mary that she was the one to write it, Shelley himself set to work upon *The Cenci*.

But all this, and the inexhaustible wealth of ancient and modern things in Rome, suddenly lost significance. The Shelleys were already accustomed to the deaths of their children and other intimates, but the boy William had been so brilliantly strong and well that they could not suspect anything would befall him. He had been their already intelligent companion; and on 7 June 1819 after a short illness, watched sleeplessly by Shelley, he lay dead. Instead of returning to Naples the father and mother hurried away to Leghorn, where they could find some relief from the calamity in the good nature of their friends John and Maria Gisborne.

It was timely, too, to receive just now and to share with the Gisbornes a novel by T.L. Peacock called *Nightmare Abbey* in which Shelley was caricatured with unerring delicacy as Scythrop Glowry. The pure humour of this characterization was at once applauded by the enthusiast reflected in it, and the whole book was assessed in the highest terms; so fine a judge as Mr. David Garnett in his recent edition of Peacock's novels agrees with Shelley, and places *Nightmare Abbey* at the top of all the series early and late. But it is to the youthful Shelley that Scythrop is related; we must leave it at that.

'I have a study here in a tower, something like Scythrop's, where I am just beginning to recover the faculties of reading and writing.' Shelley is sending Peacock his news from a country villa near Leghorn on 6 July 1819. And in this tower with its startling panorama he is writing his five-act play *The Cenci* with a pathetic confidence that Miss O'Neil, whose acting had charmed him much in the last weeks in London, will play the principal part. True, the tragedy turns on the incest committed by Count Cenci, and the revenge taken by his daughter Beatrice and others; that, although Shelley has been in-credibly skilful in leaving the incest understood but not particularized, may disconcert the theatre managers . . . It did, and the play was not acted with Miss O'Neil, or Edmund Kean, or anyone in the leading parts until long after Shelley was dead. It is probably the greatest of all the dramas in the manner of Elizabethan plays modernized, which abounded in England in the nineteenth century, and if in form it is not so original as it could have been that arises from Shelley's deliberate choice and—in this direction—practical thinking. As a published dramatic poem it had more success than his other writings, and it still insists on our being interested in the phantom of Beatrice Cenci whom the author seemed to see before him.

Life in and below the tower is thus reported to Peacock late in August 1819: 'My employments are these: I awaken usually at seven; read half-an-hour; then get up; breakfast; after breakfast ascend *my tower*; and read or write until two. Then we dine. After dinner I read Dante with Mary, gossip a little, eat grapes and figs, sometimes walk, though seldom, and at half-past five pay a visit to Mrs. Gisborne, who reads Spanish with me until near seven. We then come for Mary, and stroll about till supper time.' Shelley's Spanish studies were begun in the desire to read Calderón's plays in the original language and with the thought that a visit to Spain, recommended by the doctors, might one day be practicable. At least they produced some specimens of Calderón in English which still live and please.

It has been seen that Shelley had written what might have remained the whole of *Prometheus Unbound* and had spoken of it in letters to several friends as a finished composition; but before the year 1819 he had reconsidered it, and decided that it needed some further inventions of scene, music and idea. The additional Act IV was one of the fine things which Shelley wrote after removing from his crow's-nest near Leghorn to Florence on 2 October 1819. It may be that the spirit of delight in this new Act was partly aroused by the birth of Shelley's son Percy Florence on 12 November, a child destined to live peacefully into the days of R. L. Stevenson who was one of his many friends, literary, theatrical, or sea-going.

The removal from Leghorn interrupted the meetings with the Gisbornes, who scarcely felt the change more than their dog; on hearing of this admirer's unhappiness Shelley wrote, 'Poor Oscar! I feel a kind of remorse to think of the unequal love with which two animated beings regard each other, when I experience no such sensations for him, as those which he manifested for us. His importunate regret is, however, a type of ours, as regards you. Our memory —if you will accept so humble a metaphor—is for ever scratching at the door of your absence.' The letter goes on to the topic of 'Henry and the steam-engine,' which was prominent in Shelley's mind then and afterwards. Briefly, he had volunteered to finance Mrs. Gisborne's son Henry Reveley, a young engineer, in the construction of the first steamboat to ply between Marseilles, Genoa and Leghorn. In this project Shelley of the scientific turn of mind, and the benevolent Shelley prepared to go to great lengths for the advantage even of a new acquaintance with something of public usefulness in view, are seen persisting. The poet, as the work went on, was not merely the man with the chequebook; he spent hours in the office, he exhorted and he made suggestions; and the steamboat almost became a reality. But Reveley could not quite manage it all, and Shelley's eventual disappointment was rather over the abandonment of a cherished plan than the waste of his money.

While this hope of a modern wonder was arising Shelley was also stirred with the excitement of a new democratic power in England, notwithstanding that at first sight the suppression of that power was all a reader of newspapers might make out. The victory over Napoleon at Waterloo in 1815 led to the naming of a melancholy business at Manchester on 16 August 1819 as Peterloo; when the military attacked a Reform meeting, termed a riot, in St. Peter's Field. Shelley's long ballad *The Mask of Anarchy* then written in deep anger is not only a malediction on the masters of force and misgovernment but a prophecy of the triumph of resistance without violence—here if anywhere the poetry of socialism, its justice and its true lights, is found.

Shelley had plenty of amusing foibles, one of which was his assurance that he was a good weather-prophet, and at Florence on 25 October 1819 he predicted the oncoming of the autumnal rains, which were announced by a tempestuous wind and a thunderstorm. The facts might not interest us much today had not this seasonal change immediately found a response in Shelley's poetic nature, for that day he wrote much of the *Ode to the West Wind*. It is a poem of the past, of vanished vitality and things of glory spoiled and faded, but an appeal to the future also, springing up with the *"Spirit fierce"* of the storm and expecting regeneration out of the seeming fall.

Quite another source of inspiration increased Shelley's wish to write lyrically while the winter was closing on Florence in 1819; the ward of his uncle and aunt (Mr. and Mrs. Parker) at Maidstone was on her travels with a Welsh lady, and they became neighbours of the Shelleys for a few weeks. Sophia Stacey was Shelley's admirer from the first, and admiration from one so honest, comely and sweet-voiced was never unpleasing to the poet; it was all the more natural because of the family connection—the Parkers had never joined in the expulsion of Shelley. Among the songs written for Sophia the *Indian Serenade* is the most popular, and even if (as Newman White interprets) all of them were tributes to the power of music we can add that at a good moment Sophia arrived to reaweaken the melody in Shelley's life.

How Shelley looked to a woman's eye in 1819 it is easy to discover, for in this year the only surviving portrait of him in manhood —leaving aside sketches and other representations of more or less plausibility—was begun by Amelia Curran. This lady, whose father J. P. Curran of political fame had received Shelley in Ireland, was an amateur painter in Rome, and surely a skilful one. Her picture of Claire Clairmont is memorable, and that of Shelley although left unfinished has been reproduced times beyond counting. The original is at the National Portrait Gallery. It is spiritualized, we must deduce from written accounts of Shelley's features and expressions, but as a single impression of this poet's countenance it can never be superseded. The complaint against it is only that it has assisted (by its very beauty) to spread the legend of Shelley's being a flower-like and fairyland kind of being, which an inspection of his varied and dominating activity in an excessively burdened life must disallow.

IX. THE POET'S FULFILMENT

Prometheus Unbound, A Lyrical Drama was published in London, in succession to *The Cenci, A Tragedy*, in 1820. The myth on which it is founded, derived from the Greeks and expressed in one of the world's highest dramas by Aeschylus in the fifth century B.C., was current through Europe in the literature, art and music of the Romantic movement. That Prometheus, who taught man all the arts he knows, stole fire from heaven in order to work out his designs, and was punished by Zeus by being chained to a rock and eternally preyed upon by Zeus's eagle, was set free by Hercules after he shot the bird, is the received fable. Aeschylus, in a lost play exhibiting the liberation of Prometheus, is said to have based that liberation upon an agreement between the tyrannous Zeus and the chained rebel, who exchanged an important piece of foreknowledge for the unchaining. Shelley, of course, takes his own way, and rejects such reconciliation and barter. He leaves it to a mystery which may be allied to his god Mutability to overthrow Zeus at an 'inevitable hour,' and Prometheus is quietly released by Hercules and, in a manner, absorbed by the vast and harmonious change which grows through the universe thereafter.

For all Shelley's strenuous attempts while in England to convey his thoughts on the history of mankind and the prospects of society in poetical forms, it was in Italy that he became able to do this; the causes for his advance must have been numerous, and some of them are summed up simply in his comparative freedom from being hounded as he had been. But the education which he had gladly received since he reached Milan early in 1818, deepening his comprehension of the controlled greatness of works of art which last, bringing him into touch with masterpieces of architecture, sculpture, painting and scene again and again, and interesting him fully in the powers of music, the theatre and the dance, was one main contribution to his achieving *Prometheus Unbound*. He had never been deficient in the imaginings and allusions which a long poem requires, and now he had acquired a greater profusion still of these, but he had learned that opulent diversity only keeps the colours of life when it is sustained by a strong unity of concept or of plot.

His poem was many things, yet one. Sometimes the reader may say 'This is a kind of equivalent of a work by Mozart,' sometimes 'What a ballet is contained in this,' or again 'The only thing like this might be presented by some genius of cinematography.' The piece could be pardonably mistaken, at many points, for a bright and capricious fantasy, produced in the mood of a dreamer enjoying some wildly winding journey through dream appearances. But in a merely prosaic examination *Prometheus Unbound* cannot be judged to include much that is not selected by the writer's brain for its special effect in the combination of reasonings and appeals devoted to the creed of the coming race.

The fourth Act is in one view a sheer festivity—or it has that quality until very near its conclusion.

> Then weave the web of the mystic measure;
> From the depths of the sky and the ends of the earth
>   Come, swift Spirits of might and of pleasure,
> Fill the dance and the music of mirth,
>   As the waves of a thousand streams rush by
>   To an ocean of splendour and harmony!

In this Act, we have a sort of lyrical dialogue of love and glory between the Spirit of the Earth and the Spirit of the Moon. It is enjoyable simply as a poetical ballet, but what is said is not in the nature of a charming scene of that kind only. Shelley is at one and the same time putting on his magic figures in their delightful action and asserting a thing of the future, as one result of the Promethean course of ideas, which may yet be seen. The moon, he foretells, ceases to be a lifeless satellite; and once we permit ourselves to read what he actually says in this as in hundreds of passages as meaning something distinct and rational, instead of passing over the pages because critics have described Shelley as vague and rhetorical, we encounter a mind of the Shakespearean class, whose parable is worth our unriddling.

Shelley sees no limitation to the arts, expressions, discoveries, sciences of man—what he says in the poetry can be compared with what he says somewhere or other in his prose; but the condition on which for him all enterprise depends, as *Prometheus Unbound* shows his thought, is in one word 'love.' But that again is accompanied by other 'seals of that most firm assurance which bars the pit over Destruction's strength,' and the striking phrase dismisses any notion that Shelley is a sentimentalist. He is writing for the creation of the greater humanity in the persuasion that the artist may help to bring on that which he desires ideally, but he knows all the dangers and the chances. Above all Shelley offers no mirage of a Promethean paradise this week or the week after next; he points out that the passions remain, and chance, death, and (once again this shadowy but determined ancient) mutability.

If any poem deserved to be instantly read through Europe in 1820, *Prometheus Bound* was that poem; but Shelley was not the poet whom English reviewers with any noteworthy part to play were willing to support. He was a desperado, and if he had written *The Christian Year* it would have been sneered off or dropped into the waste-paper basket as another sinister attempt to destroy Church and State. With the passing of time his poem could be seen as one of the most profound, energetic and orchestral creations of the Romantics in any medium,—an obvious example of the abundance which goes with genius.

At the end of January 1820 Shelley transferred his household from Florence, where he felt the winter, to Pisa, where he could easily consult the fashionable Dr. Vacca. Besides, a friendly family lived there and Shelley, Mary (not quite so much) and Claire were at all times welcome. Mr. and Mrs. Mason were in fact Mr. George William Tighe and Lady Mount Cashell, whose education had been given by Mary Shelley's mother and who was independent enough by temperament apart from training. She impressed Shelley as being 'everything that is amiable and wise.' With books ancient and modern but not less with human beings, and with her garden, she was thoroughly at ease. It is recorded that Shelley's not quite convincing poem *The Sensitive Plant*, a dream with an uncertain interpretation, was occasioned by his visits to Mrs. Mason's garden. So far as the flowers and the gardening in the poem go, he could well have supplied all the details from his reminiscences of Field Place, and probably he did so.

Claire Clairmont, who had a talent for mildly wicked pen-sketches of people, included Mr. Mason among the queer sights of Pisa and even listed Shelley there—because he 'walks about reading a great quarto Encyclopaedia with another volume under his arm.' The best people at Marlow had disapproved of this habit of reading in public as he walked to the shops. But he was not merely filling in time; he had his difficulty to find time; and at Pisa he was collecting data for *A Philosophical View of Reform*. This prose treatise had to wait a hundred years for publication. It ought not to have been delayed, for it could have given some guidance as well as annoyance in the period to which its learning and argument were directed as though by a Whig M.P.

Shelley's life at Pisa was not free from disturbances which began in England, and of these the invectives and the exactions of William Godwin were the most painful. Nothing could induce Shelley, however, to abandon his philosophical veneration for the author of *Political Justice*, whom he stubbornly placed at the front of his generation when he wrote his verse *Letter to Maria Gisborne* in London, in the summer of 1820. This *Letter*, if we could take a census of reading, might prove to be very nearly the favourite of all Shelley's writings; it is a self-portrait (with a wide background) drawn with faultless good-humour and ease. It would seem to resemble Shelley's conversation, and so to explain the spell he could cast (when he did not think it an unsocial act) over his companions. For the range of theme, the amount and vividness of the observation, the sudden felicities of phrase and the negligent or desultory flings of high imagination, are all in the *Letter*; and if Shelleyan humour is an acquired taste, that is the place in which it may be acquired readily enough.

The *Letter to Maria Gisborne* can also be called an instance of the courtesy for which Shelley was admired among those who knew him; it is obviously—323 lines—a more than ordinary effort, and is an expression in its own kind of gratitude to the Gisbornes for lending the house in which Shelley sits writing.—It was near Leghorn, and nothing remarkable happened while the Shelleys occupied it. They left it in August when the hot weather affected them and then stayed at the Baths of Pisa. In this solacing retreat Mrs. Mason visited them, and made one of Shelley's audience while he read out his bardic *Ode to Liberty*. Not all to his discomfiture his performance was accompanied by the grunts of pigs out in the market pens, it being a fair-day; 'he compared it to the "chorus of frogs" in the satiric drama of Aristophanes,' and went on to imagine a burlesque play on the politics of 1820 in England with a chorus of pigs. The notion was not indeed a new one, but Shelley believed it was, and quickly wrote his lengthy joke out with the title *Œdipus Tyrannus, or Swellfoot the Tyrant*. He managed to get it published in London,

thanks to Horace Smith, but without his name; and when a busybody
of an alderman offered to have the publisher prosecuted, the edition,
almost entire, was surrendered. Shelley the humorist was no more
fortunate in his publishing than Shelley the poet and Shelley the
political philosopher.

Another long poem of much the same date can be described as
an instance of Shelley's light verse, though its nature is more delicate.
During a day's wanderings in solitude among the hills he had a
fancy which was soon expressed with ample detail as *The Witch
of Atlas*. It is again in the nature of a poetic ballet, and Shelley
requested Mary not to strip the forms therein of their light garments,
so that it may be hard on him to press for a prose abstract of his
'visionary rhyme.' But, since it is an elaborate mystification, it has
been investigated for its substance, and the scientific knowledge of
Shelley's age has been detected; within these luminous draperies
one man finds a story of electricity, another the marvels of the yet
opening age of steam. Perhaps it was the costuming and scene-
making that mattered most, and Shelley's resources for them were
profuse. One may dream of him with an experimental theatre of
his own in the material sense, and his youngest son Percy Florence
lived to have more than one such.

Assiduous as the poet was in his own compositions he was re-
markably observant of the poetry appearing month by month, and
studied the Reviews and journals for signs of it, but also obtained
as many productions as he could through his friends in London.
In the summer of 1820 John Keats was once more before the public
with the since celebrated collection *Lamia, Isabella and other Poems*.
When Shelley received a copy he appears to have been comparatively
unmoved by many of the poems there which are now considered
among the triumphs of English verse, but the fragment *Hyperion*
leapt out at him as a miraculous revelation. Though he had always
admitted that Keats was a poet he had hitherto shared the opinions
of Peacock and Hogg that the feeling and thought of his old ac-
quaintance were spoiled by his poor judgment, his suburban manner-
isms. In *Hyperion* Shelley saw Keats rising to what he believed to be
the right epic style; and from this time he lost no opportunity of
recommending this piece to his friends near and far and basing upon it
his prediction that Keats was going to emerge among the great poets.

To intensify Shelley's sympathy with Keats, first there was the
battering which Keats had been enduring from the same types of
critics who were always in the field against Shelley himself. If the
older of the two young men looked upon Keats as in need of

protection against literary blackguardism, it may have been a misunderstanding of Keats's personal character, but it was the kind of championship which Shelley was accustomed to look on as his responsibility. Next, the Gisbornes reported to Shelley, after meeting Keats, that he was extremely ill and had indeed been 'sentenced to death' by Shelley's admired medical friend Dr. Lambe.

A letter was soon sent off to Keats, inviting him to stay with the Shelleys at Pisa. In his reply, Keats showed that he was still vexed with Shelley's assumption of poetical seniority and tutorship in the Hampstead days, but grateful for the invitation and eager to keep it in prospect even though his plans were still to be made. On Keats's side Shelley's offer was not the easiest thing to receive, for his friends Taylor and Hessey, who were prominent in the urgent task of raising a fund and arranging the method of his seeking recovery in the South, were far from being friends of Shelley. Their puritanism could just stand the strain of their idolized Keats's free behaviour, but Shelley's private history as they supposed they knew it made him anathema.

At the end of October 1820 the Shelleys returned to Pisa; a flood at the Baths had invaded their house to the depth of four feet. They took a good, spacious and economical lodging, and before long their life was tolerably calm and studious. Picturesque Italian characters began to call upon them. One of these, Tommaso Sgricci, was on his way to winning an international reputation as a tragic poet who simply walked on to the stage himself and improvised a whole play in verse, sometimes on a subject proposed by a member of the audience. This peculiar proficiency in a traditional Italian skill was something near a fluency in Shelley's own expression, and Shelley attended some of Sgricci's public displays with curiosity. He presently described his own drama *Hellas*, 'written at the suggestion of the events of the moment,' as 'a mere improvise.'

And now Shelley was joined by his cousin and early schoolfellow Thomas Medwin, who had been soldiering in India and was rambling about Europe without any precise object unless it was to be a man of letters. In Thackeray's fiction the *genus* 'bore' is described with 'Captain' Medwin as the model, and Medwin ended by boring his patient kinsman; but his devotion to Shelley as a man and as a writer was worth having, and with Medwin at any rate Shelley could talk as long as he wished over the literary celebrities and characteristics of the age. The later career of Medwin seems to have been shabby and his attempts at authorship of the imaginative kind were undistinguished; but he rewarded Shelley for many kindnesses in some parts of his biographical papers. They are chaotic and they are fruitful in absurd errors, but to Medwin must be given the praise of having been among the very first to give the public an intimate account of Shelley as he was and as he conversed, besides paying to his memory a tribute of reasoned admiration which only grew more emphatic as the companionship of Pisa receded into the distant past. Medwin's poetry was duly submitted to Shelley for revision, but that penalty was one which Shelley did not wholly dislike and to which, in Italy, he became accustomed.

Of Prince Mavrocordato, 'gay, learned and full of enthusiasm for Greece' Mary had a higher estimate than Shelley, in spite of the appropriate dedication of *Hellas* when that work was ready. But Mary and her husband alike were wonderfully attracted by another new acquaintance, who was thus described by Mary in December 1820: 'Romantic and pathetic, a young girl of nineteen years of age, the daughter of a Florentine noble; very beautiful, very talented, who writes Italian with an elegance and delicacy equal to the foremost authors of the best Italian epoch. She is, however, most unhappy. Her mother is a very bad woman; and, as she is jealous of the talents and beauty of her daughter, she shuts her up in a convent where she sees nothing but the servants and idiots.' This fair solitary's name was Emilia Viviani.

X. THE YEAR OF 'ADONAIS'

Very early in 1821 Mary had some reason herself to be jealous of Emilia, for Shelley seemed to have little time or taste for any other subject. Once again he made the mistake, which was not a habit of this idealist only, of becoming quite bewildered by a new light. He tried to befriend Emilia in her troubles and was enchanted by her unsophisticated acceptance of him. In disposing of the suggestion made by Claire, that he ran a risk of involving himself in something more than a delicate friendship with Emilia, Shelley declared, 'I think her tender and true—which is always something. How many are only one of these things at a time!' Probably he would view Mary in 1821 as more true than tender, and to discover a new aim for the poetry of adoration in which he was gifted was a necessity.

Those who have watched him thus far as a working writer, delivering himself up to his daemon whenever a bold impulse came and speedily testing and selecting his large outlines of poems which he filled in from his own musical and thoughtful mind almost as fast as pen can move, will not be astonished at the result of his worship of Emilia Viviani. It seems to have taken him less than a fortnight to produce the poem in question, *Epipsychidion*, not to mention a number of fragments themselves of similar emotion and grace but excluded from the current of the song. For song it is, and yet it is a doctrine of love and a history of a man's loves. That it is wholly a spiritual essay on the subject cannot be said; it includes a passage on physical union; but in the world of Shelley's devotion the distinction between the body and the soul is exceedingly subtle, and there is no bathos.

But *Epipsychidion* even while he wrote it became like a lovely rumour from some other existence and some other sphere. In dispatching his manuscript to Ollier for a limited edition, on 16 February 1821, Shelley commented on this as simply as he could: it 'should not be considered as my own; indeed, in a certain sense, it is a production of a portion of me already dead; and in this sense the advertisement is no fiction.' The advertisement pretended that the writer of 'the following lines' had died at Florence, while he was getting ready for a voyage to a remote island—a person who by nature saw things tinged with his own ideal hues. It is a little saddening to hear from Shelley later on that he cannot bear to look at the poem, and that his fuller knowledge of Emilia and her defects has made him almost contemptuous of an exalted music in honour of love rather than any woman. But that mood also passed, when he found that even the intelligent misconceived the intention of the piece; *Epipsychidion*.' he then insisted, 'is a mystery,' using that word probably in the old sense of a play with only abstractions as dramatis personae. How beautiful it is, whatever else is to be said concerning it!

Through Medwin a more secure and unmystical friendship began for Shelley in January 1821, not it may be the deepest but the easiest and most contented of his later life. Edward Ellerker Williams who now arrived at Pisa with Jane Williams and their child Edward Medwin, had been at Eton during part of Shelley's schooldays. He had entered the navy, and then obtained a commission in the 8th Dragoons in India; his father had left him fairly well off, and he could afford to give up his career and travel in Europe. Like the Shelleys, he and Jane found it saved them many awkwardnesses to live on the Continent, for they were not legally married. Edward was a well-balanced personality, prepared to enjoy life, slow to blame it; a man of some reading and modestly inclined to authorship, an artist moreover—but above all a lively capable fellow. Jane was placid, handsome, musical, educated. They had come to Pisa with keen expectations of the society of Shelley, and were not disappointed. Williams quickly found that Shelley in daily life was not so ethereal as in his poems, and he delighted in both aspects of the man Medwin had reported so admiringly.

About now Shelley received the unusual request that he should write something for a magazine and be paid for it; but as the first number (it was *Ollier's Literary Miscellany*) was also the last, nothing came of the proposition. But the *Miscellany* had important consequences. It brought to Shelley's notice an article entitled *The Four Ages of Poetry*, which he soon knew to be the work of Peacock, in which the argument ran that poetry had had its day; necessary to barbarous antiquity, poetry was now an archaism, and men of the time had far more valuable things to write and to examine. Shelley's old passion for controversy had an obvious opening here, and moreover he had been shaping, in his prefaces for poems, towards a critical *Defence of Poetry*; he now sped to its making. He took a broader view of the term 'Poetry' than Peacock (in what was no doubt partly an intellectual joke) had allowed, and wrote both of the psychology of poetic creation and the place of it in man's life if that life is not to lose the light from heaven.

The *Defence* is a series of magnificent utterances, and one passage equally wise and well expressed shall stand for many: 'All things exist as they are perceived: at least in relation to the percipient. "The mind is its own place, and of itself can make a heaven of hell, a hell of heaven." But poetry defeats the curse which binds us to be subjected to the accident of surrounding impressions. And whether it spreads its own figured curtain, or withdraws life's dark veil from before the scene of things, it equally creates for us a being within our being. It makes us the inhabitants of a world to which the familiar world is a chaos. It reproduces the common universe of which we are portions and percipients, and it purges from our inward sight the film of familiarity which obscures from us the wonder of our being. It compels us to feel that which we perceive, and to imagine that which we know. It creates anew the universe, after it has been annihilated in our minds by the recurrence of impressions blunted by reiteration.'

Shelley was going to write a second part of his essay, so as to show how the principles which he accepted were being freshly employed in the poetry of his day, and to point out the spirit of the age chronicling itself through the poets even beyond their own conscious interpretation of it. It may be desirable to notice who would almost certainly have come into the survey. ' The electric life which burns within their words ' is a phrase evidently of special sympathy with Byron, who as a poet (but not as a prose critic) appeared to Shelley as an overwhelmingly strong original. The politics of Wordsworth had infuriated Shelley, but had not hardened him against the gentleness of the reflective poet and the majesty of the *Ode on Intimations of Immortality*. Coleridge had become (so it seemed) silent in verse, but Shelley was always stirred by his Odes and his *Ancient Mariner*. Keats would have been discussed, both in reference to *Endymion* and to *Hyperion*; Tom Moore, the writer of more subtle lyrics than his shallow reputation might suggest, Leigh Hunt, though Shelley enjoyed his prose more than his verse, and Charles Lamb as a modern consciousness in all forms of writing, might have appeared. Of a little earlier date, Robert Burns would probably have had one of his great eulogies from Shelley who has introduced him brilliantly elsewhere in his verse.

Byron's unique powers or potential magic of mind had more than once prompted Shelley's verse; in 1821 Shelley was increasingly under the spell of the prolific Childe. No reckoning of the personal trouble which he had suffered in the matter of Allegra and was still to bear, no recognition of the worse side of Byron's way with any interests but his own, diminished Shelley's idolatry for the man of genius. When he went to see him on several matters calling for decision, Shelley wrote to Mary of this other subject. It was at Ravenna where Byron 'lives in considerable splendour' that Shelley's host read to him 'one of the unpublished cantos of *Don Juan*, which is astonishingly fine. It sets him not only above, but far above, all the poets of the day—every word is stamped with immortality. I despair of rivalling Lord Byron, as well I may, and there is no other with whom it is worth contending. This canto is in style, but totally, and sustained with incredible ease and power, like the end of the second canto. There is not a word which the most rigid asserter of the dignity of human nature would desire to be cancelled. It fulfils, in a certain degree, what I have long preached of producing —something wholly new and relative to the age, and yet surpassingly beautiful. It may be vanity, but I think I see the trace of my earnest exhortations to him to create something wholly new.' Some months later the author of *Prometheus Unbound* is seen writing to John Gisborne: 'What think you of Lord Byron's last volume? In my opinion it contains finer poetry than has appeared in England since the publication of *Paradise Regained*. *Cain* is apocalyptic—it is a revelation not before communicated to man.'

Shelley's stay with Byron was disturbed by the disclosure that Byron had been made the recipient of a story believed by Mr. and Mrs. Hoppner, who had formerly seen something of Shelley and Claire together. The chief thing in this story was that Shelley had

had a child by Claire in 1818 and had packed it off at once to the Foundling Hospital at Naples. Byron had actually helped this story on its rounds, but now he appeared to be offering Shelley the opportunity of knowing what was going on and checking it. Whether he did or did not frustrate Shelley's method of causing the Hoppners to come out into the open is still an undecided point; it may be examined in more extensive memoirs of Shelley and of Byron .

At an earlier date Byron through Shelley had invited Leigh Hunt to Italy, and now (in August 1821) the invitation took a clearer though still a sketchy shape. Byron was smitten with the supposed advantages of having a periodical more or less at his disposal in Italy, for which the collaboration of a practised editor was desirable; and in his London period he had known Leigh Hunt as one such and one who had spoken out for him when such speech was rare. He urged Shelley to explain his proposal and bring Hunt out. The risk which Hunt would run by giving up his editorship of *The Examiner* without a precise document assuring him of an equally sound post was passed over in the large thought that any scheme in which Byron and Hunt should engage would yield thumping profits. Shelley counted himself simply as the go-between in this business, but had to put up the travelling money needed by Hunt all the same. For Hunt, longing to rejoin Shelley—no new wish—said he would come, and was soon on the way with his large family, to arrive if all went well at Pisa in November 1821. All did not go well. The further consequences of Hunt's luckless voyage were to be tragic.

Another voyager from England known to Hunt and Shelley enacted his tragedy's end in 1821, and Shelley did not get news in time to do what he would have undoubtedly done to moderate its miseries. Keats, on arriving at Naples, was given a letter from Shelley renewing the invitation to Pisa, but it was the fixed plan that he should go to Rome, and there on 23 February he died. At length John Gisborne was able to send some account of Keats's last months which one Robert Finch had obtained from Keats's generous companion Joseph Severn the painter. There were allegations in it against some of Keats's intimate circle which, taken with the savagery of the Reviews against him (and often said to have been one cause of his illness), aroused Shelley to a sacred rage.

Nowadays literary criticism seldom verges on the personal style of attack which was in use, particularly among Tory journalists, through the lives of Shelley and Keats; and although the *Quarterly Review* happily survives, its mildness bears no likeness to the haughty and aggressive force of its early years. Its power to hurt was then very great, for it was read by 'everybody who was anybody.' To be treated with contempt by the *Quarterly*, and all the talent which the editor Gifford commanded, was something which a man might feel went beyond his literary name; and in the case of Keats an innocent hope that his poems might bring him some much-needed guineas was practically destroyed at once. Did the *Quarterly's* injustice (combined with insolent reviews elsewhere) destroy Keats? We do not know, but it certainly affected him, and Shelley did not stand on ceremony in calling the Reviewer little better than Keats's murderer. In his lament for Keats entitled *Adonais*, that moving poem completed in June 1821, printed soon afterwards at Pisa and published with little immediate reverberation in London the same year, Shelley wrote with the destroyer's image in his mind's eye.

There was, however, accordant with Shelley's poetical character, an interfusion of other ideas in *Adonais*, which rises above an act of retribution and stands in metaphorical beauty as a proud memorial to the dead poet. It becomes also a poem on the distinct immortality of such spirits, in another sphere of being; and then, it would seem without deliberate choice but as the inspiration came, Shelley wrote a mysterious and what he might call an 'electrical' conclusion, in which we may see the precognition of the death which was actually approaching him. Arising from the reverie, he described his elegy as a 'piece of art,' which, on a close inspection of its allusion and style, it deserves to be called. In seeking to make it richly beautiful Shelley may have had in mind the advice he had received from Keats to be 'more of an artist' and to 'load every rift with ore'; it was the fitting occasion.

As the winter of 1821 came on quite a literary society of Englishmen with their ladies was forming in Pisa. The lion was of course Byron, who arrived with the Countess Guiccioli and some of her family. Medwin and his friends the Williamses returned from their excursions. The ground floor of Byron's big house was prepared for Leigh Hunt and his family, who however were still far away. A certain John Taaffe, with an ambition of translating and expounding Dante, was sometimes present. Then, early in 1822, Edward John Trelawny marched into the scene, a truly Romantic figure with the appropriate mustachios, a kind heart, a nautical hatred of flummery and a life-story equal to half a dozen life-stories of common men.

The straightforward diary of Edward Williams gives glimpses of Shelley's occupations at this time and by its mixture of simplicity and strength of mind helps to explain the friendship which soon grew. Some extracts follow:—

November 5th. Shelley read to me some passages of his *Hellas*, which are very fine, and his translation of the only Greek farce which has been handed down to us—the subject of which is the Death of Cyclop by Ulysses ... In the afternoon S. introduced me to Lord Byron, on whom we called .... So far from his being (as is generally imagined) wrapt in a melancholy gloom, he is all sunshine and good humour ..

November 11th. In the evening S. proposes to me to assist him in a continuation of the translation of Spinoza's Theologico-political tract, to which Lord B. has consented to put his name, and to give it greater currency, will write the life of that celebrated Jew to preface the work. The Countess of G. calls and Jane and Mary accompany her in her ride.

November 22nd. Walk with Jane and M., and join Lord B.'s party, with whom we practise pistol-firing. S. shot best, and I very ill.

December 12th. S. calls and tells us in consequence of the Scolari having made a disturbance, of having heard that a man was to be burnt alive at Lucca for sacrilege. He proposes that Lord Byron and a party of English shall enter the town and rescue the man by force. Lord B. objects, but wishes to draw up a memorial to the Grand Duke of Tuscany to interfere. On hearing, however, that the execution is not to take place to-morrow, Taaffe sets off for Lucca to make enquiries into the truth of the circumstances.

December 30th. Wind abated, but the weather still cloudy and cold from the tremendous rain of yesterday. After Church the Rev. Dr. Nott christened our little girl, Mary being her Godmother ... Dined with Mary and walk in the evening with S. who is thinking of a tragedy to be founded on the story of Timon of Athens, but adapted to modern times. An admirable theme for him.—

From such notes as these we gather that Shelley was quite steadily settled in Pisa and usually looking forward to his next literary plans, more of which arose than Williams records or than call for description here. Whatever he proposed his friend admired, with the reservation that Shelley often flew too high for the average person, and if he could only write as he talked he would undoubtedly win popularity. On 8 January 1822 the diarist remarks, 'As to S-'s *Charles the First* which he sat down to about 5 days since, if he continues it in the spirit of some of the lines which he read to me last night, it will doubtless take a place before any that has appeared since Shakespeare ... It is exceedingly to be regretted that Shelley does not meet with greater encouragement: a mind such as his, powerful as it is, requires *gentle leading*.'

XI. The Triumph of Life

Sometimes Shelley laid down his pen and looked away from his books and manuscripts, wondering if he ought not to find 'something better to do than furnish this jingling food for the hunger of oblivion, called verse.' Application to Peacock of the East India House concerning a possible job as political adviser to some Indian prince had produced the curt answer that only the servants of the East India Company could get such employment. So he resumed his pen and paper, or went off to play billiards, or shoot at half-crowns with Byron, and once a week to be of Byron's dinner-party. He was tolerably happy at the New Year (1822): 'My health is better—my cares are lighter; and although nothing will cure the consumption of my purse, yet it drags on a sort of life in death, very like its master, and seems, like Fortunatus's, always empty yet never exhausted.'

Delighted with the *Faust* of Goethe, and a German artist's designs for it, Shelley sent a request to the only man in England whom he deemed capable of making a translation—S.T. Coleridge. He however spent a few days in rendering some passages himself, and in spite of his low opinion of such work—for he alleges that he only turned to translation when he had 'nothing better to do'—it was his gift ever to re-create the chosen work from its depths. Hence his splendid success with fragments of *Faust*.

Trelawny, the man of action and enigma, was sincerely impressed by Shelley's methods as an author, gathering his materials so grimly from all kinds of boring books, but he was also provoked by such escapism. He did his best to reform the poet and make a man of him. Shelley performed ably enough when an emergency called, as it did on 24 March 1822. A drunken dragoon chose to gallop through the midst of Byron's party on the evening ride. Byron and Shelley caught him up and Shelley had to ward off a sabre-stroke with his cap. The dragoon waved another unsteady blow, then made off, and a servant of Byron got at him with a pitchfork down the road. The affray was unlucky; it brought on secret police attention to Shelley among the rest.

A severer strain fell on Shelley in April when he found himself in the position of having to inform Claire of what he had heard—that little Allegra was dead of typhus—and to inform her only when she was well out of Byron's way. He also acted as an intermediary with Byron concerning her wishes in this bereavement. It was decided in April that the Shelley and Williams families should spend the summer near Spezia, and at the same time use Pisa as a permanent address. Accordingly a house named Casa Magni on the seashore of Lerici was soon taken.

William's diary continues to bring Shelley into view:

February 18th. Jane unwell. S. turns physician. Wrote a few lines. Went in the boat with S. to try a new sail. Called on Lord B., who talks of getting up Othello. Laid a wager with S. that Lord B. quits Italy before six months. Chances against me ... Jane put on a Hindostanee dress, and passed the evening with Mary, who had also the Turkish costume.

March 14th. Sent the first Act (of a play) to S. He tells me if I finish as I have begun there is every chance of success. We sailed in the boat about half a mile down the river, and on our return, in passing the bridge, were hailed by the Custom House officers. Not, however, paying any attention to them (we have frequently passed without interruption) they seized the boat, threatened to imprison our servant, and without our paying fifty livres they declare it shall become their property. S. wrote to the minister of police about it.

May 2 (Lerici). Cloudy, with intervals of rain. Went out with Shelley in the boat—fished on the rocks—bad sport. Went in the evening after some wild ducks—saw nothing but sublime scenery, to which the grandeur of a storm greatly contributed. S. broke the sad news to Claire. We were seated in Jane's room, talking over the best means to be pursued, when she guessed the purpose of our meeting.—

But a more startling entry was made on 6 May, and it seems to usher in the fatal hour which was mostly concealed behind pleasant and joyful days of sea, sun, liberty and laughter: 'After tea, walking with Shelley on the terrace, and observing the effect of moonshine on the waters, he complained of being unusually nervous, and stopping short he grasped me violently by the arm, and stared steadfastly on the white surf that broke upon the beach under our feet. Observing him sensibly affected, I demanded of him if he were in pain? But he only answered by saying, "There it is again—There!" He recovered after some time, and declared that he saw, as plainly as he then saw me, a naked child (the child of a friend who had lately died) rise from the sea and clap its hands as in joy, smiling at him. This was a trance that it required some reasoning and philosophy to awaken him from, so forcibly had the vision operated on his mind.' If we reject the supernatural, the grief of Shelley for Allegra, whose fate he might feel he could have changed and who had been for some time as his own child, explains the visitation.

But soon afterwards a more welcome sight appeared on the waters. It was the new boat, the *Don Juan*, which Trelawny's friend Dan Roberts had been building for Shelley at the same time as the larger *Bolivar* for Byron. Williams's note is (12 May): 'She does indeed excite my surprise and admiration. S and I walked to Lerici and made a stretch off the land to try her, and I find she fetches whatever she looks at.—In short we have now a perfect plaything for the summer.' Jane Williams and Mary Shelley liked the new acquisition less. The depression of Mary at Casa Magni was already a trial for her and her husband. She was expecting a child, which miscarried, and her mind was dark with obscure forebodings as well as the inconveniences of the holiday house.

In contrast to Mary's persistent glumness Shelley saw Jane as a model of pleasantness and a source of serenity, and his poems of 1822 include a series almost all of delicate though pensive beauty, reflecting his feelings towards her. She and Williams were troubled at the position and his great longing for peace and ease, which at any rate have enriched poetry with *The Invitation, The Recollection* and the address to Jane in the manner of a speech by Ariel to Miranda (Ferdinand approving) with the guitar which he gave her. Altogether, the clouds were not immovable. On 18 June Shelley wrote, 'Williams is captain [of the *Don Juan*], and we drive along this delightful bay in the evening wind under the summer moon until earth appears another world. Jane brings her guitar, and if the past and future could be obliterated, the present would content me so well that I could say with Faust to the passing moment, "Remain thou, thou art so beautiful."'

It was impossible for Shelley even when he was taking a vacation to leave literary toil behind. There stood in 1822 behind Casa Magni some great ilexes, and with his preference for composing in the open air and with a sense of direct help from nature he sat there with the growing manuscript of one more poem in his line of long poems. Its title was *The Triumph of Life*, which seems to be related to Orcagna's painting known to him at Pisa, *The Triumph of Death;* if that shows how much the genius of Italy was influencing his own, so does the Dante-like tone, vision and debate of this strong and thoughtful poem on the state of man. It is a poem well worth attention in any judgment on Shelley's poetical capabilities, since he has often been looked on as incurably profuse and ornamental in style, and it is not hard to find him led away into tuneful rhetoric. But *The Triumph of Life*, just as it reports the hard observation and the acute summarizing of a Shelley of a less romantic attitude, is partly written in a style of sharp bare realism. The large fragment which is all that we have received from his papers is anything but a triumph in the ordinary use of that word, and it breaks off with a terrible suggestion that life is to no purpose. More we can hardly know of the poet's theme as he saw it in full extent. We shall nevertheless believe it improbable that Shelley, whatever his sum of experiences at the age of thirty came to, and however truly he declared himself already an older man than his grandfather, could so soon recant the creed of *Prometheus Unbound*. The second part of *The Triumph* must have proved to be on the side of human happiness and a benevolent universe.

On 20 June Shelley heard that Leigh Hunt had arrived at Genoa and the *Don Juan* was prepared for a voyage, but it was at Leghorn that Hunt's ship finally called. On 1 July Shelley, Williams and the young sailor Charles Vivian left Casa Magni at noon, and were safe in Leghorn harbour well before midnight. The reunion with the Hunt family was all that Shelley or Hunt could desire, but the awkward side of the episode was unmistakable: Byron, with his mistress, was preparing to leave Tuscany when the police had decided that the Gambas were political undesirables. Byron, in great agitation over this and other matters, hardly knew whether to transfer himself to America or only to Lucca, and as for Leigh Hunt and the project of a brilliant new Review to be published in Italy, together with all the practical matters of getting Hunt into the ways of the new country and Pisa, nothing seemed to interest him less. But Shelley, suppressing his resolve never even to seem to be asking Byron for benefits, hung on, and achieved at least a temporary understanding as to what was due to Hunt after being bidden to Italy on Byron's professional concerns.

Several days of discussion, of happier talks and of shopping and sightseeing passed, and having received from Mary a melancholy letter, Shelley was able to tell Williams (who had become impatient for the return) that on 8 July the *Don Juan* could weigh anchor. For the homeward voyage he had among other books aboard a copy of Keats's last volume, lent—since his own could not be found—by Leigh Hunt. The boat was well laden with supplies, and the voyagers had drawn money from their agents. They sailed at noon and in the afternoon could be seen by Dan Roberts with his telescope until a thundery haze hid them. Not many minutes later the *Don Juan* sank, and it never will be certainly known whether the storm did the mischief or a piratical *felucca* ran the light schooner down. Shelley made no attempt to save himself, and Williams who was a good swimmer seems also to have been drowned without delay; the sailor-boy shared their fate. The women at Casa Magni may have kept some faint hope alive until 19 July, when Trelawny, who had done everything that one man could, came to tell them that the worst had happened. The bodies of the three voyagers had been washed ashore. In one of Shelley's pockets the book of Keats's poems was found doubled back, as if hurriedly thrust away at a surprise. The news having been accepted as true, Mary and Jane left Casa Magni and returned with their children to Pisa.

Trelawny persuaded the quarantine authorities and others to allow an unusual, though classical proceeding, and so on 15 August the body of Edward Williams was cremated before a crowd of people near the mouth of the Serchio river where he and Shelley had often sailed. Next day, with Byron again among the mourners, a funeral pyre for Shelley was lighted on the shore of Via Reggio. This ceremony had as its setting a remarkably beautiful day and place, such as Shelley's spirit might praise. Haunting the spot long afterwards, the poet John Addington Symonds gave this picture: 'The sand-dunes stretch for miles between the sea and a low wood of stone pines, with the Carrara hills descending from their glittering pinnacles by long lines to the headlands of the Spezzian Gulf. The immeasurable distance was all painted in sky-blue and amethyst; then came the golden green of the dwarf firs; and then dry yellow in the grasses of the dunes; and then the many-tinted sea, with surf tossed up against the furthest cliffs. It is a wonderful and tragic view, to which no painter but the Roman Costa has done justice; and he, it may be said, has made this landscape of the Carrarese his own. The space between sand and pine-wood was covered with faint, yellow evening primroses. They flickered like little harmless flames in sun and shadow, and the spires of the Carrara range were giant flames transformed to marble. The memory of that day described by Trelawny in a passage of immortal English prose, when he and Byron and Leigh Hunt stood beside the funeral pyre, and libations were poured, and the *Cor Cordium* was found inviolate among the ashes, turned all my thoughts to flame beneath the gentle autumn sky.'

The ashes of Shelley were at last buried in the Protestant Cemetery in Rome, to be near the grave of his 'lost William'—and the magnetism of that place for Shelley, which was expressed consummately in *Adonais*, had not failed.

XII. Reflections

Mary Shelley lived until 1851. It was a consolation to her, often as she was torn with regret that she had sometimes been unable to utter or reveal her real love for Shelley, that she could lay the foundation of all editions of his writings in prose and poetry. The edict of Sir Timothy Shelley hindered her from what would have been at best a most anxious and trying task, the biography; but in those biographical notes which she intersperses through her editions of Shelley's works she accomplished something almost as valuable. In many matters she not only knew more but was better able to interpret Shelley than others, and as an imaginative writer she presents their life and its surfaces and depths too with a special illumination.

Shelley has divided opinion on many things and not least on his own character. The adversaries have been headed in the end by Matthew Arnold, since the old school of political destroyers in the *Quarterly, Blackwood's* and such camps has become obsolete. Arnold after reading the big *Life of Shelley* by Edward Dowden wrote the sarcastic study collected in the second series of *Essays in Criticism*, which shows him in confusion, for he denounces the 'inhuman want of humour and superhuman power of self-deception' ascribed to Shelley, but ends in another fashion: 'The Shelley of actual life is a vision of beauty and radiance, indeed, but availing nothing, effecting nothing. And in poetry, no less than in life, he is "a beautiful *and ineffectual* angel," beating in the void his "luminous wings in vain."' The quotation was from Arnold's own essay on Byron.

Shelley might be in some agreement with Inspector Arnold over what he had availed, what effected in 'actual life.' He had once presumed, even as a schoolboy, that he was sent into the world to do great things for its betterment, but he had not gone far in this enchantment before he felt the consequences of it. A succession of romantic errors left him willing to serve Reform without haste or gilded expectation; but he might confess that having failed to take his seat in Parliament he had missed certain practical opportunities. No man was ever more prompt to give away his fortune to causes and individuals, but he had not seen that his charity produced much lasting good. He did not live to take the responsibility of the large estates and varied agriculture which his father had supervised excellently. His steamship project was defeated, and another was only in his mind when he died. In his own circle he was again and again startling in effective promptness, and Byron could have borne witness to this; but the circle was not wide.

As for Shelley's poetry, concerning which he was modest enough, and to which he gave his strength without prudence through years of sheer hard work—his notebooks are the visible proofs—, Arnold's words are unintelligible. A poet can hardly be ineffectual or just a passing curiosity whose verse animates so immense a movement as the Labour movement in its first stirrings. The editions of Shelley's poems, collected or separate, which were printed in mean forms without respect of copyright between 1821 and 1848 were not bought by bibliophiles; they were the reading of the working man, and Shelley's own criticisms of *Queen Mab* do not count greatly against the *actual* progress of that poem as the ideal doctrine of men usually unconcerned with figurative poetry.

To another audience he submitted much of his work with the preliminary reservation that it was not meant to supply the answers to the profound questions on which he had been thinking. He might, as he said, deliver his instruction on the evolution of society in prose, and much of his wide reading in the sciences, in history, in philosophy and religion, in political economy and almost all learning was a preparation for prose writings. This reading contributed to the thoughts and the main drift of his indeed luminous poetical fables, but the function of these is surely to encourage and subtilize the liberal imagination of their readers, leaving them newly aware of their own powers and privileges of mind and soul. Even *Prometheus Unbound* is not a demonstration but an invocation, though its fancies are as true to history and natural history as Shelley can make them: the object is to kindle the love of ideals.

Besides this, the object of writers is on the whole to be read, poets not excepted; and if they gain it, as Matthew Arnold did and as Shelley did, they appear to have passed out of the 'ineffectual' category. The infelicity of Shelley's poems during his life was such as at moments to darken his own moods, but after his death when many of his shorter lyrical poems were made known in company with others already published his reward began to appear. Within ten years it was a contest among the young men at the Universities between the claims of Byron and of Shelley to the higher order of poetry, and although there can be no end to such comparisons it is true that Shelley's mind and style in his brief as in his sustained poems were the delight of the Victorian age. Perhaps none of our writers was ever chosen so often or in so many examples by anthologists as Shelley, and a glance at the still familiar *Golden Treasury of the*

Best Songs and Lyrical Poems selected by F.T. Palgrave (1861) shows him esteemed as effectual in much the same number of items as Wordsworth and Shakespeare.

Should it be reasoned that the beauty even of poems is dependent on what is called 'the climate of sensibility,' and that the variations of this climate with the shiftings of all our circumstance have weakened the radiance and illusion of Romantic poets, there is a rejoinder. It might well be that in Shelley's instance the indistinct profusion of aerial purples and crimsons and the abstract personifications (possibly more numerous because he was brought up on Thomas Gray's Odes) pass over our heads now. While this may leave some of his compositions out in the cold, yet in his versatility he has transmitted some in other styles which may obtain through the altered need or taste of our day a fuller admiration. That apparently easy everyday vein in which Shelley often wrote, as in *Julian and Maddalo*, the *Letter to Maria Gisborne*, *Peter Bell the Third* and (but with a difference) *The Triumph of Life*, may justify Shelley to our straitened period.

After every consideration, let us allow that there are no real rules governing appeal and response, compelling us as we take our several ways through literature to delight or to rejection. But we know that there are certain poets whose books contain most numerous possibilities of enjoyment and something exceeding that; and Shelley is one of these. It is the final magic of poetry to laugh at all the analytical study that we bring to it, and in its domains the laws of 'importance' do not always work. Hence, if an old reader of Shelley with a longish record of attempted criticism may allude to Arnold's 'actual life,' or consult memory, a so-called minor poem like *The Question*, *The Two Spirits*, *The Aziola* or the incomplete *Boat on the Serchio* becomes a perpetually present music and a fountain of grace beyond expression. When we read that Charles Lamb, who sourly resisted the philosophical poems of Shelley, was taken with his light-hearted *Lines to a Critic*, we merely read that poetry is an Ariel.

And that name is not wholly amiss as applied to Shelley, so far as his intimate friends defined his peculiar difference. In a forgotten poet's words, he was in this regard

> like a Passenger below
> That stays perhaps a Night or so;
> But still his native Country lies
> Beyond the Boundaries of the skies.

EDMUND BLUNDEN

ON THE SELECTION

No complete edition of Shelley's poetical works exists. His surviving notebooks and other manuscripts will continue to yield, to persevering scholars, additions and variations. Moreover, some passages at present scattered may be pieced·together into something like entire poems which he himself had not time to write out as he designed them. But at this time of day we may believe that practically all his fully achieved poems are accessible to us.

To give the best of his voluminous poetry is the object of the present book. I have met material considerations by letting extracts represent some of the longer poems, and do not feel that such a decision has taken away anything (beyond the fine line or phrase perhaps) of Shelley's best. Similarly I have set aside most of his translations—and he said that he fell to translating when he had nothing better to do. Many of his brief, swift fragments have been published, and many more will be; but for these gleanings, uncertain in their original application, I have not thought this occasion calls, with one or two exceptions.

The dates of composition are given as far as is possible, and a few notes may at least assist the reader to come at the original circumstances of some of the poems; for Shelley's poetical activities and methods now and then relate particularly to his life and times. But nothing like a systematic commentary is attempted, or else a whole classical dictionary would have tried to find room. And then the poetry is 'full of metaphysics,' which need not frighten us where it is also full of beauty and music.

E. B.

LONGER POEMS

Queen Mab

A PHILOSOPHICAL POEM

THE poem was accompanied with a large array of Notes in prose which aroused almost as much attention as the verse,—partly quotations from scientific, philosophical and theological books, partly Shelley's own compositions. One of these was substantially the famous pamphlet which had occasioned Shelley's expulsion from Oxford University, his *Necessity of Atheism*; it is desirable to know what Shelley was propounding. His Note on 'There is no God!' was, 'This negation must be understood solely to affect a creative Deity. The hypothesis of a pervading Spirit, coeternal with the universe, remains unshaken.'

The forecast of a glorious future awaiting humankind included in *Queen Mab* arose in part from Shelley's readings in astronomy. 'The poles are every year becoming more and more perpendicular to the ecliptic,' and this change was taken to imply an improvement in the seasons. 'There is no great extravagance in presuming that the progress of the perpendicularity of the poles may be as rapid as the progress of intellect; or that there should be a perfect identity between the moral and physical improvement of the human species. It is certain that wisdom is not compatible with disease, and that in the present state of the climates of the earth health, in the true and comprehensive sense of the word, is out of the reach of civilized man.'

Queen Mab is the immature union of Shelley's zeal for a vast transformation of society, freeing man from many miseries traced by him to conventions which he detested, and his admiration of 'wild and wondrous' tales in prose and in verse. In its protests against institutions and customs the effect of his exploring William Godwin's writings may be seen. The beautiful opening and other passages show the disciple of Robert Southey's poetry; *Thalaba the Destroyer* and *The Curse of Kehama* had delighted Shelley by their novelty of form and scene.

In 1821, when a knavish bookseller pirated *Queen Mab*, Shelley printed a letter in *The Examiner* to say that he had almost forgotten what the poem was about, and presumed it was crude; in 1839 Mary Shelley doubted that he would have allowed it a place in his collected poems, but she thought it too beautiful and striking to be omitted from her edition.

> *Ecrasez l'infame!—Correspondance de Voltaire*
>
> *Avia Pieridum peragro loca, nullius ante*
> *Trita solo; juvat integros accedere fontes;*
> *Atque haurire: juvatque novos decerpere flores.*

· · · · · · ·

Unde prius nulli velarint tempora musae.
Primum quod magnis doceo de rebus ; et arctis
Religionum animos nodis exsolvere pergo.

LUCRETIUS, lib. IV.

Δος που στῶ, καί κοσμον κινησω—ARCHIMEDES.

TO HARRIET *****

WHOSE is the love that, gleaming through the world,
Wards off the poisonous arrow of its scorn?
    Whose is the warm and partial praise,
    Virtue's most sweet reward?

Beneath whose looks did my reviving soul
Riper in truth and virtuous daring grow?
    Whose eyes have I gazed fondly on,
    And loved mankind the more?

HARRIET! on thine:—thou wert my purer mind;
Thou wert the inspiration of my song;
    Thine are these early wilding flowers,
    Though garlanded by me.

Then press into thy breast this pledge of love;
And know, though time may change and years may roll,
    Each floweret gathered in my heart
    It consecrates to thine.

I

How wonderful is Death,
    Death and his brother Sleep!
One, pale as yonder waning moon
    With lips of lurid blue;
The other, rosy as the morn
      When throned on ocean's wave
    It blushes o'er the world:
Yet both so passing wonderful!

Hath then the gloomy Power
Whose reign is in the tainted sepulchres
    Seized on her sinless soul?
Must then that peerless form

Which love and admiration cannot view
Without a beating heart, those azure veins
Which steal like streams along a field of snow,
   That lovely outline, which is fair
     As breathing marble, perish?
     Must putrefaction's breath
Leave nothing of this heavenly sight
     But loathsomeness and ruin?
Spare nothing but a gloomy theme,
On which the lightest heart might moralize?
   Or is it only a sweet slumber
     Stealing o'er sensation,
  Which the breath of roseate morning
     Chaseth into darkness?
   Will Ianthe wake again,
And give that faithful bosom joy
Whose sleepless spirit waits to catch
Light, life and rapture from her smile?

    Yes! she will wake again,
Although her glowing limbs are motionless,
   And silent those sweet lips,
    Once breathing eloquence,
That might have soothed a tiger's rage,
Or thawed the cold heart of a conqueror.
   Her dewy eyes are closed,
And on their lids, whose texture fine
Scarce hides the dark blue orbs beneath,
   The baby Sleep is pillowed:
   Her golden tresses shade
   The bosom's stainless pride,
Curling like tendrils of the parasite
   Aroung a marble column.

   Hark! whence that rushing sound?
    'Tis like the wondrous strain
That round a lonely ruin swells,
Which, wandering on the echoing shore,
   The enthusiast hears at evening:
'Tis softer than the west wind's sigh;
'Tis wilder than the unmeasured notes
Of that strange lyre whose strings

The genii of the breezes sweep:
  Those lines of rainbow light
Are like the moonbeams when they fall
Through some cathedral window, but the tints
    Are such as may not find
    Comparison on earth.

Behold the chariot of the Fairy Queen!
Celestial coursers paw the unyielding air;
Their filmy pennons at her word they furl,
And stop obedient to the reins of light:
    These the Queen of Spells drew in,
    She spread a charm around the spot,
And leaning graceful from the aethereal car,
    Long did she gaze, and silently,
      Upon the slumbering maid.

Oh! not the visioned poet in his dreams,
When silvery clouds float through the 'wildered brain,
When every sight of lovely, wild and grand
    Astonishes, enraptures, elevates,
      When fancy at a glance combines
      The wondrous and the beautiful,—
    So bright, so fair, so wild a shape
      Hath ever yet beheld,
As that which reined the coursers of the air,
    And poured the magic of her gaze
      Upon the maiden's sleep.

    The broad and yellow moon
      Shone dimly through her form—
    That form of faultless symmetry;
    The pearly and pellucid car
      Moved not the moonlight's line:
      'Twas not an earthly pageant:
    Those who had looked upon the sight,
      Passing all human glory,
      Saw not the yellow moon,
      Saw not the mortal scene,
      Heard not the night-wind's rush,
      Heard not an earthly sound,
      Saw but the fairy pageant,

Heard but the heavenly strains
That filled the lonely dwelling.

The Fairy's frame was slight, yon fibrous cloud,
That catches but the palest tinge of even,
And which the straining eye can hardly seize
When melting into eastern twilight's shadow,
Were scarce so thin, so slight; but the fair star
That gems the glittering coronet of morn,
Sheds not a light so mild, so powerful,
As that which, bursting from the Fairy's form,
Spread a purpureal halo round the scene,
　Yet with an undulating motion,
　Swayed to her outline gracefully.

　　From her celestial car
　　The Fairy Queen descended,
　　And thrice she waved her wand
　Circled with wreaths of amaranth:
　　Her thin and misty form
　　Moved with the moving air,
　　And the clear silver tones,
　　As thus she spoke, were such
As are unheard by all but gifted ear.

Fairy

'Stars! your balmiest influence shed!
Elements! your wrath suspend!
Sleep, Ocean, in the rocky bounds
　That circle thy domain!
Let not a breath be seen to stir
Around yon grass-grown ruin's height,
　Let even the restless gossamer
　　Sleep on the moveless air!
　　Soul of Ianthe! thou,
Judged alone worthy of the envied boon,
That waits the good and the sincere; that waits
Those who have struggled, and with resolute will
Vanquished earth's pride and meanness, burst the chains,
The icy chains of custom, and have shone
The day-stars of their age;—Soul of Ianthe!
　　Awake! arise!'

Sudden arose
Ianthe's Soul; it stood
All beautiful in naked purity,
The perfect semblance of its bodily frame.
Instinct with inexpressible beauty and grace,
Each stain of earthliness
Had passed away, it reassumed
Its native dignity, and stood
Immortal amid ruin.

Upon the couch the body lay
Wrapped in the depth of slumber;
Its features were fixed and meaningless,
Yet animal life was there,
And every organ yet performed
Its natural functions: 'twas a sight
Of wonder to behold the body and soul.
The self-same lineaments, the same
Marks of identity were there:
Yet, oh, how different! One aspires to Heaven,
Pants for its sempiternal heritage,
And ever-changing, ever-rising still,
Wantons in endless being.
The other, for a time the unwilling sport
Of circumstance and passion, struggles on;
Fleets through its sad duration rapidly:
Then, like an useless and worn-out machine,
Rots, perishes, and passes.

Fairy

'Spirit! who hast dived so deep;
Spirit! who hast soared so high;
Thou the fearless, thou the mild,
Accept the boon thy worth hath earned,
Ascend the car with me.'

Spirit

'Do I dream? Is this new feeling
But a visioned ghost of slumber?
If indeed I am a soul,
A free, a disembodied soul,
Speak again to me.'

Fairy

'I am the Fairy MAB: to me 'tis given
The wonders of the human world to keep:
The secrets of the immeasurable past,
In the unfailing consciences of men,
Those stern, unflattering chroniclers, I find:
The future, from the causes which arise
In each event, I gather: not the sting
Which retributive memory implants
In the hard bosom of the selfish man;
Nor that ecstatic and exulting throb
Which virtue's votary feels when he sums up
The thoughts and actions of a well-spent day,
Are unforeseen, unregistered by me:
And it is yet permitted me, to rend
The veil of mortal frailty, that the spirit,
Clothed in its changeless purity, may know
How soonest to accomplish the great end
For which it hath its being, and may taste
That peace, which in the end all life will share.
This is the meed of virtue; happy Soul,
        Ascend the car with me!'
    The chains of earth's immurement
        Fell from Ianthe's spirit;
They shrank and brake like bandages of straw
    Beneath a wakened giant's strength.
        She knew her glorious change,
    And felt in apprehension uncontrolled
        New raptures opening round:
    Each day-dream of her mortal life,
    Each frenzied vision of the slumbers
        That closed each well-spent day,
        Seemed now to meet reality.

    The Fairy and the Soul proceeded;
        The silver clouds disparted;
And as the car of magic they ascended,
    Again the speechless music swelled,
    Again the coursers of the air
Unfurled their azure pennons, and the Queen
        Shaking the beamy reins
        Bade them pursue their way.

The magic car moved on.
The night was fair, and countless stars
Studded Heaven's dark blue vault,—
   Just o'er the eastern wave
Peeped the first faint smile of morn:—
   The magic car moved on—
   From the celestial hoofs
The atmosphere in flaming sparkles flew,
   And where the burning wheels
Eddied above the mountain's loftiest peak,
   Was traced a line of lightning.
Now it flew far above a rock,
   The utmost verge of earth,
The rival of the Andes, whose dark brow
   Lowered o'er the silver sea.

Far, far below the chariot's path,
   Calm as a slumbering babe,
   Tremendous Ocean lay.
The mirror of its stillness showed
   The pale and waning stars,
   The chariot's fiery track,
   And the gray light of morn
   Tinging those fleecy clouds
   That canopied the dawn.
Seemed it, that the chariot's way
Lay through the midst of an immense concave,
Radiant with million constellations, tinged
   With shades of infinite colour,
   And semicircled with a belt
   Flashing incessant meteors.

The magic car moved on.
   As they approached their goal
The coursers seemed to gather speed;
The sea no longer was distinguished; earth
   Appeared a vast and shadowy sphere;
   The sun's unclouded orb
   Rolled through the black concave;
   Its rays of rapid light
Parted around the chariot's swifter course,
   And fell, like ocean's feathery spray

Dashed from the boiling surge
Before a vessel's prow.

The magic car moved on.
Earth's distant orb appeared
The smallest light that twinkles in the heaven;
Whilst round the chariot's way
Innumerable systems rolled,
And countless spheres diffused
An ever-varying glory.
It was a sight of wonder: some
Were hornèd like the crescent moon;
Some shed a mild and silver beam
Like Hesperus o'er the western sea;
Some dashed athwart with trains of flame,
Like worlds to death and ruin driven;
Some shone like suns, and, as the chariot passed,
Eclipsed all other light.

Spirit of Nature! here!
In this interminable wilderness
Of worlds, at whose immensity
Even soaring fancy staggers,
Here is thy fitting temple.
Yet not the lightest leaf
That quivers to the passing breeze
Is less instinct with thee:
Yet not the meanest worm
That lurks in graves and fattens on the dead
Less shares thy eternal breath.
Spirit of Nature! thou!
Imperishable as this scene,
Here is thy fitting temple.

II

If solitude hath ever led thy steps
To the wild Ocean's echoing shore,
And thou hast lingered there,
Until the sun's broad orb
Seemed resting on the burnished wave,
Thou must have marked the lines

Of purple gold, that motionless
    Hung o'er the sinking sphere:
Thou must have marked the billowy clouds
Edged with intolerable radiancy
    Towering like rocks of jet
    Crowned with a diamond wreath.
    And yet there is a moment,
    When the sun's highest point
Peeps like a star o'er Ocean's western edge,
When those far clouds of feathery gold,
    Shaded with deepest purple, gleam
    Like islands on a dark blue sea;
Then has thy fancy soared above the earth,
    And furled its wearied wing
    Within the Fairy's fane.

    Yet not the golden islands
    Gleaming in yon flood of light,
        Nor the feathery curtains
    Stretching o'er the sun's bright couch,
    Nor the burnished Ocean waves
        Paving that gorgeous dome,
    So fair, so wonderful a sight
As Mab's aethereal palace could afford.
Yet likest evening's vault, that faery Hall!
As Heaven, low resting on the wave, it spread
        Its floors of flashing light,
        Its vast and azure dome,
        Its fertile golden islands
        Floating on a silver sea;
Whilst suns their mingling beamings darted
Through clouds of circumambient darkness,
    And pearly battlements around
    Looked o'er the immense of Heaven.

    The magic car no longer moved.
        The Fairy and the Spirit
        Entered the Hall of Spells:
            Those golden clouds
        That rolled in glittering billows
        Beneath the azure canopy
With the aethereal footsteps trembled not:

The light and crimson mists,
Floating to strains of thrilling melody
    Through that unearthly dwelling,
Yielded to every movement of the will.
Upon their passive swell the Spirit leaned,
And, for the varied bliss that pressed around,
    Used not the glorious privilege
        Of virtue and of wisdom.

        'Spirit!' the Fairy said,
    And pointed to the gorgeous dome,
        'This is a wondrous sight
        And mocks all human grandeur;
But, were it virtue's only meed, to dwell
In a celestial palace, all resigned
To pleasurable impulses, immured
Within the prison of itself, the will
Of changeless Nature would be unfulfilled.
Learn to make others happy. Spirit, come!
This is thine high reward:—the past shall rise;
Thou shalt behold the present; I will teach
        The secrets of the future.'

        The Fairy and the Spirit
Approached the overhanging battlement.—
        Below lay stretched the universe!
        There, far as the remotest line
        That bounds imagination's flight,
        Countless and unending orbs
        In mazy motion intermingled,
        Yet still fulfilled immutably
            Eternal Nature's law.
            Above, below, around,
            The circling systems formed
        A wilderness of harmony;
        Each with undeviating aim,
In eloquent silence, through the depths of space
        Pursued its wondrous way.

        There was a little light
That twinkled in the misty distance:
        None but a spirit's eye

Might ken that rolling orb;
None but a spirit's eye,
And in no other place
But that celestial dwelling, might behold
Each action of this earth's inhabitants.
But matter, space and time
In those aëreal mansions cease to act;
And all-prevailing wisdom, when it reaps
The harvest of its excellence, o'erbounds
Those obstacles, of which an earthly soul
Fears to attempt the conquest.

The Fairy pointed to the earth.
The Spirit's intellectual eye
Its kindred beings recognized.
The thronging thousands, to a passing view,
Seemed like an ant-hill's citizens.
How wonderful! that even
The passions, prejudices, interests,
That sway the meanest being, the weak touch
That moves the finest nerve,
And in one human brain
Causes the faintest thought, becomes a link
In the great chain of Nature.

'Behold,' the Fairy cried,
'Palmyra's ruined palaces!—
Behold! where grandeur frowned;
Behold! where pleasure smiled;
What now remains?—the memory
Of senselessness and shame—
What is immortal there?
Nothing—it stands to tell
A melancholy tale, to give
An awful warning: soon
Oblivion will steal silently
The remnant of its fame.
Monarchs and conquerors there
Proud o'er prostrate millions trod—
The earthquakes of the human race;
Like them, forgotten when the ruin
That marks their shock is past.

'Beside the eternal Nile,
   The Pyramids have risen.
Nile shall pursue his changeless way:
   Those Pyramids shall fall;
Yea! not a stone shall stand to tell
   The spot whereon they stood!
Their very site shall be forgotten,
   As is their builder's name!

'Behold yon sterile spot;
Where now the wandering Arab's tent
   Flaps in the desert-blast.
There once old Salem's haughty fane
Reared high to Heaven its thousand golden domes,
   And in the blushing face of day
   Exposed its shameful glory.
Oh! many a widow, many an orphan cursed
The building of that fane; and many a father,
Worn out with toil and slavery, implored
The poor man's God to sweep it from the earth,
And spare his children the detested task
Of piling stone on stone, and poisoning
   The choicest days of life,
   To soothe a dotard's vanity.
There an inhuman and uncultured race
Howled hideous praises to their Demon-God;
They rushed to war, tore from the mother's womb
The unborn child,—old age and infancy
Promiscuous perished; their victorious arms
Left not a soul to breathe. Oh! they were fiends:
But what was he who taught them that the God
Of nature and benevolence hath given
A special sanction to the trade of blood?
His name and theirs are fading, and the tales
Of this barbarian nation, which imposture
Recites till terror credits, are pursuing
   Itself into forgetfulness.

'Where Athens, Rome, and Sparta stood,
   There is a moral desert now:
   The mean and miserable huts,
   The yet more wretched palaces,

Contrasted with those ancient fanes,
Now crumbling to oblivion;
The long and lonely colonnades,
Through which the ghost of Freedom stalks,
    Seem like a well-known tune,
Which in some dear scene we have loved to hear,
    Remembered now in sadness.
    But, oh! how much more changed,
    How gloomier is the contrast
    Of human nature there!
Where Socrates expired, a tyrant's slave,
A coward and a fool, spreads death around—
    Then, shuddering, meets his own.
Where Cicero and Antoninus lived,
  A cowled and hypocritical monk
    Prays, curses and deceives.

    'Spirit, ten thousand years
    Have scarcely passed away,
Since, in the waste where now the savage drinks
His enemy's blood, and aping Europe's sons,
    Wakes the unholy song of war,
    Arose a stately city,
Metropolis of the western continent:
    There, now, the mossy columnstone,
Indented by Time's unrelaxing grasp,
    Which once appeared to brave
    All, save its country's ruin;
    There the wide forest scene,
Rude in the uncultivated loveliness
    Of gardens long run wild,
Seems, to the unwilling sojourner, whose steps
  Chance in that desert has delayed,
Thus to have stood since earth was what it is.
    Yet once it was the busiest haunt,
Whither, as to a common centre, flocked
  Strangers, and ships, and merchandise:
    Once peace and freedom blessed
    The cultivated plain:
    But wealth, that curse of man,
Blighted the bud of its prosperity:
Virtue and wisdom, truth and liberty,

Fled, to return not, until man shall know
That they alone can give the bliss
Worthy a soul that claims
Its kindred with eternity.

'There's not one atom of yon earth
But once was living man;
Nor the minutest drop of rain,
That hangeth in its thinnest cloud,
But flowed in human veins:
And from the burning plains
Where Libyan monsters yell,
From the most gloomy glens
Of Greenland's sunless clime,
To where the golden fields
Of fertile England spread
Their harvest to the day,
Thou canst not find one spot
Whereon no city stood.

'How strange is human pride!
I tell thee that those living things,
To whom the fragile blade of grass,
That springeth in the morn
And perisheth ere noon,
Is an unbounded world;
I tell thee that those viewless beings,
Whose mansion is the smallest particle
Of the impassive atmosphere,
Think, feel and live like man;
That their affections and antipathies,
Like his, produce the laws
Ruling their moral state;
And the minutest throb
That through their frame diffuses
The slightest, faintest motion,
Is fixed and indispensable
As the majestic laws
That rule yon rolling orbs.'

The Fairy paused. The Spirit,
In ecstasy of admiration, felt

All knowledge of the past revived; the events
Of old and wondrous times,
Which dim tradition interruptedly
Teaches the credulous vulgar, were unfolded
In just perspective to the view;
Yet dim from their infinitude.
The Spirit seemed to stand
High on an isolated pinnacle;
The flood of ages combating below,
The depth of the unbounded universe
Above, and all around
Nature's unchanging harmony.

III

'FAIRY!' the Spirit said,
And on the Queen of Spells
Fixed her aethereal eyes,
'I thank thee. Thou hast given
A boon which I will not resign, and taught
A lesson not to be unlearned. I know
The past, and thence I will essay to glean
A warning for the future, so that man
May profit by his errors, and derive
Experience from his folly:
For, when the power of imparting joy
Is equal to the will, the human soul
Requires no other Heaven.'

Mab

'Turn thee, surpassing Spirit!
Much yet remains unscanned.
Thou knowest how great is man,
Thou knowest his imbecility:
Yet learn thou what he is:
Yet learn the lofty destiny
Which restless time prepares
For every living soul.

'Behold a gorgeous palace, that, amid
Yon populous city rears its thousand towers
And seems itself a city. Gloomy troops
Of sentinels, in stern and silent ranks,

Encompass it around: the dweller there
Cannot be free and happy; hearest thou not
The curses of the fatherless, the groans
Of those who have no friend? He passes on:
The King, the wearer of a gilded chain
That binds his soul to abjectness, the fool
Whom courtiers nickname monarch, whilst a slave
Even to the basest appetites—that man
Heeds not the shriek of penury; he smiles
At the deep curses which the destitute
Mutter in secret, and a sullen joy
Pervades his bloodless heart when thousands groan
But for those morsels which his wantonness
Wastes in unjoyous revelry, to save
All that they love from famine: when he hears
The tale of horror, to some ready-made face
Of hypocritical assent he turns,
Smothering the glow of shame, that, spite of him,
Flushes his bloated cheek.

                         Now to the meal
Of silence, grandeur, and excess, he drags
His palled unwilling appetite. If gold,
Gleaming around, and numerous viands culled
From every clime, could force the loathing sense
To overcome satiety,—if wealth
The spring it draws from poisons not,—or vice,
Unfeeling, stubborn vice, converteth not
Its food to deadliest venom; then that king
Is happy; and the peasant who fulfils
His unforced task, when he returns at even,
And by the blazing faggot meets again
Her welcome for whom all his toil is sped,
Tastes not a sweeter meal.

                         Behold him now
Stretched on the gorgeous couch; his fevered brain
Reels dizzily awhile: but ah! too soon
The slumber of intemperance subsides,
And conscience, that undying serpent, calls
Her venomous brood to their nocturnal task.
Listen! he speaks! oh! mark that frenzied eye—
Oh! mark that deadly visage.'

King

'No cessation!
Oh! must this last for ever? Awful Death,
I wish, yet fear to clasp thee!—Not one moment
Of dreamless sleep! O dear and blessèd peace!
Why dost thou shroud thy vestal purity
In penury and dungeons? wherefore lurkest
With danger, death, and solitude; yet shunn'st
The palace I have built thee? Sacred peace!
Oh visit me but once, but pitying shed
One drop of balm upon my withered soul.'

The Fairy

'Vain man! that palace is the virtuous heart,
And Peace defileth not her snowy robes
In such a shed as thine. Hark! yet he mutters;
His slumbers are but varied agonies,
They prey like scorpions on the springs of life.
There needeth not the hell that bigots frame
To punish those who err: earth in itself
Contains at once the evil and the cure;
And all-sufficing Nature can chastise
Those who transgress her law,—she only knows
How justly to proportion to the fault
The punishment it merits.
                              Is it strange
That this poor wretch should pride him in his woe?
Take pleasure in his abjectness, and hug
The scorpion that consumes him? Is it strange
That, placed on a conspicuous throne of thorns,
Grasping an iron sceptre, and immured
Within a splendid prison, whose stern bounds
Shut him from all that's good or dear on earth,
His soul asserts not its humanity?
That man's mild nature rises not in war
Against a king's employ? No—'tis not strange.
He, like the vulgar, thinks, feels, acts and lives
Just as his father did; the unconquered powers
Of precedent and custom interpose
Between a *king* and virtue. Stranger yet,
To those who know not Nature, nor deduce

The future from the present, it may seem,
That not one slave, who suffers from the crimes
Of this unnatural being; not one wretch,
Whose children famish, and whose nuptial bed
Is earth's unpitying bosom, rears an arm
To dash him from his throne!

                    Those gilded flies
That, basking in the sunshine of a court,
Fatten on its corruption!—what are they?
—The drones of the community; they feed
On the mechanic's labour: the starved hind ,
For them compels the stubborn glebe to yield
Its unshared harvests; and yon squalid form,
Leaner than fleshless misery, that wastes
A sunless life in the unwholesome mine,
Drags out in labour a protracted death,
To glut their grandeur; many faint with toil,
That few may know the cares and woe of sloth.

'Whence, think'st thou, kings and parasites arose?
Whence that unnatural line of drones, who heap
Toil and unvanquishable penury
On those who build their palaces, and bring
Their daily bread?—From vice, black loathsome vice;
From rapine, madness, treachery, and wrong;
From all that 'genders misery, and makes
Of earth this thorny wilderness; from lust,
Revenge, and murder . . . . And when Reason's voice,
Loud as the voice of Nature, shall have waked
The nations; and mankind perceive that vice
Is discord, war, and misery; that virtue
Is peace, and happiness and harmony;
When man's maturer nature shall disdain
The playthings of its childhood;—kingly glare
Will lose its power to dazzle; its authority
Will silently pass by; the gorgeous throne
Shall stand unnoticed in the regal hall,
Fast falling to decay; whilst falsehood's trade
Shall be as hateful and unprofitable
As that of truth is now.

                  Where is the fame
Which the vainglorious mighty of the earth

Seek to eternize? Oh! the faintest sound
From Time's light footfall, the minutest wave
That swells the flood of ages, whelms in nothing
The unsubstantial bubble. Ay! today
Stern is the tyrant's mandate, red the gaze
That flashes desolation, strong the arm
That scatters multitudes. To-morrow comes!
That mandate is a thunder-peal that died
In ages past; that gaze, a transient flash
On which the midnight closed, and on that arm
The worm has made his meal.
                                        The virtuous man,
Who, great in his humility, as kings
Are little in their grandeur; he who leads
Invincibly a life of resolute good,
And stands amid the silent dungeon-depths
More free and fearless than the trembling judge,
Who, clothed in venal power, vainly strove
To bind the impassive spirit;—when he falls,
His mild eye beams benevolence no more:
Withered the hand outstretched but to relieve;
Sunk Reason's simple eloquence, that rolled
But to appal the guilty. Yes! the grave
Hath quenched that eye, and Death's relentless frost
Withered that arm: but the unfading fame
Which Virtue hangs upon its votary's tomb;
The deathless memory of that man, whom kings
Call to their mind and tremble; the remembrance
With which the happy spirit contemplates
Its well-spent pilgrimage on earth,
Shall never pass away.

'Nature rejects the monarch, not the man;
The subject, not the citizen: for kings
And subjects, mutual foes, forever play
A losing game into each other's hands,
Whose stakes are vice and misery.
                                        The man
Of virtuous soul commands not, nor obeys.
Power, like a desolating pestilence,
Pollutes whate'er it touches; and obedience,
Bane of all genius, virtue, freedom, truth,

Makes slaves of men, and, of the human frame,
A mechanized automaton.   When Nero,
High over flaming Rome, with savage joy
Lowered like a fiend, drank with enraptured ear
The shrieks of agonizing death, beheld
The frightful desolation spread, and felt
A new-created sense within his soul
Thrill to the sight, and vibrate to the sound;
Think'st thou his grandeur had not overcome
The force of human kindness? and, when Rome,
With one stern blow, hurled not the tyrant down,
Crushed not the arm red with her dearest blood,
Had not submissive abjectness destroyed
Nature's suggestions?   Look on yonder earth:
The golden harvests spring: the unfailing sun
Sheds light and life; the fruits, the flowers, the trees,
Arise in due succession; all things speak
Peace, harmony, and love. The universe,
In Nature's silent eloquence, declares
That all fulfil the works of love and joy—,
All but the outcast, Man. He fabricates
The sword which stabs his peace; he cherisheth
The snakes that gnaw his heart; he raiseth up
The tyrant, whose delight is in his woe,
Whose sport is in his agony. Yon sun,
Lights it the great alone? Yon silver beams,
Sleep they less sweetly on the cottage thatch
Than on the dome of kings? Is mother Earth
A step-dame to her numerous sons, who earn
Her unshared gifts with unremitting toil;
A mother only to those puling babes
Who, nursed in ease and luxury, make men
The playthings of their babyhood, and mar,
In self-important childishness, that peace
Which men alone appreciate?

            'Spirit of Nature! no.
The pure diffusion of thy essence throbs
    Alike in every human heart.
            Thou, aye, erectest there

Thy throne of power unappealable:
Thou art the judge beneath whose nod
Man's brief and frail authority
    Is powerless as the wind
    That passeth idly by.
Thine the tribunal which surpasseth
  The show of human justice,
    As God surpasses man.

    'Spirit of Nature! thou
Life of interminable multitudes;
  Soul of those mighty spheres
Whose changeless paths through Heaven's deep silence lie;
  Soul of that smallest being,
    The dwelling of whose life
  Is one faint April sun-gleam;—
    Man, like these passive things,
Thy will unconsciously fulfilleth:
  Like theirs, his age of endless peace,
    Which time is fast maturing,
    Will swiftly, surely come;
And the unbounded frame, which thou pervadest,
    Will be without a flaw
  Marring its perfect symmetry.

IV

'How beautiful this night! the balmiest sigh,
Which vernal zephyrs breathe in evening's ear,
Were discord to the speaking quietude
That wraps this moveless scene.
    Heaven's ebon vault,
Studded with stars unutterably bright,
Through which the moon's unclouded grandeur rolls,
Seems like a canopy which love had spread
To curtain her sleeping world. Yon gentle hills,
Robed in a garment of untrodden snow;
Yon darksome rocks, whence icicles depend,
So stainless, that their white and glittering spires
Tinge not the moon's pure beam; yon castled steep,
Whose banner hangeth o'er the timeworn tower

So idly, that rapt fancy deemeth it
A metaphor of peace;—all form a scene
Where musing Solitude might love to lift
Her soul above this sphere of earthliness;
Where Silence undisturbed might watch alone,
So cold, so bright, so still.

                 The orb of day,
In southern climes, o'er ocean's waveless field
Sinks sweetly smiling: not the faintest breath
Steals o'er the unruffled deep; the clouds of eve
Reflect unmoved the lingering beam of day;
And vesper's image on the western main
Is beautifully still. To-morrow comes:
Cloud upon cloud, in dark and deepening mass,
Roll o'er the blackened waters; the deep roar
Of distant thunder mutters awfully;
Tempest unfolds its pinion o'er the gloom
That shrouds the boiling surge; the pitiless fiend,
With all his winds and lightnings, tracks his prey;
The torn deep yawns,—the vessel finds a grave
Beneath its jaggèd gulf.

              Ah! whence yon glare
That fires the arch of Heaven?—that dark red smoke
Blotting the silver moon? The stars are quenched
In darkness, and the pure and spangling snow
Gleams faintly through the gloom that gathers round!
Hark to that roar, whose swift and deaf'ning peals
In countless echoes through the mountains ring,
Startling pale Midnight on her starry throne!
Now swells the intermingling din; the jar
Frequent and frightful of the bursting bomb;
The falling beam, the shriek, the groan, the shout,
The ceaseless clangour, and the rush of men
Inebriate with rage:—loud, and more loud
The discord grows; till pale Death shuts the scene,
And o'er the conqueror and the conquered draws
His cold and bloody shroud.—Of all the men
Whom day's departing beam saw blooming there,
In proud and vigorous health; of all the hearts
That beat with anxious life at sunset there;
How few survive, how few are beating now!
All is deep silence, like the fearful calm

That slumbers in the storm's portentous pause;
Save when the frantic wail of widowed love
Comes shuddering on the blast, or the faint moan
With which some soul bursts from the frame of clay
Wrapped round its struggling powers.

                       The gray morn
Dawns on the mournful scene; the sulphurous smoke
Before the icy wind slow rolls away,
And the bright beams of frosty morning dance
Along the spangling snow. There tracks of blood
Even to the forest's depth, and scattered arms,
And lifeless warriors, whose hard lineaments
Death's self could change not, mark the dreadful path
Of the outsallying victors: far behind,
Black ashes note where their proud city stood.
Within yon forest is a gloomy glen—
Each tree which guards its darkness from the day,
Waves o'er a warrior's tomb.

                       I see thee shrink,
Surpassing Spirit!—wert thou human else?
I see a shade of doubt and horror fleet
Across thy stainless features: yet fear not;
This is no unconnected misery,
Nor stands uncaused, and irretrievable.
Man's evil nature, that apology
Which kings who rule, and cowards who crouch, set up
For their unnumbered crimes, sheds not the blood
Which desolates the discord-wasted land.
From kings, and priests, and statesmen, war arose,
Whose safety is man's deep unbettered woe,
Whose grandeur his debasement. Let the axe
Strike at the root, the poison-tree will fall;
And where its venomed exhalations spread
Ruin, and death, and woe, where millions lay
Quenching the serpent's famine, and their bones
Bleaching unburied in the putrid blast,
A garden shall arise, in loveliness
Surpassing fabled Eden.

                    Hath Nature's soul,
That formed this world so beautiful, that spread
Earth's lap with plenty, and life's smallest chord
Strung to unchanging unison, that gave

The happy birds their dwelling in the grove,
That yielded to the wanderers of the deep
The lovely silence of the unfathomed main,
And filled the meanest worm that crawls in dust
With spirit, thought, and love; on Man alone,
Partial in causeless malice, wantonly
Heaped ruin, vice, and slavery; his soul
Blasted with withering curses; placed afar
The meteor-happiness, that shuns his grasp,
But serving on the frightful gulf to glare,
Rent wide beneath his footsteps?

                        Nature!—no!
Kings, priests, and statesmen, blast the human flower
Even in its tender bud; their influence darts
Like subtle poison through the bloodless veins
Of desolate society. The child,
Ere he can lisp his mother's sacred name,
Swells with the unnatural pride of crime, and lifts
His baby-sword even in a hero's mood.
This infant-arm becomes the bloodiest scourge
Of devastated earth; whilst specious names,
Learned in soft childhood's unsuspecting hour,
Serve as the sophisms with which manhood dims
Bright Reason's ray, and sanctifies the sword
Upraised to shed a brother's innocent blood.
Let priest-led slaves cease to proclaim that man
Inherits vice and misery, when Force
And Falsehood hang even o'er the cradled babe,
Stifling with rudest grasp all natural good.
'Ah! to the stranger-soul, when first it peeps
From its new tenement, and looks abroad
For happiness and sympathy, how stern
And desolate a tract is this wide world!
How withered all the buds of natural good!
No shade, no shelter from the sweeping storms
Of pitiless power! On its wretched frame,
Poisoned, perchance, by the disease and woe
Heaped on the wretched parent whence it sprung
By morals, law, and custom, the pure winds
Of Heaven, that renovate the insect tribes,
May breathe not. The untainting light of day
May visit not its longings. It is bound

Ere it has life: yea, all the chains are forged
Long ere its being: all liberty and love
And peace is torn from its defencelessness;
Cursed from its birth, even from its cradle doomed
To abjectness and bondage!

'Throughout this varied and eternal world
Soul is the only element: the block
That for uncounted ages has remained
The moveless pillar of a mountain's weight
Is active, living spirit. Every grain
Is sentient both in unity and part,
And the minutest atom comprehends
A world of loves and hatreds; these beget
Evil and good: hence truth and falsehood spring;
Hence will and thought and action, all the germs
Of pain or pleasure, sympathy or hate,
That variegate the eternal universe.
Soul is not more polluted than the beams
Of Heaven's pure orb, ere round their rapid lines
The taint of earth-born atmospheres arise.

'Man is of soul and body, formed for deeds
Of high resolve, on fancy's boldest wing
To soar unwearied, fearlessly to turn
The keenest pangs to peacefulness, and taste
The joys which mingled sense and spirit yield.
Or he is formed for abjectness and woe,
To grovel on the dunghill of his fears,
To shrink at every sound, to quench the flame
Of natural love in sensualism, to know
That hour as blessed when on his worthless days
The frozen hand of Death shall set its seal,
Yet fear the cure, though hating the disease.
The one is man that shall hereafter be;
The other, man as vice has made him now.

'War is the statesman's game, the priest's delight,
The lawyer's jest, the hired assassin's trade,
And, to those royal murderers, whose mean thrones
Are bought by crimes of treachery and gore,
The bread they eat, the staff on which they lean.

Guards, garbed in blood-red livery, surround
Their palaces, participate the crimes
That force defends, and from a nation's rage
Secure the crown, which all the curses reach
That famine, frenzy, woe and penury breathe.
These are the hired bravos who defend
The tyrant's throne—the bullies of his fear:
These are the sinks and channels of worst vice,
The refuse of society, the dregs
Of all that is most vile: their cold hearts blend
Deceit with sternness, ignorance with pride,
All that is mean and villainous, with rage
Which hopelessness of good, and self-contempt,
Alone might kindle; they are decked in wealth,
Honour and power, then are sent abroad
To do their work. The pestilence that stalks
In gloomy triumph through some eastern land
Is less destroying. They cajole with gold,
And promises of fame, the thoughtless youth
Already crushed with servitude: he knows
His wretchedness too late, and cherishes
Repentance for his ruin, when his doom
Is sealed in gold and blood!
Those too the tyrant serve, who, skilled to snare
The feet of Justice in the toils of law,
Stand, ready to oppress the weaker still;
And right or wrong will vindicate for gold,
Sneering at public virtue, which beneath
Their pitiless tread lies torn and trampled, where
Honour sits smiling at the sale of truth.

'Then grave and hoary-headed hypocrites,
Without a hope, a passion, or a love,
Who, through a life of luxury and lies,
Have crept by flattery to the seats of power,
Support the system whence their honours flow....
They have three words:—well tyrants know their use,
Well pay them for the loan, with usury
Torn from a bleeding world!—God, Hell, and Heaven.
A vengeful, pitiless, and almighty fiend,
Whose mercy is a nickname for the rage
Of tameless tigers hungering for blood.

Hell, a red gulf of everlasting fire,
Where poisonous and undying worms prolong
Eternal misery to those hapless slaves
Whose life has been a penance for its crimes.
And Heaven, a meed for those who dare belie
Their human nature, quake, believe, and cringe
Before the mockeries of earthly power.

'These tools the tyrant tempers to his work,
Wields in his wrath, and as he wills destroys,
Omnipotent in wickedness: the while
Youth springs, age moulders, manhood tamely does
His bidding, bribed by short-lived joys to lend
Force to the weakness of his trembling arm.

'They rise, they fall; one generation comes
Yielding its harvest to destruction's scythe.
It fades, another blossoms: yet behold!
Red glows the tyrant's stamp-mark on its bloom,
Withering and cankering deep its passive prime.
He has invented lying words and modes,
Empty and vain as his own coreless heart;
Evasive meanings, nothings of much sound,
To lure the heedless victim to the toils
Spread round the valley of its paradise.

'Look to thyself, priest, conqueror, or prince!
Whether thy trade is falsehood, and thy lusts
Deep wallow in the earnings of the poor,
With whom thy Master was:—or thou delight'st
In numbering o'er the myriads of thy slain,
All misery weighing nothing in the scale
Against thy short-lived fame: or thou dost load
With cowardice and crime the groaning land,
A pomp-fed king. Look to thy wretched self!
Ay, art thou not the veriest slave that e'er
Crawled on the loathing earth? Are not thy days
Days of unsatisfying listlessness?
Dost thou not cry, ere night's long rack is o'er,
"When will the morning come?" Is not thy youth
A vain and feverish dream of sensualism?
Thy manhood blighted with unripe disease?

Are not thy views of unregretted death
Drear, comfortless, and horrible? Thy mind,
Is it not morbid as thy nerveless frame,
Incapable of judgement, hope, or love?
And dost thou wish the errors to survive
That bar thee from all sympathies of good,
After the miserable interest
Thou hold'st in their protraction?

                                  When the grave
Has swallowed up thy memory and thyself,
Dost thou desire the bane that poisons earth
To twine its roots around thy coffined clay,
Spring from thy bones, and blossom on thy tomb,
That of its fruit thy babes may eat and die?

V

'Thus do the generations of the earth
Go to the grave, and issue from the womb,
Surviving still the imperishable change
That renovates the world; even as the leaves
Which the keen frost-wind of the waning year
Has scattered on the forest soil, and heaped
For many seasons there—though long they choke,
Loading with loathsome rottenness the land,
All germs of promise, yet when the tall trees
From which they fell, shorn of their lovely shapes,
Lie level with the earth to moulder there,
They fertilize the land they long deformed,
Till from the breathing lawn a forest springs
Of youth, integrity, and loveliness,
Like that which gave it life, to spring and die.
Thus suicidal selfishness, that blights
The fairest feelings of the opening heart,
Is destined to decay, whilst from the soil
Shall spring all virtue, all delight, all love,
And judgement cease to wage unnatural war
With passion's unsubduable array.
Twin-sister of religion, selfishness!
Rival in crime and falsehood, aping all
The wanton horrors of her bloody play;
Yet frozen, unimpassioned, spiritless,
Shunning the light, and owning not its name.

Compelled, by its deformity, to screen
With flimsy veil of justice and of right
Its unattractive lineaments, that scare
All, save the brood of ignorance: at once
The cause and the effect of tyranny;
Unblushing, hardened, sensual, and vile;
Dead to all love but of its abjectness,
With heart impassive by more noble powers
Than unshared pleasure, sordid gain, or fame;
Despising its own miserable being,
Which still it longs, yet fears to disenthral.

'Hence commerce springs, the venal interchange
Of all that human art or nature yield;
Which wealth should purchase not, but want demand,
And natural kindness hasten to supply
From the full fountain of its boundless love,
For ever stifled, drained, and tainted now.
Commerce! beneath whose poison-breathing shade
No solitary virtue dares to spring,
But Poverty and Wealth with equal hand
Scatter their withering curses, and unfold
The doors of premature and violent death,
To pining famine and full-fed disease,
To all that shares the lot of human life,
Which poisoned, body and soul, scarce drags the chain,
That lengthens as it goes and clanks behind.

'Commerce has set the mark of selfishness,
The signet of its all-enslaving power,
Upon a shining ore, and called it gold:
Before whose image bow the vulgar great,
The vainly rich, the miserable proud,
The mob of peasants, nobles, priests, and kings,
And with blind feelings reverence the power
That grinds them to the dust of misery.
But in the temple of their hireling hearts
Gold is a living god, and rules in scorn
All earthly things but virtue.

'Since tyrants, by the sale of human life,
Heap luxuries to their sensualism, and fame

To their wide-wasting and insatiate pride,
Success has sanctioned to a credulous world
The ruin, the disgrace, the woe of war.
His hosts of blind and unresisting dupes
The despot numbers; from his cabinet
These puppets of his schemes he moves at will,
Even as the slaves by force or famine driven,
Beneath a vulgar master, to perform
A task of cold and brutal drudgery;—
Hardened to hope, insensible to fear,
Scarce living pulleys of a dead machine,
Mere wheels of work and articles of trade,
That grace the proud and noisy pomp of wealth!

'The harmony and happiness of man
Yields to the wealth of nations; that which lifts
His nature to the heaven of its pride,
Is bartered for the poison of his soul;
The weight that drags to earth his towering hopes,
Blighting all prospect but of selfish gain,
Withering all passion but of slavish fear,
Extinguishing all free and generous love
Of enterprise and daring, even the pulse
That fancy kindles in the beating heart
To mingle with sensation, it destroys,—
Leaves nothing but the sordid lust of self,
The grovelling hope of interest and gold,
Unqualified, unmingled, unredeemed
Even by hypocrisy.
                              And statesmen boast
Of wealth! The wordy eloquence, that lives
After the ruin of their hearts, can gild
The bitter poison of a nation's woe,
Can turn the worship of the servile mob
To their corrupt and glaring idol, Fame,
From Virtue, trampled by its iron tread,
Although its dazzling pedestal be raised
Amid the horrors of a limb-strewn field,
With desolated dwellings smoking round.
The man of ease, who, by his warm fireside,
To deeds of charitable intercourse,
And bare fulfilment of the common laws

Of decency and prejudice, confines
The struggling nature of his human heart,
Is duped by their cold sophistry; he sheds
A passing tear perchance upon the wreck
Of earthly peace, when near his dwelling's door
The frightful waves are driven,—when his son
Is murdered by the tyrant, or religion
Drives his wife raving mad. But the poor man,
Whose life is misery, and fear, and care;
Whom the morn wakens but to fruitless toil;
Who ever hears his famished offspring's scream,
Whom their pale mother's uncomplaining gaze
For ever meets, and the proud rich man's eye
Flashing command, and the heartbreaking scene
Of thousands like himself;—he little heeds
The rhetoric of tyranny; his hate
Is quenchless as his wrongs; he laughs to scorn
The vain and bitter mockery of words,
Feeling the horror of the tyrant's deeds,
And unrestrained but by the arm of power,
That knows and dreads his enmity.

'The iron rod of Penury still compels
Her wretched slave to bow the knee to wealth,
And poison, with unprofitable toil,
A life too void of solace to confirm
The very chains that bind him to his doom.
Nature, impartial in munificence,
Has gifted man with all-subduing will.
Matter, with all its transitory shapes,
Lies subjected and plastic at his feet,
That, weak from bondage, tremble as they tread.
How many a rustic Milton has passed by,
Stifling the speechless longings of his heart,
In unremitting drudgery and care!
How many a vulgar Cato has compelled
His energies, no longer tameless then,
To mould a pin, or fabricate a nail!
How many a Newton, to whose passive ken
Those mighty spheres that gem infinity
Were only specks of tinsel, fixed in Heaven
To light the midnights of his native town!

'Yet every heart contains perfection's germ:
The wisest of the sages of the earth,
That ever from the stores of reason drew
Science and truth, and virtue's dreadless tone,
Were but a weak and inexperienced boy,
Proud, sensual, unimpassioned, unimbued
With pure desire and universal love,
Compared to that high being, of cloudless brain,
Untainted passion, elevated will,
Which Death (who even would linger long in awe
Within his noble presence, and beneath
His changeless eyebeam) might alone subdue.
Him, every slave now dragging through the filth
Of some corrupted city his sad life,
Pining with famine, swoln with luxury,
Blunting the keenness of his spiritual sense
With narrow schemings and unworthy cares,
Or madly rushing through all violent crime,
To move the deep stagnation of his soul—
Might imitate and equal.
                              But mean lust
Has bound its chains so tight around the earth,
That all within it but the virtuous man
Is venal: gold or fame will surely reach
The price prefixed by selfishness, to all
But him of resolute and unchanging will;
Whom, nor the plaudits of a servile crowd,
Nor the vile joys of tainting luxury,
Can bribe to yield his elevated soul
To Tyranny or Falsehood, though they wield
With blood-red hand the sceptre of the world.

'All things are sold: the very light of Heaven
Is venal; earth's unsparing gifts of love,
The smallest and most despicable things
That lurk in the abysses of the deep,
All objects of our life, even life itself,
And the poor pittance which the laws allow
Of liberty, the fellowship of man,
Those duties which his heart of human love
Should urge him to perform instinctively,
Are bought and sold as in a public mart

Of undisguising selfishness, that sets
On each its price, the stamp-mark of her reign.
Even love is sold; the solace of all woe
Is turned to deadliest agony, old age
Shivers in selfish beauty's loathing arms,
And youth's corrupted impulses prepare
A life of horror from the blighting bane
Of commerce; whilst the pestilence that springs
From unenjoying sensualism, has filled
All human life with hydra-headed woes.

'Falsehood demands but gold to pay the pangs
Of outraged conscience, for the slavish priest
Sets no great value on his hireling faith:
A little passing pomp, some servile souls,
Whom cowardice itself might safely chain,
Or the spare mite of avarice could bribe
To deck the triumph of their languid zeal,
Can make him minister to tyranny.
More daring crime requires a loftier meed:
Without a shudder, the slave-soldier lends
His arm to murderous deeds, and steels his heart,
When the dread eloquence of dying men,
Low mingling on the lonely field of fame,
Assails that nature, whose applause he sells
For the gross blessings of a patriot mob,
For the vile gratitude of heartless kings,
And for a cold world's good word,—viler still!

'There is a nobler glory, which survives
Until our being fades, and, solacing
All human care, accompanies its change;
Deserts not virtue in the dungeon's gloom,
And, in the precincts of the palace, guides
Its footsteps through that labyrinth of crime;
Imbues his lineaments with dauntlessness,
Even when, from Power's avenging hand, he takes
Its sweetest, last and noblest title—death;
—The consciousness of good, which neither gold,
Nor sordid fame, nor hope of heavenly bliss
Can purchase; but a life of resolute good,
Unalterable will, quenchless desire

Of universal happiness, the heart
That beats with it in unison, the brain
Whose ever wakeful wisdom toils to change
Reason's rich stores for its eternal weal.

'This commerce of sincerest virtue needs
No mediative signs of selfishness,
No jealous intercourse of wretched gain,
No balancings of prudence, cold and long;
In just and equal measure all is weighed,
One scale contains the sum of human weal,
And one, the good man's heart.
                                                    How vainly seek
The selfish for that happiness denied
To aught but virtue! Blind and hardened, they,
Who hope for peace amid the storms of care,
Who covet power they know not how to use,
And sigh for pleasure they refuse to give,—
Madly they frustrate still their own designs;
And, where they hope that quiet to enjoy
Which virtue pictures, bitterness of soul,
Pining regrets, and vain repentances,
Disease, disgust, and lassitude, pervade
Their valueless and miserable lives.

'But hoary-headed Selfishness has felt
Its death-blow, and is tottering to the grave:
A brighter morn awaits the human day,
When every transfer of earth's natural gifts
Shall be a commerce of good words and works;
When poverty and wealth, the thirst of fame,
The fear of infamy, disease and woe,
War with its million horrors, and fierce hell
Shall live but in the memory of Time,
Who, like a penitent libertine, shall start,
Look back, and shudder at his younger years.'

VI

ALL touch, all eye, all ear,
The Spirit felt the Fairy's burning speech.
    O'er the thin texture of its frame,
The varying periods painted changing glows,
        As on a summer even,
When soul-enfolding music floats around,
    The stainless mirror of the lake
    Re-images the eastern gloom,
Mingling convulsively its purple hues
        With sunset's burnished gold.

        Then thus the Spirit spoke:
'It is a wild and miserable world!
        Thorny, and full of care,
Which every fiend can make his prey at will.
    O Fairy! in the lapse of years,
        Is there no hope in store?
        Will yon vast suns roll on
    Interminably, still illuming
    The night of so many wretched souls,
        And see no hope for them?
Will not the universal Spirit e'er
Revivify this withered limb of Heaven?'

        The Fairy calmly smiled
In comfort, and a kindling gleam of hope
    Suffused the Spirit's lineaments.
'Oh! rest thee tranquil; chase those fearful doubts,
Which ne'er could rack an everlasting soul,
That sees the chains which bind it to its doom.
Yes! crime and misery are in yonder earth,
        Falsehood, mistake, and lust;
        But the eternal world
Contains at once the evil and the cure.
Some eminent in virtue shall start up,
        Even in perversest time:
The truths of their pure lips, that never die,
Shall bind the scorpion falsehood with a wreath
        Of ever-living flame,
Until the monster sting itself to death.

'How sweet a scene will earth become!
Of purest spirits a pure dwelling-place,
Symphonious with the planetary spheres;
When man, with changeless Nature coalescing,
Will undertake regeneration's work,
When its ungenial poles no longer point
   To the red and baleful sun
   That faintly twinkles there.

  'Spirit! on yonder earth,
 Falsehood now triumphs; deadly power
Has fixed its seal upon the lip of truth!
 Madness and misery are there!
The happiest is most wretched! Yet confide,
Until pure health-drops, from the cup of joy,
Fall like a dew of balm upon the world.
Now, to the scene I show, in silence turn,
And read the blood-stained charter of all woe,
Which Nature soon, with re-creating hand,
Will blot in mercy from the book of earth.
How bold the flight of Passion's wandering wing,
How swift the step of Reason's firmer tread,
How calm and sweet the victories of life,
How terrorless the triumph of the grave!
How powerless were the mightiest monarch's arm,
Vain his loud threat, and impotent his frown!
How ludicrous the priest's dogmatic roar!
The weight of his exterminating curse
How light! and his affected charity,
To suit the pressure of the changing times,
What palpable deceit!—but for thy aid,
Religion! but for thee, prolific fiend,
Who peoplest earth with demons, Hell with men,
And Heaven with slaves!

'Thou taintest all thou look'st upon!—the stars,
Which on the cradle beamed so brightly sweet,
Were gods to the distempered playfulness
Of thy untutored infancy: the trees,
The grass, the clouds, the mountains, and the sea,
All living things that walk, swim, creep, or fly,
Were gods: the sun had homage, and the moon
Her worshipper. Then thou becam'st, a boy,

More daring in thy frenzies: every shape,
Monstrous or vast, or beautifully wild,
Which, from sensation's relics, fancy culls;
The spirits of the air, the shuddering ghost,
The genii of the elements, the powers
That give a shape to Nature's varied works,
Had life and place in the corrupt belief
Of thy blind heart: yet still thy youthful hands
Were pure of human blood. Then manhood gave
Its strength and ardour to thy frenzied brain;
Thine eager gaze scanned the stupendous scene,
Whose wonders mocked the knowledge of thy pride:
Their everlasting and unchanging laws
Reproached thine ignorance. Awhile thou stoodst
Baffled and gloomy; then thou didst sum up
The elements of all that thou didst know;
The changing seasons, winter's leafless reign,
The budding of the Heaven-breathing trees,
The eternal orbs that beautify the night,
The sunrise, and the setting of the moon,
Earthquakes and wars, and poisons and disease,
And all their causes, to an abstract point
Converging, thou didst bend and called it God!
The self-sufficing, the omnipotent,
The merciful, and the avenging God!
Who, prototype of human misrule, sits
High in Heaven's realm, upon a golden throne,
Even like an earthly king; and whose dread work,
Hell, gapes for ever the unhappy slaves
Of fate, whom He created, in his sport,
To triumph in their torments when they fell!
Earth heard the name; Earth trembled, as the smoke
Of His revenge ascended up to Heaven,
Blotting the constellations; and the cries
Of millions, butchered in sweet confidence
And unsuspecting peace, even when the bonds
Of safety were confirmed by wordy oaths
Sworn in His dreadful name, rung through the land;
Whilst innocent babes writhed on thy stubborn spear,
And thou didst laugh to hear the mother's shriek
Of maniac gladness, as the sacred steel
Felt cold in her torn entrails!

'Religion! thou wert then in manhood's prime:
But age crept on: one God would not suffice
For senile puerility; thou framedst
A tale to suit thy dotage, and to glut
Thy misery-thirsting soul, that the mad fiend
Thy wickedness had pictured might afford
A plea for sating the unnatural thirst
For murder, rapine, violence, and crime,
That still consumed thy being, even when
Thou heardst the step of Fate;—that flames might light
Thy funeral scene, and the shrill horrent shrieks
Of parents dying on the pile that burned
To light their children to thy paths, the roar
Of the encircling flames, the exulting cries
Of thine apostles, loud commingling there,
        Might sate thine hungry ear
        Even on the bed of death!

'But now contempt is mocking thy gray hairs;
Thou art descending to the darksome grave,
Unhonoured and unpitied, but by those
Whose pride is passing by like thine, and sheds,
Like thine, a glare that fades before the sun
Of truth, and shines but in the dreadful night
That long has lowered above the ruined world.

'Throughout these infinite orbs of mingling light,
Of which yon earth is one, is wide diffused
A Spirit of activity and life,
That knows no term, cessation, or decay;
That fades not when the lamp of earthly life,
Extinguished in the dampness of the grave,
Awhile there slumbers, more than when the babe
In the dim newness of its being feels
The impulses of sublunary things,
And all is wonder to unpractised sense:
But, active, steadfast, and eternal, still
Guides the fierce whirlwind, in the tempest roars,
Cheers in the day, breathes in the balmy groves,
Strengthens in health, and poisons in disease;
And in the storm of change, that ceaselessly
Rolls round the eternal universe, and shakes

Its undecaying battlement, presides,
Apportioning with irresistible law
The place each spring of its machine shall fill;
So that when waves on waves tumultuous heap
Confusion to the clouds, and fiercely driven
Heaven's lightnings scorch the uprooted ocean-fords,
Whilst, to the eye of shipwrecked mariner,
Lone sitting on the bare and shuddering rock,
All seems unlinked contingency and chance;
No atom of this turbulence fulfils
A vague and unnecessitated task,
Or acts but as it must and ought to act.
Even the minutest molecule of light,
That in an April sunbeam's fleeting glow
Fulfils its destined, though invisible work,
The universal Spirit guides; nor less,
When merciless ambition, or mad zeal,
Has led two hosts of dupes to battlefield,
That, blind, they there may dig each other's graves,
And call the sad work glory, does it rule
All passions: not a thought, a will, an act,
No working of the tyrant's moody mind,
Nor one misgiving of the slaves who boast
Their servitude, to hide the shame they feel,
Nor the events enchaining every will,
That from the depths of unrecorded time
Have drawn all-influencing virtue, pass
Unrecognized, or unforeseen by thee,
Soul of the Universe! eternal spring
Of life and death, of happiness and woe,
Of all that chequers the phantasmal scene
That floats before our eyes in wavering light,
Which gleams but on the darkness of our prison,
   Whose chains and massy walls
   We feel, but cannot see.

'Spirit of Nature! all-sufficing Power,
Necessity! thou mother of the world!
Unlike the God of human error, thou
Requir'st no prayers or praises; the caprice
Of man's weak will belongs no more to thee
Than do the changeful passions of his breast

To thy unvarying harmony: the slave,
Whose horrible lusts spread misery o'er the world,
And the good man, who lifts, with virtuous pride,
His being, in the sight of happiness,
That springs from his own works; the poison-tree,
Beneath whose shade all life is withered up,
And the fair oak, whose leafy dome affords
A temple where the vows of happy love
Are registered, are equal in thy sight:
No love, no hate thou cherishest; revenge
And favouritism, and worst desire of fame
Thou know'st not: all that the wide world contains
Are but thy passive instruments, and thou
Regard'st them all with an impartial eye,
Whose joy or pain thy nature cannot feel,
   Because thou hast not human sense,
   Because thou art not human mind.

   'Yes! when the sweeping storm of time
   Has sung its death-dirge o'er the ruined fanes
And broken altars of the almighty Fiend
Whose name usurps thy honours, and the blood
Through centuries clotted there, has floated down
The tainted flood of ages, shalt thou live
Unchangeable! A shrine is raised to thee,
   Which, nor the tempest-breath of time,
   Nor the interminable flood,
   Over earth's slight pageant rolling,
     Availeth to destroy,—
The sensitive extension of the world.
   That wondrous and eternal fane,
Where pain and pleasure, good and evil join,
To do the will of strong necessity,
   And life, in multitudinous shapes,
Still pressing forward where no term can be,
   Like hungry and unresting flame
Curls round the eternal columns of its strength.'

VII

Spirit

'I was an infant when my mother went
To see an atheist burned. She took me there:
The dark-robed priests were met around the pile;
The multitude was gazing silently;
And as the culprit passed with dauntless mien,
Tempered disdain in his unaltering eye,
Mixed with a quiet smile, shone calmly forth:
The thirsty fire crept round his manly limbs;
His resolute eyes were scorched to blindness soon;
His death-pang rent my heart! the insensate mob
Uttered a cry of triumph, and I wept,
"Weep not, child!" cried my mother, "for that man
Has said, There is no God."'

Fairy

                         'There is no God!
Nature confirms the faith his death-groan sealed:
Let heaven and earth, let man's revolving race,
His ceaseless generations tell their tale;
Let every part depending on the chain
That links it to the whole, point to the hand
That grasps its term! let every seed that falls
In silent eloquence unfold its store
Of argument; infinity within,
Infinity without, belie creation;
The exterminable spirit it contains
Is nature's only God; but human pride
Is skilful to invent most serious names
To hide its ignorance.
                         The name of God
Has fenced about all crime with holiness,
Himself the creature of His worshippers,
Whose names and attributes and passions change,
Seeva, Buddh, Foh, Jehovah, God, or Lord,
Even with the human dupes who build His shrines,
Still serving o'er the war-polluted world
For desolation's watchword; whether hosts
Stain His death-blushing chariot-wheels, as on

Triumphantly they roll, whilst Brahmins raise
A sacred hymn to mingle with the groans;
Or countless partners of His power divide
His tyranny to weakness; or the smoke
Of burning towns, the cries of female helplessness,
Unarmed old age, and youth, and infancy,
Horribly massacred, ascend to Heaven
In honour of His name; or, last and worst,
Earth groans beneath religion's iron age,
And priests dare babble of a God of peace,
Even whilst their hands are red with guiltless blood,
Murdering the while, uprooting every germ
Of truth, exterminating, spoiling all,
Making the earth a slaughter-house!

            'O Spirit! through the sense
    By which thy inner nature was apprised
        Of outward shows, vague dreams have rolled,
    And varied reminiscences have waked
            Tablets that never fade;
        All things have been imprinted there,
        The stars, the sea, the earth, the sky,
        Even the unshapeliest lineaments
            Of wild and fleeting visions
                Have left a record there
                To testify of earth.

'These are my empire, for to me is given
The wonders of the human world to keep,
And Fancy's thin creations to endow
With manner, being, and reality;
Therefore a wondrous phantom, from the dreams
Of human error's dense and purblind faith,
I will evoke, to meet thy questioning.
        Ahasuerus, rise!'

            A strange and woe-worn wight
        Arose beside the battlement,
            And stood unmoving there.
    His inessential figure cast no shade
            Upon the golden floor;
    His port and mien bore mark of many years,

And chronicles of untold ancientness
Were legible within his beamless eye:
 Yet his cheek bore the mark of youth;
Freshness and vigour knit his manly frame;
The wisdom of old age was mingled there
 With youth's primaeval dauntlessness;
  And inexpressible woe,
Chastened by fearless resignation, gave
An awful grace to his all-speaking brow.

Spirit

'Is there a God?'

Ahasuerus

'Is there a God!—ay, an almighty God,
And vengeful as almighty! Once His voice
Was heard on earth: earth shuddered at the sound;
The fiery-visaged firmament expressed
Abhorrence, and the grave of Nature yawned
To swallow all the dauntless and the good
That dared to hurl defiance at His throne.
Girt as it was with power. None but slaves
Survived,—cold-blooded slaves, who did the work
Of tyrannous omnipotence; whose souls
No honest indignation ever urged
To elevated daring, to one deed
Which gross and sensual self did not pollute.
These slaves built temples for the omnipotent Fiend,
Gorgeous and vast: the costly altars smoked
With human blood, and hideous paeans rung
Through all the long-drawn aisles. A murderer heard
His voice in Egypt, one whose gifts and arts
Had raised him to his eminence in power,
Accomplice of omnipotence in crime,
And confidant of the all-knowing one.
 These were Jehovah's words:—

'From an eternity of idleness
I, God, awoke; in seven days' toil made earth
From nothing; rested, and created man:
I placed him in a Paradise, and there
Planted the tree of evil, so that he

Might eat and perish, and My soul procure
Wherewith to sate its malice, and to turn,
Even like a heartless conqueror of the earth,
All misery to My fame. The race of men
Chosen to My honour, with impunity
May sate the lusts I planted in their heart.
Here I command thee hence to lead them on,
Until, with hardened feet, their conquering troops
Wade on the promised soil through woman's blood,
And make My name be dreaded through the land.
Yet ever-burning flame and ceaseless woe
Shall be the doom of their eternal souls,
With every soul on this ungrateful earth,
Virtuous or vicious, weak or strong,—even all
Shall perish, to fulfil the blind revenge
(Which you, to men, call justice) of their God.'

                    The murderer's brow
Quivered with horror.

                     'God omnipotent,
Is there no mercy? must our punishment
Be endless? will long ages roll away,
And see no term? Oh! wherefore hast Thou made
In mockery and wrath this evil earth?
Mercy becomes the powerful—be but just:
O God! repent and save.'

                    'One way remains:
I will beget a Son, and He shall bear
The sins of all the world; He shall arise
In an unnoticed corner of the earth,
And there shall die upon a cross, and purge
The universal crime; so that the few
On whom My grace descends, those who are marked
As vessels to the honour of their God,
May credit this strange sacrifice, and save
Their souls alive: millions shall live and die,
Who ne'er shall call upon their Saviour's name,
But, unredeemed, go to the gaping grave.
Thousands shall deem it an old woman's tale,
Such as the nurses frighten babes withal;
These in a gulf of anguish and of flame

Shall curse their reprobation endlessly,
Yet tenfold pangs shall force them to avow,
Even on their beds of torment, where they howl,
My honour, and the justice of their doom.
What then avail their virtuous deeds, their thoughts
Of purity, with radiant genius bright,
Or lit with human reason's earthly ray?
Many are called, but few will I elect.
Do thou My bidding, Moses!'

                            Even the murderer's cheek
Was blanched with horror, and his quivering lips
Scarce faintly uttered—'O almighty One,
I tremble and obey!'

'O Spirit! centuries have set their seal
On this heart of many wounds, and loaded brain,
Since the Incarnate came: humbly He came,
Veiling His horrible Godhead in the shape
Of man, scorned by the world, His name unheard,
Save by the rabble of His native town,
Even as a parish demagogue. He led
The crowd; He taught them justice, truth, and peace,
In semblance; but He lit within their souls
The quenchless flames of zeal, and blessed the sword
He brought on earth to satiate with the blood
Of truth and freedom His malignant soul.
At length His mortal frame was led to death.
I stood beside Him: on the torturing cross
No pain assailed His unterrestrial sense;
And yet He groaned. Indignantly I summed
The massacres and miseries which His name
Had sanctioned in my country, and I cried,
"Go! Go!" in mockery.
A smile of godlike malice reillumed
His fading lineaments.—"I go," He cried,
"But thou shalt wander o'er the unquiet earth
Eternally."——The dampness of the grave
Bathed my imperishable front. I fell,
And long lay tranced upon the charmèd soil.
When I awoke Hell burned within my brain,
Which staggered on its seat; for all around
The mouldering relics of my kindred lay,

Even as the Almighty's ire arrested them,
And in their various attitudes of death
My murdered children's mute and eyeless skulls
Glared ghastily upon me.
                                    But my soul,
From sight and sense of the polluting woe
Of tyranny, had long learned to prefer
Hell's freedom to the servitude of Heaven.
Therefore I rose, and dauntlessly began
My lonely and unending pilgrimage,
Resolved to wage unweariable war
With my almighty Tyrant, and to hurl
Defiance at His impotence to harm
Beyond the curse I bore. The very hand
That barred my passage to the peaceful grave
Has crushed the earth to misery, and given
Its empire to the chosen of His slaves.
These have I seen, even from the earliest dawn
Of weak, unstable and precarious power,
Then preaching peace, as now they practise war;
So, when they turned but from the massacre
Of unoffending infidels, to quench
Their thirst for ruin in the very blood
That flowed in their own veins, and pitiless zeal
Froze every human feeling, as the wife
Sheathed in her husband's heart the sacred steel,
Even whilst its hopes were dreaming of her love;
And friends to friends, brothers to brothers stood
Opposed in bloodiest battle-field, and war,
Scarce satiable by fate's last death-draught, waged,
Drunk from the winepress of the Almighty's wrath;
Whilst the red cross, in mockery of peace,
Pointed to victory! When the fray was done,
No remnant of the exterminated faith
Survived to tell its ruin, but the flesh,
With putrid smoke poisoning the atmosphere,
That rotted in the half-extinguished pile.

'Yes! I have seen God's worshippers unsheathe
The sword of His revenge, when grace descended,
Confirming all unnatural impulses,
To sanctify their desolating deeds;

And frantic priests waved the ill-omened cross
O'er the unhappy earth: then shone the sun
On showers of gore from the upflashing steel
Of safe assassination, and all crime
Made stingless by the Spirits of the Lord,
And blood-red rainbows canopied the land.

'Spirit, no year of my eventful being
Has passed unstained by crime and misery,
Which flows from God's own faith. I've marked His slaves
With tongues whose lies are venomous, beguile
The insensate mob, and, whilst one hand was red
With murder, feign to stretch the other out
For brotherhood and peace; and that they now
Babble of love and mercy, whilst their deeds
Are marked with all the narrowness and crime
That Freedom's young arm dare not yet chastise,
Reason may claim our gratitude, who now
Establishing the imperishable throne
Of truth, and stubborn virtue, maketh vain
The unprevailing malice of my Foe,
Whose bootless rage heaps torments for the brave,
Adds impotent eternities to pain,
Whilst keenest disappointment racks His breast
To see the smiles of peace around them play,
To frustrate or to sanctify their doom.

'Thus have I stood,—through a wild waste of years
Struggling with whirlwinds of mad agony,
Yet peaceful, and serene, and self-enshrined,
Mocking my powerless Tyrant's horrible curse
With stubborn and unalterable will,
Even as a giant oak, which Heaven's fierce flame
Had scathèd in the wilderness, to stand
A monument of fadeless ruin there;
Yet peacefully and movelessly it braves
The midnight conflict of the wintry storm,
    As in the sunlight's calm it spreads
    Its worn and withered arms on high
To meet the quiet of a summer's noon.'

The Fairy waved her wand:
Ahasuerus fled
Fast as the shapes of mingled shade and mist,
That lurk in the glens of a twilight grove,
Flee from the morning beam:
The matter of which dreams are made
Not more endowed with actual life
Than this phantasmal portraiture
Of wandering human thought.

VIII

The Fairy

'The Present and the Past thou hast beheld:
It was a desolate sight. Now, Spirit, learn
The secrets of the Future.—Time!
Unfold the brooding pinion of thy gloom,
Render thou up thy half-devoured babes,
And from the cradles of eternity,
Where millions lie lulled to their portioned sleep
By the deep murmuring stream of passing things,
Tear thou that gloomy shroud.—Spirit, behold
Thy glorious destiny!'

Joy to the Spirit came.
Through the wide rent in Time's eternal veil,
Hope was seen beaming through the mists of fear:
Earth was no longer Hell;
Love, freedom, health, had given
Their ripeness to the manhood of its prime,
And all its pulses beat
Symphonious to the planetary spheres:
Then dulcet music swelled
Concordant with the life-strings of the soul;
It throbbed in sweet and languid beatings there,
Catching new life from transitory death,—
Like the vague sighings of a wind at even,
That wakes the wavelets of the slumbering sea
And dies on the creation of its breath,
And sinks and rises, fails and swells by fits,
Was the pure stream of feeling
That sprung from these sweet notes,

And o'er the Spirit's human sympathies
With mild and gentle motion calmly flowed.

        Joy to the Spirit came,—
    Such joy as when a lover sees
The chosen of his soul in happiness,
        And witnesses her peace
Whose woe to him were bitterer than death,
        Sees her unfaded cheek
Glow mantling in first luxury of health,
        Thrills with her lovely eyes,
Which like two stars amid the heaving main
        Sparkle through liquid bliss.

Then in her triumph spoke the Fairy Queen:
'I will not call the ghost of ages gone
To unfold the frightful secrets of its lore;
        The present now is past,
And those events that desolate the earth
Have faded from the memory of Time,
Who dares not give reality to that
Whose being I annul. To me is given
The wonders of the human world to keep,
Space, matter, time, and mind. Futurity
Exposes now its treasure; let the sight
Renew and strengthen all thy failing hope.
O human Spirit! spur thee to the goal
Where virtue fixes universal peace,
And midst the ebb and flow of human things,
Show somewhat stable, somewhat certain still,
A lighthouse o'er the wild of dreary waves.

'The habitable earth is full of bliss;
Those wastes of frozen billows that were hurled
By everlasting snowstorms round the poles,
Where matter dared not vegetate or live,
But ceaseless frost round the vast solitude
Bound its broad zone of stillness, are unloosed;
And fragrant zephyrs there from spicy isles
Ruffle the placid-ocean deep, that rolls
Its broad, bright surges to the sloping sand,
Whose roar is wakened into echoings sweet

To murmur through the Heaven-breathing groves
And melodize with man's blest nature there.

'Those deserts of immeasurable sand,
Whose age-collected fervours scarce allowed
A bird to live, a blade of grass to spring,
Where the shrill chirp of the green lizard's love
Broke on the sultry silentness alone,
Now teem with countless rills and shady woods,
Cornfields and pastures and white cottages;
And where the startled wilderness beheld
A savage conqueror stained in kindred blood,
A tigress sating with the flesh of lambs
The unnatural famine of her toothless cubs,
Whilst shouts and howlings through the desert rang,
Sloping and smooth the daisy-spangled lawn,
Offering sweet incense to the sunrise, smiles
To see a babe before his mother's door,
        Sharing his morning's meal
      With the green and golden basilisk
        That comes to lick his feet.

'Those trackless deeps, where many a weary sail
Has seen above the illimitable plain,
Morning on night, and night on morning rise,
Whilst still no land to greet the wanderer spread
Its shadowy mountains on the sunbright sea,
Where the loud roarings of the tempest-waves
So long have mingled with the gusty wind
In melancholy loneliness, and swept
The desert of those ocean solitudes,
But vocal to the sea-bird's harrowing shriek,
The bellowing monster, and the rushing storm,
Now to the sweet and many-mingling sounds
Of kindliest human impulses respond.
Those lonely realms bright garden-isles begem,
With lightsome clouds and shining seas between,
And fertile valleys, resonant with bliss,
Whilst green woods overcanopy the wave,
Which like a toil-worn labourer leaps to shore,
To meet the kisses of the flow'rets there.

'All things are recreated, and the flame
Of consentaneous love inspires all life:
The fertile bosom of the earth gives suck
To myriads, who still grow beneath her care,
Rewarding her with their pure perfectness:
The balmy breathings of the wind inhale
Her virtues, and diffuse them all abroad:
Health floats amid the gentle atmosphere,
Glows in the fruits, and mantles on the stream:
No storms deform the beaming brow of Heaven,
Nor scatter in the freshness of its pride
The foliage of the ever-verdant trees;
But fruits are ever ripe, flowers ever fair,
And Autumn proudly bears her matron grace,
Kindling a flush on the fair cheek of Spring,
Whose virgin bloom beneath the ruddy fruit
Reflects its tint, and blushes into love.

'The lion now forgets to thirst for blood:
There might you see him sporting in the sun
Beside the dreadless kid; his claws are sheathed,
His teeth are harmless, custom's force has made
His nature as the nature of a lamb.
Like passion's fruit, the nightshade's tempting bane
Poisons no more the pleasure it bestows:
All bitterness is past: the cup of joy
Unmingled mantles to the goblet's brim,
And courts the thirsty lips it fled before.

'But chief, ambiguous Man, he that can know
More misery, and dream more joy than all:
Whose keen sensations thrill within his breast
To mingle with a loftier instinct there,
Lending their power to pleasure and to pain,
Yet raising, sharpening, and refining each;
Who stands amid the ever-varying world,
The burthen or the glory of the earth;
He chief perceives the change, his being notes
The gradual renovation, and defines
Each movement of its progress on his mind.

'Man, where the gloom of the long polar night

Lowers o'er the snow-clad rocks and frozen soil,
Where scarce the hardiest herb that braves the frost
Basks in the moonlight's ineffectual glow,
Shrank with the plants, and darkened with the night;
His chilled and narrow energies, his heart,
Insensible to courage, truth, or love,
His stunted stature and imbecile frame,
Marked him for some abortion of the earth,
Fit compeer of the bears that roamed around,
Whose habits and enjoyments were his own:
His life a feverish dream of stagnant woe,
Whose meagre wants, but scantily fulfilled,
Apprised him ever of the joyless length
Which his short being's wretchedness had reached;
His death a pang which famine, cold and toil
Long on the mind, whilst yet the vital spark
Clung to the body stubbornly, had brought:
All was inflicted here that Earth's revenge
Could wreak on the infringers of her law;
One curse alone was spared—the name of God.

'Nor where the tropics bound the realms of day
With a broad belt of mingling cloud and flame,
Where blue mists through the unmoving atmosphere
Scattered the seeds of pestilence, and fed
Unnatural vegetation, where the land
Teemed with all earthquake, tempest and disease,
Was Man a nobler being; slavery
Had crushed him to his country's blood-stained dust;
Or he was bartered for the fame of power,
Which all internal impulses destroying,
Makes human will an article of trade;
Or he was changed with Christians for their gold,
And dragged to distant isles, where to the sound
Of the flesh-mangling scourge, he does the work
Of all-polluting luxury and wealth,
Which doubly visits on the tyrants' heads
The long-protracted fulness of their woe;
Or he was led to legal butchery,
To turn to worms beneath that burning sun,
Where kings first leagued against the rights of men,
And priests first traded with the name of God.

'Even where the milder zone afforded Man
A seeming shelter, yet contagion there,
Blighting his being with unnumbered ills,
Spread like a quenchless fire; nor truth till late
Availed to arrest its progress, or create
That peace which first in bloodless victory waved
Her snowy standard o'er this favoured clime:
There man was long the train-bearer of slaves,
The mimic of surrounding misery,
The jackal of ambition's lion-rage,
The bloodhound of religion's hungry zeal.

'Here now the human being stands adorning
This loveliest earth with taintless body and mind;
Blessed from his birth with all bland impulses,
Which gently in his noble bosom wake
All kindly passions and all pure desires.
Him, still from hope to hope the bliss pursuing
Which from the exhaustless lore of human weal
Dawns on the virtuous mind, the thoughts that rise
In time-destroying infiniteness, gift
With self-enshrined eternity, that mocks
The unprevailing hoariness of age,
And man, once fleeting o'er the transient scene
Swift as an unremembered vision, stands
Immortal upon earth: no longer now
He slays the lamb that looks him in the face,
And horribly devours his mangled flesh,
Which, still avenging Nature's broken law,
Kindled all putrid humours in his frame,
All evil passions, and all vain belief,
Hatred, despair, and loathing in his mind,
The germs of misery, death, disease, and crime.
No longer now the wingèd habitants,
That in the woods their sweet lives sing away,
Flee from the form of man; but gather round,
And prune their sunny feathers on the hands
Which little children stretch in friendly sport
Towards these dreadless partners of their play.
All things are void of terror: Man has lost
His terrible prerogative, and stands
An equal amidst equals: happiness

And science dawn though late upon the earth;
Peace cheers the mind, health renovates the frame;
Disease and pleasure cease to mingle here,
Reason and passion cease to combat there;
Whilst each unfettered o'er the earth extend
Their all-subduing energies, and wield
The sceptre of a vast dominion there;
Whilst every shape and mode of matter lends
Its force to the omnipotence of mind,
Which from its dark mine drags the gem of truth
To decorate its Paradise of peace.'

IX

'O HAPPY Earth! reality of Heaven!
To which those restless souls that ceaselessly
Throng through the human universe, aspire;
Thou consummation of all mortal hope!
Thou glorious prize of blindly-working will!
Whose rays, diffused throughout all space and time,
Verge to one point and blend for ever there:
Of purest spirits thou pure dwelling-place!
Where care and sorrow, impotence and crime,
Languor, disease, and ignorance dare not come:
O happy Earth, reality of Heaven!

'Genius has seen thee in her passionate dreams,
And dim forebodings of thy loveliness
Haunting the human heart, have there entwined
Those rooted hopes of some sweet place of bliss
Where friends and lovers meet to part no more.
Thou art the end of all desire and will,
The product of all action; and the souls
That by the paths of an aspiring change
Have reached thy haven of perpetual peace,
There rest from the eternity of toil
That framed the fabric of thy perfectness.

'Even Time, the conqueror, fled thee in his fear;
That hoary giant, who, in lonely pride,
So long had ruled the world that nations fell
Beneath his silent footstep. Pyramids,

That for millenniums had withstood the tide
Of human things, his storm-breath drove in sand
Across that desert where their stones survived
The name of him whose pride had heaped them there.
Yon monarch, in his solitary pomp,
Was but the mushroom of a summer day,
That his light-wingèd footstep pressed to dust:
Time was the king of earth; all things gave way
Before him, but the fixed and virtuous will,
The sacred sympathies of soul and sense,
That mocked his fury and prepared his fall.

'Yet slow and gradual dawned the morn of love;
Long lay the clouds of darkness o'er the scene,
Till from its native Heaven they rolled away:
First, Crime triumphant o'er all hope careered
Unblushing, undisguising, bold and strong;
Whilst Falsehood, tricked in Virtue's attributes,
Long sanctified all deeds of vice and woe,
Till done by her own venomous sting to death,
She left the moral world without a law,
No longer fettering Passion's fearless wing,
Nor searing Reason with the brand of God.
Then steadily the happy ferment worked;
Reason was free; and wild though Passion went
Through tangled glens and wood-embosomed meads,
Gathering a garland of the strangest flowers,
Yet like the bee returning to her queen,
She bound the sweetest on her sister's brow,
Who meek and sober kissed the sportive child,
No longer trembling at the broken rod.

'Mild was the slow necessity of death:
The tranquil spirit failed beneath its grasp,
Without a groan, almost without a fear,
Calm as a voyager to some distant land,
And full of wonder, full of hope as he.
The deadly germs of languor and disease
Died in the human frame, and Purity
Blessed with all gifts her earthly worshippers.
How vigorous then the athletic form of age!
How clear its open and unwrinkled brow!

Where neither avarice, cunning, pride, nor care.
Had stamped the seal of gray deformity
On all the mingling lineaments of time.
How lovely the intrepid front of youth!
Which meek-eyed courage decked with freshest grace;
Courage of soul, that dreaded not a name,
And elevated will, that journeyed on
Through life's phantasmal scene in fearlessness,
With virtue, love, and pleasure, hand in hand.

'Then, that sweet bondage which is Freedom's self,
And rivets with sensation's softest tie
The kindred sympathies of human souls,
Needed no fetters of tyrannic law:
Those delicate and timid impulses
In Nature's primal modesty arose.
And with undoubted confidence disclosed
The growing longings of its dawning love,
Unchecked by dull and selfish chastity,
That virtue of the cheaply virtuous,
Who pride themselves in senselessness and frost.
No longer prostitution's venomed bane
Poisoned the springs of happiness and life;
Woman and man, in confidence and love,
Equal and free and pure together trod
The mountain-paths of virtue, which no more
Were stained with blood from many a pilgrim's feet.

'Then, where, through distant ages, long in pride
The palace of the monarch-slave had mocked
Famine's faint groan, and Penury's silent tear,
A heap of crumbling ruins stood, and threw
Year after year their stones upon the field,
Wakening a lonely echo; and the leaves
Of the old thorn, that on the topmost tower
Usurped the royal ensign's grandeur, shook
In the stern storm that swayed the topmost tower
And whispered strange tales in the Whirlwind's ear.

'Low through the lone cathedral's roofless aisles
The melancholy winds a death-dirge sung:
It were a sight of awfulness to see
The works of faith and slavery, so vast,

So sumptuous, yet so perishing withal!
Even as the corpse that rests beneath its wall.
A thousand mourners deck the pomp of death
To-day, the breathing marble glows above
To decorate its memory, and tongues
Are busy of its life: to-morrow, worms
In silence and in darkness seize their prey.

'Within the massy prison's mouldering courts,
Fearless and free the ruddy children played,
Weaving gay chaplets for their innocent brows
With the green ivy and the red wall-flower,
That mock the dungeon's unavailing gloom;
The ponderous chains, and gratings of strong iron,
There rusted amid heaps of broken stone
That mingled slowly with their native earth:
There the broad beam of day, which feebly once
Lighted the cheek of lean Captivity
With a pale and sickly glare, then freely shone
On the pure smiles of infant playfulness:
No more the shuddering voice of hoarse Despair
Pealed through the echoing vaults, but soothing notes
Of ivy-fingered winds and gladsome birds
And merriment were resonant around.

'These ruins soon left not a wreck behind:
Their elements, wide scattered o'er the globe,
To happier shapes were moulded, and became
Ministrant to all blissful impulses:
Thus human things were perfected, and earth,
Even as a child beneath its mother's love,
Was strengthened in all excellence, and grew
Fairer and nobler with each passing year.

'Now Time his dusky pennons o'er the scene
Closes in steadfast darkness, and the past
Fades from our charmèd sight. My task is done:
Thy lore is learned. Earth's wonders are thine own,
With all the fear and all the hope they bring.
My spells are passed: the present now recurs.
Ah me! a pathless wilderness remains
Yet unsubdued by man's reclaiming hand.

'Yet, human Spirit, bravely hold thy course,
Let virtue teach thee firmly to pursue
The gradual paths of an aspiring change:
For birth and life and death, and that strange state
Before the naked soul has found its home,
All tend to perfect happiness, and urge
The restless wheels of being on their way,
Whose flashing spokes, instinct with infinite life,
Bicker and burn to gain their destined goal:
For birth but wakes the spirit to the sense
Of outward shows, whose unexperienced shape
New modes of passion to its frame may lend;
Life is its state of action, and the store
Of all events is aggregated there
That variegate the eternal universe;
Death is a gate of dreariness and gloom,
That leads to azure isles and beaming skies
And happy regions of eternal hope.
Therefore, O Spirit! fearlessly bear on:
Though storms may break the primrose on its stalk,
Though frosts may blight the freshness of its bloom,
Yet Spring's awakening breath will woo the earth,
To feed with kindliest dews its favourite flower,
That blooms in mossy banks and darksome glens,
Lighting the greenwood with its sunny smile.

'Fear not then, Spirit, Death's disrobing hand,
So welcome when the tyrant is awake,
So welcome when the bigot's hell-torch burns;
'Tis but the voyage of a darksome hour,
The transient gulf-dream of a startling sleep.
Death is no foe to Virtue: earth has seen
Love's brightest roses on the scaffold bloom,
Mingling with Freedom's fadeless laurels there,
And presaging the truth of visioned bliss.
Are there not hopes within thee, which this scene
Of linked and gradual being has confirmed?
Whose stingings bade thy heart look further still,
When, to the moonlight walk by Henry led,
Sweetly and sadly thou didst talk of death?
And wilt thou rudely tear them from thy breast,
Listening supinely to a bigot's creed,

Or tamely crouching to the tyrant's rod,
Whose iron thongs are red with human gore?
Never: but bravely bearing on, thy will
Is destined an eternal war to wage
With tyranny and falsehood, and uproot
The germs of misery from the human heart.
Thine is the hand whose piety would soothe
The thorny pillow of unhappy crime,
Whose impotence an easy pardon gains,
Watching its wanderings as a friend's disease:
Thine is the brow whose mildness would defy
Its fiercest rage, and brave its sternest will,
When fenced by power and master of the world.
Thou art sincere and good; of resolute mind,
Free from heart-withering custom's cold control,
Of passion lofty, pure and unsubdued.
Earth's pride and meanness could not vanquish thee,
And therefore art thou worthy of the boon
Which thou hast now received: Virtue shall keep
Thy footsteps in the path that thou hast trod,
And many days of beaming hope shall bless
Thy spotless life of sweet and sacred love.
Go, happy one, and give that bosom joy
     Whose sleepless spirit waits to catch
     Light, life and rapture from thy smile.'

     The Fairy waves her wand of charm.
Speechless with bliss the Spirit mounts the car,
     That rolled beside the battlement,
Bending her beamy eyes in thankfulness.
     Again the enchanted steeds were yoked
     Again the burning wheels inflame
The steep descent of Heaven's untrodden way.
     Fast and far the chariot flew:
     The vast and fiery globes that rolled
     Around the Fairy's palace-gate
Lessened by slow degrees and soon appeared
Such tiny twinklers as the planet orbs
That there attendant on the solar power
With borrowed light pursued their narrower way.

Earth floated then below:
　The chariot paused a moment there;
　　The Spirit then descended:
The restless coursers pawed the ungenial soil,
Snuffed the gross air, and then, their errand done,
Unfurled their pinions to the winds of Heaven.

　The Body and the Soul united then,
A gentle start convulsed Ianthe's frame:
Her veiny eyelids quietly unclosed;
Moveless awhile the dark blue orbs remained:
She looked around in wonder and beheld
Henry, who kneeled in silence by her couch,
Watching her sleep with looks of speechless love,
　　And the bright beaming stars
　　That through the casement shone.

Alastor; or The Spirit of Solitude

The title of the poem is explained by the alternative; but the spirit is
given a bad name. An Alastor is a fury, such as waits to harass a being
over-addicted to solitude. Shelley is found in this piece to move away
from the forensic style into a more delicate relation with his reader;
he argues less, and charms more. He had been learning from the philo-
sophical gradualness of Wordsworth to think more subtly, and to suit
the rhythm and the wording of his expression to a deeper contem-
plativeness.

In *Prince Athanase* Shelley appears to approach the *Alastor* theme
again, so far as it is a study of one far from the madding crowd,
endowed with noble longings, going about the world in search of
the one woman in whom his ideal companion is recognisable. Of
Prince Athanase only detached passages remain, the last of which carries
the story to the deathbed of the Prince; and there 'the lady who can
really reply to his soul comes and kisses his lips.'

> Nondum amabam, et amare amabam, quaerebam quid
> amarem, amans amare.—*Confessions of St. Augustine.*

EARTH, ocean, air, belovèd brotherhood!
If our great Mother has imbued my soul
With aught of natural piety to feel
Your love, and recompense the boon with mine;
If dewy morn, and odorous noon, and even,
With sunset and its gorgeous ministers,
And solemn midnight's tingling silentness;
If autumn's hollow sighs in the sere wood,
And winter robing with pure snow and crowns
Of starry ice the grey grass and bare boughs;
If spring's voluptuous pantings when she breathes
Her first sweet kisses, have been dear to me;
If no bright bird, insect, or gentle beast

I consciously have injured, but still loved
And cherished these my kindred: then forgive
This boast, belovèd brethren, and withdraw
No portion of your wonted favour now!

Mother of this unfathomable world!
Favour my solemn song, for I have loved
Thee ever, and thee only; I have watched
Thy shadow, and the darkness of thy steps,
And my heart ever gazes on the depth
Of thy deep mysteries. I have made my bed
In charnels and on coffins, where black death
Keeps record of the trophies won from thee,
Hoping to still these obstinate questionings
Of thee and thine, by forcing some lone ghost
Thy messenger, to render up the tale
Of what we are. In lone and silent hours,
When night makes a weird sound of its own stillness,
Like an inspired and desperate alchymist
Staking his very life on some dark hope,
Have I mixed awful talk and asking looks
With my most innocent love, until strange tears
Uniting with those breathless kisses, made
Such magic as compels the charmèd night
To render up thy charge:... and, though ne'er yet
Thou hast unveiled thy inmost sanctuary,
Enough from incommunicable dream,
And twilight phantasms, and deep noon-day thought,
Has shone within me, that serenely now
And moveless, as a long-forgotten lyre
Suspended in the solitary dome
Of some mysterious and deserted fane,
I wait thy breath, Great Parent, that my strain
May modulate with murmurs of the air,
And motions of the forests and the sea,
And voice of living beings, and woven hymns
Of night and day, and the deep heart of man.

There was a Poet whose untimely tomb
No human hands with pious reverence reared,
But the charmed eddies of autumnal winds
Built o'er his mouldering bones a pyramid

Of mouldering leaves in the waste wilderness:—
A lovely youth,—no mourning maiden decked
With weeping flowers, or votive cypress wreath,
The lone couch of his everlasting sleep:—
Gentle, and brave, and generous,—no lorn bard
Breathed o'er his dark fate one melodious sigh:
He lived, he died, he sung, in solitude.
Strangers have wept to hear his passionate notes,
And virgins, as unknown he passed, have pined
And wasted for fond love of his wild eyes.
The fire of those soft orbs has ceased to burn,
And Silence, too enamoured of that voice,
Locks its mute music in her rugged cell.

By solemn vision, and bright silver dream,
His infancy was nurtured. Every sight
And sound from the vast earth and ambient air,
Sent to his heart its choicest impulses.
The fountains of divine philosophy
Fled not his thirsting lips, and all of great,
Or good, or lovely, which the sacred past
In truth or fable consecrates, he felt
And knew. When early youth had passed, he left
His cold fireside and alienated home
To seek strange truths in undiscovered lands.
Many a wide waste and tangled wilderness
Has lured his fearless steps; and he has bought
With his sweet voice and eyes, from savage men,
His rest and food. Nature's most secret steps
He like her shadow has pursued, where'er
The red volcano overcanopies
Its fields of snow and pinnacles of ice
With burning smoke, or where bitumen lakes
On black bare pointed islets ever beat
With sluggish surge, or where the secret caves
Rugged and dark, winding among the springs
Of fire and poison, inaccessible
To avarice or pride, their starry domes
Of diamond and of gold expand above
Numberless and immeasurable halls,
Frequent with crystal column, and clear shrines
Of pearl, and thrones radiant with chrysolite.

Nor had that scene of ampler majesty
Than gems or gold, the varying roof of heaven
And the green earth lost in his heart its claims
To love and wonder; he would linger long
In lonesome vales, making the wild his home,
Until the doves and squirrels would partake
From his innocuous hand his bloodless food,
Lured by the gentle meaning of his looks,
And the wild antelope, that starts whene'er
The dry leaf rustles in the brake, suspend
Her timid steps to gaze upon a form
More graceful than her own.
                                        His wandering step
Obedient to high thoughts, has visited
The awful ruins of the days of old:
Athens, and Tyre, and Balbec, and the waste
Where stood Jerusalem, the fallen towers
Of Babylon, the eternal pyramids,
Memphis and Thebes, and whatsoe'er of strange
Sculptured on alabaster obelisk,
Or jasper tomb, or multilated sphynx,
Dark Aethiopia in her desert hills
Conceals. Among the ruined temples there,
Stupendous columns, and wild images
Of more than man, where marble daemons watch
The Zodiac's brazen mystery, and dead men
Hang their mute thoughts on the mute walls around,
He lingered, poring on memorials
Of the world's youth, through the long burning day
Gazed on those speechless shapes, nor, when the moon
Filled the mysterious halls with floating shades
Suspended he that task, but ever gazed
And gazed, till meaning on his vacant mind
Flashed like strong inspiration, and he saw
The thrilling secrets of the birth of time.

Meanwhile an Arab maiden brought his food,
Her daily portion, from her father's tent.
And spread her matting for his couch, and stole
From duties and repose to tend his steps:—
Enamoured, yet not daring for deep awe
To speak her love:—and watched his nightly sleep,

Sleepless herself, to gaze upon his lips
Parted in slumber, whence the regular breath
Of innocent dreams arose: then, when red morn
Made paler the pale moon, to her cold home
Wildered, and wan, and panting, she returned.

The Poet wandering on, through Arabie
And Persia, and the wild Carmanian waste,
And o'er the aërial mountains which pour down
Indus and Oxus from their icy caves,
In joy and exultation held his way;
Till in the vale of Cashmire, far within
Its loneliest dell, where odorous plants entwine
Beneath the hollow rocks a natural bower,
Beside a sparkling rivulet he stretched
His languid limbs. A vision on his sleep
There came, a dream of hopes that never yet
Had flushed his cheek. He dreamed a veilèd maid
Sate near him, talking in low solemn tones.
Her voice was like the voice of his own soul
Heard in the calm of thought; its music long,
Like woven sounds of streams and breezes, held
His inmost sense suspended in its web
Of many-coloured woof and shifting hues.
Knowledge and truth and virtue were her theme,
And lofty hopes of divine liberty,
Thoughts the most dear to him, and poesy,
Herself a poet. Soon the solemn mood
Of her pure mind kindled through all her frame
A permeating fire: wild numbers then
She raised, with voice stifled in tremulous sobs
Subdued by its own pathos: her fair hands
Were bare alone, sweeping from some strange harp
Strange symphony, and in their branching veins
The eloquent blood told an ineffable tale.
The beating of her heart was heard to fill
The pauses of her music, and her breath
Tumultuously accorded with those fits
Of intermitted song. Sudden she rose,
As if her heart impatiently endured
Its bursting burthen: at the sound he turned,
And saw by the warm light of their own life

Her glowing limbs beneath the sinuous veil
Of woven wind, her outspread arms now bare,
Her dark locks floating in the breath of night,
Her beamy bending eyes, her parted lips
Outstretched, and pale, and quivering eagerly.
His strong heart sunk and sickened with excess
Of love. He reared his shuddering limbs and quelled
His gasping breath, and spread his arms to meet
Her panting bosom: ... she drew back a while,
Then, yielding to the irresistible joy,
With frantic gesture and short breathless cry
Folded his frame in her dissolving arms.
Now blackness veiled his dizzy eyes, and night
Involved and swallowed up the vision; sleep,
Like a dark flood suspended in its course,
Rolled back its impulse on his vacant brain.

Roused by the shock he started from his trance—
The cold white light of morning, the blue moon
Low in the west, the clear and garish hills,
The distinct valley and the vacant woods,
Spread round him where he stood. Whither have fled
The hues of heaven that canopied his bower
Of yesternight? The sounds that soothed his sleep,
The mystery and the majesty of Earth,
The joy, the exultation? His wan eyes
Gaze on the empty scene as vacantly
As ocean's moon looks on the moon in heaven.
The spirit of sweet human love has sent
A vision to the sleep of him who spurned
Her choicest gifts. He eagerly pursues
Beyond the realms of dream that fleeting shade;
He overleaps the bounds. Alas! Alas!
Were limbs, and breath, and being intertwined
Thus treacherously? Lost, lost, for ever lost,
In the wide pathless desert of dim sleep,
That beautiful shape! Does the dark gate of death
Conduct to thy mysterious paradise,
O Sleep? Does the bright arch of rainbow clouds,
And pendent mountains seen in the calm lake,
Lead only to a black and watery depth,
While death's blue vault, with loathliest vapours hung

Where every shade which the foul grave exhales
Hides its dead eye from the detested day,
Conduct, O sleep, to thy delightful realms?
This doubt with sudden tide flowed on his heart,
The insatiate hope which it awakened, stung
His brain even like despair.

                    While daylight held
The sky, the Poet kept mute conference
With his still soul. At night the passion came,
Like the fierce fiend of a distempered dream,
And shook him from his rest, and led him forth
Into the darkness.—As an eagle grasped
In folds of the green serpent, feels her breast
Burn with the poison, and precipitates
Through night and day, tempest, and calm, and cloud,
Frantic with dizzying anguish, her blind flight
O'er the wide aëry wilderness: thus driven
By the bright shadow of that lovely dream,
Beneath the cold glare of the desolate night,
Through tangled swamps and deep precipitous dells,
Startling with careless step the moonlight snake,
He fled. Red morning dawned upon his flight,
Shedding the mockery of its vital hues
Upon his cheek of death. He wandered on
Till vast Aornos seen from Petra's steep
Hung o'er the low horizon like a cloud;
Through Balk, and where the desolated tombs
Of Parthian kings scatter to every wind
Their wasting dust, wildly he wandered on,
Day after day a weary waste of hours,
Bearing within his life the brooding care
That ever fed on its decaying flame.
And now his limbs were lean; his scattered hair
Sered by the autumn of strange suffering
Sung dirges in the wind; his listless hand
Hung like dead bone within its withered skin;
Life, and the lustre that consumed it, shone
As in a furnace burning secretly
From his dark eyes alone. The cottagers,
Who ministered with human charity
His human wants, beheld with wondering awe
Their fleeting visitant. The mountaineer,

Encountering on some dizzy precipice
That spectral form, deemed that the Spirit of wind
With lightning eyes, and eager breath, and feet
Disturbing not the drifted snow, had paused
In its career: the infant would conceal
His troubled visage in his mother's robe
In terror at the glare of those wild eyes,
To remember their strange light in many a dream
Of after-times; but youthful maidens, taught
By nature, would interpret half the woe
That wasted him, would call him with false names
Brother, and friend, would press his pallid hand
At parting, and watch, dim through tears, the path
Of his departure from their father's door.

At length upon the lone Chorasmian shore
He paused, a wide and melancholy waste
Of putrid marshes. A strong impulse urged
His steps to the sea-shore. A swan was there,
Beside a sluggish stream among the reeds.
It rose as he approached, and with strong wings
Scaling the upward sky, bent its bright course
High over the immeasurable main.
His eyes pursued its flight.—'Thou hast a home,
Beautiful bird; thou voyagest to thine home,
Where thy sweet mate will twine her downy neck
With thine, and welcome thy return with eyes
Bright in the lustre of their own fond joy.
And what am I that I should linger here,
With voice far sweeter than thy dying notes,
Spirit more vast than thine, frame more attuned
To beauty, wasting these surpassing powers
In the deaf air, to the blind earth, and heaven
That echoes not my thoughts?' A gloomy smile
Of desperate hope wrinkled his quivering lips.
For sleep, he knew, kept most relentlessly
Its precious charge, and silent death exposed,
Faithless perhaps as sleep, a shadowy lure,
With doubtful smile mocking its own strange charms.

Startled by his own thoughts he looked around.
There was no fair fiend near him, not a sight

Or sound of awe but in his own deep mind.
A little shallop floating near the shore
Caught the impatient wandering of his gaze.
It had been long abandoned, for its sides
Gaped wide with many a rift, and its frail joints
Swayed with the undulations of the tide.
A restless impulse urged him to embark
And meet lone Death on the drear ocean's waste;
For well he knew that mighty Shadow loves
The slimy caverns of the populous deep.

The day was fair and sunny, sea and sky
Drank its inspiring radiance, and the wind
Swept strongly from the shore, blackening the waves.
Following his eager soul, the wanderer
Leaped in the boat, he spread his cloak aloft
On the bare mast, and took his lonely seat,
And felt the boat speed o'er the tranquil sea
Like a torn cloud before the hurricane.

As one that in a silver vision floats
Obedient to the sweep of odorous winds
Upon resplendent clouds, so rapidly
Along the dark and ruffled waters fled
The straining boat.—A whirlwind swept it on,
With fierce gusts and precipitating force,
Through the white ridges of the chafèd sea.
The waves arose. Higher and higher still
Their fierce necks writhed beneath the tempest's scourge
Like serpents struggling in a vulture's grasp.
Calm and rejoicing in the fearful war
Of wave ruining on wave, and blast on blast
Descending, and black flood on whirlpool driven
With dark obliterating course, he sate:
As if their genii were the ministers
Appointed to conduct him to the light
Of those belovèd eyes, the Poet sate
Holding the steady helm. Evening came on,
The beams of sunset hung their rainbow hues
High 'mid the shifting domes of sheeted spray
That canopied his path o'er the waste deep;
Twilight, ascending slowly from the east,

Entwined in duskier wreaths her braided locks
O'er the fair front and radiant eyes of day;
Night followed, clad with stars. On every side
More horribly the multitudinous streams
Of ocean's mountainous waste to mutual war
Rushed in dark tumult thundering, as to mock
The calm and spangled sky. The little boat
Still fled before the storm; still fled, like foam
Down the steep cataract of a wintry river;
Now pausing on the edge of the riven wave;
Now leaving far behind the bursting mass
That fell, convulsing ocean: safely fled—
As if that frail and wasted human form,
Had been an elemental god.

                           At midnight
The moon arose: and lo! the ethereal cliffs
Of Caucasus, whose icy summits shone
Among the stars like sunlight, and around
Whose caverned base the whirlpools and the waves
Bursting and eddying irresistibly
Rage and resound for ever.—Who shall save?—
The boat fled on,—the boiling torrent drove,—
The crags closed round with black and jaggèd arms,
The shattered mountain overhung the sea,
And faster still, beyond all human speed,
Suspended on the sweep of the smooth wave,
The little boat was driven. A cavern there
Yawned, and amid its slant and winding depths
Ingulfed the rushing sea. The boat fled on
With unrelaxing speed.—'Vision and Love!'
The Poet cried aloud, 'I have beheld
The path of thy departure. Sleep and death
Shall not divide us long!'

                         The boat pursued
The windings of the cavern. Daylight shone
At length upon that gloomy river's flow;
Now, where the fiercest war among the waves
Is calm, on the unfathomable stream
The boat moved slowly. Where the mountain, riven,
Exposed those black depths to the azure sky,
Ere yet the flood's enormous volume fell

Even to the base of Caucasus, with sound
That shook the everlasting rocks, the mass
Filled with one whirlpool all that ample chasm;
Stair above stair the eddying waters rose,
Circling immeasurably fast, and laved
With alternating dash the gnarlèd roots
Of mighty trees, that stretched their giant arms
In darkness over it. I' the midst was left,
Reflecting yet distorting every cloud,
A pool of treacherous and tremendous calm.
Seized by the sway of the ascending stream,
With dizzy swiftness, round, and round, and round,
Ridge after ridge the straining boat arose,
Till on the verge of the extremest curve,
Where, through an opening of the rocky bank,
The waters overflow, and a smooth spot
Of glassy quiet mid those battling tides
Is left, the boat paused shuddering.—Shall it sink
Down the abyss? Shall the reverting stress
Of that resistless gulf embosom it?
Now shall it fall?—A wandering stream of wind,
Breathed from the west, has caught the expanded sail,
And, lo! with gentle motion, between banks
Of mossy slope, and on a placid stream,
Beneath a woven grove it sails, and, hark!
The ghastly torrent mingles its far roar,
With the breeze murmuring in the musical woods.
Where the embowering trees recede, and leave
A little space of green expanse, the cove
Is closed by meeting banks, whose yellow flowers
For ever gaze on their own drooping eyes,
Reflected in the crystal calm. The wave
Of the boat's motion marred their pensive task,
Which nought but vagrant bird, or wanton wind,
Or falling spear-grass, or their own decay
Had e'er disturbed before. The Poet longed
To deck with their bright hues his withered hair,
But on his heart its solitude returned,
And he forbore. Not the strong impulse hid
In those flushed cheeks, bent eyes, and shadowy frame
Had yet performed its ministry: it hung
Upon his life, as lightning in a cloud

Gleams, hovering ere it vanish, ere the floods
Of night close over it.   The noonday sun
Now shone upon the forest, one vast mass
Of mingling shade, whose brown magnificence
A narrow vale embosoms. There, huge caves,
Scooped in the dark base of their aëry rocks
Mocking its moans, respond and roar for ever.
The meeting boughs and implicated leaves
Wove twilight o'er the Poet's path, as led
By love, or dream, or god, or mightier Death,
He sought in Nature's dearest haunt, some bank,
Her cradle, and his sepulchre. More dark
And dark the shades accumulate. The oak,
Expanding its immense and knotty arms,
Embraces the light beech. The pyramids
Of the tall cedar overarching, frame
Most solemn domes within, and far below,
Like clouds suspended in an emerald sky,
The ash and the acacia floating hang
Tremulous and pale. Like restless serpents, clothed
In rainbow and in fire, the parasites,
Starred with ten thousand blossoms, flow around
The grey trunks, and, as gamesome infants' eyes,
With gentle meanings, and most innocent wiles,
Fold their beams round the hearts of those that love,
These twine their tendrils with the wedded boughs
Uniting their close union; the woven leaves
Make net-work of the dark blue light of day,
And the night's noontide clearness, mutable
As shapes in the weird clouds. Soft mossy lawns
Beneath these canopies extend their swells,
Fragant with perfumed herbs, and eyed with blooms
Minute yet beautiful. One darkest glen
Sends from its woods of musk-rose, twined with jasmine,
A soul-dissolving odour, to invite
To some more lovely mystery. Through the dell,
Silence and Twilight here, twin-sisters, keep
Their noonday watch, and sail among the shades,
Like vaporous shapes half seen; beyond, a well,
Dark, gleaming, and of most translucent wave,
Images all the woven boughs above,

And each depending leaf, and every speck
Of azure sky, darting between their chasms;
Nor aught else in the liquid mirror laves
Its portraiture, but some inconstant star
Between one foliaged lattice twinkling fair,
Or painted bird, sleeping beneath the moon,
Or gorgeous insect floating motionless,
Unconscious of the day, ere yet his wings
Have spread their glories to the gaze of noon.

Hither the Poet came. His eyes beheld
Their own wan light through the reflected lines
Of his thin hair, distinct in the dark depth
Of that still fountain; as the human heart,
Gazing in dreams over the gloomy grave,
Sees its own treacherous likeness there. He heard
The motion of the leaves, the grass that sprung
Startled and glanced and trembled even to feel
An unaccustomed presence, and the sound
Of the sweet brook that from the secret springs
Of that dark fountain rose. A Spirit seemed
To stand beside him—clothed in no bright robes
Of shadowy silver or enshrining light,
Borrowed from aught the visible world affords
Of grace, or majesty, or mystery;—
But, undulating woods, and silent well,
And leaping rivulet, and evening gloom
Now deepening the dark shades, for speech assuming,
Held commune with him, as if he and it
Were all that was,—only...when his regard
Was raised by intense pensiveness, ... two eyes,
Two starry eyes, hung in the gloom of thought,
And seemed with their serene and azure smiles
To beckon him.

                 Obedient to the light
That shone within his soul, he went, pursuing
The windings of the dell.—The rivulet
Wanton and wild, through many a green ravine
Beneath the forest flowed. Sometimes it fell
Among the moss with hollow harmony
Dark and profound. Now on the polished stones

It danced; like childhood laughing as it went:
Then, through the plain in tranquil wanderings crept,
Reflecting every herb and drooping bud
That overhung its quietness.—'O stream!
Whose source is inaccessibly profound,
Whither do thy mysterious waters tend?
Thou imagest my life. Thy darksome stillness,
Thy dazzling waves, thy loud and hollow gulfs,
Thy searchless fountain, and invisible course
Have each their type in me: and the wide sky,
And measureless ocean may declare as soon
What oozy cavern or what wandering cloud
Contains thy waters, as the universe
Tell where these living thoughts reside, when stretched
Upon thy flowers my bloodless limbs shall waste
I' the passing wind!'

                  Beside the grassy shore
Of the small stream he went; he did impress
On the green moss his tremulous step, that caught
Strong shuddering from his burning limbs. As one
Roused by some joyous madness from the couch
Of fever, he did move; yet, not like him,
Forgetful of the grave, where, when the flame
Of his frail exultation shall be spent,
He must descend. With rapid steps he went
Beneath the shade of trees, beside the flow
Of the wild babbling rivulet; and now
The forest's solemn canopies were changed
For the uniform and lightsome evening sky.
Grey rocks did peep from the spare moss, and stemmed
The struggling brook: tall spires of windlestrae
Threw their thin shadows down the rugged slope,
And nought but gnarled roots of ancient pines
Branchless and blasted, clenched with grasping roots
The unwilling soil. A gradual change was here,
Yet ghastly. For, as fast years flow away,
The smooth brow gathers, and the hair grows thin
And white, and where irradiate dewy eyes
Had shone, gleam stony orbs:—so from his steps
Bright flowers departed, and the beautiful shade
Of the green groves, with all their odorous winds

And musical motions. Calm, he still pursued
The stream, that with a larger volume now
Rolled through the labyrinthine dell; and there
Fretted a path through its descending curves
With its wintry speed. On every side now rose
Rocks, which, in unimaginable forms,
Lifted their black and barren pinnacles
In the light of evening, and, its precipice
Obscuring the ravine, disclosed above,
Mid toppling stones, black gulfs and yawning caves,
Whose windings gave ten thousand various tongues
To the loud stream. Lo! where the pass expands
Its stony jaws, the abrupt mountain breaks,
And seems, with its accumulated crags,
To overhang the world: for wide expand
Beneath the wan stars and descending moon
Islanded seas, blue mountains, mighty streams,
Dim tracts and vast, robed in the lustrous gloom
Of leaden-coloured even, and fiery hills
Mingling their flames with twilight, on the verge
Of the remote horizon. The near scene,
In naked and severe simplicity,
Made contrast with the universe. A pine,
Rock-rooted, stretched athwart the vacancy
Its swinging boughs, to each inconstant blast
Yielding one only response, at each pause
In most familiar cadence, with the howl
The thunder and the hiss of homeless streams
Mingling its solemn song, whilst the broad river,
Foaming and hurrying o'er its rugged path,
Fell into that immeasurable void
Scattering its waters to the passing winds.

Yet the grey precipice and solemn pine
And torrent, were not all;—one silent nook
Was there. Even on the edge of that vast mountain,
Upheld by knotty roots and fallen rocks,
It overlooked in its serenity
The dark earth, and the bending vault of stars.
It was a tranquil spot, that seemed to smile
Even in the lap of horror. Ivy clasped
The fissured stones with its entwining arms,

And did embower with leaves for ever green,
And berries dark, the smooth and even space
Of its inviolated floor, and here
The children of the autumnal whirlwind bore,
In wanton sport, those bright leaves, whose decay,
Red, yellow, or ethereally pale,
Rivals the pride of summer. 'Tis the haunt
Of every gentle wind, whose breath can teach
The wilds to love tranquillity. One step,
One human step alone, has ever broken
The stillness of its solitude:—one voice
Alone inspired its echoes;—even that voice
Which hither came, floating among the winds,
And led the loveliest among human forms
To make their wild haunts the depository
Of all the grace and beauty that endued
Its motions, render up its majesty,
Scatter its music on the unfeeling storm,
And to the damp leaves and blue cavern mould,
Nurses of rainbow flowers and branching moss,
Commit the colours of that varying cheek,
That snowy breast, those dark and drooping eyes.

The dim and hornèd moon hung low, and poured
A sea of lustre on the horizon's verge
That overflowed its mountains. Yellow mist
Filled the unbounded atmosphere, and drank
Wan moonlight even to fulness: not a star
Shone, not a sound was heard; the very winds,
Danger's grim playmates, on that precipice
Slept, clasped in his embrace.—O, storm of death!
Whose sightless speed divides this sullen night:
And thou, colossal Skeleton, that, still
Guiding its irresistible career
In thy devastating omnipotence,
Art king of this frail world, from the red field
Of slaughter, from the reeking hospital,
The patriot's sacred couch, the snowy bed
Of innocence, the scaffold and the throne,
A mighty voice invokes thee. Ruin calls
His brother Death. A rare and regal prey
He hath prepared, prowling around the world;

Glutted with which thou mayst repose, and men
Go to their graves like flowers or creeping worms,
Nor ever more offer at thy dark shrine
The unheeded tribute of a broken heart.

When on the threshold of the green recess
The wanderer's footsteps fell, he knew that death
Was on him. Yet a little, ere it fled,
Did he resign his high and holy soul
To images of the majestic past,
That paused within his passive being now,
Like winds that bear sweet music, when they breathe
Through some dim latticed chamber. He did place
His pale lean hand upon the rugged trunk
Of the old pine. Upon an ivied stone
Reclined his languid head, his limbs did rest,
Diffused and motionless, on the smooth brink
Of that obscurest chasm;—and thus he lay,
Surrendering to their final impulses
The hovering powers of life. Hope and despair,
The torturers, slept; no mortal pain or fear
Marred his repose, the influxes of sense,
And his own being unalloyed by pain,
Yet feebler and more feeble, calmly fed
The stream of thought, till he lay breathing there
At peace, and faintly smiling:—his last sight
Was the great moon, which o'er the western line
Of the wide world her mighty horn suspended,
With whose dun beams inwoven darkness seemed
To mingle. Now upon the jaggèd hills
It rests, and still as the divided frame
Of the vast meteor sunk, the Poet's blood,
That ever beat in mystic sympathy
With nature's ebb and flow, grew feebler still:
And when two lessening points of light alone
Gleamed through the darkness, the alternate gasp
Of his faint respiration scarce did stir
The stagnate night:—till the minutest ray
Was quenched, the pulse yet lingered in his heart.
It paused—it fluttered. But when heaven remained
Utterly black, the murky shades involved
An image, silent, cold, and motionless,

As their own voiceless earth and vacant air.
Even as a vapour fed with golden beams
That ministered on sunlight, ere the west
Eclipses it, was now that wondrous frame—
No sense, no motion, no divinity—
A fragile lute, on whose harmonious strings
The breath of heaven did wander—a bright stream
Once fed with many-voicèd waves—a dream
Of youth, which night and time have quenched for ever,
Still, dark, and dry, and unremembered now.

O, for Medea's wondrous alchemy,
Which wheresoe'er it fell made the earth gleam
With bright flowers, and the wintry boughs exhale
From vernal blooms fresh fragrance! O, that God,
Profuse of poisons, would concede the chalice
Which but one living man has drained, who now,
Vessel of deathless wrath, a slave that feels
No proud exemption in the blighting curse
He bears, over the world wanders for ever,
Lone as incarnate death! O, that the dream
Of dark magician in his visioned cave,
Raking the cinders of a crucible
For life and power, even when his feeble hand
Shakes in its last decay, were the true law
Of this so lovely world! But thou art fled
Like some frail exhalation; which the dawn
Robes in its golden beams,—ah! thou hast fled!
The brave, the gentle, and the beautiful,
The child of grace and genius. Heartless things
Are done and said i' the world, and many worms
And beasts and men live on, and mighty Earth
From sea and mountain, city and wilderness,
In vesper low or joyous orison,
Lifts still its solemn voice:—but thou art fled—
Thou canst no longer know or love the shapes
Of this phantasmal scene, who have to thee
Been purest ministers, who are, alas!
Now thou art not. Upon those pallid lips
So sweet even in their silence, on those eyes
That image sleep in death, upon that form
Yet safe from the worm's outrage, let no tear

Be shed—not even in thought. Nor, when those hues
Are gone, and those divinest lineaments,
Worn by the senseless wind, shall live alone
In the frail pauses of this simple strain,
Let not high verse, mourning the memory
Of that which is no more, or painting's woe
Or sculpture, speak in feeble imagery
Their own cold powers. Art and eloquence,
And all the shows o' the world are frail and vain
To weep a loss that turns their lights to shade.
It is a woe 'too deep for tears,' when all
Is reft at once, when some surpassing Spirit,
Whose light adorned the world around it, leaves
Those who remain behind, not sobs or groans,
The passionate tumult of a clinging hope;
But pale despair and cold tranquillity,
Nature's vast frame, the web of human things,
Birth and the grave, that are not as they were.

The Revolt of Islam

A POEM IN TWELVE CANTOS

THIS long poem, apart from its theoretical nature, is a 'sensational novel.' But Shelley expected too much of his readers; the maze is too ingenious. The poet introduces the real tale with a symbolic scene of evil and good in terrible combat, then with his voyage to the Temple of the Spirit, or hall of triumphant immortals, into which come the spirits Laon and Cythna. From this point the poet retires from the stage. We now have Laon recounting his own vicissitudes, together with those of Cythna, both of them being liberators of humanity from oppression. The story is a reflection from the history of Greek independence.

Laon and Cythna have their moments of victory, their sufferings and frustrations, and their mutual love; but that consolation is destroyed in this world, like their political and moral plans, by the cunning and cleverness of the Tyrant. Laon is sent to be burned at the stake and Cythna insists on sharing his fate. He and she, as spirits, in the last stage make a voyage together with Cythna's dead child to the Temple in which the prologue showed them.

Upon this groundwork Shelley elaborates with every gift of mind, heart, fancy, utterance except that of keeping the large design distinct; the incidents and local descriptions, with the doctrines, crowd over it. If (as he hints) he revised the poem in his later years, this fault will have been what he hoped to amend; then the work must have been truly great; but such revision is not yet traced among his papers. A selection of the episodes, as the piece stands, is not an injustice to it.

FROM THE PREFACE

THE Poem which I now present to the world is an attempt from which I scarcely dare to expect success, and in which a writer of established fame might fail without disgrace. It is an experiment on the temper of the public mind, as to how far a thirst for a happier condition of moral and political society survives, among the enlightened and refined, the tempests which have shaken the age in which we live. I have sought to enlist the harmony of metrical language, the ethereal combinations of the fancy, the rapid and subtle transitions of human passion, all those elements which essentially compose a Poem, in the cause of a liberal and comprehensive morality; and in the view of kindling within the bosoms of my readers a virtuous enthusiasm for those doctrines of liberty and justice, that faith and hope in something good, which neither violence nor misrepresentation nor prejudice can ever totally extinguish among mankind.

For this purpose I have chosen a story of human passion in its most universal character, diversified with moving and romantic adventures, and appealing, in contempt of all artificial opinions or institutions, to the common sympathies of every human breast. I have made no attempt to recommend the motives which I would substitute for those at present governing mankind, by methodical and systematic argument. I would only awaken the feelings, so that the reader should see the beauty of true virtue, and be incited to those inquiries which have led to my moral and political creed, and that of some of the sublimest intellects in the world. The Poem therefore (with the exception of the first canto, which is purely introductory) is narrative, not didactic. It is a succession of pictures illustrating the growth and progress of individual mind aspiring after excellence, and devoted to the love of mankind; its influence in refining and making pure the most daring and uncommon impulses of the imagination, the understanding, and the senses; its impatience at 'all the oppressions which are done under the sun'; its tendency to awaken public hope, and to enlighten and improve mankind; the rapid effects of the application of that tendency; the awakening of an immense nation from their slavery and degradation to a true sense of moral dignity and freedom; the bloodless dethronement of their oppressors, and the unveiling of the religious frauds by which they had been deluded into submission; the tranquillity of successful patriotism, and the universal toleration and benevolence of true philanthropy; the treachery and barbarity of hired soldiers; vice not the object of punishment and hatred, but kindness and pity; the faithlessness of tyrants; the confederacy of the Rulers of the World, and the restoration of the expelled Dynasty by foreign arms; the massacre and extermination of the Patriots, and the victory of established power; the consequences of legitimate despotism,—civil war, famine, plague, superstition, and an utter extinction of the domestic affections; the judicial murder of the advocates of Liberty; the temporary triumph of oppression, that secure earnest security of its final and inevitable fall; the transient nature of ignorance and error, and the eternity of genius and virtue. Such is the series of delineations of which the Poem consists.

DEDICATION

There is no danger to a man, that knows
What life and death is: there's not any law
Exceeds his knowledge; neither is it lawful
That he should stoop to any other law.—CHAPMAN.

To Mary

So now my summer task is ended, Mary,
   And I return to thee, mine own heart's home;
As to his Queen some victor Knight of Faëry,
   Earning bright spoils for her enchanted dome;
   Nor thou disdain, that ere my fame become
A star among the stars of mortal night,
   If it indeed may cleave its natal gloom,
Its doubtful promise thus I would unite
With thy belovèd name, thou Child of love and light.

The toil which stole from thee so many an hour,
   Is ended,—and the fruit is at thy feet!
No longer where the woods to frame a bower
   With interlacèd branches mix and meet,
   Or where with sound like many voices sweet,
Waterfalls leap among wild islands green,
   Which framed for my lone boat a lone retreat
Of moss-grown trees and weeds, shall I be seen:
But beside thee, where still my heart has ever been.

Thoughts of great deeds were mine, dear Friend, when first
   The clouds which wrap this world from youth did pass.
I do remember well the hour which burst
   My spirit's sleep: a fresh May-dawn it was,
   When I walked forth upon the glittering grass,
And wept, I knew not why; until there rose
   From the near schoolroom, voices, that, alas!
Were but one echo from a world of woes—
The harsh and grating strife of tyrants and of foes.

And then I clasped my hands and looked around—
   But none was near to mock my streaming eyes.
Which poured their warm drops on the sunny ground—
   So, without shame, I spake:—'I will be wise,
   And just, and free, and mild, if in me lies
Such power, for I grow weary to behold
   The selfish and the strong still tyrannise
Without reproach or check.' I then controlled
My tears, my heart grew calm, and I was meek and bold.

And from that hour did I with earnest thought
  Heap knowledge from forbidden mines of lore,
Yet nothing that my tyrants knew or taught
  I cared to learn, but from that secret store
  Wrought linkèd armour for my soul, before
It might walk forth to war among mankind;
    Thus power and hope were strengthened more and **more**
Within me, till there came upon my mind
A sense of loneliness, a thirst with which I pined.

Alas, that love should be a blight and snare
  To those who seek all sympathies in one!—
Such once I sought in vain; then black despair,
  The shadow of a starless night, was thrown
  Over the world in which I moved alone:—
Yet never found I one not false to me,
  Hard hearts, and cold, like weights of icy stone
Which crushed and withered mine, that could not **be**
Aught but a lifeless clod, until revived by thee.

Thou Friend, whose presence on my wintry **heart**
  Fell, like bright Spring upon some herbless plain;
How beautiful and calm and free thou wert
  In thy young wisdom, when the mortal chain
  Of Custom thou didst burst and rend in twain,
And walked as free as light the clouds among,
  Which many an envious slave then breathed **in vain**
From his dim dungeon, and my spirit sprung
To meet thee from the woes which had begirt it long!

No more alone through the world's wilderness,
  Although I trod the paths of high intent,
I journeyed now: no more companionless,
  Where solitude is like despair, I went.—
  There is the wisdom of a stern content
When Poverty can blight the just and good,
  When Infamy dares mock the innocent,
And cherished friends turn with the multitude
To trample: this was ours, and we unshaken stood!

Now has descended a serener hour,
    And with inconstant fortune, friends return;
Though suffering leaves the knowledge and the power
    Which says:—Let scorn be not repaid with scorn.
    And from thy side two gentle babes are born
To fill our home with smiles, and thus are we
    Most fortunate beneath life's beaming morn;
And these delights, and thou, have been to me
The parents of the Song I consecrate to thee.

Is it, that now my inexperienced fingers
    But strike the prelude of a loftier strain?
Or must the lyre on which my spirit lingers
    Soon pause in silence, ne'er to sound again,
    Though it might shake the Anarch Custom's reign,
And charm the minds of men to Truth's own sway
    Holier than was Amphion's? I would fain
Reply in hope—but I am worn away,
And Death and Love are yet contending for their prey.

And what art thou? I know, but dare not speak:
    Time may interpret to his silent years.
Yet in the paleness of thy thoughtful cheek,
    And, in the light thine ample forehead wears,
    And in thy sweetest smiles, and in thy tears,
And in thy gentle speech, a prophecy
    Is whispered, to subdue my fondest fears:
And through thine eyes, even in thy soul I see
A lamp of vestal fire burning internally.

They say that thou wert lovely from thy birth,
    Of glorious parents, thou aspiring Child.
I wonder not—for One then left this earth
    Whose life was like a setting planet mild,
    Which clothed thee in the radiance undefiled
Of its departing glory; still her fame
    Shines on thee, through the tempests dark and wild
Which shake these latter days; and thou canst claim
The shelter, from thy Sire, of an immortal name.

One voice came forth from many a mighty spirit,
  Which was the echo of three thousand years;
And the tumultuous world stood mute to hear it,
  As some lone man who in a desert hears
  The music of his home:—unwonted fears
Fell on the pale oppressors of our race,
  And Faith, and Custom, and low-thoughted cares,
Like thunder-stricken dragons, for a space
Left the torn human heart, their food and dwelling-place.

Truth's deathless voice pauses among mankind!
  If there must be no response to my cry—
If men must rise and stamp with fury blind
  On his pure name who loves them,—thou and I,
  Sweet friend! can look from our tranquillity
Like lamps into the world's tempestuous night,—
  Two tranquil stars, while clouds are passing by
Which wrap them from the foundering seaman's sight,
That burn from year to year with unextinguished light.

From Canto I

Eagle and Serpent

When the last hope of trampled France had failed
  Like a brief dream of unremaining glory,
From visions of despair I rose, and scaled
  The peak of an aëreal promontory,
  Whose caverned base with the vexed surge was hoary;
And saw the golden dawn break forth, and waken
  Each cloud, and every wave:—but transitory
The calm: for sudden, the firm earth was shaken,
As if by the last wreck its frame were overtaken.

So as I stood, one blast of muttering thunder
  Burst in far peals along the waveless deep,
When, gathering fast, around, above, and under,
  Long trains of tremulous mist began to creep,
  Until their complicating lines did steep
The orient sun in shadow:—not a sound
  Was heard; one horrible repose did keep
The forests and the floods, and all around
Darkness more dread than night was poured upon the ground.

Hark! 'tis the rushing of a wind that sweeps
    Earth and the ocean. See! the lightnings yawn
Deluging Heaven with fire, and the lashed deeps
    Glitter and boil beneath: it rages on,
    One mighty stream, whirlwind and waves upthrown,
Lightning, and hail, and darkness eddying by.
    There is a pause—the sea-birds, that were gone
Into their caves to shriek, come forth, to spy
What calm has fall'n on earth, what light is in the sky.

For, where the irresistible storm had cloven
    That fearful darkness, the blue sky was seen
Fretted with many a fair cloud interwoven
    Most delicately, and the ocean green,
    Beneath that opening spot of blue serene,
Quivered like burning emerald: calm was spread
    On all below: but far on high, between
Earth and the upper air, the vast clouds fled,
Countless and swift as leaves on autumn's tempest shed.

For ever, as the war became more fierce
    Between the whirlwinds and the rack on high,
That spot grew more serene; blue light did pierce
    The woof of those white clouds, which seem to lie
    Far, deep, and motionless; while through the sky
The pallid semicircle of the moon
    Passed on, in slow and moving majesty;
Its upper horn arrayed in mists, which soon
But slowly fled, like dew beneath the beams of noon.

I could not choose but gaze; a fascination
    Dwelt in that moon, and sky, and clouds, which drew
My fancy thither, and in expectation
    Of what I knew not, I remained:—the hue
    Of the white moon, amid that heaven so blue,
Suddenly stained with shadow did appear;
    A speck, a cloud, a shape, approaching grew,
Like a great ship in the sun's sinking sphere
Beheld afar at sea, and swift it came anear.

Even like a bark, which from a chasm of mountains,
   Dark, vast, and overhanging, on a river
Which there collects the strength of all its fountains,
   Comes forth, whilst with the speed its frame doth quiver,
   Sails, oars, and stream, tending to one endeavour;
So, from that chasm of light a wingèd Form
   On all the winds of heaven approaching ever
Floated, dilating as it came: the storm
Pursued it with fierce blasts, and lightnings swift and warm.

A course precipitous, of dizzy speed,
   Suspending thought and breath; a monstrous sight!
For in the air do I behold indeed
   An Eagle and a Serpent wreathed in fight:—
   And now relaxing its impetuous flight,
Before the aëreal rock on which I stood,
   The Eagle, hovering, wheeled to left and right,
And hung with lingering wings over the flood,
And startled with its yells the wide air's solitude.

A shaft of light upon its wings descended,
   And every golden feather gleamed therein—
Feather and scale, inextricably blended.
   The Serpent's mailed and many-coloured skin
   Shone through the plumes its coils were twined within
By many a swoln and knotted fold, and high
   And far, the neck, receding lithe and thin,
Sustained a crested head, which warily
Shifted and glanced before the Eagle's steadfast eye.

Around, around, in ceaseless circles wheeling
   With clang of wings and scream, the Eagle sailed
Incessantly—sometimes on high concealing
   Its lessening orbs, sometimes as if it failed,
   Drooped through the air; and still it shrieked and wailed,
And casting back its eager head, with beak
   And talon unremittingly assailed
The wreathèd Serpent, who did ever seek
Upon his enemy's heart a mortal wound to wreak.

What life, what power, was kindled and arose
  Within the sphere of that appalling fray!
For, from the encounter of those wondrous foes,
  A vapour like the sea's suspended spray
  Hung gathered: in the void air, far away,
Floated the shattered plumes; bright scales did leap,
  Where'er the Eagle's talons made their way,
Like sparks into the darkness;—as they sweep,
Blood stains the snowy foam of the tumultuous deep.

Swift chances in that combat—many a check,
  And many a change, a dark and wild turmoil;
Sometimes the Snake around his enemy's neck
  Locked in stiff rings his adamantine coil,
  Until the Eagle, faint with pain and toil,
Remitted his strong flight, and near the sea
  Languidly fluttered, hopeless so to foil
His adversary, who then reared on high
His red and burning crest, radiant with victory.

Then on the white edge of the bursting surge,
  Where they had sunk together, would the Snake
Relax his suffocating grasp, and scourge
  The wind with his wild writhings; for to break
  That chain of torment, the vast bird would shake
The strength of his unconquerable wings
  As in despair, and with his sinewy neck,
Dissolve in sudden shock those linkèd rings,
Then soar—as swift as smoke from a volcano springs.

Wile baffled wile, and strength encountered strength,
  Thus long, but unprevailing:—the event
Of that portentous fight appeared at length:
  Until the lamp of day was almost spent
  It had endured, when lifeless, stark, and rent,
Hung high that mighty Serpent, and at last
  Fell to the sea, while o'er the continent,
With clang of wings and scream the Eagle passed,
Heavily borne away on the exhausted blast.

And with it fled the tempest, so that ocean
 And earth and sky shone through the atmosphere—
Only, 'twas strange to see the red commotion
 Of waves like mountains o'er the sinking sphere
 Of sunset sweep, and their fierce roar to hear
Amid the calm: down the steep path I wound
 To the sea-shore—the evening was most clear
And beautiful, and there the sea I found
Calm as a cradled child in dreamless slumber bound.

The Hall of Immortals

AND swift and swifter grew the vessel's motion,
 So that a dizzy trance fell on my brain—
Wild music woke me: we had passed the ocean
 Which girds the pole, Nature's remotest reign—
 And we glode fast o'er a pellucid plain
Of waters, azure with the noontide day.
 Ethereal mountains shone around—a Fane
 Stood in the midst, girt by green isles which lay
On the blue sunny deep, resplendent far away.

It was a Temple, such as mortal hand
 Has never built, nor ecstasy, nor dream
Reared in the cities of enchanted land:
 'Twas likest Heaven, ere yet day's purple stream
 Ebbs o'er the western forest, while the gleam
Of the unrisen moon among the clouds
 Is gathering—when with many a golden beam
The thronging constellations rush in crowds,
Paving with fire the sky and the marmoreal floods.

Like what may be conceived of this vast dome,
 When from the depths which thought can seldom pierce
Genius beholds it rise, his native home,
 Girt by the deserts of the Universe;
 Yet, nor in painting's light, or mightier verse,
Or sculpture's marble language, can invest
 That shape to mortal sense—such glooms immerse
That incommunicable sight, and rest
Upon the labouring brain and overburdened breast.

Winding among the lawny islands fair,
　　Whose blosmy forests starred the shadowy deep,
The wingless boat paused where an ivory stair
　　Its fretwork in the crystal sea did steep,
　　Encircling that vast Fane's aërial heap:
We disembarked, and through a portal wide
　　We passed—whose roof of moonstone carved did keep
A glimmering o'er the forms on every side,
Sculptures like life and thought; immovable, deep-eyed.

We came to a vast hall, whose glorious roof
　　Was diamond, which had drank the lightning's sheen
In darkness, and now poured it through the woof
　　Of spell-inwoven clouds hung there to screen
　　Its blinding splendour—through such veil was seen
That work of subtlest power, divine and rare;
　　Orb above orb, with starry shapes between,
And hornèd moons, and meteors strange and fair,
On night-black columns poised—one hollow hemisphere!

Ten thousand columns in that quivering light
　　Distinct—between whose shafts wound far away
The long and labyrinthine aisles—more bright
　　With their own radiance than the Heaven of Day;
　　And on the jasper walls around, there lay
Paintings, the poesy of mightiest thought,
　　Which did the Spirit's history display;
A tale of passionate change, divinely taught,
Which, in their wingèd dance, unconscious Genii wrought.

Beneath, there sate on many a sapphire throne,
　　The Great, who had departed from mankind,
A mighty Senate;—some, whose white hair shone
　　Like mountain snow, mild, beautiful, and blind;
　　Some, female forms, whose gestures beamed with mind;
And ardent youths, and children bright and fair;
　　And some had lyres whose strings were intertwined
With pale and clinging flames, which ever there
Waked faint yet thrilling sounds that pierced the crystal air.

FROM CANTO II
Laon's Awakening

I WANDERED through the wrecks of days departed
    Far by the desolated shore, when even
O'er the still sea and jagged islets darted
    The light of moonrise; in the northern Heaven,
    Among the clouds near the horizon driven,
The mountains lay beneath our planet pale;
    Around me, broken tombs and columns riven
Looked vast in twilight, and the sorrowing gale
Waked in those ruins gray its everlasting wail!

I knew not who had framed these wonders then,
    Nor had I heard the story of their deeds;
But dwellings of a race of mightier men,
    And monuments of less ungentle creeds
    Tell their own tale to him who wisely heeds
The language which they speak; and now, to me
    The moonlight making pale the blooming weeds,
The bright stars shining in the breathless sea,
Interpreted those scrolls of mortal mystery.

Such man has been, and such may yet become!
    Ay, wiser, greater, gentler, even than they
Who on the fragments of yon shattered dome
    Have stamped the sign of power—I felt the sway
    Of the vast stream of ages bear away
My floating thoughts—my heart beat loud and fast—
    Even as a storm let loose beneath the ray
Of the still moon, my spirit onward past
Beneath truth's steady beams upon its tumult cast.

It shall be thus no more! too long, too long,
    Sons of the glorious dead, have ye lain bound
In darkness and in ruin!—Hope is strong,
    Justice and Truth their wingèd child have found—
    Awake! arise! until the mighty sound
Of your career shall scatter in its gust
    The thrones of the oppressor, and the ground
Hide the last altar's unregarded dust,
Whose Idol has so long betrayed your impious trust!

It must be so—I will arise and waken
    The multitude, and like a sulphurous hill,
Which on a sudden from its snows has shaken
    The swoon of ages, it shall burst and fill
    The world with cleansing fire: it must, it will—
It may not be restrained!—and who shall stand
    Amid the rocking earthquake steadfast still,
But Laon? on high Freedom's desert land
A tower whose marble walls the leaguèd storms withstand!

The Child Cythna

AN orphan with my parents lived, whose eyes
    Were lodestars of delight, which drew me home
When I might wander forth; nor did I prize
    Aught human thing beneath Heaven's mighty dome
    Beyond this child: so when sad hours were come,
And baffled hope like ice still clung to me,
    Since kin were cold, and friends had now become
Heartless and false, I turned from all, to be,
Cythna, the only source of tears and smiles to thee.

What wert thou then? A child most infantine,
    Yet wandering far beyond that innocent age
In all but its sweet looks and mien divine:
    Even then, methought, with the world's tyrant rage
    A patient warfare thy young heart did wage,
When those soft eyes of scarcely conscious thought
    Some tale, or thine own fancies, would engage
To overflow with tears, or converse fraught
With passion, o'er their depths its fleeting light has wrought.

She moved upon this earth a shape of brightness,
    A power, that from its objects scarcely drew
One impulse of her being—in her lightness
    Most like some radiant cloud of morning dew,
    Which wanders through the waste air's pathless blue,
To nourish some far desert: she did seem
    Beside me, gathering beauty as she grew,
Like the bright shade of some immortal dream
Which walks, when tempest sleeps, the wave of life's dark stream.

As mine own shadow was this child to me,
    A second self, far dearer and more fair;
Which clothed in undissolving radiancy
    All those steep paths which languor and despair
    Of human things, had made so dark and bare,
But which I trod alone—nor, till bereft
    Of friends, and overcome by lonely care,
Knew I what solace for that loss was left,
Though by a bitter wound my trusting heart was cleft.

Once she was dear, now she was all I had
    To love in human life—this playmate sweet,
This child of twelve years old—so she was made
    My sole associate, and her willing feet
    Wandered with mine where earth and ocean meet,
Beyond the aëreal mountains whose vast cells
    The unreposing billows ever beat,
Through forests wide and old, and lawny dells
Where boughs of incense droop over the emerald wells.

And warm and light I felt her clasping hand
    When twined in mine: she followed where I went,
Through the lone paths of our immortal land.
    It had no waste but some memorial lent
    Which strung me to my toil—some monument
Vital with mind: then, Cythna by my side,
    Until the bright and beaming day were spent,
Would rest, with looks entreating to abide,
Too earnest and too sweet ever to be denied.

From Canto III

Laon the Captive

What followed then, I know not—for a stroke
    On my raised arm and naked head, came down,
Filling my eyes with blood—when I awoke,
    I felt that they had bound me in my swoon,
    And up a rock which overhangs the town,
By the steep path were bearing me: below,
    The plain was filled with slaughter,—overthrown
The vineyards and the harvests, and the glow
Of blazing roofs shone far o'er the white Ocean's flow.

Upon that rock a mighty column stood,
   Whose capital seemed sculptured in the sky,
Which to the wanderers o'er the solitude
   Of distant seas, from ages long gone by,
   Had made a landmark; o'er its height to fly
Scarcely the cloud, the vulture, or the blast,
   Has power—and when the shades of evening lie
On Earth and Ocean, its carved summits cast
The sunken daylight far through the aërial waste.

They bore me to a cavern in the hill
   Beneath that column, and unbound me there:
And one did strip me stark; and one did fill
   A vessel from the putrid pool; one bare
   A lighted torch, and four with friendless care
Guided my steps the cavern-paths along,
   Then up a steep and dark and narrow stair
We wound, until the torch's fiery tongue
Amid the gushing day beamless and pallid hung.

They raised me to the platform of the pile,
   That column's dizzy height:—the grate of brass
Through which they thrust me, open stood the while,
   As to its ponderous and suspended mass,
   With chains which eat into the flesh, alas!
With brazen links, my naked limbs they bound:
   The grate, as they departed to repass,
With horrid clangour fell, and the far sound
Of their retiring steps in the dense gloom were drowned.

The noon was calm and bright:—around that column
   The overhanging sky and circling sea
Spread forth in silentness profound and solemn
   The darkness of brief frenzy cast on me,
   So that I knew not my own misery:
The islands and the mountains in the day
   Like clouds reposed afar; and I could see
The town among the woods below that lay,
And the dark rocks which bound the bright and glassy bay.

It was so calm, that scarce the feathery weed
    Sown by some eagle on the topmost stone
Swayed in the air:—so bright, that noon did breed
    No shadow in the sky beside mine own—
    Mine, and the shadow of my chain alone.
Below, the smoke of roofs involved in flame
    Rested like night, all else was clearly shown
In that broad glare, yet sound to me none came,
But of the living blood that ran within my frame.

The peace of madness fled, and ah, too soon!
    A ship was lying on the sunny main,
Its sails were flagging in the breathless noon—
    Its shadow lay beyond—that sight again
    Waked, with its presence, in my trancèd brain
The stings of a known sorrow, keen and old:
    I knew that ship bore Cythna o'er the plain
Of waters, to her blighting slavery sold,
And watched it with such thoughts as must remain untold.

From Canto IV

The Hermit Speaks of Cythna

'But I, alas! am both unknown and old,
    And though the woof of wisdom I know well
To dye in hues of language, I am cold
    In seeming, and the hopes which inly dwell,
    My manners note that I did long repel;
But Laon's name to the tumultuous throng
    Were like the star whose beams the waves compel
And tempests, and his soul-subduing tongue
Were as a lance to quell the mailèd crest of wrong.

'Perchance blood need not flow, if thou at length
    Wouldst rise, perchance the very slaves would spare
Their brethren and themselves; great is the strength
    Of words—for lately did a maiden fair,
    Who from her childhood has been taught to bear
The tyrant's heaviest yoke, arise, and make
    Her sex the law of truth and freedom hear,
And with these quiet words—"For thine own sake
I prithee spare me;"—did with ruth so take

'All hearts, that even the torturer who had bound
　　Her meek calm frame, ere it was yet impaled,
Loosened her, weeping then; nor could be found
　　One human hand to harm her—unassailed
　　Therefore she walks through the great City, veiled
In virtue's adamantine eloquence,
　　'Gainst scorn, and death and pain thus trebly mailed,
And blending, in the smiles of that defence,
The Serpent and the Dove, Wisdom and Innocence.

'The wild-eyed women throng around her path:
　　From their luxurious dungeons, from the dust
Of meaner thralls, from the oppressor's wrath,
　　Or the caresses of his sated lust
　　They congregate:—in her they put their trust;
The tyrants send their armèd slaves to quell
　　Her power;—they, even like a thunder-gust
Caught by some forest, bend beneath the spell
Of that young maiden's speech, and to their chiefs rebel.

'Thus she doth equal laws and justice teach
　　To woman, outraged and polluted long:
Gathering the sweetest fruit in human reach
　　For those fair hands now free, while armèd wrong
　　Trembles before her look, though it be strong;
Thousands thus dwell beside her, virgins bright,
　　And matrons with their babes, a stately throng!
Lovers renew the vows which they did plight
In early faith, and hearts long parted now unite,

'And homeless orphans find a home near her,
　　And those poor victims of the proud, no less.
Fair wrecks, on whom the smiling world with stir,
　　Thrusts the redemption of its wickedness:—
　　In squalid huts, and in its palaces
Sits Lust alone, while o'er the land is borne
　　Her voice, whose awful sweetness doth repress
All evil, and her foes relenting turn,
And cast the vote of love in hope's abandoned urn.

FROM CANTO V

The Lonely Tyrant

THE little child stood up when we came nigh;
    Her lips and cheeks seemed very pale and wan,
But on her forehead, and within her eye
    Lay beauty, which makes hearts that feed thereon
    Sick with excess of sweetness; on the throne
She leaned;—the King, with gathered brow, and lips
    Wreathed by long scorn, did inly sneer and frown
With hue like that when some great painter dips
His pencil in the gloom of earthquake and eclipse.

She stood beside him like a rainbow braided
    Within some storm, when scarce its shadows vast
From the blue paths of the swift sun have faded;
    A sweet and solemn smile, like Cyntha's, cast
    One moment's light, which made my heart beat fast,
O'er that child's parted lips—a gleam of bliss,
    A shade of vanished days,—as the tears passed
Which wrapped it, even as with a father's kiss
I pressed those softest eyes in trembling tenderness.

The sceptred wretch then from that solitude
    i drew, and, of his change compassionate,
With words of sadness soothed his rugged mood.
    But he, while pride and fear held deep debate,
    With sullen guile of ill-dissembled hate
Glared on me as a toothless snake might glare:
    Pity, not scorn I felt, though desolate
The desolator now, and unaware
The curses which he mocked had caught him by the hair.

I led him forth from that which now might seem
    A gorgeous grave: through portals sculptured deep
With imagery beautiful as dream
    We went, and left the shades which tend on sleep
    Over its unregarded gold to keep
Their silent watch.—The child trod faintingly,
    And as she went, the tears which she did weep
Glanced in the starlight; wildered seemèd she,
And when I spake, for sobs she could not answer me.

At last the tyrant cried, 'She hungers, slave,
  Stab her, or give her bread!'—It was a tone
Such as sick fancies in a new-made grave
  Might hear. I trembled, for the truth was known;
  He with this child had thus been left alone,
And neither had gone forth for food,—but he
  In mingled pride and awe cowered near his throne,
And she a nursling of captivity
Knew nought beyond those walls, nor what such change
  might be.

And he was troubled at a charm withdrawn
  Thus suddenly; that sceptres ruled no more—
That even from gold the dreadful strength was gone,
  Which once made all things subject to its power—
  Such wonder seized him, as if hour by hour
The past had come again: and the swift fall
  Of one so great and terrible of yore,
To desolateness, in the hearts of all
Like wonder stirred, who saw such awful change befall

A mighty crowd, such as the wide land pours
  Once in a thousand years, now gathered round
The fallen tyrant;—like the rush of showers
  Of hail in spring, pattering along the ground,
  Their many footsteps fell, else came no sound
From the wide multitude: that lonely man
  Then knew the burden of his change, and found,
Concealing in the dust his visage wan,
Refuge from the keen looks which through his bosom ran.

And he was faint withal: I sate beside him
  Upon the earth, and took that child so fair
From his weak arms, that ill might none betide him
  Or her;—when food was brought to them, her share
  To his averted lips the child did bear,
But, when she saw he had enough, she ate
  And wept the while;—the lonely man's despair
Hunger then overcame, and of his state
Forgetful, on the dust as in a trance he sate.

From Canto VI

Laon and Cythna Together

AND for a space in my embrace she rested,
  Her head on my unquiet heart reposing,
While my faint arms her languid frame invested:
  At length she looked on me, and half unclosing
  Her tremulous lips, said: 'Friend, thy bands were losing
The battle, as I stood before the King
  In bonds.—I burst them then, and swiftly choosing
The time, did seize a Tartar's sword, and spring
Upon his horse, and, swift as on the whirlwind's wing,

'Have thou and I been borne beyond pursuer,
  And we are here.'—Then turning to the steed,
She pressed the white moon on his front with pure
  And rose-like lips, and many a fragrant weed
  From the green ruin plucked, that he might feed;—
But I to a stone seat that Maiden led,
  And kissing her fair eyes, said, 'Thou hast need
Of rest,' and I heaped up the courser's bed
In a green mossy nook, with mountain-flowers dispread.

Within that ruin, where a shattered portal
  Looks to the eastern stars, abandoned now
By man, to be the home of things immortal,
  Memories, like awful ghosts which come and go,
  And must inherit all he builds below,
When he is gone, a hall stood; o'er whose roof
  Fair clinging weeds with ivy pale did grow,
Clasping its gray rents with a verdurous woof,
A hanging dome of leaves, a canopy moon-proof.

The autumnal winds, as if spell-bound, had made
  A natural couch of leaves in that recess,
Which seasons none disturbed, but, in the shade
  Of flowering parasites, did Spring love to dress
  With their sweet blooms the wintry loneliness
Of those dead leaves. shedding their stars, whene'er
  The wandering wind her nurslings might caress;
Whose intertwining fingers ever there
Made music wild and soft that filled the listening air.

We know not where we go, or what sweet dream
   May pilot us through caverns strange and fair
Of far and pathless passion, while the stream
   Of life, our bark doth on its whirlpools bear,
   Spreading swift wings as sails to the dim air;
Nor should we seek to know, so the devotion
   Of love and gentle thoughts be heard still there
Louder and louder from the utmost Ocean
Of universal life, attuning its commotion.

To the pure all things are pure! Oblivion wrapped
   Our spirits, and the fearful overthrow
Of public hope was from our being snapped,
   Though linkèd years had bound it there; for now
   A power, a thirst, a knowledge, which below
All thoughts, like light beyond the atmosphere,
   Clothing its clouds with grace, doth ever flow,
Came on us, as we sate in silence there,
Beneath the golden stars of the clear azure air:—

In silence which doth follow talk that causes
   The baffled heart to speak with sighs and tears,
When wildering passion swalloweth up the pauses
   Of inexpressive speech:—the youthful years
   Which we together passed, their hopes and fears,
The blood itself which ran within our frames,
   That likeness of the features which endears
The thoughts expressed by them, our very names,
And all the wingèd hours which speechless memory claims,

Had found a voice—and ere that voice did pass,
   The night grew damp and dim, and through a rent
Of the ruin where we sate, from the morass,
   A wandering Meteor by some wild wind sent,
   Hung high in the green dome, to which it lent
A faint and pallid lustre; while the song
   Of blasts, in which its blue hair quivering bent,
Strewed strangest sounds the moving leaves among;
A wondrous light, the sound as of a spirit's tongue.

The Meteor showed the leaves on which we sate,
   And Cythna's glowing arms, and the thick ties
Of her soft hair, which bent with gathered weight
   My neck near hers, her dark and deepening eyes,
   Which, as twin phantoms of one star that lies
O'er a dim well, move, though the star reposes,
   Swam in our mute and liquid ecstasies,
Her marble brow, and eager lips, like roses,
With their own fragance pale, which Spring but half uncloses.

The Meteor to its far morass returned:
   The beating of our veins one interval
Made still; and then I felt the blood that burned
   Within her frame, mingle with mine, and fall
   Around my heart like fire; and over all
A mist was spread, the sickness of a deep
   And speechless swoon of joy, as might befall
Two disunited spirits when they leap
In union from this earth's obscure and fading sleep.

Was it one moment that confounded thus
   All thought, all sense, all feeling, into one
Unutterable power, which shielded us
   Even from our own cold looks, when we had gone
   Into a wide and wild oblivion
Of tumult and of tenderness? or now
   Had ages, such as make the moon and sun,
The seasons, and mankind their changes know,
Left fear and time unfelt by us alone below?

I know not. What are kisses whose fire clasps
   The failing heart in languishment, or limb
Twined within limb? or the quick dying gasps
   Of the life meeting, when the faint eyes swim
   Through tears of a wide mist boundless and dim,
In one caress? What is the strong control
   Which leads the heart that dizzy steep to climb,
Where far over the world those vapours roll,
Which blend two restless frames in one reposing soul?

It is the shadow which doth float unseen,
  But not unfelt, o'er blind mortality,
Whose divine darkness fled not, from that green
  And lone recess, where lapped in peace did lie
  Our linkèd frames till, from the changing sky,
That night and still another day had fled;
  And then I saw and felt. The moon was high,
And clouds, as of a coming storm, were spread
Under its orb,—loud winds were gathering overhead.

From Canto IX
Cythna the Prophetess

'We know not what will come—yet Laon, dearest,
  Cythna shall be the prophetess of Love,
Her lips shall rob thee of the grace thou wearest,
  To hide thy heart, and clothe the shapes which rove
  Within the homeless Future's wintry grove;
For I now, sitting thus beside thee, seem
  Even with thy breath and blood to live and move,
And violence and wrong are as a dream
Which rolls from steadfast truth, an unreturning stream.

'The blasts of Autumn drive the wingèd seeds
  Over the earth,—next come the snows, and rain,
And frosts, and storms, which dreary Winter leads
  Out of his Scythian cave, a savage train;
  Behold! Spring sweeps over the world again,
Shedding soft dews from her ethereal wings;
  Flowers on the mountains, fruits over the plain,
And music on the waves and woods she flings,
And love on all that lives, and calm on lifeless things.

'O Spring, of hope, and love, and youth, and gladness
  Wind-wingèd emblem! brightest, best and fairest!
Whence comest thou, when with dark Winter's sadness
  The tears that fade in sunny smiles thou sharest?
  Sister of joy, thou art the child who wearest
Thy mother's dying smile, tender and sweet;
  Thy mother Autumn, for whose grave thou bearest
Fresh flowers, and beams like flowers, with gentle feet,
Disturbing not the leaves which are her winding-sheet.

'Virtue, and Hope, and Love, like light and Heaven,
    Surround the world.—We are their chosen slaves.
Has not the whirlwind of our spirit driven
    Truth's deathless germs to thought's remotest caves?
    Lo, Winter comes!—the grief of many graves,
The frost of death, the tempest of the sword,
    The flood of tyranny, whose sanguine waves
Stagnate like ice at Faith the enchanter's word,
And bind all human hearts in its repose abhorred.

'The seeds are sleeping in the soil: meanwhile
    The Tyrant peoples dungeons with his prey,
Pale victims on the guarded scaffold smile
    Because they cannot speak; and, day by day,
    The moon of wasting Science wanes away
Among her stars, and in that darkness vast
    The sons of earth to their foul idols pray,
And gray Priests triumph, and like blight or blast
A shade of selfish care o'er human looks is cast.

'This is the winter of the world;—and here
    We die, even as the winds of Autumn fade,
Expiring in the frore and foggy air.—
    Behold! Spring comes, though we must pass, who made
    The promise of its birth,—even as the shade
Which from our death, as from a mountain, flings
    The future, a broad sunrise; thus arrayed
As with the plumes of overshadowing wings,
From its dark gulf of chains, Earth like an eagle springs.

'O dearest love! we shall be dead and cold
    Before this morn may on the world arise;
Wouldst thou the glory of its dawn behold?
    Alas! gaze not on me, but turn thine eyes
    On thine own heart—it is a paradise
Which everlasting Spring has made its own,
    And while drear Winter fills the naked skies,
Sweet streams of sunny thought, and flowers fresh-blown,
Are there, and weave their sounds and odours into one.

'In their own hearts the earnest of the hope
  Which made them great, the good will ever find;
And though some envious shades may interlope
  Between the effect and it, One comes behind,
  Who aye the future to the past will bind—
Necessity, whose sightless strength for ever
  Evil with evil, good with good must wind
In bands of union, which no power may sever:
They must bring forth their kind, and be divided never!

'The good and mighty of departed ages
  Are in their graves, the innocent and free,
Heroes, and Poets, and prevailing Sages,
  Who leave the vesture of their majesty
  To adorn and clothe this naked world;—and we
Are like to them—such perish, but they leave
  All hope, or love, or truth, or liberty,
Whose forms their mighty spirits could conceive,
To be a rule and law to ages that survive.

'So be the turf heaped over our remains
  Even in our happy youth, and that strange lot,
Whate'er it be, when in these mingling veins
  The blood is still, be ours; let sense and thought
  Pass from our being, or be numbered not
Among the things that are; let those who come
  Behind, for whom our steadfast will has bought
A calm inheritance, a glorious doom,
Insult with careless tread our undivided tomb.

'Our many thoughts and deeds, our life and love,
  Our happiness, and all that we have been,
Immortally must live, and burn and move,
  When we shall be no more;—the world has seen
  A type of peace; and—as some most serene
And lovely spot to a poor maniac's eye,
  After long years, some sweet and moving scene
Of youthful hope, returning suddenly,
Quells his long madness—thus man shall remember thee.

'And Calumny meanwhile shall feed on us,
 As worms devour the dead, and near the throne
And at the altar, most accepted thus
 Shall sneers and curses be;—what we have done
 None shall dare vouch, though it be truly known;
That record shall remain, when they must pass
 Who built their pride on its oblivion;
And fame, in human hope which sculptured was,
Survive the perished scrolls of unenduring brass.

'The while we two, belovèd, must depart,
 And Sense and Reason, those enchanters fair,
Whose wand of power is hope, would bid the heart
 That gazed beyond the wormy grave despair:
 These eyes, these lips, this blood, seems darkly there
To fade in hideous ruin; no calm sleep
 Peopling with golden dreams the stagnant air,
Seems our obscure and rotting eyes to steep
In joy;—but senseless death—a ruin dark and deep!

'These are blind fancies—reason cannot know
 What sense can neither feel, nor thought conceive;
There is delusion in the world —and woe,
 And fear, and pain—we know not whence we live,
 Or why, or how, or what mute Power may give
Their being to each plant, and star, and beast,
 Or even these thoughts.—Come near me! I do weave
A chain I cannot break—I am possessed
With thoughts too swift and strong for one lone human breast.

'Yes, yes—thy kiss is sweet, thy lips are warm—
 O! willingly, belovèd, would these eyes,
Might they no more drink being from thy form,
 Even as to sleep whence we again arise,
 Close their faint orbs in death: I fear nor prize
Aught that can now betide, unshared by thee—
 Yes, Love when Wisdom fails makes Cythna wise:
Darkness and death, if death be true, must be
Dearer than life and hope, if unenjoyed with thee.

'Alas, our thoughts flow on with streams, whose waters
   Return not to their fountain—Earth and Heaven,
The Ocean and the Sun, the Clouds their daughters,
   Winter, and Spring, and Morn, and Noon, and Even,
   All that we are or know, is darkly driven
Towards one gulf.—Lo! what a change is come
   Since I first spake—but time shall be forgiven,
Though it change all but thee!'—She ceased—night's gloom
Meanwhile had fallen on earth from the sky's sunless dome.

Though she had ceased, her countenance uplifted
   To Heaven still spake, with solemn glory bright;
Her dark deep eyes, her lips, whose motions gifted
   The air they breathed with love, her locks undight.
   'Fair star of life and love,' I cried, 'my soul's delight,
Why lookest thou on the crystalline skies?
   O, that my spirit were yon Heaven of night,
Which gazes on thee with its thousand eyes!'
She turned to me and smiled—that smile was Paradise!

From Canto XI

America

'THERE is a People mighty in its youth,
   A land beyond the Oceans of the West,
Where, though with rudest rites, Freedom and Truth
   Are worshipped; from a glorious Mother's breast,
   Who, since high Athens fell, among the rest
Sate like the Queen of Nations, but in woe,
   By inbred monsters outraged and oppressed,
Turns to her chainless child for succour now,
It draws the milk of Power in Wisdom's fullest flow.

'That land is like an Eagle, whose young gaze
   Feeds on the noontide beam, whose golden plume
Floats moveless on the storm, and in the blaze
   Of sunrise gleams when Earth is wrapped in gloom;
   An epitaph of glory for the tomb
Of murdered Europe may thy fame be made,
   Great People! as the sands shalt thou become;
Thy growth is swift as morn, when night must fade;
The multitudinous Earth shall sleep beneath thy shade.

'Yes, in the desert there is built a home
    For Freedom. Genius is made strong to rear
The monuments of man beneath the dome
    Of a new Heaven; myriads assemble there,
    Whom the proud lords of man, in rage or fear,
Drive from their wasted homes: the boon I pray
    Is this—that Cythna shall be convoyed there—
Nay, start not at the name—America!
And then to you this night Laon will I betray.

'With me do what you will. I am your foe!'
    The light of such a joy as makes the stare
Of hungry snakes like living emeralds glow,
    Shone in a hundred human eyes—'Where, where
    Is Laon? Haste! fly! drag him swiftly here!
We grant thy boon.'—'I put no trust in ye,
    Swear by the Power ye dread.'—'We swear, we swear!'
The Stranger threw his vest back suddenly,
And smiled in gentle pride, and said, Lo! I am he!'

From Canto XII

The Last Voyage

AND is this death?—The pyre has disappeared,
    The Pestilence, the Tyrant, and the throng;
The flames grow silent—slowly there is heard
    The music of a breath-suspending song,
    Which, like the kiss of love when life is young,
Steeps the faint eyes in darkness sweet and deep;
    With ever-changing notes it floats along,
Till on my passive soul there seemed to creep
A melody, like waves on wrinkled sands that leap.

The warm touch of a soft and tremulous hand
    Wakened me then; lo! Cythna sate reclined
Beside me, on the waved and golden sand
    Of a clear pool, upon a bank o'ertwined
    With strange and star-bright flowers, which to the wind
Breathed divine odour; high above was spread
    The emerald heaven of trees of unknown kind,
Whose moonlike blooms and bright fruit overhead
A shadow, which was light, upon the waters shed.

And round about sloped many a lawny mountain
    With incense-bearing forests, and vast caves
Of marble radiance, to that mighty fountain;
    And where the flood its own bright margin laves,
    Their echoes talk with its eternal waves,
Which, from the depths whose jaggèd caverns breed
    Their unreposing strife, it lifts and heaves,—
Till through a chasm of hills they roll, and feed
A river deep, which flies with smooth but arrowy speed.

As we sate gazing in a trance of wonder,
    A boat approached, borne by the musical air
Along the waves which sung and sparkled under
    Its rapid keel—a wingèd shape sate there,
    A child with silver-shining wings, so fair
That as her bark did through the waters glide,
    The shadow of the lingering waves did wear
Light, as from starry beams; from side to side,
While veering to the wind her plumes the bark did guide.

The boat was one curved shell of hollow pearl,
    Almost translucent with the light divine
Of her within; the prow and stern did curl
    Hornèd on high, like the young moon supine,
    When o'er dim twilight mountains dark with pine
It floats upon the sunset's sea of beams,
    Whose golden waves in many a purple line
Fade fast, till borne on sunlight's ebbing streams,
Dilating, on earth's verge the sunken meteor gleams.

Its keel has struck the sands beside our feet;—
    Then Cythna turned to me, and from her eyes
Which swam with unshed tears, a look more sweet
    Than happy love, a wild and glad surprise,
    Glanced as she spake: 'Ay, this is Paradise
And not a dream, and we are all united!
    Lo, that is mine own child, who in the guise
Of madness came, like day to one benighted
In lonesome woods: my heart is now too well requited!'

And then she wept aloud, and in her arms
   Clasped that bright Shape, less marvellously fair
Than her own human hues and living charms;
   Which, as she leaned in passion's silence there,
   Breathed warmth on the cold bosom of the air,
Which seemed to blush and tremble with delight;
   The glossy darkness of her streaming hair
Fell o'er that snowy child, and wrapped from sight
The fond and long embrace which did their hearts unite.

Then the bright child, the plumèd Seraph came,
   And fixed its blue and beaming eyes on mine,
And said, 'I was disturbed by tremulous shame
   When once we met, yet knew that I was thine
   From the same hour in which thy lips divine
Kindled a clinging dream within my brain,
   Which ever waked when I might sleep, to twine
Thine image with *her* memory dear—again
We meet; exempted now from mortal fear or pain.

'When the consuming flames had wrapped ye round,
   The hope which I had cherished went away;
I fell in agony on the senseless ground,
   And hid mine eyes in dust, and far astray
   My mind was gone, when bright, like dawning day,
The Spectre of the Plague before me flew,
   And breathed upon my lips, and seemed to say,
"They wait for thee, belovèd!"—then I knew
The death-mark on my breast, and became calm anew.

'It was the calm of love—for I was dying.
   I saw the black and half-extinguished pyre
In its own gray and shrunken ashes lying;
   The pitchy smoke of the departed fire
   Still hung in many a hollow dome and spire
Above the towers, like night; beneath whose shade
   Awed by the ending of their own desire
The armies stood; a vacancy was made
In expectation's depth, and so they stood dismayed.

'The frightful silence of that altered mood,
    The tortures of the dying clove alone,
Till one uprose among the multitude,
    And said—"The flood of time is rolling on,
    We stand upon its brink, whilst *they* are gone
To glide in peace down death's mysterious stream.
    Have ye done well? They moulder flesh and bone,
Who might have made this life's envenomed dream
A sweeter draught than ye will ever taste, I deem.

'"These perish as the good and great of yore
    Have perished, and their murderers will repent,—
Yes, vain and barren tears shall flow before
    Yon smoke has faded from the firmament
    Even for this cause, that ye who must lament
The death of those that made this world so fair,
    Cannot recall them now; but there is lent
To man the wisdom of a high despair,
When such can die, and he live on and linger here.

'"Ay, ye may fear not now the Pestilence,
    From fabled hell as by a charm withdrawn;
All power and faith must pass, since calmly hence
    In pain and fire have unbelievers gone;
    And ye must sadly turn away, and moan
In secret, to his home each one returning,
    And to long ages shall this hour be known;
And slowly shall its memory, ever burning,
Fill this dark night of things with an eternal morning.

'"For me the world is grown too void and cold,
    Since Hope pursues immortal Destiny
With steps thus slow—therefore shall ye behold
    How those who love, yet fear not, dare to die;
    Tell to your children this!" Then suddenly
He sheathed a dagger in his heart and fell;
    My brain grew dark in death, and yet to me
There came a murmur from the crowd, to tell
Of deep and mighty change which suddenly befell.

'Then suddenly I stood, a wingèd Thought,
   Before the immortal Senate, and the seat
Of that star-shining spirit, whence is wrought
   The strength of its dominion, good and great,
   The better Genius of this world's estate.
His realm around one mighty Fane is spread,
   Elysian islands bright and fortunate,
Calm dwellings of the free and happy dead,
Where I am sent to lead!' These wingèd words she said,

And with the silence of her eloquent smile,
   Bade us embark in her divine canoe;
Then at the helm we took our seat, the while
   Above her head those plumes of dazzling hue
   Into the winds' invisible stream she threw,
Sitting beside the prow: like gossamer
   On the swift breath of morn, the vessel flew
O'er the bright whirlpools of that fountain fair,
Whose shores receded fast, whilst we seemed lingering there;

Till down that mighty stream, dark, calm, and fleet,
   Between a chasm of cedarn mountains riven,
Chased by the thronging winds whose viewless feet
   As swift as twinkling beams, had, under Heaven,
   From woods and waves wild sounds and odours driven,
The boat fled visibly—three nights and days,
   Borne like a cloud through morn, and noon, and even,
We sailed along the winding watery ways
Of the vast stream, a long and labyrinthine maze.

A scene of joy and wonder to behold
   That river's shapes and shadows changing ever,
When the broad sunrise filled with deepening gold
   Its whirlpools, where all hues did spread and quiver;
   And where melodious falls did burst and shiver
Among rocks clad with flowers, the foam and spray
   Sparkled like stars upon the sunny river,
Or when the moonlight poured a holier day,
One vast and glittering lake around green islands lay.

Morn, noon, and even, that boat of pearl outran
    The streams which bore it, like the arrowy cloud
Of tempest, or the speedier thought of man,
    Which flieth forth and cannot make abode;
    Sometimes through forests, deep like night, we glode,
Between the walls of mighty mountains crowned
    With Cyclopean piles, whose turrets proud,
The homes of the departed, dimly frowned
O'er the bright waves which girt their dark foundations round.

Sometimes between the wide and flowering meadows,
    Mile after mile we sailed, and 'twas delight
To see far off the sunbeams chase the shadows
    Over the grass; sometimes beneath the night
    Of wide and vaulted caves, whose roofs were bright
With starry gems, we fled, whilst from their deep
    And dark-green chasms, shades beautiful and white,
Amid sweet sounds across our path would sweep,
Like swift and lovely dreams that walk the waves of sleep.

And ever as we sailed, our minds were full
    Of love and wisdom, which would overflow
In converse wild, and sweet, and wonderful,
    And in quick smiles whose light would come and go
    Like music o'er wide waves, and in the flow
Of sudden tears, and in the mute caress—
    For a deep shade was cleft, and we did know,
That virtue, though obscured on Earth, not less
Survives all mortal change in lasting loveliness.

Three days and nights we sailed, as thought and feeling
    Number delightful hours—for through the sky
The spherèd lamps of day and night, revealing
    New changes and new glories, rolled on high,
    Sun, Moon, and moonlike lamps, the progeny
Of a diviner Heaven, serene and fair:
    On the fourth day, wild as a windwrought sea
The stream became, and fast and faster bare
The spirit-wingèd boat, steadily speeding there.

Steady and swift, where the waves rolled like mountains
　　Within the vast ravine, whose rifts did pour
Tumultuous floods from their ten thousand fountains,
　　The thunder of whose earth-uplifting roar
　　Made the air sweep in whirlwinds from the shore,
Calm as a shade, the boat of that fair child
　　Securely fled, that rapid stress before,
Amid the topmost spray, and sunbows wild,
Wreathed in the silver mist: in joy and pride we smiled.

The torrent of that wide and raging river
　　Is passed, and our aëreal speed suspended.
We look behind: a golden mist did quiver
　　Where its wild surges with the lake were blended,—
　　Our bark hung there, as on a line suspended
Between two heavens,—that windless waveless lake
　　Which four great cataracts from four vales, attended
By mists, aye feed; from rocks and clouds they break,
And of that azure sea a silent refuge make.

Motionless resting on the lake awhile,
　　I saw its marge of snow-bright mountains rear
Their peaks, aloft, I saw each radiant isle,
　　And, in the midst afar, even like a sphere
　　Hung in one hollow sky, did there appear
The Temple of the Spirit; on the sound
　　Which issued thence, drawn nearer and more near,
Like the swift moon this glorious earth around,
The charmèd boat approached and there its haven found.

Prince Athanase

LOVE

THOU art the wine whose drunkenness is all
We can desire, O Love! and happy souls,
Ere from thy vine the leaves of autumn fall,

Catch thee, and feed from their o'erflowing bowls
Thousands who thirst for thine ambrosial dew;—
Thou art the radiance which where ocean rolls

Investeth it; and when the heavens are blue
Thou fillest them; and when the earth is fair
The shadow of thy moving wings imbue

Its deserts and its mountains, till they wear
Beauty like some light robe;—thou ever soarest
Among the towers of men, and as soft air

In spring, which moves the unawakened forest,
Clothing with leaves its branches bare and bleak,
Thou floatest among men; and aye implorest

That which from thee they should implore:—the weak
Alone kneel to thee, offering up the hearts
The strong have broken—yet where shall any seek

A garment whom thou clothest not? the darts
Of the keen winter storm, barbèd with frost,
Which, from the everlasting snow that parts

The Alps from Heaven, pierce some traveller lost
In the wide waved interminable snow
Ungarmented,.....

Rosalind and Helen

A MODERN ECLOGUE

It is recorded by Mary Shelley that her husband after beginning this narrative poem at Marlow in 1817 was inclined to abandon it, but that in Italy she persuaded him to go on with it. His own comment is, 'It is not an attempt in the highest style of poetry.' Indeed it is an experiment in fiction, metre being no bar to that, and as such it has originality. The theme is simple: both Rosalind and Helen have their misfortunes in love, yet these troubles, in spite of their original conflict of principle on love and conduct, at last reconcile them. The psychological world is what Shelley tries to present, and the poem has its atmosphere, like some recent 'novels' which are nearer poems; yet the realism which is essential to the introduction of the abstract and transcendental is sketchy, and Shelley probably saw the defect.

The Death of Lionel

Amid a bloomless myrtle wood,
On a green and sea-girt promontory,
Not far from where we dwelt, there stood
In record of a sweet sad story,
An altar and a temple bright
Circled by steps, and o'er the gate
Was sculptured, 'To Fidelity;'
And in the shrine an image sate,
All veiled: but there was seen the light
Of smiles, which faintly could express
A mingled pain and tenderness.
Through that ethereal drapery
The left hand held the head, the right—
Beyond the veil, beneath the skin,
You might see the nerves quivering within—
Was forcing the point of a barbèd dart
Into its side-convulsing heart.
An unskilled hand, yet one informed
With genius, had the marble warmed

With that pathetic life. This tale
It told: A dog had from the sea,
When the tide was raging fearfully,
Dragged Lionel's mother, weak and pale,
Then died beside her on the sand,
And she that temple thence had planned;
But it was Lionel's own hand
Had wrought the image. Each new moon
That lady did, in this lone fane,
The rites of a religion sweet,
Whose god was in her heart and brain;
The seasons' loveliest flowers were strewn
On the marble floor beneath her feet,
And she brought crowns of sea-buds white,
Whose odour is so sweet and faint,
And weeds, like branching chrysolite,
Woven in devices fine and quaint.
And tears from her brown eyes did stain
The altar: need but look upon
That dying statue fair and wan,
If tears should cease, to weep again:
And rare Arabian odours came,
Through the myrtle copses steaming thence
From the hissing frankincense,
Whose smoke, wool-white as ocean foam,
Hung in dense flocks beneath the dome—
That ivory dome, whose azure night
With golden stars, like heaven, was bright—
O'er the split cedar's pointed flame;
And the lady's harp would kindle there
The melody of an old air,
Softer than sleep; the villagers
Mixed their religion up with hers,
And as they listened round, shed tears.

One eve he led me to this fane:
Daylight on its last purple cloud
Was lingering gray, and soon her strain
The nightingale began; now loud,
Climbing in circles the windless sky,
Now dying music; suddenly
'Tis scattered in a thousand notes.

And now to the hushed ear it floats
Like field smells known in infancy,
Then failing, soothes the air again.
We sate within that temple lone,
Pavilioned round with Parian stone:
His mother's harp stood near, and oft
I had awakened music soft
Amid its wires: the nightingale
Was pausing in her heaven-taught tale:
'Now drain the cup,' said Lionel,
'Which the poet-bird has crowned so well
With the wine of her bright and liquid song!
Heardst thou not sweet words among
That heaven-resounding minstrelsy?
Heardst thou not, that those who die
Awake in a world of ecstasy?
That love, when limbs are interwoven,
And sleep, when the night of life is cloven,
And thought, to the world's dim boundaries clinging,
And music, when one beloved is singing,
Is death? Let us drain right joyously
The cup which the sweet bird fills for me,'
He paused, and to my lips he bent
His own: like spirit his words went
Through all my limbs with the speed of fire;
And his keen eyes, glittering through mine,
Filled me with the flame divine,
Which in their orbs was burning far,
Like the light of an unmeasured star,
In the sky of midnight dark and deep:
Yes, 'twas his soul that did inspire
Sounds, which my skill could ne'er awaken;
And first, I felt my fingers sweep
The harp, and a long quivering cry
Burst from my lips in symphony:
The dusk and solid air was shaken,
As swift and swifter the notes came
From my touch, that wandered like quick flame,
And from my bosom, labouring
With some unutterable thing:
The awful sound of my own voice made
My faint lips tremble; in some mood

Of wordless thought Lionel stood
So pale, that even beside his cheek
The snowy column from its shade
Caught whiteness: yet his countenance
Raised upward, burned with radiance
Of spirit-piercing joy, whose light,
Like the moon struggling through the night
Of whirlwind-rifted clouds, did break
With beams that might not be confined
I paused, but soon his gestures kindled
New power, as by the moving wind
The waves are lifted, and my song
To low soft notes now changed and dwindled,
And from the twinkling wires among,
My languid fingers drew and flung
Circles of life-dissolving sound,
Yet faint; in aëry rings they bound
My Lionel, who, as every strain
Grew fainter but more sweet, his mien
Sunk with the sound relaxedly;
And slowly now he turned to me,
As slowly faded from his face
That awful joy: with looks serene
He was soon drawn to my embrace,
And my wild song then died away
In murmurs: words I dare not say
We mixed, and on his lips mine fed
Till they methought felt still and cold:
'What is it with thee, love?' I said:
No word, no look, no motion! yes,
There was a change, but spare to guess,
Nor let that moment's hope be told.
I looked, and knew that he was dead,
And fell, as the eagle on the plain
Falls when life deserts her brain,
And the mortal lightning is veiled again.

Lines Written Among the Euganean Hills

For prose impressions of the Euganean Hills by a later English poet see *In the Key of Blue* by Shelley's biographer, J. A. Symonds. Like one or two earlier hill-poems, Shelley's begins with sunrise and ends with sunset. The metre and some other points in the panorama typically called *Lines* seem to show that Shelley knew the charming *Grongar Hill* by John Dyer, the eighteenth-century painter-poet. Shelley introduced the passage on Lord Byron 'the tempest-cleaving swan' as an after-thought, and has been blamed for his notion that the history of Venice might be reduced to the memory of Byron's residence there.

F. T. Palgrave found the plan of the *Lines* obscure, and yet explained it in a note. The 'island' in the sea of Shelley's life of successive troubles is the single day of serenity and freedom in a scene of natural beauty and imaginative delight.

Many a green isle needs must be
In the deep wide sea of Misery,
Or the mariner, worn and wan,
Never thus could voyage on—
Day and night, and night and day,
Drifting on his dreary way,
With the solid darkness black,
Closing round his vessel's track;
Whilst above the sunless sky,
Big with clouds, hangs heavily,
And behind the tempest fleet
Hurries on with lightning feet,
Riving sail, and cord, and plank,
Till the ship has almost drank
Death from the o'er-brimming deep:
And sinks down, down, like that sleep
When the dreamer seems to be
Weltering through eternity;

And the dim low line before
Of a dark and distant shore
Still recedes, as ever still
Longing with divided will,
But no power to seek or shun,
He is ever drifted on
O'er the unreposing wave
To the haven of the grave.
What, if there no friends will greet;
What, if there no heart will meet
His with love's impatient beat;
Wander wheresoe'er he may,
Can he dream before that day
To find refuge from distress
In friendship's smile, in love's caress?
Then 'twill wreak him little woe
Whether such there be or no:
Senseless is the breast, and cold,
Which relenting love would fold;
Bloodless are the veins and chill
Which the pulse of pain did fill;
Every little living nerve
That from bitter words did swerve
Round the tortured lips and brow,
Are like sapless leaflets now
Frozen upon December's bough.

On the beach of a northern sea
Which tempests shake eternally,
As once the wretch there lay to sleep,
Lies a solitary heap,
One white skull and seven dry bones,
On the margin of the stones,
Where a few gray rushes stand,
Boundaries of the sea and land:
Nor is heard one voice of wail
But the sea-mews, as they sail
O'er the billows of the gale:
Or the whirlwind up and down
Howling, like a slaughtered town,
When a king in glory rides
Through the pomp of fratricides:

Those unburied bones around
There is many a mournful sound;
There is no lament for him,
Like a sunless vapour, dim,
Who once clothed with life and thought
What now moves nor murmurs not.

Ay, many flowering islands lie
In the waters of wide Agony:
To such a one this morn was led,
My bark by soft winds piloted:
'Mid the mountains Euganean
I stood listening to the paean
With which the legioned rooks did hail
The sun's uprise majestical;
Gathering round with wings all hoar,
Through the dewy mist they soar
Like gray shades, till the eastern heaven
Bursts, and then, as clouds of even,
Flecked with fire and azure, lie
In the unfathomable sky,
So their plumes of purple grain,
Starred with drops of golden rain,
Gleam above the sunlight woods,
As in silent multitudes
On the morning's fitful gale
Through the broken mist they sail,
And the vapours cloven and gleaming
Follow, down the dark steep streaming,
Till all is bright, and clear, and still,
Round the solitary hill.

Beneath is spread like a green sea
The waveless plain of Lombardy,
Bounded by the vaporous air,
Islanded by cities fair;
Underneath Day's azure eyes
Ocean's nursling, Venice lies,
A peopled labyrinth of walls,
Amphitrite's destined halls,
Which her hoary sire now paves
With his blue and beaming waves.

Lo! the sun upsprings behind,
Broad, red, radiant, half-reclined
On the level quivering line
Of the waters crystalline;
And before that chasm of light,
As within a furnace bright,
Column, tower, and dome, and spire,
Shine like obelisks of fire,
Pointing with inconstant motion
From the altar of dark ocean
To the sapphire-tinted skies;
As the flames of sacrifice
From the marble shrines did rise,
As to pierce the dome of gold
Where Apollo spoke of old.

Sun-girt City, thou hast been
Ocean's child, and then his queen;
Now is come a darker day,
And thou soon must be his prey,
If the power that raised thee here
Hallow so thy watery bier.
A less drear ruin then than now.
With thy conquest-branded brow
Stooping to the slave of slaves
From thy throne, among the waves
Wilt thou be, when the sea-mew
Flies, as once before if flew,
O'er thine isles depopulate,
And all is in its ancient state,
Save where many a palace gate
With green sea-flowers overgrown
Like a rock of Ocean's own,
Topples o'er the abandoned sea
As the tides change sullenly.
The fisher on his watery way,
Wandering at the close of day,
Will spread his sail and seize his oar
Till he pass the gloomy shore,
Lest thy dead should, from their sleep
Bursting o'er the starlight deep,
Lead a rapid masque of death
O'er the waters of his path.

Those who alone thy towers behold
Quivering through aëreal gold,
As I now behold them here,
Would imagine not they were
Sepulchres, where human forms,
Like pollution-nourished worms,
To the corpse of greatness cling,
Murdering, and now mouldering:
But if Freedom should awake
In her omnipotence, and shake
From the Celtic Anarch's hold
All the keys of dungeons cold,
Where a hundred cities lie
Chained like thee, ingloriously,
Thou and all thy sister band
Might adorn this sunny land,
Twining memories of old time
With new virtues more sublime;
If not, perish thou and they!—
Clouds which stain truth's rising day
By her sun consumed away—
Earth can spare ye: while like flowers,
In the waste of years and hours,
From your dust new nations spring
With more kindly blossoming.

Perish—let there only be
Floating o'er thy hearthless sea
As the garment of thy sky
Clothes the world immortally,
One remembrance, more sublime
Than the tattered pall of time,
Which scarce hides thy visage wan;—
That a tempest-cleaving Swan
Of the songs of Albion,
Driven from his ancestral streams
By the might of evil dreams,
Found a nest in thee; and Ocean
Welcomed him with such emotion
That its joy grew his, and sprung
From his lips like music flung
O'er a mighty thunder-fit,

Chastening terror:—what though yet
Poesy's unfailing River,
Which through Albion winds forever
Lashing with melodious wave
Many a sacred Poet's grave,
Mourn its latest nursling fled?
What though thou with all thy dead
Scarce can for this fame repay
Aught thine own? oh, rather say
Though thy sins and slaveries foul
Overcloud a sunlike soul?
As the ghost of Homer clings
Round Scamander's wasting springs;
As divinest Shakespeare's might
Fills Avon and the world with light
Like omniscient power which he
Imaged 'mid mortality;
As the love from Petrarch's urn,
Yet amid yon hills doth burn,
A quenchless lamp by which the heart
Sees things unearthly;—so thou art,
Mighty spirit—so shall be
The City that did refuge thee.

Lo, the sun floats up the sky
Like thought-wingèd Liberty,
Till the universal light
Seems to level plain and height;
From the sea a mist has spread,
And the beams of morn lie dead
On the towers of Venice now,
Like its glory long ago,
By the skirts of that gray cloud
Many-domèd Padua proud
Stands, a peopled solitude,
'Mid the harvest-shining plain,
Where the peasant heaps his grain
In the garner of his foe,
And the milk-white oxen slow
With the purple vintage strain,
Heaped upon the creaking wain,
That the brutal Celt may swill

Drunken sleep with savage will;
And the sickle to the sword
Lies unchanged, though many a lord,
Like a weed whose shade is poison,
Overgrows this region's foison,
Sheaves of whom are ripe to come
To destruction's harvest-home:
Men must reap the things they sow,
Force from force must ever flow,
Or worse; but 'tis a bitter woe
That love or reason cannot change
The despot's rage, the slave's revenge,
Padua, thou within whose walls
Those mute guests at festivals,
Son and Mother, Death and Sin,
Played at dice for Ezzelin,
Till Death cried, "I win, I win!"
And Sin cursed to lose the wager,
But Death promised, to assuage her,
That he would petition for
Her to be made Vice-Emperor,
When the destined years were o'er,
Over all between the Po
And the eastern Alpine snow,
Under the mighty Austrian.
Sin smiled so as Sin only can,
And since that time, ay, long before,
Both have ruled from shore to shore,—
That incestuous pair, who follow
Tyrants as the sun the swallow,
As Repentance follows Crime,
And as changes follow Time.

In thine halls the lamp of learning,
Padua, now no more is burning;
Like a meteor, whose wild way
Is lost over the grave of day,
It gleams betrayed and to betray:
Once remotest nations came
To adore that sacred flame,
When it lit not many a hearth
On this cold and gloomy earth:

Now new fires from antique light
Spring beneath the wide world's might;
But their spark lies dead in thee,
Trampled out by Tyranny.
As the Norway woodman quells,
In the depth of piny dells,
One light flame among the brakes,
While the boundless forest shakes,
And its mighty trunks are torn
By the fire thus lowly born:
The spark beneath his feet is dead,
He starts to see the flames it fed
Howling through the darkened sky
With a myriad tongues victoriously,
And sinks down in fear: so thou,
O Tyranny, beholdest now
Light around thee, and thou hearest
The loud flames ascend, and fearest:
Grovel on the earth; ay, hide
In the dust thy purple pride!

Noon descends around me now:
'Tis the noon of autumn's glow,
When a soft and purple mist
Like a vaporous amethyst,
Or an air-dissolvèd star
Mingling light and fragrance, far
From the curved horizon's bound
To the point of Heaven's profound,
Fills the overflowing sky;
And the plains that silent lie
Underneath, the leaves unsodden
Where the infant Frost has trodden
With his morning-wingèd feet,
Whose bright print is gleaming yet;
And the red and golden vines,
Piercing with their trellised lines
The rough, dark-skirted wilderness;
The dun and bladed grass no less,
Pointing from this hoary tower
In the windless air; the flower
Glimmering at my feet; the line

Of the olive-sandalled Apennine
In the south dimly islanded;
And the Alps, whose snows are spread
High between the clouds and sun;
And of living things each one;
And my spirit which so long
Darkened this swift stream of song,—
Interpenetrated lie
By the glory of the sky:
Be it love, light, harmony,
Odour, or the soul of all
Which from Heaven like dew doth fall,
Or the mind which feeds this verse
Peopling the lone universe.

Noon descends, and after noon
Autumn's evening meets me soon,
Leading the infantine moon,
And that one star, which to her
Almost seems to minister
Half the crimson light she brings
From the sunset's radiant springs:
And the soft dreams of the morn
(Which like wingèd winds had borne
To that silent isle, which lies
Mid remembered agonies,
The frail bark of this lone being)
Pass, to other sufferers fleeing,
And its ancient pilot, Pain,
Sits beside the helm again,

Other flowering isles must be
In the sea of Life and Agony:
Other spirits float and flee
O'er that gulf: even now, perhaps,
On some rock the wild wave wraps,
With folded wings they waiting sit
For my bark, to pilot it
To some calm and blooming cove,
Where for me, and those I love,
May a windless bower be built,
Far from passion, pain, and guilt,

In a dell mid lawny hills,
Which the wild sea-murmur fills,
And soft sunshine, and the sound
Of old forests echoing round,
And the light and smell divine
Of all flowers that breathe and shine:
We may live so happy there,
That the Spirits of the Air,
Envying us, may even entice
To our healing Paradise
The polluting multitude;
But their rage would be subdued
By that clime divine and calm,
And the winds whose wings rain balm
On the uplifted soul, and leaves
Under which the bright sea heaves;
While each breathless interval
In their whisperings musical
The inspired soul supplies
With its own deep melodies,
And the love which heals all strife
Circling, like the breath of life,
All things in that sweet abode
With its own mild brotherhood:
They, not it, would change; and soon
Every sprite beneath the moon
Would repent its envy vain,
And the earth grow young again.

Julian and Maddalo

A CONVERSATION

'Do you remember in *Julian and Maddalo*, where [Byron and Shelley], looking towards the Euganean hills, see the great bell of the Insane Asylum swing in the sunset? I found the exact spot. I have seldom felt melancholy so strongly as when standing there.' So in 1861 George Meredith to Captain Maxse, and in 1862 he added, 'In Venice, read *Julian and Maddalo*. It is one of Shelley's best: admirable for simplicity of style, ease, beauty of description and local truth. The philosophy, of course, you may pass.'

Some assert that in the Madman's outbursts concerning his intimate life Shelley recalls his own life with Harriet. This is to deny his deep grief over her death, too deep almost for him ever to speak of it; and also to refuse him the poet's usual interest in observing life outside himself. Shelley told Leigh Hunt that he would recognize two actual characters in Julian and Maddalo, but the third was a study from nature modified by imagination.

> The meadows with fresh streams, the bees with thyme,
> The goats with the green leaves of budding Spring,
> Are saturated not—nor Love with tears.—VIRGIL'S *Gallus*.

Preface

COUNT MADDALO is a Venetian nobleman of ancient family and of great fortune, who, without mixing much in the society of his country-men, resides chiefly at his magnificent palace in that city. He is a person of the most consummate genius, and capable, if he would direct his energies to such an end, of becoming the redeemer of his degraded country. But it is his weakness to be proud: he derives, from a comparison of his own extraordinary mind with the dwarfish intellects that surround him, an intense apprehension of the nothingness of human life. His passions and his powers are incomparably greater than those of other men; and, instead of the latter having been employed in curbing the former, they have mutually lent each other strength. His ambition preys upon itself, for want of objects which it can consider worthy of exertion. I say that Maddalo is proud, because I can find no other word to express the concentered and impatient feelings which consume him; but it is on his own hopes and affections only that he seems to trample, for in social life no human being can be more gentle, patient, and unassuming than Maddalo. He is cheerful, frank, and witty. His more serious conversation is a sort of intoxication; men are held by it as by a spell. He has travelled much; and there is an inexpressible charm in his relation of his adventures in different countries.

Julian is an Englishman of good family, passionately attached to those philosophical notions which assert the power of man over his own mind, and the immense improvements of which, by the extinction of certain moral superstitions, human society may be yet susceptible. Without concealing the evil in the world, he is for ever speculating how good may be made superior. He is a complete infidel, and a scoffer at all things reputed holy; and Maddalo takes a wicked pleasure in drawing out his taunts against religion. What Maddalo thinks on these matters is not exactly known. Julian, in spite of his heterodox opinions, is conjectured by his friends to possess some good qualities. How far this is possible the pious reader will determine. Julian is rather serious.

Of the Maniac I can give no information. He seems, by his own account, to have been disappointed in love. He was evidently a very cultivated and amiable person when in his right senses. His story, told at length, might be like many other stories of the same kind: the unconnected exclamations of his agony will perhaps be found a sufficient comment for the text of every heart.

I RODE one evening with Count Maddalo
Upon the bank of land which breaks the flow
Of Adria towards Venice: a bare strand
Of hillocks, heaped from ever-shifting sand,
Matted with thistles and amphibious weeds.
Such as from earth's embrace the salt ooze breeds,
Is this; an uninhabited sea-side,
Which the lone fisher, when his nets are dried,
Abandons; and no other object breaks
The waste, but one dwarf tree and some few stakes
Broken and unrepaired, and the tide makes
A narrow space of level sand thereon,
Where 'twas our wont to ride while day went down.
This ride was my delight. I love all waste
And solitary places; where we taste
The pleasure of believing what we see
Is boundless, as we wish our souls to be:
And such was this wide ocean, and this shore
More barren than its billows; and yet more
Than all, with a remembered friend I love
To ride as then I rode;—for the winds drove

The living spray along the sunny air
Into our faces; the blue heavens were bare,
Stripped to their depths by the awakening north;
And, from the waves, sound like delight broke forth
Harmonising with solitude, and sent
Into our hearts aëreal merriment.
So, as we rode, we talked, and the swift thought,
Winging itself with laughter, lingered not,
But flew from brain to brain,—such glee was ours,
Charged with light memories of remembered hours,
None slow enough for sadness: till we came
Homeward, which always makes the spirit tame.
This day had been cheerful but cold, and now
The sun was sinking, and the wind also.
Our talk grew somewhat serious, as may be
Talk interrupted with such raillery
As mocks itself, because it cannot scorn
The thoughts it would extinguish:—'twas forlorn,
Yet pleasing, such as once, so poets tell,
The devils held within the dales of Hell
Concerning God, freewill and destiny:
Of all that earth has been or yet may be,
All that vain men imagine or believe,
Or hope can paint or suffering may achieve,
We descanted, and I (for ever still
Is it not wise to make the best of ill?)
Argued against despondency, but pride
Made my companion take the darker side.
The sense that he was greater than his kind
Has struck, methinks, his eagle spirit blind
By gazing on its own exceeding light.
Meanwhile the sun paused ere it should alight,
Over the horizon of the mountains;—Oh,
How beautiful is sunset, when the glow
Of Heaven descends upon a land like thee,
Thou Paradise of exiles, Italy!
Thy mountains, seas, and vineyards, and the towers
Of cities they encircle!—it was ours
To stand on thee, beholding it: and then,
Just where we had dismounted, the Count's men
Were waiting for us with the gondola.—
As those who pause on some delightful way

Though bent on pleasant pilgrimage, we stood
Looking upon the evening, and the flood
Which lay between the city and the shore,
Paved with the image of the sky ... the hoar
And aëry Alps towards the North appeared
Through mist, an heaven-sustaining bulwark reared
Between the East and West; and half the sky
Was roofed with clouds of rich emblazonry
Dark purple at the zenith, which still grew
Down the steep West into a wondrous hue
Brighter than burning gold, even to the rent
Where the swift sun yet paused in his descent
Among the many-folded hills: they were
Those famous Euganean hills, which bear,
As seen from Lido thro' the harbour piles,
The likeness of a clump of peakèd isles.
And then, as if the Earth and Sea had been
Dissolved into one lake of fire, were seen
Those mountains towering as from waves of flame
Around the vaporous sun, from which there came
The inmost purple spirit of light, and made
Their very peaks transparent. 'Ere it fade,'
Said my companion, 'I will show you soon
A better station'—so, o'er the lagune
We glided; and from that funereal bark
I leaned, and saw the city, and could mark
How from their many isles, in evening's gleam,
Its temples and its palaces did seem
Like fabrics of enchantment piled to Heaven.
I was about to speak, when—'We are even
Now at the point I meant,' said Maddalo,
And bade the gondolieri cease to row,
'Look, Julian, on the west, and listen well
If you hear not a deep and heavy bell.'
I looked, and saw between us and the sun
A building on an island; such a one
As age to age might add, for uses vile,
A windowless, deformed and dreary pile;
And on the top an open tower, where hung
A bell, which in the radiance swayed and swung;
We could just hear its hoarse and iron tongue:
The broad sun sunk behind it, and it tolled

In strong and black relief.—'What we behold
Shall be the madhouse and its belfry tower,'
Said Maddalo, 'and ever at this hour
Those who may cross the water, hear that bell
Which calls the maniacs, each one from his cell,
To vespers.'—'As much skill as need to pray
In thanks or hope for their dark lot have they
To their stern maker,' I replied. 'O ho!
You talk as in years past,' said Maddalo.
''Tis strange men change not. You were ever still
Among Christ's flock a perilous infidel,
A wolf for the meek lambs—if you can't swim
Beware of Providence.' I looked on him,
But the gay smile had faded in his eye.
'And such,'—he cried, 'is our mortality,
And this must be the emblem and the sign
Of what should be eternal and divine!—
And like that black and dreary bell, the soul,
Hung in a heaven-illumined tower, must toll
Our thoughts and our desires to meet below
Round the rent heart and pray—as madmen do
For what? they know not,—till the night of death
As sunset that strange vision, severeth
Our memory from itself, and us from all
We sought and yet were baffled.' I recall
The sense of what he said, although I mar
The force of his expressions. The broad star
Of day meanwhile had sunk behind the hill,
And the black bell became invisible,
And the red tower looked gray, and all between
The churches, ships and palaces were seen
Huddled in gloom;—into the purple sea
The orange hues of heaven sunk silently.
We hardly spoke, and soon the gondola
Conveyed me to my lodging by the way.

  The following morn was rainy, cold and dim:
Ere Maddalo arose, I called on him,
And whilst I waited with his child I played;
A lovelier toy sweet Nature never made,
A serious, subtle, wild, yet gentle being,
Graceful without design and unforeseeing,
With eyes—Oh speak not of her eyes!—which seem

Twin mirrors of Italian Heaven, yet gleam
With such deep meaning, as we never see
But in the human countenance: with me
She was a special favourite: I had nursed
Her fine and feeble limbs when she came first
To this bleak world; and she yet seemed to know
On second sight her ancient playfellow,
Less changed than she was by six months or so;
For after her first shyness was worn out
We sate there, rolling billiard balls about,
When the Count entered. Salutations past—
'The word you spoke last night might well have cast
A darkness on my spirit—if man be
The passive thing you say, I should not see
Much harm in the religions and old saws
(Tho' I may never own such leaden laws)
Which break a teachless nature to the yoke:
Mine is another faith'—thus much I spoke
And noting he replied not, added: 'See
This lovely child, blithe, innocent and free;
She spends a happy time with little care,
While we to such sick thoughts subjected are
As came on you last night—it is our will
That thus enchains us to permitted ill—
We might be otherwise—we might be all
We dream of happy, high, majestical.
Where is the love, beauty, and truth we seek
But in our mind? and if we were not weak
Should we be less in deed than in desire?'
'Ay, if we were not weak—and we aspire
How vainly to be strong!' said Maddalo:
'You talk Utopia.' 'It remains to know,'
I then rejoined, 'and those who try may find
How strong the chains are which our spirit bind;
Brittle perchance as straw ... We are assured
Much may be conquered, much may be endured,
Of what degrades and crushes us. We know
That we have power over ourselves to do
And suffer—what, we know not till we try;
But something nobler than to live and die—
So taught those kings of old philosophy
Who reigned, before Religion made men blind;

And those who suffer with their suffering kind
Yet feel their faith, religion.' 'My dear friend,'
Said Maddalo, 'my judgement will not bend
To your opinion, though I think you might
Make such a system refutation-tight
As far as words go. I knew one like you
Who to this city came some months ago,
With whom I argued in this sort, and he
Is now gone mad,—and so he answered me,—
Poor fellow! but if you would like to go
We'll visit him, and his wild talk will show
How vain are such aspiring theories.'
'I hope to prove the induction otherwise,
And that a want of that true theory, still,
Which seeks a "soul of goodness" in things ill
Or in himself or others, has thus bowed
His being—there are some by nature proud,
Who patient in all else demand but this—
To love and be beloved with gentleness;
And being scorned, what wonder if they die
Some living death? this is not destiny
But man's own wilful ill.'
                              As thus I spoke
Servants announced the gondola, and we
Through the fast-falling rain and high-wrought sea
Sailed to the island where the madhouse stands.
We disembarked. The clap of tortured hands,
Fierce yells and howlings and lamentings keen,
And laughter where complaint had merrier been,
Moans, shrieks, and curses, and blaspheming prayers
Accosted us. We climbed the oozy stairs
Into an old courtyard. I heard on high,
Then, fragments of most touching melody,
But looking up saw not the singer there—
Through the black bars in the tempestuous air
I saw, like weeds on a wrecked palace growing,
Long tangled locks flung wildly forth, and flowing,
Of those who on a sudden were beguiled
Into strange silence, and looked forth and smiled
Hearing sweet sounds.—Then I: 'Methinks there were
A cure of these with patience and kind care,
If music can thus move ...'but what is he

Whom we seek here?' 'Of his sad history
I know but this,' said Maddalo: 'he came
To Venice a dejected man, and fame
Said he was wealthy, or he had been so;
Some thought the loss of fortune wrought him woe;
But he was ever talking in such sort
As you do—far more sadly—he seemed hurt,
Even as a man with his peculiar wrong,
To hear but of the oppression of the strong,
Or those absurd deceits (I think with you
In some respects, you know) which carry through
The excellent impostors of this earth
When they outface detection—he had worth,
Poor fellow! but a humorist in his way'.
'Alas, what drove him mad?' 'I cannot say:
A lady came with him from France, and when
She left him and returned, he wandered then
About yon lonely isles of desert sand
Till he grew wild—he had no cash or land
Remaining,—the police had brought him here—
Some fancy took him and he would not bear
Removal; so I fitted up for him
Those rooms beside the sea, to please his whim,
And sent him busts and books and urns for flowers,
Which had adorned his life in happier hours,
And instruments of music—you may guess
A stranger could do little more or less
For one so gentle and unfortunate:
And those are his sweet strains which charm the weight
From madmen's chains, and make this Hell appear
A heaven of sacred silence, hushed to hear.'
'Nay, this was kind of you—he had no claim,
As the world says'—'None but the very same
Which I on all mankind were I as he
Fallen to such deep reverse;—his melody
Is interrupted—now we hear the din
Of madmen, shriek on shriek, again begin;
Let us now visit him; after this strain
He ever communes with himself again,
And sees nor hears not any.' Having said
These words we called the keeper, and he led
To an apartment opening on the sea—

There the poor wretch was sitting mournfully
Near a piano, his pale fingers twined
One with the other, and the ooze and wind
Rushed through an open casement, and did sway
His hair, and starred it with the brackish spray;
His head was leaning on a music book,
And he was muttering, and his lean limbs shook;
His lips were pressed against a folded leaf
In hue too beautiful for health, and grief
Smiled in their motions as they lay apart—
As one who wrought from his own fervid heart
The eloquence of passion, soon he raised
His sad meek face and eyes lustrous and glazed
And spoke—sometimes as one who wrote, and thought
His words might move some heart that heeded not,
If sent to distant lands: and then as one
Reproaching deeds never to be undone
With wondering self-compassion; then his speech
Was lost in grief, and then his words came each
Unmodulated, cold, expressionless,—
But that from one jarred accent you might guess
It was despair made them so uniform:
And all the while the loud and gusty storm
Hissed through the window, and we stood behind
Stealing his accents from the envious wind
Unseen. I yet remember what he said
Distinctly: such impression his words made.

'Month after month,' he cried, 'to bear this load
And as a jade urged by the whip and goad
To drag life on, which like a heavy chain
Lengthens behind with many a link of pain!—
And not to speak my grief—O, not to dare
To give a human voice to my despair,
But live and move, and, wretched thing! smile on
As if I never went aside to groan,
And wear this mask of falsehood even to those
Who are most dear—not for my own repose—
Alas! no scorn or pain or hate could be
So heavy as that falsehood is to me—
But that I cannot bear more altered faces
Than needs must be, more changed and cold embraces,

More misery, disappointment, and mistrust
To own me for their father. Would the dust
Were covered in upon my body now!
That the life ceased to toil within my brow!
And then these thoughts would at the least be fled;
Let us not fear such pain can vex the dead.

'What Power delights to torture us? I know
That to myself I do not wholly owe
What now I suffer, though in part I may.
Alas! none strewed sweet flowers upon the way
Where wandering heedlessly, I met pale Pain
My shadow, which will leave me not again—
If I have erred, there was no joy in error,
But pain and insult and unrest and terror;
I have not as some do, bought penitence
For then,—if love and tenderness and truth
Had overlived hope's momentary youth,
My creed should have redeemed me from repenting;
But loathèd scorn and outrage unrelenting
Met love excited by far other seeming
Until the end was gained: as one from dreaming
Of sweetest peace, I woke, and found my state
Such as it is.
                    'O thou, my spirit's mate,
Who, for thou art compassionate and wise,
Wouldst pity me from thy most gentle eyes
If this sad writing thou shouldst ever see—
My secret groans must be unheard by thee,
Thou wouldst weep tears bitter as blood to know
Thy lost friend's incommunicable woe.

'Ye few by whom my nature has been weighed
In friendship, let me not that name degrade
By placing on your hearts the secret load
Which crushes mine to dust. There is one road
To peace and that is truth, which follow ye!
Love sometimes leads astray to misery.
Yet think not though subdued—and I may well
Say that I am subdued—that the full Hell
Within me would infect the untainted breast
Of sacred nature with its own unrest;

As some perverted beings think to find
In scorn or hate a medicine for the mind
Which scorn or hate have wounded—O how vain!
The dagger heals not but may rend again.
Believe that I am ever still the same
In creed as in resolve, and what may tame
My heart, must leave the understanding free,
Or all would sink in this keen agony—
Nor dream that I will join the vulgar cry;
Or with my silence sanction tyranny;
Or seek a moments' shelter from my pain
In any madness which the world calls gain,
Ambition or revenge or thoughts as stern
As those which make me what I am; or turn
To avarice or misanthropy or lust.
Heap on me soon, O grave, thy welcome dust!
Till then the dungeon may demand its prey,
And Poverty and Shame may meet and say—
Halting beside me on the public way—
"That love-devoted youth is ours: let's sit
Beside him—he may live some six months yet."
Or the red scaffold, as our country bends,
May ask some willing victim, or ye friends
May fall under some sorrow which this heart
Or hand may share or vanquish or avert;
I am prepared—in truth with no proud joy—
To do or suffer aught, as when a boy
I did devote to justice and to love
My nature, worthless now!

                      'I must remove
A veil from my pent mind. 'Tis torn aside!
O, pallid as Death's dedicated bride,
Thou mockery which art sitting by my side,
Am I not wan like thee? at the grave's call
I haste, invited to thy wedding-ball
To greet the ghastly paramour for whom
Thou hast deserted me—and made the tomb
Thy bridal bed. But I beside your feet.
Will lie and watch ye from my winding sheet
Thus—wide awake tho' dead—yet stay, O stay!
Go not so soon—I know not what I say—
Hear but my reasons—I am mad, I fear,

My fancy is o'erwrought—thou art not here.
Pale art thou, 'tis most true—but thou art gone,
Thy work is finished—I am left alone!—

'Nay, was it I who wooed thee to this breast
Which, like a serpent, thou envenomest
As in repayment of the warmth it lent?
Didst thou not seek me for thine own content?
Did not thy love awaken mine? I thought
That thou wert she who said, "You kiss me not
Ever, I fear you do not love me now".
In truth I loved even to my overthrow
Her who would fain forget these words: but they
Cling to her mind, and cannot pass away.

'You say that I am proud; that when I speak
My lip is tortured with the wrongs which break
The spirit it expresses. Never one
Humbled himself before, as I have done;
Even the instinctive worm on which we tread
Turns, though it wound not—then with prostrate head
Sinks in the dusk and writhes like me—and dies;
No: wears a living death of agonies
As the slow shadows of the pointed grass
Mark the eternal periods, his pangs pass
Slow, ever-moving,—making moments be
As mine seem, each an immortality!

'That you had never seen me! never heard
My voice, and more than all had ne'er endured
The deep pollution of my loathed embrace;
That your eyes ne'er had lied love in my face!
That, like some maniac monk, I had torn out
The nerves of manhood by their bleeding root
With mine own quivering fingers, so that ne'er
Our hearts had for a moment mingled there,
To disunite in horror—these were not
With thee like some suppressed and hideous thought
Which flits athwart our musings, but can find
No rest within a pure and gentle mind.
Thou sealedst them with many a bare broad word,
And cered'st my memory o'er them,—for I heard

And can forget not—they were ministered
One after one, those curses. Mix them up
Like self-destroying poisons in one cup.
And they will make one blessing which thou ne'er
Didst imprecate for, on me,—death.

                      'It were
A cruel punishment for one most cruel,
If such can love, to make that love the fuel
Of the mind's hell; hate, scorn, remorse, despair:
But *me*, whose heart a stranger's tear might wear
As water-drops the sandy fountain-stone,
Who loved and pitied all things, and could moan
For woes which others hear not, and could see
The absent with the glance of phantasy,
And with the poor and trampled sit and weep,
Following the captive to his dungeon deep;
Me who am as a nerve o'er which do creep
The else unfelt oppressions of this earth
And was to thee the flame upon thy hearth,
When all beside was cold—that thou on me
Shouldst rain these plagues of blistering agony—
Such curses are from lips once eloquent
With love's too partial praise—let none relent
Who intend deeds too dreadful for a name
Henceforth, if an example for the same
They seek: for thou on me lookedst so, and so—
And didst speak thus and thus I live to show
How much men bear and die not.

                       'Thou wilt tell,
With the grimace of hate, how horrible
It was to meet my love when thine grew less;
Thou wilt admire how I could e'er address
Such features to love's work...this taunt, though true,
(For indeed Nature nor in form nor hue
Bestowed on me her choicest workmanship)
Shall not be thy defence: for since thy lip
Met mine first, years long past, since thine eye kindled
With soft fire under mine, I have not dwindled
Nor changed in mind or body, or in aught
But as love changes what it loveth not

After long years and many trials.
                                        'How vain
Are words; I thought never to speak again,
Not even in secret, not to my own heart—
But from my lips the unwilling accents start,
And from my pen the words flow as I write,
Dazzling my eyes with scalding tears—my sight
Is dim to see that charactered in vain
On this unfeeling leaf which burns the brain
And eats into it, blotting all things fair
And wise and good which time had written there.

'Those who inflict must suffer, for they see
The work of their own hearts, and this must be
Our chastisement or recompense—O child!
I would that thine were like to be more mild
For both our wretched sakes, for thine the most
Who feelest already all that thou hast lost
Without the power to wish it thine again;
And as slow years pass, a funereal train
Each with the ghost of some lost hope or friend
Following it like its shadow, wilt thou bend
No thought on my dead memory?
                                        'Alas, love!
Fear me not ... against thee I would not move
A finger in despite. Do I not live
That thou mayst have less bitter cause to grieve?
I give thee tears for scorn and love for hate;
And that thy lot may be less desolate
Than his on whom thou tramplest, I refrain
From that sweet sleep which medicines all pain.
Then, when thou speakest of me, never say
"He could forgive not." Here I cast away
All human passions, all revenge, all pride;
I think, speak, act no ill; I do but hide
Under these words, like embers, every spark
Of that which has consumed me—quick and dark
The grave is yawning; as its roof shall cover
My limbs with dust and worms under and over
So let Oblivion hide this grief. The air
Closes upon my accents, as despair
Upon my heart—let death upon my care!'

He ceased, and overcome leant back awhile,
Then rising, with a melancholy smile
Went to a sofa, and lay down, and slept
A heavy sleep, and in his dreams he wept
And muttered some familiar name, and we
Wept without shame in his society.
I think I never was impressed so much;
The man who were not, must have lacked a touch
Of human nature—then we lingered not,
Although our argument was quite forgot,
But calling the attendants went to dine
At Maddalo's; yet neither cheer nor wine
Could give us spirits, for we talked of him
And nothing else, till daylight made stars dim;
And we agreed his was some dreadful ill
Wrought on him boldly, yet unspeakable,
By a dear friend; some deadly change in love
Of one vowed deeply which he dreamed not of;
For whose sake he, it seemed, had fixed a blot
Of falsehood on his mind which flourished not
But in the light of all-beholding truth;
And having stamped this canker on his youth
She had abandoned him—and how much more
Might be his woe, we guessed not; he had store
Of friends and fortune once, as we could guess
From his nice habits and his gentleness;
These were now lost—it were a grief indeed
If he had changed one unsustaining reed
For all that such a man might else adorn.
The colours of his mind seemed yet unworn;
For the wild language of his grief was high,
Such as in measure were called poetry.
And I remember one remark which then
Maddalo made: he said: 'Most wretched men
Are cradled into poetry by wrong,
They learn in suffering what they teach in song.'

If I had been an unconnected man
I, from the moment, should have formed some plan
Never to leave sweet Venice, for to me
It was delight to ride by the lone sea;
And then, the town is silent—one may write

Or read in gondolas by day or night,
Having the little brazen lamp alight,
Unseen, uninterrupted; books are there,
Pictures, and casts from all those statues fair
Which were twin-born with poetry, and all
We seek in towns, with little to recall
Regrets for the green country; I might sit
In Maddalo's great palace, and his wit
And subtle talk would cheer the winter night
And make me know myself, and the firelight
Would flash upon our faces, till the day
Might dawn and make me wonder at my stay.
But I had friends in London too: the chief
Attraction here was that I sought relief
From the deep tenderness that maniac wrought
Within me—'twas perhaps an idle thought,
But I imagined that if day by day
I watched him, and but seldom went away,
And studied all the beatings of his heart
With zeal, as men study some stubborn art
For their own good, and could by patience find
An entrance to the caverns of his mind,
I might reclaim him from his dark estate.
In friendships I had been most fortunate,—
Yet never saw I one whom I would call
More willingly my friend; and this was all
Accomplished not; such dreams of baseless good
Oft come and go in crowds or solitude
And leave no trace—but what I now designed
Made for long years impression on my mind.
The following morning, urged by my affairs,
I left bright Venice.
                        After many years
And many changes I returned; the name
Of Venice and its aspect was the same;
But Maddalo was travelling far away
Among the mountains of Armenia.
His dog was dead: his child had now become
A woman; such as it has been my doom
To meet with few,—a wonder of this earth,
Where there is little of transcendent worth,—
Like one of Shakespeare's women: kindly she,

And with a manner beyond courtesy,
Received her father's friend; and when I asked
Of the lorn maniac, she her memory tasked,
And told as she had heard the mournful tale:
'That the poor sufferer's health began to fail
Two years from my departure, but that then
The lady who had left him, came again.
Her mien had been imperious, but she now
Looked meek—perhaps remorse had brought her low.
Her coming made him better, and they stayed
Together at my father's—for I played,
As I remember, with the lady's shawl—
I might be six years old—but after all
She left him'. 'Why, her heart must have been tough:
How did it end?' 'And was not this enough?
They met, they parted'—'Child, is there no more?'
'Something within that interval which bore
The stamp of *why* they parted, *how* they met:
Yet if thine agèd eyes disdain to wet
Those wrinkled cheeks with youth's remembered tears,
Ask me no more, but let the silent tears
Be closed and cered over their memory
As yon mute marble where their corpses lie.'
I urged and questioned still, she told me how
All happened—but the cold world shall not know.

Marenghi

LET those who pine in pride or in revenge,
  Or think that ill for ill should be repaid,
Who barter wrong for wrong, until the exchange
  Ruins the merchants of such thriftless trade,
Visit the tower of Vado, and unlearn
Such bitter faith beside Marenghi's urn.

★ ★ ★

Was Florence the liberticide? that band
  Of free and glorious brothers who had planted,
Like a green isle mid Aethiopian sand,
  A nation amid slaveries, disenchanted
Of many impious faiths—wise, just, do they,
Does Florence, gorge the sated tyrants' prey?

O foster-nurse of man's abandoned glory,
  Since Athens, its great mother, sunk in splendour;
Thou shadowest forth that mighty shape in story,
  As ocean its wrecked fanes, severe yet tender:—
The light-invested angel Poesy
Was drawn from the dim world to welcome thee.

And thou in painting didst transcribe all taught
  By loftiest meditations; marble knew
The sculptor's fearless soul—and as he wrought,
  The grace of his own power and freedom grew.
And more than all, heroic, just, sublime
Thou wert among the false ... was this thy crime?

Yes; and on Pisa's marble walls the twine
  Of direst weeds hangs garlanded—the snake
Inhabits its wrecked palaces;—in thine
  A beast of subtler venom new doth make
Its lair, and sits amid their glories overthrown,
And this thy victim's fate is as thine own.

The sweetest flowers are ever frail and rare,
　　And love and freedom blossom but to wither;
And good and ill like vines entangled are,
　　So that their grapes may oft be plucked together;—
Divide the vintage ere thou drink, then make
Thy heart rejoice for dead Marenghi's sake.

* * *

No record of his crime remains in story,
　　But if the morning bright as evening shone,
It was some high and holy deed, by glory
　　Pursued into forgetfulness, which won
From the blind crowd he made secure and free
The patriot's meed, toil, death, and infamy.

For when by sound of trumpet was declared
　　A price upon his life, and there was set
A penalty of blood on all who shared
　　So much of water with him as might wet
His lips, which speech divided not—he went
Alone, as you may guess, to banishment.

Amid the mountains, like a hunted beast,
　　He hid himself, and hunger, toil, and cold
Month after month endured; it was a feast
　　Whene'er he found those globes of deep-red gold
Which in the woods the strawberry-tree doth bear,
Suspended in their emerald atmosphere.

And in the roofless huts of vast morasses,
　　Deserted by the fever-stricken serf,
All overgrown with reeds and long rank grasses,
　　And hillocks heaped of moss-inwoven turf,
And where the huge and speckled aloe made,
Rooted in stones, a broad and pointed shade,

He housed himself. There is a point of strand
　　Near Vado's tower and town; and on one side
The treacherous marsh divides it from the land,
　　Shadowed by pine and ilex forests wide,
And on the other, creeps eternally
Through muddy weeds the shallow sullen sea.

Here the earth's breath is pestilence, and few
　　But things whose nature is at war with life—
Snakes and ill worms—endure its mortal dew.
　　The trophies of the clime's victorious strife—
And ringed horns which the buffalo did wear,
And the wolf's dark gray scalp who tracked him there.

And at the utmost point ... stood there
　　The relics of a reed-inwoven cot,
Thatched with broad flags. An outlawed murderer
　　Had lived seven days there: the pursuit was hot
When he was cold. The birds that were his grave
Fell dead after their feast in Vado's wave.

There must have burned within Marenghi's breast
　　That fire, more warm and bright than life and hope,
(Which to the martyr makes his dungeon ....
　　More joyous than free heaven's majestic cope
To his oppressor), warring with decay,—
Or he could ne'er have lived years, day by day.

Nor was his state so lone as you might think.
　　He had tamed every newt and snake and toad,
And every seagull which sailed down to drink
　　Those freshes ere the death-mist went abroad.
And each one, with peculiar talk and play,
Wiled, not untaught, his silent time away.

And the marsh-meteors, like tame beasts, at night
　　Came licking with blue tongues his veinèd feet;
And he would watch them, as, like spirits bright,
　　In many entangled figures quaint and sweet
To some enchanted music they would dance—
Until they vanished at the first moon-glance.

He mocked the stars by grouping on each weed
　　The summer dew-globes in the golden dawn;
And, ere the hoar-frost languished, he could read
　　Its pictured path, as on bare spots of lawn
Its delicate brief touch in silver weaves
The likeness of the wood's remembered leaves.

And many a fresh Spring morn would he awaken—
  While yet the unrisen sun made glow, like iron
Quivering in crimson fire, the peaks unshaken
  Of mountains and blue isles which did environ
With air-clad crags that plain of land and sea,—
And feel ....   liberty.

And in the moonless nights, when the dun ocean
  Heaved underneath wide heaven, star-impearled,
Starting from dreams ...
  Communed with the immeasurable world;
And felt his life beyond his limbs dilated,
Till his mind grew like that it contemplated.

His food was the wild fig and strawberry;
  The milky pine-nuts which the autumn-blast
Shakes into the tall grass; or such small fry
  As from the sea by winter-storms are cast;
And the coarse bulbs of iris-flowers he found
Knotted in clumps under the spongy ground.

And so were kindled powers and thoughts which made
  His solitude less dark. When memory came
(For years gone by leave each a deepening shade),
  His spirit basked in its internal flame,—
As, when the black storm hurries round at night,
The fisher basks beside his red firelight.

Yet human hopes and cares and faiths and errors,
  Like billows unawakened by the wind,
Slept in Marenghi still; but that all terrors,
  Weakness, and doubt, had withered in his mind.
His couch ....

.   .   .   .   .   .

And, when he saw beneath the sunset's planet
  A black ship walk over the crimson ocean,—
Its pennon streaming on the blasts that fan it,
  Its sails and ropes all tense and without motion,
Like the dark ghost of the unburied even
Striding athwart the orange-coloured heaven,—

The thought of his own kind who made the soul
  Which sped that wingèd shape through night and day,—
The thought of his own country ...

Prometheus Unbound

A LYRICAL DRAMA IN FOUR ACTS

Audisne haec Amphiaraë, sub terram abdite?

In this, the highest expression of his creed of human advancement and indeed the growing beauty, pleasure and fruitfulness of all nature Shelley employs one of the classical myths which haunted the mind of Europe in his age. Even his dreary cousin Tom Medwin grew poetical upon it; Goethe had already been one of its powerful interpreters. Prometheus, as Shelley says, in the theatre of Aeschylus, overthrew Zeus on a different plan from his own, which however is not beyond question. 'Fate, Time, Occasion, Chance and Change' defeat the alleged Oppressor.

But Shelley covers the uncertainty there by summoning the peculiar deity Demogorgon, who had previously appeared in English poetry at the call of Spenser and Milton. The other name ascribed to this unanswerable functionary is Eternity. With infallible discernment Shelley allots to him among his dramatis personæ the last profound comments and verities of his poem.

The musical creativeness and the ballet-making in *Prometheus Unbound* and all the radiant variety of the scenes-moving before the mind's eye, in fact the delightful developments of the fable itself, are said to obscure the serious argument or biological substance within. Shelley, young as he was, harmonized in his master-work the satisfactions of the innovative artist, the resources of a man of learning and the far view of a seer of history in its extent. As elsewhere he presents something of the scientist's notebook in the colours of magnificent or curious fantasy. In the beginning he seems mostly the Greek scholar, imitating Aeschylus in English. Presently he finds his freedom, and that is appropriate to the transition from Prometheus on the rock to the happiness won for life by his endurance. But there is no casual release into pure optimism, and Shelley at the close moves from lyric lightness into a solemn music.

From Shelley's Preface

THE Greek tragic writers, in selecting as their subject any portion of their national history or mythology, employed in their treatment of it a certain arbitrary discretion. They by no means conceived themselves bound to adhere to the common interpretation or to imitate in story as in title their rivals and predecessors. Such a system would have amounted to a resignation of those claims to preference over their competitors which incited the composition. The Agamemnonian story was exhibited on the Athenian theatre with as many variations as dramas.

I have presumed to employ a similar licence. The *Prometheus Unbound* of Aeschylus supposed the reconciliation of Jupiter with his victim as the price of the disclosure of the danger threatened to his empire by the consummation of his marriage with Thetis. Thetis, according to this view of the subject, was given in marriage to Peleus, and Prometheus, by the permission of Jupiter, delivered from his captivity by Hercules. Had I framed my story on this model, I should have done no more than have attempted to restore the lost drama of Aeschylus; an ambition which, if my preference to this mode of treating the subject had incited me to cherish, the recollection of the high comparison such an attempt would challenge might well abate. But, in truth, I was averse from a catastrophe so feeble as that of reconciling the Champion with the Oppressor of mankind. The moral interest of the fable, which is so powerfully sustained by the sufferings and endurance of Prometheus, would be annihilated if we could conceive of him as unsaying his high language and quailing before his sucessful and perfidious adversary. The only imaginary being resembling in any degree Prometheus, is Satan; and Prometheus is, in my judgement, a more poetical character than Satan, because, in addition to courage, and majesty, and firm and patient opposition to omnipotent force, he is susceptible of being described as exempt from the taints of ambition, envy, revenge, and a desire for personal aggrandisement; which, in the Hero of *Paradise Lost*, interfere with the interest. The character of Satan engenders in the mind a pernicious casuistry which leads us to weigh his faults with his wrongs, and to excuse the former because the latter exceed all measure. In the minds of those who consider that magnificent fiction with a religious feeling it engenders something worse. But Prometheus is, as it were, the type of the highest perfection of moral and intellectual nature, impelled by the purest and the truest motives to the best and noblest ends.

This Poem was chiefly written upon the mountainous ruins of the Baths of Caracalla, among the flowery glades, and thickets of odoriferous blossoming trees, which are extended in ever winding labyrinths upon its immense platforms and dizzy arches suspended in the air. The bright blue sky of Rome, and the effect of the vigorous awakening spring in that divinest climate, and the new life with which it drenches the spirits even to intoxication, were the inspiration of this drama.

The imagery which I have employed will be found, in many instances, to have been drawn from the operations of the human mind, or from those external actions by which they are expressed. This is unusual in modern poetry, although Dante and Shakespeare are full of instances of the same kind: Dante indeed more than any other poet, and with greater success. But the Greek poets, as writers to whom no resource of awakening the sympathy of their contemporaries was unknown, were in the habitual use of this power; and it is the study of their works (since a higher merit would probably be denied me) to which I am willing that my readers should impute this singularity.

One word is due in candour to the degree in which the study of

contemporary writings may have tinged my composition, for such
has been a topic of censure with regard to poems far more popular,
and indeed more deservedly popular, than mine. It is impossible that
any one who inhabits the same age with such writers as those who
stand in the foremost ranks of our own, can conscientiously assure
himself that his language and tone of thought may not have been
modified by the study of the productions of those extraordinary
intellects. It is true, that, not the spirit of their genius, but the forms in
which it has manifested itself, are due less to the peculiarities of their
own minds than to the peculiarity of the moral and intellectual con-
dition of the minds among which they have been produced. Thus a
number of writers possess the form whilst they want the spirit of
those whom, it is alleged, they imitate; because the former is the en-
dowment of the age in which they live, and the latter must be the
uncommunicated lightning of their own mind.

Dramatis Personæ

PROMETHEUS	APOLLO	HERCULES
DEMOGORGON	MERCURY	THE PHANTASM OF JUPITER
JUPITER	ASIA	THE SPIRIT OF THE EARTH
THE EARTH	PANTHEA } Ocean-ides	THE SPIRIT OF THE MOON
OCEAN	IONE	SPIRITS OF THE HOURS
	SPIRITS ECHOES FAUNS FURIES	

Act I

SCENE.—*A Ravine of Icy Rocks in the Indian Caucasus.* PRO-
METHEUS *is discovered bound to the Precipice.* PANTHEA *and*
IONE *are seated at his feet. Time, night. During the Scene,
morning slowly breaks.*

Prometheus. Monarch of Gods and Dæmons, and all Spirits
But One, who throng those bright and rolling worlds
Which Thou and I alone of living things
Behold with sleepless eyes! regard this Earth
Made multitudinous with thy slaves, whom thou
Requitest for knee-worship, prayer, and praise,
And toil, and hecatombs of broken hearts,
With fear and self-contempt and barren hope.
Whilst me, who am thy foe, eyeless in hate,
Hast thou made reign and triumph, to thy scorn,
O'er mine own misery and thy vain revenge.

Three thousand years of sleep-unsheltered hours,
And moments aye divided by keen pangs
Till they seemed years, torture and solitude,
Scorn and despair,—these are mine empire:—
More glorious far than that which thou surveyest
From thine unenvied throne, O Mighty God!
Almighty, had I deigned to share the shame
Of thine ill tyranny, and hung not here
Nailed to this wall of eagle-baffling mountain,
Black, wintry, dead, unmeasured; without herb,
Insect, or beast, or shape or sound of life.
Ah me! alas, pain, pain ever, for ever!

No change, no pause, no hope! Yet I endure.
I ask the Earth, have not the mountains felt?
I ask yon Heaven, the all-beholding Sun,
Has it not seen? The Sea, in storm or calm,
Heaven's ever-changing Shadow, spread below,
Have its deaf waves not heard my agony?
Ah me! alas, pain, pain ever, for ever!

The crawling glaciers pierce me with the spears
Of their moon-freezing crystals, the bright chains
Eat with their burning cold into my bones.
Heaven's wingèd hound, polluting from thy lips
His beak in poison not his own, tears up
My heart; and shapeless sights come wandering by,
The ghastly people of the realm of dream,
Mocking me: and the Earthquake-fiends are charged
To wrench the rivets from my quivering wounds
When the rocks split and close again behind:
While from their loud abysses howling throng
The genii of the storm, urging the rage
Of whirlwind, and afflict me with keen hail.
And yet to me welcome is day and night,
Whether one breaks the hoar frost of the morn,
Or starry, dim, and slow, the other climbs
The leaden-coloured east; for then they lead
The wingless, crawling hours, one among whom
—As some dark Priest hales the reluctant victim—
Shall drag thee, cruel King, to kiss the blood
From these pale feet, which then might trample thee

If they disdained not such a prostrate slave.
Disdain! Ah no! I pity thee. What ruin
Will hunt thee undefended through wide Heaven!
How will thy soul, cloven to its depth with terror,
Gape like a hell within! I speak in grief
Not exultation, for I hate no more,
As then ere misery made me wise. The curse
Once breathed on thee I would recall. Ye Mountains,
Whose many-voicèd Echoes, through the mist
Of cataracts, flung the thunder of that spell!
Ye icy Springs, stagnant with wrinkling frost,
Which vibrated to hear me, and then crept
Shuddering through India! Thou serenest Air,
Through which the Sun walks burning without beams!
And ye swift Whirlwinds, who on poisèd wings
Hung mute and moveless o'er yon hushed abyss,
As thunder, louder than your own, made rock
The orbèd world! If then my words had power,
Though I am changed so that aught evil wish
Is dead within; although no memory be
Of what is hate, let them not lose it now!
What was that curse? for ye all heard me speak.

First Voice (from the Mountains)

Thrice three hundred thousand years
    O'er the Earthquake's couch we stood:
Oft, as men convulsed with fears,
    We trembled in our multitude.

Second Voice (from the Springs)

Thunderbolts had parched our water,
    We had been stained with bitter blood,
And had run mute, 'mid shrieks of slaughter,
    Thro' a city and a solitude.

Third Voice (from the Air)

I had clothed, since Earth uprose,
    Its wastes in colours not their own,
And oft had my serene repose
    Been cloven by many a rending groan.

Fourth Voice (from the Whirlwinds)

We had soared beneath these mountains
    Unresting ages; nor had thunder,
Nor yon volcano's flaming fountains,
    Nor any power above or under
    Ever made us mute with wonder.

First Voice

But never bowed our snowy crest
As at the voice of thine unrest.

Second Voice

Never such a sound before
To the Indian waves we bore.
A pilot asleep on the howling sea
Leaped up from the deck in agony,
And heard, and cried, 'Ah, woe is me!'
And died as mad as the wild waves be.

Third Voice

By such dread words from Earth to Heaven
My still realm was never riven:
When its wound was closed, there stood
Darkness o'er the day like blood.

Fourth Voice

And we shrank back: for dreams of ruin
To frozen caves our flight pursuing
Made us keep silence—thus—and thus—
Though silence is as hell to us.

The Earth. The tongueless Caverns of the craggy hills
Cried, 'Misery!' then; the hollow Heaven replied,
'Misery!' And the Ocean's purple waves,
Climbing the land, howled to the lashing winds,
And the pale nations heard it, 'Misery!'
    Prometheus. I heard a sound of voices: not the voice
Which I gave forth. Mother, thy sons and thou
Scorn him, without whose all-enduring will
Beneath the fierce omnipotence of Jove,
Both they and thou had vanished, like thin mist
Unrolled on the morning wind. Know ye not me,

The Titan? He who made his agony
The barrier to your else all-conquering foe?
Oh, rock-embosomed lawns, and snow-fed streams,
Now seen athwart frore vapours, deep below,
Through whose o'ershadowing woods I wandered once
With Asia, drinking life from her loved eyes:
Why scorns the spirit which informs ye, now
To commune with me? me alone, who checked,
As one who checks a fiend-drawn charioteer,
The falsehood and the force of him who reigns
Supreme, and with the groans of pining slaves
Fills your dim glens and liquid wildernesses:
Why answer ye not, still? Brethren!

    The Earth.   They dare not.
    Prometheus. Who dares? for I would hear that curse again.
Ha, what an awful whisper rises up!
'Tis scarce like sound: it tingles through the frame
As lightning tingles, hovering ere it strike.
Speak, Spirit! from thine inorganic voice
I only know that thou art moving near,
And love. How cursed I him?

    The Earth.   How canst thou hear
Who knowest not the language of the dead?
    Prometheus. Thou art a living spirit; speak as they.
    The Earth. I dare not speak like life, lest Heaven's fell King
Should hear, and link me to some wheel of pain
More torturing than the one whereon I roll.
Subtle thou art and good, and though the Gods
Hear not this voice, yet thou art more than God,
Being wise and kind: earnestly hearken now.
    Prometheus. Obscurely through my brain, like shadows dim,
Sweep awful thoughts, rapid and thick. I feel
Faint, like one mingled in entwining love;
Yet 'tis not pleasure.

    The Earth.   No, thou canst not hear:
Thou art immortal, and this tongue is known
Only to those who die.

    Prometheus.   And what art thou,
O melancholy Voice?

    The Earth.   I am the Earth,
Thy mother; she within whose stony veins,
To the last fibre of the loftiest tree

Whose thin leaves trembled in the frozen air,
Joy ran, as blood within a living frame,
When thou didst from her bosom, like a cloud
Of glory, arise, a spirit of keen joy!
And at thy voice her pining sons uplifted
Their prostrate brows from the polluting dust,
And our almighty Tyrant with fierce dread
Grew pale, until his thunder chained thee here.
Then, see those million worlds which burn and roll
Around us: their inhabitants beheld
My spherèd light wane in wide Heaven; the sea
Was lifted by strange tempest, and new fire
From earthquake-rifted mountains of bright snow
Shook its portentous hair beneath Heaven's frown;
Lightning and Inundation vexed the plains;
Blue thistles bloomed in cities; foodless toads
Within voluptuous chambers panting crawled:
When Plague had fallen on man, and beast, and worm,
And Famine; and black blight on herb and tree;
And in the corn, and vines, and meadow-grass,
Teemed ineradicable poisonous weeds
Draining their growth, for my wan breast was dry
With grief; and the thin air, my breath, was stained
With the contagion of a mother's hate
Breathed on her child's destroyer; ay, I heard
Thy curse, the which, if thou rememberest not,
Yet my innumerable seas and streams,
Mountains, and caves, and winds, and yon wide air,
And the inarticulate people of the dead,
Preserve, a treasured spell. We meditate
In secret joy and hope those dreadful words,
But dare not speak them.

   Prometheus.   Venerable mother!
All else who live and suffer take from thee
Some comfort; flowers, and fruits, and happy sounds
And love, though fleeting; these may not be mine.
But mine own words, I pray, deny me not.

   The Earth. They shall be told. Ere Babylon was dust,
The Magus Zoroaster, my dead child,
Met his own image walking in the garden.
That apparition, sole of men, he saw.
For know there are two worlds of life and death:

One that which thou beholdest; but the other
Is underneath the grave, where do inhabit
The shadows of all forms that think and live
Till death unite them and they part no more;
Dreams and the light imaginings of men,
And all that faith creates or love desires,
Terrible, strange, sublime and beauteous shapes.
There thou art, and dost hang, a writhing shade,
'Mid whirlwind-peopled mountains; all the gods
Are there, and all the powers of nameless worlds,
Vast, sceptred phantoms; heroes, men, and beasts;
And Demogorgon, a tremendous gloom;
And he, the supreme Tyrant, on his throne
Of burning gold. Son, one of these shall utter
The curse which all remember. Call at will
Thine own ghost, or the ghost of Jupiter,
Hades or Typhon, or what mightier Gods
From all-prolific Evil, since thy ruin
Have sprung, and trampled on my prostrate sons.
Ask, and they must reply: so the revenge
Of the Supreme may sweep through vacant shades,
As rainy wind through the abandoned gate
Of a fallen palace.
    Prometheus.   Mother, let not aught
Of that which may be evil, pass again
My lips, or those of aught resembling me.
Phantasm of Jupiter, arise, appear!

Ione

My wings are folded o'er mine ears:
    My wings are crossèd o'er mine eyes:
Yet through their silver shade appears,
    And through their lulling plumes arise,
A Shape, a throng of sounds;
    May it be no ill to thee
  O thou of many wounds!
Near whom, for our sweet sister's sake,
Ever thus we watch and wake.

Panthea

The sound is of whirlwind underground,
　　Earthquake, and fire, and mountains cloven;
The shape is awful like the sound,
　　Clothed in dark purple, star-inwoven.
A sceptre of pale gold
　　To stay steps proud, o'er the slow cloud
His veinèd hand doth hold.
Cruel he looks, but calm and strong.
Like one who does, not suffers wrong.

Phantasm of Jupiter. Why have the secret powers of this strange world
Driven me, a frail and empty phantom, hither
On direst storms? What unaccustomed sounds
Are hovering on my lips, unlike the voice
With which our pallid race hold ghastly talk
In darkness? And, proud sufferer, who art thou?

Prometheus. Tremendous Image, as thou art must be
He whom thou shadowest forth. I am his foe,
The Titan. Speak the words which I would hear,
Although no thought inform thine empty voice.

The Earth. Listen! And though your echoes must be mute,
Gray mountains, and old woods, and haunted springs,
Prophetic caves, and isle-surrounding streams,
Rejoice to hear what yet ye cannot speak.

Phantasm. A spirit seizes me and speaks within:
It tears me as fire tears a thunder-cloud.

Panthea. See, how he lifts his mighty looks, the Heaven
Darkens above.

Ione.　　　　He speaks! O shelter me!

Prometheus. I see the curse on gestures proud and cold,
And looks of firm defiance, and calm hate,
And such despair as mocks itself with smiles,
Written as on a scroll: yet speak: Oh, speak!

Phantasm

Fiend, I defy thee! with a calm, fixed mind,
　　All that thou canst inflict I bid thee do;
Foul Tyrant both of Gods and Human-kind,
　　One only being shalt thou not subdue.
Rain then thy plagues upon me here,

Ghastly disease, and frenzying fear;
And let alternate frost and fire
Eat into me, and be thine ire
Lightning, and cutting hail, and legioned forms
Of furies, driving by upon the wounding storms.

Ay, do thy worst. Thou art omnipotent.
O'er all things but thyself I gave thee power,
And my own will. Be thy swift mischiefs sent
To blast mankind, from yon ethereal tower.
Let thy malignant spirit move
In darkness over those I love:
On me and mine I imprecate
The utmost torture of thy hate;
And thus devote to sleepless agony
This undeclining head while thou must reign on high.

But thou, who art the God and Lord: O, thou,
Who fillest with thy soul this world of woe,
To whom all things of Earth and Heaven do bow
In fear and worship: all-prevailing foe!
I curse thee! let a sufferer's curse
Clasp thee, his torturer, like remorse;
Till thine Infinity shall be
A robe of envenomed agony;
And thine Omnipotence a crown of pain,
To cling like burning gold round thy dissolving brain.

Heap on thy soul, by virtue of this Curse,
Ill deeds, then be thou damned, beholding good;
Both infinite as is the universe,
And thou, and thy self-torturing solitude.
An awful image of calm power
Though now thou sittest, let the hour
Come, when thou must appear to be
That which thou art internally;
And after many a false and fruitless crime
Scorn track thy lagging fall through boundless space and time.

Prometheus. Were these my words, O Parent?
The Earth.   They were thine.
Prometheus. It doth repent me: words are quick and vain:

Grief for awhile is blind, and so was mine.
I wish no living thing to suffer pain.

The Earth

Misery, Oh misery to me,
That Jove at length should vanquish thee.
Wail, howl aloud, Land and Sea,
The Earth's rent heart shall answer ye.
Howl, Spirits of the living and the dead,
Your refuge, your defence lies fallen and vanquishèd.

First Echo

Lies fallen and vanquishèd!

Second Echo

Fallen and vanquishèd!

Ione

Fear not: 'tis but some passing spasm,
    The Titan is unvanquished still.
But see, where through the azure chasm
    Of yon forked and snowy hill
Trampling the slant winds on high
    With golden-sandalled feet, that glow
Under plumes of purple dye,
Like rose-ensanguined ivory,
    A Shape comes now,
Stretching on high from his right hand
A serpent-cinctured wand.

Panthea

'Tis Jove's world-wandering herald, Mercury.

Ione

And who are those with hydra tresses
    And iron wings that climb the wind,
Whom the frowning God represses
    Like vapours steaming up behind,
Clanging loud, an endless crowd—

Panthea

These are Jove's tempest-walking hounds,
Whom he gluts with groans and blood,
When charioted on sulphurous cloud
    He bursts Heaven's bounds.

Ione

Are they now led, from the thin dead
On new pangs to be fed?

Panthea

The Titan looks as ever, firm, not proud.

First Fury. Ha! I scent life!
Second Fury.   Let me but look into his eyes!
Third Fury. The hope of torturing him smells like a heap
Of corpses, to a death-bird after battle.
   First Fury. Darest thou delay, O Herald? take cheer, Hounds
Of Hell: what if the Son of Maia soon
Should make us food and sport—who can please long
The Omnipotent?
   Mercury.   Back to your towers of iron,
And gnash, beside the streams of fire and wail,
Your foodless teeth. Geryon, arise! and Gorgon,
Chimæra, and thou Sphinx, subtlest of fiends
Who ministered to Thebes Heaven's poisoned wine,
Unnatural love, and more unnatural hate:
These shall perform your task.
   First Fury.   Oh, mercy! mercy!
We die with our desire: drive us not back!
   Mercury. Crouch then in silence.
                           Awful Sufferer!
To thee unwilling, most unwillingly
I come, by the great Father's will driven down,
To execute a doom of new revenge.
Alas! I pity thee, and hate myself
That I can do no more: aye from thy sight
Returning, for a season, Heaven seems Hell,
So thy worn form pursues me night and day,
Smiling reproach. Wise art thou, firm and good,
But vainly wouldst stand forth alone in strife
Against the Omnipotent; as yon clear lamps

That measure and divide the weary years
From which there is no refuge, long have taught
And long must teach. Even now thy Torturer arms
With the strange might of unimagined pains
The powers who scheme slow agonies in Hell,
And my commission is to lead them here,
Or what more subtle, foul, or savage fiends
People the abyss, and leave them to their task.
Be it not so! there is a secret known
To thee, and to none else of living things,
Which may transfer the sceptre of wide Heaven,
The fear of which perplexes the Supreme:
Clothe it in words, and bid it clasp his throne
In intercession; bend thy soul in prayer,
And like a suppliant in some gorgeous fane,
Let the will kneel within thy haughty heart:
For benefits and meek submission tame
The fiercest and the mightiest.

 Prometheus.   Evil minds
Change good to their own nature. I gave all
He has; and in return he chains me here
Years, ages, night and day: whether the Sun
Split my parched skin, or in the moony night
The crystal-wingèd snow cling round my hair:
Whilst my belovèd race is trampled down
By his thought-executing ministers.
Such is the tyrant's recompense: 'tis just:
He who is evil can receive no good;
And for a world bestowed, or a friend lost,
He can feel hate, fear, shame; not gratitude:
He but requites me for his own misdeed.
Kindness to such is keen reproach, which breaks
With bitter stings the light sleep of Revenge.
Submission, thou dost know I cannot try:
For what submission but that fatal word,
The death-seal of mankind's captivity,
Like the Sicilian's hair-suspended sword,
Which trembles o'er his crown, would he accept,
Or could I yield? Which yet I will not yield.
Let others flatter Crime, where it sits throned
In brief Omnipotence: secure are they:
For Justice, when triumphant, will weep down

Pity, not punishment, on her own wrongs,
Too much avenged by those who err. I wait,
Enduring thus, the retributive hour
Which since we spake is even nearer now.
But hark, the hell-hounds clamour: fear delay:
Behold! Heaven lowers under thy Father's frown.
   Mercury. Oh, that we might be spared: I to inflict
And thou to suffer! Once more answer me:
Thou knowest not the period of Jove's power?
   Prometheus. I know but this, that it must come.
   Mercury.   Alas!
Thou canst not count thy years to come of pain?
   Prometheus. They last while Jove must reign: nor more, nor less
Do I desire or fear.
   Mercury.   Yet pause, and plunge
Into Eternity, where recorded time,
Even all that we imagine, age on age,
Seems but a point, and the reluctant mind
Flags wearily in its unending flight,
Till it sink, dizzy, blind, lost, shelterless;
Perchance it has not numbered the slow years
Which thou must spend in torture, unreprieved?
   Prometheus. Perchance no thought can count them, yet they pass.
   Mercury. If thou might'st dwell among the Gods the while Lapped in voluptuous joy?
   Prometheus.   I would not quit
This bleak ravine, these unrepentant pains.
   Mercury. Alas! I wonder at, yet pity thee.
   Prometheus. Pity the self-despising slaves of Heaven,
Not me, within whose mind sits peace serene.
As light in the sun, throned: how vain is talk!
Call up the fiends.
   Ione.   O, sister, look! White fire
Has cloven to the roots yon huge snow-loaded cedar;
How fearfully God's thunder howls behind!
   Mercury. I must obey his words and thine: alas!
Most heavily remorse hangs at my heart!
   Panthea. See where the child of Heaven with wingèd feet,
Runs down the slanted sunlight of the dawn.
   Ione. Dear sister, close thy plumes over thine eyes

Lest thou behold and die: they come: they come
Blackening the birth of day with countless wings,
And hollow underneath, like death.

 First Fury.   Prometheus!

 Second Fury. Immortal Titan!

 Third Fury.   Champion of Heaven's slaves!

 Prometheus. He whom some dreadful voice invokes is here,
Prometheus, the chained Titan. Horrible forms,
What and who are ye? Never yet there came
Phantasms so foul through monster-teeming Hell
From the all-miscreative brain of Jove;
Whilst I behold such execrable shapes,
Methinks I grow like what I contemplate,
And laugh and stare in loathsome sympathy.

 First Fury. We are the ministers of pain, and fear,
And disappointment, and mistrust, and hate,
And clinging crime; and as lean dogs pursue
Through wood and lake some struck and sobbing fawn,
We track all things that weep, and bleed, and live,
When the great King betrays them to our will.

 Prometheus. Oh! many fearful natures in one name,
I know ye; and these lakes and echoes know
The darkness and the clangour of your wings.
But why more hideous than your loathèd selves
Gather ye up in legions from the deep?

 Second Fury. We knew not that: Sisters, rejoice, rejoice!

 Prometheus. Can aught exult in its deformity?

 Second Fury. The beauty of delight makes lovers glad,
Gazing on one another: so are we.
As from the rose which the pale priestess kneels
To gather for her festal crown of flowers
The aëreal crimson falls, flushing her cheek,
So from our victim's destined agony
The shade which is our form invests us round,
Else we are shapeless as our mother Night.

 Prometheus. I laugh your power, and his who sent you here,
To lowest scorn. Pour forth the cup of pain.

 First Fury. Thou thinkest we will rend thee bone from bone,
And nerve from nerve, working like fire within?

 Prometheus. Pain is my element, as hate is thine;
Ye rend me now: I care not.

 Second Fury.   Dost imagine

We will but laugh into thy lidless eyes?
   Prometheus. I weigh not what ye do, but what ye suffer,
Being evil.   Cruel was the power which called
You, or aught else so wretched, into light.
   Third Fury. Thou think'st we will live through thee, one by one,
Like animal life, and though we can obscure not
The soul which burns within, that we will dwell
Beside it, like a vain loud multitude
Vexing the self-content of wisest men:
That we will be dread thought beneath thy brain,
And foul desire round thine astonished heart,
And blood within thy labyrinthine veins
Crawling like agony?
   Prometheus.   Why, ye are thus now;
Yet am I king over myself, and rule
The torturing and conflicting throngs within,
As Jove rules you when Hell grows mutinous.

Chorus of Furies

From the ends of the earth, from the ends of the earth,
Where the night has its grave and the morning its birth,
        Come, come, come!
Oh, ye who shake hills with the scream of your mirth,
When cities sink howling in ruin; and ye
Who with wingless footsteps trample the sea,
And close upon Shipwreck and Famine's track,
Sit chattering with joy on the foodless wreck;
        Come, come, come!
   Leave the bed, low, cold, and red,
   Strewed beneath a nation dead;
   Leave the hatred, as in ashes
     Fire is left for future burning:
   It will burst in bloodier flashes
     When ye stir it, soon returning:
   Leave the self-contempt implanted
   In young spirits, sense-enchanted,
     Misery's yet unkindled fuel:
   Leave Hell's secrets half unchanted
     To the maniac dreamer; cruel
   More than ye can be with hate
     Is he with fear.
        Come, come, come!

We are steaming up from Hell's wide gate
And we burthen the blast of the atmosphere,
But vainly we toil till ye come here.

Ione. Sister, I hear the thunder of new wings.
Panthea. These solid mountains quiver with the sound
Even as the tremulous air: their shadows make
The space within my plumes more black than night.

First Fury

Your call was as a wingèd car
Driven on whirlwinds fast and far;
It rapt us from red gulfs of war.

Second Fury

From wide cities, famine-wasted;

Third Fury

Groans half heard, and blood untasted;

Fourth Fury

Kingly conclaves stern and cold,
Where blood with gold is bought and sold;

Fifth Fury

From the furnace, white and hot,
In which—

A Fury

Speak not: whisper not:
I know all that ye would tell,
But to speak might break the spell
Which must bend the Invincible,
    The stern of thought;
He yet defies the deepest power of Hell.

A Fury

Tear the veil!

Another Fury.

It is torn.

Chorus

                     The pale stars of the morn
Shine on a misery, dire to be borne.
Dost thou faint, mighty Titan? We laugh thee to scorn.
Dost thou boast the clear knowledge thou waken'dst for man?
Then was kindled within him a thirst which outran
Those perishing waters; a thirst of fierce fever,
Hope, love, doubt, desire, which consume him for ever.
        One came forth of gentle worth
        Smiling on the sanguine earth;
        His words outlived him, like swift poison
          Withering up truth, peace, and pity.
        Look! where round the wide horizon
          Many a million-peopled city
        Vomits smoke in the bright air.
        Hark that outcry of despair!
'Tis his mild and gentle ghost
          Wailing for the faith he kindled:
        Look again, the flames almost
          To a glow-worm's lamp have dwindled:
The survivors round the embers
    Gather in dread.
              Joy, joy, joy!
Past ages crowd on thee, but each one remembers,
And the future is dark, and the present is spread
Like a pillow of thorns for thy slumberless head.

Semichorus I

    Drops of bloody agony flow
    From his white and quivering brow.
    Grant a little respite now:
    See a disenchanted nation
    Springs like day from desolation;
    To Truth its state is dedicate,
    And Freedom leads it forth, her mate;
    A legioned band of linkèd brothers
    Whom Love calls children—

Semichorus II

                   'Tis another's;
    See how kindred murder kin:
    'Tis the vintage-time for death and sin:

> Blood, like new wine, bubbles within:
>> Till Despair smothers
> The struggling world, which slaves and tyrants win.

[All the FURIES *vanish, except one.*

Ione. Hark, sister! what a low yet dreadful groan
Quite unsuppressed is tearing up the heart
Of the good Titan, as storms tear the deep,
And beasts hear the sea moan in inland caves.
Darest thou observe how the fiends torture him?

Panthea. Alas! I looked forth twice, but will no more.

Ione. What didst thou see?

Panthea.   A woful sight: a youth
With patient looks nailed to a crucifix.

Ione. What next?

Panthea.   The heaven around, the earth below
Was peopled with thick shapes of human death,
All horrible, and wrought by human hands,
And some appeared the work of human hearts,
For men were slowly killed by frowns and smiles:
And other sights too foul to speak and live
Were wandering by. Let us not tempt worse fear
By looking forth: those groans are grief enough.

Fury. Behold an emblem: those who do endure
Deep wrongs for man, and scorn, and chains, but heap
Thousandfold torment on themselves and him.

Prometheus. Remit the anguish of that lighted stare;
Close those wan lips; let that thorn-wounded brow
Stream not with blood; it mingles with thy tears!
Fix, fix those tortured orbs in peace and death,
So thy sick throes shake not that crucifix,
So those pale fingers play not with thy gore.
O, horrible! Thy name I will not speak,
It hath become a curse. I see, I see
The wise, the mild, the lofty, and the just,
Whom thy slaves hate for being like to thee,
Some hunted by foul lies from their heart's home,
An early-chosen, late-lamented home;
As hooded ounces cling to the driven hind;
Some linked to corpses in unwholesome cells:
Some—Hear I not the multitude laugh loud?—
Impaled in lingering fire: and mighty realms
Float by my feet, like sea-uprooted isles.

Whose sons are kneaded down in common blood
By the red light of their own burning homes.
    Fury. Blood thou canst see, and fire; and canst hear groans;
Worse things, unheard, unseen, remain behind.
    Prometheus. Worse?
    Fury.   In each human heart terror survives
The ravin it has gorged: the loftiest fear
All that they would disdain to think were true:
Hypocrisy and custom make their minds
The fanes of many a worship, now outworn.
They dare not devise good for man's estate,
And yet they know not that they do not dare.
The good want power, but to weep barren tears.
The powerful goodness want: worse need for them.
The wise want love; and those who love want wisdom;
And all best things are thus confused to ill.
Many are strong and rich, and would be just,
But live among their suffering fellow-men
As if none felt: they know not what they do.
    Prometheus. Thy words are like a cloud of wingèd snakes;
And yet I pity those they torture not.
    Fury. Thou pitiest them? I speak no more! [*Vanishes.*
    Prometheus.   Ah woe!
Ah woe! Alas! pain, pain ever, for ever!
I close my tearless eyes, but see more clear
Thy works within my woe-illumèd mind,
Thou subtle tyrant! Peace is in the grave.
The grave hides all things beautiful and good:
I am a God and cannot find it there,
Nor would I seek it: for, though dread revenge,
This is defeat, fierce king, not victory.
The sights with which thou torturest gird my soul
With new endurance, till the hour arrives
When they shall be no types of things which are.
    Panthea. Alas! what sawest thou more?
    Prometheus.   There are two woes:
To speak, and to behold; thou spare me one.
Names are there, Nature's sacred watchwords, they
Were borne aloft in bright emblazonry;
The nations thronged around, and cried aloud,
As with one voice, Truth, liberty, and love!
Suddenly fierce confusion fell from heaven

Among them: there was strife, deceit, and fear:
Tyrants rushed in, and did divide the spoil.
This was the shadow of the truth I saw.

   The Earth. I felt thy torture, son, with such mixed joy
As pain and virtue give. To cheer thy state
I bid ascend those subtle and fair spirits,
Whose homes are the dim caves of human thought,
And who inhabit, as birds wing the wind,
Its world-surrounding aether: they behold
Beyond that twilight realm, as in a glass,
The future: may they speak comfort to thee!

   Panthea. Look, sister, where a troop of spirits gather,
Like flocks of clouds in spring's delightful weather,
Thronging in the blue air!

   Ione.   And see! more come,
Like fountain-vapours when the winds are dumb,
That climb up the ravine in scattered lines.
And, hark! is it the music of the pines?
Is it the lake? Is it the waterfall?

   Panthea. 'Tis something sadder, sweeter far than all.

Chorus of Spirits

From unremembered ages we
Gentle guides and guardians be
Of heaven-oppressed mortality;
And we breathe, and sicken not.
The atmosphere of human thought:
Be it dim, and dank, and gray,
Like a storm-extinguished day,
Travelled o'er by dying gleams;
  Be it bright as all between
Cloudless skies and windless streams,
  Silent, liquid, and serene;
As the birds within the wind,
  As the fish within the wave,
As the thoughts of man's own mind
  Float through all above the grave;
We make there our liquid lair,
Voyaging cloudlike and unpent
Through the boundless element:
Thence we bear the prophecy
Which begins and ends in thee!

Ione. More yet come, one by one: the air around them
Looks radiant as the air around a star.

First Spirit

On a battle-trumpet's blast
I fled hither, fast, fast, fast,
'Mid the darkness upward cast.
From the dust of creeds outworn,
From the tyrant's banner torn,
Gathering round me, onward borne,
There was mingled many a cry—
Freedom! Hope! Death! Victory!
Till they faded through the sky;
And one sound, above, around,
One sound beneath, around, above,
Was moving; 'twas the soul of Love;
'Twas the hope, the prophecy,
Which begins and ends in thee.

Second Spirit

A rainbow's arch stood on the sea,
Which rocked beneath, immovably;
And the triumphant storm did flee,
Like a conqueror, swift and proud,
Between, with many a captive cloud,
A shapeless, dark and rapid crowd,
Each by lightning riven in half:
I heard the thunder hoarsely laugh:
Mighty fleets were strewn like chaff
And spread beneath a hell of death
O'er the white waters. I alit
On a great ship lightning-split,
And speeded hither on the sigh
Of one who gave an enemy
His plank, then plunged aside to die.

Third Spirit

I sate beside a sage's bed.
And the lamp was burning red
Near the book where he had fed,
When a Dream with plumes of flame,
To his pillow hovering came,

And I knew it was the same
Which had kindled long ago
Pity, eloquence, and woe;
And the world awhile below
Wore the shade, its lustre made.
It has borne me here as fleet
As Desire's lightning feet:
I must ride it back ere morrow,
Or the sage will wake in sorrow.

Fourth Spirit

On a poet's lips I slept
Dreaming like a love-adept
In the sound his breathing kept;
Nor seeks nor finds he mortal blisses,
But feeds on the aëreal kisses
Of shapes that haunt thought's wildernesses.
He will watch from dawn to gloom
The lake-reflected sun illume
The yellow bees in the ivy-bloom,
Nor heed nor see, what things they be;
But from these create he can
Forms more real than living man,
Nursings of immortality!
One of these awakened me,
And I sped to succour thee.

Ione

Behold'st thou not two shapes from the east and west
Come, as two doves to one belovèd nest,
Twin nurslings of the all-sustaining air
On swift still wings glide down the atmosphere?
And, hark! their sweet, sad voices! 'tis despair
Mingled with love and then dissolved in sound.

Panthea. Canst thou speak, sister? all my words are drowned.
Ione. Their beauty gives me voice. See how they float
On their sustaining wings of skiey grain,
Orange and azure deepening into gold:
Their soft smiles light the air like a star's fire.

Chorus of Spirits

Hast thou beheld the form of Love?

Fifth Spirit

                 As over wide dominions
I sped, like some swift cloud that wings the wide air's wildernesses,
That planet-crested shape swept by on lightning-braided pinions,
   Scattering the liquid joy of life from his ambrosial tresses:
His footsteps paved the world with light; but as I passed 'twas fading,
   And hollow Ruin yawned behind: great sages bound in madness,
And headless patriots, and pale youths who perished, unupbraiding,
   Gleamed in the night. I wandered o'er, till thou, O King of sadness,
Turned by thy smile the worst I saw to recollected gladness.

Sixth Spirit

Ah, sister! Desolation is a delicate thing:
   It walks not on the earth, it floats not on the air,
But treads with lulling footstep, and fans with silent wing
   The tender hopes which in their hearts the best and gentlest bear;
Who, soothed to false repose by the fanning plumes above
   And the music-stirring motion of its soft and busy feet,
Dream visions of aëreal joy, and call the monster, Love,
   And wake, and find the shadow Pain, as he whom now we greet.

Chorus

   Though Ruin now Love's shadow be,
   Following him, destroyingly,
      On Death's white and wingèd steed,
    Which the fleetest cannot flee,
      Trampling down both flower and weed,
   Man and beast, and foul and fair,
   Like a tempest through the air;
   Thou shalt quell this horseman grim,
   Woundless though in heart or limb.

Prometheus. Spirits! how know ye this shall be?

Chorus

   In the atmosphere we breathe,
  As buds grow red when the snow-storms flee,
   From Spring gathering up beneath,
  Whose mild winds shake the elder brake,

And the wandering herdsmen know
That the white-thorn soon will blow:
    Wisdom, Justice, Love, and Peace,
    When they struggle to increase,
        Are to us as soft winds be
        To shepherd boys, the prophecy
        Which begins and ends in thee.

Ione. Where are the Spirits fled?
    Panthea.   Only a sense
Remains of them, like the omnipotence
Of music, when the inspired voice and lute
Languish, ere yet the responses are mute,
Which through the deep and labyrinthine soul,
Like echoes through long caverns, wind and roll.
    Prometheus. How fair these airborn shapes! and yet I feel
Most vain all hope but love; and thou art far,
Asia! who, when my being overflowed,
Wert like a golden chalice to bright wine
Which else had sunk into the thirsty dust.
All things are still: alas! how heavily
This quiet morning weighs upon my heart;
Though I should dream I could even sleep with grief
If slumber were denied not. I would fain
Be what it is my destiny to be.
The saviour and the strength of suffering man,
Or sink into the original gulf of things:
There is no agony, and no solace left;
Earth can console, Heaven can torment no more.
    Panthea. Hast thou forgotten one who watches thee
The cold dark night, and never sleeps but when
The shadow of thy spirit falls on her?
    Prometheus. I said all hope was vain but love: thou lovest.
    Panthea. Deeply in truth; but the eastern star looks white,
And Asia waits in that far Indian vale,
The scene of her sad exile; rugged once
And desolate and frozen, like this ravine;
But now invested with fair flowers and herbs,
And haunted by sweet airs and sounds, which flow
Among the woods and waters, from the aether
Of her transforming presence, which would fade
If it were mingled not with thine.   Farewell!

Act II

SCENE I.—*Morning. A lovely Vale in the Indian Caucasus.*
ASIA *alone.*

Asia. From all the blasts of heaven thou hast descended:
Yes, like a spirit, like a thought, which makes
Unwonted tears throng to the horny eyes,
And beatings haunt the desolated heart,
Which should have learnt repose: thou hast descended
Cradled in tempests; thou dost wake, O Spring!
O child of many winds! As suddenly
Thou comest as the memory of a dream,
Which now is sad because it hath been sweet;
Like genius, or like joy which riseth up
As from the earth, clothing with golden clouds
The desert of our life.
This is the season, this the day, the hour;
At sunrise thou shouldst come, sweet sister mine,
Too long desired, too long delaying, come!
How like death-worms the wingless moments crawl!
The point of one white star is quivering still
Deep in the orange light of widening morn
Beyond the purple mountains: through a chasm
Of wind-divided mist the darker lake
Reflects it: now it wanes: it gleams again
As the waves fade, and as the burning threads
Of woven cloud unravel in pale air;
'Tis lost! and through yon peaks of cloud-like snow
The roseate sunlight quivers: hear I not
The Æolian music of her sea-green plumes
Winnowing the crimson dawn?   [PANTHEA *enters.*
                       I feel, I see
Those eyes which burn through smiles that fade in tears,
Like stars half quenched in mists of silver dew.
Belovèd and most beautiful, who wearest
The shadow of that soul by which I live.
How late thou art! the spherèd sun had climbed
The sea; my heart was sick with hope, before
The printless air felt thy belated plumes.

Panthea. Pardon, great Sister! but my wings were faint
With the delight of a remembered dream.
As are the noontide plumes of summer winds
Satiate with sweet flowers.   I was wont to sleep
Peacefully, and awake refreshed and calm
Before the sacred Titan's fall, and thy
Unhappy love, had made, through use and pity,
Both love and woe familiar to my heart
As they had grown to thine: erewhile I slept
Under the glaucous caverns of old Ocean
Within dim bowers of green and purple moss,
Our young Ione's soft and milky arms
Locked then, as now, behind my dark moist hair,
While my shut eyes and cheek were pressed within
The folded depth of her life-breathing bosom:
But not as now, since I am made the wind
Which fails beneath the music that I bear
Of thy most wordless converse; since dissolved
Into the sense with which love talks, my rest
Was troubled and yet sweet; my waking hours
Too full of care and pain.
  Asia.   Lift up thine eyes,
And let me read thy dream.
  Panthea.   As I have said
With our sea-sister at his feet I slept.
The mountain mists, condensing at our voice
Under the moon, had spread their snowy flakes,
From the keen ice shielding our linkèd sleep.
Then two dreams came. One, I remember not.
But in the other his pale wound-worn limbs
Fell from Prometheus, and the azure night
Grew radiant with the glory of that form
Which lives unchanged within, and his voice fell
Like music which makes giddy the dim brain,
Faint with intoxication of keen joy:
'Sister of her whose footsteps pave the world
With loveliness—more fair than aught but her,
Whose shadow thou art—lift thine eyes on me.'
I lifted them: the overpowering light
Of that immortal shape was shadowed o'er
By love; which, from his soft and flowing limbs,
And passion-parted lips, and keen, faint eyes,

Steamed forth like vaporous fire; an atmosphere
Which wrapped me in its all-dissolving power,
As the warm aether of the morning sun
Wraps ere it drinks some cloud of wandering dew.
I saw not, heard not, moved not, only felt
His presence flow and mingle through my blood
Till it became his life, and his grew mine,
And I was thus absorbed, until it passed,
And like the vapours when the sun sinks down,
Gathering again in drops upon the pines,
And tremulous as they, in the deep night
My being was condensed; and as the rays
Of thought were slowly gathered, I could hear
His voice, whose accents lingered ere they died
Like footsteps of weak melody: thy name
Among the many sounds alone I heard
Of what might be articulate; though still
I listened through the night when sound was none.
Ione wakened then, and said to me:
'Canst thou divine what troubles me to-night?
I always knew what I desired before,
Nor ever found delight to wish in vain.
But now I cannot tell thee what I seek;
I know not; something sweet, since it is sweet
Even to desire; it is thy sport, false sister;
Thou hast discovered some enchantment old,
Whose spells have stolen my spirit as I slept
And mingled it with thine: for when just now
We kissed, I felt within thy parted lips
The sweet air that sustained me, and the warmth
Of the life-blood, for loss of which I faint,
Quivered between our intertwining arms.'
I answered not, for the Eastern star grew pale,
But fled to thee.
    Asia.   Thou speakest, but thy words
Are as the air: I feel them not: Oh, lift
Thine eyes, that I may read his written soul!
    Panthea. I lift them though they droop beneath the load
Of that they would express: what canst thou see
But thine own fairest shadow imaged there?
    Asia. Thine eyes are like the deep, blue, boundless heaven
Contracted to two circles underneath

Their long, fine lashes; dark, far, measureless,
Orb within orb, and line through line inwoven.
   Panthea. Why lookest thou as if a spirit passed?
   Asia. There is a change: beyond their inmost depth
I see a shade, a shape: 'tis He, arrayed
In the soft light of his own smiles, which spread
Like radiance from the cloud-surrounded moon.
Prometheus, it is thine! depart not yet!
Say not those smiles that we shall meet again
Within that bright pavilion which their beams
Shall build o'er the waste world? The dream is told.
What shape is that between us? Its rude hair
Roughens the wind that lifts it, its regard
Is wild and quick, yet 'tis a thing of air,
For through its gray robe gleams the golden dew
Whose stars the noon has quenched not.
   Dream.   Follow! Follow!
   Panthea. It is mine other dream.
   Asia.   It disappears.
   Panthea. It passes now into my mind. Methought
As we sate here, the flower-infolding buds
Burst on yon lightning-blasted almond-tree,
When swift from the white Scythian wilderness
A wind swept forth wrinkling the Earth with frost:
I looked, and all the blossoms were blown down;
But on each leaf was stamped, as the blue bells
Of Hyacinth tell Apollo's written grief,
O, FOLLOW, FOLLOW!
   Asia.   As you speak, your words
Fill, pause by pause, my own forgotten sleep
With shapes. Methought among these lawns together
We wandered, underneath the young gray dawn,
And multitudes of dense white fleecy clouds
Were wandering in thick flocks along the mountains
Shepherded by the slow, unwilling wind;
And the white dew on the new-bladed grass,
Just piercing the dark earth, hung silently;
And there was more which I remember not:
But on the shadows of the morning clouds,
Athwart the purple mountain slope, was written
FOLLOW, O, FOLLOW! as they vanished by;
And on each herb, from which Heaven's dew had fallen,

The like was stamped, as with a withering fire;
A wind arose among the pines; it shook
The clinging music from their boughs, and then
Low, sweet, faint sounds, like the farewell of ghosts,
Were heard: O, FOLLOW, FOLLOW, FOLLOW ME!
And then I said: 'Panthea, look on me.'
But in the depth of those belovèd eyes
Still I saw, FOLLOW, FOLLOW!
    Echo.   Follow, follow!
    Panthea. The crags, this clear spring morning, mock our voices
As they were spirit-tongued.
    Asia.   It is some being
Around the crags. What fine clear sounds! O, list!

Echoes (unseen)

Echoes we: listen!
  We cannot stay:
As dew-stars glisten
  Then fade away—
    Child of Ocean!

    Asia. Hark! Spirits speak. The liquid responses
Of their aëreal tongues yet sound.
    Panthea.   I hear.

Echoes

O, follow, follow,
  As our voice recedeth
Through the caverns hollow,
  Where the forest spreadeth;

(More distant)

O, follow, follow!
Through the caverns hollow,
As the song floats thou pursue,
Where the wild bee never flew,
Through the noontide darkness deep,
By the odour-breathing sleep
Of faint night flowers, and the waves
At the fountain-lighted caves,
While our music, wild and sweet,
Mocks thy gently falling feet,
    Child of Ocean!

Asia. Shall we pursue the sound? It grows more faint
And distant.
Panthea. List! the strain floats nearer now.

Echoes

In the world unknown
  Sleeps a voice unspoken;
By thy step alone
  Can its rest be broken;
    Child of Ocean!

Asia. How the notes sink upon the ebbing wind!

Echoes

O, follow, follow!
  Through the caverns hollow,
As the song floats thou pursue,
By the woodland noontide dew;
By the forest, lakes, and fountains,
Through the many-folded mountains;
To the rents, and gulfs, and chasms,
Where the Earth reposed from spasms,
On the day when He and thou
Parted, to commingle now;
    Child of Ocean!

Asia. Come, sweet Panthea, link thy hand in mine,
And follow, ere the voices fade away.

SCENE II.—*A Forest, intermingled with Rocks and Caverns.* ASIA
  and PANTHEA *pass into it. Two young Fauns are sitting on
  a Rock listening.*

Semichorus I of Spirits

The path through which that lovely twain
  Have passed, by cedar, pine, and yew.
  And each dark tree that ever grew
  Is curtained out from Heaven's wide blue;
Nor sun, nor moon, nor wind, nor rain,
  Can pierce its interwoven bowers,
  Nor aught, save where some cloud of dew,
Drifted along the earth-creeping breeze,
Between the trunks of the hoar trees,

    Hangs each a pearl in the pale flowers
     Of the green laurel, blown anew;
And bends, and then fades silently,
One frail and fair anemone:
Or when some star of many a one
That climbs and wanders through steep night,
Has found the cleft through which alone
Beams fall from high those depths upon
Ere it is borne away, away,
By the swift Heavens that cannot stay,
It scatters drops of golden light,
Like lines of rain that ne'er unite:
And the gloom divine is all around,
And underneath is the mossy ground.

Semichorus II

There the voluptuous nightingales,
    Are awake through all the broad noonday.
When one with bliss or sadness fails,
     And through the windless ivy-boughs,
    Sick with sweet love, droops dying away
On its mate's music-panting bosom;
Another from the swinging blosom.
     Watching to catch the languid close
    Of the last strain, then lifts on high
    The wings of the weak melody,
Till some new strain of feeling bear
    The song, and all the woods are mute;
When there is heard through the dim air
The rush of wings, and rising there
    Like many a lake-surrounded flute,
Sounds overflow the listener's brain
So sweet, that joy is almost pain.

Semichorus I

There those enchanted eddies play
     Of echoes, music-tongued, which draw,
     By Demogorgon's mighty law,
     With melting rapture, or sweet awe,
All spirits on that secret way;
     As inland boats are driven to Ocean
Down streams made strong with mountain-thaw:

And first there comes a gentle sound
To those in talk or slumber bound,
And wakes the destined, soft emotion,
Attracts, impels them; those who saw
Say from the breathing earth behind
There steams a plume-uplifting wind
Which drives them on their path, while they
Believe their own swift wings and feet
The sweet desires within obey:
And so they float upon their way,
Until, still sweet, but loud and strong,
The storm of sound is driven along,
Sucked up and hurrying: as they fleet
Behind, its gathering billows meet
And to the fatal mountain bear
Like clouds amid the yielding air.

First Faun. Canst thou imagine where those spirits live
Which make such delicate music in the woods?
We haunt within the least frequented caves
And closest coverts, and we know these wilds,
Yet never meet them, though we hear them oft:
Where may they hide themselves?

 Second Faun.   'Tis hard to tell:
I have heard those more skilled in spirits say,
The bubbles, which the enchantment of the sun
Sucks from the pale faint water-flowers that pave
The oozy bottom of clear lakes and pools,
Are the pavilions where such dwell and float
Under the green and golden atmosphere
Which noontide kindles through the woven leaves;
And when these burst, and the thin fiery air,
The which they breathed within those lucent domes,
Ascends to flow like meteors through the night,
They ride on them, and rein their headlong speed,
And bow their burning crests, and glide in fire
Under the waters of the earth again.

 First Faun. If such live thus, have others other lives,
Under pink blossoms or within the bells
Of meadow flowers, or folded violets deep,
Or on their dying odours, when they die,
Or in the sunlight of the spherèd dew?

 Second Faun. Ay, many more which we may well divine.

But, should we stay to speak, noontide would come,
And thwart Silenus find his goats undrawn,
And grudge to sing those wise and lovely songs
Of Fate, and Chance, and God, and Chaos old,
And Love, and the chained Titan's woful doom,
And how he shall be loosed, and make the earth
One brotherhood: delightful strains which cheer
Our solitary twilights, and which charm
To silence the unenvying nightingales.

SCENE III.—A PINNACLE OF ROCK AMONG MOUNTAINS.
ASIA *and* PANTHEA.

Panthea. Hither the sound has borne us—to the realm
Of Demogorgon, and the mighty portal,
Like a volcano's meteor-breathing chasm,
Whence the oracular vapour is hurled up
Which lonely men drink wandering in their youth,
And call truth, virtue, love, genius, or joy,
That maddening wine of life, whose dregs they drain
To deep intoxication; and uplift,
Like Mænads who cry loud, Evoe! Evoe!
The voice which is contagion to the world.
    Asia. Fit throne for such a Power! Magnificent!
How glorious art thou, Earth! And if thou be
The shadow of some spirit lovelier still,
Though evil stain its work, and it should be
Like its creation, weak yet beautiful,
I could fall down and worship that and thee,
Even now my heart adoreth: Wonderful!
Look, sister, ere the vapour dim thy brain:
Beneath is a wide plain of billowy mist,
As a lake, paving in the morning sky,
With azure waves which burst in silver light,
Some Indian vale. Behold it, rolling on
Under the curdling winds, and islanding
The peak whereon we stand, midway, around,
Encinctured by the dark and blooming forests,
Dim twilight-lawns, and stream-illumèd caves,
And wind-enchanted shapes of wandering mist;
And far on high the keen sky-cleaving mountains
From icy spires of sun-like radiance fling
The dawn, as lifted Ocean's dazzling spray,

From some Atlantic islet scattered up,
Spangles the wind with lamp-like water-drops.
The vale is girdled with their walls, a howl
Of cataracts from their thaw-cloven ravines,
Satiates the listening wind, continuous, vast,
Awful as silence. Hark! the rushing snow!
The sun-awakened avalanche! whose mass,
Thrice sifted by the storm, had gathered there
Flake after flake, in heaven-defying minds
As thought by thought is piled, till some great truth
Is loosened, and the nations echo round,
Shaken to their roots, as do the mountains now.

    Panthea. Look how the gusty sea of mist is breaking
In crimson foam, even at our feet! it rises
As Ocean at the enchantment of the moon
Round foodless men wrecked on some oozy isle.

    Asia. The fragments of the cloud are scattered up;
The wind that lifts them disentwines my hair;
Its billows now sweep o'er mine eyes; my brain
Grows dizzy; see'st thou shapes within the mist?

    Panthea. A countenance with beckoning smiles: **there burns**
An azure fire within its golden locks!
Another and another: hark! they **speak!**

Song of Spirits

To the deep, to the deep,
        Down, down!
Through the shade of sleep,
Through the cloudy strife
Of Death and of Life;
Through the veil and the bar
Of things which seem and are
Even to the steps of the remotest throne,
        Down, down!

While the sound whirls around,
        Down, down!
As the fawn draws the hound,
As the lightning the vapour,
As a weak moth the taper;
Death, despair; love, sorrow;
Time both; to-day, to-morrow;

As steel obeys the spirit of the stone,
                    Down, down!

Through the gray, void abysm,
                    Down, down!
Where the air is no prism,
And the moon and stars are not,
And the cavern-crags wear not
The radiance of Heaven,
Nor the gloom to Earth given,
Where there is One pervading, One alone,
                    Down, down!

In the depth of the deep,
                    Down, down!
Like veiled lightning asleep,
Like the spark nursed in embers,
The last look Love remembers,
Like a diamond, which shines
On the dark wealth of mines,
A spell is treasured but for thee alone.
                    Down, down!

We have bound thee, we guide thee;
                    Down, down!
With the bright form beside thee;
Resist not the weakness,
Such strength is in meekness
That the Eternal, the Immortal,
Must unloose through life's portal
The snake-like Doom coiled underneath his throne
                    By that alone.

SCENE IV.—THE CAVE OF DEMOGORGON. ASIA *and* PANTHEA.

Panthea. What veilèd form sits on that ebon throne?
Asia. The veil has fallen.
Panthea.   I see a mighty darkness
Filling the seat of power, and rays of gloom
Dart round, as light from the meridian sun.
—Ungazed upon and shapeless; neither limb,
Nor form, nor outline; yet we feel it is
A living Spirit.

Demogorgon. Ask what thou wouldst know.

Asia. What canst thou tell?

Demorgorgon. All things thou dar'st demand.

Asia. Who made the living world?

Demogorgon. God.

Asia. Who made all
That it contains? thought, passion, reason, will,
Imagination?

Demogorgon. God: Almighty God.

Asia. Who made that sense which, when the winds of Spring
In rarest visitation, or the voice
Of one belovèd heard in youth alone,
Fills the faint eyes with falling tears which dim
The radiant looks of unbewailing flowers,
And leaves this peopled earth a solitude
When it returns no more?

Demogorgon. Merciful God.

Asia. And who made terror, madness, crime, remorse,
Which from the links of the great chain of things,
To every thought within the mind of man
Sway and drag heavily, and each one reels
Under the load towards the pit of death;
Abandoned hope, and love that turns to hate;
And self-contempt, bitterer to drink than blood;
Pain, whose unheeded and familiar speech
Is howling, and keen shrieks, day after day;
And Hell, or the sharp fear of Hell?

Demogorgon. He reigns.

Asia. Utter his name: a world pining in pain
Asks but his name: curses shall drag him down.

Demogorgon. He reigns.

Asia. I feel, I know it: who?

Demogorgon. He reigns.

Asia. Who reigns? There was the Heaven and Earth at first,
And Light and Love; then Saturn, from whose throne
Time fell, an envious shadow: such the state
Of the earth's primal spirits beneath his sway,
As the calm joy of flowers and living leaves
Before the wind or sun has withered them
And semivital worms; but he refused
The birthright of their being, knowledge, power,
The skill which wields the elements, the thought

Which pierces this dim universe like light,
Self-empire, and the majesty of love;
For thirst of which they fainted. Then Prometheus
Gave wisdom, which is strength, to Jupiter,
And with this law alone, 'Let man be free,'
Clothed him with the dominion of wide Heaven.
To know nor faith, nor love, nor law; to be
Omnipotent but friendless is to reign;
And Jove now reigned; for on the race of man
First famine, and then toil, and then disease,
Strife, wounds, and ghastly death unseen before,
Fell; and the unseasonable seasons drove
With alternating shafts of frost and fire,
Their shelterless, pale tribes to mountain caves:
And in their desert hearts fierce wants he sent,
And mad disquietudes, and shadows idle
Of unreal good, which levied mutual war,
So ruining the lair wherein they raged.
Prometheus saw, and waked the legioned hopes
Which sleep within folded Elysian flowers,
Nepenthe, Moly, Amaranth, fadeless blooms,
That they might hide with thin and rainbow wings
The shape of Death; and Love he sent to bind
The disunited tendrils of that vine
Which bears the wine of life, the human heart;
And he tamed fire which, like some beast of prey,
Most terrible, but lovely, played beneath
The frown of man; and tortured to his will
Iron and gold, the slaves and signs of power,
And gems and poisons, and all subtlest forms
Hidden beneath the mountains and the waves.
He gave man speech, and speech created thought,
Which is the measure of the universe;
And Science struck the thrones of earth and heaven,
Which shook, but fell not; and the harmonious mind
Poured itself forth in all-prophetic song;
And music lifted up the listening spirit
Until it walked, exempt from mortal care,
Godlike, o'er the clear billows of sweet sound;
And human hands first mimicked and then mocked,
With moulded limbs more lovely than its own,
The human form, till marble grew divine;

And mothers, gazing, drank the love men see
Reflected in their race, behold, and perish.
He told the hidden power of herbs and springs,
And Disease drank and slept. Death grew like sleep.
He taught the implicated orbits woven
Of the wide-wandering stars; and how the sun
Changes his lair, and by what secret spell
The pale moon is transformed, when her broad eye
Gazes not on the interlunar sea:
He taught to rule, as life directs the limbs,
The tempest-wingèd chariots of the Ocean,
And the Celt knew the Indian. Cities then
Were built, and through their snow-like columns flowed
The warm winds, and the azure aether shone,
And the blue sea and shadowy hills were seen.
Such, the alleviations of his state,
Prometheus gave to man, for which he hangs
Withering in destined pain: but who rains down
Evil, the immedicable plague, which, while
Man looks on his creation like a God
And sees that it is glorious, drives him on,
The wreck of his own will, the scorn of earth,
The outcast, the abandoned, the alone?
Not Jove: while yet his frown shook Heaven, ay, when
His adversary from adamantine chains
Cursed him, he trembled like a slave. Declare
Who is his master? Is he too a slave?

   Demogorgon. All spirits are enslaved which serve things evil:
Thou knowest if Jupiter be such or no.

   Asia. Whom calledst thou God?

   Demogorgon.   I spoke but as ye speak,
For Jove is the supreme of living things.

   Asia. Who is the master of the slave?

   Demogorgon.   If the abysm
Could vomit forth its secrets. . . . But a voice
Is wanting, the deep truth is imageless;
For what would it avail to bid thee gaze
On the revolving world? What to bid speak
Fate, Time, Occasion, Chance, and Change? To these
All things are subject but eternal Love.

   Asia. So much I asked before, and my heart gave
The response thou hast given; and of such truths

Each to itself must be the oracle.
One more demand; and do thou answer me
As mine own soul would answer, did it know
That which I ask. Prometheus shall arise
Henceforth the sun of this rejoicing world:
When shall the destined hour arrive?

    Demogorgon.   Behold!

   Asia. The rocks are cloven, and through the purple night
I see cars drawn by rainbow-wingèd steeds
Which trample the dim winds: in each there stands
A wild-eyed charioteer urging their flight.
Some look behind, as fiends pursued them there,
And yet I see no shapes but the keen stars:
Others, with burning eyes, lean forth, and drink
With eager lips the wind of their own speed,
As if the thing they loved fled on before,
And now, even now, they clasped it. Their bright locks
Stream like a comet's flashing hair: they all
Sweep.

    Demogorgon. These are the immortal Hours,
Of whom thou didst demand. One waits for thee.

   Asia. A spirit with a dreadful countenance
Checks its dark chariot by the craggy gulf.
Unlike thy brethren, ghastly charioteer.
Who art thou? Whither wouldst thou bear me? Speak!

    Spirit. I am the shadow of a destiny
More dread than is my aspect: ere yon planet
Has set, the darkness which ascends with me
Shall wrap in lasting night heaven's kingless throne.

    Asia. What meanest thou?

    Panthea.   That terrible shadow floats
Up from its throne, as may the lurid smoke
Of earthquake-ruined cities o'er the sea.
Lo! it ascends the car; the coursers fly
Terrified: watch its path among the stars
Blackening the night!

    Asia.   Thus I am answered: strange!

    Panthea. See, near the verge, another chariot stays;
An ivory shell inlaid with crimson fire,
Which comes and goes within its sculptured rim
Of delicate strange tracery; the young spirit
That guides it has the dove-like eyes of hope;

How its soft smiles attract the soul! as light
Lures wingèd insects through the lampless air.

Spirit

My coursers are fed with the lightning,
    They drink of the whirlwind's stream,
And when the red morning is bright'ning
    They bathe in the fresh sunbeam;
    They have strength for their swiftness I deem,
Then ascend with me, daughter of Ocean.
I desire: and their speed makes night kindle;
    I fear: they outstrip the Typhoon;
Ere the cloud piled on Atlas can dwindle
    We encircle the earth and the moon:
    We shall rest from long labours at noon:
Then ascend with me, daughter of Ocean.

SCENE V.—*The Car pauses within a Cloud on the top of a snowy Mountain.*
    ASIA, PANTHEA, *and the* SPIRIT OF THE HOUR.

Spirit

On the brink of the night and the morning
    My coursers are wont to respire;
But the Earth has just whispered a warning
    That their flight must be swifter than fire:
    They shall drink the hot speed of desire!

Asia. Thou breathest on their nostrils, but my breath
Would give them swifter speed.
Spirit.   Alas! it could not.
Panthea. Oh Spirit! pause, and tell whence is the light
Which fills this cloud? the sun is yet unrisen.
    Spirit. The sun will rise not until noon. Apollo
Is held in heaven by wonder; and the light
Which fills this vapour, as the aëreal hue
Of fountain-gazing roses fills the water,
Flows from thy mighty sister.
    Panthea.   Yes, I feel—
    Asia. What is it with thee, sister? Thou art pale.
    Panthea. How thou art changed! I dare not look on thee;
I feel but see thee not. I scarce endure

The radiance of thy beauty. Some good change
Is working in the elements, which suffer
Thy presence thus unveiled. The Nereids tell
That on the day when the clear hyaline
Was cloven at thine uprise, and thou didst stand
Within a veinèd shell, which floated on
Over the calm floor of the crystal sea,
Among the Ægean isles, and by the shores
Which bear thy name; love, like the atmosphere
Of the sun's fire filling the living world,
Burst from thee, and illumined earth and heaven
And the deep ocean and the sunless caves
And all that dwells within them; till grief cast
Eclipse upon the soul from which it came:
Such art thou now; nor is it I alone,
Thy sister, thy companion, thine own chosen one,
But the whole world which seeks thy sympathy.
Hearest thou not sounds i' the air which speak the love
Of all articulate beings? Feelest thou not
The inanimate winds enamoured of thee? List!   [*Music.*

    Asia. Thy words are sweeter than aught else but his
Whose echoes they are: yet all love is sweet,
Given or returned. Common as light is love,
And its familiar voice wearies not ever.
Like the wide heaven, the all-sustaining air,
It makes the reptile equal to the God:
They who inspire it most are fortunate,
As I am now; but those who feel it most
Are happier still, after long sufferings,
As I shall soon become.

      Panthea.   List! Spirits speak.

         Voice in the Air, singing.

    Life of Life! thy lips enkindle
      With their love the breath between them;
    And thy smiles before they dwindle
      Make the cold air fire; then screen them
    In those looks, where whoso gazes
    Faints, entangled in their mazes.

    Child of Light! thy limbs are burning
      Through the vest which seems to hide them;

As the radiant lines of morning
  Through the clouds ere they divide them;
And this atmosphere divinest
Shrouds thee wheresoe'er thou shinest.

Fair are others; none beholds thee,
  But thy voice sounds low and tender
Like the fairest, for it folds thee
  From the sight, that liquid splendour,
And all feel, yet see thee never,
As I feel now, lost for ever!

Lamp of Earth! where'er thou movest
  Its dim shapes are clad with brightness,
And the souls of whom thou lovest
  Walk upon the winds with lightness,
Till they fail, as I am failing,
Dizzy, lost, yet unbewailing!

Asia

My soul is an enchanted boat,
  Which, like a sleeping swan, doth float
Upon the silver waves of thy sweet singing;
  And thine doth like an angel sit
  Beside a helm conducting it,
Whilst all the winds with melody are ringing.
  It seems to float ever, for ever,
  Upon that many-winding river,
  Between mountains, woods, abysses,
  A paradise of wildernesses!
Till, like one in slumber bound,
Borne to the ocean, I float down, around,
Into a sea profound, of ever-spreading sound:

  Meanwhile thy spirit lifts its pinions
  In music's most serene dominions;
Catching the winds that fan that happy heaven.
  And we sail on, away, afar.
  Without a course, without a star,
But, by the instinct of sweet music driven;
  Till through Elysian garden islets
  By thee, most beautiful of pilots,

Where never mortal pinnace glided,
  The boat of my desire is guided:
Realms where the air we breathe is love,
Which in the winds and on the waves doth move,
Harmonizing this earth with what we feel above.

We have passed Age's icy caves,
  And Manhood's dark and tossing waves,
And Youth's smooth ocean, smiling to betray:
    Beyond the glassy gulfs we flee
    Of shadow-peopled Infancy,
Through Death and Birth, to a diviner day;
    A paradise of vaulted bowers,
    Lit by downward-gazing flowers,
    And watery paths that wind between
  Wildernesses calm and green,
Peopled by shapes too bright to see,
And rest, having beheld; somewhat like thee;
Which walk upon the sea, and chant melodiously!

Act III

SCENE I.—*Heaven.* JUPITER *on his Throne*; THETIS *and the other Deities
              assembled.*

Jupiter. Ye congregated powers of heaven, who share
The glory and the strength of him ye serve,
Rejoice! henceforth I am omnipotent.
All else had been subdued to me; alone
The soul of man, like unextinguished fire,
Yet burns towards heaven with fierce reproach, and doubt
And lamentation, and reluctant prayer,
Hurling up insurrection, which might make
Our antique empire insecure, though built
On eldest faith, and hell's coeval, fear;
And though my curses through the pendulous air,
Like snow on herbless peaks, fall flake by flake,
And cling to it; though under my wrath's night
It climbs the crags of life, step after step,
Which wound it, as ice wounds unsandalled feet,
It yet remains supreme o'er misery,
Aspiring, unrepressed, yet soon to fall:
Even now have I begotten a strange wonder,

That fatal child, the terror of the earth,
Who waits but till the destined hour arrive,
Bearing from Demogorgon's vacant throne
The dreadful might of ever-living limbs
Which clothed that awful spirit unbeheld,
To redescend, and trample out the spark.
Pour forth heaven's wine, Idæan Ganymede,
And let it fill the Dædal cups like fire,
And from the flower-inwoven soil divine
Ye all-triumphant harmonies arise,
As dew from earth under the twilight stars:
Drink! be the nectar circling through your veins
The soul of joy, ye ever-living Gods,
Till exultation burst in one wide voice
Like music from Elysian winds.

                       And thou
Ascend beside me, veilèd in the light
Of the desire which makes thee one with me,
Thetis, bright image of eternity!
When thou didst cry, 'Insufferable might!
God! Spare me! I sustain not the quick flames,
The penetrating presence; all my being,
Like him whom the Numidian seps did thaw
Into a dew with poison, is dissolved,
Sinking through its foundations:' even then
Two mighty spirits, mingling, made a third
Mightier than either, which, unbodied now,
Between us floats, felt, although unbeheld,
Waiting the incarnation, which ascends,
(Hear ye the thunder of the fiery wheels
Griding the winds?) from Demogorgon's throne.
Victory! victory! Feel'st thou not, O world,
The earthquake of his chariot thundering up
Olympus?

    [*The Car of the Hour arrives.* DEMOGORGON *descends,*
      and moves towards the Throne of JUPITER.
              Awful shape, what art thou? Speak!
   Demogorgon. Eternity. Demand no direr name.
Descend, and follow me down the abyss.
I am thy child, as thou wert Saturn's child;
Mightier than thee: and we must dwell together
Henceforth in darkness. Lift thy lightnings not.

The tyranny of heaven none may retain,
Or reassume, or hold, succeeding thee:
Yet if thou wilt, as 'tis the destiny
Of trodden worms to writhe till they are dead,
Put forth thy might.
  Jupiter.   Detested prodigy!
Even thus beneath the deep Titanian prisons
I trample thee! thou lingerest?
          Mercy! mercy!
No pity, no release, no respite! Oh,
That thou wouldst make mine enemy my judge,
Even where he hangs, seared by my long revenge,
On Caucasus! he would not doom me thus.
Gentle, and just, and dreadless, is he not
The monarch of the world? What then art thou?
No refuge! no appeal!
        Sink with me then,
We two will sink on the wide waves of ruin,
Even as a vulture and a snake outspent
Drop, twisted in inextricable fight,
Into a shoreless sea. Let hell unlock
Its mounded oceans of tempestuous fire,
And whelm on them into the bottomless void
This desolated world, and thee, and me,
The conqueror and the conquered, and the wreck
Of that for which they combated.
           Ai! Ai!
The elements obey me not. I sink
Dizzily down, ever, for ever, down.
And, like a cloud, mine enemy above
Darkens my fall with victory! Ai! Ai!

SCENE II.—*The Mouth of a great River in the Island Atlantis.* OCEAN
 is discovered reclining near the Shore; APOLLO *stands beside him.*

  Ocean. He fell, thou sayest, beneath his conqueror's frown?
  Apollo. Ay, when the strife was ended which made dim
The orb I rule, and shook the solid stars,
The terrors of his eye illumined heaven
With sanguine light, through the thick ragged skirts
Of the victorious darkness, as he fell:
Like the last glare of day's red agony,

Which, from a rent among the fiery clouds,
Burns far along the tempest-wrinkled deep.

   Ocean. He sunk to the abyss? To the dark void?

   Apollo. An eagle so caught in some bursting cloud
On Caucasus, his thunder-baffled wings
Entangled in the whirlwind, and his eyes
Which gazed on the undazzling sun, now blinded
By the white lightning, while the ponderous hail
Beats on his struggling form, which sinks at length
Prone, and the aëreal ice clings over it.

   Ocean. Henceforth the fields of heaven-reflecting sea
Which are my realm, will heave, unstained with blood,
Beneath the uplifting winds, like plains of corn
Swayed by the summer air; my streams will flow
Round many-peopled continents, and round
Fortunate isles; and from their glassy thrones
Blue Proteus and his humid nymphs shall mark
The shadow of fair ships, as mortals see
The floating bark of the light-laden moon
With that white star, its sightless pilot's crest,
Borne down the rapid sunset's ebbing sea;
Tracking their path no more by blood and groans,
And desolation, and the mingled voice
Of slavery and command; but by the light
Of wave-reflected flowers, and floating odours,
And music soft, and mild, free, gentle voices,
And sweetest music, such as spirits love.

   Apollo. And I shall gaze not on the deeds which make
My mind obscure with sorrow, as eclipse
Darkens the sphere I guide; but list, I hear
The small, clear, silver lute of the young Spirit
That sits i' the morning star.

   Ocean.   Thou must away;
Thy steeds will pause at even, till when farewell:
The loud deep calls me home even now to feed it
With azure calm out of the emerald urns
Which stand for ever full beside my throne.
Behold the Nereids under the green sea,
Their wavering limbs borne on the wind-like stream,
Their white arms lifted o'er their streaming hair
With garlands pied and starry sea-flower crowns,
Hastening to grace their mighty sister's joy.

[*A sound of waves is heard.*

It is the unpastured sea hungering for calm.
Peace, monster; I come now. Farewell.
   Apollo.   Farewell.

SCENE III.—*Caucasus.* PROMETHEUS, HERCULES, IONE, *the* EARTH,
SPIRITS, ASIA, *and* PANTHEA, *borne in the Car with the* SPIRIT
OF THE HOUR. HERCULES *unbinds* PROMETHEUS, *who descends.*

Hercules. Most glorious among Spirits, thus doth strength
To wisdom, courage, and long-suffering love,
And thee, who art the form they animate,
Minister like a slave.
   Prometheus.   Thy gentle words
Are sweeter even than freedom long desired
And long delayed.
                   Asia, thou light of life,
Shadow of beauty unbeheld: and ye,
Fair sister nymphs, who made long years of pain
Sweet to remember, through your love and care:
Henceforth we will not part. There is a cave,
All overgrown with trailing odorous plants,
Which curtain out the day with leaves and flowers,
And paved with veinèd emerald, and a fountain
Leaps in the midst with an awakening sound.
From its curved roof the mountain's frozen tears
Like snow, or silver, or long diamond spires,
Hang downward, raining forth a doubtful light:
And there is heard the ever-moving air,
Whispering without from tree to tree, and birds,
And bees; and all around are mossy seats,
And the rough walls are clothed with long soft grass;
A simple dwelling, which shall be our own;
Where we will sit and talk of time and change,
As the world ebbs and flows, ourselves unchanged.
What can hide man from mutability?
And if ye sigh, then I will smile; and thou,
Ione, shalt chant fragments of sea-music,
Until I weep, when ye shall smile away
The tears she brought, which yet were sweet to shed.
We will entangle buds and flowers and beams

Which twinkle on the fountain's brim, and make
Strange combinations out of common things,
Like human babes in their brief innocence;
And we will search, with looks and words of love,
For hidden thoughts, each lovelier than the last,
Our unexhausted spirits; and like lutes
Touched by the skill of the enamoured wind,
Weave harmonies divine, yet ever new,
From difference sweet where discord cannot be;
And hither come, sped on the charmèd winds,
Which meet from all the points of heaven, as bees
From every flower aëreal Enna feeds,
At their known island-homes in Himera,
The echoes of the human world, which tell
Of the low voice of love, almost unheard,
And dove-eyed pity's murmured pain, and music,
Itself the echo of the heart, and all
That tempers or improves man's life, now free;
And lovely apparitions,—dim at first,
Then radiant, as the mind, arising bright
From the embrace of beauty (whence the forms
Of which these are the phantoms) casts on them
The gathered rays which are reality—
Shall visit us, the progeny immortal
Of Painting, Sculpture, and rapt Poesy,
And arts, though unimagined, yet to be.
The wandering voices and the shadows these
Of all that man becomes, the mediators
Of that best worship love, by him and us
Given and returned; swift shapes and sounds, which grow
More fair and soft as man grows wise and kind,
And, veil by veil, evil and error fall:
Such virtue has the cave and place around.
                              [*Turning to the* Spirit of the Hour.
For thee, fair Spirit, one toil remains. Ione,
Give her that curvèd shell, which Proteus old
Made Asia's nuptial boon, breathing within it
A voice to be accomplished, and which thou
Didst hide in grass under the hollow rock.
    Ione. Thou most desired Hour, more loved and lovely
Than all thy sisters, this is the mystic shell;
See the pale azure fading into silver

Lining it with a soft yet glowing light:
Looks it not like lulled music sleeping there?

 Spirit. It seems in truth the fairest shell of Ocean:
Its sound must be at once both sweet and strange.

 Prometheus. Go, borne over the cities of mankind
On whirlwind-footed coursers: once again
Outspeed the sun around the orbèd world;
And as thy chariot cleaves the kindling air,
Thou breathe into the many-folded shell,
Loosening its mighty music; it shall be
As thunder mingled with clear echoes: then
Return; and thou shalt dwell beside our cave.
And thou, O, Mother Earth!—

 The Earth.   I hear, I feel;
Thy lips are on me, and their touch runs down
Even to the adamantine central gloom
Along these marble nerves; 'tis life, 'tis joy,
And through my withered, old, and icy frame
The warmth of an immortal youth shoots down
Circling. Henceforth the many children fair
Folded in my sustaining arms; all plants,
And creeping forms, and insects rainbow-winged,
And birds, and beasts, and fish, and human shapes,
Which drew disease and pain from my wan bosom,
Draining the poison of despair, shall take
And interchange sweet nutriment; to me
Shall they become like sister-antelopes
By one fair dam, snow-white and swift as wind,
Nursed among lilies near a brimming stream.
The dew-mists of my sunless sleep shall float
Under the stars like balm: night-folded flowers
Shall suck unwithering hues in their repose:
And men and beasts in happy dreams shall gather
Strength for the coming day, and all its joy:
And death shall be the last embrace of her
Who takes the life she gave, even as a mother
Folding her child, says, 'Leave me not again.'

 Asia. Oh, mother! wherefore speak the name of death?
Cease they to love, and move, and breathe, and speak,
Who die?

 The Earth. It would avail not to reply:
Thou art immortal, and this tongue is known

But to the uncommunicating dead.
Death is the veil which those who live call life:
They sleep, and it is lifted: and meanwhile
In mild variety the seasons mild
With rainbow-skirted showers, and odorous winds,
And long blue meteors cleansing the dull night,
And the life-kindling shafts of the keen sun's
All-piercing bow, and the dew-mingled rain
Of the calm moonbeams, a soft influence mild,
Shall clothe the forests and the fields, ay, even
The crag-built deserts of the barren deep,
With ever-living leaves, and fruits, and flowers.
And thou! There is a cavern where my spirit
Was panted forth in anguish whilst thy pain
Made my heart mad, and those who did inhale it
Became mad too, and built a temple there,
And spoke, and were oracular, and lured
The erring nations round to mutual war.
And faithless faith, such as Jove kept with thee;
Which breath now rises, as amongst tall weeds
A violet's exhalation, and it fills
With a serener light and crimson air
Intense, yet soft, the rocks and woods around;
It feeds the quick growth of the serpent vine,
And the dark linkèd ivy tangling wild,
And budding, blown, or odour-faded blooms
Which star the winds with points of coloured light,
As they rain through them, and bright golden globes
Of fruit, suspended in their own green heaven,
And through their veinèd leaves and amber stems
The flowers whose purple and translucid bowls
Stand ever mantling with aëreal dew,
The drink of spirits: and it circles round,
Like the soft waving wings of noonday dreams,
Inspiring calm and happy thoughts, like mine,
Now thou art thus restored. This cave is thine.
Arise! Appear!

                    [*A* Spirit *rises in the likeness of a winged child.*
                This is my torch-bearer;
Who let his lamp out in old time with gazing
On eyes from which he kindled it anew
With love, which is as fire, sweet daughter mine,

For such is that within thine own. Run, wayward,
And guide this company beyond the peak
Of Bacchic Nysa, Mænad-haunted mountain,
And beyond Indus and its tribute rivers,
Trampling the torrent streams and glassy lakes
With feet unwet, unwearied, undelaying,
And up the green ravine, across the vale,
Beside the windless and crystalline pool,
Where ever lies, on unerasing waves,
The image of a temple, built above,
Distinct with column, arch, and architrave,
And palm-like capital, and over-wrought,
And populous with most living imagery,
Praxitelean shapes, whose marble smiles
Fill the hushed air with everlasting love.
It is deserted now, but once it bore
Thy name, Prometheus; there the emulous youths
Bore to thy honour through the divine gloom
The lamp which was thine emblem; even as those
Who bear the untransmitted torch of hope
Into the grave, across the night of life,
As thou hast borne it most triumphantly
To this far goal of Time. Depart, farewell.
Beside that temple is the destined cave.

SCENE IV.—*A Forest. In the Background a Cave.* PROMETHEUS, ASIA,
    PANTHEA, IONE, *and the* SPIRIT OF THE EARTH.

Ione. Sister, it is not earthly: how it glides
Under the leaves! how on its head there burns
A light, like a green star, whose emerald beams
Are twined with its fair hair! how, as it moves,
The splendour drops·in flakes upon the grass!
Knowest thou it?
    Panthea.   It is the delicate spirit
That guides the earth through heaven. From afar
The populous constellations call that light
The loveliest of the planets; and sometimes
It floats along the spray of the salt sea,
Or makes its chariot of a foggy cloud,
Or walks through fields or cities while men sleep,

Or o'er the mountain tops, or down the rivers,
Or through the green waste wilderness, as now,
Wondering at all it sees. Before Jove reigned
It loved our sister Asia, and it came
Each leisure hour to drink the liquid light
Out of her eyes, for which it said it thirsted
As one bit by a dipsas, and with her
It made its childish confidence, and told her
All it had known or seen, for it saw much,
Yet idly reasoned what it saw; and called her—
For whence it sprung it knew not, nor do I—
Mother, dear mother.

  The Spirit of the Earth (running to Asia). Mother, dearest mother;
May I then talk with thee as I was wont?
May I then hide my eyes in thy soft arms,
After thy looks have made them tired of joy?
May I then play beside thee the long noons,
When work is none in the bright silent air?

  Asia. I love thee, gentlest being, and henceforth
Can cherish thee unenvied: speak, I pray:
Thy simple talk once solaced, now delights.

  Spirit of the Earth. Mother, I am grown wiser, though a child
Cannot be wise like thee, within this day;
And happier too; happier and wiser both.
Thou knowest that toads, and snakes, and loathly worms,
And venomous and malicious beasts, and boughs
That bore ill berries in the woods, were ever
An hindrance to my walks o'er the green world:
And that, among the haunts of humankind,
Hard-featured men, or with proud, angry looks,
Or cold, staid gait, or false and hollow smiles,
Or the dull sneer of self-loved ignorance,
Or other such foul masks, with which ill thoughts
Hide that fair being whom we spirits call man;
And women too, ugliest of all things evil,
(Though fair, even in a world where thou art fair,
When good and kind, free and sincere like thee),
When false or frowning made me sick at heart
To pass them, though they slept, and I unseen.
Well, my path lately lay through a great city
Into the woody hills surrounding it:
A sentinel was sleeping at the gate:

When there was heard a sound, so loud, it shook
The towers amid the moonlight, yet more sweet
Than any voice but thine, sweetest of all;
A long, long sound, as it would never end:
And all the inhabitants leaped suddenly
Out of their rest, and gathered in the streets,
Looking in wonder up to Heaven, while yet
The music pealed along. I hid myself
Within a fountain in the public square,
Where I lay like the reflex of the moon
Seen in a wave under green leaves; and soon
Those ugly human shapes and visages
Of which I spoke as having wrought me pain,
Passed floating through the air, and fading still
Into the winds that scattered them; and those
From whom they passed seemed mild and lovely forms
After some foul disguise had fallen, and all
Were somewhat changed, and after brief surprise
And greetings of delighted wonder, all
Went to their sleep again: and when the dawn
Came, wouldst thou think that toads, and snakes, and efts,
Could e'er be beautiful? yet so they were,
And that with little change of shape or hue:
All things had put their evil nature off:
I cannot tell my joy, when o'er a lake
Upon a drooping bough with nightshade twined,
I saw two azure halcyons clinging downward
And thinning one bright bunch of amber berries,
With quick long beaks, and in the deep there lay
Those lovely forms imaged as in a sky;
So, with my thoughts full of these happy changes,
We meet again, the happiest change of all.

    Asia. And never will we part, till thy chaste sister
Who guides the frozen and inconstant moon
Will look on thy more warm and equal light
Till her heart thaw like flakes of April snow
And love thee.

    Spirit of the Earth. What; as Asia loves Prometheus?
    Asia. Peace, wanton, thou art yet not old enough.
Think ye by gazing on each other's eyes
To multiply your lovely selves, and fill
With spherèd fires the interlunar air?

Spirit of the Earth. Nay, mother, while my sister trims her lamp
'Tis hard I should go darkling.

    Asia.   Listen; look!

                         [*The* SPIRIT OF THE HOUR *enters.*

    Prometheus. We feel what thou hast heard and seen: yet speak

    Spirit of the Hour. Soon as the sound had ceased whose thunder filled
The abysses of the sky and the wide earth,
There was a change: the impalpable thin air
And the all-circling sunlight were transformed,
As if the sense of love dissolved in them
Had folded itself round the spherèd world.
My vision then grew clear, and I could see
Into the mysteries of the universe:
Dizzy as with delight I floated down,
Winnowing the lightsome air with languid plumes,
My coursers sought their birthplace in the sun,
Where they henceforth will live exempt from toil,
Pasturing flowers of vegetable fire;
And where my moonlike car will stand within
A temple, gazed upon by Phidian forms
Of thee, and Asia, and the Earth, and me,
And you fair nymphs looking the love we feel,—
In memory of the tidings it has borne,—
Beneath a dome fretted with graven flowers,
Poised on twelve columns of resplendent stone,
And open to the bright and liquid sky.
Yoked to it by an amphisbaenic snake
The likeness of those wingèd steeds will mock
The flight from which they find repose. Alas,
Whither has wandered now my partial tongue
When all remains untold which ye would hear?
As I have said, I floated to the earth:
It was, as it is still, the pain of bliss
To move, to breathe, to be; I wandering went
Among the haunts and dwellings of mankind,
And first was disappointed not to see
Such mighty change as I had felt within
Expressed in outward things; but soon I looked,
And behold, thrones were kingless, and men walked
One with the other even as spirits do.
None fawned, none trampled; hate, disdain, or fear,

Self-love or self-contempt, on human brows
No more inscribed, as o'er the gate of hell,
'All hope abandon ye who enter here;'
None frowned, none trembled, none with eager fear
Gazed on another's eye of cold command,
Until the subject of a tyrant's will
Became, worse fate, the abject of his own,
Which spurred him, like an outspent horse, to death.
None wrought his lips in truth-entangling lines
Which smiled the lie his tongue disdained to speak;
None, with firm sneer, trod out in his own heart
The sparks of love and hope till there remained
Those bitter ashes, a soul self-consumed,
And the wretch crept a vampire among men,
Infecting all with his own hideous ill;
None talked that common, false, cold, hollow talk
Which makes the heart deny the *yes* it breathes,
Yet question that unmeant hypocrisy
With such a self-mistrust as has no name.
And women, too, frank, beautiful, and kind
As the free heaven which rains fresh light and dew
On the wide earth, past; gentle radiant forms,
From custom's evil taint exempt and pure;
Speaking the wisdom once they could not think,
Looking emotions once they feared to feel,
And changed to all which once they dared not be,
Yet being now, made earth like heaven; nor pride,
Nor jealousy, nor envy, nor ill shame,
The bitterest of those drops of treasured gall,
Spoilt the sweet taste of the nepenthe, love.

Thrones, altars, judgement-seats, and prisons; wherein,
And beside which, by wretched men were borne
Sceptres, tiaras, swords, and chains, and tomes
Of reasoned wrong, glozed on by ignorance,
Were like those monstrous and barbaric shapes,
The ghosts of a no-more-remembered fame,
Which, from their unworn obelisks, look forth
In triumph o'er the palaces and tombs
Of those who were their conquerors: mouldering round,
These imaged to the pride of kings and priests
A dark yet mighty faith, a power as wide

As is the world it wasted, and are now
But an astonishment; even so the tools
And emblems of its last captivity,
Amid the dwellings of the peopled earth,
Stand, not o'erthrown, but unregarded now.
And those foul shapes, abhorred by god and man,—
Which, under many a name and many a form
Strange, savage, ghastly, dark and execrable,
Were Jupiter, the tyrant of the world;
And which the nations, panic-stricken, served
With blood, and hearts broken by long hope, and love
Dragged to his altars soiled and garlandless,
And slain amid men's unreclaiming tears,
Flattering the thing they feared, which fear was hate,—
Frown, mouldering fast, o'er their abandoned shrines:
The painted veil, by those who were, called life,
Which mimicked, as with colours idly spread,
All men believed or hoped, is torn aside;
The loathsome mask has fallen, the man remains
Sceptreless, free, uncircumscribed, but man
Equal, unclassed, tribeless, and nationless,
Exempt from awe, worship, degree, the king
Over himself; just, gentle, wise: but man
Passionless?——no, yet free from guilt or pain,
Which were, for his will made or suffered them,
Nor yet exempt, though ruling them like slaves,
From chance, and death, and mutability,
The clogs of that which else might oversoar
The loftiest star of unascended heaven,
Pinnacled dim in the intense inane.

Act IV

SCENE.—*A Part of the Forest near the Cave of* PROMETHEUS. PANTHEA
and IONE *are sleeping: they awaken gradually during the first Song.*

Voice of unseen Spirits

The pale stars are gone!
For the sun, their swift shepherd,
To their folds them compelling,
In the depths of the dawn.
Hastes, in meteor-eclipsing array, and they flee

Beyond his blue dwelling,
As fawns flee the leopard.
But where are ye?

A Train of dark Forms and Shadows passes by confusedly, singing

Here, oh, here:
We bear the bier
Of the Father of many a cancelled year!
Spectres we
Of the dead Hours be,
We bear Time to his tomb in eternity.

Strew, oh, strew
Hair, not yew!
Wet the dusty pall with tears, not dew!
Be the faded flowers
Of Death's bare bowers
Spread on the corpse of the King of Hours!

Haste, oh, haste!
As shades are chased,
Trembling, by day, from heaven's blue waste.
We melt away,
Like dissolving spray,
From the children of a diviner day,
With the lullaby
Of winds that die
On the bosom of their own harmony!

Ione

What dark forms were they?

Panthea

The past Hours weak and gray,
With the spoil which their toil
Raked together
From the conquest but One could foil.

Ione

Have they passed?

Panthea

                    They have passed;
They outspeeded the blast,
While 'tis said, they are fled:

Ione

Whither, oh, whither?

Panthea

To the dark, to the past, to the dead.

Voice of unseen Spirits

Bright clouds float in heaven,
Dew-stars gleam on earth,
Waves assemble on ocean,
They are gathered and driven
By the storm of delight, by the panic of glee!
They shake with emotion,
They dance in their mirth.
        But where are ye?

The pine boughs are singing
Old songs with new gladness,
The billows and fountains
Fresh music are flinging,
Like the notes of a spirit from land and from sea;
The storms mock the mountains
With the thunder of gladness.
        But where are ye?

Ione. What charioteers are these?
Panthea.   Where are their chariots?

Semichorus of Hours

The voice of the Spirits of Air and of Earth
    Have drawn back the figured curtain of sleep
Which covered our being and darkened our birth
    In the deep.

A Voice

In the deep?

Semichorus II

                    Oh, below the deep

Semichorus I

An hundred ages we had been kept
　　Cradled in visions of hate and care,
And each one who waked as his brother slept,
　　Found the truth—

Semichorus II

Worse than his visions were!

Semichorus I

We have heard the lute of Hope in sleep;
　　We have known the voice of Love in dreams;
We have felt the wand of Power, and leap—

Semichorus II

As the billows leap in the morning beams!

Chorus

Weave the dance on the floor of the breeze,
　　Pierce with song heaven's silent light,
Enchant the day that too swiftly flees,
　　To check its flight ere the cave of Night.

Once the hungry Hours were hounds
　　Which chased the day like a bleeding deer,
And it limped and stumbled with many wounds
　　Through the nightly dells of the desert year.

But now, oh weave the mystic measure
　　Of music, and dance, and shapes of light,
Let the Hours, and the spirits of might and plesaure,
　　Like the clouds and sunbeams, unite.

A Voice

　　　　　　　　　　　　Unite!

Panthea. See, where the Spirits of the human mind
Wrapped in sweet sounds, as in bright veils, approach.

Chorus of Spirits

We join the throng
Of the dance and the song,
By the whirlwind of gladness borne along;

As the flying-fish leap
From the Indian deep,
And mix with the sea-birds, half asleep.

Chorus of Hours

Whence come ye, so wild and so fleet,
For sandals of lightning are on your feet,
And your wings are soft and swift as thought,
And your eyes are as love which is veilèd not?

Chorus of Spirits

We come from the mind
Of human kind
Which was late so dusk, and obscene, and blind,
Now 'tis an ocean
Of clear emotion,
A heaven of serene and mighty motion

From that deep abyss
Of wonder and bliss,
Whose caverns are crystal palaces;
From those skiey towers
Where Thought's crowned powers
Sit watching your dance, ye happy Hours!

From the dim recesses
Of woven caresses,
Where lovers catch ye by your loose tresses;
From the azure isles,
Where sweet Wisdom smiles,
Delaying your ships with her siren wiles.

From the temples high
Of Man's ear and eye,
Roofed over Sculpture and Poesy;
From the murmurings
Of the unsealed springs
Where Science bedews her Dædal wings.

Years after years,
Through blood, and tears,
And a thick hell of hatreds, and hopes, and fears;

We waded and flew,
And the islets were few
Where the bud-blighted flowers of happiness grew.

Our feet now, every palm,
Are sandalled with calm,
And the dew of our wings is a rain of balm;
And, beyond our eyes,
The human love lies
Which makes all it gazes on Paradise.

Chorus of Spirits and Hours

Then weave the web of the mystic measure;
From the depths of the sky and the ends of the earth,
Come, swift Spirits of might and of pleasure,
Fill the dance and the music of mirth,
As the waves of a thousand streams rush by
To an ocean of splendour and harmony!

Chorus of Spirits

Our spoil is won,
Our task is done,
We are free to dive, or soar, or run;
Beyond and around,
Or within the bound
Which clips the world with darkness round.

We'll pass the eyes
Of the starry skies
Into the hoar deep to colonize:
Death, Chaos, and Night,
From the sound of our flight,
Shall flee, like mist from a tempest's might.

And Earth, Air, and Light,
And the Spirit of Might,
Which drives round the stars in their fiery flight;
And Love, Thought, and Breath,
The powers that quell Death,
Wherever we soar shall assemble beneath.

And our singing shall build
In the void's loose field
A world for the Spirit of Wisdom to wield;
We will take our plan
From the new world of man,
And our work shall be called the Promethean.

Chorus of Hours

Break the dance, and scatter the song;
Let some depart, and some remain.

Semichorus I

We, beyond heaven, are driven along:

Semichorus II

Us the enchantments of earth retain:

Semichorus I

Ceaseless, and rapid, and fierce, and free,
With the Spirits which build a new earth and sea,
And a heaven where yet heaven could never be.

Semichorus II

Solemn, and slow, and serene, and bright,
Leading the Day and outspeeding the Night,
With the powers of a world of perfect light.

Semichorus I

We whirl, singing loud, round the gathering sphere,
Till the trees, and the beasts, and the clouds appear
From its chaos made calm by love, not fear.

Semichorus II

We encircle the ocean and mountains of earth,
And the happy forms of its death and birth
Change to the music of our sweet mirth.

Chorus of Hours and Spirits

Break the dance, and scatter the song,
Let some depart, and some remain,
Wherever we fly we lead along
In leashes, like starbeams, soft yet strong,
The clouds that are heavy with love's sweet rain.

Panthea. Ha! they are gone!

Ione.   Yet feel you no delight
From the past sweetness?

Panthea.   As the bare green hill
When some soft cloud vanishes into rain,
Laughs with a thousand drops of sunny water
To the unpavilioned sky!

Ione.   Even whilst we speak
New notes arise. What is that awful sound?

Panthea. 'Tis the deep music of the rolling world
Kindling within the strings of the waved air
Æolian modulations.

Ione.   Listen too,
How every pause is filled with under-notes,
Clear, silver, icy, keen, awakening tones,
Which pierce the sense, and live within the soul,
As the sharp stars pierce winter's crystal air
And gaze upon themselves within the sea.

Panthea. But see where through two openings in the forest
Which hanging branches overcanopy,
And where two runnels of a rivulet,
Between the close moss violet-inwoven,
Have made their path of melody, like sisters
Who part with sighs that they may meet in smiles,
Turning their dear disunion to an isle
Of lovely grief, a wood of sweet sad thoughts;
Two visions of strange radiance float upon
The ocean-like enchantment of strong sound,
Which flows intenser, keener, deeper yet
Under the ground and through the windless air.

Ione. I see a chariot like that thinnest boat,
In which the Mother of the Months is borne
By ebbing light into her western cave,
When she upsprings from interlunar dreams;
O'er which is curved an orblike canopy
Of gentle darkness, and the hills and woods,
Distinctly seen through that dusk aery veil,
Regard like shapes in an enchanter's glass;
Its wheels are solid clouds, azure and gold,
Such as the genii of the thunderstorm
Pile on the floor of the illumined sea
When the sun rushes under it; they roll

And move and grow as with an inward wind;
Within it sits a wingèd infant, white
Its countenance, like the whiteness of bright snow,
Its plumes are as feathers of sunny frost,
Its limbs gleam white, through the wind-flowing folds
Of its white robe, woof of ethereal pearl.
Its hair is white, the brightness of white light
Scattered in strings; yet its two eyes are heavens
Of liquid darkness, which the Deity
Within seems pouring, as a storm is poured
From jaggèd clouds, out of their arrowy lashes,
Tempering the cold and radiant air around,
With fire that is not brightness; in its hand
It sways a quivering moonbeam, from whose point
A guiding power directs the chariot's prow
Over its wheelèd clouds, which as they roll
Over the grass, and flowers, and waves, wake sounds,
Sweet as a singing rain of silver dew.
   Panthea. And from the other opening in the wood
Rushes, with loud and whirlwind harmony,
A sphere, which is as many thousand spheres,
Solid as crystal, yet through all its mass
Flow, as through empty space, music and light:
Ten thousand orbs involving and involved,
Purple and azure, white, and green, and golden,
Sphere within sphere; and every space between
Peopled with unimaginable shapes,
Such as ghosts dream dwell in the lampless deep,
Yet each inter-transpicuous, and they whirl
Over each other with a thousand motions,
Upon a thousand sightless axles spinning,
And with the force of self-destroying swiftness,
Intensely, slowly, solemnly roll on,
Kindling with mingled sounds, and many tones,
Intelligible words and music wild.
With mighty whirl the multitudinous orb
Grinds the bright brook into an azure mist
Of elemental subtlety, like light:
And the wild odour of the forest flowers,
The music of the living grass and air,
The emerald light of leaf-entangled beams
Round its intense yet self-conflicting speed,

Seem kneaded into one aëreal mass
Which drowns the sense. Within the orb itself,
Pillowed upon its alabaster arms,
Like to a child o'erwearied with sweet toil,
On its own folded wings, and wavy hair,
The Spirit of the Earth is laid asleep,
And you can see its little lips are moving,
Amid the changing light of their own smiles,
Like one who talks of what he loves in dream.

   Ione. 'Tis only mocking the orb's harmony.

   Panthea. And from a star upon its forehead, shoot,
Like swords of azure fire, or golden spears
With tyrant-quelling myrtle overtwined,
Embleming heaven and earth united now,
Vast beams like spokes of some invisible wheel
Which whirl as the orb whirls, swifter than thought,
Filling the abyss with sun-like lightenings,
And perpendicular now, and now transverse,
Pierce the dark soil, and as they pierce and pass,
Make bare the secrets of the earth's deep heart;
Infinite mines of adamant and gold,
Valueless stones, and unimagined gems,
And caverns on crystalline columns poised
With vegetable silver overspread;
Wells of unfathomed fire and water springs
Whence the great sea, even as a child is fed,
Whose vapours clothe earth's monarch mountain-tops
With kingly, ermine snow. The beams flash on
And make appear the melancholy ruins
Of cancelled cycles; anchors, beaks of ships;
Planks turned to marble; quivers, helms, and spears,
And gorgon-headed targes, and the wheels
Of scythèd chariots, and the emblazonry
Of trophies, standards, and armorial beasts,
Round which death laughed, sepulchred emblems
Of dead destruction, ruin within ruin!
The wrecks beside of many a city vast,
Whose population which the earth grew over
Was mortal, but not human; see, they lie,
Their monstrous works, and uncouth skeletons,
Their statues, homes and fanes; prodigious shapes
Huddled in gray annihilation, split,

Jammed in the hard, black deep; and over these,
The anatomies of unknown wingèd things,
And fishes which were isles of living scale,
And serpents, bony chains, twisted around
The iron crags, or within heaps of dust
To which the tortuous strength of their last pangs
Had crushed the iron crags; and over these
The jaggèd alligator, and the might
Of earth-convulsing behemoth, which once
Were monarch beasts, and on the slimy shores,
And weed-overgrown continents of earth,
Increased and multiplied like summer worms
On an abandoned corpse, till the blue globe
Wrapped deluge round it like a cloak, and they
Yelled, gasped, and were abolished; or some God
Whose throne was in a comet, passed, and cried,
'Be not!' And like my words they were no more.

The Earth

The joy, the triumph, the delight, the madness!
    The boundless, overflowing, bursting gladness,
The vaporous exultation not to be confined!
    Ha! ha! the animation of delight
    Which wraps me, like an atmosphere of light,
And bears me as a cloud is borne by its own wind.

The Moon

Brother mine, calm wanderer,
    Happy globe of land and air,
Some Spirit is darted like a beam from thee,
    Which penetrates my frozen frame,
    And passes with the warmth of flame,
With love, and odour, and deep melody
        Through me, through me!

The Earth

Ha! ha! the caverns of my hollow mountains,
    My cloven fire-crags, sound-exulting fountains
Laugh with a vast and inextinguishable laughter.
    The oceans, and the deserts, and the abysses,
    And the deep air's unmeasured wildernesses,
Answer from all their clouds and billows, echoing after.

They cry aloud as I do. Sceptred curse,
　Who all our green and azure universe
Threatenedst to muffle round with black destruction, sending
　A solid cloud to rain hot thunderstones,
　And splinter and knead down my children's bones,
All I bring forth, to one void mass battering and blending,

　Until each crag-like tower, and storied column,
　Palace, and obelisk, and temple solemn,
My imperial mountains crowned with cloud, and snow, and fire;
　My sea-like forests, every blade and blossom
　Which finds a grave or cradle in my bosom,
Were stamped by thy strong hate into a lifeless mire:

　How art thou sunk, withdrawn, covered, drunk up
　By thirsty nothing, as the brackish cup
Drained by a desert-troop, a little drop for all;
　And from beneath, around, within, above,
　Filling thy void annihilation, love
Burst in like light on caves cloven by the thunder-ball.

The Moon

　The snow upon my lifeless mountains
　Is loosened into living fountains,
My solid oceans flow, and sing, and shine:
　A spirit from my heart bursts forth,
　It clothes with unexpected birth
My cold bare bosom: Oh! it must be thine
　　On mine, on mine!

　Gazing on thee I feel, I know
　Green stalks burst forth, and bright flowers grow,
And living shapes upon my bosom move:
　Music is in the sea and air,
　Wingèd clouds soar here and there,
Dark with the rain new buds are dreaming of:
　　'Tis love, all love!

The Earth

It interpenetrates my granite mass,
　　Through tangled roots and trodden clay doth pass
Into the utmost leaves and delicatest flowers;
　　Upon the winds, among the clouds 'tis spread,
　　It wakes a life in the forgotten dead,
They breathe a spirit up from their obscurest bowers.

　　And like a storm bursting its cloudy prison
　　With thunder, and with whirlwind, has arisen
Out of the lampless caves of unimagined being:
　　With earthquake shock and swiftness making shiver
　　Thought's stagnant chaos, unremoved for ever,
Till hate, and fear, and pain, light-vanquished shadows, fleeing,

　　Leave Man, who was a many-sided mirror,
　　Which could distort to many a shape of error,
This true fair world of things, a sea reflecting love;
　　Which over all his kind, as the sun's heaven
　　Gliding o'er ocean, smooth, serene, and even,
Darting from starry depths radiance and life, doth move:

　　Leave Man, even as a leprous child is left,
　　Who follows a sick beast to some warm cleft
Of rocks, through which the might of healing springs is poured;
　　Then when it wanders home with rosy smile,
　　Unconscious, and its mother fears awhile
It is a spirit, then, weeps on her child restored.

　　Man, oh, not men! a chain of linkèd thought,
　　Of love and might to be divided not,
Compelling the elements with adamantine stress;
　　As the sun rules, even with a tyrant's gaze,
　　The unquiet republic of the maze
Of planets, struggling fierce towards heaven's free wilderness.

　　Man, one harmonious soul of many a soul,
　　Whose nature is its own divine control,
Where all things flow to all, as rivers to the sea;
　　Familiar acts are beautiful through love;
　　Labour, and pain, and grief, in life's green grove
Sport like tame beasts, none knew how gentle they could be!

His will, with all mean passions, bad delights,
And selfish cares, its trembling satellites,
A spirit ill to guide, but mighty to obey,
Is as a tempest-wingèd ship, whose helm
Love rules, through waves which dare not overwhelm,
Forcing life's wildest shores to own its sovereign sway.

All things confess his strength. Through the cold mass
Of marble and of colour his dreams pass;
Bright threads whence mothers weave the robes their children
          wear;
Language is a perpetual Orphic song,
Which rules with Dædal harmony a throng
Of thoughts and forms, which else senseless and shapeless were.

The lightning is his slave; heaven's utmost deep
Gives up her stars, and like a flock of sheep
They pass before his eye, are numbered, and roll on!
The tempest is his steed, he strides the air;
And the abyss shouts from her depth laid bare,
Heaven, hast thou secrets? Man unveils me; I have none.

The Moon

The shadow of white death has passed
From my path in heaven at last,
A clinging shroud of solid frost and sleep;
And through my newly-woven bowers,
Wander happy paramours,
Less mighty, but as mild as those who keep
          Thy vales more deep.

The Earth

As the dissolving warmth of dawn may fold
A half unfrozen dew-globe, green, and gold,
And crystalline, till it becomes a wingèd mist,
And wanders up the vault of the blue day,
Outlives the moon, and on the sun's last ray
Hangs o'er the sea, a fleece of fire and amethyst.

The Moon

Thou art folded, thou art lying
In the light which is undying
Of thine own joy, and heaven's smile divine;
All suns and constellations shower
On thee a light, a life, a power
Which doth array thy sphere; thou pourest thine
On mine, on mine!

The Earth

I spin beneath my pyramid of night,
Which points into the heavens dreaming delight,
Murmuring victorious joy in my enchanted sleep;
As a youth lulled in love-dreams faintly sighing,
Under the shadow of his beauty lying,
Which round his rest a watch of light and warmth doth keep.

The Moon

As in the soft and sweet eclipse,
When soul meets soul on lovers' lips,
High hearts are calm, and brightest eyes are dull;
So when thy shadow falls on me,
Then am I mute and still, by thee
Covered; of thy love, Orb most beautiful,
Full, oh, too full!

Thou art speeding round the sun
Brightest world of many a one;
Green and azure sphere which shinest
With a light which is divinest
Among all the lamps of Heaven
To whom life and light is given;
I, thy crystal paramour
Borne beside thee by a power
Like the polar Paradise,
Magnet-like of lovers' eyes;
I, a most enamoured maiden
Whose weak brain is overladen
With the pleasure of her love,
Maniac-like around thee move
Gazing, an insatiate bride,
On thy form from every side

Like a Mænad, round the cup
Which Agave lifted up
In the weird Cadmæan forest.
Brother, wheresoe'er thou soarest
I must hurry, whirl and follow
Through the heavens wide and hollow,
Sheltered by the warm embrace
Of thy soul from hungry space,
Drinking from thy sense and sight
Beauty, majesty, and might,
As a lover or a chameleon
Grows like what it looks upon,
As a violet's gentle eye
Gazes on the azure sky
Until its hue grows like what it beholds,
As a gray and watery mist
Glows like solid amethyst
Athwart the western mountain it enfolds,
When the sunset sleeps
Upon its snow—

The Earth

And the weak day weeps
That it should be so.
Oh, gentle Moon, the voice of thy delight
Falls on me like thy clear and tender light
Soothing the seaman, borne the summer night
Through isles for ever calm;
Oh, gentle Moon, thy crystal accents pierce
The caverns of my pride's deep universe,
Charming the tiger joy, whose tramplings fierce
Made wounds which need thy balm.
Panthea. I rise as from a bath of sparkling water,
A bath of azure light, among dark rocks,
Out of the stream of sound.
Ione.   Ah me! sweet sister,
The stream of sound has ebbed away from us,
And you pretend to rise out of its wave,
Because your words fall like the clear soft dew
Shaken from a bathing wood-nymph's limbs and hair.
Panthea. Peace! peace! A mighty Power which is as darkness
Is rising out of Earth, and from the sky

Is showered like night, and from within the air
Bursts, like eclipse which had been gathered up
Into the pores of sunlight: the bright visions,
Wherein the singing spirits rode and shone,
Gleam like pale meteors through a watery night.
   Ione. There is a sense of words upon mine ear.
   Panthea. An universal sound like words: Oh, list!

Demogorgon

Thou, Earth, calm empire of a happy soul,
   Sphere of divinest shapes and harmonies,
Beautiful orb! gathering as thou dost roll
   The love which paves thy path along the skies:

The Earth

   I hear: I am as a drop of dew that dies.

Demogorgon

Thou, Moon, which gazest on the nightly Earth
   With wonder, as it gazes upon thee;
Whilst each to men, and beasts, and the swift birth
   Of birds, is beauty, love, calm, harmony:

The Moon

   I hear: I am a leaf shaken by thee!

Demogorgon

Ye Kings of suns and stars, Dæmons and Gods,
   Aetherial Dominations, who possess
Elysian, windless, fortunate abodes
   Beyond Heaven's constellated wilderness:

A Voice from above

   Our great Republic hears, we are blest, and bless.

Demogorgon

Ye happy Dead, whom beams of brightest verse
   Are clouds to hide, not colours to portray,
Whether your nature is that universe
   Which once ye saw and suffered—

A Voice from beneath

                     Or as they
Whom we have left, we change and pass away.

Demogorgon

Ye elemental Genii, who have homes
   From man's high mind even to the central stone
Of sullen lead; from heaven's star-fretted domes
   To the dull weed some sea-worm battens on:

A confused Voice

We hear: thy words waken Oblivion.

Demogorgon

Spirits, whose homes are flesh: ye beasts and birds,
   Ye worms, and fish; ye living leaves and buds;
Lightning and wind; and ye untameable herds,
   Meteors and mists, which throng air's solitudes:

A Voice

Thy voice to us·is wind among still woods.

Demogorgon

Man, who wert once a despot and a slave;
   A dupe and a deceiver; a decay;
A traveller from the cradle to the grave
   Through the dim night of this immortal day:

All

Speak: thy strong words may never pass away.

Demogorgon

This is the day, which down the void abysm
At the Earth-born's spell yawns for Heaven's despotism,
   And Conquest is dragged captive through the deep:
Love, from its awful throne of patient power
In the wise heart, from the last giddy hour
   Of dread endurance, from the slippery, steep,
And narrow verge of crag-like agony, springs
And folds over the world its healing wings.

Gentleness, Virtue, Wisdom, and Endurance,
These are the seals of that most firm assurance
   Which bars the pit over Destruction's strength;
And if, with infirm hand, Eternity,
Mother of many acts and hours, should free
   The serpent that would clasp her with his length;
These are the spells by which to reassume
An empire o'er the disentangled doom.

To suffer woes which Hope thinks infinite;
To forgive wrongs darker than death or night;
   To defy Power, which seems omnipotent;
To love, and bear; to hope till Hope creates
From its own wreck the thing it contemplates;
   Neither to change, nor falter, nor repent;
This, like thy glory, Titan, is to be
Good, great and joyous, beautiful and free;
This is alone Life, Joy, Empire, and Victory.

The Cenci

A TRAGEDY IN FIVE ACTS

THE principal part was written with the thought that Miss O'Neil might take it. Shelley was among her warmest admirers, in her tragic characters at least. She was not even permitted to inspect the manuscript. However dexterously Shelley avoided all precise indication of the ultimate crime of Count Cenci, the subject was one which London theatre managers could not then touch. The Elizabethan stage could have accepted it, and since 1821 the piece has had some trials in the theatre, in England and America, and nobody has died of it. In 1820 Leigh Hunt described it as 'to say the least of it' undoubtedly the greatest dramatic production of the day; he was thinking of the profusion of quasi-Elizabethan plays then being performed. Shelley himself reckoned *The Cenci* as good as any of them for the theatre apart from Coleridge's *Remorse*, 1813, and this is a fair judgment.

Preface

A MANUSCRIPT was communicated to me during my travels in Italy, which was copied from the archives of the Cenci Palace at Rome, and contains a detailed account of the horrors which ended in the extinction of one of the noblest and richest families of that city during the Pontificate of Clement VIII, in the year 1599. The story is, that an old man having spent his life in debauchery and wickedness, conceived at length an implacable hatred towards his children; which showed itself towards one daughter under the form of an incestuous passion, aggravated by every circumstance of cruelty and violence. This daughter, after long and vain attempts to escape from what she considered a perpetual contamination both of body and mind, at length plotted with her mother-in-law and brother to murder their common tyrant. The young maiden, who was urged to this tremendous deed by an impulse which overpowered its horror, was evidently a most gentle and amiable being, a creature formed to adorn and be admired, and thus violently thwarted from her nature by the necessity of circumstance and opinion. The deed was quickly discovered, and, in spite of the most earnest prayers made to the Pope by the highest persons in Rome, the criminals were put to death. The old man had during his life repeatedly bought his pardon from the Pope for capital crimes of the most enormous and unspeakable kind, at the price of a hundred thousand crowns; the death therefore of his victims can scarcely be accounted for by the love of justice. The Pope, among other motives for severity, probably felt that whoever killed the Count Cenci deprived his treasury of a certain and copious source of revenue. Such a story, if told so as to present to the reader all the feelings of those who once acted it, their hopes and fears, their confidences and misgivings, their various interests, passions, and opinions, acting upon and with each other, yet all conspiring to one tremendous end, would be as a light to make apparent some of the most dark and secret caverns of the human heart.

***

I have endeavoured as nearly as possible to represent the characters as they probably were, and have sought to avoid the error of making them actuated by my own conceptions of right or wrong, false or true: thus under a thin veil converting names and actions of the sixteenth century into cold impersonations of my own mind. They are represented as Catholics, and as Catholics deeply tinged with religion. To a Protestant apprehension there will appear something unnatural in the earnest and perpetual sentiment of the relations between God and men which pervade the tragedy of the Cenci. It will especially be startled at the combination of an undoubting persuasion of the truth of the popular religion with a cool and determined perseverance in enormous guilt. But religion in Italy is not, as in Protestant countries, a cloak to be worn on particular days; or a passport which those who do not wish to be railed at carry with them to exhibit; or a gloomy passion for penetrating the impenetrable mysteries of our being, which terrifies its possessor at the darkness of the abyss to the brink of which it has conducted him. Religion coexists, as it were, in the mind of an Italian Catholic, with a faith in that of which all men have the most certain knowledge. It is interwoven with the whole fabric of life. It is adoration, faith, submission, penitence, blind admiration; not a rule for moral conduct. It has no necessary connection with any one virtue. The most atrocious villain may be rigidly devout, and without any shock to established faith, confess himself to be so. Religion pervades intensely the whole frame of society, and is according to the temper of the mind which it inhabits, a passion, a persuasion, an excuse, a refuge; never a check. Cenci himself built a chapel in the court of his Palace, and dedicated it to St. Thomas the Apostle, and established masses for the peace of his soul. Thus in the first scene of the fourth act Lucretia's design in exposing herself to the consequences of an expostulation with Cenci after having administered the opiate, was to induce him by a feigned tale to confess himself before death; this being esteemed by Catholics as essential to salvation; and she only relinquishes her purpose when she perceives that her perseverance would expose Beatrice to new outrages.

I have avoided with great care in writing this play the introduction of what is commonly called mere poetry, and I imagine there will scarcely be found a detached simile or a single isolated description, unless Beatrice's description of the chasm appointed for her father's murder should be judged to be of that nature.

Dramatis Personæ

COUNT FRANCESCO CENCI.

GIACOMO, } *his Sons.*
BERNARDO,

CARDINAL CAMILLO.

ORSINO, *a Prelate.*

SAVELLA, *the Pope's Legate.*

OLIMPIO, } *Assassins.*
MARZIO,

ANDREA, *Servant to Cenci.*

Nobles, Judges, Guards, Servants.

LUCRETIA, *Wife of* CENCI, *and Step-mother of his children.*

BEATRICE, *his Daughter.*

The SCENE lies principally in Rome, but changes during the Fourth
    Act to Petrella, a castle among the Apulian Apennines.

TIME. During the Pontificate of Clement VIII.

Act I

SCENE I.—*An Apartment in the Cenci Palace.*
Enter COUNT CENCI, *and* CARDINAL CAMILLO.

Camillo. That matter of the murder is hushed up
If you consent to yield his Holiness
Your fief that lies beyond the Pincian gate.—
It needed all my interest in the conclave
To bend him to this point: he said that you
Bought perilous impunity with your gold;
That crimes like yours if once or twice compounded
Enriched the Church, and respited from hell
An erring soul which might repent and live:—
But that the glory and the interest
Of the high throne he fills, little consist
With making it a daily mart of guilt
As manifold and hideous as the deeds
Which you scarce hide from men's revolted eyes,
    Cenci. The third of my possessions—let it go!
Ay, I once heard the nephew of the Pope
Had sent his architect to view the ground,
Meaning to build a villa on my vines
The next time I compounded with his uncle:
I little thought he should outwit me so!
Henceforth no witness—not the lamp—shall see

That which the vassal threatened to divulge
Whose throat is choked with dust for his reward.
The deed he saw could not have rated higher
Than his most worthless life:—it angers me!
Respited me from Hell!—So may the Devil
Respite their souls from Heaven. No doubt Pope Clement,
And his most charitable nephews, pray
That the Apostle Peter and the Saints
Will grant for their sake that I long enjoy
Strength, wealth, and pride, and lust, and length of days
Wherein to act the deeds which are the stewards
Of their revenue.—But much yet remains
To which they show no title.
    Camillo.   Oh, Count Cenci!
So much that thou mightst honourably live
And reconcile thyself with thine own heart
And with thy God, and with the offended world.
How hideously look deeds of lust and blood
Through those snow white and venerable hairs!—
Your children should be sitting round you now,
But that you fear to read upon their looks
The shame and misery you have written there.
Where is your wife? Where is your gentle daughter?
Methinks her sweet looks, which make all things else
Beauteous and glad, might kill the fiend within you.
Why is she barred from all society
But her own strange and uncomplaining wrongs?
Talk with me, Count,—you know I mean you well.
I stood beside your dark and fiery youth
Watching its bold and bad career, as men
Watch meteors, but it vanished not—I marked
Your desperate and remorseless manhood; now
Do I behold you in dishonoured age
Charged with a thousand unrepented crimes.
Yet I have ever hoped you would amend,
And in that hope have saved your life three times.
    Cenci. For which Aldobrandino owes you now
My fief beyond the Pincian.—Cardinal,
One thing, I pray you, recollect henceforth,
And so we shall converse with less restraint.
A man you knew spoke of my wife and daughter—
He was accustomed to frequent my house;

So the next day *his* wife and daughter came
And asked if I had seen him; and I smiled:
I think they never saw him any more.

   Camillo. Thou execrable man, beware!—
   Cenci.   Of thee?
Nay this is idle:—We should know each other.
As to my character for what men call crime
Seeing I please my senses as I list,
And vindicate that right with force or guile,
It is a public matter, and I care not
If I discuss it with you. I may speak
Alike to you and my own conscious heart—
For you give out that you have half reformed me,
Therefore strong vanity will keep you silent
If fear should not; both will, I do not doubt.
All men delight in sensual luxury,
All men enjoy revenge; and most exult
Over the tortures they can never feel—
Flattering their secret peace with others' pain.
But I delight in nothing else. I love
The sight of agony, and the sense of joy,
When this shall be another's, and that mine.
And I have no remorse and little fear,
Which are, I think, the checks of other men.
This mood has grown upon me, until now
Any design my captious fancy makes
The picture of its wish, and it forms none
But such as men like you would start to know,
Is as my natural food and rest debarred
Until it be accomplished.

   Camillo.   Art thou not
Most miserable?

   Cenci.   Why, miserable?—
No.—I am what your theologians call
Hardened;—which they must be in impudence,
So to revile a man's peculiar taste.
True, I was happier than I am, while yet
Manhood remained to act the thing I thought:
While lust was sweeter than revenge; and now
Invention palls:—Ay, we must all grow old—
And but that there yet remains a deed to act
Whose horror might make sharp an appetite

Duller than mine—I'd do—I know not what.
When I was young I thought of nothing else
But pleasure; and I fed on honey sweets:
Men, by St. Thomas! cannot live like bees,
And I grew tired:—yet, till I killed a foe,
And heard his groans, and heard his children's groans,
Knew I not what delight was else on earth,
Which now delights me little. I the rather
Look on such pangs as terror ill conceals,
The dry fixed eyeball; the pale quivering lip,
Which tell me that the spirit weeps within
Tears bitterer than the bloody sweat of Christ.
I rarely kill the body, which preserves.
Like a strong prison, the soul within my power,
Wherein I feed it with the breath of fear
For hourly pain.
    Camillo.   Hell's most abandoned fiend
Did never, in the drunkenness of guilt,
Speak to his heart as now you speak to me;
I thank my God that I believe you not.

Enter ANDREA.

    Andrea. My Lord, a gentleman from Salamanca
Would speak with you.
    Cenci.   Bid him attend me in
The grand saloon.   [*Exit* ANDREA
    Camillo.   Farewell; and I will pray
Almighty God that thy false, impious words
Tempt not his spirit to abandon thee.   [*Exit* CAMILLO.
    Cenci. The third of my possessions! I must use
Close husbandry, or gold, the old man's sword,
Falls from my withered hand. But yesterday
There came an order from the Pope to make
Fourfold provision for my cursèd sons;
Whom I had sent from Rome to Salamanca,
Hoping some accident might cut them off;
And meaning if I could to starve them there.
I pray thee, God, send some quick death upon them!
Bernardo and my wife could not be worse
If dead and damned:—then, as to Beatrice—
                [*Looking around him suspiciously*
I think they cannot hear me at that door;

What if they should? And yet I need not speak
Though the heart triumphs with itself in words.
O, thou most silent air, that shalt not hear
What now I think! Thou, pavement, which I tread
Towards her chamber,—let your echoes talk
Of my imperious step scorning surprise,
But not of my intent!—Andrea!

Enter ANDREA.

 Andrea.   My lord?
 Cenci. Bid Beatrice attend me in her chamber
This evening:—no, at midnight and alone.   [*Exeunt.*

SCENE II.—*A Garden of the Cenci Palace. Enter* BEATRICE *and* ORSINO,
as in conversation.

Beatrice. Pervert not truth.
Orsino. You remember where we held
That conversation;—nay, we see the spot
Even from this cypress;—two long years are past
Since, on an April midnight, underneath
The moonlight ruins of mount Palatine,
I did confess to you my secret mind.
 Orsino. You said you loved me then.
 Beatrice.   You are a Priest,
Speak to me not of love.
 Orsino.   I may obtain
The dispensation of the Pope to marry.
Because I am a Priest do you believe
Your image, as the hunter some struck deer,
Follows me not whether I wake or sleep?
 Beatrice. As I have said, speak to me not of love;
Had you a dispensation I have not;
Nor will I leave this home of misery
Whilst my poor Bernard, and that gentle lady
To whom I owe life, and these virtuous thoughts,
Must suffer what I still have strength to share.
Alas, Orsino! All the love that once
I felt for you, is turned to bitter pain.
Ours was a youthful contract, which you first
Broke, by assuming vows no Pope will loose.

And thus I love you still, but holily,
Even as a sister or a spirit might;
And so I swear a cold fidelity.
And it is well perhaps we shall not marry.
You have a sly, equivocating vein
That suits me not.—Ah, wretched that I am!
Where shall I turn? Even now you look on me
As you were not my friend, and as if you
Discovered that I thought so, with false smiles
Making my true suspicion seem your wrong.
Ah, no! forgive me; sorrow makes me seem
Sterner than else my nature might have been;
I have a weight of melancholy thoughts,
And they forbode,—but what can they forbode
Worse than I now endure?

    Orsino.   All will be well.
Is the petition yet prepared? You know
My zeal for all you wish, sweet Beatrice;
Doubt not but I will use my utmost skill
So that the Pope attend to your complaint.

    Beatrice. Your zeal for all I wish;—Ah me, you are cold!
Your utmost skill . . . speak but one word . . . *(aside)* Alas!
Weak and deserted creature that I am,
Here I stand bickering with my only friend! [*To* ORSINO.
This night my father gives a sumptuous feast,
Orsino; he has heard some happy news
From Salamanca, from my brothers there,
And with this outward show of love he mocks
His inward hate. 'Tis bold hypocrisy,
For he would gladlier celebrate their deaths,
Which I have heard him pray for on his knees:
Great God! that such a father should be mine!
But there is mighty preparation made,
And all our kin, the Cenci, will be there,
And all the chief nobility of Rome.
And he has bidden me and my pale Mother
Attire ourselves in festival array.
Poor lady! She expects some happy change
In his dark spirit from this act; I none.
At supper I will give you the petition:
Till when—farewell.

    Orsino. Farewell. (*Exit* BEATRICE.) I know the Pope

Will ne'er absolve me from my priestly vow
But by absolving me from the revenue
Of many a wealthy see; and, Beatrice,
I think to win thee at an easier rate.
Nor shall he read her eloquent petition:
He might bestow her on some poor relation
Of his sixth cousin, as he did her sister,
And I should be debarred from all access.
Then as to what she suffers from her father,
In all this there is much exaggeration:—
Old men are testy and will have their way;
A man may stab his enemy, or his vassal,
And live a free life as to wine or women,
And with a peevish temper may return
To a dull home, and rate his wife and children;
Daughters and wives call this foul tyranny.
I shall be well content if on my conscience
There rest no heavier sin than what they suffer
From the devices of my love—a net
From which she shall escape not. Yet I fear
Her subtle mind, her awe-inspiring gaze,
Whose beams anatomize me nerve by nerve
And lay me bare, and make me blush to see
My hidden thoughts.—Ah, no! A friendless girl
Who clings to me, as to her only hope:—
I were a fool, not less than if a panther
Were panic-stricken by the antelope's eye,
If she escape me.   [*Exit.*

SCENE III.—*A Magnificent Hall in the Cenci Palace. A Banquet. Enter*
CENCI, LUCRETIA, BEATRICE, ORSINO, CAMILLO, NOBLES.

Cenci. Welcome, my friends and kinsmen; welcome ye,
Princes and Cardinals, pillars of the church,
Whose presence honours our festivity.
I have too long lived like an anchorite,
And in my absence from your merry meetings
An evil word is gone abroad of me;
But I do hope that you, my noble friends,
When you have shared the entertainment here,
And heard the pious cause for which 'tis given,

And we have pledged a health or two together,
Will think me flesh and blood as well as you;
Sinful indeed, for Adam made all so,
But tender-hearted, meek and pitiful.

    First Guest. In truth, my Lord, you seem too light of heart,
Too sprightly and companionable a man.
To act the deeds that rumour pins on you.
(*To his Companion.*) I never saw such blithe and open cheer
In any eye!

    Second Guest. Some most desired event,
In which we all demand a common joy,
Has brought us hither; let us hear it, Count.

    Cenci. It is indeed a most desired event.
If, when a parent from a parent's heart
Lifts from this earth to the great Father of all
A prayer, both when he lays him down to sleep,
And when he rises up from dreaming it;
One supplication, one desire, one hope,
That he would grant a wish for his two sons,
Even all that he demands in their regard—
And suddenly beyond his dearest hope
It is accomplished, he should then rejoice,
And call his friends and kinsmen to a feast,
And task their love to grace his merriment,—
Then honour me thus far—for I am he.

    Beatrice (*To* LUCRETIA). Great God! How horrible! Some
        dreadful ill
Must have befallen my brothers.

    Lucretia.   Fear not, Child,
He speaks too frankly.

    Beatrice.   Ah! My blood runs cold.
I fear that wicked laughter round his eye,
Which wrinkles up the skin even to the hair.

    Cenci. Here are the letters brought from Salamanca;
Beatrice, read them to your mother, God!
I thank thee! In one night didst thou perform,
By ways inscrutable, the thing I sought.
My disobedient and rebellious sons
Are dead!—Why, dead!—What means this change of cheer?
You hear me not, I tell you they are dead;
And they will need no food or raiment more:
The tapers that did light them the dark way

Are their last cost. The Pope, I think, will not
Expect I should maintain them in their coffins.
Rejoice with me—my heart is wondrous glad.

[*Lucretia sinks, half fainting;* Beatrice *supports her.*

Beatrice. It is not true!—Dear lady, pray look up.
Had it been true, there is a God in Heaven,
He would not live to boast of such a boon.
Unnatural man, thou knowest that it is false.

Cenci. Ay, as the word of God; whom here I call
To witness that I speak the sober truth:—
And whose most favouring Providence was shown
Even in the manner of their deaths. For Rocco
Was kneeling at the mass, with sixteen others,
When the church fell and crushed him to a mummy,
The rest escaped unhurt. Cristofano
Was stabbed in error by a jealous man,
Whilst she he loved was sleeping with his rival;
All in the self-same hour of the same night;
Which shows that Heaven has special care of me.
I beg those friends who love me, that they mark
The day a feast upon their calendars.
It was the twenty-seventh of December:
Ay, read the letters if you doubt my oath.

[*The Assembly appears confused; several of the guests rise.*

First Guest. Oh, horrible! I will depart—
Second Guest.   And I.—
Third Guest.   No, stay!
I do believe it is some jest; though faith!
'Tis mocking us somewhat too solemnly.
I think his son has married the Infanta,
Or found a mine of gold in El Dorado;
'Tis but to season some such news; stay, stay!
I see 'tis only raillery by his smile.

Cenci (*filling a bowl of wine, and lifting it up*). Oh, thou bright
                wine whose purple splendour leaps
And bubbles gaily in this golden bowl
Under the lamplight, as my spirits do,
To hear the death of my accursèd sons!
Could I believe thou wert their mingled blood,
Then would I taste thee like a sacrament,
And pledge with thee the mighty Devil in Hell,
Who, if a father's curses, as men say,

Climb with swift wings after their children's souls,
And drag them from the very throne of Heaven,
Now triumphs in my triumph!—But thou art
Superfluous; I have drunken deep of joy,
And I will taste no other wine to-night.
Here, Andrea! Bear the bowl around.

    A Guest (rising).   Thou wretch!
Will none among this noble company
Check the abandoned villain?

    Camillo.   For God's sake
Let me dismiss the guests! You are insane,
Some ill will come of this.

    Second Guest.   Seize, silence him!
    First Guest. I will!
    Third Guest.   And I!
    Cenci (addressing those who rise with a threatening gesture).
                      Who moves? Who speaks?
                  (turning to the Company)
                  'tis nothing,
Enjoy yourselves.—Beware! For my revenge
Is as the sealed commission of a king
That kills, and none dare name the murderer.

    [*The Banquet is broken up; several of the Guests are departing.*

    Beatrice. I do entreat you, go not, noble guests;
What, although tyranny and impious hate
Stand sheltered by a father's hoary hair?
What, if 'tis he who clothed us in these limbs
Who tortures them, and triumphs? What, if we,
The desolate and the dead, were his own flesh,
His children and his wife, whom he is bound
To love and shelter? Shall we therefore find
No refuge in this merciless wide world?
O think what deep wrongs must have blotted out
First love, then reverence in a child's prone mind,
Till it thus vanquish shame and fear! O think!
I have borne much, and kissed the sacred hand
Which crushed us to the earth, and thought its stroke
Was perhaps some paternal chastisement!
Have excused much, doubted; and when no doubt
Remained, have sought by patience, love, and tears
To soften him, and when this could not be
I have knelt down through the long sleepless nights

And lifted up to God, the Father of all,
Passionate prayers: and when these were not heard
I have still borne,—until I meet you here,
Princes and kinsmen, at this hideous feast
Given at my brothers' deaths. Two yet remain,
His wife remains and I, whom if ye save not,
Ye may soon share such merriment again
As fathers make over their children's graves.
O Prince Colonna, thou art our near kinsman,
Cardinal, thou art the Pope's chamberlain,
Camillo, thou art chief justiciary,
Take us away!

    Cenci. (*He has been conversing with* CAMILLO *during the first
        part of* BEATRICE'S *speech; he hears the conclusion, and now
        advances.*)   I hope my good friends here
Will think of their own daughters—or perhaps
Of their own throats—before they lend an ear
To this wild girl.

    Beatrice (*not noticing the words of Cenci*). Dare no one look
        on me?
None answer? Can one tyrant overbear
The sense of many best and wisest men?
Or is it that I sue not in some form
Of scrupulous law, that ye deny my suit?
O God! That I were buried with my brothers!
And that the flowers of this departed spring
Were fading on my grave! And that my father
Were celebrating now one feast for all!

    Camillo. A bitter wish for one so young and gentle;
Can we do nothing?

    Colonna.   Nothing that I see.
Count Cenci were a dangerous enemy:
Yet I would second any one.

    A Cardinal.   And I.

    Cenci. Retire to your chamber, insolent girl!

    Beatrice. Retire thou, impious man! Ay, hide thyself
Where never eye can look upon thee more!
Wouldst thou have honour and obedience
Who art a torturer? Father, never dream
Though thou mayst overbear this company,
But ill must come of ill.—Frown not on me!
Haste, hide thyself, lest with avenging looks

My brothers' ghosts should hunt thee from thy seat!
Cover thy face from every living eye,
And start if thou but hear a human step:
Seek out some dark and silent corner, there,
Bow thy white head before offended God,
And we will kneel around, and fervently
Pray that he pity both ourselves and thee.

   Cenci. My friends, I do lament this insane girl
Has spoilt the mirth of our festivity.
Good night, farewell; I will not make you longer
Spectators of our dull domestic quarrels.
Another time.—   *[Exeunt all but* CENCI *and* BEATRICE.
                My brain is swimming round;
Give me a bowl of wine!   *[To* BEATRICE.
                  Thou painted viper!
Beast that thou art! Fair and yet terrible!
I know a charm shall make thee meek and tame,
Now get thee from my sight!   *[Exit* BEATRICE.
                Here, Andrea,
Fill up this goblet with Greek wine. I said
I would not drink this evening; but I must;
For, strange to say, I feel my spirits fail
With thinking what I have decreed to do.—
                    [Drinking the wine.
Be thou the resolution of quick youth
Within my veins, and manhood's purpose stern,
And age's firm, cold, subtle villainy;
As if thou wert indeed my children's blood
Which I did thirst to drink! The charm works well;
It must be done; it shall be done, I swear!   *[Exit.*

Act II

SCENE I.—*An Apartment in the Cenci Palace. Enter* LUCRETIA
and BERNARDO.

   Lucretia. Weep not, my gentle boy; he struck but me
Who have borne deeper wrongs. In truth, if he
Had killed me, he had done a kinder deed.
O God, Almighty, do Thou look upon us,
We have no other friend but only Thee!
Yet weep not; though I love you as my own,
I am not your true mother.

 Bernardo.   O more, more,
Than ever mother was to any child,
That have you been to me! Had he not been
My father, do you think that I should weep!
 Lucretia. Alas! Poor boy, what else couldst thou have done?

Enter BEATRICE

 Beatrice (*in a hurried voice*). Did he pass this way? Have you
   seen him, brother?
Ah, no! that is his step upon the stairs;
'Tis nearer now; his hand is on the door;
Mother, if I to thee have ever been
A duteous child, now save me! Thou, great God,
Whose image upon earth a father is,
Dost Thou indeed abandon me? He comes;
The door is opening now; I see his face;
He frowns on others, but he smiles on me,
Even as he did after the feast last night.

Enter a Servant.

Almighty God, how merciful Thou art!
'Tis but Orsino's servant.—Well, what news?
 Servant. My master bids me say, the Holy Father
Has sent back your petition thus unopened. [*Giving a paper.*
And he demands at what hour 'twere secure
To visit you again?
 Lucretia.   At the Ave Mary.   [*Exit Servant.*
So, daughter, our last hope has failed; Ah me!
How pale you look; you tremble, and you stand
Wrapped in some fixed and fearful meditation,
As if one thought were over strong for you:
Your eyes have a chill glare; O, dearest child!
Are you gone mad? If not, pray speak to me.
 Beatrice. You see I am not mad: I speak to you.
 Lucretia. You talked of something that your father did
After that dreadful feast? Could it be worse
Than when he smiled, and cried, 'My sons are dead!'
And every one looked in his neighbour's face
To see if others were as white as he?
At the first word he spoke I felt the blood
Rush to my heart, and fell into a trance;
And when it passed I sat all weak and wild;

Whilst you alone stood up, and with strong words
Checked his unnatural pride; and I could see
The devil was rebuked that lives in him.
Until this hour thus have you ever stood
Between us and your father's moody wrath
Like a protecting presence: your firm mind
Has been our only refuge and defence:
What can have thus subdued it? What can now
Have given you that cold melancholy look,
Succeeding to your unaccustomed fear?

   Beatrice. What is it that you say? I was just thinking
'Twere better not to struggle any more.
Men, like my father, have been dark and bloody,
Yet never—Oh! Before worse comes of it
'Twere wise to die: it ends in that at last.

   Lucretia. Oh, talk not so, dear child! Tell me at once
What did your father do or say to you?
He stayed not after that accursèd feast
One moment in your chamber.—Speak to me.

   Bernardo. Oh, sister, sister, prithee, speak to us!

   Beatrice (speaking very slowly with a forced calmness). It was
      one word, Mother, one little word;
One look, one smile. (*Wildly.*) Oh! He has trampled me
Under his feet, and made the blood stream down
My pallid cheeks. And he has given us all
Ditch-water, and the fever-stricken flesh
Of buffaloes, and bade us eat or starve,
And we have eaten.—He has made me look
On my beloved Bernardo, when the rust
Of heavy chains has gangrened his sweet limbs,
And I have never yet despaired—but now!
What could I say?   [*Recovering herself.*
         Ah, no! 'tis nothing new.
The sufferings we all share have made me wild:
He only struck and cursed me as he passed;
He said, he looked, he did;—nothing at all
Beyond his wont, yet it disordered me.
Alas! I am forgetful of my duty.
I should preserve my senses for your sake.

   Lucretia. Nay, Beatrice; have courage, my sweet girl,
If any one despairs it should be I
Who loved him once, and now must live with him

Till God in pity call for him or me.
For you may, like your sister, find some husband,
And smile, years hence, with children round your knees;
Whilst I, then dead, and all this hideous coil
Shall be remembered only as a dream.

   Beatrice. Talk not to me, dear lady, of a husband.
Did you not nurse me when my mother died?
Did you not shield me and that dearest boy?
And had we any other friend but you
In infancy, with gentle words and looks,
To win our father not to murder us?
And shall I now desert you? May the ghost
Of my dead Mother plead against my soul
If I abandon her who filled the place
She left, with more, even, than a mother's love!

   Bernardo. And I am of my sister's mind. Indeed
I would not leave you in this wretchedness,
Even though the Pope should make me free to live
In some blithe place, like others of my age,
With sports, and delicate food, and the fresh air.
Oh, never think that I will leave you, Mother!

   Lucretia. My dear, dear children!

              Enter CENCI, *suddenly.*

   Cenci.   What, Beatrice here!
Come hither!   *[She shrinks back, and covers her face.*
            Nay, hide not your face, 'tis fair;
Look up! Why, yesternight you dared to look
With disobedient insolence upon me,
Bending a stern and an inquiring brow
On what I meant; whilst I then sought to hide
That which I came to tell you—but in vain.

   Beatrice (*wildly, staggering towards the door*). O that the earth
        would gape! Hide me, O God!

   Cenci. Then it was I whose inarticulate words
Fell from my lips, and who with tottering steps
Fled from your presence, as you now from mine.
Stay, I command you—from this day and hour
Never again, I think, with fearless eye,
And brow superior, and unaltered cheek,
And that lip made for tenderness or scorn,
Shalt thou strike dumb the meanest of mankind;
Me least of all. Now get thee to thy chamber!

Thou too, loathed image of thy cursèd mother,

                           [To BERNARDO.

Thy milky, meek face makes me sick with hate!

                    [Exeunt BEATRICE *and* BERNARDO.

    (*Aside.*) So much has passed between us as must make
Me bold, her fearful.—'Tis an awful thing
To touch such mischief as I now conceive:
So men sit shivering on the dewy bank,
And try the chill stream with their feet; once in ...
How the delighted spirit pants for joy!

    Lucretia (*advancing timidly towards him*). O husband! Pray
        forgive poor Beatrice.
She meant not any ill.

    Cenci.   Nor you perhaps?
Nor that young imp, whom you have taught by rote
Parricide with his alphabet? Nor Giacomo?
Nor those two most unnatural sons, who stirred
Enmity up against me with the Pope?
Whom in one night merciful God cut off:
Innocent lambs! They thought not any ill.
You were not here conspiring? You said nothing
Of how I might be dungeoned as a madman;
Or be condemned to death for some offence,
And you would be the witnesses?—This failing,
How just it were to hire assassins, or
Put sudden poison in my evening drink?
Or smother me when overcome by wine?
Seeing we had no other judge but God,
And He had sentenced me, and there were none
But you to be the executioners
Of His decree enregistered in Heaven?
Oh, no! You said not this?

    Lucretia.   So help me God,
I never thought the things you charge me with!

    Cenci. If you dare speak that wicked lie again
I'll kill you. What! It was not by your counsel
That Beatrice disturbed the feast last night?
You did not hope to stir some enemies
Against me, and escape, and laugh to scorn
What every nerve of you now trembles at?
You judged that men were bolder than they are;
Few dare to stand between their grave and me.

Lucretia. Look not so dreadfully! By my salvation
I knew not aught that Beatrice designed;
Nor do I think she designed any thing
Until she heard you talk of her dead brothers.
    Cenci. Blaspheming liar! You are damned for this!
But I will take you where you may persuade
The stones you tread on to deliver you:
For men shall there be none but those who dare
All things—not question that which I command.
On Wednesday next I shall set out: you know
That savage rock, the Castle of Petrella:
'Tis safely walled, and moated round about:
Its dungeons underground, and its thick towers
Never told tales; though they have heard and seen
What might make dumb things speak.—Why do you linger?
Make speediest preparation for the journey! [*Exit* LUCRETIA.
The all-beholding sun yet shines; I hear
A busy stir of men about the streets;
I see the bright sky through the window panes;
It is a garish, broad, and peering day;
Loud, light, suspicious, full of eyes and ears,
And every little corner, nook, and hole
Is penetrated with the insolent light.
Come darkness! Yet, what is the day to me?
And wherefore should I wish for night, who do
A deed which shall confound both night and day?
'Tis she shall grope through a bewildering mist
Of horror: if there be a sun in heaven
She shall not dare to look upon its beams;
Nor feel its warmth. Let her then wish for night;
The act I think shall soon extinguish all
For me: I bear a darker deadlier gloom
Than the earth's shade, or interlunar air,
Or constellations quenched in murkiest cloud,
In which I walk secure and unbeheld
Towards my purpose.—Would that it were done! [*Exit*

SCENE II.—*A Chamber in the Vatican. Enter* CAMILLO *and* GIACOMO, *in conversation.*

Camillo. There is an obsolete and doubtful law
By which you might obtain a bare provision
Of food and clothing—
   Giacomo.   Nothing more? Alas!
Bare must be the provision which strict law
Awards, and agèd, sullen avarice pays.
Why did my father not apprentice me
To some mechanic trade? I should have then
Been trained in no highborn necessities
Which I could meet not by my daily toil.
The eldest son of a rich nobleman
Is heir to all his incapacities;
He has wide wants, and narrow powers. If you,
Cardinal Camillo, were reduced at once
From thrice-driven beds of down, and delicate food,
An hundred servants, and six palaces,
To that which nature doth indeed require?—
   Camillo. Nay, there is reason in your plea; 'twere hard.
   Giacomo. 'Tis hard for a firm man to bear: but I
Have a dear wife, a lady of high birth,
Whose dowry in ill hour I lent my father
Without a bond or witness to the deed:
And children, who inherit her fine senses,
The fairest creatures in this breathing world;
And she and they reproach me not. Cardinal,
Do you not think the Pope would interpose
And stretch authority beyond the law?
   Camillo. Though your peculiar case is hard, I know
The Pope will not divert the course of law.
After that impious feast the other night
I spoke with him, and urged him then to check
Your father's cruel hand; he frowned and said,
'Children are disobedient, and they sting
Their fathers' hearts to madness and despair,
Requiting years of care with contumely.
I pity the Count Cenci from my heart;
His outraged love perhaps awakened hate,
And thus he is exasperated to ill.

In the great war between the old and young
I, who have white hairs and a tottering body,
Will keep at least blameless neutrality.'

Enter ORSINO.

You, my good Lord Orsino, heard those words.
   Orsino. What words?
   Giacomo.   Alas, repeat them not again!
There then is no redress for me, at least
None but that which I may achieve myself,
Since I am driven to the brink.—But, say,
My innocent sister and my only brother
Are dying underneath my father's eye.
The memorable torturers of this land,
Galeaz Visconti, Borgia, Ezzelin,
Never inflicted on the meanest slave
What these endure; shall they have no protection?
   Camillo. Why, if they would petition to the Pope
I see not how he could refuse it—yet
He holds it of most dangerous example
In aught to weaken the paternal power,
Being, as 'twere, the shadow of his own.
I pray you now excuse me. I have business
That will not bear delay.   *[Exit* CAMILLO.
   Giacomo.   But you, Orsino,
Have the petition: wherefore not present it?
   Orsino. I have presented it, and backed it with
My earnest prayers, and urgent interest;
It was returned unanswered. I doubt not
But that the strange and execrable deeds
Alleged in it—in truth they might well baffle
Any belief—have turned the Pope's displeasure
Upon the accusers from the criminal:
So I should guess from what Camillo said.
   Giacomo. My friend, that palace-walking devil Gold
Has whispered silence to his Holiness:
And we are left, as scorpions ringed with fire.
What should we do but strike ourselves to death?
For he who is our murderous persecutor
Is shielded by a father's holy name,
Or I would—   *[Stops abruptly.*
   Orsino.   What? Fear not to speak your thought.

Words are but holy as the deeds they cover:
A priest who has forsworn the God he serves;
A judge who makes Truth weep at his decree;
A friend who should weave counsel, as I now,
But as the mantle of some selfish guile;
A father who is all a tyrant seems,
Were the profaner for his sacred name.

   Giacomo. Ask me not what I think; the unwilling brain
Feigns often what it would not; and we trust
Imagination with such phantasies
As the tongue dares not fashion into words,
Which have no words, their horror makes them dim
To the mind's eye.—My heart denies itself
To think what you demand.

   Orsino.   But a friend's bosom
Is as the inmost cave of our own mind
Where we sit shut from the wide gaze of day,
And from the all-communicating air.
You look what I suspected—

   Giacomo.   Spare me now!
I am as one lost in a midnight wood,
Who dares not ask some harmless passenger
The path across the wilderness, lest he,
As my thoughts are, should be—a murderer.
I know you are my friend, and all I dare
Speak to my soul that will I trust with thee.
But now my heart is heavy, and would take
Lone counsel from a night of sleepless care.
Pardon me, that I say farewell—farewell!
I would that to my own suspected self
I could address a word so full of peace.

   Orsino. Farewell!—Be your thoughts better or more bold.
                           [*Exit* GIACOMO.
I had disposed the Cardinal Camillo
To feed his hope with cold encouragement:
It fortunately serves my close designs
That 'tis a trick of this same family
To analyse their own and other minds.
Such self-anatomy shall teach the will
Dangerous secrets: for it tempts our powers,
Knowing what must be thought, and may be done,
Into the depth of darkest purposes:

So Cenci fell into the pit; even I,
Since Beatrice unveiled me to myself,
And made me shrink from what I cannot shun,
Show a poor figure to my own esteem,
To which I grow half reconciled. I'll do
As little mischief as I can; that thought
Shall fee the accuser conscience.

    (After a pause.)   Now what harm
If Cenci should be murdered?—Yet, if murdered,
Wherefore by me? And what if I could take
The profit, yet omit the sin and peril
In such an action? Of all earthly things
I fear a man whose blows outspeed his words;
And such is Cenci: and while Cenci lives
His daughter's dowry were a secret grave
If a priest wins her.—Oh, fair Beatrice!
Would that I loved thee not, or loving thee
Could but despise danger and gold and all
That frowns between my wish and its effect,
Or smiles beyond it! There is no escape . . .
Her bright form kneels beside me at the altar,
And follows me to the resort of men,
And fills my slumber with tumultuous dreams,
So when I wake my blood seems liquid fire;
And if I strike my damp and dizzy head
My hot palm scorches it: her very name,
But spoken by a stranger, makes my heart
Sicken and pant; and thus unprofitably
I clasp the phantom of unfelt delights
Till weak imagination half possesses
The self-created shadow. Yet much longer
Will I not nurse this life of feverous hours:
From the unravelled hopes of Giacomo
I must work out my own dear purposes.
I see, as from a tower, the end of all:
Her father dead; her brother bound to me
By a dark secret, surer than the grave;
Her mother scared and unexpostulating
From the dread manner of her wish achieved:
And she!—Once more take courage, my faint heart;
What dares a friendless maiden matched with thee?
I have such foresight as assures success:

Some unbeheld divinity doth ever,
When dread events are near, stir men's minds
To black suggestions; and he prospers best,
Not who becomes the instrument of ill,
But who can flatter the dark spirit, that makes
Its empire and its prey of other hearts
Till it become his slave . . . as I will do.   [*Exit.*

Act III

SCENE I.—*An Apartment in the Cenci palace.* LUCRETIA, *to her enter*
BEATRICE.

Beatrice. (*She enters staggering, and speaks wildly.*) Reach me
    that handkerchief!—My brain is hurt;
My eyes are full of blood; just wipe them for me . . .
I see but indistinctly . . .
    Lucretia.   My sweet child,
You have no wound; 'tis only a cold dew
That starts from your dear brow . . . Alas! Alas!
What has befallen?
    Beatrice.   How comes this hair undone?
Its wandering strings must be what blind me so,
And yet I tied it fast.—O, horrible!
The pavement sinks under my feet! The walls
Spin round! I see a woman weeping there,
And standing calm and motionless, whilst I
Slide giddily as the world reels . . . My God!
The beautiful blue heaven is flecked with blood!
The sunshine on the floor is black! The air
Is changed to vapours such as the dead breathe
In charnel pits! Pah! I am choked! There creeps
A clinging, black, contaminating mist
About me . . . 'tis substantial, heavy, thick,
I cannot pluck it from me, for it glues
My fingers and my limbs to one another,
And eats into my sinews, and dissolves
My flesh to a pollution, poisoning
The subtle, pure, and inmost spirit of life!
My God! I never knew what the mad felt
Before; for I am mad beyond all doubt!
(*More wildly.*) No, I am dead! These putrefying limbs

Shut round and sepulchre the panting soul
Which would burst forth into the wandering air!   (*A pause.*)
What hideous thought was that I had even now?
'Tis gone; and yet its burthen remains here
O'er these dull eyes ... upon this weary heart!
O, world! O, life! O, day! O, misery!
   Lucretia. What ails thee, my poor child? She answers not:
Her spirit apprehends the sense of pain,
But not its cause; suffering has dried away
The source from which it sprung ...
   Beatrice (*franticly*).   Like Parricide ...
Misery has killed its father: yet its father
Never like mine ... O, God! What thing am I?
   Lucretia. My dearest child, what has your father done?
   Beatrice (*doubtfully*). Who art thou, questioner? I have no
       father.
(*Aside.*) She is the madhouse nurse who tends on me,
It is a piteous office.   [*To* LUCRETIA, *in a slow, subdued voice.*
               Do you know
I thought I was that wretched Beatrice
Men speak of, whom her father sometimes hales
From hall to hall by the entangled hair;
At others, pens up naked in damp cells
Where scaly reptiles crawl, and starves her there,
Till she will eat strange flesh. This woful story
So did I overact in my sick dreams,
That I imagined ... no, it cannot be!
Horrible things have been in this wide world,
Prodigious mixtures, and confusions strange
Of good and ill; and worse have been conceived
Than ever there was found a heart to do.
But never fancy imaged such a deed
As ...   [*Pauses, suddenly recollecting herself.*
        Who art thou? Swear to me, ere I die
With fearful expectation, that indeed
Thou art not what thou seemest ... Mother!
   Lucretia.   Oh!
My sweet child, know you ...
   Beatrice.   Yet speak it not:
For then if this be truth, that other too
Must be a truth, a firm enduring truth,
Linked with each lasting circumstance of life,

Never to change, never to pass away.
Why so it is. This is the Cenci Palace;
Thou art Lucretia; I am Beatrice.
I have talked some wild words, but will no more.
Mother, come near me: from this point of time,
I am . . .   [*Her voice dies away faintly.*
   Lucretia. Alas! What has befallen thee, child?
What has thy father done?
   Beatrice.   What have I done?
Am I not innocent? Is it my crime
That one with white hair, and imperious brow,
Who tortured me from my forgotten years,
As parents only dare, should call himself
My father, yet should be!—Oh, what am I?
What name, what place, what memory shall be mine?
What retrospects, outliving even despair?
   Lucretia. He is a violent tyrant, surely, child:
We know that death alone can make us free;
His death or ours. But what can he have done
Of deadlier outrage or worse injury?
Thou art unlike thyself; thine eyes shoot forth
A wandering and strange spirit. Speak to me,
Unlock those pallid hands whose fingers twine
With one another.
   Beatrice.   'Tis the restless life
Tortured within them. If I try to speak
I shall go mad. Ay, something must be done;
What, yet I know not . . . something which shall make
The thing that I have suffered but a shadow
In the dread lightning which avenges it;
Brief, rapid, irreversible, destroying
The consequence of what it cannot cure.
Some such thing is to be endured or done:
When I know what, I shall be still and calm,
And never anything will move me more.
But now!—O blood, which art my father's blood,
Circling through these contaminated veins,
If thou, poured forth on the polluted earth,
Could wash away the crime, and punishment
By which I suffer . . . no, that cannot be!
Many might doubt there were a God above
Who sees and permits evil, and so die:

That faith no agony shall obscure in me.

 Lucretia. It must indeed have been some bitter wrong;
Yet what, I dare not guess. Oh, my lost child,
Hide not in proud impenetrable grief
Thy sufferings from my fear.

 Beatrice.   I hide them not.
What are the words which you would have me speak?
I, who can feign no image in my mind
Of that which has transformed me: I, whose thought
Is like a ghost shrouded and folded up
In its own formless horror: of all words,
That minister to mortal intercourse,
Which wouldst thou hear? For there is none to tell
My misery: if another ever knew
Aught like to it, she died as I will die.
And left it, as I must, without a name.
Death! Death! Our law and our religion call thee
A punishment and a reward . . . Oh, which
Have I deserved?

 Lucretia.   The peace of innocence;
Till in your season you be called to heaven.
Whate'er you may have suffered, you have done
No evil. Death must be the punishment
Of crime, or the reward of trampling down
The thorns which God has strewed upon the path
Which leads to immortality.

 Beatrice.   Ay, death . . .
The punishment of crime. I pray thee, God,
Let me not be bewildered while I judge.
If I must live day after day, and keep
These limbs, the unworthy temple of Thy spirit,
As a foul den from which what Thou abhorrest
May mock Thee, unavenged . . . it shall not be!
Self-murder . . . no, that might be no escape,
For Thy decree yawns like a Hell between
Our will and it:—O! In this mortal world
There is no vindication and no law
Which can adjudge and execute the doom
Of that through which I suffer.

Enter ORSINO.

(*She approaches him solemnly.*) Welcome, Friend!

I have to tell you that, since last we met,
I have endured a wrong so great and strange,
That neither life nor death can give me rest.
Ask me not what it is, for there are deeds
Which have no form, sufferings which have no tongue.

  Orsino. And what is he who has thus injured you?

  Beatrice. The man they call my father: a dread name.

  Orsino. It cannot be . . .

  Beatrice.   What it can be, or not,
Forbear to think. It is, and it has been;
Advise me how it shall not be again.
I thought to die; but a religious awe
Restrains me, and the dread lest death itself
Might be no refuge from the consciousness
Of what is yet unexpiated. Oh, speak!

  Orsino. Accuse him of the deed, and let the law
Avenge thee.

  Beatrice.   Oh, ice-hearted counsellor!
If I could find a word that might make known
The crime of my destroyer; and that done,
My tongue should like a knife tear out the secret
Which cankers my heart's core; ay, lay all bare
So that my unpolluted fame should be
With vilest gossips a stale mouthèd story;
A mock, a byword, an astonishment:—
If this were done, which never shall be done,
Think of the offender's gold, his dreaded hate,
And the strange horror of the accuser's tale,
Baffling belief, and overpowering speech;
Scarce whispered, unimaginable, wrapped
In hideous hints . . . Oh, most assured redress!

  Orsino. You will endure it then?

  Beatrice.   Endure?—Orsino,
It seems your counsel is small profit.

                 [Turns from him, and speaks half to herself.
                  Ay,
All must be suddenly resolved and done.
What is this undistinguishable mist
Of thoughts, which rise, like shadow after shadow,
Darkening each other?

  Orsino.   Should the offender live?
Triumph in his misdeed? and make, by use,

His crime, whate'er it is, dreadful no doubt,
Thine element; until thou mayst become
Utterly lost; subdued even to the hue
Of that which thou permittest?
  Beatrice (to herself).   Mighty death!
Thou double-visaged shadow? Only judge!
Rightfullest arbiter!   [*She retires absorbed in thought.*
  Lucretia. If the lightning
Of God has e'er descended to avenge . . .
  Orsino. Blaspheme not! His high Providence commits
Its glory on this earth, and their own wrongs
Into the hands of men; if they neglect
To punish crime . . .
  Lucretia.   But, if one like this wretch,
Should mock, with gold, opinion, law, and power?
If there be no appeal to that which makes
The guiltiest tremble? If because our wrongs,
For that they are unnatural, strange, and monstrous,
Exceed all measure of belief? O God!
If, for the very reasons which should make
Redress most swift and sure, our injurer triumphs?
And we, the victims, bear worse punishment
Than that appointed for their torturer?
  Orsino.   Think not
But that there is redress where there is wrong,
So we be bold enough to seize it.
  Lucretia.   How?
If there were any way to make all sure,
I know not . . . but I think it might be good
To . . .
  Orsino. Why, his late outrage to Beatrice;
For it is such, as I but faintly guess,
As makes remorse dishonour, and leaves her
Only one duty, how she may avenge:
You, but one refuge from ills ill endured;
Me, but one counsel . . .
  Lucretia.   For we cannot hope
That aid, or retribution, or resource
Will arise thence, where every other one
Might find them with less need. [*Beatrice advances.*
  Orsino.   Then . . .
  Beatrice.   Peace, Orsino!

And, honoured Lady, while I speak, I pray,
That you put off, as garments overworn,
Forbearance and respect, remorse and fear,
And all the fit restraints of daily life,
Which have been borne from childhood, but which now
Would be a mockery to my holier plea.
As I have said, I have endured a wrong,
Which, though it be expressionless, is such
As asks atonement; both for what is past,
And lest I be reserved, day after day,
To load with crimes an overburthened soul,
And be . . . what ye can dream not. I have prayed
To God, and I have talked with my own heart,
And have unravelled my entangled will,
And have at length determined what is right.
Art thou my friend, Orsino? False or true?
Pledge thy salvation ere I speak.
   Orsino.   I swear
To dedicate my cunning, and my strength,
My silence, and whatever else is mine,
To thy commands.
   Lucretia.   You think we should devise
His death?
   Beatrice. And execute what is devised,
And suddenly. We must be brief and bold.
   Orsino. And yet most cautious.
   Lucretia.   For the jealous laws
Would punish us with death and infamy
For that which it became themselves to do.
   Beatrice. Be cautious as ye may, but prompt. Orsino,
What are the means?
   Orsino.   I know two dull, fierce outlaws,
Who think man's spirit as a worm's, and they
Would trample out, for any slight caprice,
The meanest or the noblest life. This mood
Is marketable here in Rome. They sell
What we now want.
   Lucretia.   To-morrow before dawn,
Cenci will take us to that lonely rock,
Petrella, in the Apulian Apennines.
If he arrive there . . .
   Beatrice.   He must not arrive.

 Orsino. Will it be dark before you reach the tower?
 Lucretia. The sun will scarce be set.
 Beatrice.   But I remember
Two miles on this side of the fort, the road
Crosses a deep ravine; 'tis rough and narrow,
And winds with short turns down the precipice;
And in its depth there is a mighty rock,
Which has, from unimaginable years,
Sustained itself with terror and with toil
Over a gulf, and with the agony
With which it clings seems slowly coming down;
Even as a wretched soul hour after hour,
Clings to the mass of life; yet clinging, leans;
And leaning, makes more dark the dread abyss
In which it fears to fall: beneath this crag
Huge as despair, as if in weariness,
The melancholy mountain yawns . . . below,
You hear but see not an impetuous torrent
Raging among the caverns, and a bridge
Crosses the chasm; and high above there grow,
With intersecting trunks, from crag to crag,
Cedars, and yews, and pines; whose tangled hair
Is matted in one solid roof of shade
By the dark ivy's twine. At noonday here
'Tis twilight, and at sunset blackest night.
 Orsino. Before you reach that bridge make some excuse
For spurring on your mules, or loitering
Until . . .
 Beatrice. What sound is that?
 Lucretia. Hark! No, it cannot be a servant's step
It must be Cenci, unexpectedly
Returned . . . Make some excuse for being here.
 Beatrice. (*To* ORSINO, *as she goes out.*) That step we hear
  approach must never pass
The bridge of which we spoke.
        [*Exeunt* LUCRETIA *and* BEATRICE.
 Orsino.   What shall I do?
Cenci must find me here, and I must bear
The imperious inquisition of his looks
As to what brought me hither: let me mask
Mine own in some inane and vacant smile.

Enter GIACOMO, *in a hurried manner.*

How! Have you ventured hither? Know you then
That Cenci is from home?

    Giacomo.   I sought him here;
And now must wait till he returns.

    Orsino.   Great God!
Weigh you the danger of this rashness?

    Giacomo.   Ay!
Does my destroyer know his danger? We
Are now no more, as once, parent and child,
But man to man; the oppressor to the oppressed;
The slanderer to the slandered; foe to foe:
He has cast Nature off, which was his shield,
And Nature casts him off, who is her shame;
And I spurn both. Is it a father's throat
Which I will shake, and say, I ask not gold;
I ask not happy years; nor memories
Of tranquil childhood; nor home-sheltered love;
Though all these hast thou torn from me, and more;
But only my fair fame; only one hoard
Of peace, which I thought hidden from thy hate,
Under the penury heaped on me by thee,
Or I will . . . God can understand and pardon,
Why should I speak with man?

    Orsino.   Be calm, dear friend.

    Giacomo. Well, I will calmly tell you what he did.
This old Francesco Cenci, as you know,
Borrowed the dowry of my wife from me,
And then denied the loan; and left me so
In poverty, the which I sought to mend
By holding a poor office in the state.
It had been promised to me, and already
I bought new clothing for my raggèd babes,
And my wife smiled; and my heart knew repose.
When Cenci's intercession, as I found,
Conferred this office on a wretch, whom thus
He paid for vilest service. I returned
With this ill news, and we sate sad together
Solacing our despondency with tears
Of such affection and unbroken faith
As temper life's worst bitterness; when he,
As he is wont, came to upbraid and curse,

Mocking our poverty, and telling us
Such was God's scourge for disobedient sons.
And then, that I might strike him dumb with shame,
I spoke of my wife's dowry; but he coined
A brief yet specious tale, how I had wasted
The sum in secret riot; and he saw
My wife was touched, and he went smiling forth.
And when I knew the impression he had made,
And felt my wife insult with silent scorn
My ardent truth, and look averse and cold,
I went forth too: but soon returned again;
Yet not so soon but that my wife had taught
My children her harsh thoughts, and they all cried,
'Give us clothes, father! Give us better food!
What you in one night squander were enough
For months!' I looked, and saw that home was hell.
And to that hell will I return no more
Until mine enemy has rendered up
Atonement, or, as he gave life to me
I will, reversing Nature's law . . .
    Orsino.   Trust me,
The compensation which thou seekest here
Will be denied.
    Giacomo.   Then . . . Are you not my friend?
Did you not hint at the alternative,
Upon the brink of which you see I stand,
The other day when we conversed together?
My wrongs were then less. That word parricide,
Although I am resolved, haunts me like fear.
    Orsino. It must be fear itself, for the bare word
Is hollow mockery. Mark, how wisest God
Draws to one point the threads of a just doom,
So sanctifying it: what you devise
Is, as it were, accomplished.
    Giacomo.   Is he dead?
    Orsino. His grave is ready. Know that since we met
Cenci has done an outrage to his daughter.
    Giacomo. What outrage?
    Orsino.   That she speaks not, but you may
Conceive such half conjectures as I do,
From her fixed paleness, and the lofty grief
Of her stern brow bent on the idle air,

And her severe unmodulated voice,
Drowning both tenderness and dread; and last
From this; that whilst her step-mother and I,
Bewildered in our horror, talked together
With obscure hints; both self-misunderstood
And darkly guessing, stumbling, in our talk,
Over the truth, and yet to its revenge,
She interrupted us, and with a look
Which told before she spoke it, he must die: ...

    Giacomo. It is enough. My doubts are well appeased;
There is a higher reason for the act
Than mine; there is a holier judge than me,
A more unblamed avenger. Beatrice,
Who in the gentleness of thy sweet youth
Hast never trodden on a worm, or bruised
A living flower, but thou hast pitied it
With needless tears! Fair sister, thou in whom
Men wondered how such loveliness and wisdom
Did not destroy each other! Is there made
Ravage of thee? O, heart, I ask no more
Justification! Shall I wait, Orsino,
Till he return, and stab him at the door?

    Orsino. Not so; some accident might interpose
To rescue him from what is now most sure;
And you are unprovided where to fly.
How to excuse or to conceal. Nay, listen:
All is contrived; success is so assured
That ...

                Enter BEATRICE.

    Beatrice. 'Tis my brother's voice! You know me not?
    Giacomo. My sister, my lost sister!
    Beatrice.   Lost indeed!
I see Orsino has talked with you, and
That you conjecture things too horrible
To speak, yet far less than the truth. Now, stay not,
He might return: yet kiss me; I shall know
That then thou hast consented to his death.
Farewell, farewell! Let piety to God,
Brotherly love, justice and clemency,
And all things that make tender hardest hearts
Make thine hard, brother. Answer not ... farewell.
                                [Exeunt severally.

Scene II.—*A mean Apartment in* Giacomo's *House.*
                    Giacomo *alone.*

Giacomo. 'Tis midnight, and Orsino comes not yet.
                    [*Thunder, and the sound of a storm.*
What! can the everlasting elements
Feel with a worm like man? If so, the shaft
Of mercy-wingèd lightning would not fall
On stones and trees. My wife and children sleep:
They are now living in unmeaning dreams:
But I must wake, still doubting if that deed
Be just which is most necessary. O,
Thou unreplenished lamp! whose narrow fire
Is shaken by the wind, and on whose edge
Devouring darkness hovers! Thou small flame,
Which, as a dying pulse rises and falls,
Still flickerest up and down, how very soon.
Did I not feed thee, wouldst thou fail and be
As thou hadst never been! So wastes and sinks
Even now, perhaps, the life that kindled mine:
But that no power can fill with vital oil
That broken lamp of flesh. Ha! 'tis the blood
Which fed these veins that ebbs till all is cold:
It is the form that moulded mine that sinks
Into the white and yellow spasms of death:
It is the soul by which mine was arrayed
In God's immortal likeness which now stands
Naked before Heaven's judgement seat!   [*A bell strikes.*
                                        One! Two!
The hours crawl on; and when my hairs are white,
My son will then perhaps be waiting thus,
Tortured between just hate and vain remorse;
Chiding the tardy messenger of news
Like those which I expect. I almost wish
He be not dead, although my wrongs are great;
Yet . . . 'tis Orsino's step . . .

                    Enter Orsino.

                              Speak!
    Orsino.   I am come
To say he has escaped.
        Giacomo.   Escaped!

Orsino.   And safe
Within Petrella. He passed by the spot
Appointed for the deed an hour too soon.

Giacomo. Are we the fools of such contingencies?
And do we waste in blind misgivings thus
The hours when we should act? Then wind and thunder,
Which seemed to howl his knell, is the loud laughter
With which Heaven mocks our weakness! I henceforth
Will ne'er repent of aught designed or done
But my repentance.

Orsino.   See, the lamp is out.

Giacomo. If no remorse is ours when the dim air
Has drank this innocent flame, why should we quail
When Cenci's life, that light by which ill spirits
See the worst deeds they prompt, shall sink for ever?
No, I am hardened.

Orsino.   Why, what need of this?
Who feared the pale intrusion of remorse
In a just deed? Although our first plan failed,
Doubt not but he will soon be laid to rest.
But light the lamp; let us not talk i' the dark.

   Giacomo (lighting the lamp). And yet once quenched I cannot
          thus relume
My father's life: do you not think his ghost
Might plead that argument with God?

Orsino.   Once gone
You cannot now recall your sister's peace;
Your own extinguished years of youth and hope;
Nor your wife's bitter words; nor all the taunts
Which, from the prosperous, weak misfortune takes;
Nor your dead mother; nor . . .

Giacomo.   O, speak no more!
I am resolved, although this very hand
Must quench the life that animated it.

Orsino. There is no need of that. Listen: you know
Olimpio, the castellan of Petrella
In old Colonna's time; him whom your father
Degraded from his post? And Marzio,
That desperate wretch, whom he deprived last year
Of a reward of blood, well earned and due?

Giacomo, I knew Olimpio; and they say he hated
Old Cenci so, that in his silent rage

His lips grew white only to see him pass.
Of Marzio I know nothing.
  Orsino.   Marzio's hate
Matches Olimpio's. I have sent these men,
But in your name, and as at your request,
To talk with Beatrice and Lucretia.
  Giacomo. Only to talk?
  Orsino.   The moments which even now
Pass onward to to-morrow's midnight hour
May memorize their flight with death: ere then
They must have talked, and may perhaps have done,
And made an end . . .
  Giacomo.   Listen! What sound is that?
  Orsino. The house-dog moans, and the beams crack: nought
   else.
  Giacomo. It is my wife complaining in her sleep:
I doubt not she is saying bitter things
Of me; and all my children round her dreaming
That I deny them sustenance.
  Orsino.   Whilst he
Who truly took it from them, and who fills
Their hungry rest with bitterness, now sleeps
Lapped in bad pleasures, and triumphantly
Mocks thee in visions of successful hate
Too like the truth of day.
  Giacomo.   If e'er he wakes
Again, I will not trust to hireling hands . . .
  Orsino. Why, that were well. I must be gone; good-night.
When next we meet—may all be done!
  Giacomo.   And all
Forgotten: Oh, that I had never been!   [*Exeunt.*

Act IV

Scene I.—*An Apartment in the Castle of Petrella.*
Enter Cenci.

Cenci. She comes not; yet I left her even now
Vanquished and faint. She knows the penalty
Of her delay: yet what if threats are vain?
Am I not now within Petrella's moat?
Or fear I still the eyes and ears of Rome?

Might I not drag her by the golden hair?
Stamp on her? Keep her sleepless till her brain
Be overworn? Tame her with chains and famine?
Less would suffice. Yet so to leave undone
What I most seek! No, 'tis her stubborn will
Which by its own consent shall stoop as low
As that which drags it down.

Enter LUCRETIA.

                              Thou loathèd wretch!
Hide thee from my abhorrence: fly, begone!
Yet stay! Bid Beatrice come hither.

   Lucretia.   Oh,
Husband! I pray for thine own wretched sake
Heed what thou dost. A man who walks like thee
Through crimes, and through the danger of his crimes,
Each hour may stumble o'er a sudden grave.
And thou art old; thy hairs are hoary gray;
As thou wouldst save thyself from death and hell,
Pity thy daughter; give her to some friend
In marriage: so that she may tempt thee not
To hatred, or worse thoughts, if worse there be.

   Cenci. What! like her sister who has found a home
To mock my hate from with prosperity?
Strange ruin shall destroy both her and thee
And all that yet remain. My death may be
Rapid, her destiny outspeeds it. Go,
Bid her come hither, and before my mood
Be changed, lest I should drag her by the hair.

   Lucretia. She sent me to thee, husband. At thy presence
She fell, as thou dost know, into a trance;
And in that trance she heard a voice which said,
'Cenci must die! Let him confess himself!
Even now the accusing Angel waits to hear
If God, to punish his enormous crimes,
Harden his dying heart!'

   Cenci.   Why—such things are . . .
No doubt divine revealings may be made.
'Tis plain I have been favoured from above.
For when I cursed my sons they died.—Ay . . . so . . .
As to the right or wrong, that's talk . . . repentance . . .
Repentance is an easy moment's work
And more depends on God than me. Well . . . well . . .

I must give up the greater point, which was
To poison and corrupt her soul.

                    [*A pause;* LUCRETIA *approaches anxiously, and
                             then shrinks back as he speaks.*

                                      One, two;

Ay ... Rocco and Cristofano my curse
Strangled: and Giacomo, I think, will find
Life a worse Hell than that beyond the grave:
Beatrice shall, if there be skill in hate,
Die in despair, blashpeming: to Bernardo,
He is so innocent, I will bequeath
The memory of these deeds, and make his youth
The sepulchre of hope, where evil thoughts
Shall grow like weeds on a neglected tomb.
When all is done, out in the wide Campagna,
I will pile up my silver and my gold;
My costly robes, paintings and tapestries;
My parchments and all records of my wealth,
And make a bonfire in my joy, and leave
Of my possessions nothing but my name;
Which shall be an inheritance to strip
Its wearer bare as infamy. That done,
My soul, which is a scourge, will I resign
Into the hands of him who wielded it;
Be it for its own punishment or theirs,
He will not ask it of me till the lash
Be broken in its last and deepest wound;
Until its hate be all inflicted. Yet,
Lest death outspeed my purpose, let me make
Short work and sure ...   [*Going.*

    Lucretia. (*Stops him.*) Oh, stay! It was a feint:
She had no vision, and she heard no voice.
I said it but to awe thee.
      Cenci.   That is well.
Vile palterer with the sacred truth of God,
Be thy soul choked with that blaspheming lie!
For Beatrice worse terrors are in store
To bend her to my will.
      Lucretia.   Oh! to what will?
What cruel sufferings more than she has known
Canst thou inflict?
      Cenci.   Andrea! Go call my daughter,

And if she comes not tell her that I come.
What sufferings? I will drag her, step by step,
Through infamies unheard of among men:
She shall stand shelterless in the broad noon
Of public scorn, for acts blazoned abroad,
One among which shall be ... What? Canst thou guess?
She shall become (for what she most abhors
Shall have a fascination to entrap
Her loathing will) to her own conscious self
All she appears to others; and when dead,
As she shall die unshrived and unforgiven,
A rebel to her father and her God,
Her corpse shall be abandoned to the hounds;
Her name shall be the terror of the earth;
Her spirit shall approach the throne of God
Plague-spotted with my curses. I will make
Body and soul a monstrous lump of ruin.

Enter ANDREA.

 Andrea. The Lady Beatrice ...
 Cenci.   Speak, pale slave! What
Said she?
 Andrea. My Lord, 'twas what she looked; she said:
'Go tell my father that I see the gulf
Of Hell between us two, which he may pass,
I will not.'   [*Exit* ANDREA.
 Cenci. Go thou quick, Lucretia,
Tell her to come; yet let her understand
Her coming is consent: and say, moreover,
That if she come not I will curse her. [*Exit* LUCRETIA.
             Ha!
With what but with a father's curse doth God
Panic-strike armèd victory, and make pale
Cities in their prosperity? The world's Father
Must grant a parent's prayer against his child,
Be he who asks even what men call me.
Will not the deaths of her rebellious brothers
Awe her before I speak? For I on them
Did imprecate quick ruin, and it came.

Enter LUCRETIA.

Well; what? Speak, wretch!

   Lucretia.   She said, 'I cannot come;
Go tell my father that I see a torrent
Of his own blood raging between us.'
   Cenci (kneeling).   God!
Hear me! If this most specious mass of flesh,
Which Thou hast made my daughter; this my blood,
This particle of my divided being;
Or rather, this my bane and my disease,
Whose sight infects and poisons me; this devil
Which sprung from me as from a hell, was meant
To aught good use; if her bright loveliness
Was kindled to illumine this dark world;
If nursed by Thy selectest dew of love
Such virtues blossom in her as should make
The peace of life, I pray Thee for my sake,
As Thou the common God and Father art
Of her, and me, and all; reverse that doom!
Earth, in the name of God, let her food be
Poison, until she be encrusted round
With leprous stains! Heaven, rain upon her head
The blistering drops of the Maremma's dew,
Till she be speckled like a toad; parch up
Those love-enkindled lips, warp those fine limbs
To loathèd lameness! All-beholding sun,
Strike in thine envy those life-darting eyes
With thine own blinding beams!
   Lucretia.   Peace! Peace!
For thine own sake unsay those dreadful words.
When high God grants He punishes such prayers.
   Cenci (leaping up, and throwing his right hand towards
                               Heaven).

       He does His will, I mine! This in addition,
That if she have a child . . .
   Lucretia.   Horrible thought!
   Cenci. That if she ever have a child; and thou,
Quick Nature! I adjure thee by thy God,
That thou be fruitful in her, and increase
And multiply, fulfilling his command,
And my deep imprecation! May it be
A hideous likeness of herself, that as
From a distorting mirror, she may see
Her image mixed with what she most abhors,

Smiling upon her from her nursing breast.
And that the child may from its infancy
Grow, day by day, more wicked and deformed,
Turning her mother's love to misery:
And that both she and it may live until
It shall repay her care and pain with hate,
Or what may else be more unnatural.
So he may hunt her through the clamorous scoffs
Of the loud world to a dishonoured grave.
Shall I revoke this curse? Go, bid her come,
Before my words are chronicled in Heaven.

                                        [*Exit* LUCRETIA.

I do not feel as if I were a man,
But like a fiend appointed to chastise
The offences of some unremembered world.
My blood is running up and down my veins;
A fearful pleasure makes it prick and tingle:
I feel a giddy sickness of strange awe;
My heart is beating with an expectation
Of horrid joy.

                    Enter LUCRETIA.

             What? Speak!
    Lucretia.   She bids thee curse;
And if thy curses, as they cannot do,
Could kill her soul . . .
       Cenci.   She would not come. 'Tis well,
I can do both: first take what I demand,
And then extort concession. To thy chamber!
Fly ere I spurn thee: and beware this night
That thou cross not my footsteps. It were safer
To come between the tiger and his prey. [*Exit* LUCRETIA.
It must be late; mine eyes grow weary dim
With unaccustomed heaviness of sleep.
Conscience! Oh, thou most insolent of lies!
They say that sleep, that healing dew of Heaven,
Steeps not in balm the foldings of the brain
Which thinks thee an impostor. I will go
First to belie thee with an hour of rest,
Which will be deep and calm, I feel: and then . . .
O, multitudinous Hell, the fiends will shake
Thine arches with the laughter of their joy!

There shall be lamentation heard in Heaven
As o'er an angel fallen; and upon Earth
All good shall droop and sicken, and ill things
Shall with a spirit of unnatural life
Stir and be quickened . . . even as I am now.   [*Exit.*

SCENE II.—*Before the Castle of Petrella. Enter* BEATRICE *and*
LUCRETIA *above on the Ramparts.*

    Beatrice. They come not yet.
    Lucretia.   'Tis scarce midnight.
    Beatrice.   How slow
Behind the course of thought, even sick with speed,
Lags leaden-footed time!
    Lucretia.   The minutes pass . . .
If he should wake before the deed is done?
    Beatrice. O, mother! He must never wake again.
What thou hast said persuades me that our act
Will but dislodge a spirit of deep hell
Out of a human form.
    Lucretia.   'Tis true he spoke
Of death and judgment with strange confidence
For one so wicked; as a man believing
In God, yet recking not of good or ill.
And yet to die without confession! . . .
    Beatrice.   Oh!
Believe that Heaven is merciful and just,
And will not add our dread necessity
To the amount of his offences.

             Enter OLIMPIO *and* MARZIO, *below.*

    Lucretia.   See,
They come.
    Beatrice. All mortal things must hasten thus
To their dark end. Let us go down.
                [*Exeunt* LUCRETIA *and* BEATRICE *from above.*
    Olimpio. How feel you to this work?
    Marzio.   As one who thinks
A thousand crowns excellent market price
For an old murderer's life. Your cheeks are pale.
    Olimpio. It is the white reflection of your own,
Which you call pale.

Marzio.   Is that their natural hue?
Olimpio. Or 'tis my hate and the deferred desire
To wreak it, which extinguishes their blood.
   Marzio. You are inclined then to this business?
   Olimpio.   Ay.
If one should bribe me with a thousand crowns
To kill a serpent which had stung my child,
I could not be more willing.

     Enter BEATRICE *and* LUCRETIA, *below.*
                   Noble ladies!

   Beatrice. Are ye resolved?
   Olimpio.   Is he asleep?
Marzio.   Is all
Quiet?
   Lucretia. I mixed an opiate with his drink:
He sleeps so soundly . . .
   Beatrice.   That his death will be
But as a change of sin-chastising dreams
A dark continuance of the Hell within him,
Which God extinguish! But ye are resolved?
Ye know it is a high and holy deed?
   Olimpio. We are resolved.
   Marzio.   As to the how this act
Be warranted, it rests with you.
   Beatrice.   Well, follow!
   Olimpio. Hush! Hark! What noise is that?
   Marzio.   Ha! some one comes!
   Beatrice. Ye conscience-stricken cravens, rock to rest
Your baby hearts. It is the iron gate,
Which ye left open, swinging to the wind.
That enters whistling as in scorn. Come, follow!
And be your steps like mine, light, quick and bold.   [*Exeunt.*

SCENE III.—*An Apartment in the Castle. Enter* BEATRICE *and* LUCRETIA

   Lucretia. They are about it now.
   Beatrice.   Nay, it is done.
   Lucretia. I have not heard him groan.
   Beatrice.   He will not groan.
   Lucretia. What sound is that?
   Beatrice.   List! 'tis the tread of feet
About his bed.

Lucretia.   My God!
If he be now a cold stiff corpse . . .
          Beatrice.   O, fear not
What may be done, but what is left undone:
The act seals all.

                    Enter OLIMPIO *and* MARZIO.

                    Is it accomplished?
     Marzio.   What?
     Olimpio Did you not call?
     Beatrice.   When?
     Olimpio.   Now.
     Beatrice.   I ask if all is over?
     Olimpio. We dare not kill an old and sleeping man;
His thin gray hair, his stern and reverend brow,
His veinèd hands crossed on his heaving breast,
And the calm innocent sleep in which he lay,
Quelled me. Indeed, indeed, I cannot do it.
     Marzio. But I was bolder; for I chid Olimpio,
And bade him bear his wrongs to his own grave
And leave me the reward. And now my knife
Touched the loose wrinkled throat, when the old man
Stirred in his sleep, and said, 'God! hear, O, hear,
A father's curse! What, art Thou not our Father?'
And then he laughed. I knew it was the ghost
Of my dead father speaking through his lips,
And could not kill him.
     Beatrice.   Miserable slaves!
Where, if ye dare not kill a sleeping man,
Found ye the boldness to return to me
With such a deed undone? Base palterers!
Cowards and traitors! Why, the very conscience
Which ye would sell for gold and for revenge
Is an equivocation: it sleeps over
A thousand daily acts disgracing men;
And when a deed where mercy insults Heaven . . .
Why do I talk?
                    [*Snatching a dagger from one of them and raising it.*
                    Hadst thou a tongue to say,
'She murdered her own father!'—I must do it!
But never dream ye shall outlive him long!
     Olimpio. Stop, for God's sake!

Marzio.   I will go back and kill him.
Olimpio. Give me the weapon, we must do thy will.
Beatrice. Take it! Depart! Return!

                          [*Exeunt* OLIMPIO *and* MARZIO.
                                          How pale thou art!
We do but that which 'twere a deadly crime
To leave undone.
     Lucretia.   Would it were done!
     Beatrice.   Even whilst
That doubt is passing through your mind, the world
Is conscious of a change. Darkness and Hell
Have swallowed up the vapour they sent forth
To blacken the sweet light of life. My breath
Comes, methinks, lighter, and the jellied blood
Runs freely through my veins. Hark!

               Enter OLIMPIO *and* MARZIO.
                                          He is . . .
     Olimpio.   Dead!
     Marzio. We strangled him that there might be no blood;
And then we threw his heavy corpse i' the garden
Under the balcony; 'twill seem it fell.

     Beatrice (*giving them a bag of coin*). Here, take this gold, and
          hasten to your homes.
And, Marzio, because thou wast only awed
By that which made me tremble, wear thou this!

                          [*Clothes him in a rich mantle.*
It was the mantle which my grandfather
Wore in his high prosperity, and men
Envied his state: so may they envy thine.
Thou wert a weapon in the hand of God
To a just use. Live long and thrive! And, mark,
If thou hast crimes, repent: this deed is none.

                          [*A horn is sounded.*
     Lucretia. Hark, 'tis the castle horn; my God! it sounds
Like the last trump.
     Beatrice.   Some tedious guest is coming.
     Lucretia. The drawbridge is let down; there is a tramp
Of horses in the court; fly, hide yourselves!

                          [*Exeunt* OLIMPIO *and* MARZIO.
     Beatrice. Let us retire to counterfeit deep rest;
I scarcely need to counterfeit it now;
The spirit which doth reign within these limbs

Seems strangely undisturbed. I could even sleep
Fearless and calm: all ill is surely past.   [*Exeunt.*

SCENE IV.—*Another Apartment in the Castle. Enter on one side the*
LEGATE SAVELLA, *introduced by a Servant, and on the
other* LUCRETIA *and* BERNARDO.

Savella. Lady, my duty to his Holiness
Be my excuse that thus unseasonably
I break upon your rest. I must speak with
Count Cenci; doth he sleep?
    Lucretia (*in a hurried and confused manner*). I think he sleeps;
Yet wake him not, I pray, spare me awhile,
He is a wicked and a wrathful man;
Should he be roused out of his sleep to-night,
Which is, I know, a hell of angry dreams,
It were not well; indeed it were not well.
Wait till day break . . . (*aside*) O, I am deadly sick!
    Savella. I grieve thus to distress you, but the Count
Must answer charges of the gravest import,
And suddenly; such my commission is.
    Lucretia (*with increased agitation*). I dare not rouse him: I
        know none who dare . . .
'Twere perilous; . . . you might as safely waken
A serpent; or a corpse in which some fiend
Were laid to sleep.
    Savella.   Lady, my moments here
Are counted. I must rouse him from his sleep,
Since none else dare.
    Lucretia (*aside*).   O, terror! O, despair!
(*To* BERNARDO). Bernardo, conduct you the Lord Legate to
Your father's chamber.   [*Exeunt* SAVELLA *and* BERNARDO.

Enter BEATRICE.

    Beatrice.   'Tis a messenger
Come to arrest the culprit who now stands
Before the throne of unappealable God.
Both Earth and Heaven, consenting arbiters,
Acquit our deed.
    Lucretia.   Oh, agony of fear!
Would that he yet might live! Even now I heard
The Legate's followers whisper as they passed
They had a warrant for his instant death.

All was prepared by unforbidden means
Which we must pay so dearly, having done.
Even now they search the tower, and find the body;
Now they suspect the truth; now they consult
Before they come to tax us with the fact;
O, horrible, 'tis all discovered!
   Beatrice.   Mother,
What is done wisely, is done well. Be bold
As thou art just. 'Tis like a truant child
To fear that others know what thou hast done,
Even from thine own strong consciousness, and **thus**
Write on unsteady eyes and altered cheeks
All thou wouldst hide. Be faithful to thyself,
And fear no other witness but thy fear.
For if, as cannot be, some circumstance
Should rise in accusation, we can blind
Suspicion with such cheap astonishment,
Or overbear it with such guiltless pride,
As murderers cannot feign. The deed is done.
And what may follow now regards not me.
I am as universal as the light;
Free as the earth-surrounding air; as firm
As the world's centre. Consequence, to me,
Is as the wind which strikes the solid rock
But shakes it not.   *[A cry within and tumult.*
   Voices.   Murder! Murder! Murder!

Enter BERNARDO *and* SAVELLA.

   Savella (to his followers). Go search the castle round;
      sound the alarm;
Look to the gates that none escape!
   Beatrice.   What now?
   Bernardo. I know not what to say . . . my father's dead.
   Beatrice. How; dead! he only sleeps; you mistake, brother.
His sleep is very calm, very like death;
'Tis wonderful how well a tyrant sleeps.
He is not dead?
   Bernardo.   Dead; murdered.
   Lucretia (with extreme agitation).   Oh no, no,
He is not murdered though he may be dead;
I have alone the keys of those apartments.
   Savella. Ha! Is it so?

Beatrice.　　　　　My Lord, I pray excuse us;
We will retire; my mother is not well:
She seems quite overcome with this strange horror.

　　　　　　　　　　　　[*Exeunt* LUCRETIA *and* BEATRICE.

Savella. Can you suspect who may have murdered him?
Bernardo. I know not what to think.
Savella.　　　　　　　　Can you name any
Who had an interest in his death?
Bernardo.　　　　　　　Alas!
I can name none who had not, and those most
Who most lament that such a deed is done;
My mother, and my sister, and myself.
Savella. 'Tis strange! There were clear marks of violence.
I found the old man's body in the moonlight
Hanging beneath the window of his chamber,
Among the branches of a pine: he could not
Have fallen there, for all his limbs lay heaped
And effortless; 'tis true there was no blood ...
Favour me, Sir; it much imports your house,
That all should be made clear; to tell the ladies
That I request their presence.　　　[*Exit* BERNARDO.

　　　　Enter GUARDS *bringing in* MARZIO.

Guard.　　　　　　　We have one.
Officer. My Lord, we found this ruffian and another
Lurking among the rocks; there is not doubt
But that they are the murderers of Count Cenci:
Each had a bag of coin: this fellow wore
A gold-inwoven robe, which shining bright
Under the dark rocks to the glimmering moon
Betrayed them to our notice: the other fell
Desperately fighting.
Savella.　　　　　What does he confess?
Officer. He keeps firm silence; but these lines found on him
May speak.
Savella. Their language is at least sincere.　　[*Reads.*

　　'*To the Lady Beatrice.*
　　'*That the atonement of what my nature sickens to conjecture may
soon arrive. I send thee, at thy brother's desire, those who will speak
and do more than I dare write...*

　　　　　　　　　'*Thy devoted servant, Orsino.*'

Enter LUCRETIA, BEATRICE, *and* BERNARDO.

Knowest thou this writing, Lady?

    Beatrice.   No.

    Savella.   Nor thou?

    Lucretia. (*Her conduct throughout the scene is marked by extreme
        agitation.*) Where was it found? What is it! It should be
Orsino's hand! It speaks of that strange horror
Which never yet found utterance, but which made
Between that hapless child and her dead father
A gulf of obscure hatred.

    Savella.   Is it so?
Is it true, Lady, that thy father did
Such outrages as to awaken in thee
Unfilial hate?

    Beatrice.   Not hate, 'twas more than hate:
This is most true, yet wherefore question me?

    Savella. There is a deed demanding question done;
Thou hast a secret which will answer not.

    Beatrice. What sayest? My Lord, your words are bold and
        rash.

    Savella. I do arrest all present in the name
Of the Pope's Holiness. You must to Rome.

    Lucretia. O, not to Rome! Indeed we are not guilty.

    Beatrice. Guilty! Who dares talk of guilt? My Lord,
I am more innocent of parricide
Than is a child born fatherless . . . Dear mother,
Your gentleness and patience are no shield
For this keen-judging world, this two-edged lie,
Which seems, but is not. What! will human laws,
Rather will ye who are their ministers,
Bar all access to retribution first,
And then, when Heaven doth interpose to do
What ye neglect, arming familiar things
To the redress of an unwonted crime,
Make ye the victims who demanded it
Culprits? 'Tis ye are culprits! That poor wretch
Who stands so pale, and trembling, and amazed,
If it be true he murdered Cenci, was
A sword in the right hand of justest God.
Wherefore should I have wielded it? Unless
The crimes which mortal tongue dare never name
God therefore scruples to avenge.

   Savella.   You own
That you desired his death?
   Beatrice.   It would have been
A crime no less than his, if for one moment
That fierce desire had faded in my heart.
'Tis true I did believe, and hope, and pray,
Ay, I even knew . . . for God is wise and just,
That some strange sudden death hung over him.
'Tis true that this did happen, and most true
There was no other rest for me on earth,
No other hope in Heaven . . . now what of this?
   Savella. Strange thoughts beget strange deeds; and here are
both: I judge thee not.
   Beatrice.   And yet, if you arrest me
You are the judge and executioner
Of that which is the life of life: the breath
Of accusation kills an innocent name,
And leaves for lame acquittal the poor life
Which is a mask without it. 'Tis most false
That I am guilty of foul parricide;
Although I must rejoice, for justest cause,
That other hands have sent my father's soul
To ask the mercy he denied to me.
Now leave us free; stain not a noble house
With vague surmises of rejected crime;
Add to our sufferings and your own neglect
No heavier sum: let them have been enough:
Leave us the wreck we have.
   Savella.   I dare not, Lady.
I pray that you prepare yourselves for Rome:
There the Pope's further pleasure will be known.
   Lucretia. O, not to Rome! O, take us not to Rome!
   Beatrice. Why not to Rome, dear mother? There as here
Our innocence is as an armèd heel
To trample accusation. God is there
As here, and with His shadow ever clothes
The innocent, the injured and the weak;
And such are we. Cheer up, dear Lady, lean
On me; collect your wandering thoughts. My Lord,
As soon as you have taken some refreshment,
And had all such examinations made
Upon the spot, as may be necessary

To the full understanding of this matter,
We shall be ready. Mother; will you come?
   Lucretia. Ha! they will bind us to the rack, and wrest
Self-accusation from our agony!
Will Giacomo be there? Orsino? Marzio?
All present; all confronted; all demanding
Each from the other's countenance the thing
Which is in every heart! O, misery!

                            [She faints, and is borne out.
   Savella. She faints: an ill appearance this.
   Beatrice.   My Lord,
She knows not yet the uses of the world.
She fears that power is as a beast which grasps
And loosens not: a snake whose look transmutes
All things to guilt which is its nutriment.
She cannot know how well the supine slaves
Of blind authority read the truth of things
When written on a brow of guilelessness:
She sees not yet triumphant Innocence
Stand at the judgement-seat of mortal man,
A judge and an accuser of the wrong
Which drags it there. Prepare yourself, my Lord;
Our suite will join yours in the court below.   *[Exeunt.*

Act V

SCENE I.—*An Apartment in* ORSINO'S *Palace. Enter* ORSINO *and*
GIACOMO.

   Giacomo. Do evil deeds thus quickly come to end?
O, that the vain remorse which must chastise
Crimes done, had but as loud a voice to warn
As its keen sting is mortal to avenge!
O, that the hour when present had cast off
The mantle of its mystery, and shown
The ghastly form with which it now returns
When its scared game is roused, cheering the hounds
Of conscience to their prey! Alas! Alas!
It was a wicked thought, a piteous deed,
To kill an old and hoary-headed father.
   Orsino. It has turned out unluckily, in truth.
   Giacomo. To violate the sacred doors of sleep;

To cheat kind Nature of the placid death
Which she prepares for overwearied age;
To drag from Heaven an unrepentant soul
Which might have quenched in reconciling prayers
A life of burning crimes . . .
    Orsino.   You cannot say
I urged you to the deed.
    Giacomo.   O, had I never
Found in thy smooth and ready countenance
The mirror of my darkest thoughts; hadst thou
Never with hints and questions made me look
Upon the monster of my thought, until
It grew familiar to desire . . .
    Orsino.   'Tis thus
Men cast the blame of their unprosperous acts
Upon the abettors of their own resolve;
Or anything but their weak, guilty selves.
And yet, confess the truth, it is the peril
In which you stand that gives you this pale sickness
Of penitence; confess 'tis fear disguised
From its own shame that takes the mantle now
Of thin remorse. What if we yet were safe?
    Giacomo. How can that be? Already Beatrice,
Lucretia and the murderer are in prison.
I doubt not officers are, whilst we speak,
Sent to arrest us.
    Orsino.   I have all prepared
For instant flight. We can escape even now,
So we take fleet occasion by the hair.
    Giacomo. Rather expire in tortures, as I may.
What! will you cast by self-accusing flight
Assured conviction upon Beatrice?
She, who alone in this unnatural work,
Stands like God's angel ministered upon
By fiends; avenging such a nameless wrong
As turns black parricide to piety;
Whilst we for basest ends . . . I fear, Orsino,
While I consider all your words and looks,
Comparing them with your proposal now,
That you must be a villain. For what end
Could you engage in such a perilous crime,
Training me on with hints, and signs, and smiles,

Even to this gulf? Thou art no liar? No,
Thou art a lie! Traitor and murderer!
Coward and slave! But, no, defend thyself;   [*Drawing.*
Let the sword speak what the indignant tongue
Disdains to brand thee with.

    Orsino.   Put up your weapon.
Is it the desperation of your fear
Makes you thus rash and sudden with a friend,
Now ruined for your sake? If honest anger
Have moved you, know, that what I just proposed
Was but to try you. As for me, I think,
Thankless affection led me to this point,
From which, if my firm temper could repent,
I cannot now recede. Even whilst we speak
The ministers of justice wait below:
They grant me these brief moments. Now if you
Have any word of melancholy comfort
To speak to your pale wife, 'twere best to pass
Out at the postern, and avoid them so.

    Giacomo. O, generous friend! How canst thou pardon me?
Would that my life could purchase thine!

    Orsino.   That wish
Now comes a day too late. Haste; fare thee well!
Hear'st thou not steps along the corridor? [*Exit* GIACOMO.
I'm sorry for it; but the guards are waiting
At his own gate, and such was my contrivance
That I might rid me both of him and them.
I thought to act a solemn comedy
Upon the painted scene of this new world,
And to attain my own peculiar ends
By some such plot of mingled good and ill
As others weave; but there arose a Power
Which grasped and snapped the threads of my device
And turned it to a net of ruin . . . Ha! [*A shout is heard.*
Is that my name I hear proclaimed abroad?
But I will pass, wrapped in a vile disguise;
Rags on my back, and a false innocence
Upon my face, through the misdeeming crowd
Which judges by what seems. 'Tis easy then
For a new name and for a country new,
And a new life, fashioned on old desires,
To change the honours of abandoned Rome.

And these must be the masks of that within,
Which must remain unaltered . . . Oh, I fear
That what is past will never let me rest!
Why, when none else is conscious, but myself,
Of my misdeeds, should my own heart's contempt
Trouble me? Have I not the power to fly
My own reproaches? Shall I be the slave
Of . . . what? A word? which those of this false world
Employ against each other, not themselves;
As men wear daggers not for self-offence.
But if I am mistaken, where shall I
Find the disguise to hide me from myself,
As now I skulk from every other eye?   [*Exit.*

SCENE II.—*A Hall of Justice.* CAMILLO, JUDGES, *&c., are discovered
seated;* MARZIO *is led in.*

First Judge. Accused, do you persist in your denial?
I ask you, are you innocent, or guilty?
I demand who were the participators
In your offence? Speak truth and the whole truth.
   Marzio. My God! I did not kill him; I know nothing;
Olimpio sold the robe to me from which
You would infer my guilt.
   Second Judge.   Away with him!
   First Judge. Dare you, with lips yet white from the rack's kiss
Speak false? Is it so soft a questioner,
That you would bandy lover's talk with it
Till it wind out your life and soul? Away!
   Marzio. Spare me! O, spare! I will confess.
   First Judge.   Then speak.
   Marzio. I strangled him in his sleep.
   First Judge.   Who urged you to it?
   Marzio. His own son Giacomo, and the young prelate
Orsino sent me to Petrella; there
The ladies Beatrice and Lucretia
Tempted me with a thousand crowns, and I
And my companion forthwith murdered him.
Now let me die.
   First Judge.   This sounds as bad as truth. Guards, there,
Lead forth the prisoner!

Enter LUCRETIA, BEATRICE, *and* GIACOMO, *guarded*

And beg from your tormentors, like that slave,
The refuge of dishonourable death.
I pray thee, Cardinal, that thou assert
My innocence.
    Camillo (much moved). What shall we think, my Lords?
Shame on these tears! I thought the heart was frozen
Which is their fountain. I would pledge my soul
That she is guiltless.
    Judge.   Yet she must be tortured.
    Camillo. I would as soon have tortured mine own nephew
(If he now lived he would be just her age;
  His hair, too, was her colour, and his eyes
Like hers in shape, but blue and not so deep)
As that most perfect image of God's love
That ever came sorrowing upon the earth.
She is as pure as speechless infancy!
    Judge. Well, be her purity on your head, my Lord,
If you forbid the rack. His Holiness
Enjoined us to pursue this monstrous crime
By the severest forms of law; nay even
To stretch a point against the criminals.
The prisoners stand accused of parricide
Upon such evidence as justifies
Torture.
    Beatrice. What evidence? This man's ?
    Judge.   Even so.
    Beatrice (to MARZIO). Come near. And who art thou thus
      chosen forth
Out of the multitude of living men
To kill the innocent?
    Marzio.   I am Marzio,
Thy father's vassal.
    Beatrice.   Fix thine eyes on mine;
Answer to what I ask.   [*Turning to the* JUDGES.
                I prithee mark
His countenance: unlike bold calumny
Which sometimes dares not speak the thing it looks,
He dares not look the thing he speaks, but bends
His gaze on the blind earth.
(*To* MARZIO.)   What! wilt thou say
That I did murder my own father?
    Marzio.   Oh!

       Look upon this man;
When did you see him last?
  Beatrice.   We never saw him.
  Marzio. You know me too well, Lady Beatrice.
  Beatrice. I know thee! How? where? when?
  Marzio.   You know 'twas I
Whom you did urge with menaces and bribes
To kill your father. When the thing was done
You clothed me in a robe of woven gold
And bade me thrive: how I have thriven, you see.
You, my Lord Giacomo, Lady Lucretia,
You know that what I speak is true.

       [BEATRICE *advances towards him; he covers*
        his face, and shrinks back.
            Oh, dart
The terrible resentment of those eyes
On the dead earth! Turn them away from me!
They wound: 'twas torture forced the truth. My Lords,
Having said this let me be led to death.
  Beatrice. Poor wretch, I pity thee: yet stay awhile.
  Camillo. Guards, lead him not away.
  Beatrice.   Cardinal Camillo.
You have a good repute for gentleness
And wisdom: can it be that you sit here
To countenance a wicked farce like this?
When some obscure and trembling slave is dragged
From sufferings which might shake the sternest heart
And bade to answer, not as he believes,
But as those may suspect or do desire
Whose questions thence suggest their own reply:
And that in peril of such hideous torments
As merciful God spares even the damned. Speak now
The thing you surely know, which is that you,
If your fine frame were stretched upon that wheel,
And you were told: 'Confess that you did poison
Your little nephew; that fair blue-eyed child
Who was the lodestar of your life:—and though
All see, since his most swift and piteous death,
That day and night, and heaven and earth, and time,
And all the things hoped for or done therein
Are changed to you, through your exceeding grief,
Yet you would say, 'I confess anything:'

Spare me! My brain swims round . . . I cannot speak . . .
It was that horrid torture forced the truth.
Take me away! Let her not look on me!
I am a guilty miserable wretch;
I have said all I know; now, let me die!

    Beatrice. My Lords, if by my nature I had been
So stern, as to have planned the crime alleged,
Which your suspicions dictate to this slave,
And the rack makes him utter, do you think
I should have left this two-edged instrument
Of my misdeed; this man, this bloody knife
With my own name engraven on the heft,
Lying unsheathed amid a world of foes,
For my own death? That with such horrible need
For deepest silence, I should have neglected
So trivial a precaution, as the making
His tomb the keeper of a secret written
On a thief's memory? What is his poor life?
What are a thousand lives? A parricide
Had trampled them like dust; and, see, he lives!
(*Turning to* MARZIO.) And thou . . .

    Marzio.   Oh, spare me! Speak to me no more!
That stern yet piteous look, those solemn tones,
Wound worse than torture.

    (*To the* JUDGES.)   I have told it all;
For pity's sake lead me away to death.

    Camillo. Guards, lead him nearer the Lady Beatrice,
He shrinks from her regard like autumn's leaf
From the keen breath of the serenest north.

    Beatrice. O thou who tremblest on the giddy verge
Of life and death, pause ere thou answerest me;
So mayst thou answer God with less dismay:
What evil have we done thee? I, alas!
Have lived but on this earth a few sad years,
And so my lot was ordered, that a father
First turned the moments of awakening life
To drops, each poisoning youth's sweet hope; and then
Stabbed with one blow my everlasting soul;
And my untainted fame; and even that peace
Which sleeps within the core of the heart's heart;
But the wound was not mortal; so my hate
Became the only worship I could lift

To our great father, who in pity and love,
Armed thee, as thou dost say, to cut him off;
And thus his wrong becomes my accusation;
And art thou the accuser? If thou hopest
Mercy in heaven, show justice upon earth:
Worse than a bloody hand is a hard heart.
If thou hast done murders, made thy life's path
Over the trampled laws of God and man,
Rush not before thy Judge, and say: 'My maker,
I have done this and more; for there was one
Who was most pure and innocent on earth;
And because she endured what never any
Guilty or innocent endured before:
Because her wrongs could not be told, not thought;
Because thy hand at length did rescue her;
I with my words killed her and all her kin.'
Think, I adjure you, what it is to slay
The reverence living in the minds of men
Towards our ancient house, and stainless fame!
Think what it is to strangle infant pity,
Cradled in the belief of guileless looks,
Till it become a crime to suffer. Think
What 'tis to blot with infamy and blood
All that which shows like innocence, and is,
Hear me, great God! I swear, most innocent,
So that the world lose all discrimination
Between the sly, fierce, wild regard of guilt,
And that which now compels thee to reply
To what I ask: Am I, or am I not
A parricide?
   Marzio.   Thou art not!
   Judge.   What is this?
   Marzio. I here declare those whom I did accuse
Are innocent. 'Tis I alone am guilty.
   Judge. Drag him away to torments; let them be
Subtle and long drawn out, to tear the folds
Of the heart's inmost cell. Unbind him not
Till he confess.
   Marzio.   Torture me as ye will:
A keener pang has wrung a higher truth
From my last breath. She is most innocent!
Bloodhounds, not men, glut yourselves well with me;

I will not give you that fine piece of nature
To rend and ruin.   [*Exit* MARZIO, *guarded.*
   Camillo.   What say ye now, my Lords?
   Judge. Let tortures strain the truth till it be white
As snow thrice sifted by the frozen wind.
   Camillo. Yet stained with blood.
   Judge (*to* BEATRICE).   Know you this paper, Lady?
   Beatrice. Entrap me not with questions. Who stands here
As my accuser? Ha! wilt thou be he,
Who art my judge? Accuser, witness, judge,
What, all in one? Here is Orsino's name;
Where is Orsino? Let his eye meet mine.
What means this scrawl? Alas! ye know not what,
And therefore on the chance that it may be
Some evil, will ye kill us?

Enter an Officer.

   Officer.   Marzio's dead.
   Judge. What did he say?
   Officer.   Nothing. As soon as we
Had bound him on the wheel, he smiled on us,
As one who baffles a deep adversary;
And holding his breath, died.
   Judge.   There remains nothing
But to apply the question to those prisoners,
Who yet remain stubborn.
   Camillo.   I overrule
Further proceedings, and in the behalf
Of these most innocent and noble persons
Will use my interest with the Holy Father.
   Judge. Let the Pope's pleasure then be done. Meanwhile
Conduct these culprits each to separate cells;
And be the engines ready: for this night
If the Pope's resolution be as grave,
Pious, and just as once, I'll wring the truth
Out of those nerves and sinews, groan by groan.   [*Exeunt.*

Scene III.—*The Cell of a Prison.* Beatrice *is discovered asleep on a couch. Enter* Bernardo.

Bernardo. How gently slumber rests upon her face,
Like the last thoughts of some day sweetly spent
Closing in night and dreams, and so prolonged.
After such torments as she bore last night,
How light and soft her breathing comes. Ay me!
Methinks that I shall never sleep again.
But I must shake the heavenly dew of rest
From this sweet folded flower, thus . . . wake! awake!
What, sister, canst thou sleep?
    Beatrice (awaking).   I was just dreaming
That we were all in Paradise. Thou knowest
This cell seems like a kind of Paradise
After our father's presence.
    Bernardo.   Dear, dear sister.
Would that thy dream were not a dream! O God!
How shall I tell?
    Beatrice.   What wouldst thou tell, sweet brother?
    Bernardo. Look not so calm and happy, or even whilst
I stand considering what I have to say
My heart will break.
    Beatrice.   See now, thou mak'st me weep:
How very friendless thou wouldst be, dear child,
If I were dead. Say what thou hast to say.
    Bernardo. They have confessed; they could endure no more
The tortures . . .
    Beatrice.   Ha! What was there to confess?
They must have told some weak and wicked lie
To flatter their tormentors. Have they said
That they were guilty? O white innocence,
That thou shouldst wear the mask of guilt to hide
Thine awful and serenest countenance
From those who know thee not!

    Enter Judge *with* Lucretia *and* Giacomo, *guarded.*

                       Ignoble hearts!
For some brief spasms of pain, which are at least
As mortal as the limbs through which they pass,
Are centuries of high splendour laid in dust?
And that eternal honour which should live
Sunlike, above the reek of mortal fame.

Changed to a mockery and a byword? What!
Will you give up these bodies to be dragged
At horses' heels, so that our hair should sweep
The footsteps of the vain and senseless crowd,
Who, that they may make our calamity
Their worship and their spectacle, will leave
The churches and the theatres as void
As their own hearts? Shall the light multitude
Fling, at their choice, curses of faded pity,
Sad funeral flowers to deck a living corpse,
Upon us as we pass to pass away,
And leave . . . what memory of our having been?
Infamy, blood, terror, despair? O thou,
Who wert a mother to the parentless,
Kill not thy child! Let not her wrongs kill thee!
Brother, lie down with me upon the rack,
And let us each be silent as a corpse;
It soon will be as soft as any grave.
'Tis but the falsehood it can wring from fear
Makes the rack cruel.

    Giacomo.   They will tear the truth
Even from thee at last, those cruel pains:
For pity's sake say thou art guilty now.

    Lucretia. Oh, speak the truth! Let us all quickly die;
And after death, God is our judge, not they;
He will have mercy on us.

    Bernardo.   If indeed
It can be true, say so, dear sister mine;
And then the Pope will surely pardon you,
And all be well.

    Judge.   Confess, or I will warp
Your limbs with such keen tortures . . .

    Beatrice.   Tortures! Turn
The rack henceforth into a spinning-wheel!
Torture your dog, that he may tell when last
He lapped the blood his master shed . . . not me!
My pangs are of the mind, and of the heart,
And of the soul; ay, of the inmost soul,
Which weeps within tears as of burning gall
To see, in this ill world where none are true,
My kindred false to their deserted selves.
And with considering all the wretched life

Which I have lived, and its now wretched end,
And the small justice shown by Heaven and Earth
To me or mine; and what a tyrant thou art,
And what slaves these; and what a world we make,
The oppressor and the oppressed... such pangs compel
My answer. What is it thou wouldst with me?

   Judge. Art thou not guilty of thy father's death?

   Beatrice. Or wilt thou rather tax high-judging God
That He permitted such an act as that
Which I have suffered, and which He beheld;
Made it unutterable, and took from it
All refuge, all revenge, all consequence,
But that which thou hast called my father's death?
Which is or is not what men call a crime,
Which either I have done, or have not done;
Say what ye will. I shall deny no more.
If ye desire it thus, thus let it be,
And so an end of all. Now do your will;
No other pains shall force another word.

   Judge. She is convicted, but has not confessed.
Be it enough. Until their final sentence
Let none have converse with them. You, young Lord,
   Linger not here!

   Beatrice.   Oh, tear him not away!

   Judge. Guards, do your duty.

   Bernardo (embracing BEATRICE*).* Oh! would ye divide
Body from soul?

   Officer.   That is the headsman's business.

        [*Exeunt all but* LUCRETIA, BEATRICE, *and* GIACOMO.

   Giacomo. Have I confessed? Is it all over now?
No hope! No refuge! O weak, wicked tongue
Which hast destroyed me, would that thou hadst been
Cut out and thrown to dogs first! To have killed
My father first, and then betrayed my sister;
Ay, thee! the one thing innocent and pure
In this black guilty world, to that which I
So well deserve! My wife! my little ones!
Destitute, helpless, and I... Father! God!
Canst Thou forgive even the unforgiving,
When their full hearts break thus, thus!..[*Covers his face and weeps.*

   Lucretia.   O my child!
To what a dreadful end are we all come!

Why did I yield? Why did I not sustain
Those torments? Oh, that I were all dissolved
Into these fast and unavailing tears,
Which flow and feel not!

Beatrice.   What 'twas weak to do,
'Tis weaker to lament, once being done;
Take cheer! The God who knew my wrong, and made
Our speedy act the angel of His wrath,
Seems, and but seems, to have abandoned us.
Let us not think that we shall die for this.
Brother, sit near me; give me your firm hand,
You had a manly heart. Bear up! Bear up!
O dearest Lady, put your gentle head
Upon my lap, and try to sleep awhile:
Your eyes look pale, hollow and overworn,
With heaviness of watching and slow grief.
Come, I will sing you some low, sleepy tune,
Not cheerful, not yet sad; some dull old thing,
Some outworn and unused monotony,
Such as our country gossips sing and spin,
Till they almost forget they live: lie down!
So, that will do. Have I forgot the words?
Faith! They are sadder than I thought they were.

SONG

Ⅰ

False friend, wilt thou smile or weep
When my life is laid asleep?
Little cares for a smile or a tear
The clay-cold corpse upon the bier!
        Farewell! Heigho!
        What is this whispers low?
There is a snake in thy smile, my dear;
And bitter poison within thy tear.

Sweet sleep, were death like to thee,
Or if thou couldst mortal be,
I would close these eyes of pain;
When to wake? Never again.
        O World! Farewell!
        Listen to the passing bell!
It says, thou and I must part,
With a light and a heavy heart. [*The scene closes.*

SCENE IV.—*A Hall of the Prison.* Enter CAMILLO *and* BERNARDO.

Camillo. The Pope is stern; not to be moved or bent.
He looked as calm and keen as is the engine
Which tortures and which kills, exempt itself
From aught that it inflicts; a marble form,
A rite, a law, a custom: not a man.
He frowned, as if to frown had been the trick
Of his machinery, on the advocates
Presenting the defences, which he tore
And threw behind, muttering with hoarse, harsh voice:
'Which among ye defended their old father
Killed in his sleep?' Then to another: 'Thou
Dost this in virtue of thy place; 'tis well.'
He turned to me then, looking deprecation,
And said these three words, coldly: 'They must die.'
   Bernardo. And yet you left him not?
   Camillo.   I urged him still;
Pleading, as I could guess, the devilish wrong
Which prompted your unnatural parent's death.
And he replied: 'Paolo Santa Croce
Murdered his mother yester evening,
And he is fled. Parricide grows so rife
That soon, for some just cause no doubt, the young
Will strangle us all, dozing in our chairs.
Authority, and power, and hoary hair
Are grown crimes capital. You are my nephew,
You come to ask their pardon; stay a moment;
Here is their sentence; never see me more
Till, to the letter, it be all fulfilled.'
   Bernardo. O God, not so! I did believe indeed
That all you said was but sad preparation
For happy news. Oh, there are words and looks
To bend the sternest purpose! Once I knew them,
Now I forget them at my dearest need.
What think you if I seek him out, and bathe
His feet and robe with hot and bitter tears?
Importune him with prayers, vexing his brain
With my perpetual cries, until in rage
He strike me with his pastoral cross, and trample
Upon my prostrate head, so that my blood
May stain the senseless dust on which he treads,

And remorse waken mercy? I will do it!
Oh, wait till I return!   [*Rushes out.*

   Camillo.   Alas! poor boy!
A wreck-devoted seaman thus might pray
To the deaf sea.

   Enter LUCRETIA, BEATRICE, *and* GIACOMO, *guarded.*

   Beatrice.   I hardly dare to fear
That thou bring'st other news than a just pardon.
   Camillo. May God in heaven be less inexorable
To the Pope's prayers, than he has been to mine.
Here is the sentence and the warrant.
   Beatrice (wildly).   O
My God! Can it be possible I have
To die so suddenly? So young to go
Under the obscure, cold, rotting, wormy ground!
To be nailed down into a narrow place;
To see no more sweet sunshine; hear no more
Blithe voice of living thing; muse not again
Upon familiar thoughts, sad, yet thus lost—
How fearful! to be nothing! Or to be...
What? Oh, where am I? Let me not go mad!
Sweet Heaven, forgive weak thoughts! If there should be
No God, no Heaven, no Earth in the void world;
The wide, gray, lampless, deep, unpeopled world!
If all things then should be... my father's spirit,
His eye, his voice, his touch surrounding me;
The atmosphere and breath of my dead life!
If sometimes, as a shape more like himself,
Even the form which tortured me on earth,
Masked in gray hairs and wrinkles, he should come
And wind me in his hellish arms, and fix
His eyes on mine, and drag me down, down, down!
For was he not alone omnipotent
On Earth, and ever present? Even though dead,
Does not his spirit live in all that breathe,
And work for me and mine still the same ruin,
Scorn, pain, despair? Who ever yet returned
To teach the laws of Death's untrodden realm?
Unjust perhaps as those which drive us now,
Oh, whither, whither?
   Lucretia.   Trust in God's sweet love,

The tender promises of Christ: ere night,
Think, we shall be in Paradise.
    Beatrice.   'Tis past!
Whatever comes my heart shall sink no more.
And yet, I know not why, your words strike chill:
How tedious, false and cold seem all things. I
Have met with much injustice in this world;
No difference has been made by God or man,
Or any power moulding my wretched lot,
'Twixt good or evil, as regarded me.
I am cut off from the only world I know,
From light, and life, and love, in youth's sweet prime.
You do well telling me to trust in God,
I hope I do trust in Him. In whom else
Can any trust? And yet my heart is cold.
           [*During the latter speeches* GIACOMO *has retired conversing*
              with CAMILLO, *who now goes out;* GIACOMO *advances.*
    Giacomo. Know you not, Mother... Sister, know you not?
Bernardo even now is gone to implore
The Pope to grant our pardon.
    Lucretia.   Child, perhaps
It will be granted. We may all then live
To make these woes a tale for distant years:
Oh, what a thought! It gushes to my heart
Like the warm blood.
    Beatrice.   Yet both will soon be cold.
Oh, trample out that thought! Worse than despair,
Worse than the bitterness of death, is hope:
It is the only ill which can find place
Upon the giddy, sharp narrow hour
Tottering beneath us. Plead with the swift frost
That it should spare the eldest flower of spring:
Plead with awakening earthquake, o'er whose couch
Even now a city stands, strong, fair, and free;
Now stench and blackness yawn, like death. Oh, plead
With famine, or wind-walking Pestilence,
Blind lightning, or the deaf sea, not with man!
Cruel, cold, formal man; righteous in words,
In deeds a Cain. No, Mother, we must die:
Since such is the reward of innocent lives;
Such the alleviation of worst wrongs.
And whilst our murderers live, and hard, cold men,

Smiling and slow, walk through a world of tears
To death as to life's sleep; 'twere just the grave
Were some strange joy for us. Come, obscure Death,
And wind me in thine all-embracing arms!
Like a fond mother hide me in thy bosom,
And rock me to the sleep from which none wake.
Live ye, who live, subject to one another
As we were once, who now . . .

BERNARDO *rushes in.*

Bernardo.   Oh, horrible!
That tears, that looks, that hope poured forth in prayer,
Even till the heart is vacant and despairs,
Should all be vain! The ministers of death
Are waiting round the doors. I thought I saw
Blood on the face of one . . . What if 'twere fancy?
Soon the heart's blood of all I love on earth
Will sprinkle him, and he will wipe it off
As if 'twere only rain. O life! O world!
Cover me! let me be no more! To see
That perfect mirror of pure innocence
Wherein I gazed, and grew happy and good,
Shivered to dust! To see thee, Beatrice,
Who made all lovely thou didst look upon . . .
Thee, light of life . . . dead, dark! while I say, sister,
To hear I have no sister; and thou, Mother,
Whose love was as a bond to all our loves . . .
Dead! The sweet bond broken!

Enter CAMILLO *and Guards.*

                                  They come! Let me
Kiss those warm lips before their crimson leaves
Are blighted . . . white . . . cold. Say farewell, before
Death chokes that gentle voice! Oh, let me hear
You speak!
    Beatrice. Farewell, my tender brother. Think
Of our sad fate with gentleness, as now:
And let mild, pitying thoughts lighten for thee
Thy sorrow's load. Err not in harsh despair,
But tears and patience. One thing more, my child:
For thine own sake be constant to the love
Thou bearest us; and to the faith that I,

Though wrapped in a strange cloud of crime and shame,
Lived ever holy and unstained. And though
Ill tongues shall wound me, and our common name
Be as a mark stamped on thine innocent brow
For men to point at as they pass, do thou
Forbear, and never think a thought unkind
Of those, who perhaps love thee in their graves.
So mayest thou die as I do; fear and pain
Being subdued. Farewell! Farewell! Farewell!
    Bernardo. I cannot say, farewell!
    Camillo.   Oh, Lady Beatrice!
    Beatrice. Give yourself no unnecessary pain,
My dear Lord Cardinal. Here, Mother, tie
My girdle for me, and bind up this hair
In any simple knot; ay, that does well.
And yours I see is coming down. How often
Have we done this for one another; now
We shall not do it any more. My Lord,
We are quite ready. Well, 'tis very well.

The Mask of Anarchy

WRITTEN ON THE OCCASION OF THE MASSACRE AT
MANCHESTER

In August 1819 military forces fired on a Reform meeting at St. Peter's Field, Manchester. The action was ironically called Peterloo. The news inevitably stirred Shelley into writing his *Mask*, which he sent to *The Examiner*; his friend Leigh Hunt as editor, having been several times prosecuted for political libel, did not then print it. In 1832, when Reform had made big advances, he edited it with a noble preface. An unauthorized cheap reprint is dated 1842.

'The poem', Hunt remarked 'though written purposely in a lax and familiar measure, is highly characteristical of the author. It has the usual ardour of his tone, the unbounded sensibility by which he combines the most domestic with the most remote and fanciful images, and the patience, so beautifully checking, and, in fact, produced by, the extreme impatience of his moral feeling. His patience is the deposit of many impatiences, acting upon an equal measure of understanding and moral taste.' Hunt printed in italics the three stanzas beginning 'Let the laws of your own land' because they 'marked out the sober, lawful and charitable mode of proceeding advocated and anticipated by this supposed reckless innovator.'

Lord Eldon (stanza 4) delivered the judgment depriving Shelley of the control of his children Ianthe and Charles.

> As I lay asleep in Italy
> There came a voice from over the Sea,
> And with great power it forth led me
> To walk in the visions of Poesy.
>
> I met Murder on the way—
> He had a mask like Castlereagh—
> Very smooth he looked, yet grim;
> Seven blood-hounds followed him:
>
> All were fat; and well they might
> Be in admirable plight,
> For one by one, and two by two,
> He tossed them human hearts to chew
> Which from his wide cloak he drew.

Next came Fraud, and he had on,
Like Lord Eldon, an ermined gown;
His big tears, for he wept well,
Turned to mill-stones as they fell.

And the little children, who
Round his feet played to and fro,
Thinking every tear a gem,
Had their brains knocked out by them.

Clothed with the Bible, as with light,
And the shadows of the night,
Like Sidmouth, next, Hypocrisy
On a crocodile rode by.

And many more Destructions played
In this ghastly masquerade,
All disguised, even to the eyes,
Like Bishops, lawyers, peers, and spies.

Last came Anarchy: he rode
On a white horse, splashed with blood;
He was pale even to the lips,
Like Death in the Apocalypse.

And he wore a kingly crown;
And in his grasp a sceptre shone;
On his brow this mark I saw—
'I AM GOD, AND KING, AND LAW!'

With a pace stately and fast,
Over English land he passed,
Trampling to a mire of blood
The adoring multitude.

And a mighty troop around
With their trampling shook the ground,
Waving each a bloody sword,
For the service of their Lord.

And with glorious triumph they
Rode through England proud and gay,
Drunk as with intoxication
Of the wine of desolation.

O'er fields and towns, from sea to sea,
Passed the Pageant swift and free,
Tearing up, and trampling down;
Till they came to London town.

And each dweller, panic-stricken,
Felt his heart with terror sicken
Hearing the tempestuous cry
Of the triumph of Anarchy.

For from pomp to meet him came,
Clothed in arms like blood and flame,
The hired murderers, who did sing
'Thou art God, and Law, and King.

'We have waited weak and lone
For thy coming, Mighty One!
Our purses are empty, our swords are cold,
Give us glory, and blood, and gold.'

Lawyers and priests, a motley crowd,
To the earth their pale brows bowed;
Like a bad prayer not over loud,
Whispering—'Thou art Law and God.'—

Then all cried with one accord,
'Thou art King, and God, and Lord;
Anarchy, to thee we bow,
Be thy name made holy now!'

And Anarchy, the Skeleton,
Bowed and grinned to every one,
As well as if his education
Had cost ten millions to the nation.

For he knew the Palaces
Of our Kings were rightly his;
His the sceptre, crown, and globe,
And the gold-inwoven robe.

So he sent his slaves before
To seize upon the Bank and Tower,
And was proceeding with intent
To meet his pensioned Parliament

When one fled past, a maniac maid,
And her name was Hope, she said:
But she looked more like Despair,
And she cried out in the air:

'My father Time is weak and gray
With waiting for a better day;
See how idiot-like he stands,
Fumbling with his palsied hands!

'He has had child after child,
And the dust of death is piled
Over every one but me—
Misery, oh, Misery!'

Then she lay down in the street,
Right before the horses feet,
Expecting, with a patient eye,
Murder, Fraud, and Anarchy.

When between her and her foes
A mist, a light, an image rose.
Small at first, and weak, and frail
Like the vapour of a vale:

Till as clouds grow on the blast,
Like tower-crowned giants striding fast,
And glare with lightnings as they fly,
And speak in thunder to the sky,

It grew—a Shape arrayed in mail
Brighter than the viper's scale,
And upborne on wings whose grain
Was as the light of sunny rain.

On its helm, seen far away,
A planet, like the Morning's, lay;
And those plumes its light rained through
Like a shower of crimson dew.

With step as soft as wind it passed
O'er the heads of men—so fast
That they knew the presence there,
And looked,—but all was empty air.

As flowers beneath May's footstep waken,
As stars from Night's loose hair are shaken,
As waves arise when loud winds call,
Thoughts sprung where'er that step did fall.

And the prostrate multitude
Looked—and ankle-deep in blood,
Hope, that maiden most serene,
Was walking with a quiet mien:

And Anarchy, the ghastly birth,
Lay dead earth upon the earth;
The Horse of Death tameless as wind
Fled, and with his hoofs did grind
To dust the murderers thronged behind.

A rushing light of clouds and splendour,
A sense awakening and yet tender
Was heard and felt—and at its close
These words of joy and fear arose

As if their own indignant Earth
Which gave the sons of England birth
Had felt their blood upon her brow,
And shuddering with a mother's throe

Had turned every drop of blood
By which her face had been bedewed
To an accent unwithstood,—
As if her heart cried out aloud:

'Men of England, heirs of Glory,
Heroes of unwritten story,
Nurslings of one mighty Mother,
Hopes of her, and one another;

'Rise like Lions after slumber
In unvanquishable number.
Shake your chains to earth like dew
Which in sleep had fallen on you—
Ye are many—they are few.

'What is Freedom?—ye can tell
That which slavery is, too well—
For its very name has grown
To an echo of your own.

''Tis to work and have such pay
As just keeps life from day to day
In your limbs, as in a cell
For the tyrants' use to dwell,

'So that ye for them are made
Loom, and plough, and sword, and spade,
With or without your own will bent
To their defence and nourishment.

''Tis to see your children weak
With their mothers pine and peak,
When the winter winds are bleak,—
They are dying whilst I speak.

''Tis to hunger for such diet
As the rich man in his riot
Casts to the fat dogs that lie
Surfeiting beneath his eye;

"'Tis to let the Ghost of Gold
Take from Toil a thousandfold
More than e'er its substance could
In the tyrannies of old.

'Paper coin—that forgery
Of the title-deeds, which ye
Hold to something from the worth
Of the inheritance of Earth.

"'Tis to be a slave in soul
And to hold no strong control
Over your own wills, but be
All that others make of ye.

'And at length when ye complain
With a murmur weak and vain
'Tis to see the Tyrant's crew
Ride over your wives and you—
Blood is on the grass like dew.

"Then it is to feel revenge
Fiercely thirsting to exchange
Blood for blood—and wrong for wrong—
Do not thus when ye are strong.

'Birds find rest, in narrow nest
When weary of their wingèd quest;
Beasts find fare, in woody lair
When storm and snow are in the air.

'Horses, oxen, have a home,
When from daily toil they come;
Household dogs, when the wind roars,
Find a home within warm doors.'

'Asses, swine, have litter spread
And with fitting food are fed;
All things have a home but one—
Thou, Oh, Englishman, hast none!

'This is Slavery—savage men,
Or wild beasts within a den
Would endure not as ye do—
But such ills they never knew.

'What art thou, Freedom? O! could slaves
Answer from their living graves
This demand—tyrants would flee
Like a dream's imagery:

'Thou art not, as impostors say,
A shadow soon to pass away,
A superstition, and a name
Echoing from the cave of Fame.

'For the labourer thou art bread,
And a comely table spread
From his daily labour come
In a neat and happy home.

'Thou art clothes, and fire, and food
For the trampled multitude—
No—in countries that are free
Such starvation cannot be
As in England now we see.

'To the rich thou art a check,
When his foot is on the neck
Of his victim, thou dost make
That he treads upon a snake.

'Thou art Justice—ne'er for gold
May thy righteous laws be sold
As laws are in England—thou
Shield'st alike both high and low.

'Thou art Wisdom—Freemen never
Dream that God will damn for ever
All who think those things untrue
Of which Priests make such ado.

'Thou art Peace—never by thee
Would blood and treasure wasted be
As tyrants wasted them, when all
Leagued to quench thy flame in Gaul.

'What if English toil and blood
Was poured forth, even as a flood?
It availed, Oh, Liberty,
To dim, but not extinguish thee.

'Thou art Love—the rich have kissed
Thy feet, and like him following Christ,
Give their substance to the free
And through the rough world follow thee,

'Or turn their wealth to arms, and make
War for thy belovèd sake
On wealth, and war, and fraud—whence they
Drew the power which is their prey.

'Science, Poetry, and Thought
Are thy lamps; they make the lot
Of the dwellers in a cot
So serene, they curse it not.

'Spirit, Patience, Gentleness,
All that can adorn and bless
Art thou—let deeds, not words, express
Thine exceeding loveliness.

'Let a great Assembly be
Of the fearless and the free
On some spot of English ground
Where the plains stretch wide around.

'Let the blue sky overhead,
The green earth on which ye tread,
All that must eternal be
Witness the solemnity.

'From the corners uttermost
Of the bounds of English coast;
From every hut, village, and town
Where those who live and suffer moan
For others' misery or their own,

'From the workhouse and the prison
Where pale as corpses newly risen,
Women, children, young and old
Groan for pain, and weep for cold—

'From the haunts of daily life
Where is waged the daily strife
With common wants and common cares
Which sows the human heart with tares—

'Lastly from the palaces
Where the murmur of distress
Echoes, like the distant sound
Of a wind alive around

'Those prison halls of wealth and fashion.
Where some few feel such compassion
For those who groan, and toil, and wail
As must make their brethren pale—

'Ye who suffer woes untold,
Or to feel, or to behold
Your lost country bought and sold
With a price of blood and gold—

'Let a vast assembly be,
And with great solemnity
Declare with measured words that ye
Are, as God has made ye, free—

'Be your strong and simple words
Keen to wound as sharpened swords,
And wide as targes let them be,
With their shade to cover ye.

'Let the tyrants pour around
With a quick and startling sound,
Like the loosening of a sea,
Troops of armed emblazonry.

'Let the charged artillery drive
Till the dead air seems alive
With the clash of clanging wheels,
And the tramp of horses' heels.

'Let the fixèd bayonet
Gleam with sharp desire to wet
Its bright point in English blood
Looking keen as one for food.

'Let the horsemen's scimitars
Wheel and flash, like sphereless stars
Thirsting to eclipse their burning
In a sea of death and mourning.

'Stand ye calm and resolute,
Like a forest close and mute,
With folded arms and looks which are
Weapons of unvanquished war,

'And let Panic, who outspeeds
The career of armèd steeds
Pass, a disregarded shade
Through your phalanx undismayed.

'Let the laws of your own land,
Good or ill, between ye stand
Hand to hand, and foot to foot,
Arbiters of the dispute,

'The old laws of England—they
Whose reverend heads with age are gray,
Children of a wiser day;
And whose solemn voice must be
Thine own echo—Liberty!

'On those who first should violate
Such sacred heralds in their state
Rest the blood that must ensue,
And it will not rest on you.

'And if then the tyrants dare
Let them ride among you there,
Slash, and stab, and maim, and hew,—
What they like, that let them do.

'With folded arms and steady eyes,
And little fear, and less surprise,
Look upon them as they slay
Till their rage has died away.

'Then they will return with shame
To the place from which they came.
And the blood thus shed will speak
In hot blushes on their cheek.

'Every woman in the land
Will point at them as they stand—
They will hardly dare to greet
Their acquaintance in the street.

'And the bold, true warriors
Who have hugged Danger in wars
Will turn to those who would be free,
Ashamed of such base company.

'And that slaughter to the Nation
Shall steam up like inspiration,
Eloquent, oracular;
A volcano heard afar.

'And these words shall then become
Like Oppression's thundered doom
Ringing through each heart and brain.
Heard again—again—again—

'Rise like Lions after slumber
In unvanquishable number—
Shake your chains to earth like dew
Which in sleep had fallen on you—
Ye are many—they are few.'

The Sensitive Plant

WHILE this poem is said to have had its origin in the garden of Shelley's friend Mrs Mason in Italy, Shelley's flowers may be looked for rather in his father's ampler gardens at Field Place. The Lady in his later opinion resembled Jane Williams, but he had never seen her when he wrote the poem. The keenness of the figurative details denoting the advance of winter has a seventeenth-century look and recalls Charles Cotton's Ode on that subject; but Shelley had lived much among trees, flowers, and herbs and felt their presences.

The Sensitive Plant was in favour with cultured people in Shelley's time. Romney painted a head of Lady Hamilton and called it Sensibility. His friend Hayley urged him to improve the significance; to 'introduce the shrub mimosa' growing in a vase, and a hand approaching its leaves. Romney agreed, and Hayley hurried 'to an eminent nurseryman at Hammersmith' to buy a good specimen of the mystical mimosa.

PART FIRST

A SENSITIVE Plant in a garden grew,
And the young winds fed it with silver dew,
And it opened its fan-like leaves to the light,
And closed them beneath the kisses of Night.

And the Spring arose on the garden fair,
Like the Spirit of Love felt everywhere;
And each flower and herb on Earth's dark breast
Rose from the dreams of its wintry rest.

But none ever trembled and panted with bliss
In the garden, the field, or the wilderness,
Like a doe in the noontide with love's sweet want,
As the companionless Sensitive Plant.

The snowdrop, and then the violet,
Arose from the ground with warm rain wet,
And their breath was mixed with fresh odour, sent
From the turf, like the voice and the instrument.

Then the pied wind-flowers and the tulip tall,
And narcissi, the fairest among them all,
Who gaze on their eyes in the stream's recess,
Till they die of their own dear loveliness;

And the Naiad-like lily of the vale,
Whom youth makes so fair and passion so pale
That the light of its tremulous bells is seen
Through their pavilions of tender green;

And the hyacinth purple, and white, and blue,
Which flung from its bells a sweet peal anew
Of music so delicate, soft, and intense,
It was felt like an odour within the sense;

And the rose like a nymph to the bath addressed,
Which unveiled the depth of her glowing breast,
Till, fold after fold, to the fainting air
The soul of her beauty and love lay bare:

And the wand-like lily, which lifted up,
As a Maenad, its moonlight-coloured cup,
Till the fiery star, which is its eye,
Gazed through clear dew on the tender sky;

And the jessamine faint, and the sweet tuberose,
The sweetest flower for scent that blows;
And all rare blossoms from every clime
Grew in that garden in perfect prime.

And on the stream whose inconstant bosom
Was pranked, under boughs of embowering blossom,
With golden and green light, slanting through
Their heaven of many a tangled hue,

Broad water-lilies lay tremulously,
And starry river-buds glimmered by,
And around them the soft stream did glide and dance
With a motion of sweet sound and radiance.

And the sinuous paths of lawn and of moss,
Which led through the garden along and across,
Some open at once to the sun and the breeze,
Some lost among bowers of blossoming trees,

Were all paved with daisies and delicate bells
As fair as the fabulous asphodels,
And flow'rets which, drooping as day drooped too,
Fell into pavilions, white, purple, and blue,
To roof the glow-worm from the evening dew.

And from this undefilèd Paradise
The flowers (as an infant's awakening eyes
Smile on its mother, whose singing sweet
Can first lull, and at last must awaken it),

When Heaven's blithe winds had unfolded them,
As mine-lamps enkindle a hidden gem,
Shone smiling to Heaven, and every one
Shared joy in the light of the gentle sun;

For each one was interpenetrated
With the light and the odour its neighbour shed,
Like young lovers whom youth and love make dear
Wrapped and filled by their mutual atmosphere.

But the Sensitive Plant which could give small fruit
Of the love which it felt from the leaf to the root,
Received more than all, it loved more than ever,
Where none wanted but it, could belong to the giver,—

For the Sensitive Plant has no bright flower;
Radiance and odour are not its dower;
It loves, even like Love, its deep heart is full,
It desires what it has not, the Beautiful!

The light winds which from unsustaining wings
Shed the music of many murmurings;
The beams which dart from many a star
Of the flowers whose hues they bear afar;

The plumèd insects swift and free,
Like golden boats on a sunny sea,
Laden with light and odour, which pass
Over the gleam of the living grass;

The unseen clouds of the dew, which lie
Like fire in the flowers till the sun rides high,
Then wander like spirits among the spheres,
Each cloud faint with the fragrance it bears;

The quivering vapours of dim noontide,
Which like a sea o'er the warm earth glide,
In which every sound, and odour, and beam,
Move, as reeds in a single stream;

Each and all like ministering angels were
For the Sensitive Plant sweet joy to bear,
Whilst the lagging hours of the day went by
Like windless clouds o'er a tender sky.

And when evening descended from Heaven above,
And the Earth was all rest, and the air was all love,
And delight, though less bright, was far more deep,
And the day's veil fell from the world of sleep,

And the beasts, and the birds, and the insects were drowned
In an ocean of dreams without a sound;
Whose waves never mark, though they ever impress
The light sand which paves it, consciousness;

(Only overhead the sweet nightingale
Ever sang more sweet as the day might fail,
And snatches of its Elysian chant
Were mixed with the dreams of the Sensitive Plant):—

The Sensitive Plant was the earliest
Upgathered into the bosom of rest;
A sweet child weary of its delight,
The feeblest and yet the favourite,
Cradled within the embrace of Night.

PART SECOND

There was a Power in this sweet place,
An Eve in this Eden; a ruling Grace
Which to the flowers, did they waken or dream,
Was as God is to the starry scheme.

A Lady, the wonder of her kind,
Whose form was upborne by a lovely mind
Which, dilating, had moulded her mien and motion
Like a sea-flower unfolded beneath the ocean,

Tended the garden from morn to even:
And the meteors of that sublunar Heaven.
Like the lamps of the air when Night walks forth,
Laughed round her footsteps up from the Earth!

She had no companion of mortal race.
But her tremulous breath and her flushing face
Told, whilst the morn kissed the sleep from her eyes,
That her dreams were less slumber than Paradise:

As if some bright Spirit for her sweet sake
Had deserted Heaven while the stars were awake,
As if yet around her he lingering were,
Though the veil of daylight concealed him from her.

Her step seemed to pity the grass it pressed;
You might hear by the heaving of her breast,
That the coming and going of the wind
Brought pleasure there and left passion behind.

And wherever her aëry footstep trod,
Her trailing hair from the grassy sod
Erased its light vestige, with shadowy sweep,
Like a sunny storm o'er the dark green deep.

I doubt not the flowers of that garden sweet
Rejoiced in the sound of her gentle feet;
I doubt not they felt the spirit that came
From her glowing fingers through all their frame.

She sprinkled bright water from the stream
On those that were faint with the sunny beam;
And out of the cups of the heavy flowers
She emptied the rain of the thunder-showers.

She lifted their heads with her tender hands,
And sustained them with rods and osier-bands;
If the flowers had been her own infants, she
Could never have nursed them more tenderly.

And all killing insects and gnawing worms,
And things of obscene and unlovely forms,
She bore, in a basket of Indian woof,
Into the rough woods far aloof,—

In a basket, of grasses and wild-flowers full,
The freshest her gentle hands could pull
For the poor banished insects, whose intent,
Although they did ill, was innocent.

But the bee and the beamlike ephemeris
Whose path is the lightning's, and soft moths that kiss
The sweet lips of the flowers, and harm not, did she
Make her attendant angels be.

And many an antenatal tomb,
Where butterflies dream of the life to come,
She left clinging round the smooth and dark
Edge of the odorous cedar bark.

This fairest creature from earliest Spring
Thus moved through the garden ministering
All the sweet season of Summertide,
And ere the first leaf looked brown—she died!

PART THIRD

Three days the flowers of the garden fair,
Like stars when the moon is awakened, were,
Or the waves of Baiae, ere luminous
She floats up through the smoke of Vesuvius.

And on the fourth, the Sensitive Plant
Felt the sound of the funeral chant,
And the steps of the bearers, heavy and slow,
And the sobs of the mourners, deep and low;

The weary sound and the heavy breath,
And the silent motions of passing death,
And the smell, cold, oppressive, and dank,
Sent through the pores of the coffin-plank;

The dark grass, and the flowers among the grass,
Were bright with tears as the crowd did pass;
From their sighs the wind caught a mournful tone,
And sate in the pines, and gave groan for groan.

The garden, once fair, became cold and foul,
Like the corpse of her who had been its soul,
Which at first was lovely as if in sleep,
Then slowly changed, till it grew a heap
To make men tremble who never weep.

Swift Summer into the Autumn flowed,
And frost in the mist of the morning rode,
Though the noonday sun looked clear and bright,
Mocking the spoil of the secret night.

The rose-leaves, like flakes of crimson snow,
Paved the turf and the moss below.
The lilies were drooping, and white, and wan,
Like the head and the skin of a dying man.

And Indian plants, of scent and hue
The sweetest that ever were fed on dew,
Leaf by leaf, day after day,
Were massed into the common clay.

And the leaves, brown, yellow, and gray, and red,
And white with the whiteness of what is dead,
Like troops of ghosts on the dry wind passed;
Their whistling noise made the birds aghast.

And the gusty winds waked the wingèd seeds,
Out of their birthplace of ugly weeds,
Till they clung round many a sweet flower's stem,
Which rotted into the earth with them.

The water-blooms under the rivulet
Fell from the stalks on which they were set;
And the eddies drove them here and there,
As the winds did those of the upper air.

Then the rain came down, and the broken stalks
Were bent and tangled across the walks;
And the leafless network of parasite bowers
Massed into ruin; and all sweet flowers.

Between the time of the wind and the snow
All loathliest weeds began to grow,
Whose coarse leaves were splashed with many a speck,
Like the water-snake's belly and the toad's back.

And thistles, and nettles, and darnels rank,
And the dock, and henbane, and hemlock dank,
Stretched out its long and hollow shank,
And stifled the air till the dead wind stank.

And plants, at whose names the verse feels loath,
Filled the place with a monstrous undergrowth,
Prickly, and pulpous, and blistering, and blue,
Livid, and starred with a lurid dew.

And agarics, and fungi, with mildew and mould
Started like mist from the wet ground cold;
Pale, fleshy, as if the decaying dead
With a spirit of growth had been animated!

Spawn, weeds, and filth, a leprous scum,
Made the running rivulet thick and dumb,
And at its outlet flags huge as stakes
Dammed it up with roots knotted like water-snakes.

And hour by hour, when the air was still,
The vapours arose which have strength to kill;
At morn they were seen, at noon they were felt,
At night they were darkness no star could melt.

And unctuous meteors from spray to spray
Crept and flitted in broad noonday
Unseen; every branch on which they alit
By a venomous blight was burned and bit.

The Sensitive Plant, like one forbid,
Wept, and the tears within each lid
Of its folded leaves, which together grew,
Were changed to a blight of frozen glue.

For the leaves soon fell, and the branches soon
By the heavy axe of the blast were hewn;
The sap shrank to the root through every pore
As blood to a heart that will beat no more.

For Winter came: the wind was his whip:
One choppy finger was on his lip:
He had torn the cataracts from the hills
And they clanked at his girdle like manacles;

His breath was a chain which without a sound
The earth, and the air, and the water bound;
He came, fiercely driven, in his chariot-throne
By the tenfold blasts of the Arctic zone.

Then the weeds which were forms of living death
Fled from the frost to the earth beneath.
Their decay and sudden flight from frost
Was but like the vanishing of a ghost!

And under the roots of the Sensitive Plant
The moles and the dormice died for want:
The birds dropped stiff from the frozen air
And were caught in the branches naked and bare.

First there came down a thawing rain
And its dull drops froze on the boughs again;
Then there steamed up a freezing dew
Which to the drops of the thaw-rain grew;

And a northern whirlwind, wandering about
Like a wolf that had smelt a dead child out,
Shook the boughs thus laden, and heavy, and stiff,
And snapped them off with his rigid griff.

When Winter had gone and Spring came back
The Sensitive Plant was a leafless wreck;
But the mandrakes, and toadstools, and docks, and darnels,
Rose like the dead from their ruined charnels.

CONCLUSION

Whether the Sensitive Plant, or that
Which within its boughs like a Spirit sat,
Ere its outward form had known decay,
Now felt this change, I cannot say.

Whether that Lady's gentle mind,
No longer with the form combined
Which scattered love, as stars do light,
Found sadness, where it left delight,

I dare not guess; but in this life
Of error, ignorance, and strife,
Where nothing is, but all things seem,
And we the shadows of the dream,

It is a modest creed, and yet
Pleasant if one considers it,
To own that death itself must be,
Like all the rest, a mockery.

That garden sweet, that lady fair,
And all sweet shapes and odours there,
In truth have never passed away:
'Tis we, 'tis ours, are changed; not they.

For love, and beauty, and delight,
There is no death, no change: their might
Exceeds our organs, which endure
No light being themselves obscure.

March 1820

A Vision of the Sea

THE poet, who did not himself publish many of his 'minor poems, published this fragment; what completion was possible he perhaps did not know. He had a high opinion of Coleridge's *Ancient Mariner*, and here and there the *Vision* may have Coleridgean circumstance; yet its Sea is not the same. Its terror is brilliant and tigerish. It might be Herman Melville's latitudes. The late Newman White conjectured that it might signify Mary Shelley's 'withdrawal into herself'!

'TIS the terror of tempest. The rags of the sail
Are flickering in ribbons within the fierce gale:
From the stark night of vapours the dim rain is driven,
And when lightning is loosed, like a deluge from Heaven,
She sees the black trunks of the waterspouts spin
And bend, as if Heaven was ruining in,
Which they seemed to sustain with their terrible mass
As if ocean had sunk from beneath them: they pass
To their graves in the deep with an earthquake of sound,
And the waves and the thunders, made silent around,
Leave the wind to its echo. The vessel, now tossed
Through the low-trailing rack of the tempest, is lost
In the skirts of the thunder-cloud: now down the sweep
Of the wind-cloven wave to the chasm of the deep
It sinks, and the walls of the watery vale
Whose depths of dread calm are unmoved by the gale,
Dim mirrors of ruin, hang gleaming about;
While the surf, like a chaos of stars, like a rout
Of death-flames, like whirlpools of fire-flowing iron,
With splendour and terror the black ship environ,
Or like sulphur-flakes hurled from a mine of pale fire
In fountains spout o'er it. In many a spire
The pyramid-billows with white points of brine
In the cope of the lightning inconstantly shine,

As piercing the sky from the floor of the sea.
The great ship seems splitting! it cracks as a tree,
While an earthquake is splintering its root, ere the blast
Of the whirlwind that stripped it of branches has passed.
The intense thunder-balls which are raining from Heaven
Have shattered its mast, and it stands black and riven.
The chinks suck destruction. The heavy dead hulk
On the living sea rolls an inanimate bulk,
Like a corpse on the clay which is hungering to fold
Its corruption around it. Meanwhile, from the hold,
One deck is burst up by the waters below,
And it splits like the ice when the thaw-breezes blow
O'er the lakes of the desert! Who sit on the other?
Is that all the crew that lie burying each other,
Like the dead in a breach, round the foremast? Are those
Twin tigers, who burst, when the waters arose,
In the agony of terror, their chains in the hold;
(What now makes them tame, is what then made them bold;)
Who crouch, side by side, and have driven, like a crank,
The deep grip of their claws through the vibrating plank:—
Are these all? Nine weeks the tall vessel had lain
On the windless expanse of the watery plain,
Where the death-darting sun cast no shadow at noon,
And there seemed to be fire in the beams of the moon,
Till a lead-coloured fog gathered up from the deep,
Whose breath was quick pestilence; then, the cold sleep
Crept, like blight through the ears of a thick field of corn,
O'er the populous vessel. And even and morn,
With their hammocks for coffins the seamen aghast
Like dead men the dead limbs of their comrades cast
Down the deep, which closed on them above and around,
And the sharks and the dogfish their grave-clothes unbound,
And were glutted like Jews with this manna rained down
From God on their wilderness. One after one
The mariners died; on the eve of this day,
When the tempest was gathering in cloudy array,
But seven remained. Six the thunder has smitten,
And they lie black as mummies on which Time has written
His scorn of the embalmer; the seventh, from the deck
An oak-splinter pierced through his breast and his back,
And hung out to the tempest, a wreck on the wreck.
No more? At the helm sits a woman more fair

Than Heaven, when, unbinding its star-braided hair,
It sinks with the sun on the earth and the sea.
She clasps a bright child on her upgathered knee;
It laughs at the lightning, it mocks the mixed thunder
Of the air and the sea, with desire and with wonder
It is beckoning the tigers to rise and come near,
It would play with those eyes where the radiance of fear
Is outshining the meteors; its bosom beats high,
The heart-fire of pleasure has kindled its eye,
While its mother's is lustreless. 'Smile not, my child,
But sleep deeply and sweetly, and so be beguiled
Of the pang that awaits us, whatever that be,
So dreadful since thou must divide it with me!
Dream, sleep! This pale bosom, thy cradle and bed,
Will it rock thee not, infant? 'Tis beating with dread!
Alas! what is life, what is death, what are we,
That when the ship sinks we no longer may be?
What! to see thee no more, and to feel thee no more?
To be after life what we have been before?
Not to touch those sweet hands? Not to look on those eyes,
Those lips, and that hair,—all the smiling disguise
Thou yet wearest, sweet Spirit, which I, day by day,
Have so long called my child, but which now fades away
Like a rainbow, and I the fallen shower?'—Lo! the ship
Is settling, it topples, the leeward ports dip;
The tigers leap up when they feel the slow brine
Crawling inch by inch on them; hair, ears, limbs, and eyne,
Stand rigid with horror; a loud, long, hoarse cry
Bursts at once from their vitals tremendously,
And 'tis borne down the mountainous vale of the wave,
Rebounding, like thunder, from crag to cave,
Mixed with the clash of the lashing rain,
Hurried on by the might of the hurricane:
The hurricane came from the west, and passed on
By the path of the gate of the eastern sun,
Transversely dividing the stream of the storm;
As an arrowy serpent, pursuing the form
Of an elephant, bursts through the brakes of the waste.
Black as a cormorant the screaming blast,
Between Ocean and Heaven, like an ocean, passed,
Till it came to the clouds on the verge of the world
Which, based on the sea and to Heaven upcurled,

Like columns and walls did surround and sustain
The dome of the tempest; it rent them in twain,
As a flood rends its barriers of mountainous crag:
And the dense clouds in many a ruin and rag,
Like the stones of a temple ere earthquake has passed,
Like the dust of its fall, on the whirlwind are cast;
They are scattered like foam on the torrent; and where
The wind has burst out through the chasm, from the air
Of clear morning the beams of the sunrise flow in
Unimpeded, keen, golden, and crystalline,
Banded armies of light and of air; at one gate
They encounter, but interpenetrate.
And that breach in the tempest is widening away,
And the caverns of cloud are torn up by the day,
And the fierce winds are sinking with weary wings,
Lulled by the motion and murmurings
And the long glassy heave of the rocking sea,
And overhead, glorious but dreadful to see,
The wrecks of the tempest like vapours of gold
Are consuming in sunrise. The heaped waves behold
The deep calm of blue Heaven dilating above,
And like passions made still by the presence of Love
Beneath the clear surface reflecting it, slide,
Tremulous with soft influence; extending its tide
From the Andes to Atlas, round mountain and isle,
Round sea-birds and wrecks, paved with Heaven's azure smile,
The wide world of waters is vibrating. Where
Is the ship? On the verge of the wave where it lay
One tiger is mingled in ghastly affray
With a sea-snake. The foam and the smoke of the battle
Stain the clear air with sunbows; the jar, and the rattle
Of solid bones crushed by the infinite stress
Of the snake's adamantine voluminousness;
And the hum of the hot blood that spouts and rains
Where the gripe of the tiger has wounded the veins
Swollen with rage, strength, and effort; the whirl and the splash
As of some hideous engine whose brazen teeth smash
The thin winds and soft waves into thunder; the screams
And hissings crawl fast o'er the smooth ocean-streams,
Each sound like a centipede. Near this commotion,
A blue shark is hanging within the blue ocean,
The fin-wingèd tomb of the victor. The other

Is winning his way from the fate of his brother
To his own with the speed of despair. Lo! a boat
Advances; twelve rowers with the impulse of thought
Urge on the keen keel,—the brine foams. At the stern
Three marksmen stand levelling. Hot bullets burn
In the breast of the tiger, which yet bears him on
To his refuge and ruin. One fragment alone,—
'Tis dwindling and sinking, 'tis now almost gone,—
Of the wreck of the vessel peers out of the sea.
With her left hand she grasps it impetuously,
With her right she sustains her fair infant. Death, Fear,
Love, Beauty, are mixed in the atmosphere,
Which trembles and burns with the fervour of dread
Around her wild eyes, her bright hand, and her head,
Like a meteor of light o'er the waters! her child
Is yet smiling, and playing, and murmuring; so smiled
The false deep ere the storm. Like a sister and brother
The child and the ocean still smile on each other,
Whilst——

April 1820

Letter to Maria Gisborne

A COURTEOUS poem; Shelley is reporting 'all's well' from the Gisborne's house in Italy. In London Mr and Mrs Gisborne met besides the interesting persons whom Shelley names a silent John Keats, 'under sentence of death from Dr. Lambe.' The Henry of Shelley's 'Letter' is Henry Reveley, Mrs Gisborne's son, a young engineer; Shelley was paying him money for the construction of a steamship partly designed by the financier, and Henry ungratefully attributed the failure of the scheme not to his own inadequacy but to Shelley's cumbrous design. The Letter makes us wish Shelley had written twenty such, so easily does he discourse, taking everything that comes to his mind for humorous, affectionate or imaginative communication.

THE spider spreads her webs, whether she be
In poet's tower, cellar, or barn, or tree;
The silk-worm in the dark green mulberry leaves
His winding sheet and cradle ever weaves;
So I, a thing whom moralists call worm,
Sit spinning still round this decaying form,
From the fine threads of rare and subtle thought—
No net of words in garish colours wrought
To catch the idle buzzers of the day—
But a soft cell, where when that fades away,
Memory may clothe in wings my living name
And feed it with the asphodels of fame,
Which in those hearts which must remember me
Grow, making love an immortality.

Whoever should behold me now, I wist,
Would think I were a mighty mechanist,
Bent with sublime Archimedean art
To breathe a soul into the iron heart
Of some machine portentous, or strange gin,

Which by the force of figured spells might win
Its way over the sea, and sport therein;
For round the walls are hung dread engines, such
As Vulcan never wrought for Jove to clutch
Ixion or the Titan:—or the quick
Wit of that man of God, St. Dominic,
To convince Atheist, Turk, or Heretic,
Or those in philanthropic council met,
Who thought to pay some interest for the debt
They owed to Jesus Christ for their salvation,
By giving a faint foretaste of damnation
To Shakespeare, Sidney, Spenser, and the rest
Who made our land an island of the blest.
When lamp-like Spain, who now relumes her fire
On Freedom's hearth, grew dim with Empire:—
With thumbscrews, wheels, with tooth and spike and jag,
Which fishers found under the utmost crag
Of Cornwall and the storm-encompassed isles,
Where to the sky the rude sea rarely smiles
Unless in treacherous wrath, as on the morn
When the exulting elements in scorn,
Satiated with destroyed destruction, lay
Sleeping in beauty on their mangled prey,
As panthers sleep;—and other strange and dread
Magical forms the brick floor overspread,—
Proteus transformed to metal did not make
More figures, or more strange: nor did he take
Such shapes of unintelligible brass,
Or heap himself in such a horrid mass
Of tin and iron not to be understood;
And forms of unimaginable wood,
To puzzle Tubal Cain and all his brood:
Great screws, and cones, and wheels, and groovèd blocks,
The elements of what will stand the shocks
Of wave and wind and time.—Upon the table
More knacks and quips there be than I am able
To catalogize in this verse of mine:—
A pretty bowl of wood—not full of wine,
But quicksilver; that dew which the gnomes drink
When at their subterranean toil they swink,
Pledging the demons of the earthquake, who
Reply to them in lava—cry halloo!

And call out to the cities o'er their head,—
Roofs, towers, and shrines, the dying and the dead,
Crash through the chinks of earth—and then all quaff
Another rouse, and hold their sides and laugh.
This quicksilver no gnome has drunk—within
The walnut bowl it lies, veinèd and thin,
In colour like the wake of light that stains
The Tuscan deep, when from the moist moon rains
The inmost shower of its white fire—the breeze
Is still—blue Heaven smiles over the pale seas.
And in this bowl of quicksilver—for I
Yield to the impulse of an infancy
Outlasting manhood—I have made to float
A rude idealism of a paper boat:—
A hollow screw with cogs—Henry will know
The thing I mean and laugh at me,—if so
He fears not I should do more mischief.—Next
Lie bills and calculations much perplexed,
With steam-boats, frigates, and machinery quaint
Traced over them in blue and yellow paint.
Then comes a range of mathematical
Instruments, for plans nautical and statical;
A heap of rosin, a queer broken glass
With ink in it;—a china cup that was
What it will never be again, I think,—
A thing from which sweet lips were wont to drink
The liquor doctors rail at—and which I
Will quaff in spite of them—and when we die
We'll toss up who died first of drinking tea,
And cry out,—'Heads or tails?' where'er we be.
Near that a dusty paint-box, some odd hooks.
A half-burnt match, an ivory block, three books,
Where conic sections, spherics, logarithms.
To great Laplace, from Saunderson and Sims,
Lie heaped in their harmonious disarray
Of figures,—disentangle them who may.
Baron de Tott's Memoirs beside them lie,
And some odd volumes of old chemistry.
Near those a most inexplicable thing.
With lead in the middle—I'm conjecturing
How to make Henry understand; but no—
I'll leave, as Spenser says, with many moe,

This secret in the pregnant womb of time,
Too vast a matter for so weak a rhyme.

And here like some weird Archimage sit I,
Plotting dark spells, and devilish enginery,
The self-impelling steam-wheels of the mind
Which pump up oaths from clergymen, and grind
The gentle spirit of our meek reviews
Into a powdery foam of salt abuse,
Ruffling the ocean of their self-content;—
I sit—and smile or sigh as is my bent,
But not for them—Libeccio rushes round
With an inconstant and an idle sound,
I heed him more than them—the thunder-smoke
Is gathering on the mountains, like a cloak
Folded athwart their shoulders broad and bare;
The ripe corn under the undulating air
Undulates like an ocean:—and the vines
Are trembling wide in all their trellised lines—
The murmur of the awakening sea doth fill
The empty pauses of the blast;—the hill
Looks hoary through the white electric rain,
And from the glens beyond, in sullen strain,
The interrupted thunder howls; above
One chasm of Heaven smiles, like the eye of Love
On the unquiet world;—while such things are,
How could one worth your friendship heed the war
Of worms? the shriek of the world's carrion jays,
Their censure, or their wonder, or their praise?

You are not here! the quaint witch Memory secs,
In vacant chairs, your absent images,
And points where once you sat, and now should be
But are not.—I demand if ever we
Shall meet as then we met;—and she replies,
Veiling in awe her second-sighted eyes;
'I know the past alone—but summon home
My sister Hope,—she speaks of all to come.'
But I, an old diviner, who knew well
Every false verse of that sweet oracle,
Turned to the sad enchantress once again,
And sought a respite from my gentle pain,

In citing every passage o'er and o'er
Of our communion—how on the sea-shore
We watched the ocean and the sky together
Under the roof of blue Italian weather;
How I ran home through last year's thunder-storm,
And felt the transverse lightning linger warm
Upon my cheek—and how we often made
Feasts for each other, where good will outweighed
The frugal luxury of our country cheer,
As well it might, were it less firm and clear
Than ours must ever be;—and how we spun
A shroud of talk to hide us from the sun
Of this familiar life, which seems to be
But is not:—or is but quaint mockery
Of all we would believe, and sadly blame
The jarring and inexplicable frame
Of this wrong world:—and then anatomize
The purposes and thoughts of men whose eyes
Were closed in distant years;—or widely guess
The issue of the earth's great business,
When we shall be as we no longer are—
Like babbling gossips safe, who hear the war
Of winds, and sigh, but tremble not;—or how
You listened to some interrupted flow
Of visionary rhyme,—in joy and pain
Struck from the inmost fountains of my brain,
With little skill perhaps;—or how we sought
Those deepest wells of passion or of thought
Wrought by wise poets in the waste of years,
Staining their sacred waters with our tears;
Quenching a thirst ever to be renewed!
Or how I, wisest lady! then endued
The language of a land which now is free,
And, winged with thoughts of truth and majesty,
Flits round the tyrant's sceptre like a cloud,
And bursts the peopled prisons, and cries aloud,
'My name is Legion!'—that majestic tongue
Which Calderon over the desert flung
Of ages and of nations; and which found
An echo in our hearts, and with the sound
Startled oblivion;—thou wert then to me
As is a nurse—when inarticulately

A child would talk as its grown parents do.
If living winds the rapid clouds pursue,
If hawks chase doves through the aethereal way,
Huntsmen the innocent deer, and beasts their prey,
Why should not we rouse with the spirit's blast
Out of the forest of the pathless past
These recollected pleasures?
                              You are now
In London, that great sea, whose ebb and flow
At once is deaf and loud, and on the shore
Vomits its wrecks, and still howls on for more.
Yet in its depth what treasures! You will see
That which was Godwin,—greater none than he
Though fallen—and fallen on evil times—to stand
Among the spirits of our age and land,
Before the dread tribunal of *to come*
The foremost,—while Rebuke cowers pale and dumb.
You will see Coleridge—he who sits obscure
In the exceeding lustre and the pure
Intense irradiation of a mind,
Which, with its own internal lightning blind,
Flags wearily through darkness and despair—
A cloud-encircled meteor of the air,
A hooded eagle among blinking owls.—
You will see Hunt—one of those happy souls
Which are the salt of the earth, and without whom
This world would smell like what it is—a tomb;
Who is, what others seem; his room no doubt
Is still adorned with many a cast from Shout,
With graceful flowers tastefully placed about;
And coronals of bay from ribbons hung,
And brighter wreaths in neat disorder flung;
The gifts of the most learned among some dozens
Of female friends, sisters-in-law, and cousins.
And there is he with his eternal puns,
Which beat the dullest brain for smiles, like duns
Thundering for money at a poet's door;
Alas! it is no use to say, 'I'm poor!'
Or oft in graver mood, when he will look
Things wiser than were ever read in book,
Except in Shakespeare's wisest tenderness.—
You will see Hogg,—and I cannot express

His virtues,—though I know that they are great,
Because he locks, then barricades the gate
Within which they inhabit;—of his wit
And wisdom, you'll cry out when you are bit.
He is a pearl within an oyster shell,
One of the richest of the deep;—and there
Is English Peacock, with his mountain Fair,
Turned into a Flamingo;—that shy bird
That gleams i' the Indian air—have you not heard
When a man marries, dies, or turns Hindoo,
His best friends hear no more of him?—but you
Will see him, and will like him too, I hope,
With the milk-white Snowdonian Antelope
Matched with this cameleopard—his fine wit
Makes such a wound, the knife is lost in it;
A strain too learnèd for a shallow age,
Too wise for selfish bigots; let his page,
Which charms the chosen spirits of the time,
Fold itself up for the serener clime
Of years to come, and find its recompense
In that just expectation.—Wit and sense,
Virtue and human knowledge; all that might
Make this dull world a business of delight,
Are all combined in Horace Smith.—And these,
With some exceptions, which I need not tease
Your patience by descanting on,—are all
You and I know in London.
                I recall
My thoughts, and bid you look upon the night.
As water does a sponge, so the moonlight
Fills the void, hollow, universal air—
What see you?—unpavilioned Heaven is fair,
Whether the moon, into her chamber gone,
Leaves midnight to the golden stars, or wan
Climbs with diminished beams the azure steep;
Or whether clouds sail o'er the inverse deep,
Piloted by the many-wandering blast,
And the rare stars rush through them dim and fast:—
All this is beautiful in every land.—
But what see you beside?—a shabby stand
Of Hackney coaches—a brick house or wall
Fencing some lonely court, white with the scrawl

Of our unhappy politics;—or worse—
A wretched woman reeling by, whose curse
Mixed with the watchman's, partner of her trade,
You must accept in place of serenade—
Or yellow-haired Pollonia murmuring
To Henry some unutterable thing.
I see a chaos of green leaves and fruit
Built round dark caverns, even to the root
Of the living stems that feed them—in whose bowers
There sleep in their dark dew the folded flowers;
Beyond, the surface of the unsickled corn
Trembles not in the slumbering air, and borne
In circles quaint, and ever-changing dance,
Like wingèd stars the fire-flies flash and glance,
Pale in the open moonshine, but each one
Under the dark trees seems a little sun,
A meteor tamed; a fixed star gone astray
From the silver regions of the milky way;—
Afar the Contadino's song is heard,
Rude, but made sweet by distance—and a bird
Which cannot be the Nightingale, and yet
I know none else that sings so sweet as it
At this late hour;—and then all is still—
Now—Italy or London, which you will!

Next winter you must pass with me; I'll have
My house by that time turned into a grave
Of dead despondence and low-thoughted care.
And all the dreams which our tormentors are;
Oh! that Hunt, Hogg, Peacock, and Smith were there,
With everything belonging to them fair!—
We will have books, Spanish, Italian, Greek;
And ask one week to make another week
As like his father, as I'm unlike mine,
Which is not his fault, as you may divine.
Though we eat little flesh and drink no wine,
Yet let's be merry: we'll have tea and toast;
Custards for supper, and an endless host
Of syllabubs and jellies and mince-pies,
And other such lady-like luxuries,—
Feasting on which we will philosophize!
And we'll have fires out of the Grand Duke's wood,

To thaw the six weeks' winter in our blood.
And then we'll talk;—what shall we talk about?
Oh! there are themes enough for many a bout
Of thought-entangled descant;—as to nerves—
With cones and parallelograms and curves
I've sworn to strangle them if once they dare
To bother me—when you are with me there.
And they shall never more sip laudanum,
From Helicon or Himeros; —well, come,
And in despite of God and of the devil,
We'll make our friendly philosophic revel
Outlast the leafless time; till buds and flowers
Warn the obscure inevitable hours,
Sweet meeting by sad parting to renew;—
'To-morrow to fresh woods and pastures new.'

The Witch of Atlas

HERE also the conversation of Shelley sounds through the verse, which is as he says, 'light' verse; but the riddle which he is setting is elaborate enough. He appears to be entertaining those who will give him their time with a poetical bioscope. He does not wish us to solve the enigma of his Witch's name and nature in too certain terms, but she is evidently a feminine relation of Prometheus, and a good fairy for all faithful Reformists. Some part of the spectacle in which she is a Queen of such exquisite grace and wit is said by S.B.P. in *Notes and Queries* to signify the steamboat which was still a modern miracle at the time of the poem—and the marvels of electricity may also be the explanation of some of the display. The poem is in any case a holiday diversion, even while it continues Shelley's most urgent theme of revolutions of all kinds.

To Mary

ON HER OBJECTING TO THE FOLLOWING POEM, UPON THE
SCORE OF ITS CONTAINING NO HUMAN INTEREST

How, my dear Mary,—are you critic-bitten
    (For vipers kill, though dead) by some review,
That you condemn these verses I have written,
    Because they tell no story, false or true?
What, though no mice are caught by a young kitten,
    May it not leap and play as grown cats do,
Till its claws come? Prithee, for this one time,
Content thee with a visionary rhyme.

What hand would crush the silken-wingèd fly,
    The youngest of inconstant April's minions,
Because it cannot climb the purest sky,
    Where the swan sings, amid the sun's dominions?
Not thine. Thou knowest 'tis its doom to die,
    When Day shall hide within her twilight pinions
The lucent eyes, and the eternal smile,
Serene as thine, which lent it life awhile.

To thy fair feet a wingèd Vision came,
　　Whose date should have been longer than a day,
And o'er thy head did beat its wings for fame,
　　And in thy sight its fading plumes display;
The watery bow burned in the evening flame,
　　But the shower fell, the swift Sun went his way—
And that is dead.—O, let me not believe
That anything of mine is fit to live!

Wordsworth informs us he was nineteen years
　　Considering and retouching Peter Bell;
Watering his laurels with the killing tears
　　Of slow, dull care, so that their roots to Hell
Might pierce, and their wide branches blot the spheres
　　Of Heaven, with dewy leaves and flowers; this well
May be, for Heaven and Earth conspire to foil
The over-busy gardener's blundering toil.

My Witch indeed is not so sweet a creature
　　As Ruth or Lucy, whom his graceful praise
Clothes for our grandsons—but she matches Peter,
　　Though he took nineteen years, and she three days
In dressing. Light the vest of flowing metre
　　She wears; he, proud as dandy with his stays,
Has hung upon his wiry limbs a dress
Like King Lear's 'looped and windowed raggedness.'

If you strip Peter, you will see a fellow
　　Scorched by Hell's hyperequatorial climate
Into a kind of a sulphureous yellow:
　　A lean mark, hardly fit to fling a rhyme at;
In shape a Scaramouch, in hue Othello.
　　If you unveil my Witch, no priest nor primate
Can shrive you of that sin,—if sin there be
In love, when it becomes idolatry.

The Witch of Atlas

BEFORE those cruel Twins, whom at one birth
   Incestuous Change bore to her father Time,
Error and Truth, had hunted from the Earth
   All those bright natures which adorned its prime,
And left us nothing to believe in, worth
   The pains of putting into learnèd rhyme,
A lady-witch there lived on Atlas' mountain
Within a cavern, by a secret fountain.

Her mother was one of the Atlantides:
   The all-beholding Sun had ne'er beholden
In his wide voyage o'er continents and seas
   So fair a creature, as she lay enfolden
In the warm shadow of her loveliness;—
   He kissed her with his beams, and made all golden
The chamber of gray rock in which she lay—
She, in that dream of joy, dissolved away.

'Tis said, she first was changed into a vapour,
   And then into a cloud, such clouds as flit,
Like splendour-wingèd moths about a taper,
   Round the red west when the sun dies in it:
And then into a meteor, such as caper
   On hill-tops when the moon is in a fit:
Then, into one of those mysterious stars
Which hide themselves between the Earth and Mars.

Ten times the Mother of the Months had bent
   Her bow beside the folding-star, and bidden
With that bright sign the billows to indent
   The sea-deserted sand—like children chidden,
At her command they ever came and went—
   Since in that cave a dewy splendour hidden
Took shape and motion: with the living form
Of this embodied Power, the cave grew warm.

A lovely lady garmented in light
   From her own beauty—deep her eyes, as are
Two openings of unfathomable night
   Seen through a Temple's cloven roof—her hair

Dark—the dim brain whirls dizzy with delight.
  Picturing her form; her soft smiles shone afar,
And her low voice was heard like love, and drew
All living things towards this wonder new.

And first the spotted cameleopard came,
  And then the wise and fearless elephant;
Then the sly serpent, in the golden flame
  Of his own volumes intervolved;—all gaunt
And sanguine beasts her gentle looks made tame.
  They drank before her at her sacred fount;
And every beast of beating heart grew bold,
Such gentleness and power even to behold.

The brinded lioness led forth her young,
  That she might teach them how they should forego
Their inborn thirst of death; the pard unstrung
  His sinews at her feet, and sought to know
With looks whose motions spoke without a tongue
  How he might be as gentle as the doe.
The magic circle of her voice and eyes
All savage natures did imparadise.

And old Silenus, shaking a green stick
  Of lilies, and the wood-gods in a crew
Came, blithe, as in the olive copses thick
  Cicadae are, drunk with the noonday dew:
And Dryope and Faunus followed quick,
  Teasing the God to sing them something new;
Till in this cave they found the lady lone,
Sitting upon a seat of emerald stone.

And universal Pan, 'tis said, was there,
  And though none saw him,—through the adamant
Of the deep mountains, through the trackless air,
  And through those living spirits, like a want,
He passed out of his everlasting lair
  Where the quick heart of the great world doth pant,
And felt that wondrous lady all alone,—
And she felt him, upon her emerald throne.

And every nymph of stream and spreading tree,
    And every shepherdess of Ocean's flocks,
Who drives her white waves over the green sea,
    And Ocean with the brine on his gray locks,
And quaint Priapus with his company,
    All came, much wondering how the enwombèd rocks
Could have brought forth so beautiful a birth;—
Her love subdued their wonder and their mirth.

The herdsmen and the mountain maidens came,
    And the rude kings of pastoral Garamant—
Their spirits shook within them, as a flame
    Stirred by the air under a cavern gaunt:
Pigmies, and Polyphemes, by many a name,
    Centaurs, and Satyrs, and such shapes as haunt
Wet clefts,—and lumps neither alive nor dead,
Dog-headed, bosom-eyed, and bird-footed.

For she was beautiful—her beauty made
    The bright world dim, and everything beside
Seemed like the fleeting image of a shade:
    No thought of living spirit could abide,
Which to her looks had ever been betrayed,
    On any object in the world so wide,
On any hope within the circling skies,
But on her form, and in her inmost eyes.

Which when the lady knew, she took her spindle
    And twined three threads of fleecy mist, and three
Long lines of light, such as the dawn may kindle
    The clouds and waves and mountains with; and she
As many star-beams, ere their lamps could dwindle
    In the belated moon, wound skilfully;
And with these threads a subtle veil she wove—
A shadow for the splendour of her love.

The deep recesses of her odorous dwelling
    Were stored with magic treasures—sounds of air,
Which had the power all spirits of compelling,
    Folded in cells of crystal silence there;

Such as we hear in youth, and think the feeling
   Will never die—yet ere we are aware,
The feeling and the sound are fled and gone,
And the regret they leave remains alone.

And there lay Visions swift, and sweet, and quaint,
   Each in its thin sheath, like a chrysalis,
Some eager to burst forth, some weak and faint
   With the soft burthen of intensest bliss
It was its work to bear to many a saint
   Whose heart adores the shrine which holiest is.
Even Love's;—and others white, green, gray, and black,
And of all shapes—and each was at her beck.

And odours in a kind of aviary
   Of ever-blooming Eden-trees she kept,
Clipped in a floating net, a love-sick Fairy
   Had woven from dew-beams while the moon yet slept;
As bats at the wired window of a dairy,
   They beat their vans; and each was an adept,
When loosed and missioned, making wings of winds,
To stir sweet thoughts or sad, in destined minds.

And liquors clear and sweet, whose healthful might
   Could medicine the sick soul to happy sleep,
And change eternal death into a night
   Of glorious dreams—or if eyes needs must weep,
Could make their tears all wonder and delight,
   She in her crystal vials did closely keep:
If men could drink of those clear vials, 'tis said
The living were not envied of the dead.

Her cave was stored with scrolls of strange device,
   The works of some Saturnian Archimage,
Which taught the expiations at whose price
   Men from the Gods might win that happy age
Too lightly lost, redeeming native vice;
   And which might quench the Earth-consuming rage
Of gold and blood—till men should live and move
Harmonious as the sacred stars above;

And how all things that seem untameable,
  Not to be checked and not to be confined,
Obey the spells of Wisdom's wizard skill;
  Time, earth, and fire—the ocean and the wind,
And all their shapes—and man's imperial will;
  And other scrolls whose writings did unbind
The inmost lore of Love—let the profane
Tremble to ask what secrets they contain.

And wondrous works of substances unknown,
  To which the enchantment of her father's power
Had changed those ragged blocks of savage stone,
  Were heaped in the recesses of her bower;
Carved lamps and chalices, and vials which shone
  In their own golden beams—each like a flower,
Out of whose depth a fire-fly shakes his light
Under a cypress in a starless night.

At first she lived alone in this wild home,
  And her own thoughts were each a minister,
Clothing themselves, or with the ocean foam,
  Or with the wind, or with the speed of fire,
To work whatever purposes might come
  Into her mind; such power her mighty Sire
Had girt them with, whether to fly or run,
Through all the regions which he shines upon.

The Ocean-nymphs and Hamadryades,
  Oreads and Naiads, with long weedy locks,
Offered to do her bidding through the seas,
  Under the earth, and in the hollow rocks,
And far beneath the matted roots of trees,
  And in the gnarlèd heart of stubborn oaks,
So they might live for ever in the light
Of her sweet presence—each a satellite.

'Tis may not be,' the wizard maid replied;
  'The fountains where the Naiades bedew
Their shining hair, at length are drained and dried;
  The solid oaks forget their strength, and strew

Their latest leaf upon the mountains wide;
  The boundless ocean like a drop of dew
Will be consumed—the stubborn centre must
Be scattered, like a cloud of summer dust.

'And ye with them will perish, one by one;—
  If I must sigh to think that this shall be,
If I must weep when the surviving Sun
  Shall smile on your decay—oh, ask not me
To love you till your little race is run;
  I cannot die as ye must—over me
Your leaves shall glance—the streams in which ye dwell
Shall be my paths henceforth, and so—farewell!'—

She spoke and wept:—the dark and azure well
  Sparkled beneath the shower of her bright tears,
And every little circlet where they fell
  Flung to the cavern-roof inconstant spheres
And intertangled lines of light:—a knell
  Of sobbing voices came upon her ears
From those departing Forms, o'er the serene
Of the white streams and of the forest green.

All day the wizard lady sate aloof,
  Spelling out scrolls of dread antiquity,
Under the cavern's fountain-lighted roof;
  Or broidering the pictured poesy
Of some high tale upon her growing woof,
  Which the sweet splendour of her smiles could dye
In hues outshining heaven—and ever she
Added some grace to the wrought poesy.

While on her hearth lay blazing many a piece
  Of sandal wood, rare gums, and cinnamon;
Men scarcely know how beautiful fire is—
  Each flame of it is as a precious stone
Dissolved in ever-moving light, and this
  Belongs to each and all who gaze upon.
The Witch beheld it not, for in her hand
She held a woof that dimmed the burning brand.

This lady never slept, but lay in trance
   All night within the fountain—as in sleep.
Its emerald crags glowed in her beauty's glance;
   Through the green splendour of the water deep
She saw the constellations reel and dance
   Like fire-flies—and withal did ever keep
The tenour of her contemplations calm,
With open eyes, closed feet, and folded palm.

And when the whirlwinds and the clouds descended
   From the white pinnacles of that cold hill,
She passed at dewfall to a space extended,
   Where in a lawn of flowering asphodel
Amid a wood of pines and cedars blended,
   There yawned an inextinguishable well
Of crimson fire—full even to the brim,
And overflowing all the margin trim.

Within the which she lay when the fierce war
   Of wintry winds shook that innocuous liquor
In many a mimic moon and bearded star
   O'er woods and lawns;—the serpent heard it flicker
In sleep, and dreaming still, he crept afar—
   And when the windless snow descended thicker
Than autumn leaves, she watched it as it came
Melt on the surface of the level flame.

She had a boat, which some say Vulcan wrought
   For Venus, as the chariot of her star;
But it was found too feeble to be fraught
   With all the ardours in that sphere which are,
And so she sold it, and Apollo bought
   And gave it to this daughter: from a car
Changed to the fairest and the lightest boat
Which ever upon mortal stream did float.

And others say, that, when but three hours old,
   The first-born Love out of his cradle lept,
And clove dun Chaos with his wings of gold,
   And like a horticultural adept,

Stole a strange seed, and wrapped it up in mould,
　　And sowed it in his mother's star, and kept
Watering it all the summer with sweet dew,
And with his wings fanning it as it grew.

The plant grew strong and green, the snowy flower
　　Fell, and the long and gourd-like fruit began
To turn the light and dew by inward power
　　To its own substance; woven tracery ran
Of light firm texture, ribbed and branching, o'er
　　The solid rind, like a leaf's veinèd fan—
Of which Love scooped this boat—and with soft motion
Piloted it round the circumfluous ocean.

This boat she moored upon her fount, and lit
　　A living spirit within all its frame,
Breathing the soul of swiftness into it.
　　Couched on the fountain like a panther tame,
One of the twain at Evan's feet that sit—
　　Or as on Vesta's sceptre a swift flame—
Or on blind Homer's heart a wingèd thought,--
In joyous expectation lay the boat.

Then by strange art she kneaded fire and snow
　　Together, tempering the repugnant mass
With liquid love—all things together grow
　　Through which the harmony of love can pass;
And a fair Shape out of her hands did flow—
　　A living Image, which did far surpass
In beauty that bright shape of vital stone
Which drew the heart out of Pygmalion.

A sexless thing it was, and in its growth
　　It seemed to have developed no defect
Of either sex, yet all the grace of both,—
　　In gentleness and strength its limbs were decked;
The bosom swelled lightly with its full youth,
　　The countenance was such as might select
Some artist that his skill should never die,
Imaging forth such perfect purity.

From its smooth shoulders hung two rapid wings,
    Fit to have borne it to the seventh sphere,
Tipped with the speed of liquid lightenings,
    Dyed in the ardours of the atmosphere:
She led her creature to the boiling springs
    Where the light boat was moored, and said: 'Sit here!'
And pointed to the prow, and took her seat
Beside the rudder, with opposing feet.

And down the streams which clove those mountains vast,
    Around their inland islets, and amid
The panther-peopled forests, whose shade cast
    Darkness and odours, and a pleasure hid
In melancholy gloom, the pinnace passed;
    By many a star-surrounded pyramid
Of icy crag cleaving the purple sky,
And caverns yawning round unfathomably.

The silver noon into that winding dell,
    With slanted gleam athwart the forest tops,
Tempered like golden evening, feebly fell;
    A green and glowing light, like that which drops
From folded lilies in which glow-worms dwell,
    When Earth over her face Night's mantle wraps;
Between the severed mountains lay on high,
Over the stream, a narrow rift of sky.

And ever as she went, the Image lay
    With folded wings and unawakened eyes;
And o'er its gentle countenance did play
    The busy dreams, as thick as summer flies,
Chasing the rapid smiles that would not stay,
    And drinking the warm tears, and the sweet sighs
Inhaling, which, with busy murmur vain,
They had aroused from that full heart and brain.

And ever down the prone vale, like a cloud
    Upon a stream of wind, the pinnace went:
Now lingering on the pools, in which abode
    The calm and darkness of the deep content

In which they paused; now o'er the shallow road
   Of white and dancing waters, all besprent
With sand and polished pebbles:—mortal boat
In such a shallow rapid could not float.

And down the earthquaking cataracts which shiver
   Their snow-like waters into golden air,
Or under chasms unfathomable ever
   Sepulchre them, till in their rage they tear
A subterranean portal for the river,
   It fled—the circling sunbows did upbear
Its fall down the hoar precipice of spray,
Lighting it far upon its lampless way.

And when the wizard lady would ascend
   The labyrinths of some many-winding vale,
Which to the inmost mountain upward tend—
   She called 'Hermaphroditus!'—and the pale
And heavy hue which slumber could extend
   Over its lips and eyes, as on the gale
A rapid shadow from a slope of grass,
Into the darkness of the stream did pass.

And it unfurled its heaven-coloured pinions,
   With stars of fire spotting the stream below;
And from above into the Sun's dominions
   Flinging a glory, like the golden glow
In which Spring clothes her emerald-wingèd minions,
   All interwoven with fine feathery snow
And moonlight splendour of intensest rime,
With which frost paints the pines in winter time.

And then it winnowed the Elysian air
   Which ever hung about that lady bright,
With its aethereal vans—and speeding there,
   Like a star up the torrent of the night,
Of a swift eagle in the morning glare
   Breasting the whirlwind with impetuous flight,
The pinnace, oared by those enchanted wings,
Clove the fierce streams towards their upper springs.

The water flashed, like sunlight by the prow
  Of a noon-wandering meteor flung to Heaven;
The still air seemed as if its waves did flow
  In tempest down the mountains; loosely driven
The lady's radiant hair streamed to and fro:
  Beneath, the billows having vainly striven
Indignant and impetuous, roared to feel
The swift and steady motion of the keel.

Or, when the weary moon was in the wane,
  Or in the noon of interlunar night,
The lady-witch in visions could not chain
  Her spirit; but sailed forth under the light
Of shooting stars, and bade extend amain
  Its storm-outspeeding wings, the Hermaphrodite;
She to the Austral waters took her way,
Beyond the fabulous Thamondocana,—

Where, like a meadow which no scythe has shaven,
  Which rain could never bend, or whirl-blast shake,
With the Antarctic constellations paven,
  Canopus and his crew, lay the Austral lake—
There she would build herself a windless haven
  Out of the clouds whose moving turrets make
The bastions of the storm, when through the sky
The spirits of the tempest thundered by:

A haven beneath whose translucent floor
  The tremulous stars sparkled unfathomably,
And around which the solid vapours hoar,
  Based on the level waters, to the sky
Lifted their dreadful crags, and like a shore
  Of wintry mountains, inaccessibly
Hemmed in with rifts and precipices gray,
And hanging crags, many a cove and bay.

And whilst the outer lake beneath the lash
  Of the wind's scourge, foamed like a wounded thing,
And the incessant hail with stony clash
  Ploughed up the waters, and the flagging wing

Of the roused cormorant in the lightning flash
   Looked like the wreck of some wind-wandering
Fragment of inky thunder-smoke—this haven
Was as a gem to copy Heaven engraven,—

On which that lady played her many pranks,
   Circling the image of a shooting star,
Even as a tiger on Hydaspes' banks
   Outspeeds the antelopes which speediest are,
In her light boat; and many quips and cranks
   She played upon the water, till the car
Of the late moon, like a sick matron wan,
To journey from the misty east began.

And then she called out of the hollow turrets
   Of those high clouds, white, golden and vermilion,
The armies of her ministering spirits—
   In mighty legions, million after million,
They came, each troop emblazoning its merits
   On meteor flags; and many a proud pavilion
Of the intertexture of the atmosphere
They pitched upon the plain of the calm mere.

They framed the imperial tent of their great Queen
   Of woven exhalations, underlaid
With lambent lightning-fire, as may be seen
   A dome of thin and open ivory inlaid
With crimson silk—cressets from the serene
   Hung there, and on the water for her tread
A tapestry of fleece-like mist was strewn,
Dyed in the beams of the ascending moon.

And on a throne o'erlaid with starlight, caught
   Upon those wandering isles of aëry dew,
Which highest shoals of mountain shipwreck not,
   She sate, and heard all that had happened new
Between the earth and moon, since they had brought
   The last intelligence—and now she grew
Pale as that moon, lost in the watery night—
And now she wept, and now she laughed outright.

These were tame pleasures; she would often climb
   The steepest ladder of the crudded rack
Up to some beakèd cape of cloud sublime,
   And like Arion on the dolphin's back
Ride singing through the shoreless air;—oft-time
   Following the serpent lightning's winding track,
She ran upon the platforms of the wind,
And laughed to hear the fire-balls roar behind.

And sometimes to those streams of upper air
   Which whirl the earth in its diurnal round,
She would ascend, and win the spirits there
   To let her join their chorus. Mortals found
That on those days the sky was calm and fair,
   And mystic snatches of harmonious sound
Wandered upon the earth where'er she passed,
And happy thoughts of hope, too sweet to last.

But her choice sport was, in the hours of sleep,
   To glide adown old Nilus, where he threads
Egypt and Aethiopia, from the steep
   Of utmost Axumè, until he spreads,
Like a calm flock of silver-fleecèd sheep,
   His waters on the plain: and crested heads
Of cities and proud temples gleam amid,
And many a vapour-belted pyramid.

By Moeris and the Mareotid lakes,
   Strewn with faint blooms like bridal chamber floors,
Where naked boys bridling tame water-snakes.
   Or charioteering ghastly alligators,
Had left on the sweet waters mighty wakes
   Of those huge forms—within the brazen doors
Of the great Labyrinth slept both boy and beast,
Tired with the pomp of their Osirian feast.

And where within the surface of the river
   The shadows of the massy temples lie,
And never are erased—but tremble ever
   Like things which every cloud can doom to die,

Through lotus-paven canals, and wheresoever
   The works of man pierced that serenest sky
With tombs, and towers, and fanes, 'twas her delight
To wander in the shadow of the night.

With motion like the spirit of that wind
   Whose soft step deepens slumber, her light feet
Passed through the peopled haunts of humankind,
   Scattering sweet visions from her presence sweet,
Through fane, and palace-court, and labyrinth mined
   With many a dark and subterranean street
Under the Nile, through chambers high and deep
She passed, observing mortals in their sleep.

A pleasure sweet doubtless it was to see
   Mortals subdued in all the shapes of sleep.
Here lay two sister twins in infancy;
   There, a lone youth who in his dreams did weep;
Within, two lovers linkèd innocently
   In their loose locks which over both did creep
Like ivy from one stem;—and there lay calm
Old age with snow-bright hair and folded palm.

But other troubled forms of sleep she saw,
   Not to be mirrored in a holy song—
Distortions foul of supernatural awe,
   And pale imaginings of visioned wrong;
And all the code of Custom's lawless law
   Written upon the brows of old and young:
'This,' said the wizard maiden, 'is the strife
Which stirs the liquid surface of man's life.'

And little did the sight disturb her soul.—
   We, the weak mariners of that wide lake
Where'er its shores extend or billows roll,
   Our course unpiloted and starless make
O'er its wild surface to an unknown goal:—
   But she in the calm depths her way could take,
Where in bright bowers immortal forms abide
Beneath the weltering of the restless tide.

And she saw princes couched under the glow
   Of sunlike gems; and round each temple-court
In dormitories ranged, row after row,
   She saw the priests asleep—all of one sort—
For all were educated to be so.—
   The peasants in their huts, and in the port
The sailors she saw cradled on the waves,
And the dead lulled within their dreamless graves.

And all the forms in which those spirits lay
   Were to her sight like the diaphanous
Veils, in which those sweet ladies oft array
   Their delicate limbs, who would conceal from us
Only their scorn of all concealment: they
   Move in the light of their own beauty thus.
But these and all now lay with sleep upon them,
And little thought a Witch was looking on them.

She, all those human figures breathing there,
   Beheld as living spirits—to her eyes
The naked beauty of the soul lay bare,
   And often through a rude and worn disguise
She saw the inner form most bright and fair—
   And then she had a charm of strange device,
Which, murmured on mute lips with tender tone,
Could make that spirit mingle with her own.

Alas! Aurora, what wouldst thou have given
   For such a charm when Tithon became gray?
Or how much, Venus, of thy silver heaven
   Wouldst thou have yielded, ere Proserpina
Had half (oh! why not all?) the debt forgiven
   Which dear Adonis had been doomed to pay,
To any witch who would have taught you it?
The Heliad doth not know its value yet.

'Tis said in after times her spirit free
   Knew what love was, and felt itself alone—
But holy Dian could not chaster be
   Before she stooped to kiss Endymion,

Than now this lady—like a sexless bee
    Tasting all blossoms, and confined to none,
Among those mortal forms, the wizard-maiden
Passed with an eye serene and heart unladen.

To those she saw most beautiful, she gave
    Strange panacea in a crystal bowl:—
They drank in their deep sleep of that sweet wave,
    And lived thenceforward as if some control,
Mightier than life, were in them; and the grave
    Of such, when death oppressed the weary soul,
Was as a green and overarching bower
Lit by the gems of many a starry flower.

For on the night when they were buried, she
    Restored the embalmers' ruining, and shook
The light out of the funeral lamps, to be
    A mimic day within that deathy nook;
And she unwound the woven imagery
    Of second childhood's swaddling bands, and took
The coffin, its last cradle, from its niche,
And threw it with contempt into a ditch.

And there the body lay, age after age,
    Mute, breathing, beating, warm, and undecaying,
Like one asleep in a green hermitage,
    With gentle smiles about its eyelids playing,
And living in its dreams beyond the rage
    Of death or life; while they were still arraying
In liveries ever new, the rapid, blind
And fleeting generations of mankind.

And she would write strange dreams upon the brain
    Of those who were less beautiful, and make
All harsh and crooked purposes more vain
    Than in the desert is the serpent's wake
Which the sand covers—all his evil gain
    The miser in such dreams would rise and shake
Into a beggar's lap;—the lying scribe
Would his own lies betray without a bribe.

The priests would write an explanation full,
    Translating hieroglyphics into Greek,
How the God Apis really was a bull,
    And nothing more; and bid the herald stick
The same against the temple doors, and pull
    The old cant down; they licensed all to speak
Whate'er they thought of hawks, and cats, and geese,
By pastoral letters to each diocese.

The king would dress an ape up in his crown
    And robes, and seat him on his glorious seat,
And on the right hand of the sunlike throne
    Would place a gaudy mock-bird to repeat
The chatterings of the monkey.—Every one
    Of the prone courtiers crawled to kiss the feet
Of their great Emperor, when the morning came,
And kissed—alas, how many kiss the same!

The soldiers dreamed that they were blacksmiths, and
    Walked out of quarters in somnambulism;
Round the red anvils you might see them stand
    Like Cyclopses in Vulcan's sooty abysm,
Beating their swords to ploughshares;—in a band
    The gaolers sent those of the liberal schism
Free through the streets of Memphis, much, I wis,
To the annoyance of king Amasis.

And timid lovers who had been so coy,
    They hardly knew whether they loved or not,
Would rise out of their rest, and take sweet joy,
    To the fulfilment of their inmost thought;
And when next day the maiden and the boy
    Met one another, both, like sinners caught,
Blushed at the thing which each believed was done
Only in fancy—till the tenth moon shone;

And then the Witch would let them take no ill:
    Of many thousand schemes which lovers find,
The Witch found one,—and so they took their fill
    Of happiness in marriage warm and kind.

Friends who, by practice of some envious skill,
　　Were torn apart—a wide wound, mind from mind!—
She did unite again with visions clear
Of deep affection and of truth sincere.

These were the pranks she played among the cities
　　Of mortal men, and what she did to Sprites
And Gods, entangling them in her sweet ditties
　　To do her will, and show their subtle sleights,
I will declare another time; for it is
　　A tale more fit for the weird winter nights
Than for these garish summer days, when we
Scarcely believe much more than we can see.

Epipsychidion

PERHAPS the title only means 'a little book concerning the soul.' Shelley describes the piece as private poetry, and says that those who wish to work out his enigma in commonplace terms should begin trying their skill on Shakespeare's Sonnets.

Epipsychidion is autobiographical to the extent that Shelley for a time idolized Emilia Viviani, and that he depicts his earlier adorations of woman, but when he calls the poem 'mystery' he means that he is using figures and not portraits. Yet those who will may identify Mary Shelley ('the orphan one' of the first line and 'the cold chaste Moon' later) and possibly other actual people. The dangerous lady under the nightshade by the well remains unnamed. 'Marina, Vanna, Primus' are presumably Mary, Jane and Edward Williams.

Though *Epipsychidion* is a great attempt to find words for the ecstasy of love, it is also one more of Shelley's excursions into the pleasures of wishing for earthly paradises.

Advertisement

THE Writer of the following lines died at Florence, as he was preparing for a voyage to one of the wildest of the Sporades, which he had bought, and where he had fitted up the ruins of an old building, and where it was his hope to have realised a scheme of life, suited perhaps to that happier and better world of which he is now an inhabitant, but hardly practicable in this. His life was singular; less on account of the romantic vicissitudes which diversified it, than the ideal tinge which it received from his own character and feelings. The present Poem, like the *Vita Nuova* of Dante, is sufficiently intelligible to a certain class of readers without a matter-of-fact history of the circumstances to which it relates; and to a certain other class it must ever remain incomprehensible, from a defect of a common organ of perception for the ideas of which it treats. Not but that *gran vergogna sarebbe a colui, che rimasse cosa sotto veste di figura, o di colore rettorico : e domandato non sapesse denudare le sue parole da cotal veste, in guisa che avessero verace intendimento.*

The present poem appears to have been intended by the Writer as the dedication to some longer one. The stanza on the opposite page is almost a literal translation from Dante's famous Canzone

Voi, ch' intendendo, il terzo ciel movete, etc.

The presumptuous application of the concluding lines to his own composition will raise a smile at the expense of my unfortunate friend: be it a smile not of contempt, but pity.

S.

Verses addressed to the noble and unfortunate lady, Emilia V——

NOW IMPRISONED IN THE CONVENT OF —

L'anima amante si slancia fuori del creato, e si crea nell' infinito un Mondo tutto per essa, diverso assai da questo oscuro e pauroso baratro.

HER OWN WORDS

> MY Song, I fear that thou wilt find but few
> Who fitly shall conceive thy reasoning,
> Of such hard matter dost thou entertain;
> Whence, if by misadventure, chance should bring
> Thee to base company (as chance may do),
> Quite unaware of what thou dost contain,
> I prithee, comfort thy sweet self again,
> My last delight! tell them that they are dull,
> And bid them own that thou art beautiful.

Epipsychidion

SWEET Spirit! Sister of that orphan one,
Whose empire is the name thou weepest on,
In my heart's temple I suspend to thee
These votive wreaths of withered memory.

Poor captive bird! who, from thy narrow cage,
Pourest such music, that it might assuage
The ruggèd hearts of those who prisoned thee,
Were they not deaf to all sweet melody;
This song shall be thy rose: its petals pale
Are dead, indeed, my adored Nightingale!
But soft and fragrant is the faded blossom,
And it has no thorn left to wound thy bosom.

High, spirit-wingèd Heart! who dost for ever
Beat thine unfeeling bars with vain endeavour,
Till those bright plumes of thought, in which arrayed
It over-soared this low and worldly shade,

Lie shattered; and thy panting, wounded breast
Stains with dear blood its unmaternal nest!
I weep vain tears: blood would less bitter be,
Yet poured forth gladlier, could it profit thee.

Seraph of Heaven! too gentle to be human,
Veiling beneath that radiant form of Woman
All that is insupportable in thee
Of light, and love, and immortality!
Sweet Benediction in the eternal Curse!
Veiled Glory of this lampless Universe!
Thou Moon beyond the clouds! Thou living Form
Among the Dead! Thou Star above the Storm!
Thou Wonder, and thou Beauty, and thou Terror!
Thou Harmony of Nature's art! Thou Mirror
In whom, as in the splendour of the Sun,
All shapes look glorious which thou gazest on!
Ay, even the dim words which obscure thee now
Flash, lightning-like, with unaccustomed glow;
I pray thee that thou blot from this sad song
All of its much mortality and wrong,
With those clear drops, which start like sacred dew
From the twin lights thy sweet soul darkens through,
Weeping, till sorrow becomes ecstasy:
Then smile on it, so that it may not die.

I never thought before my death to see
Youth's vision thus made perfect. Emily,
I love thee; thou the world by no thin name
Will hide that love from its unvalued shame.
Would we two had been twins of the same mother!
Or, that the name my heart lent to another
Could be a sister's bond for her and thee,
Blending two beams of one eternity!
Yet were one lawful and the other true,
These names, though dear, could paint not, as is due,
How beyond refuge I am thine. Ah me!
I am not thine: I am a part of *thee*.

Sweet Lamp! my moth-like Muse has burned its wings
Or, like a dying swan who soars and sings,
Young Love should teach Time, in his own gray style,
All that thou art. Art thou not void of guile,

A lovely soul formed to be blessed and bless?
A well of sealed and secret happiness,
Whose waters like blithe light and music are,
Vanquishing dissonance and gloom? A Star
Which moves not in the moving heavens, alone?
A Smile amid dark frowns? a gentle tone
Amid rude voices? a belovèd light?
A Solitude, a Refuge, a Delight?
A Lute, which those whom Love has taught to play
Make music on, to soothe the roughest day
And lull fond Grief asleep? a buried treasure?
A cradle of young thoughts of wingless pleasure?
A violet-shrouded grave of Woe?—I measure
The world of fancies, seeking one like thee,
And find—alas! mine own infirmity.

She met me, Strange, upon life's rough way,
And lured me towards sweet Death; as Night by Day,
Winter by Spring, or Sorrow by swift Hope,
Led into light, life, peace. An antelope,
In the suspended impulse of its lightness,
Were less aethereally light: the brightness
Of her divinest presence trembles through
Her limbs, as underneath a cloud of dew
Embodied in the windless heaven of June
Amid the splendour-wingèd stars, the Moon
Burns, inextinguishably beautiful:
And from her lips, as from a hyacinth full
Of honey-dew, a liquid murmur drops,
Killing the sense with passion; sweet as stops
Of planetary music heard in trance.
In her mild lights the starry spirits dance,
The sunbeams of those wells which ever leap
Under the lightnings of the soul—too deep
For the brief fathom-line of thought or sense.
The glory of her being, issuing thence,
Stains the dead, blank, cold air with a warm shade
Of unentangled intermixture, made
By Love, of light and motion: one intense
Diffusion, one serene Omnipresence,
Whose flowing outlines mingle in their flowing,
Around her cheeks and utmost fingers glowing

With the unintermitted blood, which there
Quivers, (as in a fleece of snow-like air
The crimson pulse of living morning quiver,)
Continuously prolonged, and ending never,
Till they are lost, and in that Beauty furled
Which penetrates and clasps and fills the world;
Scarce visible from extreme loveliness.
Warm fragrance seems to fall from her light dress
And her loose hair; and where some heavy tress
The air of her own speed has disentwined,
The sweetness seems to satiate the faint wind;
And in the soul a wild odour is felt,
Beyond the sense, like fiery dews that melt
Into the bosom of a frozen bud.—
See where she stands! a mortal shape indued
With love and life and light and deity,
And motion which may change but cannot die;
An image of some bright Eternity;
A shadow of some golden dream; a Splendour
Leaving the third sphere pilotless; a tender
Reflection of the eternal Moon of Love
Under whose motions life's dull billows move;
A Metaphor of Spring and Youth and Morning;
A Vision like incarnate April, warning,
With smiles and tears, Frost the Anatomy
Into his summer grave.
                              Ah, woe is me!
What have I dared? where am I lifted? how
Shall I descend, and perish not? I know
That Love makes all things equal: I have heard
By mine own heart this joyous truth averred:
The spirit of the worm beneath the sod
In love and worship, blends itself with God.

Spouse! Sister! Angel! Pilot of the Fate
Whose course has been so starless! O too late
Belovèd! O too soon adored, by me!
For in the fields of Immortality
My spirit should at first have worshipped thine,
A divine presence in a place divine;
Or should have moved beside it on this earth,
A shadow of that substance, from its birth;

But not as now:—I love thee; yes, I feel
That on the fountain of my heart a seal
Is set, to keep its waters pure and bright
For thee, since in those *tears* thou hast delight.
We—are we not formed, as notes of music are,
For one another, though dissimilar;
Such difference without discord, as can make
Those sweetest sounds, in which all spirits shake
As trembling leaves in a continuous air?

Thy wisdom speaks in me, and bids me dare
Beacon the rocks on which high hearts are wrecked.
I never was attached to that great sect,
Whose doctrine is, that each one should select
Out of the crowd a mistress or a friend,
And all the rest, though fair and wise, commend
To cold oblivion, though it is in the code
Of modern morals, and the beaten road
Which those poor slaves with weary footsteps tread,
Who travel to their home among the dead
By the broad highway of the world, and so
With one chained friend, perhaps a jealous foe,
The dreariest and the longest journey go.

True Love in this differs from gold and clay,
That to divide is not to take away.
Love is like understanding, that grows bright,
Gazing on many truths; 'tis like thy light,
Imagination! which from earth and sky,
And from the depths of human fantasy,
As from a thousand prisms and mirrors, fills
The Universe with glorious beams, and kills
Error, the worm, with many a sun-like arrow
Of its reverberated lightning. Narrow
The heart that loves, the brain that contemplates,
The life that wears, the spirit that creates
One object, and one form, and builds thereby
A sepulchre for its eternity.

Mind from its object differs most in this:
Evil from good; misery from happiness;
The baser from the nobler; the impure
And frail, from what is clear and must endure.

If you divide suffering and dross, you may
Diminish till it is consumed away;
If you divide pleasure and love and thought,
Each part exceeds the whole; and we know not
How much, while any yet remains unshared,
Of pleasure may be gained, of sorrow spared:
This truth is that deep well, whence sages draw
The unenvied light of hope; the eternal law
By which those live, to whom this world of life
Is as a garden ravaged, and whose strife
Tills for the promise of a later birth
The wilderness of this Elysian earth.

There was a Being whom my spirit oft
Met on its visioned wanderings, far aloft,
In the clear golden prime of my youth's dawn,
Upon the fairy isles of sunny lawn,
Amid the enchanted mountains, and the caves
Of divine sleep, and on the air-like waves
Of wonder-level dream, whose tremulous floor
Paved her light steps;—on an imagined shore,
Under the gray beak of some promontory
She met me, robed in such exceeding glory,
That I beheld her not. In solitudes
Her voice came to me through the whispering woods,
And from the fountains, and the odours deep
Of flowers, which, like lips murmuring in their sleep
Of the sweet kisses which had lulled them there,
Breathed but of *her* to the enamoured air;
And from the breezes whether low or loud,
And from the rain of every passing cloud,
And from the singing of the summer-birds,
And from all sounds, all silence. In the words
Of antique verse and high romance,—in form,
Sound, colour—in whatever checks that Storm
Which with the shattered present chokes the past;
And in that best philosophy, whose taste
Makes this cold common hell, our life, a doom
As glorious as a fiery martyrdom;
Her Spirit was the harmony of truth.—

Then, from the caverns of my dreamy youth
I sprang, as one sandalled with plumes of fire,
And towards the lodestar of my one desire,
I flitted, like a dizzy moth, whose flight
Is as a dead leaf's in the owlet light,
When it would seek in Hesper's setting sphere
A radiant death, a fiery sepulchre,
As if it were a lamp of earthly flame.—
But She, whom prayers or tears then could not tame,
Passed, like a God throned on a wingèd planet,
Whose burning plumes to tenfold swiftness fan it,
Into the dreary cone of our life's shade;
And as a man with mighty loss dismayed,
I would have followed, though the grave between
Yawned like a gulf whose spectres are unseen:
When a voice said:—'O thou of hearts the weakest,
The phantom is beside thee whom thou seekest.'
Then I—'Where?'—the world's echo answered 'where?'
And in that silence, and in my despair,
I questioned every tongueless wind that flew
Over my tower of mourning, if it knew
Whither 'twas fled, this soul out of my soul;
And murmured names and spells which have control
Over the sightless tyrants of our fate;
But neither prayer nor verse could dissipate
The night which closed on her; nor uncreate
That world within this Chaos, mine and me,
Of which she was the veiled Divinity,
The world I say of thoughts that worshipped her:
And therefore I went forth, with hope and fear
And every gentle passion sick to death,
Feeding my course with expectation's breath,
Into the wintry forest of our life;
And struggling through its error with vain strife,
And stumbling in my weakness and my haste,
And half bewildered by new forms, I passed,
Seeking among those untaught foresters
If I could find one form resembling hers,
In which she might have masked herself from me.
There,—One, whose voice was venomed melody
Sate by a well, under blue nightshade bowers:
The breath of her false mouth was like faint flowers,

Her touch was as electric poison,—flame
Out of her looks into my vitals came,
And from her living cheeks and bosom flew
A killing air, which pierced like honey-dew
Into the core of my green heart, and lay
Upon its leaves; until, as hair grown gray
O'er a young brow, they hid its unblown prime
With ruins of unseasonable time.

In many mortal forms I rashly sought
The shadow of that idol of my thought.
And some were fair—but beauty dies away:
Others were wise—but honeyed words betray:
And One was true—oh! why not true to me?
Then, as a hunted deer that could not flee.
I turned upon my thoughts, and stood at bay,
Wounded and weak and panting; the cold day
Trembled, for pity of my strife and pain.
When, like a noonday dawn, there shone again
Deliverance. One stood on my path who seemed
As like the glorious shape which I had dreamed
As is the Moon, whose changes ever run
Into themselves, to the eternal Sun;
The cold chaste Moon, the Queen of Heaven's bright isles,
Who makes all beautiful on which she smiles,
That wandering shrine of soft yet icy flame
Which ever is transformed, yet still the same.
And warms not but illumines. Young and fair
As the descended Spirit of that sphere,
She hid me, as the Moon may hide the night
From its own darkness, until all was bright
Between the Heaven and Earth of my calm mind,
And, as a cloud charioted by the wind,
She led me to a cave in that wild place,
And sate beside me, with her downward face
Illumining my slumbers, like the Moon
Waxing and waning o'er Endymion.
And I was laid asleep, spirit and limb,
And all my being became bright or dim
As the Moon's image in a summer sea,
According as she smiled or frowned on me;
And there I lay, within a chaste cold bed:

Alas, I then was nor alive nor dead:—
For at her silver voice came Death and Life,
Unmindful each of their accustomed strife,
Masked like twin babes, a sister and a brother,
The wandering hopes of one abandoned mother,
And through the cavern without wings they flew,
And cried 'Away, he is not of our crew,'
I wept, and though it be a dream, I weep.

What storms then shook the ocean of my sleep,
Blotting that Moon, whose pale and waning lips
Then shrank as in the sickness of eclipse;—
And how my soul was as a lampless sea,
And who was then its Tempest; and when She,
The Planet of that hour, was quenched, what frost
Crept o'er those waters, till from coast to coast
The moving billows of my being fell
Into a death of ice, immovable;—
And then—what earthquakes made it gape and split,
The white Moon smiling all the while on it,
These words conceal:—If not, each word would be
The key of staunchless tears. Weep not for me!

At length, into the obscure Forest came
The Vision I had sought through grief and shame.
Athwart that wintry wilderness of thorns
Flashed from her motion splendour like the Morn's,
And from her presence life was radiated
Through the gray earth and branches bare and dead;
So that her way was paved, and roofed above
With flowers as soft as thoughts of budding love;
And music from her respiration spread
Like light,—all other sounds were penetrated
By the small, still, sweet spirit of that sound,
So that the savage winds hung mute around;
And odours warm and fresh fell from her hair
Dissolving the dull cold in the frore air:
Soft as an Incarnation of the Sun,
When light is changed to love, this glorious One
Floated into the cavern where I lay,
And called my Spirit, and the dreaming clay
Was lifted by the thing that dreamed below

As smoke by fire, and in her beauty's glow
I stood, and felt the dawn of my long night
Was penetrating me with living light:
I knew it was the Vision veiled from me
So many years—that it was Emily.

Twin Spheres of light who rule this passive Earth,
This world of love, this *me*; and into birth
Awaken all its fruits and flowers, and dart
Magnetic might into its central heart;
And lift its billows and its mists, and guide
By everlasting laws, each wind and tide
To its fit cloud, and its appointed cave;
And lull its storms, each in the craggy grave
Which was its cradle, luring to faint bowers
The armies of the rainbow-wingèd showers;
And, as those married lights, which from the towers
Of Heaven look forth and fold the wandering globe
In liquid sleep and splendour, as a robe;
And all their many-mingled influence blend,
If equal, yet unlike, to one sweet end;—
So ye, bright regents, with alternate sway
Govern my sphere of being, night and day!
Thou, not disdaining even a borrowed might;
Thou, not eclipsing a remoter light;
And, through the shadow of the seasons three,
From Spring to Autumn's sere maturity,
Light it into the Winter of the tomb,
Where it may ripen to a brighter bloom.
Thou too, O Comet beautiful and fierce,
Who drew the heart of this frail Universe
Towards thine own; till, wrecked in that convulsion,
Alternating attraction and repulsion,
Thine went astray and that was rent in twain;
Oh, float into our azure heaven again!
Be there Love's folding-star at thy return;
The living Sun will feed thee from its urn
Of golden fire; the Moon will veil her horn
In thy last smiles; adoring Even and Morn
Will worship thee with incense of calm breath
And lights and shadows; as the star of Death
And Birth is worshipped by those sisters wild

Called Hope and Fear—upon the heart are piled
Their offerings,—of this sacrifice divine
A World shall be the altar.
                                        Lady mine,
Scorn not these flowers of thought, the fading birth
Which from its heart of hearts that plant puts forth
Whose fruit, made perfect by thy sunny eyes,
Will be as of the trees of Paradise.

The day is come, and thou wilt fly with me.
To whatsoe'er of dull mortality
Is mine, remain a vestal sister still;
To the intense, the deep, the imperishable,
Not mine but me, henceforth be thou united
Even as a bride, delighting and delighted.
The hour is come:—the destined Star has risen
Which shall descend upon a vacant prison.
The walls are high, the gates are strong, thick set
The sentinels—but true Love never yet
Was thus constrained: it overleaps all fence:
Like lightning, with invisible violence
Piercing its continents; like Heaven's free breath,
Which he who grasps can hold not; liker Death,
Who rides upon a thought, and makes his way
Through temple, tower, and palace, and the array
Of arms: more strength has Love than he or they;
For it can burst his charnel, and make free
The limbs in chains, the heart in agony,
The soul in dust and chaos.
                                        Emily,
A ship is floating in the harbour now,
A wind is hovering o'er the mountain's brow;
There is a path on the sea's azure floor,
No keel has ever ploughed that path before;
The halcyons brood around the foamless isles;
The treacherous Ocean has forsworn its wiles;
The merry mariners are bold and free:
Say, my heart's sister, wilt thou sail with me?
Our bark is as an albatross, whose nest
Is a far Eden of the purple East;
And we between her wings will sit, while Night,
And Day, and Storm, and Calm, pursue their flight,

Our ministers, along the boundless Sea,
Treading each other's heels, unheededly.
It is an isle under Ionian skies,
Beautiful as a wreck of Paradise,
And, for the harbours are not safe and good,
This land would have remained a solitude
But for some pastoral people native there,
Who from the Elysian, clear, and golden air
Draw the last spirit of the age of gold,
Simple and spirited; innocent and bold.
The blue Aegean girds this chosen home.
With ever-changing sound and light and foam,
Kissing the sifted sands, and caverns hoar;
And all the winds wandering along the shore
Undulate with the undulating tide:
There are thick woods where sylvan forms abide;
And many a fountain, rivulet, and pond,
As clear as elemental diamond,
Or serene morning air; and far beyond,
The mossy tracks made by the goats and deer
(Which the rough shepherd treads but once a year)
Pierce into glades, caverns, and bowers, and halls
Built round with ivy, which the waterfalls
Illumining, with sound that never fails
Accompany the noonday nightingales;
And all the place is peopled with sweet airs;
The light clear element which the isle wears
Is heavy with the scent of lemon-flowers,
Which floats like mist laden with unseen showers,
And falls upon the eyelids like faint sleep;
And from the moss violets and jonquils peep,
And dart their arrowy odour through the brain
Till you might faint with that delicious pain.
And every motion, odour, beam, and tone,
With that deep music is in unison:
Which is a soul within the soul—they seem
Like echoes of an antenatal dream.—
It is an isle 'twixt Heaven, Air, Earth, and Sea,
Cradled, and hung in clear tranquillity;
Bright as that wandering Eden Lucifer,
Washed by the soft blue Oceans of young air.
It is a favoured place. Famine or Blight,

Pestilence, War and Earthquake, never light
Upon its mountain-peaks; blind vultures, they
Sail onward far upon their fatal way:
The wingèd storms, chanting their thunder-psalm
To other lands, leave azure chasms of calm
Over this isle, or weep themselves in dew,
From which its fields and woods ever renew
Their green and golden immortality.
And from the sea there rise, and from the sky
There fall, clear exhalations, soft and bright,
Veil after veil, each hiding some delight,
Which Sun or Moon or zephyr draw aside,
Till the isle's beauty, like a naked bride
Glowing at once with love and loveliness,
Blushes and trembles at its own excèss:
Yet, like a buried lamp, a Soul no less
Burns in the heart of this delicious isle,
An atom of th' Eternal, whose own smile
Unfolds itself, and may be felt, not seen
O'er the gray rocks, blue waves, and forests green,
Filling their bare and void interstices.—
But the chief marvel of the wilderness
Is a lone dwelling, built by whom or how
None of the rustic island-people know:
'Tis not a tower of strength, though with its height
It overtops the woods; but, for delight,
Some wise and tender Ocean-King, ere crime
Had been invented, in the world's young prime,
Reared it, a wonder of that simple time,
An envy of the isles, a pleasure-house
Made sacred to his sister and his spouse.
It scarce seems now a wreck of human art,
But, as it were Titanic; in the heart
Of Earth having assumed its form, then grown
Out of the mountains, from the living stone,
Lifting itself in caverns light and high:
For all the antique and learnèd imagery
Has been erased, and in the place of it
The ivy and the wild-vine interknit
The volumes of their many-twining stems;
Parasite flowers illume with dewy gems
The lampless halls, and when they fade, the sky

Peeps through their winter-woof of tracery
With moonlight patches, or star atoms keen,
Or fragments of the day's intense serene;—
Working mosaic on their Parian floors.
And, day and night, aloof, from the high towers
And terraces, the Earth and Ocean seem
To sleep in one another's arms, and dream
Of waves, flowers, clouds, woods, rocks, and all that we
Read in their smiles, and call reality.

This isle and house are mine, and I have vowed
Thee to be lady of the solitude.—
And I have fitted up some chambers there
Looking towards the golden Eastern air,
And level with the living winds, which flow
Like waves above the living waves below.—
I have sent books and music there, and all
Those instruments with which high Spirits call
The future from its cradle, and the past
Out of its grave, and make the present last
In thoughts and joys which sleep, but cannot die,
Folded within their own eternity.
Our simple life wants little, and true taste
Hires not the pale drudge Luxury, to waste
The scene it would adorn, and therefore still,
Nature with all her children haunts the hill.
The ring-dove, in the embowering ivy, yet
Keeps up her love-lament, and the owls flit
Round the evening tower, and the young stars glance
Between the quick bats in their twilight dance;
The spotted deer bask in the fresh moonlight
Before our gate, and the slow, silent night
Is measured by the pants of their calm sleep.
Be this our home in life, and when years heap
Their withered hours, like leaves, on our decay,
Lest us become the overhanging day,
The living soul of this Elysian isle,
Conscious, inseparable, one. Meanwhile
We two will rise, and sit, and walk together,
Under the roof of blue Ionian weather,
And wander in the meadows, or ascend
The mossy mountains, where the blue heavens bend

With lightest winds, to touch their paramour;
Or linger, where the pebble-paven shore,
Under the quick, faint kisses of the sea
Trembles and sparkles as with ecstasy,—
Possessing and possessed by all that is
Within that calm circumference of bliss,
And by each other, till to love and live
Be one:—or, at the noontide hour, arrive
Where some old cavern hoar seems yet to keep
The moonlight of the expired night asleep,
Through which the awakened day can never peep;
A veil for our seclusion, close as night's,
Where secure sleep may kill thine innocent lights;
Sleep, the fresh dew of languid love, the rain
Whose drops quench kisses till they burn again.
And we will talk, until thought's melody
Become too sweet for utterance, and it die
In words, to live again in looks, which dart
With thrilling tone into the voiceless heart,
Harmonizing silence without a sound.
Our breath shall intermix, our bosoms bound,
And our veins beat together; and our lips
With other eloquence than words, eclipse
The soul that burns between them, and the wells
Which boil under our being's inmost cells,
The fountains of our deepest life, shall be
Confused in Passion's golden purity,
As mountain-springs under the morning sun.
We shall become the same, we shall be one
Spirit within two frames, on! wherefore two?
One passion in twin-hearts, which grows and grew,
Till like two meteors of expanding flame,
Those spheres instinct with it become the same,
Touch, mingled, are transfigured; ever still
Burning, yet ever inconsumable:
In one another's substance finding food,
Like flames too pure and light and unimbued
To nourish their bright lives with baser prey,
Which point to Heaven and cannot pass away:
One hope within two wills, one will beneath
Two overshadowing minds, one life, one death,
One Heaven, one Hell, one immortality,

And one annihilation. Woe is me!
The wingèd words on which my soul would pierce
Into the height of Love's rare Universe,
Are chains of lead around its flight of fire—
I pant, I sink, I tremble, I expire!

Weak Verses, go, kneel at your Sovereign's feet,
And say:—'We are the masters of thy slave;
What wouldest thou with us and ours and thine?'
Then call your sisters from Oblivion's cave,
All singing loud: 'Love's very pain is sweet,
But its reward is in the world divine
Which, if not here, it builds beyond the grave.'
So shall ye live when I am there. Then haste
Over the hearts of men, until ye meet
Marina, Vanna, Primus, and the rest,
And bid them love each other and be blessed:
And leave the troop which errs, and which reproves,
And come and be my guest,—for I am Love's.

Adonais

AN ELEGY ON THE DEATH OF JOHN KEATS

'Αστὴρ πρὶν μὲν ἔλαμπες ἐνὶ ζωοῖσιν ῾Εῷος·
νῦν δὲ θανὼν λάμπεις ῾῾Εσπερος ἐν φθιμένοις—PLATO

REGARDING Keats as a young genius whose true inspiration came from ancient Greece, Shelley naturally chose to write in lament for his death and in honour of his immortality in the tradition of Greek poetry. The allusions to particular elegies there are distinct, and Shelley in another way writes appropriately, bringing in memories of some of Keats's poems, like the *Ode to a Nightingale*, and to a *Grecian Urn*. If he insists erroneously on the savagery of Keats's literary enemies, he was going on the best information that he could get—and surely the Reviewers did try to 'destroy' the poet Keats.

The contemporary poets ('the mountain shepherds') whom Shelley's imagination brings together to mourn for Keats are Byron, Thomas Moore, Shelley himself, and Leigh Hunt. He had some trouble to collect a worthy company. Among the many fine stanzas which he discarded some attempt to include other names, such as Horace Smith, and Wordsworth.

On reading that Keats had wished for a certain line to be engraved on his tomb,—a line now famous, as it is melancholy,—Shelley drafted a stanza which may have been intended for one version or another of *Adonais*. It may not have been completed:—

> 'Here lieth One whose name was writ on water.
> But ere the breath that could erase it blew,
> Death, in remorse for that fell slaughter,
> Death the immortalizing winter flew
> Athwart the stream,—and time's printless torrent grew
> A scroll of crystal, blazoning the name
> Of Adonais!

Preface

Φάρμακον ἦλθε, Βίων, ποτὶ σὸν στόμα, φάρμακον εἶδες.
πῶς τευ τοῖς χείλεσσι ποτέδραμε, κοὐκ ἐγλυκάνθη;
τίς δὲ βροτὸς τοσσοῦτον ἀνάμερος, ἢ κεράσαι τοι,
ἢ δοῦναι λαλέοντι τὸ φάρμακον; ἔκφυγεν ᾠδάν.

—MOSCHUS, EPITAPH. BION.

IT is my intention to subjoin to the London edition of this poem a criticism upon the claims of its lamented object to be classed among the writers of the highest genius who have adorned our age. My known repugnance to the narrow principles of taste on which several of his earlier compositions were modelled proves at least that I am an impartial judge. I consider the fragment of *Hyperion* as second to nothing that was ever produced by a writer of the same years.

John Keats died at Rome of a consumption, in his twenty-fourth year, on the——of——1821; and was buried in the romantic and lonely cemetery of the Protestants in that city, under the pyramid which is the tomb of Cestius, and the massy walls and towers, now mouldering and desolate, which formed the circuit of ancient Rome. The cemetery is an open space among the ruins, covered in winter with violets and daisies. It might make one in love with death, to think that one should be buried in so sweet a place.

The genius of the lamented person to whose memory I have dedicated these unworthy verses was not less delicate and fragile than it was beautiful; and where cankerworms abound, what wonder if its young flower was blighted in the bud? The savage criticism on his *Endymion*, which appeared in the *Quarterly Review*, produced the most violent effect on his susceptible mind; the agitation thus originated ended in the rupture of a blood-vessel in the lungs; a rapid consumption ensued, and the succeeding acknowledgements from more candid critics of the true greatness of his powers were ineffectual to heal the wound thus wantonly inflicted.

It may be well said that these wretched men know not what they do. They scatter their insults and their slanders without heed as to whether the poisoned shaft lights on a heart made callous by many blows or one like Keats's composed of more penetrable stuff. One of their associates is, to my knowledge, a most base and unprincipled calumniator. As to *Endymion*, was it a poem, whatever might be its defects, to be treated contemptuously by those who had celebrated, with various degrees of complacency and panegyric, *Paris*, and *Woman*, and a *Syrian Tale*, and Mrs. Lefanu, and Mr. Barrett, and Mr. Howard Payne, and a long list of the illustrious obscure? Are these the men who in their venal good nature presumed to draw a parallel between the Rev. Mr. Milman and Lord Byron? What gnat did they strain at here, after having swallowed all those camels? Against what woman taken in adultery dares the foremost of these literary prostitutes to cast his opprobrious stone? Miserable man! you, one of the meanest, have wantonly defaced one of the noblest specimens of the workmanship of God. Nor shall it be your excuse, that, murderer as you are, you have spoken daggers, but used none.

The circumstances of the closing scene of poor Keats's life were not made known to me until the *Elegy* was ready for the press. I am given to understand that the wound which his sensitive spirit had received from the criticism of *Endymion* was exasperated by the bitter sense of unrequited benefits; the poor fellow seems to have been hooted from the stage of life, no less by those on whom he had wasted the promise of his genius, than those on whom he had lavished his fortune and his care. He was accompanied to Rome, and attended in his last illness by Mr. Severn, a young artist of the highest promise, who, I have been informed, 'almost risked his own life, and sacrificed every prospect to unwearied attendance upon his dying friend.' Had I known these circumstances before the completion of my poem, I should have been tempted to add my feeble tribute of applause to the more solid recompense which the virtuous man finds in the recollection of his own motives. Mr. Severn can dispense with a reward from 'such stuff as dreams are made of.' His conduct is a golden augury of the success of his future career—may the unextinguished Spirit of his illustrious friend animate the creations of his pencil, and plead against Oblivion for his name!

Adonais

I weep for Adonais—he is dead!
O, weep for Adonais! though our tears
Thaw not the frost which binds so dear a head!
And thou, sad Hour, selected from all years
To mourn our loss, rouse thy obscure compeers,
And teach them thine own sorrow, say: 'With me
Died Adonais; till the Future dares
Forget the Past, his fate and fame shall be
An echo and a light unto eternity!'

Where wert thou, mighty Mother, when he lay,
When thy Son lay, pierced by the shaft which flies
In darkness? where was lorn Urania
When Adonais died? With veilèd eyes,
'Mid listening Echoes, in her Paradise
She sate, while one, with soft enamoured breath,
Rekindled all the fading melodies,
With which, like flowers that mock the corse beneath,
He had adorned and hid the coming bulk of Death.

Oh, weep for Adonais—he is dead!
Wake, melancholy Mother, wake and weep!
Yet wherefore? Quench within their burning bed
Thy fiery tears, and let thy loud heart keep
Like his, a mute and uncomplaining sleep;
For he is gone, where all things wise and fair
Descend;—oh, dream not that the amorous Deep
Will yet restore him to the vital air;
Death feeds on his mute voice, and laughs at our despair.

Most musical of mourners, weep again!
Lament anew, Urania!—He died,
Who was the Sire of an immortal strain,
Blind, old, and lonely, when his country's pride,
The priest, the slave, and the liberticide,
Trampled and mocked with many a loathèd rite
Of lust and blood; he went, unterrified,
Into the gulf of death; but his clear Sprite
Yet reigns o'er earth; the third among the sons of light.

Most musical of mourners, weep anew!
Not all to that bright station dared to climb;
And happier they their happiness who knew,
Whose tapers yet burn through that night of time
In which suns perished; others more sublime,
Struck by the envious wrath of man or god,
Have sunk, extinct in their refulgent prime;
And some yet live, treading the thorny road,
Which leads, through toil and hate, to Fame's serene abode.

But now, thy youngest, dearest one, has perished—
The nursling of thy widowhood, who grew,
Like a pale flower by some sad maiden cherished,
And fed with true-love tears, instead of dew;
Most musical of mourners, weep anew!
Thy extreme hope, the loveliest and the last.
The bloom, whose petals nipped before they blew
Died on the promise of the fruit, is waste;
The broken lily lies—the storm is overpast.

To that high Capital, where kingly Death
Keeps his pale court in beauty and decay,
He came; and bought, with price of purest breath,
A grave among the eternal.—Come away!
Haste, while the vault of blue Italian day
Is yet his fitting charnel-roof! while still
He lies, as if in dewy sleep he lay;
Awake him not! surely he takes his fill
Of deep and liquid rest, forgetful of all ill.

He will awake no more, oh, never more!—
Within the twilight chamber spreads apace
The shadow of white Death, and at the door
Invisible Corruption waits to trace
His extreme way to her dim dwelling-place;
The eternal Hunger sits, but pity and awe
Soothe her pale rage, nor dares she to deface
So fair a prey, till darkness, and the law
Of change, shall o'er his sleep the mortal curtain draw.

Oh, weep for Adonais!—The quick Dreams,
The passion-wingèd Ministers of thought,
Who were his flocks, whom near the living streams
Of his young spirit he fed, and whom he taught
The love which was its music, wander not,—
Wander no more, from kindling brain to brain,
But droop there, whence they sprung; and mourn their lot
Round the cold heart, where, after their sweet pain,
They ne'er will gather strength, or find a home again.

And one with trembling hands clasps his cold head,
And fans him with her moonlight wings, and cries;
'Our love, our hope, our sorrow, is not dead;
See, on the silken fringe of his faint eyes,
Like dew upon a sleeping flower, there lies
A tear some Dream has loosened from his brain.'
Lost Angel of a ruined Paradise!
She knew not 'twas her own; as with no stain
She faded, like a cloud which had outwept its rain.

One from a lucid urn of starry dew
Washed his light limbs as if embalming them;
Another clipped her profuse locks, and threw
The wreath upon him, like an anadem,
Which frozen tears instead of pearls begem;
Another in her wilful grief would break
Her bow and wingèd reeds, as if to stem
A greater loss with one which was more weak;
And dull the barbèd fire against his frozen cheek.

Another Splendour on his mouth alit,
That mouth, whence it was wont to draw the breath
Which gave it strength to pierce the guarded wit,
And pass into the panting heart beneath
With lightning and with music: the damp death
Quenched its caress upon his icy lips;
And, as a dying meteor stains a wreath
Of moonlight vapour, which the cold night clips,
It flushed through his pale limbs, and passed to its eclipse.

And others came . . . Desires and Adorations,
Wingèd Persuasions and veiled Destinies,
Splendours, and Glooms, and glimmering Incarnations
Of hopes and fears, and twilight Phantasies;
And Sorrow, with her family of Sighs,
And Pleasure, blind with tears, led by the gleam
Of her own dying smile instead of eyes,
Came in slow pomp;—the moving pomp might seem
Like pageantry of mist on an autumnal stream.

All he had loved, and moulded into thought,
From shape, and hue, and odour, and sweet sound,
Lamented Adonais. Morning sought
Her eastern watch-tower, and her hair unbound,
Wet with the tears which should adorn the ground,
Dimmed the aëreal eyes that kindle day;
Afar the melancholy thunder moaned,
Pale Ocean in unquiet slumber lay,
And the wild winds flew round, sobbing in their dismay.

Lost Echo sits amid the voiceless mountains,
And feeds her grief with his remembered lay,
And will not more reply to winds or fountains,
Or amorous birds perched on the young green spray,
Or herdsman's horn, or bell at closing day;
Since she can mimic not his lips, more dear
Than those for whose disdain she pined away
Into a shadow of all sounds:—a drear
Murmur, between their songs, is all the woodmen hear.

Grief made the young Spring wild, and she threw down
Her kindling buds, as if she Autumn were,
Or they dead leaves; since her delight is flown,
For whom should she have waked the sullen year?
To Phoebus was not Hyacinth so dear
Nor to himself Narcissus, as to both
Thou, Adonais: wan they stand and sere
Amid the faint companions of their youth,
With dew all turned to tears; odour, to sighing ruth.

Thy spirit's sister, the lorn nightingale
Mourns not her mate with such melodious pain;
Not so the eagle, who like thee could scale
Heaven, and could nourish in the sun's domain
Her mighty youth with morning, doth complain,
Soaring and screaming round her empty nest,
As Albion wails for thee: the curse of Cain
Light on his head who pierced thy innocent breast,
And scared the angel soul that was its earthly guest!

Ah, woe is me! Winter is come and gone,
But grief returns with the revolving year;
The airs and streams renew their joyous tone;
The ants, the bees, the swallows reappear;
Fresh leaves and flowers deck the dead Seasons' bier;
The amorous birds now pair in every brake,
And build their mossy homes in field and brere;
And the green lizard, and the golden snake,
Like unimprisoned flames, out of their trance awake.

Through wood and stream and field and hill and Ocean
A quickening life from the Earth's heart has burst
As it has ever done, with change and motion,
From the great morning of the world when first
God dawned on Chaos; in its stream immersed.
The lamps of Heaven flash with a softer light;
All baser things pant with life's sacred thirst;
Diffuse themselves; and spend in love's delight,
The beauty and the joy of their renewèd might.

The leprous corpse, touched by this spirit tender,
Exhales itself in flowers of gentle breath;
Like incarnations of the stars, when splendour
Is changed to fragrance, they illumine death
And mock the merry worm that wakes beneath;
Nought we know, dies. Shall that alone which knows
Be as a sword consumed before the sheath
By sightless lightning?—the intense atom glows
A moment, then is quenched in a most cold repose.

Alas! that all we loved of him should be,
But for our grief, as if it had not been,
And grief itself be mortal! Woe is me!
Whence are we, and why are we? of what scene
The actors or spectators? Great and mean
Meet massed in death, who lends what life must borrow.
As long as skies are blue, and fields are green,
Evening must usher night, night urge the morrow,
Month follow month with woe, and year wake year to sorrow.

He will awake no more, oh, never more!
'Wake thou,' cried Misery, 'childless Mother, rise
Out of thy sleep, and slake, in thy heart's core.
A wound more fierce than his, with tears and sighs.'
And all the Dreams that watched Urania's eyes,
And all the Echoes whom their sister's song
Had held in holy silence, cried: 'Arise!'
Swift as a Thought by the snake Memory stung,
From her ambrosial rest the fading Splendour sprung.

She rose like an autumnal Night, that springs
Out of the East, and follows wild and drear
The golden Day, which, on eternal wings,
Even as a ghost abandoning a bier,
Had left the Earth a corpse. Sorrow and fear
So struck, so roused, so rapt Urania;
So saddened round her like an atmosphere
Of stormy mist; so swept her on her way
Even to the mournful place where Adonais lay.

Out of her secret Paradise she sped,
Through camps and cities rough with stone, and steel,
And human hearts, which to her aery tread
Yielding not, wounded the invisible
Palms of her tender feet where'er they fell:
And barbèd tongues, and thoughts more sharp than they,
Rent the soft Form they never could repel,
Whose sacred blood, like the young tears of May,
Paved with eternal flowers that undeserving way.

In the death-chamber for a moment Death,
Shamed by the presence of that living Might,
Blushed to annihilation, and the breath
Revisited those lips, and Life's pale light
Flashed through those limbs, so late her dear delight.
'Leave me not wild and drear and comfortless,
As silent lightning leaves the starless night!
Leave me not!' cried Urania: her distress
Roused Death: Death rose and smiled, and met her vain caress.

'Stay yet awhile! speak to me once again;
Kiss me, so long but as a kiss may live;
And in my heartless breast and burning brain
That word, that kiss, shall all thoughts else survive,
With food of saddest memory kept alive,
Now thou art dead, as if it were a part
Of thee, my Adonais! I would give
All that I am to be as thou now art!
But I am chained to Time, and cannot thence depart!

'O gentle child, beautiful as thou wert,
Why didst thou leave the trodden paths of men
Too soon, and with weak hands though mighty heart
Dare the unpastured dragon in his den?
Defenceless as thou wert, oh, where was then
Wisdom the mirrored shield, or scorn the spear?
Or hadst thou waited the full cycle, when
Thy spirit should have filled its crescent sphere,
The monsters of life's waste had fled from thee like deer.

'The herded wolves, bold only to pursue;
The obscene ravens, clamorous o'er the dead;
The vultures to the conqueror's banner true
Who feed where Desolation first has fed.
And whose wings rain contagion;—how they fled,
When, like Apollo, from his golden bow
The Pythian of the age one arrow sped
And smiled!—The spoilers tempt no second blow,
They fawn on the proud feet that spurn them lying low.

'The sun comes forth, and many reptiles spawn;
He sets, and each ephemeral insect then
Is gathered into death without a dawn,
And the immortal stars awake again;
So is it in the world of living men:
A godlike mind soars forth, in its delight
Making earth bare and veiling heaven, and when
It sinks, the swarms that dimmed or shared its light
Leave to its kindred lamps the spirit's awful night.'

Thus ceased she: and the mountain shepherds came,
Their garlands sere, their magic mantles rent;
The Pilgrim of Eternity, whose fame
Over his living head like Heaven is bent,
An early but enduring monument,
Came, veiling all the lightnings of his song
In sorrow; from her wilds Ierne sent
The sweetest lyrist of her saddest wrong,
And Love taught Grief to fall like music from his tongue.

Midst others of less note, came one frail Form,
A phantom among men; companionless
As the last cloud of an expiring storm
Whose thunder is its knell; he, as I guess,
Had gazed on Nature's naked loveliness,
Actaeon-like, and now he fled astray
With feeble steps o'er the world's wilderness,
And his own thoughts, along that rugged way,
Pursued, like raging hounds, their father and their prey.

A pardlike Spirit beautiful and swift—
A Love in desolation masked;—a Power
Girt round with weakness;—it can scarce uplift
The weight of the superincumbent hour;
It is a dying lamp, a falling shower,
A breaking billow;—even whilst we speak
Is it not broken? On the withering flower
The killing sun smiles brightly: on a cheek
The life can burn in blood, even while the heart may break.

His head was bound with pansies overblown,
And faded violets, white, and pied, and blue;
And a light spear topped with a cypress cone,
Round whose rude shaft dark ivy-tresses grew
Yet dripping with the forest's noonday dew,
Vibrated, as the ever-beating heart
Shook the weak hand that grasped it; of that crew
He came the last, neglected and apart;
A herd-abandoned deer struck by the hunter's dart.

All stood aloof, and at his partial moan
Smiled through their tears; well knew that gentle band
Who in another's fate now wept his own,
As in the accents of an unknown land
He sung new sorrow; sad Urania scanned
The Stranger's mien, and murmured: 'Who art thou?'
He answered not, but with a sudden hand
Made bare his branded and ensanguined brow,
Which was like Cain's or Christ's—oh! that it should be so!

What softer voice is hushed over the dead?
Athwart what brow is that dark mantle thrown?
What form leans sadly o'er the white death-bed,
In mockery of monumental stone,
The heavy heart heaving without a moan?
If it be He, who, gentlest of the wise,
Taught, soothed, loved, honoured the departed one,
Let me not vex, with inharmonious sighs,
The silence of that heart's accepted sacrifice.

Our Adonais has drunk poison—oh!
What deaf and viperous murderer could crown
Life's early cup with such a draught of woe?
The nameless worm would not itself disown:
It felt, yet could escape, the magic tone
Whose prelude held all envy, hate, and wrong,
But what was howling in one breast alone,
Silent with expectation of the song,
Whose master's hand is cold, whose silver lyre unstrung.

Live thou, whose infamy is not thy fame!
Live! fear no heavier chastisement from me,
Thou noteless blot on a remembered name!
But be thyself, and know thyself to be!
And ever at thy season be thou free
To spill the venom when thy fangs o'erflow:
Remorse and Self-contempt shall cling to thee;
Hot Shame shall burn upon thy secret brow,
And like a beaten hound tremble thou shalt—as now.

Nor let us weep that our delight is fled
Far from these carrion kites that scream below;
He wakes or sleeps with the enduring dead;
Thou canst not soar where he is sitting now—
Dust to the dust! but the pure spirit shall flow
Back to the burning fountain whence it came,
A portion of the Eternal, which must glow
Through time and change, unquenchably the same,
Whilst thy cold embers choke the sordid hearth of shame.

Peace, peace! he is not dead, he doth not sleep—
He hath awakened from the dream of life—
'Tis we, who lost in stormy visions, keep
With phantoms an unprofitable strife,
And in mad trance, strike, with our spirit's knife
Invulnerable nothings.—*We* decay
Like corpses in a charnel; fear and grief
Convulse us and consume us day by day,
And cold hopes swarm like worms within our living clay.

He has outsoared the shadow of our night;
Envy and calumny and hate and pain,
And that unrest which men miscall delight,
Can touch him not and torture not again;
From the contagion of the world's slow stain
He is secure, and now can never mourn
A heart grown cold, a head grown gray in vain;
Nor, when the spirit's self has ceased to burn,
With sparkless ashes load an unlamented urn.

He lives, he wakes—'tis Death is dead, not he;
Mourn not for Adonais.—Thou young Dawn,
Turn all thy dew to splendour, for from thee
The spirit thou lamentest is not gone;
Ye caverns and ye forests, cease to moan!
Cease, ye faint flowers, and fountains and thou Air,
Which like a mourning veil thy scarf hadst thrown
O'er the abandoned Earth, now leave it bare
Even to the joyous stars which smile on its despair!

He is made one with Nature: there is heard
His voice in all her music, from the moan
Of thunder, to the song of night's sweet bird;
He is a presence to be felt and known
In darkness and in light, from herb and stone,
Spreading itself where'er that Power may move
Which has withdrawn his being to its own;
Which wields the world with never-wearied love,
Sustains it from beneath, and kindles it above.

He is a portion of the loveliness
Which once he made more lovely: he doth bear
His part, while the one Spirit's plastic stress
Sweeps through the dull dense world, compelling there,
All new successions to the forms they wear;
Torturing th' unwilling dross that checks its flight
To its own likeness, as each mass may bear;
And bursting in its beauty and its might
From trees and beasts and men into the Heaven's light.

The splendours of the firmament of time
May be eclipsed, but are extinguished not;
Like stars to their appointed height they climb,
And death is a low mist which cannot blot
The brightness it may veil. When lofty thought
Lifts a young heart above its mortal lair,
And love and life contend in it, for what
Shall be its earthly doom, the dead live there
And move like winds of light on dark and stormy air.

The inheritors of unfulfilled renown
Rose from their thrones, built beyond mortal thought,
Far in the Unapparent. Chatterton
Rose pale,—his solemn agony had not
Yet faded from him; Sidney, as he fought
And as he fell and as he lived and loved
Sublimely mild, a Spirit without spot,
Arose; and Lucan, by his death approved:
Oblivion as they rose shrank like a thing reproved.

And many more, whose names on Earth are dark,
But whose transmitted effluence cannot die
So long as fire outlives the parent spark,
Rose, robed in dazzling immortality.
'Thou art become as one of us,' they cry,
'It was for thee yon kingless sphere has long
Swung blind in unascended majesty,
Silent alone amid an Heaven of Song.
Assume thy wingèd throne, thou Vesper of our throng!'

Who mourns for Adonais? Oh, come forth,
Fond wretch! and know thyself and him aright.
Clasp with thy panting soul the pendulous Earth;
As from a centre, dart thy spirit's light
Beyond all worlds, until its spacious might
Satiate the void circumference: then shrink
Even to a point within our day and night;
And keep thy heart light lest it make thee sink
When hope has kindled hope, and lured thee to the brink.

Or go to Rome, which is the sepulchre,
Oh, not of him, but of our joy: 'tis nought
That ages, empires, and religions there
Lie buried in the ravage they have wrought;
For such as he can lend,—they borrow not
Glory from those who made the world their prey;
And he is gathered to the kings of thought
Who waged contention with their time's decay,
And of the past are all that cannot pass away.

Go thou to Rome,—at once the Paradise,
The grave, the city, and the wilderness;
And where its wrecks like shattered mountains rise,
And flowering weeds, and fragrant copses dress
The bones of Desolation's nakedness
Pass, till the spirit of the spot shall lead
Thy footsteps to a slope of green access
Where, like an infant's smile, over the dead
A light of laughing flowers along the grass is spread;

And gray walls moulder round, on which dull Time
Feeds, like slow fire upon a hoary brand;
And one keen pyramid with wedge sublime,
Pavilioning the dust of him who planned
This refuge for his memory, doth stand
Like flame transformed to marble; and beneath,
A field is spread, on which a newer band
Have pitched in Heaven's smile their camp of death,
Welcoming him we lose with scarce extinguished breath.

Here pause: these graves are all too young as yet
To have outgrown the sorrow which consigned
Its charge to each; and if the seal is set,
Here, on one fountain of a mourning mind,
Break it not thou! too surely shalt thou find
Thine own well full, if thou returnest home,
Of tears and gall. From the world's bitter wind
Seek shelter in the shadow of the tomb.
What Adonais is, why fear we to become?

The One remains, the many change and pass;
Heaven's light forever shines, Earth's shadows fly;
Life, like a dome of many-coloured glass,
Stains the white radiance of Eternity,
Until Death tramples it to fragments.—Die,
If thou wouldst be with that which thou dost seek!
Follow where all is fled!—Rome's azure sky,
Flowers, ruins, statues, music, words, are weak
The glory they transfuse with fitting truth to speak.

Why linger, why turn back, why shrink, my Heart?
Thy hopes are gone before: from all things here
They have departed; thou shouldst now depart!
A light is passed from the revolving year,
And man, and woman; and what still is dear
Attracts to crush, repels to make thee wither.
The soft sky smiles,—the low wind whispers near:
'Tis Adonais calls! oh, hasten thither,
No more let Life divide what Death can join together.

That Light whose smile kindles the Universe,
That Beauty in which all things work and move,
That Benediction which the eclipsing Curse
Of birth can quench not, that sustaining Love
Which through the web of being blindly wove
By man and beast and earth and air and sea,
Burns bright or dim, as each are mirrors of
The fire for which all thirst; now beams on me,
Consuming the last clouds of cold mortality.

The breath whose might I have invoked in song
Descends on me; my spirit's bark is driven,
Far from the shore, far from the trembling throng
Whose sails were never to the tempest given;
The massy earth and spherèd skies are riven!
I am borne darkly, fearfully, afar;
Whilst, burning through the inmost veil of Heaven,
The soul of Adonais, like a star,
Beacons from the abode where the Eternal are.

Hellas

Μάντις εἰμ' ἐσθλῶν ἀγώνων.—OEDIPUS AT COLONUS.

AT the date when Shelley wrote this prophetic play, almost with the speed of the writer of a leading article on the latest gazettes, England was not politically supporting the Greek cause against Turkey. He did not live to see English policy altered.

For Chorus he thought of a group of Greek captive women, and the lyrics written for their expression are the celebrated distinction of his play. The last of these he annotates as being 'indistinct and obscure, as the event of the living drama whose arrival it foretells. Prophecies of wars, and rumours of wars, etc., may safely be made by poet or prophet in any age, but to anticipate however darkly a period of regeneration and happiness is a more hazardous exercise of the faculty which bards possess or feign.' There we see the common-sense of Shelley who nevertheless did possess something more of the said faculty than most men.

As our selection shows, *Hellas* perpetuates the essential admiration of Jesus Christ which Shelley after boyish sallies knew he felt; but one of his notes emphasises his rejection of the Jehovah of the Old Testament and his hostility to established Christianity as a supposed source of human discontents.

From the Preface

THE poem of *Hellas*, written at the suggestion of the events of the moment, is a mere improvise, and derives its interest (should it be found to possess any) solely from the intense sympathy which the Author feels with the cause he would celebrate.

The subject, in its present state, is insusceptible of being treated otherwise than lyrically, and if I have called this poem a drama from the circumstance of its being composed in dialogue, the licence is not greater than that which has been assumed by other poets who have called their productions epics, only because they have been divided into twelve or twenty-four books.

* * *

Common fame is the only authority which I can allege for the details which form the basis of the poem, and I must trespass upon the forgiveness of my readers for the display of newspaper erudition to which I have been reduced. Undoubtedly, until the conclusion of the war, it will be impossible to obtain an account of it sufficiently authentic for historical materials; but poets have their privilege, and it is unquestionable that actions of the most exalted courage have been performed by the Greeks—that they have gained more than one naval victory, and that their defeat in Wallachia was signalized by circumstances of heroism more glorious even than victory.

The apathy of the rulers of the civilised world to the astonishing circumstance of the descendants of that nation to which they owe their civilisation, rising as it were from the ashes of their ruin, is something perfectly inexplicable to a mere spectator of the shows of this mortal scene. We are all Greeks. Our laws, our literature, our religion, our arts have their root in Greece. But for Greece—Rome, the instructor, the conqueror, or the metropolis of our ancestors, would have spread no illumination with her arms, and we might still have been savages and idolaters; or, what is worse, might have arrived at such a stagnant and miserable state of social institution as China and Japan possess.

Chorus: Freedom

In the great morning of the world,
The Spirit of God with might unfurled
The flag of Freedom over Chaos,
 And all its banded anarchs fled,
Like vultures frighted from Imaus,
 Before an earthquake's tread.—
So from Time's tempestuous dawn
Freedom's splendour burst and shone:—
Thermopylae and Marathon
Caught, like mountains beacon-lighted,
 The springing Fire.—The wingèd glory
On Philippi half-alighted,
 Like an eagle on a promontory.
Its unwearied wings could fan
The quenchless ashes of Milan.
From age to age, from man to man,
 It lived; and lit from land to land
 Florence, Albion, Switzerland.

Then night fell; and, as from night,
Reassuming fiery flight,
From the West swift Freedom came,
 Against the course of Heaven and doom,
A second sun arrayed in flame,
 To burn, to kindle, to illume.
From far Atlantis its young beams
Chased the shadows and the dreams.

France, with all her sanguine steams,
   Hid, but quenched it not; again
    Through clouds its shafts of glory rain
   From utmost Germany to Spain.
As an eagle fed with morning
Scorns the embattled tempest's warning,
When she seeks her aerie hanging
   In the mountain-cedar's hair,
And her brood expect the clanging
   Of her wings through the wild air,
Sick with famine:—Freedom, so
To what of Greece remaineth now
Returns; her hoary ruins glow
Like Orient mountains lost in day;
   Beneath the safety of her wings
Her renovated nurslings prey,
   And in the naked lightenings
Of truth they purge dazzled eyes.
Let Freedom leave—where'er she flies,
A Desert, or a Paradise:
   Let the beautiful and the brave
   Share her glory, or a grave.

Chorus: Christ

Worlds on worlds are rolling ever
   From creation to decay,
Like the bubbles on a river
   Sparkling, bursting, borne away.
   But they are still immortal
   Who, through birth's orient portal
And death's dark chasm hurrying to and fro.
   Clothe their unceasing flight
   In the brief dust and light
Gathered around their chariots as they go;
   New shapes they still may weave,
   New gods, new laws receive,
Bright or dim are they as the robes they last
   On Death's bare ribs had cast.

A power from the unknown God,
   A Promethean conqueror, came;
Like a triumphal path he trod

  The thorns of death and shame.
  A mortal shape to him
  Was like the vapour dim
Which the orient planet animates with light;
  Hell, Sin, and Slavery came,
  Like bloodhounds mild and tame,
Nor preyed, until their Lord had taken flight;
  The moon of Mahomet
  Arose, and it shall set:
While blazoned as on Heaven's immortal noon
  The cross leads generations on.

  Swift as the radiant shapes of sleep
   From one whose dreams are Paradise
  Fly, when the fond wretch wakes to weep,
   And Day peers forth with her blank eyes;
   So fleet, so faint, so fair,
   The Powers of earth and air
Fled from the folding-star of Bethlehem:
   Apollo, Pan, and Love,
   And even Olympian Jove
Grew weak, for killing Truth had glared on them;
   Our hills and seas and streams,
   Dispeopled of their dreams,
Their waters turned to blood, their dew to tears,
   Wailed for the golden years.

Chorus: The Voices of War

O Slavery! thou frost of the world's prime,
  Killing its flowers and leaving its thorns bare!
Thy touch has stamped these limbs with crime,
  These brows thy branding garland bear,
   But the free heart, the impassive soul
    Scorn thy control!

Semichorus I

  Let there be light! said Liberty,
  And like sunrise from the sea,
  Athens arose!—Around her born,
  Shone like mountains in the morn
  Glorious states;—and are they now
  Ashes, wrecks, oblivion?

Semichorus II

Go,
Where Thermae and Asopus swallowed
  Persia, as the sand does foam;
Deluge upon deluge followed,
  Discord, Macedon, and Rome:
And lastly thou!

Semichorus I

Temples and towers,
  Citadels and marts, and they
Who live and die there, have been ours,
  And may be thine, and must decay;
But Greece and her foundations are
Built below the tide of war,
Based on the crystàlline sea
Of thought and its eternity;
Her citizens, imperial spirits,
  Rule the present from the past,
On all this world of men inherits
  Their seal is set.

Semichorus II

Hear ye the blast,
  Whose Orphic thunder thrilling calls
From ruin her Titanian walls?
Whose spirit shakes the sapless bones
  Of Slavery? Argos, Corinth, Crete
Hear, and from their mountain thrones
  The daemons and the nymphs repeat
The harmony.

Semichorus I

I hear! I hear!

Semichorus II

The world's eyeless charioteer,
  Destiny, is hurrying by!
What faith is crushed, what empire bleeds
Beneath her earthquake-footed steeds?
What eagle-wingèd victory sits

At her right hand? what shadow flits
   Before? what splendour rolls behind?
     Ruin and renovation cry
'Who but We?'

Semichorus I

     I hear! I hear!
The hiss as of a rushing wind,
The roar as of an ocean foaming,
The thunder as of earthquake coming.
      I hear! I hear!
The crash as of an empire falling,
The shrieks as of a people calling
'Mercy! mercy!'—How they thrill!
Then a shout of 'kill! kill! kill!'
And then a small still voice, thus—

Semichorus II

                Fear,
Revenge and Wrong bring forth their kind,
  The foul cubs like their parents are,
Their den is in the guilty mind,
  And Conscience feeds them with despair.

Semichorus I

In sacred Athens, near the fane
Of Wisdom, Pity's altar stood:
Serve not the unknown God in vain,
But pay that broken shrine again,
  Love for hate and tears for blood.

Enter MAHMUD *and* AHASUERUS.

Mahmud. Thou art a man, thou sayest, even as we.
Ahasuerus. No more!
Mahmud.   But raised above thy fellow-men
By thought, as I by power.
Ahasuerus.   Thou sayest so.
Mahmud. Thou art an adept in the difficult lore
Of Greek and Frank philosophy; thou numberest
The flowers, and thou measurest the stars;
Thou severest element from element;
Thy spirit is present in the Past, and sees

The birth of this old world through all its cycles
Of desolation and of loveliness,
And when man was not, and how man became
The monarch and the slave of this low sphere,
And all its narrow circles—it is much—
I honour thee, and would be what thou art
Where I not what I am; but the unborn hour,
Cradled in fear and hope, conflicting storms,
Who shall unveil? Nor thou, nor I, nor any
Mighty or wise. I apprehended not
What thou hast taught me, but I now perceive
That thou art no interpreter of dreams;
Thou dost not own that art, device, or God,
Can make the Future present—let it come!
Moreover thou disdainest us and ours;
Thou art as God, whom thou contemplatest.

  Ahasuerus. Disdain thee?—not the worm beneath thy feet!
The Fathomless has care for meaner things
Than thou canst dream, and has made pride for those
Who would be what they may not, or would seem
That which they are not. Sultan! talk no more
Of thee and me, the Future and the Past;
But look on that which cannot change—the One,
The unborn and the undying. Earth and ocean,
Space, and the isles of life or light that gem
The sapphire floods of interstellar air,
This firmament pavilioned upon chaos,
With all its cressets of immortal fire,
Whose outwall, bastioned impregnably
Against the escape of boldest thoughts, repels them
As Calpe the Atlantic clouds—this Whole
Of suns, and worlds, and men, and beasts, and flowers,
With all the silent or tempestuous workings
By which they have been, are, or cease to be,
Is but a vision;—all that it inherits
Are motes of a sick eye, bubbles and dreams;
Thought is its cradle and its grave, nor less
The Future and the Past are idle shadows
Of thought's eternal flight—they have no being:
Nought is but that which feels itself to be.

  Mahmud. What meanest thou? Thy words stream like a
   tempest

Of dazzling mist within my brain—they shake
The earth on which I stand, and hang like night
On Heaven above me. What can they avail?
They cast on all things surest, brightest, best,
Doubt, insecurity, astonishment.

 Ahasuerus. Mistake me not! All is contained in each.
Dodona's forest to an acorn's cup
Is that which has been, or will be, to that
Which is—the absent to the present. Thought
Alone, and its quick elements, Will, Passion,
Reason, Imagination, cannot die;
They are, what that which they regard appears,
The stuff whence mutability can weave
All that it hath dominion o'er, worlds, worms,
Empires, and superstitions. What has thought
To do with time, or place, or circumstance?
Wouldst thou behold the Future?—ask and have!
Knock and it shall be opened—look, and lo!
The coming age is shadowed on the Past
As on a glass.

 Mahmud. Wild, wilder thoughts convulse
My spirit—Did not Mahomet the Second
Win Stamboul?

 Ahasuerus. Thou wouldst ask that giant spirit
The written fortunes of thy house and faith.
Thou wouldst cite one out of the grave to tell
How what was born in blood must die.

 Mahmud.   Thy words
Have power on me! I see——

 Ahasuerus. What hearest thou?

 Mahmud. A far whisper——
Terrible silence.

 Ahasuerus. What succeeds?

 Mahmud.   The sound
As of the assault of an imperial city.
The hiss of inextinguishable fire,
The roar of giant cannon; the earthquaking
Fall of vast bastions and precipious towers,
The shock of crags shot from strange enginery,
The clash of wheels, and clang of armèd hoofs,
And crash of brazen mail as of the wreck
Of adamantine mountains—the mad blast

Of trumpets, and the neigh of raging steeds,
The shrieks of women whose thrill jars the blood,
And one sweet laugh, most horrible to hear,
As of a joyous infant waked and playing
With its dead mother's breast, and now more loud
The mingled battle-cry,—ha! hear I not
'Ἐν τούτῳ νίκη!' 'Allah-illa-Allah!'?

    Ahasuerus. The sulphurous mist is raised—thou seest—
    Mahmud.   A chasm,
As of two mountains, in the wall of Stamboul;
And in that ghastly breach the Islamites,
Like giants on the ruins of a world,
Stand in the light of sunrise. In the dust
Glimmers a kingless diadem, and one
Of regal port has cast himself beneath
The stream of war. Another proudly clad
In golden arms spurs a Tartarian barb
Into the gap, and with his iron mace
Directs the torrent of that tide of men,
And seems—he is—Mahomet!

    Ahasuerus.   What thou seest
Is but the ghost of thy forgotten dream.
A dream itself, yet less, perhaps, than that
Thou call'st reality. Thou mayst behold
How cities, on which Empire sleeps enthroned,
Bow their towered crests to mutability.
Poised by the flood, e'en on the height thou holdest,
Thou mayst now learn how the full tide of power
Ebbs to its depths.—Inheritor of glory,
Conceived in darkness, born in blood, and nourished
With tears and toil, thou seest the mortal throes
Of that whose birth was but the same. The Past
Now stands before thee like an Incarnation
Of the To-come; yet wouldst thou commune with
That portion of thyself which was ere thou
Didst start for this brief race whose crown is death,
Dissolve with that strong faith and fervent passion
Which called it from the uncreated deep,
Yon cloud of war, with its tempestuous phantoms
Of raging death; and draw with mighty will
The imperial shade hither.   [*Exit* AHASUERUS. *The
               Phantom of* MAHOMET THE SECOND *appears.*

Mahmud.   Approach!
Phantom.   I come
Thence whither thou must go! The grave is fitter
To take the living than give up the dead;
Yet has thy faith prevailed, and I am here.
The heavy fragments of the power which fell
When I arose, like shapeless crags and clouds,
Hang round my throne on the abyss, and voices
Of strange lament soothe my supreme repose,
Wailing for glory never to return.—
    A later Empire nods in its decay:
The autumn of a greener faith is come,
And wolfish change, like winter, howls to strip
The foliage in which Fame, the eagle, built
Her aerie, while Dominion whelped below.
The storm is in its branches, and the frost
Is on its leaves, and the blank deep expects
Oblivion on oblivion, spoil on spoil,
Ruin on ruin:—Thou art slow, my son;
The Anarchs of the world of darkness keep
A throne for thee, round which thine empire lies
Boundless and mute; and for thy subjects thou,
Like us, shalt rule the ghosts of murdered life,
The phantoms of the powers who rule thee now—
Mutinous passions, and conflicting fears,
And hopes that sate themsleves on dust, and die!—
Stripped of their mortal strength, as thou of thine.
Islam must fall, but we will reign together
Over its ruins in the world of death:—
And if the trunk be dry, yet shall the seed
Unfold itself even in the shape of that
Which gathers birth in its decay. Woe! woe!
To the weak people tangled in the grasp
Of its last spasms.
    Mahmud.   Spirit, woe to all!
Woe to the wronged and the avenger! Woe
To the destroyer, woe to the destroyed!
Woe to the dupe, and woe to the deceiver!
Woe to the oppressed, and woe to the oppressor!
Woe both to those that suffer and inflict;
Those who are born and those who die! but say,
Imperial shadow of the thing I am,

When, how, by whom, Destruction must accomplish
Her consummation!
    Phantom.   Ask the cold pale Hour,
Rich in reversion of impending death,
When *he* shall fall upon whose ripe gray hairs
Sit Care, and Sorrow, and Infirmity—
The weight which Crime, whose wings are plumed with years,
Leaves in his flight from ravaged heart to heart
Over the heads of men, under which burthen
They bow themselves unto the grave: fond wretch!
He leans upon his crutch, and talks of years
To come, and how in hours of youth renewed
He will renew lost joys, and——
    Voice without.   Victory! Victory!
                        [*The Phantom vanishes.*
    Mahmud. What sound of the importunate earth has broken
My mighty trance?
    Voice without.   Victory! Victory!
    Mahmud. Weak lightning before darkness! poor faint smile
Of dying Islam! Voice which art the response
Of hollow weakness! Do I wake and live?
Were there such things, or may the unquiet brain,
Vexed by the wise mad talk of the old Jew,
Have shaped itself these shadows of its fear?
It matters not!—for nought we see or dream,
Possess, or lose, or grasp at, can be worth
More than it gives or teaches. Come what may,
The Future must become the Past, and I
As they were to whom once this present hour,
This gloomy crag of time to which I cling,
Seemed an Elysian isle of peace and joy
Never to be attained.—I must rebuke
This drunkenness of triumph ere it die,
And dying, bring despair. Victory! poor slaves!
                           [*Exit* MAHMUD.

      Semichorus I: The Future
Darkness has dawned in the East
    On the noon of time:
The death-birds descend to their feast
    From the hungry clime.
Let Freedom and Peace flee far

To a sunnier strand,
And follow Love's folding-star
To the Evening land!

Semichorus II

The young moon has fed
Her exhausted horn
With the sunset's fire:
The weak day is dead,
But the night is not born;
And, like loveliness panting with wild desire
While it trembles with fear and delight,
Hesperus flies from awakening night,
And pants in its beauty and speed with light
Fast-flashing, soft, and bright.
Thou beacon of love! thou lamp of the free!
Guide us far, far away,
To climes where now veiled by the ardour of day
Thou art hidden
From waves on which weary Noon
Faints in her summer swoon,
Between kingless continents sinless as Eden,
Around mountains and islands inviolably
Pranked on the sapphire sea.

Semichorus I

Through the sunset of hope,
Like the shapes of a dream,
What Paradise islands of glory gleam!
Beneath Heaven's cope,
Their shadows more clear float by—
The sound of their oceans, the light of their sky,
The music and fragrance their solitudes breathe
Burst, like morning on dream, or like Heaven on death,
Through the walls of our prison;
And Greece, which was dead, is arisen!

Chorus

The world's great age begins anew,
The golden years return,
The earth doth like a snake renew
Her winter weeds outworn:
Heaven smiles, and faiths and empires gleam,
Like wrecks of a dissolving dream.

A brighter Hellas rears its mountains
    From waves serener far;
A new Peneus rolls his fountains
    Against the morning star.
Where fairer Tempes bloom, there sleep
Young Cyclads on a sunnier deep.

A loftier Argo cleaves the main,
    Fraught with a later prize;
Another Orpheus sings again,
    And loves, and weeps, and dies.
A new Ulysses leaves once more
Calypso for his native shore.

Oh, write no more the tale of Troy,
    If earth Death's scroll must be!
Nor mix with Laian rage the joy
    Which dawns upon the free:
Although a subtler Sphinx renew
Riddles of death Thebes never knew.

Another Athens shall arise,
    And to remoter time
Bequeath, like sunset to the skies,
    The splendour of its prime;
And leave, if nought so bright may live,
All earth can take or Heaven can give.

Saturn and Love their long repose
    Shall burst, more bright and good
Than all who fell, than One who rose,
    Than many unsubdued:
Not gold, not blood, their altar dowers,
But votive tears and symbol flowers.

Oh, cease! must hate and death return?
    Cease! must men kill and die?
Cease! drain not to its dregs the urn
    Of bitter prophecy.
The world is weary of the past,
Oh, might it die or rest at last!

Charles I

UNFINISHED, and perhaps intended to remain so. The fragments never-theless give the idea of an exalted historical play, no doubt needing excisions. Archy is the only good 'sweet and bitter Fool' in the neo-Elizabethan drama. The large clear imagery of London and Westminster is a reminder of Shelley's being a notable Londoner.

Part of Act I Scene II

    Laud. Hazlerig, Hampden, Pym, young Harry Vane,
Cromwell, and other rebels of less note,
Intend to sail with the next favouring wind
For the Plantations.
    Archy.   Where they think to found
  A commonwealth like Gonzalo's in the play,
    Gynaecocoenic and pantisocratic.
    King. What's that, sirrah?
    Archy.   New devil's politics.
Hell is the pattern of all commonwealths:
Lucifer was the first republican.
Will you hear Merlin's prophecy, how three [posts?]
    'In one brainless skull, when the whitethorn is full,
      Shall sail round the world, and come back again:
    Shall sail round the world in a brainless skull,
      And come back again when the moon is at full:'—
When, in spite of the Church,
They will hear homilies of whatever length
Or form they please.
    [*Cottington?*] So please your Majesty to sign this order
For their detention.
    Archy. If your Majesty were tormented night and day by fever, gout, rheumatism, and stone, and asthma, etc., and you found these diseases had secretly entered into a conspiracy to abandon you, should

you think it necessary to lay an embargo on the port by which they
meant to dispeople your unquiet kingdom of man?

King. If fear were made for kings, the Fool mocks wisely; But in
this case——(*writing*). Here, my lord, take the warrant,
And see it duly executed forthwith.—
That imp of malice and mockery shall be punished.

[*Exeunt all but* KING, QUEEN, *and* ARCHY.

Archy. Ay, I am the physician of whom Plato prophesied, who
was to be accused by the confectioner before a jury of children, who
found him guilty without waiting for the summing-up, and hanged
him without benefit of clergy. Thus Baby Charles, and the Twelfth-
night Queen of Hearts, and the overgrown schoolboy Cottington,
and that little urchin Laud—who would reduce a verdict of 'guilty,
death,' by famine, if it were impregnable by composition—all im-
pannelled against poor Archy for presenting them bitter physic the
last day of the holidays.

Queen. Is the rain over, sirrah?

King.   When it rains
And the sun shines, 'twill rain again to-morrow:
And therefore never smile till you've done crying.

Archy. But 'tis all over now: like the April anger of woman, the
gentle sky has wept itself serene.

Queen. What news abroad? how looks the world this morning?

Archy. Gloriously as a grave covered with virgin flowers. There's
a rainbow in the sky. Let your Majesty look at it, for

'A rainbow in the morning
Is the shepherd's warning;'

and the flocks of which you are the pastor are scattered among the
mountain-tops, where every drop of water is a flake of snow, and
the breath of May pierces like a January blast.

King. The sheep have mistaken the wolf for their shepherd, my
poor boy; and the shepherd, the wolves for their watchdogs.

Queen. But the rainbow was a good sign, Archy: it says that the
waters of the deluge are gone, and can return no more.

Archy. Ay, the salt-water one: but that of tears and blood must yet
come down, and that of fire follow, if there be any truth in lies.—The
rainbow hung over the city with all its shops, . . . and churches, from
north to south, like a bridge of congregated lightning pieced by the
masonry of heaven—like a balance in which the angel that distributes
the coming hour was weighing that heavy one whose poise is now

felt in the lightest hearts, before it bows the proudest heads under the meanest feet.

Queen. Who taught you this trash, sirrah?

Archy. A torn leaf out of an old book trampled in the dirt.—But for the rainbow. It moved as the sun moved, and . . . until the top of the Tower . . . of a cloud through its left-hand tip, and Lambeth Palace look as dark as a rock before the other. Methought I saw a crown figured upon one tip, and a mitre on the other. So, as I had heard treasures were found where the rainbow quenches its points upon the earth, I set off, and at the Tower—— But I shall not tell your Majesty what I found close to the closet-window on which the rainbow had glimmered.

King. Speak: I will make my Fool my conscience.

Archy. Then conscience is a fool.—I saw there a cat caught in a rat-trap. I heard the rats squeak behind the wainscots: it seemed to me that the very mice were consulting on the manner of her death.

Queen. Archy is shrewd and bitter.

Archy.   Like the season,
So blow the winds.—But at the other end of the rainbow, where the gray rain was tempered along the grass and leaves by a tender interfusion of violet and gold in the meadows beyond Lambeth, what think you that I found instead of a mitre?

King. Vane's wits perhaps.

Archy.   Something as vain. I saw
a gross vapour hovering in a stinking ditch over the carcass of a dead ass, some rotten rags, and broken dishes—the wrecks of what once administered to the stuffing-out and the ornament of a worm of worms. His Grace of Canterbury expects to enter the New Jerusalem some Palm Sunday in triumph on the ghost of this ass.

Queen. Enough, enough! Go desire Lady Jane
She place my lute, together with the music
Mari received last week from Italy,
In my boudoir, and——   [*Exit* ARCHY.

King.   I'll go in.

Queen.   My beloved lord,
Have you not noted that the Fool of late
Has lost his careless mirth, and that his words
Sound like the echoes of our saddest fears?
What can it mean? I should be loth to think
Some factious slave had tutored him.

King.   Oh, no!
He is but Occasion's pupil. Partly 'tis

That our minds piece the vacant intervals
Of his wild words with their own fashioning,—
As in the imagery of summer clouds,
Or coals of the winter fire, idlers find
The perfect shadows of their teeming thoughts:
And partly, that the terrors of the time
Are sown by wandering Rumour in all spirits;
And in the lightest and the least, may best
Be seen the current of the coming wind.

    Queen. Your brain is overwrought with these deep thoughts.
Come, I will sing to you; let us go try
These airs from Italy; and, as we pass
The gallery, we'll decide where that Correggio
Shall hang—the Virgin Mother
With her child, born the King of heaven and earth,
Whose reign is men's salvation. And you shall see
A cradled miniature of yourself asleep,
Stamped on the heart by never-erring love;
Liker than any Vandyke ever made,
A pattern to the unborn age of thee,
Over whose sweet beauty I have wept for joy
A thousand times, and now should weep for sorrow,
Did I not think that after we were dead
Our fortunes would spring high in him, and that
The cares we waste upon our heavy crown
Would make it light and glorious as a wreath
Of Heaven's beams for his dear innocent brow.

    King. Dear Henrietta!

A later Scene

HAMPDEN, PYM, CROMWELL, *his Daughter, and young* SIR HARRY VANE.

    Hampden. England, farewell! thou, who hast been my cradle,
Shalt never be my dungeon or my grave!
I held what I inherited in thee
As pawn for that inheritance of freedom
Which thou hast sold for thy despoiler's smile:
How can I call thee England, or my country?—
Does the wind hold?

    Vane.   The vanes sit steady
Upon the Abbey towers. The silver lightnings
Of the evening star, spite of the city's smoke,

Tell that the north wind reigns in the upper air.
Mark too that flock of fleecy-wingèd clouds
Sailing athwart St. Margaret's.
    Hampden.   Hail, fleet herald
Of tempest! that rude pilot who shall guide
Hearts free as his, to realms as pure as thee.
Beyond the shot of tyranny,
Beyone the webs of that swoln spider . . .
Beyond the curses, calumnies, and [lies?]
Of atheist priests!   And thou
Fair star, whose beam lies on the wide Atlantic,
Athwart its zones of tempest and of calm,
Bright as the path to a belovèd home,
Oh, light us to the isles of the evening land!
Like floating Edens cradled in the glimmer
Of sunset, through the distant mist of years
Touched by departing hope, they gleam! lone regions,
Where Power's poor dupes and victims yet have never
Propitiated the savage fear of kings
With purest blood of noblest hearts; whose dew
Is yet unstained with tears of those who wake
To weep each day the wrongs on which it dawns;
Whose sacred silent air owns yet no echo
Of formal blasphemies: nor impious rites
Wrest man's free worship, from the God who loves,
To the poor worm who envies us His love!
Receive, thou young   of Paradise.
These exiles from the old and sinful world!

   .   .   .   .   .   .

This glorious clime, this firmament, whose lights
Dart mitigated influence through their veil
Of pale blue atmosphere; whose tears keep green
The pavement of this moist all-feeding earth;
This vaporous horizon, whose dim round
Is bastioned by the circumfluous sea,
Repelling invasion from the sacred towers,
Presses upon me like a dungeon's grate,
A low dark roof, a damp and narrow wall.
The boundless universe
Becomes a cell too narrow for the soul
That owns no master; while the loathliest ward
Of this wide prison, England, is a nest

Of cradling peace built on the mountain tops,—
To which the eagle spirits of the free.
Which range through heaven and earth, and scorn the storm
Of time, and gaze upon the light of truth,
Return to brood on thoughts that cannot die
And cannot be repelled.
Like eaglets floating in the heaven of time,
They soar above their quarry, and shall stoop
Through palaces and temples thunderproof.

The Fool Sings

Archy. I'll go live under the ivy that overgrows the terrace, and
count the tears shed on its old [roots?] as the [wind?] plays the song of

'A widow bird sate mourning
Upon a wintry bough.'

[Sings]

Heigho! the lark and the owl!
    One flies the morning, and one lulls the night:—
Only the nightingale, poor fond soul,
    Sings like the fool through darkness and light.
'A widow bird sate mourning for her love
    Upon a wintry bough;
The frozen wind crept on above,
    The freezing stream below.

'There was no leaf upon the forest bare,
    No flower upon the ground,
And little motion in the air
    Except the mill-wheel's sound.'

1822

Scenes from 'Faust'

In earlier years Shelley had made word-for-word translations from Goethe's play as part of his German exercises. In the spring of 1822 his delight in the original was increased by the illustrations to it—the sharp outlines of Moritz Retzsch—which were obtaining European popularity. Selected scenes in English were given in the London edition of these outlines but they seemed to Shelley to be very poor. His own renderings were not undertaken to demonstrate that he could produce a final perfection; he declared that Coleridge and nobody else could translate *Faust*; his own labour was to serve as the basis for 'a paper' to appear in Byron's projected periodical. The *Scenes* were printed there (*The Liberal*) after Shelley's death.

SCENE I.—PROLOGUE IN HEAVEN. *The* LORD *and the* HOST *of* HEAVEN.

Enter three ARCHANGELS.

Raphael

THE sun makes music as of old
    Amid the rival spheres of Heaven,
On its predestined circle rolled
    With thunder speed: the Angels even
Draw strength from gazing on its glance,
    Though none its meaning fathom may:—
The world's unwithered countenance
    Is bright as at Creation's day.

Gabriel

And swift and swift, with rapid lightness,
    The adornèd Earth spins silently,
Alternating Elysian brightness
    With deep and dreadful night; the sea
Foams in broad billows from the deep
    Up to the rocks, and rocks and Ocean,
Onward, with spheres which never sleep,
    Are hurried in eternal motion.

469

Michael

And tempests in contention roar
  From land to sea, from sea to land;
And, raging, weave a chain of power,
  Which girds the earth, as with a band.—
A flashing desolation there,
  Flames before the thunder's way;
But Thy servants, Lord, revere
  The gentle changes of Thy day.

Chorus of the Three

The Angels draw strength from Thy glance,
  Though no one comprehend Thee may:—
Thy world's unwithered countenance
  Is bright as on Creation's day.

Enter MEPHISTOPHELES.

Mephistopheles. As thou, O Lord, once more art kind enough
To interest Thyself in our affairs,
And ask, 'How goes it with you there below?'
And as indulgently at other times
Thou tookest not my visits in ill part,
Thou seest me here once more among Thou household.
Though I should scandalize this company,
You will excuse me if I do not talk
In the high style which they think fashionable;
My pathos certainly would make You laugh too,
Had You not long since given over laughing.
Nothing know I to say of suns and worlds;
I observe only how men plague themselves;—
The little god o' the world keeps the same stamp,
As wonderful as on creation's day:—
A little better would he live, hadst Thou
Not given him a glimpse of Heaven's light
Which he calls reason, and employs it only
To live more beastlily than any beast.
With reverence to Your Lordship be it spoken,
He's like one of those long-legged grasshoppers,
Who flits and jumps about, and sings for ever
The same old song i' the grass. There let him lie,
Burying his nose in every heap of dung.
    The Lord. Have you no more to say? Do you come here

Always to scold, and cavil, and complain?
Seems nothing ever right to you on earth?
   Mephistopheles. No, Lord! I find all there, as ever, bad at best.
Even I am sorry for man's days of sorrow;
I could myself almost give up the pleasure
Of plaguing the poor things.
   The Lord.   Knowest thou Faust?
   Mephistopheles. The Doctor?
   The Lord.   Ay; My servant Faust.
   Mephistopheles.   In truth
He serves You in a fashion quite his own;
And the fool's meat and drink are not of earth.
His aspirations bear him on so far.
That he is half aware of his own folly,
For he demands from Heaven its fairest star,
And from the earth the highest joy it bears,
Yet all things far, and all things near, are vain
To calm the deep emotions of his breast.
   The Lord. Though he now serves Me in a cloud of error,
I will soon lead him forth to the clear day.
When trees look green, full well the gardener knows
That fruits and blooms will deck the coming year.
   Mephistopheles. What will You bet?—now I am sure of
      winning—
Only, observe You give me full permission
To lead him softly on my path.
   The Lord.   As long
As he shall live upon the earth, so long
Is nothing unto thee forbidden—Man
Must err till he has ceased to struggle.
   Mephistopheles.   Thanks.
And that is all I ask; for willingly
I never make acquaintance with the dead.
The full fresh cheeks of youth are food for me,
And if a corpse knocks, I am not at home.
For I am like a cat—I like to play
A little with the mouse before I eat it.
   The Lord. Well, well! it is permitted thee. Draw thou
His spirit from its springs; as thou find'st power,
Seize him and lead him on thy downward path;
And stand ashamed when failure teaches thee
That a good man, even in his darkest longings,

Is well aware of the right way.

    Mephistopheles.   Well and good.
I am not in much doubt about my bet,
And if I lose, then 'tis Your turn to crow;
Enjoy Your triumph then with a full breast.
Ay; dust shall he devour, and that with pleasure,
Like my old paramour, the famous Snake.

    The Lord. Pray come here when it suits you; for I never
Had much dislike for people of your sort.
And, among all the Spirits who rebelled,
The knave was ever the least tedious to Me.
The active spirit of man soon sleeps, and soon
He seeks unbroken quiet; therefore I
Have given him the Devil for a companion,
Who may provoke him to some sort of work,
And must create forever.—But ye, pure
Children of God, enjoy eternal beauty;—
Let that which ever operates and lives
Clasp you within the limits of its love;
And seize with sweet and melancholy thoughts
The floating phantoms of its loveliness.

                [Heaven closes; the Archangels exeunt.

    Mephistopheles. From time to time I visit the old fellow,
And I take care to keep on good terms with Him.
Civil enough is the same God Almighty,
To talk so freely with the Devil himself.

SCENE II.—MAY-DAY NIGHT. *The Hartz Mountain, a desolate Country.*
            FAUST, MEPHISTOPHELES.

    Mephistopheles. Would you not like a broomstick? As for me
I wish I had a good stout ram to ride;
For we are still far from the appointed place.

    Faust. This knotted staff is help enough for me,
Whilst I feel fresh upon my legs. What good
Is there in making short a pleasant way?
To creep along the labyrinths of the vales,
And climb those rocks, where ever-babbling springs,
Precipitate themselves in waterfalls,
Is the true sport that seasons such a path.
Already Spring kindles the birchen spray,
And the hoar pines already feel her breath:
Shall she not work also within our limbs?

Mephistopheles. Nothing of such an influence do I feel.
My body is all wintry, and I wish
The flowers upon our path were frost and snow.
But see how melancholy rises now,
Dimly uplifting her belated beam.
The blank unwelcome round of the red moon,
And gives so bad a light, that every step
One stumbles 'gainst some crag. With your permission,
I'll call on Ignis-fatuus to our aid:
I see one yonder burning jollily.
Halloo, my friend! may I request that you
Would favour us with your bright company?
Why should you blaze away there to no purpose?
Pray be so good as light us up this way.

   Ignis-fatuus. With reverence be it spoken, I will try
To overcome the lightness of my nature;
Our course, you know, is generally zigzag.

   Mephistopheles. Ha, ha! your worship thinks you have to deal
With men. Go straight on, in the Devil's name,
Or I shall puff your flickering life out.

   Ignis-fatuus.   Well,
I see you are the master of the house;
I will accommodate myself to you.
Only consider that to-night this mountain
Is all enchanted, and if Jack-a-lantern
Shows you his way, though you should miss your own,
You ought not to be too exact with him.

FAUST, MEPHISTOPHELES, *and* IGNIS-FATUUS, *in alternate Chorus.*

     The limits of the sphere of dream,
       The bounds of true and false, are past.
     Lead us on, thou wandering Gleam,
       Lead us onward, far and fast.
       To the wide, the desert waste.

     But see, how swift advance and shift
       Trees behind trees, row by row,—
     How, clift by clift, rocks bend and lift
       Their frowning foreheads as we go.
       The giant-snouted crags, ho! ho!
       How they snort, and how they blow!

Through the mossy sods and stones,
   Stream and streamlet hurry down—
     A rushing throng! A sound of song
    Beneath the vault of Heaven is blown!
Sweet notes of love, the speaking tones
Of this bright day, sent down to say
   That Paradise on Earth is known,
Resound around, beneath, above.
All we hope and all we love
Finds a voice in this blithe strain,
   Which wakens hill and wood and rill,
     And vibrates far o'er field and vale,
     And which Echo, like the tale
Of old times, repeats again.

To-whoo! to-whoo! near, nearer now
The sound of song, the rushing throng!
Are the screech, the lapwing, and the jay,
All awake as if 'twere day?
See, with long legs and belly wide,
   A salamander in the brake!
   Every root is like a snake,
And along the loose hillside,
With strange contortions through the night,
Curls, to seize or to affright;
And, animated, strong, and many,
They dart forth polypus-antennae,
To blister with their poison spume
The wanderer. Through the dazzling gloom
The many-coloured mice, that thread
The dewy turf beneath our tread,
In troops each other's motions cross,
Through the heath and through the moss;
And, in legions intertangled,
   The fire-flies flit, and swarm, and throng,
Till all the mountain depths are spangled.

Tell me, shall we go or stay?
   Shall we onward? Come along!
   Everything around is swept
Forward, onward, far away!
Trees and masses intercept

The sight, and wisps on every side
Are puffed up and multiplied.

Mephistopheles. Now vigorously seize my skirt, and gain
This pinnacle of isolated crag.
One may observe with wonder from this point,
How Mammon glows among the mountains.
 Faust.   Ay—
And strangely through the solid depth below
A melancholy light, like the red dawn,
Shoots from the lowest gorge of the abyss
Of mountains, lightning hitherward: there rise
Pillars of smoke, here clouds float gently by;
Here the light burns soft as the enkindled air,
Or the illumined dust of golden flowers;
And now it glides like tender colours spreading;
And now bursts forth in fountains from the earth;
And now it winds, one torrent of broad light,
Through the far valley with a hundred veins;
And now once more within that narrow corner
Masses itself into intensest splendour.
And near us, see, sparks spring out of the ground,
Like golden sand scattered upon the darkness;
The pinnacles of that black wall of mountains
That hems us in are kindled.
 Mephistopheles.   Rare: in faith!
Does not Sir Mammon gloriously illuminate
His palace for this festival?—it is
A pleasure which you had not known before.
I spy the boisterous guests already.
 Faust.   How
The children of the wind rage in the air!
With what fierce strokes they fall upon my neck!

Mephistopheles

Cling tightly to the old ribs of the crag.
 Beware! for if with them thou warrest
  In their fierce flight towards the wilderness,
Their breath will sweep thee into dust, and drag
  Thy body to a grave in the abyss.
 A cloud thickens the night.
  Hark! how the tempest crashes through the forest!

The owls fly out in strange affright;
The columns of the evergreen palaces
   Are split and shattered;
  The roots creak, and stretch, and groan;
And ruinously overthrown,
   The trunks are crushed and shattered
By the fierce blast's unconquerable stress.
Over each other crack and crash they all
In terrible and intertangled fall;
And through the ruins of the shaken mountain
  The airs hiss and howl—
It is not the voice of the fountain,
  Nor the wolf in his midnight prowl.
    Dost thou not hear?
     Strange accents are ringing
   Aloft, afar, anear?
    The witches are singing!
The torrent of a raging wizard song
  Streams the whole mountain along.

Chorus of Witches

The stubble is yellow, the corn is green,
  Now to the Brocken the witches go;
The mighty multitude here may be seen
  Gathering, wizard and witch, below.
Sir Urian is sitting aloft in the air;
  Hey over stock! and hey over stone!
'Twixt witches and incubi, what shall be done?
Tell it who dare! tell it who dare!

A Voice

Upon a sow-swine, whose farrows were nine,
  Old Baubo rideth alone.

Chorus

Honour her, to whom honour is due,
Old mother Baubo, honour to you!
An able sow, with old Baubo upon her.
Is worthy of glory, and worthy of honour!
The legion of witches is coming behind,
Darkening the night, and outspeeding the wind—

A Voice

Which way comest thou?

A Voice

Over Ilsenstein;

The owl was awake in the white moonshine;
  I saw her at rest in her downy nest,
And she stared at me with her broad, bright eyne.

Voices

And you may now as well take your course on to Hell,
Since you ride by so fast on the headlong blast.

A Voice

She dropped poison upon me as I passed.
Here are the wounds——

Chorus of Witches

Come away! come along!

The way is wide, the way is long,
But what is that for a Bedlam throng?
Stick with the prong, and scratch with the broom.
The child in the cradle lies strangled at home,
And the mother is clapping her hands.—

Semichorus of Wizards I

We glide in

  Like snails when the women are all away;
And from a house once given over to sin
  Woman has a thousand steps to stray.

Semichorus II

A thousand steps must a woman take,
Where a man but a single spring will make.

Voices above

Come with us, come with us, from Felsensee.

Voices below

With what joy would we fly through the upper sky!
We are washed, we are 'nointed, stark naked are we;
  But our toil and our pain are forever in vain.

Both Choruses

The wind is still, the stars are fled,
The melancholy moon is dead;
The magic notes, like spark on spark,
Drizzle, whistling through the dark.
        Come away!

Voices below

Stay, Oh, stay!

Voices above

Out of the crannies of the rocks
Who calls?

Voices below

        Oh, let me join your flocks!
I, three hundred years have striven
To catch your skirt and mount to Heaven,—
And still in vain. Oh, might I be
With company akin to me!

Both Choruses

Some on a ram and some on a prong,
On poles and on broomsticks we flutter along;
Forlorn is the wight who can rise not to-night.

A Half-Witch below

I have been tripping this many an hour:
Are the others already so far before?
No quiet at home, and no peace abroad!
And less methinks is found by the road.

Chorus of Witches

Come onward, away! aroint thee, aroint!
A witch to be strong must anoint—anoint—
Then every trough will be boat enough;
With a rag for a sail we can sweep through the sky,
Who flies not to-night, when means he to fly?

Both Choruses

We cling to the skirt, and we strike on the ground;
Witch-legions thicken around and around;
Wizard-swarms cover the heath all over.   [*They descend*

Mephistopheles

What thronging, dashing, raging, rustling;
What whispering, babbling, hissing, bustling;
What glimmering, spurting, stinking, burning,
As Heaven and Earth were overturning.
There is a true witch element about us;
Take hold on me, or we shall be divided:—
Where are you?

Faust (*from a distance*). Here!
Mephistopheles.   What!
I must exert my authority in the house.
Place for young Voland! pray make way, good people.
Take hold on me, doctor, and with one step
Let us escape from this unpleasant crowd:
They are too mad for people of my sort.
Just there shines a peculiar kind of light—
Something attracts me in those bushes. Come
This way: we shall slip down there in a minute.
    Faust. Spirit of Contradiction! Well, lead on—
'Twere a wise feat indeed to wander out
Into the Brocken upon May-day night,
And then to isolate oneself in scorn,
Disgusted with the humours of the time.
    Mephistopheles. See yonder, round a many-coloured flame
A merry club is huddled altogether:
Even with such little people as sit there
One would not be alone.
    Faust.   Would that I were
Up yonder in the glow and whirling smoke,
Where the blind million rush impetuously
To meet the evil ones; there might I solve
Many a riddle that torments me!
    Mephistopheles.   Yet
Many a riddle there is tied anew
Inextricably. Let the great world rage!
We will stay here safe in the quiet dwellings.
'Tis an old custom. Men have ever built

Their own small world in the great world of all.
I see young witches naked there, and old ones
Wisely attired with greater decency.
Be guided now by me, and you shall buy
A pound of pleasure with a dram of trouble.
I hear them tune their instruments—one must
Get used to this damned scraping. Come, I'll lead you
Among them; and what there you do and see,
As a fresh compact 'twixt us two shall be.
How say you now? this space is wide enough—
Look forth, you cannot see the end of it—
An hundred bonfires burn in rows, and they
Who throng around them seem innumerable:
Dancing and drinking, jabbering, making love,
And cooking, are at work. Now tell me, friend,
What is there better in the world than this?

   Faust. In introducing us, do you assume
The character of Wizard or of Devil?

   Mephistopheles. In truth, I generally go about
In strict incognito; and yet one likes
To wear one's orders upon gala days.
I have no ribbon at my knee; but here
At home, the cloven foot is honourable.
See you that snail there?—she comes creeping up,
And with her feeling eyes hath smelt out something.
I could not, if I would, mask myself here.
Come now, we'll go about from fire to fire:
I'll be the Pimp, and you shall be the Lover.
       [*To some old Women, who are sitting round a heap of*
          glimmering coals.
Old gentlewomen, what do you do out here?
You ought to be with the young rioters
Right in the thickest of the revelry—
But every one is best content at home.

General

Who dare confide in right or a just claim?
   So much as I had done for them! and now—
With women and the people 'tis the same,
   Youth will stand foremost ever,—age may go
To the dark grave unhonoured.

Minister

Nowadays
People assert their rights: they go too far;
But as for me, the good old times I praise;
Then we were all in all—'twas something worth
One's while to be in place and wear a star;
That was indeed the golden age on earth.

Parvenu

We too are active, and we did and do
What we ought not, perhaps; and yet we now
Will seize, whilst all things are whirled round and round,
A spoke of Fortune's wheel, and keep our ground

Author

Who now can taste a treatise of deep sense
And ponderous volume? 'tis impertinence
To write what none will read, therefore will I
To please the young and thoughtless people try.

 Mephistopheles (who at once appears to have grown very old). I
find the people ripe for the last day,
Since I last came up to the wizard mountain;
And as my little cask runs turbid now,
So is the world drained to the dregs.

 Pedlar-witch.   Look here,
Gentlemen; do not hurry on so fast;
And lose the chance of a good pennyworth.
I have a pack full of the choicest wares
Of every sort, and yet in all my bundle
Is nothing like what may be found on earth;
Nothing that in a moment will make rich
Men and the world with fine malicious mischief—
There is no dagger drunk with blood; no bowl
From which consuming poison may be drained
By innocent and healthy lips; no jewel,
The price of an abandoned maiden's shame;
No sword which cuts the bond it cannot loose,
Or stabs the wearer's enemy in the back;
No——

 Mephistopheles. Gossip, you know little of these times.
What has been, has been; what is done, is past,
They shape themselves into the innovations

They breed, and innovation drags us with it.
The torrent of the crowd sweeps over us:
You think to impel, and are yourself impelled.
   Faust. What is that yonder?
   Mephistopheles.   Mark her well. It is
Lilith.
   Faust. Who?
   Mephistopheles. Lilith, the first wife of Adam.
Beware of her fair hair, for she excels
All women in the magic of her locks;
And when she winds them round a young man's neck,
She will not ever set him free again.

Faust

There sit a girl and an old woman—they
Seem to be tired with pleasure and with play.

Mephistopheles

There is no rest to-night for any one:
When one dance ends another is begun;
Come, let us to it. We shall have rare fun.
[FAUST *dances and sings with a girl, and* MEPHISTOPHELES *with
   an old Woman.*

Faust

    I had once a lovely dream
      In which I saw an apple-tree,
   Where two fair apples with their gleam
      To climb and taste attracted me.

The Girl

    She with apples you desired
      From Paradise came long ago:
    With you I feel that if required,
      Such still within my garden grow.

   Procto-Phantasmist. What is this cursèd multitude about?
Have we not long since proved to demonstration
That ghosts move not on ordinary feet?
But these are dancing just like men and women.
   The Girl. What does he want then at our ball?
   Faust.   Oh! he
Is far above us all in his conceit:

Whilst we enjoy, he reasons of enjoyment;
And any step which in our dance we tread,
If it be left out of his reckoning,
Is not to be considered as a step.
There are few things that scandalize him not:
And when you whirl round in the circle now,
As he went round the wheel in his old mill,
He says that you go wrong in all respects,
Especially if you congratulate him
Upon the strength of the resemblance.

    Procto-Phantasmist.   Fly!
Vanish! Unheard-of impudence! What, still there!
In this enlightened age too, since you have been
Proved not to exist!—But this infernal brood
Will hear no reason and endure no rule.
Are we so wise, and is the *pond* still haunted?
How long have I been sweeping out this rubbish
Of superstition, and the world will not
Come clean with all my pains!—it is a case
Unheard of!

    The Girl.   Then leave off teasing us so.

    Procto-Phantasmist. I tell you, spirits, to your faces now,
That I should not regret this despotism
Of spirits, but that mine can wield it not.
To-night I shall make poor work of it,
Yet I will take a round with you, and hope
Before my last step in the living dance
To beat the poet and the devil together.

    Mephistopheles. At last he will sit down in some foul puddle;
That is his way of solacing himself;
Until some leech, diverted with his gravity.
Cures him of spirits and the spirit together.

                    [*To* FAUST, *who has seceded from the dance.*
Why do you let that fair girl pass from you,
Who sung so sweetly to you in the dance?

    Faust. A red mouse in the middle of her singing
Sprung from her mouth.

    Mephistopheles.   That was all right, my friend:
Be it enough that the mouse was not gray.
Do not disturb your hour of happiness
With close consideration of such trifles.

Faust. Then saw I——

Mephistopheles.   What?

Faust.   Seest thou not a pale,
Fair girl, standing alone, far, far away?
She drags herself now forward with slow steps
And seems as if she moved with shackled feet:
I cannot overcome the thought that she
Is like poor Margaret.

Mephistopheles.   Let it be—pass on—
No good can come of it—it is not well
To meet it—it is an enchanted phantom,
A lifeless idol; with its numbing look,
It freezes up the blood of man; and they
Who meet its ghastly stare are turned to stone,
Like those who saw Medusa.

Faust.   Oh, too true!
Her eyes are like the eyes of a fresh corpse
Which no belovèd hand has closed, alas!
That is the breast which Margaret yielded to me—
Those are the lovely limbs which I enjoyed!

Mephistopheles. It is all magic, poor deluded fool!
She looks to every one like his first love.

Faust. Oh, what delight! what woe! I cannot turn
My looks from her sweet piteous countenance.
How strangely does a single blood-red line,
Not broader than the sharp edge of a knife,
Adorn her lovely neck!

Mephistopheles.   Ay, she can carry
Her head under her arm upon occasion;
Perseus has cut it off for her. These pleasures
End in delusion.—Gain this rising ground,
It is as airy here as in a . . .
And if I am not mightily deceived,
I see a theatre.—What may this mean?

Attendant. Quite a new piece, the last of seven, for 'tis
The custom now to represent that number.
'Tis written by a Dilettante, and
The actors who perform are Dilettanti;
Excuse me, gentlemen; but I must vanish.
I am a Dilettante curtain-lifter.

1822

The Triumph of Life

THIS title has the implication of a public spectacle or as Shelley says of pageantry. It is a sort of picture well practised among the Italian painters, and reflected in Italian poetry. But among the plays of Beaumont and Fletcher which appealed to Shelley's sensibility and thought we see one called *Four Plays, or Moral Representations, in One;* these four are *The Triumph of Honour, The Triumph of Love, The Triumph of Death* and *The Triumph of Time.* These titles, it may be, throw light on the title and the spirit of Shelley's last and, but for its interruption, his most important poetical essay. The hardened style and the sterner observation appear to announce a new phase in his verse, and one which might have seized thinkers who found even *Prometheus Unbound* too much in the air.

> SWIFT as a spirit hastening to his task
> Of glory and of good, the Sun sprang forth
> Rejoicing in his splendour, and the mask
>
> Of darkness fell from the awakened Earth—
> The smokeless altars of the mountain snows
> Flamed above crimson clouds, and at the birth
>
> Of light, the Ocean's orison arose,
> To which the birds tempered their matin lay.
> All flowers in field or forest which unclose
>
> Their trembling eyelids to the kiss of day,
> Swinging their censers in the element,
> With orient incense lit by the new ray
>
> Burned slow and inconsumably, and sent
> Their odorous sighs up to the smiling air;
> And, in succession due, did continent,

Isle, ocean, and all things that in them wear
The form and character of mortal mould,
Rise as the Sun their father rose, to bear

Their portion of the toil, which he of old
Took as his own, and then imposed on them:
But I, whom thoughts which must remain untold

Had kept as wakeful as the stars that gem
The cone of night, now they were laid asleep
Stretched my faint limbs beneath the hoary stem

Which an old chestnut flung athwart the steep
Of a green Apennine: before me fled
The night; behind me rose the day; the deep

Was at my feet, and Heaven above my head,—
When a strange trance over my fancy grew
Which was not slumber, for the shade it spread

Was so transparent, that the scene came through
As clear as when a veil of light is drawn
O'er evening hills they glimmer; and I knew

That I had felt the freshness of that dawn,
Bathed in the same cold dew my brow and hair,
And sate as thus upon that slope of lawn

Under the self-same bough, and heard as there
The birds, the fountains and the ocean hold
Sweet talk in music through the enamoured air,
And then a vision on my brain was rolled.

.   .   .   .   .   .

As in that trance of wondrous thought I lay,
This was the tenour of my walking dream:—
Methought I sate beside a public way

Thick strewn with summer dust, and a great stream
Of people there was hurrying to and fro,
Numerous as gnats upon the evening gleam,

All hastening onward, yet none seemed to know
Whither he went, or whence he came, or why
He made one of the multitude, and so

Was borne amid the crowd, as through the sky
One of the million leaves of summer's bier;
Old age and youth, manhood and infancy,

Mixed in one mighty torrent did appear,
Some flying from the thing they feared, and some
Seeking the object of another's fear;

And others, as with steps towards the tomb,
Pored on the trodden worms that crawled beneath,
And others mournfully within the gloom

Of their own shadow walked, and called it death;
And some fled from it as it were a ghost,
Half fainting in the affliction of vain breath:

But more, with motions which each other crossed,
Pursued or shunned the shadows the clouds threw,
Or birds within the noonday aether lost,

Upon that path where flowers never grew,—
And, weary with vain toil and faint for thirst,
Heard not the fountains, whose melodious dew

Out of their mossy cells forever burst;
Nor felt the breeze which from the forest told
Of grassy paths and wood-lawns interspersed

With overarching elms and caverns cold,
And violet banks where sweet dreams brood, but they
Pursued their serious folly as of old.

And as I gazed, methought that in the way
The throng grew wilder, as the woods of June
When the south wind shakes the extinguished day.

And a cold glare, intenser than the noon,
But icy cold, obscured with blinding light
The sun, as he the stars. Like the young moon—

When on the sunlit limits of the night
Her white shell trembles amid crimson air,
And whilst the sleeping tempest gathers might—

Doth, as the herald of its coming, bear
The ghost of its dead mother, whose dim form
Bends in dark aether from her infant's chair,—

So came a chariot on the silent storm
Of its own rushing splendour, and a Shape
So sate within, as one whom years deform,

Beneath a dusky hood and double cape,
Crouching within the shadow of a tomb;
And o'er what seemed the head a cloud-like crape

Was bent, a dun and faint aethereal gloom
Tempering the light. Upon the chariot-beam
A Janus-visaged Shadow did assume

The guidance of that wonder-wingèd team;
The shapes which drew it in thick lightenings
Were lost:—I heard alone on the air's soft stream

The music of their ever-moving wings.
All the four faces of that Charioteer
Had their eyes banded; little profit brings

Speed in the van and blindness in the rear,
Nor then avail the beams that quench the sun,—
Or that with banded eyes could pierce the sphere

Of all that is, has been or will be done;
So ill was the car guided—but it passed
With solemn speed majestically on.

The crowd gave way, and I arose aghast,
Or seemed to rise, so mighty was the trance,
And saw, like clouds upon the thunder-blast,

The million with fierce song and maniac dance
Raging around—such seemed the jubilee
As when to greet some conqueror's advance

Imperial Rome poured forth her living sea
From senate-house, and forum, and theatre,
When   upon the free

Had bound a yoke, which soon they stooped to bear.
Nor wanted here the just similitude
Of a triumphal pageant, for where'er

The chariot rolled, a captive multitude
Was driven;—all those who had grown old in power
Or misery,—all who had their age subdued

By action or by suffering, and whose hour
Was drained to its last sand in weal or woe,
So that the trunk survived both fruit and flower;—

All those whose fame or infamy must grow
Till the great winter lay the form and name
Of this green earth with them for ever low;—

All but the sacred few who could not tame
Their spirits to the conquerors—but as soon
As they had touched the world with living flame,

Fled back like eagles to their native noon,
Or those who put aside the diadem
Of earthly thrones or gems . . .

Were there of Athens or Jerusalem,
Were neither 'mid the mighty captives seen,
Nor 'mid the ribald crowd that followed them,

Nor those who went before fierce and obscene.
The wild dance maddens in the van, and those
Who lead it—fleet as shadows on the green,

Outspeed the chariot, and without repose
Mix with each other in tempestuous measure
To savage music, wilder as it grows,

They, tortured by their agonizing pleasure,
Convulsed and on the rapid whirlwinds spun
Of that fierce Spirit, whose unholy leisure

Was soothed by mischief since the world begun,
Throw back their heads and loose their streaming hair;
And in their dance round her who dims the sun,

Maidens and youths fling their wild arms in air
As their feet twinkle; they recede, and now
Bending within each other's atmosphere,

Kindle invisibly—and as they glow,
Like moths by light attracted and repelled,
Oft to their bright destruction come and go,

Till like two clouds into one vale impelled,
That shake the mountains when their lightnings mingle
And die in rain—the fiery band which held

Their natures, snaps—while the shock still may tingle.
One falls and then another in the path
Senseless—nor is the desolation single,

Yet ere I can say *where*—the chariot hath
Passed over them—nor other trace I find
But as of foam after the ocean's wrath

Is spent upon the desert shore;—behind,
Old men and women foully disarrayed,
Shake their gray hairs in the insulting wind,

And follow in the dance, with limbs decayed,
Seeking to reach the light which leaves them still
Farther behind and deeper in the shade.

But not the less with impotence of will
They wheel, though ghastly shadows interpose
Round them and round each other, and fulfil

Their work, and in the dust from whence they rose
Sink, and corruption veils them as they lie.
And past in these performs what   in those.

Struck to the heart by this sad pageantry,
Half to myself I said—'And what is this?
Whose shape is that within the car? And why—'

I would have added—'is all here amiss?—'
But a voice answered—'Life!'—I turned, and knew
(O Heaven, have mercy on such wretchedness!)

That what I thought was an old root which grew
To strange distortion out of the hill side,
Was indeed one of those deluded crew,

And that the grass, which methought hung so wide
And white, was but his thin discoloured hair,
And that the holes he vainly sought to hide,

Were or had been eyes:—'If thou canst, forbear
To join the dance, which I had well forborne!.
Said the grim Feature (of my thought aware).

'I will unfold that which to this deep scorn
Led me and my companions, and relate
The progress of the pageant since the morn;

'If thirst of knowledge shall not then abate,
Follow it thou even to the night, but I
Am weary.'—Then like one who with the weight

Of his own words is staggered, wearily
He paused; and ere he could resume, I cried:
'First, who art thou?'—'Before thy memory,

'I feared, loved, hated, suffered, did and died,
And if the spark with which Heaven lit my spirit
Had been with purer nutriment supplied,

'Corruption would not now thus much inherit
Of what was once Rousseau,—nor this disguise
Stained that which ought to have disdained to wear it;

'If I have been extinguished, yet there rise
A thousand beacons from the spark I bore'—
'And who are those chained to the car?'—'The wise,

'The great, the unforgotten,—they who wore
Mitres and helms and crowns, or wreaths of light,
Signs of thought's empire over thought—their lore

'Taught them not this, to know themselves; their might
Could not repress the mystery within,
And for the morn of truth they feigned, deep night

'Caught them ere evening.'—'Who is he with chin
Upon his breast, and hands crossed on his chain?'—
'The child of a fierce hour; he sought to win

'The world, and lost all that it did contain
Of greatness, in its hope destroyed; and more
Of fame and peace than virtue's self can gain

'Without the opportunity which bore
Him on its eagle pinions to the peak
From which a thousand climbers have before

'Fallen, as Napoleon fell.'—I felt my cheek
Alter, to see the shadow pass away,
Whose grasp had left the giant world so weak

That every pigmy kicked it as it lay;
And much I grieved to think how power and will
In opposition rule our mortal day,

And why God made irreconcilable
Good and the means of good; and for despair
I half disdained mine eyes' desire to fill

With the spent vision of the times that were
And scarce have ceased to be.—'Dost thou behold,'
Said my guide. 'those spoilers spoiled, Voltaire,

'Frederick, and Paul, Catherine, and Leopold,
And hoary anarchs, demagogues, and sage—
        names which the world thinks always old,

'For in the battle Life and they did wage,
She remained conqueror. I was overcome
By my own heart alone, which neither age,

'Nor tears, nor infamy, nor now the tomb
Could temper to its object.'—'Let them pass,'
I cried, 'the world and its mysterious doom

'Is not so much more glorious than it was,
That I desire to worship those who drew
New figures on its false and fragile glass

'As the old faded.'—'Figures ever new
Rise on the bubble, paint them as you may;
We have but thrown, as those before us threw,

'Our shadows on it as it passed away.
But mark how chained to the triumphal chair
The mighty phantoms of an elder day;

'All that is mortal of great Plato there
Expiates the joy and woe his master knew not;
The star that ruled his doom was far too fair.

'And life, where long that flower of Heaven grew not,
Conquered that heart by love, which gold, or pain,
Or age, or sloth, or slavery could subdue not.

'And near him walk the   twain,
The tutor and his pupil, whom Dominion
Followed as tame as vulture in a chain.

'The world was darkened beneath either pinion
Of him whom from the flock of conquerors
Fame singled out for her thunder-bearing minion;

'The other long outlived both woes and wars,
Throned in the thoughts of men, and still had kept
The jealous key of Truth's eternal doors,

'If Bacon's eagle spirit had not leapt
Like lightning out of darkness—he compelled
The Proteus shape of Nature as it slept

'To wake, and lead him to the caves that held
The treasure of the secrets of its reign.
See the great bards of elder time, who quelled

'The passions which they sung, as by their strain
May well be known: their living melody
Tempers its own contagion to the vein

'Of those who are infected with it—I
Have suffered what I wrote, or viler pain!
And so my words have seeds of misery—

'Even as the deeds of others, not as theirs.'
And then he pointed to a company

'Midst whom I quickly recognized the heirs
Of Caesar's crime, from him to Constantine;
The anarch chiefs, whose force and murderous snares

Had founded many a sceptre-bearing line,
And spread the plague of gold and blood abroad:
And Gregory and John, and men divine,

Who rose like shadows between man and God;
Till that eclipse, still hanging over heaven,
Was worshipped by the world o'er which they strode,

For the true sun it quenched—'Their power was given
But to destroy,' replied the leader:—'I
Am one of those who have created, even

'If it be but a world of agony.'—
'Whence camest thou? and whither goest thou?
How did thy course begin?' I said, 'and why?

'Mine eyes are sick of this perpetual flow
Of people, and my heart sick of one sad thought—
Speak!'—'Whence I am, I partly seem to know,

'And how and by what paths I have been brought
To this dread pass, methinks even thou mayst guess;—
Why this should be, my mind can compass not;

'Whither the conqueror hurries me, still less;—
But follow thou, and from spectator turn
Actor or victim in this wretchedness,

'And what thou wouldst be taught I then may learn
From thee. Now listen:—In the April prime,
When all the forest-tips began to burn

'With kindling green, touched by the azure clime
Of the young season, I was laid asleep
Under a mountain, which from unknown time

'Had yawned into a cavern, high and deep;
And from it came a gentle rivulet,
Whose water, like clear air, in its calm sweep

'Bent the soft grass, and kept for ever wet
The stems of the sweet flowers, and filled the grove
With sounds, which whoso hears must needs forget

'All pleasure and all pain, all hate and love,
Which they had known before that hour of rest;
A sleeping mother then would dream not of

'Her only child who died upon the breast
At eventide—a king would mourn no more
The crown of which his brows were dispossessed

'When the sun lingered o'er his ocean floor
To gild his rival's new prosperity.
Thou wouldst forget thus vainly to deplore

'Ills, which if ills can find no cure from thee,
The thought of which no other sleep will quell,
Nor other music blot from memory,

'So sweet and deep is the oblivious spell;
And whether life had been before that sleep
The Heaven which I imagine, or a Hell

'Like this harsh world in which I wake to weep,
I know not. I arose, and for a space
The scene of woods and waters seemed to keep,

'Though it was now broad day, a gentle trace
Of light diviner than the common sun
Sheds on the common earth, and all the place

'Was filled with magic sounds woven into one
Oblivious melody, confusing sense
Amid the gliding waves and shadows dun;

'And, as I looked, the bright omnipresence
Of morning through the orient cavern flowed,
And the sun's image radiantly intense

'Burned on the waters of the well that glowed
Like gold, and threaded all the forest's maze
With winding paths of emerald fire; there stood

'Amid the sun, as he amid the blaze
Of his own glory, on the vibrating
Floor of the fountain, paved with flashing rays,

'A Shape all light, which with one hand did fling
Dew on the earth, as if she were the dawn,
And the invisible rain did ever sing

'A silver music on the mossy lawn;
And still before me on the dusky grass,
Iris her many-coloured scarf had drawn:

'In her right hand she bore a crystal glass,
Mantling with bright Nepenthe; the fierce splendour
Fell from her as she moved under the mass

'Of the deep cavern, and with palms so tender,
Their tread broke not the mirror of its billow,
Glided along the river, and did bend her

'Head under the dark boughs, till like a willow
Her fair hair swept the bosom of the stream
That whispered with delight to be its pillow.

'As one enamoured is upborne in dream
O'er lily-paven lakes, mid silver mist,
To wondrous music, so this shape might seem

'Partly to tread the waves with feet which kissed
The dancing foam; partly to glide along
The air which roughened the moist amethyst,

'Or the faint morning beams that fell among
The trees, or the soft shadows of the trees;
And her feet, ever to the ceaseless song

'Of leaves, and winds, and waves, and birds, and bees,
And falling drops, moved in a measure new
Yet sweet, as on the summer evening breeze,

'Up from the lake a shape of golden dew
Between two rocks, athwart the rising moon,
Dances i' the wind, where never eagle flew;

'And still her feet, no less than the sweet tune
To which they moved, seemed as they moved to blot
The thoughts of him who gazed on them; and soon

'All that was, seemed as if it had been not;
And all the gazer's mind was strewn beneath
Her feet like embers; and she, thought by thought,

'Trampled its sparks into the dust of death;
As day upon the threshold of the east
Treads out the lamps of night, until the breath

'Of darkness re-illumine even the least
Of heaven's living eyes—like day she came,
Making the night a dream; and ere she ceased

'To move, as one between desire and shame
Suspended, I said—If, as it doth seem,
Thou comest from the realm without a name

'Into this valley of perpetual dream,
Show whence I came, and where I am, and why—
Pass not away upon the passing stream.

'Arise and quench thy thirst, was her reply.
And as a shut lily stricken by the wand
Of dewy morning's vital alchemy,

'I rose; and, bending at her sweet command,
Touched with faint lips the cup she raised,
And suddenly my brain became as sand

'Where the first wave had more than half erased
The track of deer on desert Labrador;
Whilst the wolf, from which they fled amazed,

'Leaves his stamp visibly upon the shore,
Until the second bursts;—so on my sight
Burst a new vision, never seen before,

'And the fair shape waned in the coming light,
As veil by veil the silent splendour drops
From Lucifer, amid the chrysolite

'Of sunrise, ere it tinge the mountain-tops;
And as the presence of that fairest planet,
Although unseen, is felt by one who hopes

'That his day's path may end as he began it,
In that star's smile, whose light is like the scent
Of a jonquil when evening breezes fan it,

'Or the soft note in which his dear lament
The Brescian shepherd breathes, or the caress
That turned his weary slumber to content;

'So knew I in that light's severe excess
The presence of that Shape which on the stream
Moved, as I moved along the wilderness,

'More dimly than a day-appearing dream,
The ghost of a forgotten form of sleep;
A light of heaven, whose half-extinguished beam

'Through the sick day in which we wake to weep
Glimmers, for ever sought, for ever lost;
So did that shape its obscure tenour keep

'Beside my path, as silent as a ghost;
But the new Vision, and the cold bright car,
With solemn speed and stunning music, crossed

'The forest, and as if from some dread war
Triumphantly returning, the loud million
Fiercely extolled the fortune of her star.

'A moving arch of victory, the vermilion
And green and azure plumes of Iris had
Built high over her wind-wingèd pavilion,

'And underneath aethereal glory clad
The wilderness, and far before her flew
The tempest of the splendour, which forbade

'Shadow to fall from leaf and stone; the crew
Seemed in that light, like atomies to dance
Within a sunbeam;—some upon the new

'Embroidery of flowers, that did enhance
The grassy vesture of the desert, played,
Forgetful of the chariot's swift advance;

'Others stood gazing, till within the shade
Of the great mountain its light left them dim;
Others outspeeded it; and others made

'Circles around it, like the clouds that swim
Round the high moon in a bright sea of air;
And more did follow, with exulting hymn,

'The chariot and the captives fettered there:—
But all like bubbles on an eddying flood
Fell into the same track at last, and were

'Borne onward.—I among the multitude
Was swept—me, sweetest flowers delayed not long;
Me, not the shadow nor the solitude;

'Me, not that falling stream's Lethean song;
Me, not the phantom of that early form
Which moved upon its motion—but among

'The thickest billows of that living storm
I plunged, and bared my bosom to the clime
Of that cold light, whose airs too soon deform.

'Before the chariot had begun to climb
The opposing steep of that mysterious dell,
Behold a wonder worthy of the rhyme

'Of him who from the lowest depths of hell,
Through every paradise and through all glory,
Love led serene, and who returned to tell

'The words of hate and awe; the wondrous story
How all things are transfigured except Love;
For deaf as is a sea, which wrath makes hoary,

'The world can hear not the sweet notes that move
The sphere whose light is melody to lovers—
A wonder worthy of his rhyme.—The grove

'Grew dense with shadows to its inmost covers,
The earth was gray with phantoms, and the air
Was peopled with dim forms, as when there hovers

'A flock of vampire-bats before the glare
Of the tropic sun, bringing, ere evening,
Strange night upon some Indian isle;—thus were

'Phantoms diffused around; and some did fling
Shadows of shadows, yet unlike themselves,
Behind them; some like eaglets on the wing

'Were lost in the white day; others like elves
Danced in a thousand unimagined shapes
Upon the sunny streams and grassy shelves;

'And others sate chattering like restless apes
On vulgar hands, . . .
Some made a cradle of the ermined capes

'Of kingly mantles; some across the tiar
Of pontiffs sate like vultures; others played
Under the crown which girt with empire

'A baby's or an idiot's brow, and made
Their nests in it. The old anatomies
Sate hatching their bare broods under the shade

'Of daemon wings, and laughed from their dead eyes
To reassume the delegated power,
Arrayed in which those worms did monarchize,

'Who made this earth their charnel. Others more
Humble, like falcons, sate upon the fist
Of common men, and round their heads did soar;

'Or like small gnats and flies, as thick as mist
On evening marshes, thronged about the brow
Of lawyers, statesmen, priest and theorist;—

'And others, like discoloured flakes of snow
On fairest bosoms and the sunniest hair,
Fell, and were melted by the youthful glow

'Which they extinguished; and, like tears, they were
A veil to those from whose faint lids they rained
In drops of sorrow. I became aware

'Of whence those forms proceeded which thus stained
The track in which we moved. After brief space,
From every form the beauty slowly waned;

'From every firmest limb and fairest face
The strength and freshness fell like dust, and left
The action and the shape without the grace

'Of life. The marble brow of youth was cleft
With care; and in those eyes where once hope shone,
Desire, like a lioness bereft

'Of her last cub, glared ere it died; each one
Of that great crowd sent forth incessantly
These shadows, numerous as the dead leaves blown

'In autumn evening from a poplar tree.
Each like himself and like each other were
At first; but some distorted seemed to be

'Obscure clouds, moulded by the casual air;
And of this stuff the car's creative ray
Wrought all the busy phantoms that were there,

'As the sun shapes the clouds; thus on the way
Mask after mask fell from the countenance
And form of all; and long before the day

'Was old, the joy which waked like heaven's glance
The sleepers in the oblivious valley, died;
And some grew weary of the ghastly dance,

'And fell, as I have fallen, by the wayside;—
Those soonest from whose forms most shadows passed,
And least of strength and beauty did abide.

Then, what is life? I cried.'—

1822

ODES

Hymn to Intellectual Beauty

THE awful shadow of some unseen Power
  Floats though unseen among us,—visiting
  This various world with as inconstant wing
As summer winds that creep from flower to flower,—
Like moonbeams that behind some piny mountain shower,
    It visits with inconstant glance
    Each human heart and countenance;
Like hues and harmonies of evening,—
    Like clouds in starlight widely spread,—
    Like memory of music fled,—
    Like aught that for its grace may be
Dear, and yet dearer for its mystery.

Spirit of BEAUTY, that dost consecrate
  With thine own hues all thou dost shine upon
  Of human thought or form,—where art thou gone?
Why dost thou pass away and leave our state,
This dim vast vale of tears, vacant and desolate?
    Ask why the sunlight not for ever
    Weaves rainbows o'er yon mountain-river.
Why aught should fail and fade that once is shown,
    Why fear and dream and death and birth
    Cast on the daylight of this earth
    Such gloom,—why man has such a scope
For love and hate, despondency and hope?

No voice from some sublimer world hath ever
  To sage or poet these responses given—
  Therefore the names of Demon, Ghost, and Heaven,
Remain the records of their vain endeavour.
Frail spells—whose uttered charm might not avail to sever,
    From all we hear and all we see,
    Doubt, chance, and mutability.

Thy light alone—like mist o'er mountains driven,
    Or music by the night-wind sent
    Through strings of some still instrument,
    Or moonlight on a midnight stream,
Gives grace and truth to life's unquiet dream.

Love, Hope, and Self-esteem, like clouds depart
    And come, for some uncertain moments lent.
    Man were immortal, and omnipotent,
Didst thou, unknown and awful as thou art,
Keep with thy glorious train firm state within his heart.
      Thou messenger of sympathies,
      That wax and wane in lovers' eyes—
Thou—that to human thought art nourishment,
      Like darkness to a dying flame!
      Depart not as thy shadow came,
      Depart not—lest the grave should be,
Like life and fear, a dark reality.

While yet a boy I sought for ghosts, and sped
    Through many a listening chamber, cave and ruin,
    And starlight wood, with fearful steps pursuing
Hopes of high talk with the departed dead.
I called on poisonous names with which our youth is fed;
      I was not heard—I saw them not—
      When musing deeply on the lot
Of life, at that sweet time when winds are wooing
      All vital things that wake to bring
      News of birds and blossoming,—
      Sudden, thy shadow fell on me;
I shrieked, and clasped my hands in ecstasy!

I vowed that I would dedicate my powers
      To thee and thine—have I not kept the vow?
      With beating heart and streaming eyes, even now
I call the phantoms of a thousand hours
Each from his voiceless grave: they have in visioned bowers
      Of studious zeal or love's delight
      Outwatched with me the envious night—
They know that never joy illumed my brow
      Unlinked with hope that thou wouldst free
      This world from its dark slavery,

That thou—O awful LOVELINESS,
Wouldst give whate'er these words cannot express.

The day becomes more solemn and serene
  When noon is past—there is a harmony
  In autumn, and a lustre in its sky,
Which through the summer is not heard or seen,
As if it could not be, as if it had not been!
      Thus let thy power, which like the truth
      Of nature on my passive youth
    Descended, to my onward life supply
      Its calm—to one who worships thee,
      And every form containing thee,
      Whom, SPIRIT fair, thy spells did bind
    To fear himself, and love all human kind.

Mont Blanc

THE everlasting universe of things
Flows through the mind, and rolls its rapid waves,
Now dark—now glittering—now reflecting gloom—
Now lending splendour, where from secret springs
The source of human thought its tribute brings
Of waters,—with a sound but half its own,
Such as a feeble brook will oft assume
In the wild woods, among the mountains lone,
Where waterfalls around it leap for ever,
Where woods and winds contend, and a vast river
Over its rocks ceaselessly bursts and raves.

Thus thou, Ravine of Arve—dark, deep Ravine—
Thou many-coloured, many-voicèd vale,
Over whose pines, and crags, and caverns sail
Fast cloud-shadows and sunbeams: awful scene,
Where Power in likeness of the Arve comes down
From the ice-gulfs that gird his secret throne,
Bursting through these dark mountains like the flame
Of lightning through the tempest;—thou dost lie,
Thy giant brood of pines around thee clinging,
Children of elder time, in whose devotion
The chainless winds still come and ever came
To drink their odours, and their mighty swinging
To hear—an old and solemn harmony;
Thine earthly rainbows stretched across the sweep
Of the aethereal waterfall, whose veil
Robes some unsculptured image; the strange sleep
Which when the voices of the desert fail
Wraps all in its own deep eternity;—
Thy caverns echoing to the Arve's commotion,
A loud, lone sound no other sound can tame;

Thou art pervaded with that ceaseless motion,
Thou art the path of that unresting sound—
Dizzy Ravine! and when I gaze on thee
I seem as in a trance sublime and strange
To muse on my own separate fantasy,
My own, my human mind, which passively
Now renders and receives fast influencings,
Holding an unremitting interchange
With the clear universe of things around;
One legion of wild thoughts, whose wandering wings
Now float above thy darkness, and now rest
Where that or thou art no unbidden guest,
In the still cave of the witch Poesy,
Seeking among the shadows that pass by
Ghost of all things that are, some shade of thee,
Some phantom, some faint image; till the breast
From which they fled recalls them, thou art there!

Some say that gleams of a remoter world
Visit the soul in sleep,—that death is slumber,
And that its shapes the busy thoughts outnumber
Of those who wake and live.—I look on high;
Has some unknown omnipotence unfurled
The veil of life and death? or do I lie
In dream, and does the mightier world of sleep
Spread far around and inaccessibly
Its circles? For the very spirit fails,
Driven like a homeless cloud from steep to steep
That vanishes among the viewless gales!
Far, far above, piercing the infinite sky,
Mont Blanc appears,—still, snowy, and serene—
Its subject mountains their unearthly forms
Pile around it, ice and rock; broad vales between
Of frozen floods, unfathomable deeps,
Blue as the overhanging heaven, that spread
And wind among the accumulated steeps;
A desert peopled by the storms alone,
Save when the eagle brings some hunter's bone,
And the wolf tracks her there—how hideously
Its shapes are heaped around! rude, bare, and high,
Ghastly, and scarred, and riven.—Is this the scene
Where the old Earthquake-daemon taught her young

Ruin? Were these their toys? or did a sea
Of fire envelop once this silent snow?
None can reply—all seems eternal now.
The wilderness has a mysterious tongue
Which teaches awful doubt, or faith so mild,
So solemn, so serene, that man may be,
But for such faith, with nature reconciled;
Thou hast a voice, great Mountain, to repeal
Large codes of fraud and woe; not understood
By all, but which the wise, and great, and good
Interpret, or make felt, or deeply feel.

The fields, the lakes, the forests, and the streams,
Ocean, and all the living things that dwell
Within the daedal earth; lightning, and rain,
Earthquake, and fiery flood, and hurricane.
The torpor of the year when feeble dreams
Visit the hidden buds, or dreamless sleep
Holds every future leaf and flower;—the bound
With which from that detested trance they leap;
The works and ways of man, their death and birth,
And that of him and all that his may be;
All things that move and breathe with toil and sound
Are born and die; revolve, subside, and swell.
Power dwells apart in its tranquillity,
Remote, serene, and inaccessible:
And *this*, the naked countenance of earth,
On which I gaze, even these primaeval mountains
Teach the adverting mind. The glaciers creep
Like snakes that watch their prey, from their far fountains,
Slow rolling on; there, many a precipice,
Frost and the Sun in scorn of mortal power
Have piled: dome, pyramid, and pinnacle,
A city of death, distinct with many a tower
And wall impregnable of beaming ice.
Yet not a city, but a flood of ruin
Is there, that from the boundaries of the sky
Rolls its perpetual stream; vast pines are strewing
Its destined path, or in the mangled soil
Branchless and shattered stand; the rocks, drawn down
From yon remotest waste, have overthrown
The limits of the dead and living world,

Never to be reclaimed. The dwelling-place
Of insects, beasts, and birds, becomes its spoil;
Their food and their retreat for ever gone,
So much of life and joy is lost. The race
Of man flies far in dread; his work and dwelling
Vanish, like smoke before the tempest's stream,
And their place is not known. Below, vast caves
Shine in the rushing torrents' restless gleam,
Which from those secret chasms in tumult welling
Meet in the vale, and one majestic River,
The breath and blood of distant lands, for ever
Rolls its loud waters to the ocean-waves,
Breathes its swift vapours to the circling air.

Mont Blanc yet gleams on high:—the power is there,
The still and solemn power of many sights,
And many sounds, and much of life and death.
In the calm darkness of the moonless nights,
In the lone glare of day, the snows descend
Upon that Mountain; none beholds them there,
Nor when the flakes burn in the sinking sun,
Or the star-beams dart through them:—Winds contend
Silently there, and heap the snow with breath
Rapid and strong, but silently! Its home
The voiceless lightning in these solitudes
Keeps innocently, and like vapour broods
Over the snow. The secret Strength of things
Which governs thought, and to the infinite dome
Of Heaven is as a law, inhabits thee!
And what were thou, and earth, and stars, and sea,
If to the human mind's imaginings
Silence and solitude were vacancy?

July 23, 1816

Ode to Heaven

First Spirit

PALACE-ROOF of cloudless nights!
Paradise of golden lights!
 Deep, immeasurable, vast,
Which art now, and which wert then
 Of the Present and the Past,
Of the eternal Where and When,
 Presence-chamber, temple, home,
 Ever-canopying dome,
 Of acts and ages yet to come!

Glorious shapes have life in thee,
Earth, and all earth's company;
 Living globes which ever throng
Thy deep chasms and wildernesses;
 And green worlds that glide along;
And swift stars with flashing tresses;
 And icy moons most cold and bright,
 And mighty suns beyond the night,
 Atoms of intensest light.

Even thy name is as a god,
Heaven! for thou art the abode
 Of that Power which is the glass
Wherein man his nature sees.
 Generations as they pass
Worship thee with bended knees.
 Their unremaining gods and they
 Like a river roll away:
 Thou remainest such—alway!—

Second Spirit

Thou art but the mind's first chamber,
Round which its young fancies clamber,
  Like weak insects in a cave,
Lighted up by stalactites;
  But the portal of the grave,
Where a world of new delights
    Will make thy best glories seem
    But a dim and noonday gleam
    From the shadow of a dream!

Third Spirit

Peace! the abyss is wreathed with scorn
At your presumption, atom-born!
  What is Heaven? and what are ye
Who its brief expanse inherit?
  What are suns and spheres which flee
  With the instinct of that Spirit
    Of which ye are but a part?
    Drops which Nature's mighty heart
    Drives through thinnest veins! Depart!

What is Heaven? a globe of dew,
Filling in the morning new
  Some eyed flower whose young leaves waken
On an unimagined world:
  Constellated suns unshaken,
Orbits measureless, are furled
    In that frail and fading sphere,
    With ten millions gathered there,
    To tremble, gleam, and disappear.

Ode to the West Wind

In Shelley's notebook, presented by Sir John Shelley-Rolls to the Bodleian Library, this Ode begins under the simple heading 'October 25.' His own published note on it amounts to an instance of his success as a weather-prophet (and Mary Shelley thought him a good one) with a word on marine botany. In the draft the much-quoted final line was in the form of an assertion; as a question it is far superior. If any literary model was in Shelley's mind as he wrote, it will have been Coleridge's *Ode on the Departing Year*, which however is largely inspired by the political upheavals of Europe. Shelley's is so much of a personal 'confession' that even the withered leaves round him are compared with his own early grey hairs.

O WILD West Wind, thou breath of Autumn's being,
Thou, from whose unseen presence the leaves dead
Are driven, like ghosts from an enchanter fleeing,

Yellow, and black, and pale, and hectic red,
Pestilence-stricken multitudes: O thou,
Who chariotest to their dark wintry bed

The wingèd seeds, where they lie cold and low,
Each like a corpse within its grave, until
Thine azure sister of the Spring shall blow

Her clarion o'er the dreaming earth, and fill
(Driving sweet buds like flocks to feed in air)
With living hues and odours plain and hill:

Wild Spirit, which art moving everywhere;
Destroyer and preserver; hear, oh, hear!

Thou on whose stream, mid the steep sky's commotion,
Loose clouds like earth's decaying leaves are shed,
Shook from the tangled boughs of Heaven and Ocean,

Angels of rain and lightning: there are spread
On the blue surface of thine aëry surge,
Like the bright hair uplifted from the head

Of some fierce Maenad, even from the dim verge
Of the horizon to the zenith's height,
The locks of the approaching storm. Thou dirge

Of the dying year, to which this closing night
Will be the dome of a vast sepulchre,
Vaulted with all thy congregated might

Of vapours, from whose solid atmosphere
Black rain, and fire, and hail will burst: oh, hear!

Thou who didst waken from his summer dreams
The blue Mediterranean, where he lay,
Lulled by the coil of his crystàlline streams,

Beside a pumice isle in Baiae's bay,
And saw in sleep old palaces and towers
Quivering within the wave's intenser day,

All overgrown with azure moss and flowers
So sweet, the sense faints picturing them! Thou
For whose path the Atlantic's level powers

Cleave themselves into chasms, while far below
The sea-blooms and the oozy woods which wear
The sapless foliage of the ocean, know

Thy voice, and suddenly grow gray with fear,
And tremble and despoil themselves: oh, hear!

If I were a dead leaf thou mightest bear;
If I were a swift cloud to fly with thee;
A wave to pant beneath thy power, and share

The impulse of thy strength, only less free
Than thou, O uncontrollable! If even
I were as in my boyhood, and could be

The comrade of thy wanderings over Heaven,
As then, when to outstrip thy skiey speed
Scarce seemed a vision; I would ne'er have striven

As thus with thee in prayer in my sore need.
Oh, lift me as a wave, a leaf, a cloud!
I fall upon the thorns of life! I bleed!

A heavy weight of hours has chained and bowed
One too like thee: tameless, and swift, and proud.

Make me thy lyre, even as the forest is:
What if my leaves are falling like its own!
The tumult of thy mighty harmonies

Will take from both a deep, autumnal tone,
Sweet though in sadness. Be thou, Spirit fierce,
My spirit! Be thou me, impetuous one!

Drive my dead thoughts over the universe
Like withered leaves to quicken a new birth!
And, by the incantation of this verse,

Scatter, as from an unextinguished hearth
Ashes and sparks, my words among mankind!
Be through my lips to unawakened earth

The trumpet of a prophecy! O, Wind,
If Winter comes, can Spring be far behind?

October 1819

Ode to Liberty

Yet freedom, yet, thy banner, torn but flying
Streams like a thunder-storm against the wind.
BYRON

A glorious people vibrated again
   The lightning of the nations: Liberty
From heart to heart, from tower to tower, o'er Spain,
   Scattering contagious fire into the sky,
Gleamed. My soul spurned the chains of its dismay,
     And in the rapid plumes of song
     Clothed itself, sublime and strong,
(As a young eagle soars the morning clouds among,)
   Hovering in verse o'er its accustomed prey;
     Till from its station in the Heaven of fame
     The Spirit's whirlwind rapt it, and the ray
     Of the remotest sphere of living flame
Which paves the void was from behind it flung,
   As foam from a ship's swiftness, when there came
   A voice out of the deep: I will record the same.

The Sun and the serenest Moon sprang forth:
The burning stars of the abyss were hurled
Into the depths of Heaven. The daedal earth,
   That island in the ocean of the world,
Hung in its cloud of all-sustaining air:
     But this divinest universe
     Was yet a chaos and a curse,
For thou wert not: but, power from worst producing worse
   The spirit of the beasts was kindled there,
     And of the birds, and of the watery forms,
   And there was war among them, and despair
     Within them, raging without truce or terms:
The bosom of their violated nurse
   Groaned, for beasts warred on beasts, and worms on worms,
   And men on men; each heart was as a hell of storms.

Man, the imperial shape, then multiplied
   His generations under the pavilion
Of the Sun's throne: palace and pyramid,
   Temple and prison, to many a swarming million
Were, as to mountain-wolves their raggèd caves.
      This human living multitude
      Was savage, cunning, blind, and rude,
For thou wert not; but o'er the populous solitude,
   Like one fierce cloud over a waste of waves,
    Hung Tyranny; beneath, sate deified
   The sister-pest, congregator of slaves;
    Into the shadow of her pinions wide
Anarchs and priests, who feed on gold and blood
Till with the stain their inmost souls are dyed,
Drove the astonished herds of men from every side.

The nodding promontories, and blue isles,
   And cloud-like mountains, and dividuous waves
Of Greece, basked glorious in the open smiles
   Of favouring Heaven: from their enchanted caves
Prophetic echoes flung dim melody.
      On the unapprehensive wild
      The vine, the corn, the olive mild.
Grew savage yet, to human use unreconciled;
   And, like unfolded flowers beneath the sea,
    Like the man's thought dark in the infant's brain,
   Like aught that is which wraps what is to be,
    Art's deathless dreams lay veiled by many a vein
Of Parian stone; and, yet a speechless child,
   Verse murmured, and Philosophy did strain
   Her lidless eyes for thee; when o'er the Aegean main

Athens arose: a city such as vision
   Builds from the purple crags and silver towers
Of battlemented cloud, as in derision
   Of kingliest masonry: the ocean-floors
Pave it; the evening sky pavilions it;
      Its portals are inhabited
      By thunder-zonèd winds, each head
Within its cloudy wings with sun-fire garlanded,—
   A divine work! Athens, diviner yet,
    Gleamed with its crest of columns, on the will

Of man, as on a mount of diamond, set;
 For thou wert, and thine all-creative skill
Peopled, with forms that mock the eternal dead
 In marble immortality, that hill
 Which was thine earliest throne and latest oracle.

Within the surface of Time's fleeting river
 Its wrinkled image lies, as then it lay
Immovably unquiet, and for ever
 It trembles, but it cannot pass away!
The voices of thy bards and sages thunder
  With an earth-awakening blast
  Through the caverns of the past:
(Religion veils her eyes; Oppression shrinks aghast:)
 A wingèd sound of joy, and love, and wonder,
  Which soars where Expectation never flew,
 Rending the veil of space and time asunder!
  One ocean feeds the clouds, and streams, and dew;
One Sun illumines Heaven; one Spirit vast
 With life and love makes chaos ever new,
 As Athens doth the world with thy delight renew.

Then Rome was, and from thy deep bosom fairest,
 Like a wolf-cub from a Cadmaean Maenad,
She drew the milk of greatness, though thy dearest
 From that Elysian food was yet unweanèd;
And many a deed of terrible uprightness
  By thy sweet love was sanctified;
  And in thy smile, and by thy side,
Saintly Camillus lived, and firm Atilius died.
 But when tears stained thy robe of vestal whiteness,
  And gold profaned thy Capitolian throne,
  Thou didst desert, with spirit-wingèd lightness,
  The senate of the tyrants: they sunk prone
Slaves of one tyrant: Palatinus sighed
 Faint echoes of Ionian song; that tone
 Thou didst delay to hear, lamenting to disown.

From what Hyrcanian glen or frozen hill,
 Or piny promontory of the Arctic main,
Or utmost islet inaccessible,
 Didst thou lament the ruin of thy reign,

Teaching the woods and waves, and desert rocks,
    And every Naiad's ice-cold urn,
      To talk in echoes sad and stern
Of that sublimest lore which man had dared unlearn?
  For neither didst thou watch the wizard flocks
    Of the Scald's dreams, nor haunt the Druid's sleep.
  What if the tears rained through thy shattered locks
    Were quickly dried? for thou didst groan, not weep,
When from its sea of death, to kill and burn,
  The Galilean serpent forth did creep,
  And made thy world an undistinguishable heap.

A thousand years the Earth cried, 'Where art thou?'
  And then the shadow of thy coming fell
On Saxon Alfred's olive-cinctured brow:
  And many a warrior-peopled citadel,
Like rocks which fire lifts out of the flat deep,
    Arose in sacred Italy,
    Frowning o'er the tempestuous sea
Of kings, and priests, and slaves, in tower-crowned majesty;
  That multitudinous anarchy did sweep
And burst around their walls, like idle foam,
  Whilst from the human spirit's deepest deep
    Strange melody with love and awe struck dumb
Dissonant arms; and Art, which cannot die,
  With divine wand traced on our earthly home
  Fit imagery to pave Heaven's everlasting dome.

Thou huntress swifter than the Moon! thou terror
  Of the world's wolves! thou bearer of the quiver,
Whose sunlike shafts pierce tempest-wingèd Error,
  As light may pierce the clouds when they dissever
In the calm regions of the orient day!
    Luther caught thy wakening glance;
    Like lightning, from his leaden lance
Reflected, it dissolved the visions of the trance
  In which, as in a tomb, the nations lay;
And England's prophets hailed thee as their queen,
  In songs whose music cannot pass away,
    Though it must flow forever: not unseen
Before the spirit-sighted countenance
  Of Milton didst thou pass, from the sad scene
  Beyond whose night he saw, with a dejected mien.

The eager hours and unreluctant years
   As on a dawn-illumined mountain stood,
Trampling to silence their loud hopes and fears,
   Darkening each other with their multitude,
And cried aloud, 'Liberty!' Indignation
      Answered Pity from her cave;
      Death grew pale within the grave,
And Desolation howled to the destroyer, Save!
   When like Heaven's Sun girt by the exhalation
     Of its own glorious light, thou didst arise,
   Chasing thy foes from nation unto nation
     Like shadows: as if day had cloven the skies
At dreaming midnight o'er the western wave,
   Men started, staggering with a glad surprise,
   Under the lightnings of thine unfamiliar eyes.

Thou Heaven of earth! what spells could pall thee then
   In ominous eclipse? a thousand years
Bred from the slime of deep Oppression's den,
   Dyed all thy liquid light with blood and tears,
Till thy sweet stars could weep the stain away;
      How like Bacchanals of blood
      Round France, the ghastly vintage, stood
Destruction's sceptred slaves, and Folly's mitred brood!
   When one, like them, but mightier far than they,
     The Anarch of thine own bewildered powers,
   Rose: armies mingled in obscure array,
     Like clouds with clouds. darkening the sacred bowers
Of serene Heaven. He, by the past pursued,
   Rests with those dead, but unforgotten hours,
   Whose ghosts scare victor kings in their ancestral towers

England yet sleeps: was she not called of old?
   Spain calls her now, as with its thrilling thunder
Vesuvius wakens Aetna, and the cold
   Snow-crags by its reply are cloven in sunder:
O'er the lit waves every Aeolian isle
      From Pithecusa to Pelorus
      Howls, and leaps, and glares in chorus:
They cry, 'Be dim; ye lamps of Heaven suspended o'er us!'
   Her chains are threads of gold, she need but smile
     And they dissolve; but Spain's were links of steel,

Till bit to dust by virtue's keenest file.
   Twins of a single destiny! appeal
To the eternal years enthroned before us
   In the dim West; impress us from a seal,
   All ye have thought and done! Time cannot dare conceal.

Tomb of Arminius! render up thy dead
   Till, like a standard from a watch-tower's staff,
His soul may stream over the tyrant's head;
   Thy victory shall be his epitaph,
Wild Bacchanal of truth's mysterious wine,
         King-deluded Germany,
         His dead spirit lives in thee.
Why do we fear or hope? thou art already free!
   And thou, lost Paradise of this divine
      And glorious world! thou flowery wilderness!
   Thou island of eternity! thou shrine
      Where Desolation, clothed with loveliness,
Worships the thing thou wert! O Italy,
   Gather thy blood into thy heart; repress
   The beasts who make their dens thy sacred palaces.

Oh, that the free would stamp the impious name
   Of KING into the dust! or write it there,
So that this blot upon the page of fame
   Were as a serpent's path, which the light air
Erases, and the flat sands close behind!
         Ye the oracle have heard:
         Lift the victory-flashing sword,
And cut the snaky knots of this foul gordian word,
   Which, weak itself as stubble, yet can bind
      Into a mass, irrefragably firm,
   The axes and the rods which awe mankind;
      The sound has poison in it, 'tis the sperm
Of what makes life foul, cankerous, and abhorred;
   Disdain not thou, at thine appointed term,
   To set thine armèd heel on this reluctant worm.

Oh, that the wise from their bright minds would kindle
   Such lamps within the dome of this dim world,
That the pale name of PRIEST might shrink and dwindle
   Into the hell from which it first was hurled,

A scoff of impious pride from fiends impure;
　　　Till human thoughts might kneel alone,
　　　Each before the judgement-throne
Of its own aweless soul, or of the Power unknown!
　　Oh, that the words which make the thoughts obscure
　　　From which they spring, as clouds of glimmering dew
From a white lake blot Heaven's blue portraiture,
　　Were stripped of their thin masks and various hue
And frowns and smiles and splendours not their own,
　　Till in the nakedness of false and true
　　They stand before their Lord, each to receive its due!

He who taught man to vanquish whatsoever
　　Can be between the cradle and the grave
Crowned him the King of Life. Oh, vain endeavour!
　　If on his own high will, a willing slave,
He has enthroned the oppression and the oppressor.
　　　What if earth can clothe and feed
　　　Amplest millions at their need,
And power in thought be as the tree within the seed?
　　Or what if Art, an ardent intercessor,
　　　Driving on fiery wings to Nature's throne,
　　Checks the great mother stooping to caress her,
　　　And cries: 'Give me, thy child, dominion
Over all height and depth'? if Life can breed
　　New wants, and wealth from those who toil and groan,
　　Rend of thy gifts and hers a thousandfold for one!

Come thou, but lead out of the inmost cave
　　Of man's deep spirit, as the morning-star
Beckons the Sun from the Eoan wave,
　　Wisdom. I hear the pennons of her car
Self-moving, like cloud chariored by flame;
　　　Comes she not, and come ye not,
　　　Rulers of eternal thought,
To judge, with solemn truth, life's ill-apportioned lot?
　　Blind Love, and equal Justice, and the Fame
　　　Of what has been, the Hope of what will be?
O Liberty! if such could be thy name
　　　Wert thou disjoined from these, or they from thee:
If thine or theirs were treasures to be bought
　　By blood or tears, have not the wise and free
　　Wept tears, and blood like tears?—The solemn harmony

Paused, and the Spirit of that mighty singing
    To its abyss was suddenly withdrawn;
Then, as a wild swan, when sublimely winging
    Its path athwart the thunder-smoke of dawn,
Sinks headlong through the aëreal golden light
        On the heavy-sounding plain,
        When the bolt has pierced its brain;
As summer clouds dissolve, unburthened of their rain;
    As a far taper fades with fading night,
        As a brief insect dies with dying day,—
    My song, its pinions disarrayed of might,
        Drooped; o'er it closed the echoes far away
Of the great voice which did its flight sustain,
    As waves which lately paved his watery way
    Hiss round a drowner's head in their tempestuous play.

Ode to Naples

All the local and historical allusions would need a long commentary. Shelley was overjoyed at the news that a Constitutional Government was proclaimed at Naples; and this news became associated with his memories of a visit to Pompeii, the scene of the opening lines. The 'Anarchs of the North' are the Austrians. Shelley lived in hopes of the overthrow of their military occupation of Italy, as indeed of the uprising of the champions of liberty everywhere. His poems, nevertheless, are to be regarded as wishes and spiritual affirmations rather than as metrical forecasts of campaigns and achievements. His capabilities in realism, looking facts in the face and admitting the odds against the patriots in Italy and in Greece, can be studied through Mrs. Shelley's notes on *Hellas*.

I STOOD within the City disinterred;
   And heard the autumnal leaves like light footfalls
Of spirits passing through the streets; and heard
    The Mountain's slumberous voice at intervals
      Thrill through those roofless halls;
The oracular thunder penetrating shook
    The listening soul in my suspended blood;
I felt that Earth out of her deep heart spoke—
    I felt, but heard not:—through white columns glowed
      The isle-sustaining ocean-flood,
A plane of light between two heavens of azure!
   Around me gleamed many a bright sepulchre
Of whose pure beauty, Time, as if his pleasure
Were to spare Death, had never made erasure;
    But every living lineament was clear
    As in the sculptor's thought; and there
The wreaths of stony myrtle, ivy, and pine,
    Like winter leaves o'ergrown by moulded snow,
      Seemed only not to move and grow
Because the crystal silence of the air

Weighed on their life; even as the Power divine
Which then lulled all things, brooded upon mine.

Then gentle winds arose
With many a mingled close
Of wild Aeolian sound, and mountain-odours keen;
And where the Baian ocean
Welters with airlike motion,
Within, above, around its bowers of starry green,
Moving the sea-flowers in those purple caves,
Even as the ever stormless atmosphere
Floats o'er the Elysian realm,
It bore me, like an Angel, o'er the waves
Of sunlight, whose swift pinnace of dewy air
No storm can overwhelm.
I sailed, where ever flows
Under the calm Serene
A spirit of deep emotion
From the unknown graves
Of the dead Kings of Melody.
Shadowy Aornos darkened o'er the helm
The horizontal aether; Heaven stripped bare
Its depth over Elysium, where the prow
Made the invisible water white as snow;
From that Typhaean mount, Inarime.
There streamed a sunbright vapour, like the standard
Of some aethereal host;
Whilst from all the coast,
Louder and louder, gathering round, there wandered
Over the oracular woods and divine sea
Prophesyings which grew articulate—
They seize me—I must speak them!—be they fate!

Naples! thou Heart of men which ever pantest
Naked, beneath the lidless eye of Heaven!
Elysian City, which to calm enchantest
The mutinous air and sea! they round thee, even
As sleep round Love, are driven!
Metropolis of a ruined Paradise
Long lost, late won, and yet but half regained!
Bright Altar of the bloodless sacrifice,
Which armèd Victory offers up unstained

To Love, the flower-enchained!
Thou which wert one, and then didst cease to be,
Now art, and henceforth ever shalt be, free,
If Hope, and Truth, and Justice can avail,—
Hail. hail, all hail!

Thou youngest giant birth
Which from the groaning earth
Leap'st, clothed in armour of impenetrable scale!
Last of the Intercessors!
Who 'gainst the Crowned Transgressors
Pleadest before God's love! Arrayed in Wisdom's mail,
Wave thy lightning lance in mirth
Nor let thy high heart fail,
Though from their hundred gates the leagued Oppressors
With hurried legions move!
Hail, hail, all hail!

What though Cimmerian Anarchs dare blaspheme
Freedom and thee? thy shield is as a mirror
To make their blind slaves see, and with fierce gleam
To turn his hungry sword upon the wearer;
A new Actaeon's error
Shall theirs have been—devoured by their own hounds!
Be thou like the imperial Basilisk
Killing thy foe with unapparent wounds!
Gaze on Oppression, till at that dread risk
Aghast she pass from the Earth's disk:
Fear not, but gaze—for freemen mightier grow,
And slaves more feeble, gazing on their foe:—
If Hope, and Truth, and Justice may avail,
Thou shalt be great—All hail!

From Freedom's form divine,
From Nature's inmost shrine,
Strip every impious gawd, rend Error veil by veil;
O'er Ruin desolate,
O'er Falsehood's fallen state,
Sit thou sublime, unawed; be the Destroyer pale!
And equal laws be thine,
And wingèd words let sail,
Freighted with truth even from the throne of God:

That wealth, surviving fate,
Be thine.—All hail!

Didst thou not start to hear Spain's thrilling paean
From land to land re-echoed solemnly,
Till silence became music? From the Aeaean
To the cold Alps, eternal Italy
Starts to hear thine! The Sea
Which paves the desert streets of Venice laughs
In light and music; widowed Genoa wan
By moonlight spells ancestral epitaphs,
Murmuring, 'Where is Doria?' fair Milan.
Within whose veins long ran
The viper's palsying venom, lifts her heel
To bruise his head. The signal and the seal
(If Hope and Truth and Justice can avail)
Art thou of all these hopes.—O hail!

Florence! beneath the sun,
Of cities fairest one,
Blushes within her bower for Freedom's expectation:
From eyes of quenchless hope
Rome tears the priestly cope,
As ruling once by power, so now by admiration,—
An athlete stripped to run
From a remoter station
For the high prize lost on Philippi's shore:—
As then Hope, Truth, and Justice did avail,
So now may Fraud and Wrong! O hail!

Hear ye the march as of the Earth-born Forms
Arrayed against the ever-living Gods?
The crash and darkness of a thousand storms
Bursting their inaccessible abodes
Of crags and thunder-clouds?
See ye the banners blazoned to the day,
Inwrought with emblems of barbaric pride?
Dissonant threats kill Silence far away,
The serene Heaven which wraps our Eden wide
With iron light is dyed;
The Anarchs of the North lead forth their legions
Like Chaos o'er creation, uncreating;

An hundred tribes nourished on strange religions
And lawless slaveries,—down the aëreal regions
    Of the white Alps, desolating,
      Famished wolves that bide no waiting,
Blotting the glowing footsteps of old glory,
Trampling our columned cities into dust,
      Their dull and savage lust
    On Beauty's corse to sickness satiating—
They come! The fields they tread look black and hoary
With fire—from their red feet the streams run gory!

      Great Spirit, deepest Love!
      Which rulest and dost move
All things which live and are, within the Italian shore;
    Who spreadest Heaven around it,
    Whose woods, rocks, waves, surround it;
Who sittest in thy star, o'er Ocean's western floor;
Spirit of beauty! at whose soft command
    The sunbeams and the showers distil its foison
      From the Earth's bosom chill;
Oh, bid those beams be each a blinding brand
    Of lightning! bid those showers be dews of poison!
      Bid the Earth's plenty kill!
      Bid thy bright Heaven above,
      Whilst light and darkness bound it,
      Be their tomb who planned
      To make it ours and thine!
    Or, with thine harmonizing ardours fill
And raise thy sons, as o'er the prone horizon
Thy lamp feeds every twilight wave with fire—
Be man's high hope and unextinct desire
The instrument to work thy will divine!
    Then clouds from sunbeams, antelopes from leopards,
      And frowns and fears from thee,
      Would not more swiftly flee
    Than Celtic wolves from the Ausonian shepherds.—
Whatever, Spirit, from thy starry shrine
    Thou yieldest or withholdest, oh, let be
    This city of thy worship ever free!

August 1820

POEMS CHIEFLY LYRICAL

The Retrospect

CWM ELAN, 1812

Evening, To Ianthe and this passage are favourable examples of the verse written by Shelley in his best days with Harriet. Cwm Elan, now in part a reservoir, was the Welsh Estate of his uncle by marriage, Thomas Grove. In 1811 Shelley had stayed there in great perplexity and apprehension, but returning in 1812 with Harriet as his wife he felt that the darkness was past. *Evening* is one of his birthday poems to his young wife, and like the sonnet to their daughter Ianthe it deepens the difficulty of understanding what changed their union, between 1813 and 1814. Their friend and guest T.L. Peacock saw at the end of 1813 no omens of such a revulsion from the sweet security of these domestic poems.

> YE jagged peaks that frown sublime,
> Mocking the blunted scythe of Time,
> Whence I would watch its lustre pale
> Steal from the moon o'er yonder vale:
>
> Thou rock, whose bosom black and vast,
> Bared to the stream's unceasing flow,
> Ever its giant shade doth cast
> On the tumultuous surge below:
>
> Woods, to whose depths retires to die
> The wounded Echo's melody,
> And whither this lone spirit bent
> The footstep of a wild intent:
>
> Meadows! whose green and spangled breast
> These fevered limbs have often pressed,
> Until the watchful fiend Despair
> Slept in the soothing coolness there!

Have not your varied beauties seen
The sunken eye, the withering mien,
Sad traces of the unuttered pain
That froze my heart and burned my brain.
How changed since Nature's summer form
Had last the power my grief to charm,
Since last ye soothed my spirit's sadness,
Strange chaos of a mingled madness!
Changed!—not the loathsome worm that fed
In the dark mansions of the dead,
Now soaring through the fields of air,
And gathering purest nectar there,
A butterfly, whose million hues
The dazzled eye of wonder views,
Long lingering on a work so strange,
Has undergone so bright a change.
How do I feel my happiness?
I cannot tell, but they may guess
Whose every gloomy feeling gone,
Friendship and passion feel alone;
Who see mortality's dull clouds
Before affection's murmur fly,
Whilst the mild glances of her eye
Pierce the thin veil of flesh that shrouds
The spirit's inmost sanctuary.
O thou! whose virtues latest known,
First in this heart yet claim'st a throne;
Whose downy sceptre still shall share
The gentle sway with virtue there;
Thou fair in form, and pure in mind,
Whose ardent friendship rivets fast
The flowery band our fates that bind,
Which incorruptible shall last
When duty's hard and cold control
Has thawed around the burning soul,—
The gloomiest retrospects that bind
With crowns of thorn the bleeding mind,
The prospects of most doubtful hue
That rise on Fancy's shuddering view,—
Are gilt by the reviving ray
Which thou hast flung upon my day.

Stanzas

APRIL, 1814

Autobiographical as these beautiful *Stanzas* are they have some manner of a
poem in a romantic novel, such as abounded at their date. Certainly they
relate to a crisis, not recorded in detail, in Shelley's feelings about his first
marriage. He stayed at Bracknell with Mrs. Boinville and her married
daughter Cornelia Turner, and these must be the originals of the two ladies
in the poem. But in fact Cornelia had no love affair with Shelley, and Mrs.
Boinville was not likely to be ungentle to one whom she understood so well
though she might be advisory. The *Stanzas* are surely a dramatisation.

  Mutability can be referred to Shelley's personal story in 1814, but does not
depend on it; it is an elegiac poem in which the writer's survey goes far be-
yond his own case.

Away! the moor is dark beneath the moon,
  Rapid clouds have drank the last pale beam of even:
Away! the gathering winds will call the darkness soon,
  And profoundest midnight shroud the serene lights of heaven.

Pause not! The time is past! Every voice cries, Away!
  Tempt not with one last tear thy friend's ungentle mood:
Thy lover's eye, so glazed and cold, dares not entreat thy stay
  Duty and dereliction guide thee back to solitude.

Away, away! to thy sad and silent home;
  Pour bitter tears on its desolated hearth;
Watch the dim shades as like ghosts they go and come,
  And complicate strange webs of melancholy mirth.

The leaves of wasted autumn woods shall float around thine head:
  The blooms of dewy spring shall gleam beneath thy feet:
But thy soul or this world must fade in the frost that binds the dead,
  Ere midnight's frown and morning's smile, ere thou and peace may
                                                              [meet.

The cloud shadows of midnight possess their own repose,
  For the weary winds are silent, or the moon is in the deep:
Some respite to its turbulence unresting ocean knows;
  Whatever moves, or toils, or grieves, hath its appointed sleep.

Thou in the grave shalt rest—yet till the phantoms flee
  Which that house and heath and garden made dear to thee erewhile,
Thy remembrance, and repentance, and deep musings are not free
  From the music of two voices and the light of one sweet smile.

Mutability

WE are as clouds that veil the midnight moon;
  How restlessly they speed, and gleam, and quiver,
Streaking the darkness radiantly!—yet soon
  Night closes round, and they are lost for ever:

Or like forgotten lyres, whose dissonant strings
  Give various response to each varying blast,
To whose frail frame no second motion brings
  One mood or modulation like the last.

We rest.—A dream has power to poison sleep;
  We rise.—One wandering thought pollutes the day;
We feel, conceive or reason, laugh or weep;
  Embrace fond woe, or cast our cares away:

It is the same!—For, be it joy or sorrow,
  The path of its departure still is free:
Man's yesterday may ne'er be like his morrow;
  Nought may endure but Mutability.

1814

A Summer Evening Churchyard

LECHLADE, GLOUCESTERSHIRE

THE wind has swept from the wide atmosphere
Each vapour that obscured the sunset's ray;
And pallid Evening twines its beaming hair
In duskier braids around the languid eyes of Day:
Silence and Twilight, unbeloved of men,
Creep hand in hand from yon obscurest glen.

They breathe their spells towards the departing day.
Encompassing the earth, air, stars, and sea;
Light, sound, and motion own the potent sway,
Responding to the charm with its own mystery.
The winds are still, or the dry church-tower grass
Knows not their gentle motions as they pass.

Thou too, aëreal Pile! whose pinnacles
Point from one shrine like pyramids of fire,
Obeyest in silence their sweet solemn spells,
Clothing in hues of heaven thy dim and distant spire,
Around whose lessening and invisible height
Gather among the stars the clouds of night.

The dead are sleeping in their sepulchres:
And, mouldering as they sleep, a thrilling sound,
Half sense, half thought, among the darkness stirs,
Breathed from their wormy beds all living things around,
And mingling with the still night and mute sky
Its awful hush is felt inaudibly.

Thus solemnized and softened, death is mild
And terrorless as this serenest night:
Here could I hope, like some inquiring child
Sporting on graves, that death did hide from human sight
Sweet secrets, or beside its breathless sleep
That loveliest dreams perpetual watch did keep.

1815

To—

Δάκρυσι διοίσω πότμον ἄποτμον

COLERIDGE, in Mrs. Shelley's opinion, is addressed in this poem. Shelley
never met him though he apparently corresponded with him. It is
likely that he associates his own qualities and paradoxes with those
of Coleridge, if he really refers to the older poet.

OH! there are spirits of the air,
    And genii of the evening breeze,
And gentle ghosts, with eyes as fair
    As star-beams among twilight trees:—
Such lovely ministers to meet
Oft hast thou turned from men thy lonely feet.

With mountain winds, and babbling springs,
    And moonlight seas, that are the voice
Of these inexplicable things,
    Thou didst hold commune, and rejoice
When they did answer thee; but they
Cast, like a worthless boon, thy love away.

And thou hast sought in starry eyes
   Beams that were never meant for thine,
Another's wealth:—tame sacrifice
   To a fond faith! still dost thou pine?
Still dost thou hope that greeting hands,
Voice, looks, or lips, may answer thy demands?

Ah! wherefore didst thou build thine hope
   On the false earth's inconstancy?
Did thine own mind afford no scope
   Of love, or moving thoughts to thee?
That natural scenes of human smiles
Could steal the power to wind thee in their wiles?

Yes, all the faithless smiles are fled
   Whose falsehood left thee broken-hearted;
The glory of the moon is dead;
   Night's ghosts and dreams have now departed;
Thine own soul still is true to thee,
But changed to a foul fiend through misery.

This fiend, whose ghastly presence ever
   Beside thee like thy shadow hangs,
Dream not to chase;—the mad endeavour
   Would scourge thee to severer pangs.
Be as thou art. Thy settled fate,
Dark as it is, all change would aggravate.

1815

Lines

THESE are dated 5 November 1815, and the manuscript makes it certain
that they are connected with those of 5 November 1817—'That time
is dead for ever, child!' But we have no information to help in seeing
what these dates signified to Shelley and why they produced such
strange and painful verses.

> THE cold earth slept below,
>   Above the cold sky shone;
> And all around, with a chilling sound,
>   From caves of ice and fields of snow,
>   The breath of night like death did flow
>   Beneath the sinking moon.

The wintry hedge was black,
  The green grass was not seen,
The birds did rest on the bare thorn's breast,
  Whose roots, beside the pathway track,
  Had bound their folds o'er many a crack
    Which the frost had made between.

Thine eyes glowed in the glare
  Of the moon's dying light;
As a fen-fire's beam on a sluggish stream
  Gleams dimly, so the moon shone there,
  And it yellowed the strings of thy raven hair,
    That shook in the wind of night.

The moon made thy lips pale, beloved—
  The wind made thy bosom chill—
The night did shed on thy dear head
  Its frozen dew, and thou didst lie
  Where the bitter breath of the naked sky
    Might visit thee at will.

November 5, 1815

To Constantia Singing

Constantia is understood to stand for Claire Clairmont. The poem was printed in a country newspaper, but that text has not been recovered and the MSS leave uncertainties. The order of the stanzas and here and there the wording which I have chosen are my own notion of what Shelley intended; those who demur may easily consult Mrs. Shelley's arrangement and selection of readings.

Her voice is hovering o'er my soul—it lingers
  O'ershadowing it with soft and lulling wings,
The blood and life within those snowy fingers
  Teach witchcraft to the instrumental strings.
My brain is wild, my breath comes quick—
  The blood is listening in my frame,
And thronging shadows, fast and thick,

Fall on my overflowing eyes;
My heart is quivering like a flame;
   As morning dew, that in the sunbeam dies,
   I am dissolved in these consuming ecstasies.

I have no life, Constantia, now, but thee,
   Whilst, like the world-surrounding air, thy song
Flows on, and fills all things with melody.—
   Now is thy voice a tempest swift and strong,
On which, like one in trance upborne,
   Secure o'er rocks and waves I sweep,
Rejoicing like a cloud of morn.
   Now 'tis the breath of summer night,
Which when the starry waters sleep,
   Round western isles, with incense-blossoms bright,
   Lingering, suspends my soul in its voluptuous flight.

A deep and breathless awe, like the swift change
   Of dreams unseen yet felt in youthful slumbers,
Wild, sweet, but uncommunicably strange,
   Thou breathest now in fast ascending numbers.
The cope of heaven seems rent and cloven
   By the enchantment of thy strain,
And on my shoulders wings are woven,
   To follow its sublime career
Beyond the mighty moons that wane
   Upon the verge Nature's utmost sphere,
   Till the world's shadowy walls are past and disappear.

Cease, cease—for such wild lessons madmen learn.
   Thus to be lost, and thus to sink and die,
Perchance were death indeed!—Constantia, turn
   In thy dark eyes a power like light doth lie
     Even though the sounds its voice that were
      Between [thy] lips are laid to sleep:
     Within thy breath, and on thy hair
     Like odour, it is [lingering] yet
      And from thy touch like fire doth leap—
   Even while I write, my burning cheeks are wet—
   Alas, that the torn heart can bleed but not forget.

1817

To William Shelley

The billows on the beach are leaping around it,
  The bark is weak and frail,
The sea looks black, and the clouds that bound it
  Darkly strew the gale
Come with me, thou delightful child,
Come with me, though the wave is wild,
And the winds are loose, we must not stay,
Or the slaves of the law may rend thee away.

They have taken thy brother and sister dear,
  They have made them unfit for thee;
They have withered the smile and dried the tear
  Which should have been sacred to me.
To a blighting faith and a cause of crime
They have bound them slaves in youthly prime,
And they will curse my name and thee
Because we fearless are and free.

Come thou, belovèd as thou art;
  Another sleepeth still
Near thy sweet mother's anxious heart,
  Which thou with joy shalt fill,
With fairest smiles of wonder thrown
On that which is indeed our own,
And which in distant lands will be
The dearest playmate unto thee.

Fear not the tyrants will rule for ever,
  Or the priests of the evil faith;
They stand on the brink of that raging river,
  Whose waves they have tainted with death.
It is fed from the depth of a thousand dells,
Around them it foams and rages and swells;
And their swords and their sceptres I floating see,
Like wrecks on the surge of eternity.

Rest, rest, and shrink not, thou gentle child!
  The rocking of the boat thou fearest,
And the cold spray and the clamour wild?—
  There, sit between us two, thou dearest—

Me and thy mother—well we know
The storm at which thou tremblest so,
With all its dark and hungry graves,
Less cruel than the savage slaves
Who hunt us o'er these sheltering waves.

This hour will in thy memory
    Be a dream of days forgotten long,
We soon shall dwell by the azure sea
Of serene and golden Italy,
Or Greece, the Mother of the free;
    And I will teach thine infant tongue
To call upon those heroes old
In their own language, and will mould
Thy growing spirit in the flame
Of Grecian lore, that by such name
A patriot's birthright thou mayst claim!

On Fanny Godwin

The stanza printed by Mary Shelley and now reprinted is part of an
unfinished poem. In Italy, under the shadow of his son William's
unexpected death, Shelley turned to the manuscript of his verses on
Fanny Godwin's last meeting with him, and added:

Thy little footsteps on the sands
    Of a remote and linely shore;
The twinkling of thine infant hands,
    Where now the worm will feed no more,
Thy mingled look of love and glee
When we returned to gaze on thee—

Thy footsteps on the sands are fled,
    Thine eyes are dark, thy hands are cold,
And she is dead, and thou art dead,
    And the

He was probably unable through keen emotion to use the pen further.

HER voice did quiver as we parted,
    Yet knew I not that heart was broken
From which it came, and I departed
    Heeding not the words then spoken.
        Misery—O Misery,
        This world is all too wide for thee.

Lines

THAT time is dead for ever, child!
Drowned, frozen, dead for ever!
　　We look on the past
　　And stare aghast
At the spectres wailing, pale and wild
Of hopes which thou and I beguiled
　　To death on life's dark river.

The stream we gazed on then, rolled by;
Its waves are unreturning;
　　But we yet stand
　　In a lone land,
Like tombs to mark the memory
Of hopes and fears, which fade and flee,
　　Mary blest, life's brief

November 5, 1817

The Past

WILT thou forget the happy hours
Which we buried in Love's sweet bowers,
Heaping over their corpses cold
Blossoms and leaves, instead of mould?
　Blossoms which were the joys that fell,
　　And leaves, the hopes that yet remain.

Forget the dead, the past? Oh, yet
There are ghosts that may take revenge for it,
Memories that make the heart a tomb,
Regrets which glide through the spirit's gloom,
　And with ghastly whispers tell
　　That joy, once lost, is pain.

1818

To Mary

O MARY dear, that you were here
With your brown eyes bright and clear,
And your sweet voice, like a bird
Singing love to its lone mate
In the ivy bower disconsolate;
Voice the sweetest ever heard!
And your brow more . . .
Than the   sky
Of this azure Italy.
Mary dear, come to me soon,
I am not well whilst thou art far;
As sunset to the spherèd moon,
As twilight to the western star,
Thou, belovèd, art to me.

O Mary dear, that you were here;
The Castle echo whispers 'Here!'

1818

Invocation to Misery

COME, be happy!—sit near me,
Shadow-vested Misery:
Coy, unwilling, silent bride,
Mourning in thy robe of pride,
Desolation—deified!

Come, be happy!—sit near me:
Sad as I may seem to thee,
I am happier far than thou,
Lady, whose imperial brow
Is endiademed with woe.

Misery! we have known each other,
Like a sister and a brother
Living in the same lone home,
Many years—we must live some
Hours or ages yet to come.

'Tis an evil lot, and yet
Let us make the best of it;
If love can live when pleasure dies,
We two will love, till in our eyes
This heart's Hell seem Paradise.

Come, be happy!—lie thee down
On the fresh grass newly mown,
Where the Grasshopper doth sing
Merrily—one joyous thing
In a world of sorrowing!

There our tent shall be the willow,
And mine arm shall be thy pillow;
Sound and odours, sorrowful
Because they once were sweet, shall lull
Us to slumber, deep and dull.

Ha! thy frozen pulses flutter
With a love thou darest not utter.
Thou art murmuring—thou art weeping—
Is thine icy bosom leaping
While my burning heart lies sleeping?

Kiss me;—oh! thy lips are cold:
Round my neck thine arms enfold—
They are soft, but chill and dead;
And thy tears upon my head
Burn like points of frozen lead.

Hasten to the bridal bed—
Underneath the grave 'tis spread:
In darkness may our love be hid,
Oblivion be our coverlid—
We may rest, and none forbid.

Clasp me till our hearts be grown
Like two shadows into one;
Till this dreadful transport may
Like a vapour fade away,
In the sleep that lasts alway.

We may dream, in that long sleep,
That we are not those who weep;
E'en as Pleasure dreams of thee,
Life-deserting Misery,
Thou mayst dream of her with me.

Let us laugh, and make our mirth,
At the shadows of the earth,
As dogs bay the moonlight clouds.
Which, like spectres wrapped in shrouds,
Pass o'er night in multitudes.

All the wide world, beside us,
Show like multitudinous
Puppets passing from a scene;
What but mockery can they mean,
Where I am—where thou hast been?

1818

Stanzas

WRITTEN IN DEJECTION, NEAR NAPLES

THE sun is warm, the sky is clear,
    The waves are dancing fast and bright,
Blue isles and snowy mountains wear
    The purple noon's transparent might,
    The breath of the moist earth is light,
Around its unexpanded buds;
    Like many a voice of one delight,
    The winds, the birds, the ocean floods,
The City's voice itself, is soft like Solitude's.

I see the Deep's untrampled floor
    With green and purple seaweeds strown;
I see the waves upon the shore,
    Like light dissolved in star-showers, thrown:
    I sit upon the sands alone,—
The lightning of the noontide ocean
    Is flashing round me, and a tone
Arises from its measured motion,
How sweet! did any heart now share in my emotion.

Alas! I have nor hope nor health,
    Nor peace within nor calm around,
Nor that content surpassing wealth
    The sage in meditation found,
    And walked with inward glory crowned—
Nor fame, nor power, nor love, nor leisure.
    Others I see whom these surround—
Smiling they live, and call life pleasure;—
To me that cup has been dealt in another measure.

Yet now despair itself is mild,
    Even as the winds and waters are;
I could lie down like a tired child,
    And weep away the life of care
    Which I have borne and yet must bear,
Till death like sleep might steal on me,
    And I might feel in the warm air
My cheek grow cold, and hear the sea
Breathe o'er my dying brain its last monotony.

Some might lament that I were cold,
    As I, when this sweet day is gone,
Which my lost heart, too soon grown old,
    Insults with this untimely moan;
    They might lament—for I am one
Whom men love not,—and yet regret,
    Unlike this day, which, when the sun
Shall on its stainless glory set,
Will linger, thou enjoyed, like joy in memory yet.

December 1818

The Woodman and the Nightingale

A WOODMAN whose rough heart was out of tune
(I think such hearts yet never came to good)
Hated to hear, under the stars or moon,

One nightingale in an interfluous wood
Satiate the hungry dark with melody;—
And as a vale is watered by a flood,

Or as the moonlight fills the open sky
Struggling with darkness—as a tuberose
Peoples some Indian dell with scents which lie

Like clouds above the flower from which they rose,
The singing of that happy nightingale
In this sweet forest, from the golden close

Of evening till the star of dawn may fail,
Was interfused upon the silentness;
The folded roses and the violets pale

Heard her within their slumbers, the abyss
Of heaven with all its planets; the dull ear
Of the night-cradled earth; the loneliness

Of the circumfluous waters,—every sphere
And every flower and beam and cloud and wave,
And every wind of the mute atmosphere,

And every beast stretched in its ruggèd cave,
And every bird lulled on its mossy bough,
And every silver moth fresh from the grave

Which is its cradle—ever from below
Aspiring like one who loves too fair, too far,
To be consumed within the purest glow

Of one serene and unapproachèd star,
As if it were a lamp of earthly light,
Unconscious, as some human lovers are,

Itself how low, how high beyond all height
The heaven where it would perish!—and every form
That worshipped in the temple of the night

Was awed into delight, and by the charm
Girt as with an interminable zone,
Whilst that sweet bird, whose music was a storm

Of sound, shook forth the dull oblivion
Out of their dreams; harmony became love
In every soul but one.

.   .   .   .

And so this man returned with axe and saw
At evening close from killing the tall treen,
The soul of whom by Nature's gentle law

Was each a wood-nymph, and kept ever green
The pavement and the roof of the wild copse,
Chequering the sunlight of the blue serene

With jaggèd leaves,—and from the forest tops
Singing the winds to sleep—or weeping oft
Fast showers of aëreal water-drops

Into their mother's bosom, sweet and soft,
Nature's pure tears which have no bitterness;—
Around the cradles of the birds aloft

They spread themselves into the loveliness
Of fan-like leaves, and over pallid flowers
Hang like moist clouds:—or, where high branches kiss,

Make a green space among the silent bowers,
Like a vast fane in a metropolis,
Surrounded by the columns and the towers

All overwrought with branch-like traceries
In which there is religion—and the mute
Persuasion of unkindled melodies,

Odours and gleams and murmurs, which the lute
Of the blind pilot-spirit of the blast
Stirs as it sails, now grave and now acute,

Wakening the leaves and waves, ere it has passed
To such brief unison as on the brain
One tone, which never can recur, has cast,
One accent never to return again.

   .   .   .   .   .   .

The world is full of Woodmen who expel
Love's gentle Dryads from the haunts of life,
And vex the nightingales in every dell.

1818

Song to the Men of England

MEN of England, wherefore plough
For the lords who lay ye low?
Wherefore weave with toil and care
The rich robes your tyrants wear?

Wherefore feed, and clothe, and save,
From the cradle to the grave,
Those ungrateful drones who would
Drain your sweat—nay, drink your blood?

Wherefore, Bees of England, forge
Many a weapon, chain, and scourge,
That these stingless drones may spoil
The forced produce of your toil?

Have ye leisure, comfort, calm,
Shelter, food, love's gentle balm?
Or what is it ye buy so dear
With your pain and with your fear?

The seed ye sow, another reaps;
The wealth ye find, another keeps;
The robes ye weave, another wears;
The arms ye forge, another bears.

Sow seed,—but let no tyrant reap;
Find wealth,—let no impostor heap;
Weave robes,—let not the idle wear;
Forge arms,—in your defence to bear.

Shrink to your cellars, holes, and cells;
In halls ye deck another dwells.
Why shake the chains ye wrought?
     Ye see
The steel ye tempered glance on ye.

With plough and spade, and hoe and loom,
Trace your grave, and build your tomb,
And weave your winding-sheet, till fair
England be your sepulchre.

1819

An Exhortation

CHAMELEONS feed on light and air:
  Poet's food is love and fame:
If in this wide world of care
  Poets could but find the same
With as little toil as they,
  Would they ever change their hue
    As the light chameleons do,
Suiting it to every ray
    Twenty times a day?

Poets are on this cold earth,
  As chameleons might be,
Hidden from their early birth
  In a cave beneath the sea:
Where light is, chameleons change:
  Where love is not, poets do:
  Fame is love disguised: if few
Find either, never think it strange
    That poets range.

Yet dare not stain with wealth or power
    A poet's free and heavenly mind:
If bright chameleons should devour
    Any food but beams and wind
They would grow as earthly soon
    As their brother lizards are.
    Children of a sunnier star,
Spirits from beyond the moon,
    Oh, refuse the boon!

1819

To Sophia

THOU art fair, and few are fairer
  Of the Nymphs of earth or ocean;
They are robes that fit the wearer—
  Those soft limbs of thine, whose motion
Ever falls and shifts and glances
As the life within them dances.

Thy deep eyes, a double Planet,
  Gaze the wisest into madness
With soft clear fire,—the winds that fan it
  Are those thoughts of tender gladness
Which, like zephyrs on the billow,
Make thy gentle soul their pillow.

If, whatever face thou paintest
  In those eyes, grows pale with pleasure,
If the fainting soul is faintest
  When it hears thy harp's wild measure,
Wonder not that when thou speakest
Of the weak my heart is weakest.

As dew beneath the wind of morning,
  As the sea which whirlwinds waken,
As the birds at thunder's warning,
  As aught mute yet deeply shaken,
As one who feels an unseen spirit
Is my heart when thine is near it.

1819

To William Shelley

I

My lost William, thou in whom
  Some bright spirit lived, and did
That decaying robe consume
  Which its lustre faintly hid,—
Here its ashes find a tomb,
  But beneath this pyramid
Thou art not—if a thing divine
Like thee can die, thy funeral shrine
Is thy mother's grief and mine.

II

Where art thou, my gentle child?
  Let me think thy spirit feeds,
With its life intense and mild,
  The love of living leaves and weeds
Among these tombs and ruins wild;—
  Let me think that through low seeds
Of sweet flowers and sunny grass
Into their hues and scents may pass
A portion——

1819

On The Medusa of Leonardo da Vinci in the
Florentine Gallery

SINCE Shelley described it the picture has ceased to be ascribed to
Leonardo. It is of 17th century origin.

It lieth, gazing on the midnight sky,
  Upon the cloudy mountain-peak supine;
Below, far lands are seen tremblingly;
  Its horror and its beauty are divine.
Upon its lips and eyelids seems to lie
  Loveliness like a shadow, from which shine,
Fiery and lurid, struggling underneath,
The agonies of anguish and of death.

Yet it is less the horror than the grace
   Which turns the gazer's spirit into stone,
Whereon the lineaments of that dead face
   Are graven, till the characters be grown
Into itself, and thought no more can trace;
   'Tis the melodious hue of beauty thrown
Athwart the darkness and the glare of pain,
Which humanize and harmonize the strain.

And from its head as from one body grow,
   As   grass out of a watery rock,
Hairs which are vipers, and they curl and flow
   And their long tangles in each other lock,
And with unending involutions show
   Their mailèd radiance, as it were to mock
The torture and the death within, and saw
The solid air with many a raggèd jaw.

And, from a stone beside, a poisonous eft
   Peeps idly into those Gorgonian eyes;
Whilst in the air a ghastly bat, bereft
   Of sense, has flitted with a mad surprise
Out of the cave this hideous light had cleft,
   And he comes hastening like a moth that hies
After a taper; and the midnight sky
Flares, a light more dread than obscurity.

'Tis the tempestuous loveliness of terror;
   For from the serpents gleams a brazen glare
Kindled by that inextricable error,
   Which makes a thrilling vapour of the air
Become a   and ever-shifting mirror
   Of all the beauty and the terror there—
A woman's countenance, with serpent-locks,
Gazing in death on Heaven from those wet rocks.

1819

Love's Philosophy

THE alternative title *An Anacreontic* shows where Shelley derived the fancy thus prettily presented, or rather the type of fancy; for he seems to write a parallel to the Anacreontic drinking-song translated by Cowley,

> *The thirsty earth soaks up the rain.*
> *And drinks, and gapes for drink again.*
> &c.

THE fountains mingle with the river
 And the rivers with the Ocean,
The winds of Heaven mix for ever
 With a sweet emotion;
Nothing in the world is single;
 All things by a law divine
In one spirit meet and mingle.
 Why not I with thine?—

See the mountains kiss high Heaven
 And the waves clasp one another;
No sister-flower would be forgiven
 If it disdained its brother;
And the sunlight clasps the earth
 And the moonbeams kiss the sea:
What is all this sweet work worth
 If thou kiss not me?

The Cloud

SHELLEY'S unification of joy in the living thing and interest in the principles of life is found here, for his cloud is electrical and is traced scientifically, while the first word 'I' announces that he, the poet, merges himself in its adventure as a conscious creation. Tennyson follows the example in letting his 'Brook' speak in the first person. Shelley's metre, new with the poem, is exactly right for the poem; much copied by later Romantics on other topics it slips into sing-song.

I BRING fresh showers for the thirsting flowers,
    From the seas and the streams;
I bear light shade for the leaves when laid
    In their noonday dreams.
From my wings are shaken the dews that waken
    The sweet buds every one,
When rocked to rest on their mother's breast,
    As she dances about the sun.
I wield the flail of the lashing hail,
    And whiten the green plains under,
And then again I dissolve it in rain,
    And laugh as I pass in thunder.

I sift the snow on the mountains below,
    And their great pines groan aghast;
And all the night 'tis my pillow white,
    While I sleep in the arms of the blast.
Sublime on the towers of my skiey bowers,
    Lightning my pilot sits;
In a cavern under is fettered the thunder,
    It struggles and howls at fits;
Over earth and ocean, with gentle motion,
    This pilot is guiding me,
Lured by the love of the genii that move
    In the depths of the purple sea;
Over the rills, and the crags, and the hills,
    Over the lakes and the plains,
Wherever he dream, under mountain or stream,
    The Spirit he loves remains;
And I all the while bask in Heaven's blue smile,
    Whilst he is dissolving in rains.

The sanguine Sunrise, with his meteor eyes,
    And his burning plumes outspread,
Leaps on the back of my sailing rack,
    When the morning star shines dead;
As on the jag of a mountain crag,
    Which an earthquake rocks and swings,
An eagle alit one moment may sit
    In the light of its golden wings.
And when Sunset may breathe, from the lit sea beneath,
    Its ardours of rest and of love,

And the crimson pall of eve may fall
    From the depth of Heaven above,
With wings folded I rest, on mine aëry nest,
    As still as a brooding dove.

That orbèd maiden with white fire laden,
    Whom mortals the Moon,
Glides glimmering o'er my fleece-like floor,
    By the midnight breezes strewn;
And wherever the beat of her unseen feet,
    Which only the angels hear,
May have broken the woof of my tent's thin roof,
    The stars peep behind her and peer;
And I laugh to see them whirl and flee,
    Like a swarm of golden bees,
When I widen the rent in my wind-built tent,
    Till the calm rivers, lakes, and seas,
Like strips of the sky fallen through me on high,
    Are each paved with the moon and these.

I bind the Sun's throne with a burning zone,
    And the Moon's with a girdle of pearl;
The volcanoes are dim, and the stars reel and swim,
    When the whirlwinds my banner unfurl.
From cape to cape, with a bridge-like shape,
    Over a torrent sea,
Sunbeam-proof, I hang like a roof,—
    The mountains its columns be.
The triumphal arch through which I march
    With hurricane, fire, and snow,
When the Powers of the air are chained to my chair,
    Is the million-coloured bow;
The sphere-fires above its soft colours wove,
    While the moist Earth was laughing below.

I am the daughter of Earth and Water,
    And the nursling of the Sky;
I pass through the pores of the ocean and shores;
    I change, but I cannot die.
For after the rain when with never a stain
    The pavilion of Heaven is bare,
And the winds and sunbeams with their convex gleams
    Build up the blue dome of air,

I silently laugh at my own cenotaph,
    And out of the caverns of rain,
Like a child from the womb, like a ghost from the tomb,
    I arise and unbuild it again.

1820

To a Skylark

THE Anacreontic poem 'The Grasshopper' translated by Cowley,—

> *Happy Insect! what can be*
> *In happiness compared to thee?*
> *Fed with nourishment divine,*

and so on,—may have assisted in the inception of this brilliant song.
The best skylarks in English poetry, which rings with them, are those
of Shakespeare, Milton, Wordsworth, Coleridge, John Clare, and
George Meredith, with Shelley's the blithest of all. If the opinion seem,
presumptuous I take refuge behind Thomas Hardy's lovely poem
written in allusion to Shelley's and in the neighbourhood where Shelley
hailed his *Sprite, or Bird.*

HAIL to thee, blithe Spirit!
    Bird thou never wert,
That from Heaven, or near it,
    Pourest thy full heart
In profuse strains of unpremeditated art.

Higher still and higher
    From the earth thou springest
Like a cloud of fire;
    The blue deep thou wingest,
And singing still dost soar,
        and soaring ever singest.

In the golden lightning
    Of the sunken sun,
O'er which clouds are bright'ning,
    Thou dost float and run;
Like an unbodied joy
        whose race is just begun.

The pale purple even
  Melts around thy flight;
Like a star of Heaven,
  In the broad daylight
Thou art unseen, but yet I hear thy shrill delight,

Keen as are the arrows
  Of that silver sphere,
Whose intense lamp narrows
  In the white dawn clear
Until we hardly see—we feel that it is there.

All the earth and air
  With thy voice is loud,
As, when night is bare,
  From one lonely cloud
The moon rains out her beams,
  and Heaven is overflowed.

What thou art we know not;
  What is most like thee?
From rainbow clouds there flow not
  Drops so bright to see
As from thy presence showers a rain of melody.

Like a Poet hidden
  In the light of thought,
Singing hymns unbidden,
  Till the world is wrought
To sympathy with hopes and fears it heeded not.

Like a high-born maiden
  In a palace-tower,
Soothing her love-laden
  Soul in secret hour
With music sweet as love,
  which overflows her bower:

Like a glow-worm golden
  In a dell of dew,
Scattering unbeholden
  Its aëreal hue
Among the flowers and grass,
  which screen it from the view!

Like a rose embowered
In its own green leaves,
By warm winds deflowered,
Till the scent it gives
Makes faint with too much sweet
those heavy-wingèd thieves:

Sound of vernal showers
On the twinkling grass,
Rain-awakened flowers,
All that ever was
Joyous, and clear, and fresh,
thy music doth surpass:

Teach us, Sprite or Bird,
What sweet thoughts are thine:
I have never heard
Praise of love or wine
That panted forth a flood
of rapture so divine.

Chorus Hymeneal,
Or triumphal chant,
Matched with thine would be all
But an empty vaunt,
A thing wherein we feel
there is some hidden want.

What objects are the fountains
Of thy happy strain?
What fields, or waves, or mountains?
What shapes of sky or plain?
What love of thine own kind?
what ignorance of pain?

With thy clear keen joyance
Languor cannot be:
Shadow of annoyance
Never came near thee:
Thou lovest—but ne'er knew
love's sad satiety.

Waking or asleep,
   Thou of death must deem
Things more true and deep
   Than we mortals dream,
Or how could thy notes flow
      in such a crystal stream?

We look before and after,
   And pine for what is not:
Our sincerest laughter
   With some pain is fraught;
Our sweetest songs are those
      that tell of saddest thought.

Yet if we could scorn
   Hate, and pride, and fear;
If we were things born
   Not to shed a tear,
I know not how thy joy
      we ever should come near.

Better than all measures
   Of delightful sound,
Better than all treasures
   That in books are found,
Thy skill to poet were,
      thou scorner of the ground!

Teach me half the gladness
   That thy brain must know,
Such harmonious madness
   From my lips would flow
The world should listen
      then—as I am listening now.

1820

To—

I FEAR thy kisses, gentle maiden,
   Thou needest not fear mine;
My spirit is too deeply laden
   Even to burthen thine.

I fear thy mien, thy tone, thy motion,
    Thou needest not fear mine;
Innocent is the heart's devotion
    With which I worship thine.

1820

The Question

THE region where the dreamer found himself could be the Sussex
country where the river Arun winds. That is Shelley's old home, still
portrayed in these lines. This, I fancy, may yield the clue to the person
in Shelley's mind and the sad daylight meaning of the whole poem.

I DREAMED that, as I wandered by the way,
    Bare Winter suddenly was changed to Spring,
And gentle odours led my steps astray,
    Mixed with a sound of waters murmuring
Along a shelving bank of turf, which lay
    Under a copse, and hardly dared to fling
Its green arms round the bosom of the stream,
But kissed it and then fled, as thou mightest in dream.

There grew pied wind-flowers and violets,
    Daisies, those pearled Arcturi of the earth,
The constellated flower that never sets;
    Faint oxslips; tender bluebells, at whose birth
The sod scarce heaved; and that tall flower that wets——
    Like a child, half in tenderness and mirth—
Its mother's face with Heaven's collected tears,
When the low wind, its playmate's voice, it hears.

And in the warm hedge grew lush eglantine,
    Green cowbind and the moonlight-coloured may,
And cherry-blossoms, and white cups, whose wine
    Was the bright dew, yet drained not by the day;
And wild roses, and ivy serpentine,
    With its dark buds and leaves, wandering astray;
And flowers azure, black, and streaked with gold,
Fairer than any wakened eyes behold.

And nearer to the river's trembling edge
   There grew broad flag-flowers, purple pranked with white,
And starry river buds among the sedge,
   And floating water-lilies, broad and bright,
Which lit the oak that overhung the hedge
   With moonlight beams of their own watery light;
And bulrushes, and reeds of such deep green
As soothed the dazzled eye with sober sheen.

Methought that of these visionary flowers
   I made a nosegay, bound in such a way
That the same hues, which in their natural bowers
   Were mingled or opposed, the like array
Kept these imprisoned children of the Hours
   Within my hand,—and then, elate and gay,
I hastened to the spot whence I had come,
That I might there present it!—Oh! to whom?

1820

The Two Spirits

AN ALLEGORY

UNDER this title Mary Shelley brought together the two passages
given. Subsequent editors, lacking MSS., have followed her. Shelley
may have meant the second passage as a metrical experiment; it is,
apart from the music, distinct from the allegory.

First Spirit

O THOU, who plumed with strong desire
   Wouldst float above the earth, beware!
A Shadow tracks thy flight of fire—
      Night is coming!
Bright are the regions of the air,
And among the winds and beams
   It were delight to wander there—
      Night is coming!

Second Spirit

The deathless stars are bright above;
   If I would cross the shade of night
Within my heart is the lamp of love,
      And that is day!

And the moon will smile with gentle light
On my golden plumes where'er they move;
   The meteors will linger round my flight,
      And make night day.

First Spirit

But if the whirlwinds of darkness waken
   Hail, and lightning, and stormy rain;
    See, the bounds of the air are shaken—
      Night is coming!
   The red swift clouds of the hurricane
Yon declining sun have overtaken,
    The clash of the hail sweeps over the plain—
      Night is coming!

Second Spirit

I see the light, and I hear the sound;
   I'll sail on the flood of the tempest dark,
With the calm within and the light around
    Which makes night day:
   And thou, when the gloom is deep and stark,
Look from thy dull earth, slumber-bound,
    My moon-like flight thou then mayst mark
      On high, far away.

      * * *

Some say there is a precipice
   Where one vast pine is frozen to ruin
O'er piles of snow and chasms of ice
    Mid Alpine mountains;
   And that the languid storm pursuing
That wingèd shape, for ever flies
   Round those hoar branches, aye renewing
    Its aëry fountains.

Some say when nights are dry and clear,
   And the death-dews sleep on the morass,
Sweet whispers are heard by the traveller,
    Which make night day:
   And a silver shape like his early love doth pass
Upborne by her wild and glittering hair,
   And when he awakes on the fragrant grass,
    He finds night day.

1820

The Waning Moon

AND like a dying lady, lean and pale,
Who totters forth, wrapped in a gauzy veil,
Out of her chamber, led by the insane
And feeble wanderings of her fading brain,
The moon arose up in the murky East,
A white and shapeless light—

1820

To the Moon

ART thou pale for weariness
Of climbing heaven and gazing on the earth,
    Wandering companionless
Among the stars that have a different birth,—
And ever changing, like a joyless eye
That finds no object worth its constancy?

1820

Summer and Winter

IT was a bright and cheerful afternoon,
Towards the end of the sunny month of June,
When the north wind congregates in crowds
The floating mountains of the silver clouds
From the horizon—and the stainless sky
Opens beyond them like eternity.
All things rejoiced beneath the sun; the weeds,
The river, and the corn-fields, and the reeds;
The willow leaves that glanced in the light breeze,
And the firm foliage of the larger trees.

It was a winter such as when birds die
In the deep forests; and the fishes lie
Stiffened in the translucent ice, which makes
Even the mud and slime of the warm lakes
A wrinkled clod as hard as brick; and when,
Among their children, comfortable men
Gather about great fires, and yet feel cold:
[Alas, then, for the homeless beggar old!]

1820

The World's Wanderers

TELL me, thou Star, whose wings of light
Speed thee in thy fiery flight,
In what cavern of the night
      Will thy pinions close now?

Tell me, Moon, thou pale and gray
Pilgrim of Heaven's homeless way,
In what depth of night or day
      Seekest thou repose now?

Weary Wind, who wanderest
Like the world's rejected guest,
Hast thou still some secret nest
      On the tree or billow?

1820

Time Long Past

LIKE the ghost of a dear friend dead
      Is Time long past.
A tone which is now forever fled,
A hope which is now forever past,
A love so sweet it could not last,
      Was Time long past.

There were sweet dreams in the night
   Of Time long past:
And, was it sadness or delight,
Each day a shadow onward cast
Which made us wish it yet might last—
   That Time long past.

There is regret, almost remorse,
   For Time long past.
'Tis like a child's belovèd corse
A father watches, till at last
Beauty is like remembrance, cast
   From Time long past.

To Night

SWIFTLY walk o'er the western wave,
   Spirit of Night!
Out of the misty eastern cave,
Where, all the long and lone daylight,
Thou wovest dreams of joy and fear,
Which make thee terrible and dear,—
   Swift be thy flight!

Wrap thy form in a mantle gray,
   Star-inwrought!
Blind with thine hair the eyes of Day;
Kiss her until she be wearied out,
Then wander o'er city, and sea, and land,
Touching all with thine opiate wand—
   Come, long-sought!

When I arose and saw the dawn,
   I sighed for thee;
When light rode high, and the dew was gone,
And noon lay heavy on flower and tree,
And the weary Day turned to his rest,
Lingering like an unloved guest,
   I sighed for thee.

Thy brother Death came, and cried,
   Wouldst thou me?
Thy sweet child Sleep, the filmy-eyed,
Murmured like a noontide bee,
Shall I nestle near thy side?
Wouldst thou me?—And I replied,
   No, not thee!

Death will come when thou art dead,
   Soon, too soon—
Sleep will come when thou art fled;
Of neither would I ask the boon
I ask of thee, belovèd Night—
Swift be thine approaching flight,
   Come soon, soon!

1821

Time

UNFATHOMABLE Sea! whose waves are years,
  Ocean of Time, whose waters of deep woe
Are brackish with the salt of human tears!
  Thou shoreless flood, which in thy ebb and flow
Claspest the limits of mortality,
And sick of prey, yet howling on for more,
Vomitest thy wrecks on its inhospitable shore;
  Treacherous in calm, and terrible in storm,
   Who shall put forth on thee,
   Unfathomable Sea?

1821

From the Arabic:

AN IMITATION

My faint spirit was sitting in the light
  Of thy looks, my love;
It panted for thee like the hind at noon
  For the brooks, my love.
Thy barb whose hoofs outspeed the tempest's flight
  Bore thee far from me;
My heart, for my weak feet were weary soon,
  Did companion thee.

Ah! fleeter far than fleetest storm or steed,
　　　Or the death they bear,
The heart which tender thought clothes like a dove
　　　With the wings of care;
In the battle, in the darkness, in the need,
　　　Shall mine cling to thee,
Nor claim one smile for all the comfort, love,
　　　It may bring to thee.

1821

To Emilia Viviani

MADONNA, wherefore hast thou sent to me
　　　Sweet-basil and mignonette?
Embleming love and health, which never yet
In the same wreath might be.
　　　Alas, and they are wet!
Is it with thy kisses or thy tears?
　　　For never rain or dew
　　　Such fragrance drew
From plant or flower—the very doubt endears
　　　My sadness ever new,
The sighs I breathe, the tears I shed for thee.

Send the stars light, but send not love to me,
　　　In whom love ever made
Health like a heap of embers soon to fade—

1821

The Fugitives

IN the very popular poem *Lord Ullin's Daughter* Thomas Campbell
had used a similar theme. Shelley goes far beyond him in *effects*, the
clanging of great bells and the flashes from the batteries; the father on
the top turret is a Count Cenci.

THE waters are flashing,
The white hail is dashing,
The lightnings are glancing,
The hoar-spray is dancing—
    Away!

The whirlwind is rolling,
The thunder is tolling,
The forest is swinging,
The minster bells ringing—
    Come away!

The Earth is like Ocean,
Wreck-strewn and in motion:
Bird, beast, man and worm
Have crept out of the storm—
    Come away!

'Our boat has one sail,
And the helmsman is pale:—
A bold pilot I trow,
Who should follow us now,'—
    Shouted he—

And she cried: 'Ply the oar!
Put off gaily from shore!'—
As she spoke, bolts of death
Mixed with hail, specked their path
    O'er the sea.

And from isle, tower and rock,
The blue beacon-cloud broke,
And though dumb in the blast,
The red cannon flashed fast
    From the lee.

And 'Fear'st thou ?' and 'Fear'st thou?'
And 'Seest thou?' and 'Hear'st thou?'
And 'Drive we not free
O'er the terrible sea,
    I and thou?'

One boat-cloak did cover
The loved and the lover—
Their blood beats one measure,
They murmur proud pleasure
    Soft and low;—

While around the lashed Ocean,
Like mountains in motion,
Is withdrawn and uplifted,
Sunk, shattered and shifted
    To an fro.

In the court of the fortress
Beside the pale portress.
Like a bloodhound well beaten
The bridegroom stands, eaten
    By shame;

On the topmost watch-turret,
As a death-boding spirit,
Stands the gray tyrant father,
To his voice the mad weather
    Seems tame;

And with curses as wild
As e'er clung to child,
He devotes to the blast.
The best, loveliest and last
    Of his name!

1821

To—

Music, when soft voices die,
Vibrates in the memory—
Odours, when sweet violets sicken,
Live within the sense they quicken.

Rose leaves, when the rose is dead,
Are heaped for the belovèd's bed;
And so thy thoughts, when thou art gone,
Love itself shall slumber on.

1821

Song

Rarely, rarely, comest thou,
    Spirit of Delight!
Wherefore hast thou left me now
    Many a day and night?
Many a weary night and day
'Tis since thou art fled away.

How shall ever one like me
    Win thee back again?
With the joyous and the free
    Thou wilt scoff at pain.
Spirit false! thou hast forgot
    All but those who need thee not.

As a lizard with the shade
    Of a trembling leaf,
Thou with sorrow art dismayed;
    Even the sighs of grief
Reproach thee, that thou art not near,
And reproach thou wilt not hear.

Let me set my mournful ditty
    To a merry measure;
Thou wilt never come for pity,
    Thou wilt come for pleasure;
Pity then will cut away
Those cruel wings, and thou wilt stay.

I love all that thou lovest,
  Spirit of Delight!
The fresh Earth in new leaves dressed,
  And the starry night;
Autumn evening, and the morn
When the golden mists are born.

I love snow, and all the forms
  Of the radiant frost;
I love waves, and winds, and storms,
  Everything almost
Which is Nature's, and may be
Untainted by man's misery.

I love tranquil solitude,
  And such society
As is quiet, wise, and good;
  Between thee and me
What difference? but thou dost possess
  The things I seek, not love them less.

I love Love—though he has wings,
  And like light can flee,
But above all other things,
  Spirit, I love thee—
Thou art love and life! Oh, come,
Make once more my heart thy home.

1821

Mutability

THE flower that smiles to-day
    To-morrow dies;
All that we wish to stay
    Tempts and then flies.
What is this world's delight?
Lightning that mocks the night,
    Brief even as bright.

Virtue, how frail it is!
                Friendship how rare!
Love, how it sells poor bliss
                For proud despair!
But we, though soon they fall,
Survive their joy, and all
                Which ours we call.

Whilst skies are blue and bright,
                Whilst flowers are gay,
Whilst eyes that change ere night
                Make glad the day;
Whilst yet the calm hours creep,
Dream thou—and from thy sleep
                Then wake to weep.

1821

Lines Written on Hearing the News of the Death of Napoleon

WHAT! alive and so bold, O Earth?
    Art thou not overbold?
    What! leapest thou forth as of old
In the light of thy morning mirth,
The last of the flock of the starry fold?
Ha! leapest thou forth as of old?
Are not the limbs still when the ghost is fled,
And canst thou move, Napoleon being dead?

How! is not thy quick heart cold?
    What spark is alive on thy hearth?
How! is not *his* death-knell knolled?
    And livest *thou* still, Mother Earth?
Thou wert warming thy fingers old
O'er the embers covered and cold
Of that most fiery spirit, when it fled—
What, Mother, do you laugh now he is dead?

'Who has known me of old,' replied Earth,
  'Or who has my story told?
  It is thou who art overbold.'
And the lightning of scorn laughed forth
As she sung, 'To my bosom I fold
All my sons when their knell is knolled,
And so with living motion all are fed,
And the quick spring like weeds out of the dead.

'Still alive and still bold,' shouted Earth,
  'I grow bolder and still more bold.
  The dead fill me ten thousandfold
Fuller of speed, and splendour, and mirth.
I was cloudy, and sullen, and cold,
Like a frozen chaos uprolled,
Till by the spirit of the mighty dead
My heart grew warm. I feed on whom I fed.

'Ay, alive and still bold,' muttered Earth,
  'Napoleon's fierce spirit rolled,
  In terror and blood and gold,
A torrent of ruin to death from his birth.
Leave the millions who follow to mould
The metal before it be cold;
And weave into his shame, which like the dead
Shrouds me, the hopes that from his glory fled.'

1821

The Aziola

'Do you not hear the Aziola cry?
  Methinks she must be nigh,'
    Said Mary, as we sate
In dusk, ere stars were lit, or candles brought;
    And I, who thought
  This Aziola was some tedious woman,
    Asked, 'Who is Aziola?' How elate
  I felt to know that it was nothing human,

No mockery of myself to fear or hate:
    And Mary saw my soul,
And laughed, and said, 'Disquiet yourself not;
    'Tis nothing but a little downy owl.'

Sad Aziola! many an eventide
    Thy music I had heard
By wood and stream, meadow and mountain-side,
    And fields and marshes wide,—
Such as nor voice, nor lute, nor wind, nor bird,
    The soul ever stirred;
Unlike and far sweeter than them all.
Sad Aziola! from that moment I
    Loved thee and thy sad cry.

1821

A Lament

O WORLD! O life! O time!
On whose last steps I climb,
    Trembling at that where I had stood before;
When will return the glory of your prime?
        No more—Oh, never more!

Out of the day and night
A joy has taken flight;
    Fresh spring, and summer, and winter hoar,
Move my faint heart with grief, but with delight
        No more—Oh, never more!

1821

Remembrance

SWIFTER far than summer's flight—
Swifter far than youth's delight—
Swifter far than happy night,
        Art thou come and gone—
As the earth when leaves are dead,
As the night when sleep is sped,
As the heart when joy is fled,
        I am left lone, alone.

The swallow summer comes again—
The owlet night resumes her reign—
But the wild-swan youth is fain
     To fly with thee, false as thou.—
My heart each day desires the morrow;
Sleep itself is turned to sorrow;
Vainly would my winter borrow
     Sunny leaves from any bough.

Lilies for a bridal bed—
Roses for a matron's head—
Violets for a maiden dead—
     Pansies let *my* flowers be:
On the living grave I bear
Scatter them without a tear—
Let no friend, however dear,
     Waste one hope, one fear for me.

1821

To Edward Williams

THE serpent is shut out from Paradise.
    The wounded deer must seek the herb no more
      In which its heart-cure lies:
    The widowed dove must cease to haunt a bower
Like that from which its mate with feignèd sighs
      Fled in the April hour.
    I too must seldom seek again
Near happy friends a mitigated pain.

Of hatred I am proud,—with scorn content;
    Indifference, that once hurt me, now is grown
      Itself indifferent;
    But, not to speak of love, pity alone
Can break a spirit already more than bent.

The miserable one
Turns the mind's poison into food,—
Its medicine is tears,—its evil good.

Therefore, if now I see you seldomer,
        Dear friends, dear *friend*! know that I only fly
            Your looks, because they stir
            Griefs that should sleep, and hopes that cannot die:
The very comfort that they minister
        I scarce can bear, yet I,
            So deeply is the arrow gone,
Should quickly perish if it were withdrawn.

When I return to my cold home, you ask
        Why I am not as I have ever been.
            You spoil me for the task
            Of acting a forced part in life's dull scene,—
Of wearing on my brow the idle mask
        Of author, great or mean,
            In the world's carnival. I sought
Peace thus, and but in you I found it not.

Full half an hour, to-day, I tried my lot
        With various flowers, and every one still said,
            'She loves me—loves me not.'
            And if this meant a vision long since fled—
If it meant fortune, fame, or peace of thought—
        If it meant,—but I dread
            To speak what you may know too well:
Still there was truth in the sad oracle.

The crane o'er seas and forests seeks her home;
        No bird so wild but has its quiet nest,
            When it no more would roam;
            The sleepless billows on the ocean's breast
Break like a bursting heart, and die in foam,
        And thus at length find rest:
            Doubtless there is a place of peace
Where *my* weak heart and all its throbs will cease.

I asked her, yesterday, if she believed
    That I had resolution. One who *had*
      Would ne'er have thus relieved
His heart with words,—but what his judgement bade
Would do, and leave the scorner unrelieved.
      These verses are too sad
    To send to you, but that I know,
Happy yourself, you feel another's woe.

1821

To—

ONE word is too often profaned
    For me to profane it,
One feeling too falsely disdained
    For thee to disdain it;
One hope is too like despair
    For prudence to smother,
And pity from thee more dear
    Than that from another.

I can give not what men call love,
    But wilt thou accept not
The worship the heart lifts above
    And the Heavens reject not,—
The desire of the moth for the star,
    Of the night for the morrow,
The devotion to something afar
    From the sphere of our sorrow?

1821

To—

WHEN passion's trance is overpast,
If tenderness and truth could last,
Or live, whilst all wild feelings keep
Some mortal slumber, dark and deep,
I should not weep, I should not weep!

It were enough to feel, to see,
Thy soft eyes gazing tenderly,
And dream the rest—and burn and be
The secret food of fires unseen,
Couldst thou but be as thou hast been.

After the slumber of the year
The woodland violets reappear;
All things revive in field or grove,
And sky and sea, but two, which move
And form all others, life and love.

1821

Evening: Ponte al Mare, Pisa

THE sun is set; the swallows are asleep;
    The bats are flitting fast in the gray air;
The slow soft toads out of damp corners creep,
    And evening's breath, wandering here and there
Over the quivering surface of the stream,
Wakes not one ripple from its summer dream.

There is no dew on the dry grass to-night,
    Nor damp within the shadow of the trees;
The wind is intermitting, dry, and light;
    And in the inconstant motion of the breeze
The dust and straws are driven up and down,
And whirled about the pavement of the town.

Within the surface of the fleeting river
  The wrinkled image of the city lay,
Immovably unquiet, and forever
  It trembles, but it never fades away;
Go to the . . .
You, being changed, will find it then as now.

The chasm in which the sun has sunk is shut
  By darkest barriers of cinereous cloud,
Like mountain over mountain huddled—but
  Growing and moving upwards in a crowd,
And over it a space of watery blue,
Which the keen evening star is shining through.

1821

The Boat on the Serchio

LIKE many poems of Shelley, this is still being re-assembled from the
disorder of his notebooks. Perhaps he never made a fair copy, or wrote
the conclusion. As it is printed the conversation between the two
Englishmen includes alternative passages. The reader may choose
between them. See an article by Mr. Neville Rogers, *Times Literary
Supplement*, August 1951.

The boat, of course, was not that in which Shelley and Williams met
their death but its smaller predecessor. The allusion to Eton has its
own interest, and does not agree with Shelley's once usual tone of
embittered memory of his school life.

OUR boat is asleep on Serchio's stream,
Its sails are folded like thoughts in a dream,
The helm sways idly, hither and thither;
  Dominic, the boatman, has brought the mast,
  And the oars, and the sails; but 'tis sleeping fast,
Like a beast, unconscious of its tether.

The stars burnt out in the pale blue air,
And the thin white moon lay withering there;
To tower, and cavern, and rift, and tree,
The owl and the bat fled drowsily.
Day had kindled the dewy woods,
  And the rocks above and the stream below,

And the vapours in their multitudes,
    And the Apennines' shroud of summer snow,
And clothed with light of aëry gold
The mists in their eastern caves uprolled.

Day had awakened all things that be,
The lark and the thrush and the swallow free,
    And the milkmaid's song and the mower's scythe,
And the matin-bell and the mountain bee:
Fireflies were quenched on the dewy corn,
    Glow-worms went out on the river's brim,
    Like lamps which a student forgets to trim:
The beetle forgot to wind his horn,
    The crickets were still in the meadow and hill:
Like a flock of rooks at a farmer's gun
Night's dreams and terrors, every one,
Fled from the brains which are their prey
From the lamp's death to the morning ray.

All rose to do the task He set to each,
    Who shaped us to His ends and not our own;
The million rose to learn, and one to teach
    What none yet ever knew or can be known.
        And many rose
    Whose woe was such that fear became desire;—
Melchior and Lionel were not among those;
They from the throng of men had stepped aside,
And made their home under the green hill-side.
It was that hill, whose intervening brow
    Screens Lucca from the Pisan's envious eye,
Which the circumfluous plain waving below,
    Like a wide lake of green fertility,
With streams and fields and marshes bare,
    Divides from the far Apennines—which lie
Islanded in the immeasurable air.

'What think you, as she lies in her green cove,
Our little sleeping boat is dreaming of?'
'If morning dreams are true, why I should guess
That she was dreaming of our idleness,
And of the miles of watery way
We should have led her by this time of day.'—

'Never mind,' said Lionel,
'Give care to the winds, they can bear it well
About yon poplar-tops; and see
The white clouds are driving merrily,
And the stars we miss this morn will light
More willingly our return to-night.—
List, my dear fellow; the breeze blows fair:
How it whistles, Dominic's long black hair!
Hear how it sings into the air—'

—'Of us and of our lazy motions,'
    Impatiently said Melchior,
'If I can guess a boat's emotions;
    And how we ought, two hours before,
To have been the devil knows where.'
And then, in such transalpine Tuscan
As would have killed a Della-Cruscan,

.   .   .   .   .

So, Lionel according to his art
    Weaving his idle words, Melchior said:
'She dreams that we are not yet out of bed;
We'll put a soul into her, and a heart
Which like a dove chased by a dove shall beat.'

.   .   .   .   .

        'Ay, heave the ballast overboard,
    And stow the eatables in the aft locker.'
'Would not this keg be best a little lowered?'
'No, now all's right.' 'Those bottles of warm tea—
(Give me some straw)—must be stowed tenderly;
Such as we used, in summer after six,
To cram in greatcoat pockets, and to mix
Hard eggs and radishes and rolls at Eton,
And, couched on stolen hay in those green harbours
Farmers called gaps, and we schoolboys called arbours,
Would feast till eight.'

.   .   .   .   .

        With a bottle in one hand,
    As if his very soul were at a stand,
Lionel stood—when Melchior brought him steady:—
'Sit at the helm—fasten this sheet—all ready!'

The chain is loosed, the sails are spread,
  The living breath is fresh behind,
As, with dews and sunrise fed,
  Comes the laughing morning wind;—
The sails are full, the boat makes head
Against the Serchio's torrent fierce,
Then flags with intermitting course,
  And hangs upon the wave, and stems
  The tempest of the . . .
Which fervid from its mountain source
Shallow, smooth and strong doth come,—
Swift as fire, tempestuously
It sweeps into the affrighted sea;
In morning's smile its eddies coil,
Its billows sparkle, toss and boil,
Torturing all its quiet light
Into columns fierce and bright.

    The Serchio, twisting forth
Between the marble barriers which it clove
  At Ripafratta, leads through the dread chasm
The wave that died the death which lovers love,
  Living in what it sought; as if this spasm
Had not yet passed, the toppling mountains cling,
  But the clear stream in full enthusiasm
Pours itself on the plain, then wandering
  Down one clear path of effluence crystalline
Sends its superfluous waves, that they may fling
  At Arno's feet tribute of corn and wine;
Then, through the pestilential deserts wild
  Of tangled marsh and woods of stunted pine,
It rushes to the Ocean.

1821

Lines

WHEN the lamp is shattered
The light in the dust lies dead—
　When the cloud is scattered
The rainbow's glory is shed.
　When the lute is broken,
Sweet tones are remembered not;
　When the lips have spoken,
Loved accents are soon forgot.

　As music and splendour
Survive not the lamp and the lute,
　The heart's echoes render
No song when the spirit is mute:—
　No song but sad dirges,
Like the wind through a ruined cell,
　Or the mournful surges
That ring the dead seaman's knell.

　When hearts have once mingled
Love first leaves the well-built nest;
　The weak one is singled
To endure what it once possessed.
　O Love! who bewailest
The frailty of all things here,
　Why choose you the frailest
For your cradle, your home, and your bier?

　Its passions will rock thee
As the storms rock the ravens on high;
　Bright reason will mock thee,
Like the sun from a wintry sky.
　From thy nest every rafter
Will rot, and thine eagle home
　Leave thee naked to laughter,
When leaves fall and cold winds come.

1822

To Jane: The Invitation

BEST and brightest, come away!
Fairer far than this fair Day,
Which like thee to those in sorrow
Comes to bid a sweet good-morrow
To the rough Year just awake
In its cradle on the brake.
The brightest hour of unborn Spring,
Through the winter wandering,
Found, it seems, the halcyon Morn
To hoar February born.
Bending from Heaven, in azure mirth,
It kissed the forehead of the Earth,
And smiled upon the silent sea,
And bade the frozen streams be free,
And waked to music all their fountains,
And breathed upon the frozen mountains,
And like a prophetess of May
Strewed flowers upon the barren way,
Making the wintry world appear
Like one on whom thou smilest, dear.

Away, away, from men and towns,
To the wild wood and the downs—
To the silent wilderness
Where the soul need not repress
Its music lest it should not find
An echo in another's mind,
While the touch of Nature's art
Harmonizes heart to heart,
I leave this notice on my door
For each accustomed visitor:—
'I am gone into the fields
To take what this sweet hour yields;—
Reflection, you may come to-morrow,
Sit by the fireside with Sorrow.—
You with the unpaid bill, Despair,—
You, tiresome verse-reciter, Care,—

I will pay you in the grave,—
Death will listen to your stave.
Expectation too, be off!
To-day is for itself enough;
Hope, in pity mock not Woe
With smiles, nor follow where I go;
Long having lived on thy sweet food,
At length I find one moment's good
After long pain—with all you love,
This you never told me of.'

Radiant Sister of the Day,
Awake! arise! and come away!
To the wild woods and the plains,
And the pools where winter rains
Image all their roof of leaves,
Where the pine its garland weaves
Of sapless green and ivy dun
Round stems that never kiss the sun;
Where the lawns and pastures be,
And the sandhills of the sea;—
Where the melting hoar-frost wets
The daisy-star that never sets,
And wind-flowers, and violets,
Which yet join not scent to hue,
Crown the pale year weak and new;
When the night is left behind
In the deep east, dun and blind,
And the blue noon is over us,
And the multitudinous
Billows murmur at our feet,
Where the earth and ocean meet,
And all things seem only one
In the universal sun.

1820

To Jane: The Recollection

Now the last day of many days,
    All beautiful and bright as thou,
        The loveliest and the last, is dead,
Rise, Memory, and write its praise!
    Up to thy wonted work! come, trace
        The epitaph of glory fled,—
For now the Earth has changed its face
    A frown is on the Heaven's brow.

We wandered to the Pine Forest
    That skirts the Ocean's foam,
The lightest wind was in its nest,
    The tempest in its home.
The whispering waves were half asleep,
    The clouds were gone to play,
And on the bosom of the deep
    The smile of Heaven lay;
It seemed as if the hour were one
    Sent from beyond the skies,
Which scattered from above the sun
    A light of Paradise.

We paused amid the pines that stood
    The giants of the waste,
Tortured by storms to shapes as rude
    As serpents interlaced,
And soothed by every azure breath
    That under Heaven is blown,
To harmonies and hues beneath,
    As tender as its own;
Now all the tree-tops lay asleep,
    Like green waves on the sea,
As still as in the silent deep
    The ocean woods may be.

How calm it was!—the silence there
   By such a chain was bound
That even the busy woodpecker
   Made stiller by her sound
The inviolable quietness;
   The breath of peace we drew
With its soft motion made not less
   The calm that round us grew.
There seemed from the remotest seat
   Of the white mountain waste,
To the soft flower beneath our feet,
   A magic circle traced,
A spirit interfused around,
   A thrilling, silent life,
To momentary peace it bound
   Our mortal nature's strife;
And still I felt the centre of
   The magic circle there
Was one fair form that filled with love
   The lifeless atmosphere.

We paused beside the pools that lie
   Under the forest bough,—
Each seemed as 'twere a little sky
   Gulfed in a world below;
A firmament of purple light
   Which in the dark earth lay,
More boundless than the depth of night,
   And purer than the day—
In which the lovely forests grew,
   As in the upper air,
More perfect both in shape and hue
   Than any spreading there.
There lay the glade and neighbouring lawn,
   And through the dark green wood
The white sun twinkling like the dawn
   Out of a speckled cloud.
Sweet views which in our world above
   Can never well be seen
Were imaged by the water's love
   Of that fair forest green.
And all was interfused beneath

With an Elysian glow,
An atmosphere without a breath,
A softer day below.
Like one beloved the scene had lent
To the dark water's breast,
Its every leaf and lineament
With more than truth expressed;
Until an envious wind crept by,
Like an unwelcome thought,
Which from the mind's too faithful eye
Blots one dear image out.
Though thou art ever fair and kind,
The forests ever green,
Less oft is peace in Shelley's mind
Than calm in water seen.

1822

With a Guitar, to Jane

ARIEL to Miranda:—Take
This slave of Music, for the sake
Of him who is the slave of thee,
And teach it all the harmony
In which thou canst, and only thou,
Make the delighted spirit glow,
Till joy denies itself again,
And, too intense, is turned to pain;
For by permission and command
Of thine own Prince Ferdinand,
Poor Ariel sends this silent token
Of more than ever can be spoken;
Your guardian spirit, Ariel, who,
From life to life, must still pursue
Your happiness—for thus alone
Can Ariel ever find his own—
From Prospero's enchanted cell,
As the mighty verses tell,
To the throne Of Naples, he
Lit you o'er the trackless sea,
Flitting on, you prow before,
Like a living meteor.

When you die, the silent Moon,
In her interlunar swoon,
Is not sadder in her cell
Than deserted Ariel.
When you live again on earth,
Like an unseen star of birth,
Ariel guides you o'er the sea
Of life from your nativity.
Many changes have been run
Since Ferdinand and you begun
Your course of love, and Ariel still
Has tracked your steps, and served your will;
Now, in humbler, happier lot,
This is all remembered not;
And now, alas! the poor sprite is
Imprisoned, for some fault of his,
In a body like a grave;—
From you he only dares to crave,
For his service and his sorrow,
A smile to-day, a song to-morrow.

The artist who this idol wrought,
To echo all harmonious thought,
Felled a tree, while on the steep
The woods were in their winter sleep,
Rocked in that repose divine
On the wind-swept Apennine;
And dreaming, some of Autumn past,
And some of Spring approaching fast,
And some of April buds and showers,
And some of songs in July bowers,
And all of love; and so this tree,—
O that such our death may be!—
Died in sleep, and felt no pain,
To live in happier form again:
From which, beneath Heaven's fairest star,
The artist wrought this loved Guitar,
And taught it justly to reply,
To all who question skilfully,
In language gentle as thine own;
Whispering in enamoured tone

Sweet oracles of woods and dells,
And summer winds in sylvan cells:
For it had learned all harmonies
Of the plains and of the skies,
Of the forests and the mountains,
And the many-voicèd fountains;
The clearest echoes of the hills,
The softest notes of falling rills,
The melodies of birds and bees,
The murmuring of summer seas,
And pattering rain, and breathing dew,
And airs of evening; and it knew
That seldom-heard mysterious sound,
Which, driven on its diurnal round,
As it floats through boundless day,
Our world enkindles on its way.—
All this it knows, but will not tell
To those who cannot question well
The Spirit that inhabits it;
It talks according to the wit
Of its companions; and no more
Is heard than has been felt before,
By those who tempt it to betray
These secrets of an elder day:
But, sweetly as its answers will
Flatter hands of perfect skill,
It keeps its highest, holiest tone
For our belovèd Jane alone.

1822

Epitaph

These are two friends whose lives were undivided;
So let their memory be, now they have glided
Under the grave; let not their bones be parted,
For their two hearts in life were single-hearted.

1822

SONNETS

Sonnets

ALL told (some early ones are not yet published) Shelley was fonder of writing sonnets than is always seen. Leigh Hunt judged that the form was too narrow for his energies, but Shelley was not always gigantic. It has been maintained that the Ode to the West Wind is actually a sonnet sequence, a theory which may be left to readers according to their sense of the main ondrive of that invocation. The poem is included, with critical arguments in defence of its inclusion, in D.M. Main's unsurpassed 'Treasury of English Sonnets', 1880.

Evening

TO HARRIET

O THOU bright Sun! beneath the dark blue line
   Of western distance that sublime descendest,
   And, gleaming lovelier as thy beams decline,
   Thy million hues to every vapour lendest,
And, over cobweb lawn and grove and stream
   Sheddest the liquid magic of thy light,
   Till calm Earth, with the parting splendour bright,
   Shows like the vision of a beauteous dream;
What gazer now with astronomic eye
   Could coldly count the spots within thy sphere?
   Such were thy lover, Harriet, could he fly
The thoughts of all that makes his passion dear,
   And, turning senseless from thy warm caress,
   Pick flaws in our close-woven happiness.

July 31, 1813

To Ianthe

I LOVE thee, Baby! for thine own sweet sake;
   Those azure eyes, that faintly dimpled cheek,
   Thy tender frame, so eloquently weak,
   Love in the sternest heart of hate might wake:
But more when o'er thy fitful slumber bending
   Thy mother folds thee to her wakeful heart,
   Whilst love and pity, in her glances blending,
   All that thy passive eyes can feel impart:
More, when some feeble lineaments of her,
   Who bore thy weight beneath her spotless bosom,
   As with deep love I read thy face, recur,—
More dear art thou, O fair and fragile blossom;
   Dearest when most thy tender traits express
The image of thy mother's loveliness.

September 1813

To Wordsworth

IN condemning Wordsworth for having abandoned his youthful sympathies with Revolution and settling into Toryism Shelley goes the same way as Hazlitt, Hunt and Keats. Later on ('Just for a handful of silver he left us') Browning said the same sort of thing without letting us know if his Lost Leader was Wordsworth or only a historical type.

Poet of Nature, thou hast wept to know
That things depart which never may return:
Childhood and youth, friendship and love's first glow,
Have fled like sweet dreams, leaving thee to mourn.
These common woes I feel. One loss is mine
Which thou too feel'st, yet I alone deplore.
Thou wert as a lone star, whose light did shine
On some frail bark in winter's midnight roar;
Thou hast like to a rock-built refuge stood
Above the blind and battling multitude:
In honoured poverty thy voice did weave
Songs consecrate to truth and liberty,—
Deserting these, thou leavest me to grieve,
Thus having been, that thou shouldst cease to be.

1815

Feelings of a Republican on the Fall of Bonaparte

I HATED thee, fallen tyrant! I did groan
To think that a most unambitious slave,
Like thou, shouldst dance and revel on the grave
Of Liberty. Thou mightst have built thy throne
Where it had stood even now: thou didst prefer
A frail and bloody pomp which Time has swept
In fragments towards Oblivion. Massacre,
For this I prayed, would on thy sleep have crept,
Treason and Slavery, Rapine, Fear, and Lust,
And stifled thee, their minister. I know
Too late, since thou and France are in the dust,
That Virtue owns a more eternal foe
Than Force or Fraud: old Custom, legal Crime,
And bloody Faith the foulest birth of Time.

1815

Ozymandias

WRITTEN probably in competition with Horace Smith (whose sonnet
is extant, but does not name Ozymandias), as Shelley's Nile sonnet
arose from a friendly contest with Keats and Leigh Hunt.

I MET a traveller from an antique land
Who said: Two vast and trunkless legs of stone
Stand in the desert . . . Near them, on the sand,
Half sunk, a shattered visage lies, whose frown,
And wrinkled lip, and sneer of cold command,
Tell that its sculptor well those passions read
Which yet survive, stamped on these lifeless things,
The hand that mocked them, and the heart that fed:
And on the pedestal these words appear:
'My name is Ozymandias, king of kings:
Look on my works, ye Mighty, and despair!'
Nothing beside remains. Round the decay
Of that colossal wreck, boundless and bare
The lone and level sands stretch far away.

December 1817

To the Nile

MONTH after month the gathered rains descend
Drenching yon secret Aethiopian dells,
And from the desert's ice-girt pinnacles
Where Frost and Heat in strange embraces blend
On Atlas, fields of moist snow half depend.
Girt there with blasts and meteors Tempest dwells
By Nile's aëreal urn, with rapid spells
Urging those waters to their mighty end.
O'er Egypt's land of Memory floods are level
And they are thine, O Nile—and well thou knowest
That soul-sustaining airs and blasts of evil
And fruits and poisons spring where'er thou flowest.
Beware, O Man—for knowledge must to thee,
Like the great flood to Egypt, ever be.

February 4, 1818

Sonnet

LIFT not the painted veil which those who live
Call Life: though unreal shapes be pictured there,
And it but mimic all we would believe
With colours idly spread,—behind, lurk Fear
And Hope, twin Destinies; who ever weave
Their shadows, o'er the chasm, sightless and drear.
I knew one who had lifted it—he sought,
For his lost heart was tender, things to love,
But found them not, alas! nor was there aught
The world contains, the which he could approve.
Through the unheeding many he did move,
A splendour among shadows, a bright blot
Upon this gloomy scene, a Spirit that strove
For truth, and like the Preacher found it not.

1818

Sonnet: England in 1819

An old, mad, blind, despised, and dying king,—
Princes, the dregs of their dull race, who flow
Through public scorn,—mud from a muddy spring,—
Rulers who neither see, nor feel, nor know,
But leech-like to their fainting country cling,
Till they drop, blind in blood, without a blow,—
A people starved and stabbed in the untilled field,—
An army, which liberticide and prey
Makes as a two-edged sword to all who wield,—
Golden and sanguine laws which tempt and slay;
Religion Christless, Godless—a book sealed;
A Senate,—Time's worst statute unrepealed,—
Are graves, from which a glorious Phantom may
Burst, to illumine our tempestuous day.

Sonnet

Ye hasten to the grave! What seek ye there,
Ye restless thoughts and busy purposes
Of the idle brain, which the world's livery wear?
O thou quick heart, which pantest to possess
All that pale Expectation feigneth fair!
Thou vainly curious mind which wouldest guess
Whence thou didst come, and whither thou must go,
And all that never yet was known would know—
Oh, whither hasten ye, that thus ye press,
With such swift feet life's green and pleasant path,
Seeking, alike from happiness and woe,
A refuge in the cavern of gray death?
O heart, and mind, and thoughts! what thing do you
Hope to inherit in the grave below?

1820

Political Greatness

Nor happiness, nor majesty, nor fame,
Nor peace, nor strength, nor skill in arms and arts,
Shepherd those herds whom tyranny makes tame;
Verse echoes not one beating of their hearts,
History is but the shadow of their shame,
Art veils her glass, or from the pageant starts
As to oblivion their blind millions fleet,
Staining that Heaven with obscene imagery
Of their own likeness. What are members knit
By force or custom? Man who man would be,
Must rule the empire of himself; in it
Must be supreme, establishing his throne
On vanquished will, quelling the anarchy
Of hopes and fears, being himself alone.

1821

To Byron

The genius which Shelley acclaimed in *Childe Harold* and *Don Juan* was not all that excited him; the cosmic outlook which Byron temporarily had in *Cain* and *Heaven and Earth* and elsewhere astonished him as this sonnet reveals. Shelley himself was rapid in his mighty imaginings but he thought he saw in Byron a power truly daemonic, and he wished to stimulate it.

If I esteemed you less, Envy would kill
Pleasure, and leave to Wonder and Despair
The ministration of the thoughts that fill
The mind which, like a worm whose life may share
A portion of the Unapproachable,
Marks your creations rise as fast and fair
As perfect worlds at the Creator's will,
And bows itself before the godhead there.
But such is my regard that nor your fame
Cast on the present by the coming hour
Nor your well-won prosperity and power
Move one regret for his unhonoured name
Who dares these words:—the worm beneath the sod
May lift itself in worship to the God.

1821

SONGS FOR MUSIC OR IN PLAYS

The Indian Serenade

ONE thing at least is sure concerning this well known trifle: Shelley wrote it some time before the arrival of Jane Williams with her Indian recollections. The air, if Indian it really was, is unidentified.

The three pieces following were supplied for their proper contexts in masques by Mary Shelley, *Proserpine* and *Midas* (edited by A. Koszul, Oxford, 1922); and *A Bridal Song*, several varying texts of which are preserved, was to be sung in Edward Williams's play *The Promise; or, A Year, A Month and a Day*. The two *Dirges* have the appearance of having been composed for a like occasion in the theatre. To generalize, a number of Shelley's lyrics may well have been written either as words for music he had heard or for some musician to set. *To Jane* is placed in this section because T. Medwin entitles it *An Ariette for Music*, and its cadences and emphases indicate that purpose.

I ARISE from dreams of thee
In the first sweet sleep of night,
When the winds are breathing low,
And the stars are shining bright:
I arise from dreams of thee,
And a spirit in my feet
Hath led me—who knows how?
To thy chamber window, Sweet!

The wandering airs they faint
On the dark, the silent stream—
The Champak odours pine
Like sweet thoughts in a dream;
The nightingale's complaint,
It dies upon her heart;—
As I must on thine,
Oh, belovèd as thou art!

Oh lift me from the grass!
I die! I faint! I fail!
Let thy love in kisses rain
On my lips and eyelids pale.
My cheek is cold and white, alas!
My heart beats laud and fast;—
Oh! press it to thine own again,
Where it will break at last.

1819

Arethusa

ARETHUSA arose
From her couch of snows
In the Acroceraunian mountains,—
From cloud and from crag,
With many a jag.
Shepherding her bright fountains.
She leapt down the rocks,
With her rainbow locks
Streaming among the streams;—
Her steps paved with green
The downward ravine
Which slopes to the western gleams;
And gliding and springing
She went, ever singing,
In murmurs as soft as sleep;
The Earth seemed to love her,
And Heaven smiled above her.
As she lingered towards the deep.

Then Alpheus bold,
On his glacier cold,
With his trident the mountains strook;
And opened a chasm
In the rocks—with the spasm
All Erymanthus shook.
And the black south wind
It unsealed behind

The urns of the silent snow,
  And earthquake and thunder
  Did rend in sunder
The bars of the springs below.
  And the beard and the hair
  Of the River-god were
Seen through the torrent's sweep,
  As he followed the light
  Of the fleet nymph's flight
To the brink of the Dorian deep.

  'Oh, save me! Oh, guide me!
  And bid the deep hide me,
For he grasps me now by the hair!'
  The loud Ocean heard,
  To its blue depth stirred,
And divided at her prayer;
  And under the water
  The Earth's white daughter
Fled like a sunny beam;
  Behind her descended
  Her billows, unblended
With the brackish Dorian stream:—
  Like a gloomy stain
  On the emerald main
Alpheus rushed behind,—
  As an eagle pursuing
  A dove to its ruin
Down the streams of the cloudy wind.

  Under the bowers
  Where the Ocean Powers
Sit on their pearlèd thrones;
  Through the coral woods
  Of the weltering floods,
Over heaps of unvalued stones;
  Through the dim beams
  Which amid the streams
Weave a network of coloured light;
  And under the caves,
  Where the shadowy waves
Are as green as the forest's night:—

    Outspeeding the shark,
    And the sword-fish dark,
Under the Ocean's foam,
    And up through the rifts
    Of the mountain clifts
They passed to their Dorian home.

    And now from their fountains
    In Enna's mountains,
Down one vale where the morning basks,
    Like friends once parted
    Grown single-hearted,
They ply their watery tasks.
    At sunrise they leap
    From their cradles steep
In the cave of the shelving hill;
    At noontide they flow
    Through the woods below
And the meadows of asphodel;
    And at night they sleep
    In the rocking deep
Beneath the Ortygian shore;—
    Like spirits that lie
    In the azure sky
When they love but live no more.

Hymn of Apollo

THE sleepless Hours who watch me as I lie,
    Curtained with star-inwoven tapestries
From the broad moonlight of the sky,
    Fanning the busy dreams from my dim eyes,—
Waken me when their Mother, the gray Dawn,
Tells them that dreams and that the moon is gone.

Then I arise, and climbing Heaven's blue dome,
    I walk over the mountains and the waves,
Leaving my robe upon the ocean foam;
    My footsteps pave the clouds with fire; the caves
Are filled with my bright presence, and the air
Leaves the green Earth to my embraces bare.

The sunbeams are my shafts, with which I kill
   Deceit, that loves the night and fears the day:
All men who do or even imagine ill
   Fly me, and from the glory of my ray
Good minds and open actions take new might,
Until diminished by the reign of Night.

I feed the clouds, the rainbows and the flowers
   With their aethereal colours; the moon's globe
And the pure stars in their eternal bowers
   Are cinctured with my power as with a robe;
Whatever lamps on Earth or Heaven may shine
Are portions of one power, which is mine.

I stand at noon upon the peak of Heaven,
   Then with unwilling steps I wander down
Into the clouds of the Atlantic even;
   For grief that I depart they weep and frown:
What look is more delightful than the smile
With which I soothe them from the western isle?

I am the eye with which the Universe
   Beholds itself and knows itself divine;
All harmony of instrument or verse,
   All prophecy, all medicine is mine,
All light of art or nature;—to my song
Victory and praise in its own right belong.

Hymn of Pan

FROM the forests and highlands
   We come, we come;
From the river-girt islands,
   Where loud waves are dumb
     Listening to my sweet pipings.
The wind in the reeds and the rushes,
   The bees on the bells of thyme,
The birds on the myrtle bushes,
   The cicale above in the lime,

And the lizards below in the grass,
Were as silent as ever old Tmolus was
　　Listening to my sweet pipings.

Liquid Peneus was flowing,
　And all dark Tempe lay
In Pelion's shadow, outgrowing
　The light of the dying day,
　　Speeded by my sweet pipings.
The Sileni, and Sylvans, and Fauns,
　And the Nymphs of the woods and the waves,
To the edge of the moist river-lawns,
　And the brink of the dewy caves,
And all that did then attend and follow,
Were silent with love, as you now, Apollo,
　　With envy of my sweet pipings.

I sang of the dancing stars.
　I sang of the daedal Earth,
And of Heaven—and the giant wars,
　And Love, and Death, and Birth,—
　　And then I changed my pipings,—
Singing how down the vale of Maenalus
　I pursued a maiden and clasped a reed.
Gods and men, we are all deluded thus!
　It breaks in our bosom and then we bleed:
All wept, as I think both ye now would,
If envy or age had not frozen your blood,
　　At the sorrow of my sweet-pipings.

1820

Autumn: A Dirge

THE warm sun is failing, the black wind is wailing,
The bare boughs are sighing, the pale flowers are dying,
　　And the Year
On the earth her death-bed, in a shroud of leaves dead,
　　Is lying.

Come, Months, come away,
From November to May,
In your saddest array;
Follow the bier
Of the dead cold Year,
And like dim shadows watch by her sepulchre.

The chill rain is falling, the nipped worm is crawling,
The rivers are swelling, the thunder is knelling
                    For the Year;
The blithe swallows are flown, and the lizards each gone
                    To his dwelling;
Come, Months, come away;
Put on white, black, and gray;
Let your light sisters play—
Ye, follow the bier
Of the dead cold Year.
And make her grave green with tear on tear.

1820

Dirge for the Year

ORPHAN Hours, the Year is dead,
  Come and sigh, come and weep!
Merry Hours, smile instead,
  For the Year is but asleep.
See, it smiles as it is sleeping.
Mocking your untimely weeping.

As an earthquake rocks a corse
  In its coffin in the clay,
So White Winter, that rough nurse,
  Rocks the death-cold Year to-day;
Solemn Hours! wail aloud
For your mother in her shroud.

As the wild air stirs and sways
  The tree-swung cradle of a child,
So the breath of these rude days
  Rocks the Year:—be calm and mild,

Trembling Hours, she will arise
With new love within her eyes.

January gray is here,
   Like a sexton by her grave;
February bears the bier,
   March with grief doth howl and rave,
And April weeps—but, O ye Hours!
Follow with May's fairest flowers.

A Bridal Song

THE golden gates of Sleep unbar
   Where Strength and Beauty, met together,
Kindle their image like a star
   In a sea of glassy weather!
Night, with all thy stars look down,—
   Darkness, weep thy holiest dew,—
Never smiled the inconstant moon
   On a pair so true.
Let eyes not see their own delight;—
Haste, swift Hour, and thy flight
   Oft renew.

Fairies, sprites, and angels, keep her!
   Holy stars, permit no wrong!
And return to wake the sleeper,
   Dawn,—ere it be long!
O joy! O fear! what will be done
In the absence of the sun?
   Come along!

1821

To Jane

THE keen stars were twinkling,
And the fair moon was rising among them,
   Dear Jane!
  The guitar was tinkling,
But the notes were not sweet till you sung them
   Again.

  As the moon's soft splendour
O'er the faint cold starlight of Heaven
   Is thrown,
  So your voice most tender
To the strings without soul had then given
   Its own.

  The stars will awaken,
Though the moon sleep a full hour later,
   To-night;
  No leaf will be shaken
Whilst the dews of your melody scatter
   Delight.

  Though the sound overpowers,
Sing again, with your dear voice revealing
   A tone
  Of some world far from ours
Where music and moonlight and feeling
   Are one.

1822

A Dirge

ROUGH wind, that moanest loud
    Grief too sad for song;
Wild wind, when sullen cloud
    Knells all the night long;
Sad storm, whose tears are vain,
Bare woods, whose branches strain,
Deep caves and dreary main,—
    Wail, for the world's wrong!

1822

MISCELLANEOUS PIECES

To the Lord Chancellor

SIR Thomas Lawrence's portrait of John Scott, first Earl of Eldon (1751–1838) is at the National Portrait Gallery, and provides a means of seeing him through Shelley's eyes. His suave politeness is ridiculed in H. B.'s series of *Political Sketches*. Some casual words of his on an official occasion made Shelley think that Eldon meditated depriving him of the custody of his children by Mary as well as the others; that apprehension underlies the poem *To William Shelley*.

THY country's curse is on thee, darkest crest
　　Of that foul, knotted, many-headed worm
Which rends our Mother's bosom—Priestly Pest!
　　Masked Resurrection of a buried Form!

Thy country's curse is on thee! Justice sold,
　　Truth trampled, Nature's landmarks overthrown,
And heaps of fraud-accumulated gold,
　　Plead, loud as thunder, at Destruction's throne.

And, whilst that sure slow Angel which aye stands
　　Watching the beck of Mutability
Delays to execute her high commands,
　　And, though a nation weeps, spares thine and thee,

Oh, let a father's curse be on thy soul,
　　And let a daughter's hope be on thy tomb;
Be both, on thy gray head, a leaden cowl
　　To weigh thee down to thine approaching doom!

I curse thee by a parent's outraged love,
  By hopes long cherished and too lately lost,
By gentle feelings thou couldst never prove.
  By griefs which thy stern nature never crossed;

By those infantine smiles of happy light,
  Which were a fire within a stranger's hearth,
Quenched even when kindled, in untimely night
  Hiding the promise of a lovely birth:

By those unpractised accents of young speech,
  Which he who is a father thought to frame
To gentlest lore, such as the wisest teach—
  Thou strike the lyre of mind!—oh, grief and shame!

By all the happy see in children's growth—
  That undeveloped flower of budding years—
Sweetness and sadness interwoven both,
  Source of the sweetest hopes and saddest fears—

By all the days, under an hireling's care,
  Of dull constraint and bitter heaviness,—
O wretched ye if ever any were,—
  Sadder than orphans, yet not fatherless!

By the false cant which on their innocent lips
  Must hang like poison on an opening bloom,
By the dark creeds which cover with eclipse
  Their pathway from the cradle to the tomb—

By thy most impious Hell, and all its terror;
By all the grief, the madness, and the guilt
Of thine impostures, which must be their error—
  That sand on which thy crumbling power is built—

By thy complicity with lust and hate—
  Thy thirst for tears—thy hunger after gold—
The ready frauds which ever on thee wait—
  The servile arts in which thou hast grown old—

By thy most killing sneer, and by thy smile—
 By all the arts and snares of thy black den,
And—for thou canst outweep the crocodile—
 By thy false tears—those millstones braining men—

By all the hate which checks a father's love—
 By all the scorn which kills a father's care—
By those most impious hands which dared remove
 Nature's high bounds—by thee—and by despair—

Yes, the despair which bids a father groan,
 And cry, 'My children are no longer mine—
The blood within those veins may be mine own,
 But—Tyrant—their polluted souls are thine;—

I curse thee—though I hate thee not.—O slave!
 If thou couldst quench the earth-consuming Hell
Of which thou art a daemon, on thy grave
 This curse should be a blessing. Fare thee well!

1817

Lines to a Critic

IN 1820 Shelley played with this topic again in *Lines to a Reviewer*
which won a good word even from that oddly inimical observer
of his course, Charles Lamb.

> Alas, good friend, what profit can you see
> In hating such a hateless thing as me?
> There is no sport in hate where all the rage;
> Is on one side: in vain would you assuage
> Your frowns upon an unresisting smile,
> In which not even contempt lurks to beguile
> Your heart, by some faint sympathy of hate.
> Oh conquer what you cannot satiate!
> For to your passion I am far more coy
> Than ever yet was coldest maid or boy
> In winter noon. Of your antipathy
> If I am the Narcissus, you are free
> To pine into a sound with hating me.

HONEY from silkworms who can gather,
    Or silk from the yellow bee?
The grass may grow in winter weather
    As soon as hate in me.

Hate men who cant, and men who pray,
    And men who rail like thee;
An equal passion to repay
    They are not coy like me.

Or seek some slave of power and gold
    To be thy dear heart's mate;
Thy love will move that bigot cold
    Sooner than me, thy hate.

A passion like the one I prove
    Cannot divided be;
I hate thy want of truth and love—
    How should I then hate thee?

Similes for Two Political Characters of 1819

As from an ancestral oak
    Two empty ravens sound their clarion,
Yell by yell, and croak by croak,
When they scent the noonday smoke
    Of fresh human carrion:—

As two gibbering night-birds flit
    From their bowers of deadly yew
Through the night to frighten it,
When the moon is in a fit,
    And the stars are none, or few:—

As a shark and dog-fish wait
    Under an Atlantic isle,
For the negro-ship, whose freight
Is the theme of their debate,
    Wrinkling their red gills the while—

Are ye, two vultures sick for battle,
 Two scorpions under one wet stone,
Two bloodless wolves whose dry throats rattle,
Two crows perched on the murrained cattle,
  Two vipers tangled into one.

FROM

Peter Bell the Third

BY MICHING MALLECHO, ESQ.

J. H. REYNOLDS's parody of Wordsworth was published and ran through an edition or two, but Shelley's remained long in manuscript. It passes from time to time into something more than comicality, and reveals that side of Shelley which does not fit the definition of a beautiful angel in the void. Shelley in Pall Mall is as historical as Shelley in cloudland.

Hell

HELL is a city much like London—
 A populous and a smoky city;
There are all sorts of people undone,
And there is little or no fun done;
 Small justice shown, and still less pity.

There is a Castles, and a Canning,
 A Cobbett, and a Castlereagh;
All sorts of caitiff corpses planning
All sorts of cozening for trepanning
 Corpses less corrupt than they.

There is a***, who has lost
 His wits, or sold them, none knows which;
He walks about a double ghost,
And though as thin as Fraud almost—
 Ever grows more grim and rich.

There is a Chancery Court; a King;
 A manufacturing mob; a set
Of thieves who by themselves are sent
Similar thieves to represent;
 An army; and a public debt.

Which last is a scheme of paper money,
    And means—being interpreted—
'Bees, keep your wax—give us the honey,
And we will plant, while skies are sunny,
    Flowers, which in winter serve instead.'

There is a great talk of revolution—
    And a great chance of despotism—
German soldiers—camps—confusion—
Tumults—lotteries—rage—delusion—
    Gin—suicide—and methodism;

Taxes too, on wine and bread,
    And meat, and beer, and tea, and cheese,
From which those patriots pure are fed,
Who gorge before they reel to bed
    The tenfold essence of all these.

There are mincing women, mewing,
    (Like cats, who *amant miserè*,)
Of their own virtue, and pursuing
Their gentler sisters to that ruin,
    Without which—what were chastity?

Lawyers—judges—old hobnobbers
    Are there—bailiffs—chancellors—
Bishops—great and little robbers—
Rhymesters—pamphleteers—stockjobbers—
    Men of glory in the wars,—

Things whose trade is, over ladies
    To lean, and flirt, and stare, and simper,
Till all that is divine in woman
Grows cruel, courteous, smooth, inhuman,
    Crucified 'twixt a smile and whimper.

Thrusting, toiling, wailing, moiling,
    Frowning, preaching—such a riot!
Each with never-ceasing labour,
Whilst he thinks he cheats his neighbour,
    Cheating his own heart of quiet.

And all these meet at levees;—
   Dinners convivial and political;—
Suppers of epic poets;—teas,
Where small talk dies in agonies;—
   Breakfasts professional and critical;

Lunches and snacks so aldermanic
   That one would furnish forth ten dinners,
Where reigns a Cretan-tonguèd panic,
Lest news Russ, Dutch, or Alemannic
   Should make some losers, and some winners;—

At conversazioni—balls—
   Conventicles—and drawing-rooms—
Courts of law—committees—calls
Of a morning—clubs—book-stalls—
   Churches—masquerades—and tombs.

And this is Hell—and in this smother
   All are damnable and damned;
Each one damning, damns the other;
They are damned by one another.
By none other are they damned.

'Tis a lie to say, 'God damns!'
   Where was Heaven's Attorney General
When they first gave out such flams?
Let there be an end of shams,
   They are mines of poisonous mineral.

Statesmen damn themselves to be
   Cursed; and lawyers damn their souls
To the auction of a fee;
Churchmen damn themselves to see
   God's sweet love in burning coals.

The rich are damned, beyond all cure,
   To taunt, and starve, and trample on
The weak and wretched; and the poor
Damn their broken hearts to endure
   Stripe on stripe, with groan on groan.

Sometimes the poor are damned indeed
   To take,—not means for being blessed,—
But Cobbett's snuff, revenge; that weed
From which the worms that it doth feed
   Squeeze less than they before possessed.

And some few, like we know who,
   Damned—but God alone knows why—
To believe their minds are given
To make this ugly Hell a Heaven;
   In which faith they live and die.

Thus, as in a town, plague-stricken,
   Each man be he sound or no
Must indifferently sicken;
As when day begins to thicken,
   None knows a pigeon from a crow,—

So good and bad, sane and mad,
   The oppressor and the oppressed;
Those who weep to see what others
Smile to inflict upon their brothers;
   Lovers, haters, worst and best;

All are damned—they breathe an air,
   Thick, infected, joy-dispelling:
Each pursues what seems most fair,
Mining like moles, through mind, and there
Scoop palace-caverns vast, where Care
   In thronèd state is ever dwelling.

Peter Bell's Poetry

At night he oft would start and wake
   Like a lover, and began
In a wild measure songs to make
On moor, and glen, and rocky lake,
   And on the heart of man—

And on the universal sky—
   And the wide earth's bosom green,—
And the sweet, strange mystery
Of what beyond these things may lie,
   And yet remain unseen.

For in his thought he visited
   The spots in which, ere dead and damned,
He his wayward life had led;
Yet knew not whence the thoughts were fed
   Which thus his fancy crammed.

And these obscure remembrances
   Stirred such harmony in Peter,
That, whensoever he should please,
He could speak of rocks and trees
   In poetic metre.

For though it was without a sense
   Of memory, yet he remembered well
Many a ditch and quick-set fence;
Of lakes he had intelligence,
   He knew something of heath and fell.

He had also dim recollections
   Of pedlars tramping on their rounds;
Milk-pans and pails; and odd collections
Of saws, and proverbs; and reflections
   Old parsons make in burying-grounds.

But Peter's verse was clear, and came
   Announcing from the frozen hearth
Of a cold age, that none might tame
The soul of that diviner flame
   It augured to the Earth:

Like gentle rains, on the dry plains,
   Making that green which late was gray,
Or like the sudden moon, that stains
Some gloomy chamber's window-panes
   With a broad light like day.

FROM

Oedipus Tyrannus

or Swellfoot the Tyrant

A TRAGEDY IN TWO ACTS

TRANSLATED FROM THE ORIGINAL DORIC

AT the Baths of Lucca, while Shelley sat reading his new *Ode to Liberty* to his little circle, he was accompanied by the gruntings of pigs brought to the market beneath the windows. Not at all put out by this contribution he started up the notion of a satire on the dispute then raging between George IV and Queen Caroline; it should have the form of a Greek drama and the pigs should be the popular chorus. The joke was not left as mere talk, but no sooner was the 'drama' published in London than an informer interfered, and the edition was suppressed. A pity, for the piece should have taken its turn in that period of caricature and burlesque.

Scene.—Thebes

Act I

SCENE I.—*A magnificent Temple, built of thigh-bones and death's-heads, and tiled with scalps. Over the Altar the statue of Famine, veiled; a number of Boars, Sows, and Sucking-Pigs, crowned with thistle, shamrock, and oak, sitting on the steps, and clinging round the Altar of the Temple.*

Enter SWELLFOOT, *in his Royal robes, without perceiving the* PIGS.

Swellfoot. Thou supreme Goddess! by whose power divine
These graceful limbs are clothed in proud array
     [*He contemplates himself with satisfaction.*
Of gold and purple, and this kingly paunch
Swells like a sail before a favouring breeze,
And these most sacred nether promontories
Lie satisfied with layers of fat; and these
Boeotian cheeks, like Egypt's pyramid,
(Nor with less toil were their foundations laid),
Sustain the cone of my untroubled brain,
That point, the emblem of a pointless nothing!
Thou to whom Kings and laurelled Emperors,
Radical-butchers, Paper-money-millers,

Bishops and Deacons, and the entire army
Of those fat martyrs to the persecution
Of stifling turtle-soup, and brandy-devils,
Offer their secret vows! Thou plenteous Ceres
Of their Eleusis, hail!

 The Swine. Eigh! eigh! eigh! eigh!
 Swellfoot.   Ha! what are ye,
Who, crowned with leaves devoted to the Furies,
Cling round this sacred shrine?

 Swine. Aigh! aigh! aigh!
 Swellfoot.   What! ye that are
The very beasts that, offered at her altar
With blood and groans, salt-cake, and fat, and inwards,
Ever propitiate her reluctant will
When taxes are withheld?

 Swine. Ugh! ugh! ugh!
 Swellfoot.   What! ye who grub
With filthy snouts my red potatoes up
In Allan's rushy bog? Who eat the oats
Up, from my cavalry in the Hebrides?
Who swill the hog-wash soup my cooks digest
From bones, and rags, and scraps of shoe-leather,
Which should be given to cleaner Pigs than you?

The Swine—Semichorus I

The same, alas! the same;
Though only now the name
 Of Pig remains to me.

Semichorus II

If 'twere your kingly will
Us wretched Swine to kill,
 What should we yield to thee?

Swellfoot. Why, skin and bones, and some few hairs for mortar.

Chorus of Swine

I have heard your Laureate sing,
 That pity was a royal thing;
Under your mighty ancestors, we Pigs
Were bless'd as nightingales on myrtle sprigs,
Or grasshoppers that live on noonday dew,
And sung, old annals tell, as sweetly too;

But now our sties are fallen in, we catch
   The murrain and the mange, the scab and itch;
Sometimes your royal dogs tear down our thatch,
   And then we seek the shelter of a ditch;
Hog-wash or grains, or ruta-baga, none
Has yet been ours since your reign begun.

First Sow

My Pigs, 'tis in vain to tug.

Second Sow

I could almost eat my litter.

First Pig

I suck, but no milk will come from the dug.

Second Pig

Our skin and our bones would be bitter.

The Boars

We fight for this rag of greasy rug
   Though a trough of wash would be fitter.

Semichorus

   Happier Swine were they than we,
     Drowned in the Gadarean sea—
I wish that pity would drive out the devils,
Which in your royal bosom hold their revels,
And sink us in the waves of your compassion!
Alas! the Pigs are an unhappy nation!
Now if your Majesty would have our bristles
   To bind your mortar with, or fill our colons
With rich blood, or make brawn out of our gristles,
   In policy—ask else your royal Solons—
You ought to give us hog-wash and clean straw,
And sties well thatched; besides it is the law!

Swellfoot. This is sedition, and rank blasphemy!
Ho! there, my guards!

Enter a GUARD.

Guard.   Your sacred Majesty.

Swellfoot. Call in the Jews, Solomon the court porkman,
Moses the sow-gelder, and Zephaniah
The hog-butcher.
  Guard.   They are in waiting, Sire.

  Enter SOLOMON, MOSES, *and* ZEPHANIAH.

Swellfoot. Out with your knife, old Moses, and spay those Sow.
         [*The* PIGS *run about in consternation.*
That load the earth with Pigs; cut close and deep
Moral restraint I see has no effect,
Nor prostitution, nor our own example,
Starvation, typhus-fever, war, nor prison—
This was the art which the arch-priest of Famine
Hinted at in his charge to the Theban clergy—
Cut close and deep, good Moses.
  Moses.   Let your Majesty
Keep the Boars quiet, else——
  Swellfoot.   Zephaniah, cut
That fat Hog's throat, the brute seems overfed;
Seditious hunks! to whine for want of grains.
  Zephaniah. Your sacred Majesty, he has the dropsy;—
We shall find pints of hydatids in 's liver,
He has not half an inch of wholesome fat
Upon his carious ribs——
  Swellfoot.   'Tis all the same,
He'll serve instead of riot money, when
Our murmuring troops bivouac in Thebes' streets;
And January winds, after a day
Of butchering, will make them relish carrion.
Now, Solomon, I'll sell you in a lump
The whole kit of them.
  Solomon.   Why, your Majesty,
I could not give——
  Swellfoot.   Kill them out of the way,
That shall be price enough, and let me hear
Their everlasting grunts and whines no more!
        [*Exeunt, driving in the* SWINE.

* * *

SCENE II.—*The interior of the Temple of Famine. The statue of the Goddess, a skeleton clothed in parti-coloured rags, seated upon a heap of skulls and loaves intermingled. A number of exceedingly fat Priests in black garments arrayed on each side, with marrow-bones and cleavers in their hands. A flourish of trumpets.*

Enter MAMMON *as arch-priest,* SWELLFOOT, DAKRY, PURGANAX, LAOCTONOS, *followed by* IONA TAURINA *guarded. On the other side enter the* SWINE.

Chorus of PRIESTS, *accompanied by the* COURT PORKMAN *on marrow-bones and cleavers.*

> GODDESS bare, and gaunt, and pale,
> Empress of the world, all hail!
> What though Cretans old called thee
> City-crested Cybele?
> We call thee FAMINE!
> Goddess of fasts and feasts, starving and cramming!
> Through thee, for emperors, kings, and priests and lords,
> Who rule by viziers, sceptres, bank-notes, words,
> The earth pours forth its plenteous fruits,
> Corn, wool, linen, flesh, and roots—
> Those who consume these fruits through thee grow fat,
> Those who produce these fruits through thee grow lean,
> Whatever change takes place, oh, stick to that!
> And let things be as they have ever been;
> At least while we remain thy priests,
> And proclaim thy fasts and feasts.
> Through thee the sacred SWELLFOOT dynasty
> Is based upon a rock amid that sea
> Whose waves are Swine—so let it ever be!

[SWELLFOOT, *etc., seat themselves at a table magnificently covered at the upper end of the Temple. Attendants pass over the stage with hog-wash in pails. A number of* PIGS, *exceedingly lean, follow them licking up the wash.*

> *Mammon.* I fear your sacred Majesty has lost
> The appetite which you were used to have.
> Allow me now to recommend this dish—
> A simple kickshaw by your Persian cook,

Such as is served at the great King's second table.
The price and pains which its ingredients cost
Might have maintained some dozen families
A winter or two—not more—so plain a dish
Could scarcely disagree.—

 Swellfoot.   After the trial,
And these fastidious Pigs are gone, perhaps
I may recover my lost appetite,—
I feel the gout flying about my stomach—
Give me a glass of Maraschino punch.

 Purganax (*filling his glass, and standing up*). The glorious
   Constitution of the Pigs!

 All. A toast! a toast! stand up, and three times three!

 Dakry. No heel-taps—darken daylights!—

 Laoctonos.   Claret, somehow,
Puts me in mind of blood, and blood of claret!

 Swellfoot. Laoctonos is fishing for a compliment,
But 'tis his due. Yes, you have drunk more wine,
And shed more blood, than any man in Thebes.

             [*To* PURGANAX.
For God's sake stop the grunting of those Pigs!

 Purganax. We dare not, Sire, 'tis Famine's privilege.

1820

INDEX OF FIRST LINES

BIBLIOGRAPHY

INDEX OF FIRST LINES

BIBLIOGRAPHY

Shelley's Principal Publications (Verse)

1813   *Queen Mab; a Philosophical Poem*
        (Privately printed. Unauthorized edition, 1821)

1816   *Alastor; or, The Spirit of Solitude; and other Poems*

1818   *Laon and Cythna . . . A Vision of the Nineteenth Century*
        (Modified as *The Revolt of Islam.* 1818)

1819   *Rosalind and Helen, A Modern Eclogue: With other Poems*
        The Cenci. A Tragedy, in Five Acts. (2nd ed., 1821)

1820   *Prometheus Unbound, A Lyrical Drama, in Four Acts*
        *Oedipus Tyrannus; or, Swellfoot the Tyrant. A Tragedy. In
        Two Acts.* (Suppressed.)

1821   *Epipsychidion. Verses Addressed to the Noble and Unfortunate
        Lady Emilia V——*
        Adonais. An Elegy on the Death of John Keats
        (Printed at Pisa)

1822   *Hellas. A Lyrical Drama*

1824   *Posthumous Poems of Percy Bysshe Shelley (soon withdrawn)*
        (The first collected edition of Shelley's Poems was published
        by Messrs. Galignani in Paris, 1829)

1832   *The Masque of Anarchy* . . . With a Preface by Leigh Hunt

1833   *The Shelley Papers* . . . By T. Medwin
        (Contains new poems by Shelley)

1839   *The Poetical Works of Percy Bysshe Shelley*
        Edited by Mrs. Shelley. In Four Volumes
        (A revised edition in one volume, containing the omitted
        passages of *Queen Mab*, the burlesque *Oedipus Tyrannus* and
        Peter Bell the Third, and other additions, appeared in 1840)

COLLECTED EDITIONS:
The Poetical Works of Percy Bysshe Shelley. 2 vols. 1870. (The earliest
    of the modern editions; it was by W. M. Rossetti)

Many other elaborate editions followed—by H. Buxton Forman, W. M. Rossetti, G. E. Woodberry, C. D. Locock and others, culminating in the *Julian Shelley* by Roger Ingpen and Walter Peck. Even so, many of Shelley's earliest poems remain unpublished.

The most practical 'complete edition' is that by Thomas Hutchinson in *Oxford Standard Authors*, in one volume. *Verse and Prose* from Shelley's MSS. edited (1934) by Sir John Shelley Rolls and Roger Ingpen, forms an interesting supplement.

Shelley's prose writings, first edited in 1840 by Mary Shelley, are fully collected in the *Julian Shelley,* and have been selected by Ernest Rhys (Camelot Classics, 1886) and others. His *Philosophical View of Reform* was first edited by T. W. Rolleston, 1920).

LETTERS (*A Selection*)

 The Letters collected and edited by R. Ingpen (2 volumes, 1914)

 Shelley Correspondence in the Bodleian Library edited by R. H. Hill (1926, 1982)

 Letters selected, with introduction by R. Brimley Johnson (1929)

 Shelley's Lost Letters to Harriet edited with an introduction by Leslie Hotson (1930, 1982)

 Mary Shelley's Letters by Frederick L. Jones (1944)

 New Shelley Letters edited by W. S. Scott (1948)

 My Best Mary: The Selected Letters of Mary Wollstonecraft Shelley, edited by Muriel Spark and Derek Stanford (1953)

CRITICAL AND BIOGRAPHICAL STUDIES (*A Selection*)

 Lord Byron and Some of His Contemporaries by Leigh Hunt (1828)

 The Life of Percy Bysshe Shelley by T. Medwin (2 volumes 1847, 1913)

 The Life of Percy Bysshe Shelley by Thomas Jefferson Hogg (2 volumes 1858, 1906)

 Memoirs of Shelley by Thomas Love Peacock (1858)

 Recollections of the Last Days of Shelley and Byron by Edward John Trelawney (1858, 1906)

 Shelley Memorials edited by Lady Shelley (1859)

 Shelley's Early Life by D. F. MacCarthy (1872)

 Shelley by J. A. Symons (1878; revised 1887)

 Place of Shelley Among the English Poets of His Time by R. P. Scott (1878, 1982)

 Life of Percy Bysshe Shelley by E. Dowden (2 volumes 1886, 1896, 1920, 1966)

 The Life of Percy Bysshe Shelley by William Sharp (1887, 1972)

 A Shelley Primer by Henry Stephens Salt (1887, 1969)

Shelley at Oxford by Thomas Jefferson Hogg (1904)

Shelley's Vegetarianism by William Axon (1908, 1982)

Shelley, The Man and the Poet by Arthur Clutton-Brock (1910, 1923)

Shelley in England by R. Ingpen (1917)

Shelley in Edinburgh by W. E. Peck (1922)

Shelley by Oliver Elton (1924)

Shelley and the Unromantics by O. W. Campbell (1924, 1982)

Shelley and Keats as They Struck Their Contemporaries by Edmund Blunden (1925)

Shelley: His Life and Work by W. E. Peck (2 volumes 1927)

Shelley and Leigh Hunt: How Friendship Made History edited by R. Brimley Johnson (1929, 1982)

A Newton Among Poets by Carl H. Grabo (1930)

The Life of Percy Bysshe Shelley, Introduction by H. Wolfe (2 volumes 1933)

Shelley by R. Bailey (1934)

In Defence of Shelley and Other Essays by Sir Herbert Read (1936)

The Unextinguished Hearth edited by Newman I. White (1838, 1966)

Mary Shelley: A Biography by R. Glynn Grylls (1938, 1982)

Shelley by Newman I. White (2 volumes, New York 1940; London 1947)

Shelley: A Life Story by Edmund Blunden (1946)

Mary Shelley's Journal edited by Frederick L. Jones (1947)

Shelley's Major Poetry by C. H. Baker (1948)

The Imagery of Keats and Shelley by Richard H. Fogle (1949)

The Young Shelley by Kenneth Neill Cameron (1951)

Shelley (in 'Writers and Their Work' series) by Stephen Spender (1952)

Child of Light by Muriel Spark (1952)

Two Gentlemen of Rome: The Story of Keats and Shelley by Ernest Raymond (1952)

Shelley: The Last Phase by Ivan Roe (1953)

Flight of the Skylark by Sylvia Normand (1954)

Byron, Shelley and their Pisan Circle by C. L. Cline (1955)

Shelley at Work: A Critical Enquiry by Neville Rogers (1956)

Shelley: His Thoughts and Work by Desmond King-Hele (1959, 1984)

Shelley and His Circle, 1733-1822 edited by Kenneth Neill Cameron (2 volumes 1961, 2 volumes 1970) and Donald H. Reiman (2 volumes 1974)

Shelley's 'Prometheus Unbound': A Critical Reading by Earl R. Wasserman (1966)

Fabric of a Vision: Shelley's Major Poetry by Carlos Baker (new edition 1966)

Shelley: The Golden Years by Kenneth Neill Cameron (1974)
Violet in the Crucible: Shelley and Translation by Timothy Webb (1977
Harriet Shelley: Five Long Years by Louise Boas (1979)
Sexuality and Feminism in Shelley by Nathaniel Brown (1979)
Unacknowledge Legislator: Shelley and Politics by P. M. S. Dawson (1980
Shelley's Poetic Thought by R. Cronin (1981)
Essays on Shelley edited by Miriam Allott (1982)
Shelley in Dublin by Brendan Kennelly (1982)
Shelley and the Romantic Revolution by F. A. Lea (1982)
Shelley in America in the Nineteenth Century by Julia Power (1982)
Keats, Shelley and Rome by Neville Rogers (1982)
Desire and Restraint in Shelley by Floyd Stovall (1982)
Red Shelley by Paul Foot (1984)
Shelley and the Sublime by Angela Leighton (1984)
Shelley's Style by William Keach (1985)